# Maximize Utility

## The Decline of
## Monetary & Macroeconomics
## *and*
## the Rise of Microeconomics

## By Christopher M. McHugh

© 2017

## Acknowledgments

Research assistant Redmond Siu did extensive editing, basic research and data compilation for *Maximize Utility*. Brandy L. Chetsas edited the manuscript. Jordan T. Bean (Tufts University class of 2016), Eric C. Sporel and Alberto A. Troccoli (both Boston College class of 2018) reviewed the book. Many friends, colleagues and students listened to my recitations on monetary economics, macroeconomics and financial markets. All content and any errors are my responsibility. The cover was designed by Jen Fleisher of Charmed Designworks (www.charmedworks.com).

# Brief Table of Contents

## Part I: The Economic Output Mode de Vie

## Part II: The New M&M Canon

## Part III: Use of Knowledge

# Detailed Table of Contents

# Part I: The Economic Output Mode de Vie

## I.1. Who Are We, and What Are We Striving For?

These might seem like unnecessary questions. We Americans are just a people, pursuing lives and livelihoods with the usual national struggles, successes and achievements that have always been the hallmark of America. In contrast to preceding decades, we recently experienced unusually tough national economic conditions. The deep recession of 2008 staggered our incomes, asset values and overall economic standard of living. In a sense, this adverse change happened for no fundamental reason—other than corporate greed and an out of control banking sector. It also happened against the reasonable intentions of our populace. We are perturbed yet not angry, and we are willing to laugh off blame and pay for losses. We are equally willing to sacrifice and work harder to get our economy back on track. This turn in fortunes took America by surprise, but we will not be fooled again. We called on the government for a little special temporary help and for continuing vigilance and increased government involvement in our economy. Indeed, we are succeeding. The United States appears to maintain the highest standard of living, the greatest economic growth (among its peers) and the admiration of world nations for its prudent policy.

Could the reality be entirely different? Are we a profligate people perpetually consuming beyond our means? Due to our fortunate place in time (post World War II era of high productivity growth), certain favorable factors (like a population pyramid) and copious borrowing we have lived beyond our means for many decades. We exaggerate our prosperity and future wealth, typically biasing any analysis in favor of our unending economic success. We feign economic struggle and innocence. We engage in an economic gambit to borrow from the future, yet we remain fairly certain we can fob our debts off on later generations and foreigners. We run to the government for bailouts more than other nations' peoples. We deny our detractors and continue to support those intellectual aiders and abettors among our great leaders.

We are the latter, and oblivious to any non-glorious economic scenario. We maintain the false economic preeminence buttressed by an equally false intellectual underpinning that by managing our economy and moving economic pieces around in time and place, we are the masters of our macroeconomy. We can lower interest rates, further overspend budgets and extricate ourselves from economic realities. We pull this trick off better than any country on the planet. This national pathos of economic control rests on the intellectual framework of "Monetary and Macroeconomics," the study of national economies.

Indeed there is a villain in our economic story, but it is not the banks or the corporations. It is the American people and their leaders who are gullible and eager to believe stories of economic output without heavy lifting. We are the Macro people, disciples of our great M&M theories. We are the "Lower the Rate" and "Aggregate Demand" populace. We are also the Time Value of Money society, prostrate to the idea that a dollar today is worth more—much more—than a dollar tomorrow. Countless experts–over a million in the U.S.–wake up every day and devote their entire efforts to scheming the increase of our national economic output. We wait on our central bank head to grant us largesse. Almost all that is expected on the people's side is to consume. We emphasize "making it economically," conscious of every penny—be it the rate of return on our savings or our mortgage rate. The government ceaselessly and steadfastly assists the effort. We are the most economically-obsessed society in the world.

## I.1.A. The Monetary & Macro People

"It's the economy, stupid," is a famous and recurring line from our national politics. Indeed, we are economic creatures. This is not new. People have always engaged economic husbandry, using resources to provide for needs. People will work hard if they can realize the benefits. Markets will set prices for goods and services and if they are competitive and open they will usually engender economic growth. These microeconomic motivations and underpinnings are omnipresent in time and place. In modern times, people, in America and elsewhere, have superimposed a peculiar and extreme macroeconomic compulsion over our individual economic behavior. We are the "monetary and macro" people: lowering interest rates and spending beyond our means, and expecting, and even depending upon, rises in asset values to fund our expenses.

Today's predominant, virtually singular, governmental goal for society is "economic." We crave ever-growing incomes and assets. This growth is achieved via continual and ever-growing spending which we call "Consumption" (or "Aggregate Demand" in economic models), and to the layman it is simply a "Strong Economy." The primary duty, perhaps the prohibitive duty, of our elected officials is vigilance over this economic pie, which we incessantly measure and count when it is expanding and agonize over and recount even more when it is contracting. Even in good times, we want more. President Obama termed it the "New Economic Patriotism." This necessitates experimental, prolonged economic policies like ZIRP (zero interest rate policy) for years and years or patchwork semi-fanatical actions, like releasing oil from our strategic reserves (as we did in summer 2011) to stimulate the economy by lowering the price of gas.

Unlike an earlier generation that endured the Great Depression, World War II and the Cold War, America's younger generations have no national goals nor any common national experience. We will fight foreign wars, but mainly for economic motivations, like oil. We gladly fund wars, if our economic interests are deemed to be greater. Our soldiers are paid in full. We have established our national psyche as coveting income and consumption and our biggest macro aggregate of all: gross domestic product ("GDP"). This goal is a very present time concern with little look to the past or the future. Such focus on today's GDP undermines goals of moderation and thrift, and, thereby, also frees us from culpability for waste and materialism.

As noted above, America asks little accountability of its people, mainly requiring one duty— consume. Whether it is Paul Krugman or Arthur Laffer, the *New York Times* or *Fox,* Donald Trump or Barack Obama, they all speak glowingly about the virtuous, hard-working American people, vehemently denying our culpability for financial excess. It is time for our leaders and people to be uncompromising. Perhaps we should embrace our ethos with some edits:

> *I pledge allegiance to the flag of the United States of America*
> *And to the governmentally-managed economy for which it stands*
> *One consuming nation, in debt,*
> *With low interest rates and aggregate demand for all.*

We think macro, not micro. We want high house prices for the asset-driven stimulus it gives to the economy (supposedly through wealth effects), even though high prices are disadvantageous for buyers. We fear deflation, another macro quantity, even though the lower prices reflects the progress of our economic lives through higher productivity. We believe low rates make us better off, yet thrifty people seemingly have a lot to lose from low rates. We view a lower value of our currency as helping us export and increasing our GDP, yet that lower currency means we are poorer. The U.S. is not the only country that schemes a macro existence, but we do it as much, and perhaps even more, than our peers do.

Of course, the economic well-being of our citizenry is paramount and a growing macroeconomy creates wealth and income. I do not want to be poor, unemployed or worried that the money in my bank is at risk. Of course, I also appreciate the people and institutions that protect my economy; yet there is something unnerving and dishonorable about our national pursuit of GDP/economic output.

## I.1.B. Seduced by M&M

Monetary & Macroeconomics ("M&M") is the analysis and measurement of the national economy; the set of models and empirical facts and figures about the economy; and the federal macroeconomic policies and central bank policies used to manage our economy. After using M&M adroitly for thirty years, we seemingly beat the odds by maintaining a close to best-in-class (among developed nations) average GDP growth. Despite the derision often heaped on economists and their faulty theories, we had a straightforward and apparently successful M&M system that worked through 2006 and even seemingly continued to succeed under extreme conditions like the Great Recession. Our M&M is constituted of a general Keynesian belief that we can manage the economy. Some combination of fiscal and, more importantly, monetary policy, can be used to keep the economy growing at its full potential and mitigate recession. The monetary policy component is the more timely and often more daring, but we also believe the fiscal component and, in general, accept the entire Keynesian package.

## I.1.B.a. Government in the Economy

At least since the 1960s the United States has had extensive government involvement in our economic lives. What role should our government have in making our economy efficient? Literally hundreds of thousands, if not millions, of highly educated people devote their lives to pondering our economic pie and how to increase it and allocate it among our people.

Government serves many functions. First and foremost a government protects the people from foreign enemies. Its next fundamental role is to establish and run the legal framework and provide for protection of citizens in basic ways. Aside from these functions a case can be made that citizens should otherwise be free to engage among themselves as they please. Of course, we also believe that government is essential in a wide variety of tasks that a people collectively want done and need the government to perform. These include large-scale projects like mail delivery, roads, airports, telecommunications, basic research, regulating standards, etc. We also recognize government as an equalizer and guarantor of certain services like aid to the indigent. We agree that such tasks require taxing richer and more fortunate citizens. All those roles of government make sense to average citizens; however, people become confused about the macroeconomic roles of government. People think the government keeps the economy going, but they do not know how or why.

Listed below is a brief round-up of all the economic roles of government and their respective M&M "effects." First, we provide five hefty examples—interest rates, housing, health care, citizenship and education—of the muddle of what our government economic policies are. Later in the text, we provide precise analysis of monetary policy and its effects.

- Interest rate policy by our central bank is omnipresent in our economy. From 2008 to the present, the U.S., through its central bank maintained very low rates. Most people can conceive that lower rates can result in more borrowing and spending. They might view it as a temporary maneuver, however, and wonder about the ultimate effects of low rates for a long time. Most economists would argue that the net effect of low rates was beneficial to our economy. Some analysts contend that low rates distort the price of capital, causing misallocation of resources. Low rates also impact savers adversely. It is a debate for which there is no answer. Policy proponents argue the former. U.S. Fed head Janet Yellen, for example, would aver many times that without low rates households would have been worse off through job losses, lower home values and lower pension fund values.[1] Which side is right?

- A house is a place to live. A home represents one of the biggest expenses of a person's life and should be a personal choice. Some people spend an inordinate amount of time and money maintaining a big property while others choose not to own a home. A multitude of government subsidies of the housing sector, however, grossly affect our housing decisions. In the years following 2008, housing policy was perhaps the most important way that the government attempted to affect the growth rate of the economy. It is presumed that housing stimulates other parts of the economy, both in the short and long run.
- Health care spending is an end in itself. People go to the doctor if they are ill. Since health care is costly and some people need more medical attention than others through no fault of their own, we charge our government with the task of subsidizing health care in many ways. Ostensibly, though, there is no pretense of supporting the economy through these expenditures, except to the extent that good health aids our lives. In some cases, though, our government justifies additional health care spending for its spillover effects on the macroeconomy.
- We like to think that immigration policies are humanitarian. As the phrase associated with the Statue of Liberty goes, "Give me your tired, your poor, your huddled masses yearning to be free." Of course, any nation would also want immigration that contributed to a broad long-run economic and social well-being of the nation. Should immigration be motivated by short-run M&M effects? Our immigration policy is often proposed front and center as a temporary antidote for poor economic growth. At one point in the financial crisis of 2008, many analysts looked to immigrants and, in particular, *immigrants buying housing*, as a short-run solution to our economic problems. These immigrants would promptly buy property and true up the all-important housing market—which, in turn, would spillover to spending on housing accoutrements, the hiring of worthy working men and ultimately to making homeowners feel rich, secure and willing to spend even more.
- Long ago in America, we deemed that every person should have a basic education. We established a public school system and, in a less extensive way, also extended government support to higher education. This cost has risen so greatly and we have created a serpentine higher education finance system to accommodate the expenditure. Student loans now represent so much outstanding debt that they have now become a potential M&M policy objective. Originally, government-subsidized student loans were intended to help young people develop human capital for a lifetime of employment. Now, we talk about government sponsored sweeping changes to a large pool of student loans that will substantially alter major facets of our lives—like job choice, earnings, housing purchases, family formation, etc.

From the above examples you can see that peoples' economic decisions are not determined solely by their own cost-benefit analyses. M&M effects are integral in every aspect of our lives.

## I.1.B.a.i. Government Economic Roles

Our federal government does about $4 trillion in spending and state and local do about $3 trillion. Collectively, governments engage in myriad tasks: border protection, military, student loans, Social Security, research, prisons, Amtrak, citizenship services, foreign aid, courts, highways, regulation, health care services,

---

[1] "Yellen Defends Seven Years of Low Interest Rates in Letter to Nader," by Christopher Condon, *Bloomberg.com*, November 23, 2015, http://www.bloomberg.com/news/articles/2015-11-23/yellen-defends-seven-years-of-zero-interest-in-letter-to-nader

public assistance, education, etc. What are the economic underpinnings for government control of these tasks? The first key distinction is that certain government spending has little pretense of shaping the macroeconomy. This spending is solely for the goods and services deemed needed through government. Most state and local spending, such as spending on education, is perceived of this way. Federal spending may ultimately be for goods and services consumed by the citizenry but federal spending can also be conceived of as having a macroeconomic impact on the growth rate of the economy.

People do believe in M&M effects, or at least that big time government economic intervention is more likely to be a net economic benefit than a cost. No doubt, levels of conviction on this belief do vary greatly. Average citizens and business people are generally more skeptical, while politicians are the quickest to believe—followed by the press, certain academics and liberal-leaning people who like to envision a salutary role of government in economic affairs in general. To give an example, *The Boston Globe*, editorializes definitively, "A fact: Stimulus created jobs,"[2] and denounces anyone who disagrees. The once free-market leaning publication *The Economist* now sees government involvement as the key to economic success.[3] Ultimately, their belief in beneficial government macroeconomic policy comes from decades of faculty M&M instruction ranging from the greatest scholars at Harvard down to part-time instructors at Podunk Community College. People believe that the M&M body of models and empirical evidence may not be perfect, but it sustains enough evidence and theory about business cycles, government policy, multipliers, the potency of the Fed, etc. to justify making the U.S. a government town. To put it another way, people think they could go to any college and ask the M&M teacher and receive confirmation that M&M is right.

Belief is facile, faith-like, hard to argue against and ubiquitous whether the source is a layman or an M&M specialist. To demonstrate this mindset, prominent economist Allen Sinai, said, "When the Fed sprinkles happy dust on the economy, we always respond. The happy dust has been out there a long, long time, and I think it finally may be settling in some places."[4]

When considering the micro v. macro role of government, you must first recognize a key distinction of government functions or provision of goods and services that we believe should be provided by government because that role is economically efficient. For some reason, private markets will not produce those particular goods as efficiently as the government. We can call this the Microeconomic role of government. Conversely, the other major government economic role relates to policies designed to stimulate the economy. The latter example is known as Macroeconomics and includes Monetary Economics.

## I.1.B.a.ii. Government Economic Roles: Microeconomic

There are strict microeconomic roles for government to enhance the efficiency of market outcomes. Under most circumstances, economists theorize that markets allocate efficiently. In other words, consumers purchase the desired amount of goods and services that producers supply at the lowest possible cost. However, there are circumstances in which markets do not attain the greatest efficiency and the government can improve outcomes. There are three specific categories that demonstrate this:

- **Public Goods**: A public good is a good or service that would not be produced by individuals through

---

[2] Editorial February 21, 2010.

[3] The lead editorial of October 18, 2008, "Capitalism at bay," composed during the peak the 2008 crisis states that since its founding, "*The Economist* has been on the side of economic liberty," but soon after states, "…defending capitalism means, paradoxically, state intervention." Read the hundreds of editorials since then and you will find the, "We support freedom, but in this case the government must take over for market," over and over. *The Economist* errs on the side of government intervention as much as my local, liberal newspaper, *The Boston Globe*.

[4] *Bloomberg.com*, "Easy-money policy may be finally paying off," December 23, 2011.

market interactions even though it is desired by people and worth its cost. The key to a public good is that it is non-excludable. The party purchasing or creating the good cannot exclude other parties from its consumption. Another way of putting it is that public goods have a freeloader aspect. A common textbook example of a public good is the lighthouse. If I build a lighthouse other people can consume its services. Other examples of public goods include national defense, a fireworks show and certain types of basic research.[5] Many goods that people might think of as public goods, like Amtrak and the U.S. Postal Service, are not genuine public goods by microeconomic definitions. In the real world, true public goods are uncommon.

- **Externalities**: An externality is when the production or consumption of a good or service has an effect on a third party who is neither the buyer nor seller. A classic example of this would be a factory disposing of waste in the river. People, like farmers, who use the downstream water have higher production costs due to the factory's effluence. This illustrates a negative externality. For society as a whole in this example, too much of the factory's output and too little of the farmers' is being produced. Externalities are usually described as negative externalities, but we can also have positive ones. If I paint my house and landscape my yard, my actions benefit neighbors by making their properties more attractive and valuable. To optimize through government subsidize positive externalities and tax negative ones. Another way to solve the problem is to incorporate the different parties' costs and benefits into one optimization problem.

- **Imperfect Competition**: When markets are not competitive we hypothesize that not enough of the goods are produced and/or the goods are produced at too high of a cost. Another way of describing the problem is that a dead weight loss, i.e., a loss to all, occurs. Examples of imperfect competition are cable television, electricity and railway service.

The above categories describe specific scenarios in which more efficiency can be attained if government steps in. Greater output means that everyone can benefit. We can theorize another microeconomic role or justification for government:

- **Redistribution**: Sharing of income through government mandated taxes, transfers, subsidies, etc. is considered a correct government role, however, in this case, we do not attain more efficiency and may indeed lose it. The justification for this role of government assumes a social objective that attaches value to redistribution. The pooling of society's economic resources makes us feel better collectively. In blunt terms, we tax the rich and give income or services (like food stamps) to the poor because we think that is the right action to take. There is not much pretense for getting additional output from the economy with such programs except to the extent that they provide for a better and fairer society. Health care, public pensions (including Social Security), public assistance, education spending, research spending, etc. fall under this category. Most of our government spending emanates from redistribution. We are left with bigger government and perhaps waste, but presumably, we accept it. In all of these government microeconomic roles—at least in principle— there is no pretense, as yet, of a macro role.

### I.1.B.a.iii. Government Economic Roles: Macroeconomic

The macroeconomic role for government is subtle and prejudicial. There is no easier way to explain

---

[5] The non-excludability is not the only facet that demarcates public goods but that is usually the way economists define it. For example, I can hold a fireworks show and non-exclude people from seeing but I may do it anyway. In a more general sense a public good is something big that consumers would buy collectively but not individually.

macroeconomic roles of government than a brief listing of concepts:

- **Traditional (pre-2008) Demand-Side Macro**: Demand-side macroeconomics is what most frequently comes to mind when you hear the term macro. Most of the talk, models, classroom instruction, etc. in the world of macroeconomics is the idea that demand for goods and services makes the world go round. Demand-side M&M has two policy pillars: (1) fiscal policy- government spending and taxation and (2) monetary policy - manipulating interest rates and money supplies. Also, for these two policies we hypothesize two time frames: (1) the short run, in which economies can be out-of-equilibrium, e.g., in a recession and may be in need of government stimulus; and (2) the long run, in which markets return to their potential. In the long run, economists contend that markets operate at efficient levels and are impervious to government policy, which can only affect the economy in the short run. Until recently, the consensus among economists was that fiscal policy was useless for stabilization both in the short and long run because of lags in policy effects. We also believed that monetary policy did not work in the long run: the famous, "long-run neutrality of money." Monetary policy did work in the short run, however. Intellectually, short-run monetary policy ruled from about 1980 through 2007.
- **Recent (post-2008) Developments in Traditional Demand-Side Macro**: Since 2008, we have reevaluated M&M. Monetary policy has become more extensive in scope, magnitudes and duration. We now engage in many unconventional monetary policies that are unlike the previous straightforward changing of interest rates or money supplies. Fiscal policy, which we had abandoned, has seen a rebirth as being effective.
- **Effects:** The pivotal aspect is the impact of demand-side policy. Does active policy increase economic output? For example, does the most typical policy of lowering interest rates create more growth? If yes, how much and in what time frame? Which particular policies work best? Most mainstream economists would confirm effects of some magnitude. For example, leading academic and Fed Board Member Stanley Fischer would speak of the state of the economy in recent years as being better due to years of lower rates that resulted in greater investment and spending that rippled through the economy. The key to "effects" is that the ultimate economy is affected and not just that the level of tools. That the government can "lower" borrowing cost (or weaken a currency) by buying assets is pretty certain but whether that affects real spending is questionable. For example, following the recession of 2008 governments lowered borrowing costs. GDP grew also, but did it grow due to the policy or was it that economies recover on their own following recessions?
- **Keynesian**: Demand-side macro is the Keynesian story. Keynesian can have many meanings depending upon context and the specific model or point. Sometimes Keynesianism refers specifically to fiscal policy and not monetary policy. In more general terms Keynesianism means believing in policy effects from both types of policy. Keynesianism assumes spillover effects, commonly called multiplier effects, from aggregate demand changes. Our post-2008 monetary policy can best be described as Keynesian central banking. It seeks to create aggregate demand.
- **Classical or Neo-Classical**: These are terms that describe the school of thought that denies policy effects, at least in efficacious ways.
- **Policy Timing**: As above, we hypothesized a long run in which the market economy tended towards optimality and efficiency by itself.[6] There could be a short run in which markets went

---

[6] Economics also has a very important microeconomic concept of short run and long run. The long run is the time that the capital of a firm can be altered. It is also the time period in which firms can enter or exit an industry. We hypothesize a short run in which there can be excess profits or losses. If the former, firms enter. If the latter, they leave. By entry and exit, excess profits are eroded. The micro concept is precise in a way but it is also a variable and situation specific concept. For example, the long

awry, typically a recession. Short-run monetary policy could be used to restore the economy to a long-run equilibrium. The time span of the short run was never precise and was usually thought of as quarters or one year or perhaps even two years, but generally not multiple years. Now policy is usually described either over a "Medium Term" or as happening at the time of the announcement of policy, i.e., "Immediate Term." These Medium and Immediate terms are both semi-ridiculous and untenable concepts. The Medium Term (which we will discuss at length later) essentially translates to admitting that policy does not ostensibly behave the way it should in the short run accompanied by a lack of any conviction that it will get the economy back on track in the long run. Rather, policy proponents hypothesize some intermediary time frame in which the effects of policy work the way they were intended. Concerning effects at the point of announcement, this is a capitulation to markets and private parties being able to anticipate policy effects rendering policy ineffective.

- **More Policy Timing - Announcement/Signal or Effectuation**: Another key distinction of policy impact concerns whether they are due to the actual effectuation of policy or just its announcement (sometimes we say signal). In textbooks and most inculcation, it must be the former. It should be that changes in policy variables cause real spending, investment and ultimately GDP growth. In reality, though, and especially given the size and efficiency of our financial markets, parties anticipate policy change so quickly and completely that many analysts believe that effects mostly play on the announcement of a policy. In this latter case, the story of the textbook becomes unwound and ridiculous. Front-runners—primarily big money managers—game the policy, and others jump on the bandwagon. Many of the policies commenced following 2008 (like different rounds of quantitative easing) apparently worked on announcement. For another example, in March 2015 when the European Central Bank ("ECB") began its quantitative easing ("QE"), bond prices indeed went up and yields declined. The value of the euro also depreciated.

- **Supply-Side Macroeconomics**: Supply-side is typically a reduction of taxes and government spending on the belief that getting more resources in private hands will mean more efficiency and more economic growth—and ultimately more output for everybody. Supply-side can also be seen with the government subsidizing certain activities, like small business or tax advantages to having children. Supply-side is a macro doctrine related to the effects of government policies. Supply-side is more of a long-run rather than short-run story, although supply-side effects do not belabor timing the way traditional demand-side effects do. Supply-side rose to prominence in the early 1980s and reappears from time to time usually associated with conservative economists and politicians.

- **Long-Run Effects**: A whole different study of the macroeconomy, sometimes called growth theory, has to do with the economy's growth over an extended period of time, like years or decades. Government policies or investments can change the long-run growth trend. Sometimes we call these structural policies. The demand-side policies were short run or stabilization policies. The former should be determined by cost-benefit analysis (i.e., are they worth it?) and should not be touted for short-run benefits of creating jobs and having multiplier spending effects. Economists of all stripes usually agree that long-run of investments in the economy (in education or infrastructure, for example) will subsequently contribute to greater economic growth. Some analysts also tout favorable spillover effects now. Often, the two effects are muddled.

- **Capsule History of Effects**: We were fearful that capitalist economies would not perform well after the Depression and World War II and gradually adopted the general Keynesian idea that fiscal policy and monetary policy could control the economy. We built theoretical and empirical models

---

run for nuclear power producers might be ten years. The long run for a newspaper delivery boy is the time it takes him to buy a bike.

of this government-managed economy. By about the early 1960s we started managing the macroeconomy. It appeared successful for a short while but in the 1970s we ended up with high inflation. All we could agree on was that bad monetary policy caused high inflation. Intellectual belief in M&M waned. Fiscal policy would be late or hard to target, and long-run monetary policy would be ineffective, only causing inflation if we tried to keep monetary policy stimulative. We did have conviction that monetary policy had effects, including adverse ones like high inflation if we tried to stimulate the economy over the long term; but it also had potentially useful, counter-cyclical effects if applied adeptly in the short term.

- **A Great Irony**: Following the ostensibly poor economic policy of the 1970s, we fell back on short-run monetary policy as effective. The conviction for monetary policy effects was largely due to one person: Milton Friedman. Ironically, the same man who believed that government management of an economy was highly disadvantageous laid the foundation for the economic policy that people use to justify modern monetary policy. Friedman's work was premised on the belief that monetary policy would primarily affect the economy adversely—sometimes greatly so, like contracting the money supply during the Depression. He did not intend to endorse active monetary policy, but policy proponents capitalized on his finding and used it to justify grooming the economy at all times. With some conviction since the 1980s, M&M economists and policy makers indulged short-run monetary policy. Teaching M&M was a cinch, simply explaining how open market operations affected the fed funds rate, which "transmitted" through various economic channels in the short run to the rest of the economy. The often dramatic and once triumphant term of Alan Greenspan as Fed Chairman was almost exclusively based on this philosophy. Coming into the 1990s, Wall Street and Main Street acutely bought into the idea that sapient use of short-run monetary policy mattered. A classic monetary policy example found in almost every text was the Fed's response in the latter half of 1998 to the Russian bond default and the resultant financial markets shakeout in the U.S. and elsewhere. The Fed engaged in three quarter-point reductions of the fed funds target rate (a total of less than 1%) and supposedly saved the economy.

- **Why and How of Policy Effects**: At all times, economists struggled with the extent and timing of short-run monetary policy effects and how or why the tail (a few billion dollars in open market operations) could wag the dog (the ten to twenty trillion dollar annual economy). We have never been too explicit about how it works. Great policy economists like James Tobin talked about a "shuffling and reshuffling" of portfolios. The empirical evidence for short-run effects of monetary policy is certain econometric analyses, which are of debatable validity, and sundry case studies of cause and effect. The case studies are episodes in extremis like the Great Depression and the Volcker money supply contraction of 1981. These types of events are rare and hardly convincing for normal times. Another often cited set of case studies relies on episodes from the 1950s that focus only on Fed policy rate raises rather than reductions. Again, this is not convincing either for current modern times or in light of the reality that interest rate reduction (i.e., stimulation) is the pivotal policy. The bottom line is that we do not have much evidence.

- **Any Effects**: To many analysts, including both non-economists and professionals, effects are simply any observable or even conceivable economic result that follows after a policy action done by the government. This is the last gasp of policy believers. It can be very minor effects, effects in a general direction or even immediate (but perhaps completely unrelated) effects. For example, a stock market rally following a policy action is confirmation of policy effects. To a policy die-hard, any effect is "worth it." Costs or unintended effects of policy are to be dismissed or thought of as payable later when the economy is strong.

- **Intention of Government's Economic Spendings**: Perhaps we should just admit that we simply prefer to conduct a greater fraction of our economic lives via government, like European countries have done for decades. Such spending by government may add little to GDP growth and indeed is not intended to, yet we couch any spendings in terms of how much they add to GDP growth. For example, we often favor greater environmental regulation and government spending on the environment, but we then characterize the spendings as creating new industries, engendering spillover spendings and ultimately creating jobs.

- **Directions and Magnitudes of Effects**: In general, a policy is supposed to work in a certain direction and with a certain magnitude. Unintended effects of policy may occur, and they may go in the same direction or in the opposite direction. Policy proponents assume that intended effects dominate but economists do not know the relative magnitudes.

- **Evidence of Effects and Arbiters of Effects**: We have no counter-examples, or "counter-factuals," to judge policy initiatives against. We cannot do controlled experiments for our macroeconomy. We mostly break on prejudices and interpret history as we please. Ben Bernanke would always state that the net economic benefits of the post-2008 monetary policy outweighed the costs. Even people who ostensibly came out as big losers from activist monetary policy, like a person who lost significant interest on his bank savings, was a net beneficiary because the economy he lived in was much more prosperous.

- **Prejudices**: Those who believe in government policy see effects in significant magnitudes and the requisite direction. Those who do not believe in government doubt effects and highlight potentially large, but also difficult to initially see, adverse effects. For example, the many economic stimulus programs following 2008 were viewed optimistically by proponents. The JOBS (Jumpstart Our Business Startups) Act of 2012 provided relatively minor economic incentives but was highly touted by proponents as creating jobs. Then, simultaneous government policies of raising taxes and increasing regulation were disregarded by policy believers as having little or no negative effect. These proponents would contend that entrepreneurs would not substantially change their work and investment efforts due to higher taxes and increased regulation. For another example, at the start of 2013 the U.S. went over the "Fiscal Cliff," which was cuts in government spending and higher taxes, both representing detractions from aggregate demand. Over the next years, the economy grew at about the same rate as before. Keynesians had contended the Fiscal Cliff would hurt the economy severely. When it did not many argued that monetary policy of the third round of quantitative easing by the U.S. Fed[7], which had commenced a few months earlier, in September 2012, had picked up the slack. Anti-policy proponents believed that quantitative easing would have no substantial beneficial economic effects and only distortionary effects. Then, they believed that the Fiscal Cliff would have little effect too. As the years played out, each side could make a case for its beliefs and diminish the other side's beliefs.

- **Plethora of Effects**: One of the very difficult aspects of M&M for average people reading the financial press is that economists and other analysts can select effects pretty much as they please. For example, the post-2008 stimulative policy was accompanied by an increase in the stock market. The former caused the latter, policy proponents could contend, and a growing stock market was good for everybody because it was good for the system.

- **Focus on Certain Effects**: Every expert can cite his own view of cause and effect, and you encounter

---

[7] Quantitative easing ("QE") is the buying of assets by the central bank beyond what it usually purchases for normal interest rate setting. Assets purchased under QE also include assets in addition to government bonds. We will discuss QE at length since it represented the main unconventional monetary policy of the post-2008 period.

this capricious aspect of M&M when teaching. Economics' professors are overwhelmed when explaining the overall effects of government economic involvement and cannot make a list like we are doing here. They are prone to lecture from sources that purport to identify all important causes and effects.

- **"Out Of Thin Air"**: As camp as this phrase may be, it best describes the condition for real policy effects. The credit created by the central bank or the fiscal spending from the government must come from "out of thin air," i.e., from nowhere and with no offset, to have an effect. If the central bank gives banks reserves but takes away banks' other assets that they were lending against, no net credit will be created. If the government issues bonds to pay for a new fiscal spending program but those are bonds are purchased by buyers who sell other debt to get the bonds, no net effect should occur.

## I.1.B.a.iv. Government Economic Roles: Assessment

Perhaps the greatest intellectual endeavor of modern times is the search for Keynesian effects. From the incipient modeling of Keynesian ideas in the 1930s all the way through the innovative policies of today like QE, negative interest rates and helicopter money, economists have searched for devices to get more economic output out of our macroeconomic system. The search for Keynesian effects is truly the lifeblood of many great minds.

Since 2008 we have engaged in unconventional and greatly extended M&M policies like the large-scale asset purchases made in the U.S. and other countries and the negative policy interest rates implemented in many countries. The questions about what policy effects are, in both theory and magnitude, altogether more intricate. This is the heart of M&M, and we will continue to discuss it at length on the following pages. At least one improvement can be attempted at this stage. When discussing the effects of government economic policies with a specialist, insist on some precision in his proposal. Ask the following questions, Is he describing: (1) a macro policy designed solely for stimulating the economy in the short run; (2), a micro policy which has no intention of Keynesian spillover but is justified as a public good, externality, etc.; or (3) or a pure expansion of the government for some social redistribution purpose and little or no effect on the path of GDP growth?

## I.1.C. An American Pathology & the Ego-Stroking Macro Yarns

In America today we "bias the economic case in our favor." We count up and embellish our economic advantages and downplay shortcomings, making praiseful assumptions about our economic capacity, people, government, rates of returns on investment, industriousness, business acumen, exceptional leadership, etc. We admit certain economic shortcomings, of course, and that we veer from sound policies at times; but in the end, we are "number one." This philosophy of modern-day American exceptionalism is backed intellectually by M&M. A variety of feel-good economic stories, assumptions and beliefs largely grounded in M&M are integral support of our pathology. A few of those stories—and their contrary realities—are listed below:

| Favorable Economic Tale | Reality |
| --- | --- |
| Front and center is our assumption about how much economic capacity we have now and will have in the future. Our gross domestic product ("GDP") and its growth rate are inviolate. Our GDP is great and | In general, the great, continually growing GDP concept rests on flimsy theory and optimistic reading of history. This is a pathology peculiar to America. We, most of all, remain sure of our |

| | |
|---|---|
| diversified and our GDP growth is persistent and relatively high. We believe in long periods of economic "recovery" with high average GDP growth (like a little over 3% real growth per year) and brief and infrequent recessions. | superior GDP growth. In the years 2012 to 2015, we boasted that we achieved great GDP growth and lower unemployment that accompanied it. We are oblivious to counter cases that our GDP growth is well-below 3% and our per capita GDP growth not higher than that of others. (Of course, the current and future state of our GDP is a complicated topic which we will discuss extensively throughout the book.) |
| Macroeconomic policy, including both monetary policy and Keynesianism, works for the U.S. The concept that we can buy our way out of debt is considered valid in America more than almost anywhere else. Our success in policy stems from our cleverness and our earnest intentions. Also, due to our size and extraordinary national economic union, policy works better than it does in smaller nations or in economic unions like Eurozone. In recent years we have touted our record of successful, pro-active macro policy. Our economy successfully recovered while competitors' economies wallowed. | Neither our recent foray nor the longer record of increased government involvement in the economy have proven successful. Macro policy merely gets us deeper and deeper into debt. Our boast of a superior recovery from the recession 2008, compared to our peers, is invalid. Our GDP grew more greatly but when adjusted for population growth it grew about the same. Our decrease in unemployment, when adjusted for our adverse change in labor force participation, is not much better than Eurozone's or Japan's. |
| The United States is home to an industrious, entrepreneurial, highly educated populace that is willing to take risk and bear losses. We readily migrate within our nation to areas with superior economic opportunities. We work hard and—if we work hard enough—our economy rewards us with increased output. Our entrepreneurial advantage stems from many special factors: deepest capital markets, best business schools, penchant for risk taking, culture and history of entrepreneurship, strict legal system, individual hard work and self-reliance, etc. | We are not that tough and independent and are prone to solicit government assistance. |
| Although we squabble politically, Americans pull together when necessary. If we do cooperate, our economic output is sufficient to pay for our needs. | We are not unified. Moreover, our economic problems are so grave that, even if we do compromise politically, we have shortfalls. |
| We care about our children and readily sacrifice for their future. | We have consciously chosen present day consumption over our children's future needs. |
| We are superior to our competitors, many of which are chronically doctrinaire, disorganized and corrupt. We are quick to highlight other societies' shortcomings and have scorn for the nations that have chosen to pool their resources, like Sweden. | Many competitor economies have caught up with us. They deride our economic bluster and highlight our economic failures, including heavy debt load and various grave microeconomic problems like the percentage of Americans that rely on public |

| | assistance. |
|---|---|
| We herald a miracle of capitalism. Free markets possess some internal dynamism that guarantees economic growth, and America is the singular capitalist society. "Let markets perform their magic," we say. | Free markets may make the most of any society's resources but they do not guarantee 3% GDP growth. Also we face competition from a multitude of new and improved capitalists and we are not singular capitalists since we impose so many limitations on our markets. |
| Small business is a great driver of economies and new business formation is perennial, regardless of increases in taxes and regulations along with other impediments to small business formation like higher minimum wages. | We have seen a marked decrease in small business activity in almost every measurement. |
| Americans' marginal products (the microeconomic term for productivity of workers and equivalent wage levels) are high due to our significant stock of intellectual capital. In other words, we are highly educated. Thus, we are the great designers, financiers, creators, researchers, educators, etc.; and America is an outsized exporter of high mark-up services. | We are simply not that great a workforce and in many ways we have lower marginal products today than our parents and grandparents did. |
| We are prodigious housing people, and housing makes us wealthier. Buy a big house, build an extension or buy a second home—these expenditures increase our economy's GDP. House values increase over time, creating an investment return over and above the value of the housing services received. Our government assists the housing market ensuring the salutary economic effects of housing. | Spending on housing neither stimulates the economy nor creates wealth. This is a prime example of an M&M fallacy, by the way. If we really believe that buildings that wear down every day are going to give us maybe 3%, 5% or even 7% return per year (estimated returns common among real estate professionals and homeowners circa 2014), we are indeed misguided. |
| Free trade is advantageous for the economy and society, and we are outstanding at maintaining free trade. | Free trade has tradeoffs and certain Americans will suffer significantly from free trade. We are not on the cutting edge of free trade policies. |
| Immigrants bring wealth and net economic gains, and America will always be a preferred destination for immigrants. | Today's immigrants represent nowhere near as much net gain to society as in the past. Talented international individuals and companies will avoid America if it has high taxes and regulation. |
| Our economy is characterized by a business cycle that recurs over time and is bounded by its ups and downs. This cycle typically shows much longer recovery periods than downswings. We are adept at discerning and controlling our business cycle, including minimizing the downswings and always achieving recovery. | The business cycle is nowhere near as predictable or controllable as we like to believe. Our economic growth path is dominated by long-term trends and random shocks and we have little control and bad prospects concerning those. |
| Inflation is controllable by our central bank. We believe we can control high inflation. We have done | We are not in control of inflation and it can rise dramatically suddenly. Presently (circa 2016) in a |

| it in the past. | precarious inflation situation: (1) Either inflation will remain low, as it has been for most of the post-2008 period; but it reflects lower wage increases and a weak economy or (2) Inflation will increase and become too high leading to represent significant loss of buying power and erosion of savings. If the latter our central bank may have a hard time keeping inflation under control. Our only case of controlling high inflation reduction is that of the early 1980s, which came at a grievous cost to our society. |
|---|---|
| U.S. government debt is risk-free and will always be in demand due to the perception of U.S. economic strength. Our debt is large and liquid which adds to its desirability. Our debt is also U.S. dollar denominated and the dollar is the world's reserve currency. | U.S. debt is not risk-free. It is large in volume, but that is not necessarily an advantage. Large U.S. debt and deficit and/or high inflation could result in a sudden reversal of the demand for U.S. debt. It is not unprecedented in modern times: In 1978 when economic conditions in the U.S. were adverse (mainly high inflation), we had to issue government debt denominated in Swiss francs. |
| The U.S. dollar will always remain the world's reserve currency because the U.S. is currently, and will always remain, the only nation economically diverse and strong enough to merit the role of reserve currency. | The U.S. could lose reserve currency status, in whole or in part. |
| The U.S. is a large fiscal union with natural advantages over smaller nations and entities comprised of disparate economies, like Eurozone. | Our large political union represents many economic costs and inefficiencies that will become more apparent in the future. |
| We boast a favorable demography, primarily with a population that will grow, with both native fertility and economically-desirable immigration. | Basics of demography work against us. Our native population will not grow. Our immigrants will not create significant net economic benefits. Our life expectancy is growing, which is economically costly and even additionally burdensome due to our general morbidity in terms of weak health and illness. Our population's mobility is greatly diminished. While we snicker at countries with low fertility rates (like Italy) and xenophobic societies (like Japan), our basic population/people attributes are no better. |
| America's money managers design large portfolios of stocks, bonds and other assets that can maintain high average rates of return. | An extraordinary period of high returns is over. Returns to financial portfolios are destined to be much lower. The money managers merely add costly and useless fees. |

The list above reflects just some of the economic fairy tales we cite. Americans are steadfast that economic success is our birthright.

### I.1.D. Omnipotent Time Value & Optimistic Rates of Return to Assets

We believe that time has value: One dollar today is worth more tomorrow. We say "Time Value of Money" ("TVM"). We believe in positive rates of return, on average, for investments and for risk-free holdings like bank deposits and government bonds. TVM means that if we defer a dollar of present consumption and save or invest it for a period, we will have more consumption in the future. If we invest with risk at a higher rate, for example at 7% per year as some experts contend you can get in equities, we could enjoy more abundant future consumption. However, suppose the true rate we can get and should rely upon is lower—like 1%. Then, it is a very different scenario. So which is it? In America we assume, and we bet the future of our children on, the premise of hefty TVM.[8]

TVM is one of most commonly taught concepts in higher education, even in high school. The premise that a dollar is more valuable today than tomorrow is perhaps the greatest iron law in social science. Although we do not have one specific interest rate for time value we generally assume pretty high rates, rendering time value not merely existent but hefty. We teach this concept repeatedly and with relish. We prostrate ourselves to the following equation:

$$PV = \frac{FV}{(1 + i)^n}$$

In demonstrations of the equation, $i$ is almost always hefty enough to make future obligations greatly diminish. Now, let us return to the example above using a 7% rate of return, as we use in many pension systems. To fund a pension of $1,000 due next year, only $935.58 is needed now. Here is an example that illustrates the power of time value and how it has changed: In my adult lifetime, since about 1980, a 1-year U.S. treasury, which represents risk-free investing, has yielded about 2% over inflation annually. Over the last few years that same return has been less than zero—perhaps even as low as -1.5%.

The text I use in my Monetary Economics class introduces time value analysis with a multiple-paragraph tirade concerning the historical condemnation of lending money at interest, and the contention that such suspicion of interest continues today: "Most people still take a dim view of the fact that lenders charge interest."[9] The textbook's authors sound as if they lived a hundred years ago. The truth is that nobody dislikes interest. Not only do people accept it, they relish it. I have never met an undergrad who does not think that time has value. In fact, I cannot recall any person ever expressing any reservation about making money on money. Young people today are enlightened—and indoctrinated—at an early age about TVM's glorious math and economics.

There is nothing economically inaccurate about the existence of TVM. That we can take resources today and through ingenuity, enterprise and hard work combine them in innovative ways to produce greater output in the future is confirmed by our entire history. This is called progress and progress has the

---

[8] We are considering real rates of return here, i.e., with the effects of inflation removed or not present at all. This distinction is simple, but often very hard to convey. Inflation, of course, is the increase in the average price level of all goods and services. Inflation has been omnipresent in our lives. Perhaps because of this, students assume inflation is relevant to any lecture point, yet many lectures assume a world without inflation. In most macro discussions though we are considering a world with inflation. In many of these cases, inflation is the key facet; however, sometimes it is not. The reader or student has to be savvy about the context or inquire bluntly.

[9] Stephen Cecchetti and Kermit Schoenholtz, *Money, Banking, and Financial Markets,* p. 75 in the 4th edition, 2015.

usual situation in history.[10] It will continue in the future too but the question is the magnitude and whether we can extrapolate TVM magnitudes from the last fifty years for investments, both with and without risk, over the next fifty years. In modern times, we have seemingly maintained a 2 to 4% TVM for riskless investments and maybe 5 to 10% for risky (both after inflation, for example, assuming average inflation of about 2% our riskless might have been 4 to 6% and risky 7 to 12%). Going forward, given the increasingly large fraction of the world's population holding increasingly large amounts of assets for their time value, how much return can we all get on average?

The severe intellectual predicament today is not that people think interest is wrong, but that they think interest is automatic and guaranteed—and generally at a substantial rate of return. People expect a return to both risk-free and risky assets. Low rates, like we have now, are seen as an aberration. Many people expect that their bank savings will again pay few percent of interest. As for returns to risky investments, many of today's adults believe high rates are more normal than not. They base their belief on the events of the last few decades. During the 1980s through early 2000s, asset markets of all kinds rose greatly with long enough streaks of very substantial gains to embed the resounding idea of high returns. For example, during the five-year period from 1995 to 1999, the stock market was up about 30% per year, and bonds were also up significantly (long-term U.S. bonds rose about 12% per year). Such rates of return were unnaturally high, yet the recipients of those high asset-based returns did not feel uneasy. There was no moral outrage.

TVM as a theoretical construct is important to teach but we must dedicate more effort to pondering the empirical level of time value for our times. We apply TVM pervasively and are generous with the rate we use. TVM applies to a multitude of rates of return that we bandy about in many ways. We uniformly feel good about those rates being so high and talk about yield or yield-to-maturity (bonds), internal rate of return (enterprises), discount rate (streams of income), investments return (stocks, mutual funds, hedge funds, etc.), dividend yield (stocks), cost of capital (enterprises), growth rate, expected return (the hurdle return on investment in one asset given opportunities in comparable investments), opportunity cost, etc. For example, the dividend-discount model, which is the basic model for the price of a stock, hinges primarily on a discount rate. When we teach the model in business and social science courses we usually use a high rate of discount, ranging from about 5 to 10%. This yields a high value for stocks. Also, the high discount rate makes it possible to assume that the price of the stock in the future goes to zero in a relatively short period, about fifteen years. Therefore, that future price can be ignored. If we used a lower rate, like 4%, the model gives much lower value and the future price becomes less insubstantial. For another example, pensions use high rates of discounting the future (or, equivalently, high rates for returns to assets in pension portfolios). Their average rate is about 7%. It should probably be about 2%.

The high rate is one long-standing and probably spurious facet about rates of return. Another pathology is that we often assume a higher rate of return to our savings compared to the rate for our borrowings, making us instantly richer. For example, I have a mortgage at 4% and hold my retirement savings at an assumed 8%, giving me an automatic and substantial net gain.

Before the 20th century, GDP grew very slowly. For a thousand years up until about 1800 per capita GDP growth was about 0.1% per year and total GDP growth was about zero to 0.2% per year for the world as a whole.[11] Growth accelerated in the 1800s. Since about 1900, real GDP has grown about 3% per year and per capita has grown about 2% per year, at least in the countries with market economies. Today, we extrapolate our future with the same 3% total GDP growth we got in the last century. We do a similar

---

[10] Another theoretical rationale for positive time value is "impatience." Regardless of whether there is progress or not, if people are impatient they may be willing to pay interest for money provided now.

[11] "Estimating World GDP, One Million B.C. – Present," Website of Professor J. Bradford DeLong of U.C. Berkeley.

extrapolation of asset returns. For a thousand years, risk-free interest rates have been less than 1% and risk premiums, as best we can calculate them, have been very high (the risk premium is the amount of additional return investors desire to partake in investing, including equity or fixed income). Again, in more recent times certain asset markets have generated much higher rates of return, like 5 to 10%, and we extrapolate those returns. To top it off, we also typically assume little risk due to diversification and/or a tacit ultimate backing of all our financial markets by the government via a powerful and prescient central bank.

I infrequently meet a college student who does not know the idea of present value. Many know the idea that a stock's value equals the present discount value of its future dividends. In contrast, when I was twenty years old such concepts were less commonly known.

## I.1.D.a. 0 to 1% for Risk-Free & 3 to 5% for Ricky Portfolio

If you are averse to holding risky assets, expect something around 0%, or a little more, for your rate of return. This would apply to bank savings, certificates of deposit and money market funds. With inflation at around 1 to 2% you will get a slight negative rate of return. Put another way, as economists say, "Defer $1 of consumption today" and figure it will give you about $1 of consumption in the future. The main risk-free vessel for institutions, the 10-year U.S. note, might yield about 2.5% or about 1% real. Add in taxes and returns are even lower. Taken altogether, safe cash minus inflation yields around 0%.

There is a wide variety of risky investments. The usual tradeoff is greater risk gets greater return. There is no sure way of predicting exact returns in any year. For example, in 2013 the stock market rose over 30% and the housing market rose about 10 to 20% (variously depending on which housing data or sector in question). That means $1 in either of those assets became $1.30 and about $1.15, respectively. That's a good economic return for just holding assets over time. What can we say about future returns on average to assets like stocks, bonds, real estate, precious metals and more complicated assets like alternatives, commodities, derivatives, timber, etc. High rates of return in major asset classes from the 1980s through the early 2000s have left us with a warped idea of how much economic output we really have to spend on a going basis. Let's look at potential returns to the major asset classes, which we will discuss at length later in the book:

- **Cash**: 0% nominal; negative real. If cash' nominal rate increases, inflation will increase in step.
- **Gold**: Unpredictable; if gold's rate of return is high, high inflation is likely.
- **Housing or Real Estate**: Individuals' homes will lose value over time. They will have a negative rate of return. Investments in real estate assets and businesses may produce some rate of return but commensurate with that of stocks (see below).
- **Bonds**: Currently bonds are so highly priced[12] and interest rates so low that it is unlikely bonds will have anything other than a very low, or even negative, rates of return. Bond portfolios with long duration (long maturity) could be subject to large drops in price if general interest rates rise.
- **Stocks**: Stocks are also highly priced.[13] Specialists debate whether stock prices can rise and it depends on a multitude of factors. My guess is that stock rates of return will be about 3%, in real

---

[12] What does it mean for a bond to be highly priced? Why does a bond's price vary from its face, or par, value? Assume a thirty-year bond with a coupon rate of 5% was issued at par a few years ago. Over the years interest rates have tended down such the same kind of company can now issue debt at 3%. The price of our 5% coupon bond should have risen to about $166 such that its coupon divided by the bond price is about 3%. That is what has happened in recent years. Since general rates are low you must pay a high price to get the interest payments of bonds.

terms (or about 5% nominal). (We will examine returns to equities at length later, but a major theme of this treatise is: Stocks will generate modest returns because their returns depend on net earnings. Net earnings will be lower because taxes will be higher, and taxes will be higher because America is running chronic deficits and piling up debt.) Some experts recommend preferred stocks for higher yields, contending that dividend yields of certain preferred stocks or mutual funds of preferred stocks of 5 to 6% are available.[14] Such packages of preferreds are not too numerous, often undiversified and the dividends are not guaranteed. Preferreds, indeed, may be senior to common stock but they are not as secure as bonds. Preferreds may be overvalued presently and could drop in value significantly just like common stocks.

- **Alternatives**: Hedge funds, private equity, commodities, venture capital, collectibles, etc. offer no higher return without risk. Alternatives may have had some record of outsized returns in the past, but as more assets are invested in alternatives, as generally is the case, they end up buying the same stocks, bonds and claims, and returns converge on those for stocks, bonds and claims. Great amounts of money have been invested in alternatives. For example, in 2015 the very large Government Pension Investment Fund of Japan planned greatly increased allocations to alternatives. Rates of return to alternatives cannot be assumed to be high.

- **Real Assets**: Investments in land, infrastructure, commodities, timber, collectibles and other assets that have an outward appearance of greater longevity and substance than paper assets might appeal to some investors but real assets may have no better rates of return.

- **Labor Income**: In the sense of the return to education that leads to lucrative employment with potential wage growth (or even as mercenary as it might sound, investing in the educations of children whose earnings constitute an option payable to you in the future under certain circumstances). Children could also be constant burdens into their adulthood, but the parent can choose to ignore their needs as adults. My main comment is that even professions that currently represent job security and high pay—like nursing, engineering, computer work, various financial services like accounting, etc.—can easily be undermined in today's global economy. Therefore, the rate of increase of wages for those jobs may be very low.

The asset classes of cash, gold and housing represent minimal rate of return (or a bet, in the case of gold). Adding bonds, stocks and alternatives to your portfolio might provide a rate of return perhaps a bit above inflation. Assuming nominal rates of 5% on stocks or alternatives, 2% on bonds and about 0% on cash, gold and housing, then subtracting about 2% for inflation, people should get about 0 to 3% in real terms. Average people who use cash and housing might get closer to 0% while richer people might get returns at the higher end.

This new low rate of return reality compares to the post-1980 three decade-long run of positive returns in most asset classes. During this time even the faultless asset class of U.S. bonds, with no default risk and plenty of liquidity, had real returns in the positive range. People will scoff at this low rate scenario: It is terrifying and completely undermines the cozy and triumphant future we have planned for ourselves and believed to be bequeathed to our children. Financial planners and spokespersons for companies that manage people's money, including reputable names like Fidelity, Schwab, PIMCO and

---

[13] What does it mean for a stock to be highly priced? Compare the price of a share of a stock to the per share earnings. This is known as the P/E ratio. The higher this ratio the more you are paying for a stream of earnings. Specialists argue about the level of the P/E in markets today but it is easy to make the case that it is very high. We discuss the valuation of stocks later.
[14] "The 'Preferred' Path to Higher Returns," by Burton Malkiel, *The Wall Street Journal*, June 20, 2015. http://www.wsj.com/articles/the-preferred-path-to-higher-returns-1466374302

Vanguard, usually project nominal rates of return at greater than 5% per year for equities. (They do not commit and typically make projections in ranges. Examine their websites or read the commentary from their Chief Investment Officers, etc.). Canned financial planning software typically presents rates of return of 5% to 10% during your earning years and 4% to 8% during your retirement. Given such high rates, financial planners can recommend to their clients that an asset amount of about $1.7 million at retirement, at an age around mid-60s, would secure a comfortable retirement. At 1%, however, even with the hefty amount of $1.7 million, you would not have a luxurious retirement. Pension funds are relying on a rate of around 7.5%. Their proponents will say such rate can be hit with a diversified portfolio including stocks and bonds and, perhaps, some higher earning asset classes like real estate and private equity. The biggest promise maker of all, the U.S. government, assumes favorable rates of growth to support its entitlement programs.

Of course, the ultimate rate, upon which all other rates depend is GDP growth; and, as we have maintained, we consider that hefty. The GDP growth rate is built into most of the projections we make, both for government budgeting and for widespread valuing of assets as done by money managers (GDP growth determines top-line, i.e., revenue, growth for companies). Current leaders, including policy figureheads and Wall Street leaders, envision hefty GDP growth as probable, but they are just looking at their own lives. We will talk about GDP growth and its future level at great length later.

Our acceptance of high rates of return is prevalent not just among private investors but among all institutions and worker groups. I reiterate my earlier point: It is not that we despise high rates of return for assets. Instead, we believe in and count on high rates. For example, for many years the Harvard University endowment grew at large percentages and the school became extremely wealthy. This was widely viewed as normal and deserved. It was a source of great pride to the Boston area, demonstrating the brilliance of the professional population within this city of many great universities. Even the superb faculty of Harvard, including the most liberal sociology, history and English professors, did not decry the year after year of double-digit returns. The faculty grumbled a little about the fees that the money managers of Harvard's endowment received, and they also clamored for the school to divest from dirty industry holdings like fossil fuels. They did not, however, criticize high returns in general. Today, even after the sobering up period of 2008, big-time endowments expect hefty returns. Chief Investment Officers of university endowments set a benchmark around 8% as minimum rate of return.

We are gradually incorporating lower returns. Now that certain yields have been low for a protracted time, their low levels get embedded in many calculations. For example, when we calculate lost wages or lost business profits we discount. In the case of wages, think of a person who died prematurely losing years of annual earnings at some level. In the business example think of a business that loses claim to a stream of profit. With wages, courts usually discount by a risk-free rate, like a 10-year U.S. treasury (the exact term of the risk-free varies by the type of claim). They would either use the current rate or a historical average. Since rates have been low for many years, both current and historical averages are low. For business profit losses, we typically use a risk-free rate and add some risk premium germane to the specific case. The graphic below illustrates the dramatic difference that rates of return constitute for how savings grow over time.

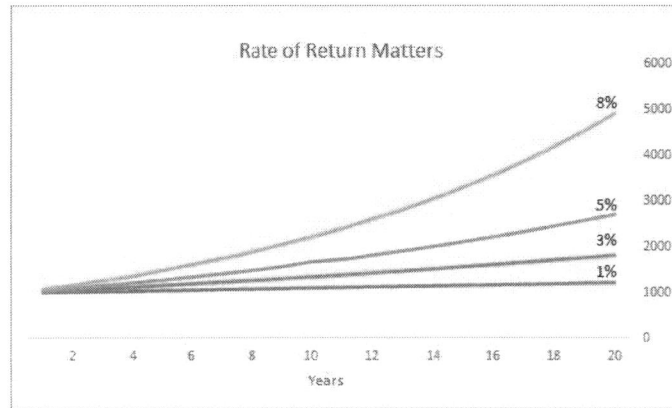

Rate of Return Matters

A $1,000 investment increasing in value at 8% per year adds up to nearly $5,000 over twenty years but at 1% per year it becomes only about $1,220.

## I.1.E. "Yields Rise When Prices Fall," The Great Fixed Income Truism, Is Obsolete

An exceedingly common line in articles on financial markets is, "Yields rise when prices fall." You also might hear varieties like, "The price of a bond and its yield are inversely related," or, "Increases in interest rates cause bond price to do down." Often, you will find statements like these as the single sentence of a paragraph in an article, emphasizing how fundamental the idea is. Strictly speaking, there is nothing inaccurate with these statements. They reflect a valid mathematical facet of bond valuation.[15] Yet this most often proclaimed relationship requires some reflection. First, there is something unnatural about the frequency and prominence in the way we invoke it. It implies a great and constant importance of the effects of changing interest rates on values of bond portfolios. It also seems to provide a cause and effect that we can benefit from. For example, if we anticipate changes in rates, we can construct bond portfolios that change in price in our favor. However, in general, investment in bonds should be primarily for coupon interest and not price changes. A bond portfolio should reward us roughly equal to the average of the coupon rates of the bonds in the portfolio.

Our economic experience in the last few decades (due to varying inflation and interest rates) has resulted in great price change in bonds. We have become accustomed to and obsessed with bond portfolio price changes. The incessant stating that "bond prices move inversely with rates" highlights our expectation of entitlement to high returns in bond portfolios due to price changes. We do not even mention coupon levels. For example, a typical article[16] describes municipal bond portfolios returning about 9% through approximately ten months of 2014. Coupons of bonds in municipal bond portfolios at the time averaged about 4 to 5%. Furthermore, since most of those bonds are priced over par their yields are even lower than the 4 to 5%. These facts are not mentioned in the article. The hefty 9% is understood to be due to bond prices going up. In this case, the bond prices happen to be increasing due primarily to the reaching for yield by managers of big bond portfolios. The article focuses on the allegedly strong balance sheets of

---

[15] For completeness I will explain the concept in simple terms. A naïve person would wonder why a change in general interest rates would affect the interest rate of the bond he already holds. After all, isn't the rate on his bond set? Indeed the coupon rate is fixed; however, his bond (if he attempted to sell it in the new interest rate environment) would vary in value. For example, if interest rates had increased the coupon payments on his bonds would be lower than those of new bonds so he would have to lower the price of his bond if you wanted to sell it.

[16] Brian Chappatta,"Munis Beating All Debt Shows Faith in Local Government," *Bloomberg.com*, November 4, 2014.

state and local governments as reasons underlying high returns though. The reader cannot discern the source of the bonds' high returns and, indeed, is given the impression that such high returns are normal.[17]

The punchline is that, going forward, investors should expect to get nothing more than approximately the weighted average of the coupons of their bond portfolios, and that weighted average will be low unless investors take risk by holding high coupon debt.

## I.1.F.a. 2008: Did We Avoid a Depression & Restore Economic Growth?

The average American may not have noticed, but today's America (since about 2010) boasts one of the greatest national achievements in modern times. We, unlike hesitant Europeans and Japanese and peoples of developing nations, prevailed in M&M. We avoided a depression after 2008 and restored our GDP growth to growth greater than that of peer nations, and we accomplished this with determined, sapient, pro-active policy. This is certainly the opinion of the U.S. media, the Academy, the majority of economic pundits and most politicians. This is also the prevalent thinking of the people currently in charge, the Baby Boom generation, who think they have done a good job providing for their progeny.

What has transpired since 2008 is an involved story with different interpretations. U.S. GDP growth held up a little better than that of certain comparable economies yet in per capita terms we did no better. Also, our debt increased more. The Keynesian promise of multiples of economic output from one piece of borrowing did not materialize. Our stock and housing markets recovered in value, but this can be viewed as an essential economic outcome making us truly better off or merely the froth of asset markets supported by expansionary monetary policy. Our unemployment rate went down, but our labor market in many respects is worse off than before. The drop in labor force participation negates our claim to a low rate of unemployment. We contend our policy worked as planned, but that is a post-hoc rationalization. If asked in 2008 what would happen over the ensuing years, our policy proponents would have said the labor market and real business investment would be the great beneficiary of policy, but the truth is that those sectors have struggled.

Did our Fed merely save financial derelicts and forestall a day of reckoning? In the meantime, the detrimental economic factors—like low rates on savings by the thrifty, lower wages, reduced job opportunities, etc.—were just too hard to see. The U.S. went from being relatively solvent to being virtually broke, but again, that is difficult to see until the day default happens. Did the Fed create much of the crisis itself? When Lehman Brothers collapsed in 2008, some analysts believe that the Fed added to a panic, causing additional commerce to retract with markets reacting largely on the cue of the Fed. The Fed itself became a lucky recipient in the crisis by swooping in and acquiring assets at cheap prices, which it would unload later at gains.

For another contemporary example of a dramatic v. prosaic story of M&M policy, consider the case of Japan. From early 2013 continuing into 2014, under new, invigorated political leadership, Japan embarked on bold economic policy. This included monetary, fiscal and even structural policy designed to revive the economy with the intention of getting GDP growth up and breaking the cycle of deflation. This was a break from supposedly tentative policy of the. It received plaudits for its boldness. Many policy proponents and a large part of the financial press touted the policy as a success with financial markets responding favorably and economic data showing some improvement. In reality, Japan ostensibly achieved

---

[17] Returns can go both ways. For example, during 2014 the high-yield bond market rose but only due to coupon payments. The Bank of American Merrill Lynch High Yield Index was up about 2.4% for the year, yet bond prices were down 4.1%, and interest accounted for 6.5% of the yield.

nothing new because the new policy was not much more than a devaluing of its currency to engender more exporting.

## I.1.F.b. Or Deepen Indebtedness and Weaken Our Already Waning Economy?

*We are broke!* We are in debt and running chronic large deficits increasing our debt every year. U.S. debt is weighty even when using the conventional measures of debt, which have flaws. If we do a truer accounting, like an accrual set of books (i.e., taking future taxes and spendings into consideration), our nation is altogether much more in debt, and we will develop this case later. It does not take a lot to get much larger true debt (we call it the fiscal gap) numbers like $50 trillion or more. Almost every trend—government budgets at all levels, population, education, etc.—look poised to exacerbate our debt problem. Official economic projections are overly favorable: We have long tolerated a biasing of the case in our favor. In U.S. official projections, we have total fertility at two (in other words, two children per each woman), GDP growth at 2%, immigration at over 1,000,000 per year and life expectancy at about 85 years. All those numbers could easily be estimated to be much less favorable. It is hard, of course, to project out far into the future and it might be a disservice to be overly conservative; yet we are committing our children to obligations based on these estimates.

The realization of this decline became acute with the economic events commencing about 2008 (which I often refer to as "2008 ff" to signify the continuing economic decline and the policy response to it as opposed to the formal recession of 2008 to 2009). Although touted as saving us from worse and achieving that desired M&M function of beating back the trough of business cycles, our crisis policy that played out mainly 2009 through 2012, has done nothing but hide and hasten our general economic decline. The federal government is broke, and our big states are, too. Jobs and real wages are down. Our central bank, recently with a solid balance sheet of nearly $1 trillion in net assets (only currency, a liability that never gets called, as its main liability), now is a multi-trillion dollar entity with a mix of assets and liabilities that can cast doubt on the bank's long-term solvency. Pensions are altogether more insolvent. Housing values and equity are reduced in many sectors and for much of the populace. Just to pay for what we got before, our taxes must go up.

The heightened competition sometimes appears overwhelming and iconic notions add to the struggle—for example, ideas like that we are the leading superpower, which perhaps only burdens us as the world's cop, and that our currency is the world's reserve currency, which perhaps makes us borrow too freely. Ultimately, we are more prone to "Solutionism": an assumption that a prompt solution to fundamental problems exists, and we need not engage in sacrifice or long-term planning. Our solutionism creates further economic loss.

We are suckers for lucky breaks and general good fortune, like 8% annual rates of return to investments. Leading financial figureheads blithely cite such rates. We persist in economic comfort like believing that our economy is not below its 3% GDP trend growth and that our debt position is not that severe. Also, we have plenty of time and resources to rectify problems. In general, we are confident we can turn it around when we need to. We arc gullible for pipe dreams like that the housing market has recovered and high prices of housing in certain markets being a source of great GDP growth. As I propose, the underlying intellectual pin is M&M: the fallacy that our magic men can lower rates and/or stimulate the economy back to prosperity.

## I.1.G. Solutions Forever

Perhaps more than any people on the planet, Americans never doubt a way out. There is always a solution—nay a multitude of solutions–and anyone who says differently is a not thinking correctly and/or lacks compassion for his fellow citizens. We can "clever" our way out of an economic problem by getting more economic output through mastery of M&M and great entrepreneurship. Every day we wake up with the privilege to scheme to tackle problems again, even if nothing has changed. You see this in popular discourse. For example, in book reviews it is very common that the reviewer will state that an author does a good job of relating current problems, but falls short in proposing solutions. People are seemingly convinced that there must be (new) solutions. Often people scold me for not proposing an alternative solution or advise me that publishers will not accept a book unless it has a conclusion with positive actions to take. Journalists consider solutions integral. When Edward Prescott and Finn Kydland won the economics Nobel Prize in 2004 they were disparaged by *Business Week* columnist Peter Coy that their contributions did not propose activist macro. Coy apparently believed that the activist M&M case was fact and economists with good intentions have positive impact on our society.[18]

In macroeconomic matters, we typically contend two major routes of solution: (1) the conservative choice of less government spending, which means hardship for the poor but prosperity for the rest and (2) the liberal choice, which means more government spending and perhaps higher taxes for the rich to pay for it. You might call the first austerity and the second Keynesianism. The key, however, is that one or the other must work, assuming we really get behind it, and indeed we can choose—if we stop squabbling. I experience this in teaching college students. A few classes into the semester, after doubting the beneficial outcomes of both the Keynesian solution and of the austerity solution, the question comes (usually from one of the earnest students sitting in the front row): "Then…," with an importuning look on her face, "what is the solution?"

In class, I sometimes invoke the microeconomic truism, "There are no solutions, only tradeoffs." I spike that with a statement about our current macroeconomic situation that we have to take a write-down in our standard of living. For example, most people agree one "solution" to the growing cost of our entitlements programs is to adjust Social Security payments to a measure of inflation that will rise less in the future.[19] Yet even if it decreases the cost of Social Security, it represents a tradeoff to Social Security recipients and prospective recipients who likely already figured in generous adjustments for inflation. Someone comes out a loser: there is no "solution" that makes everyone better off.

A recent example of our gullibility for solutions and failure to acknowledge tradeoffs is student loans. Since about 2008, outstanding student loan debt has increased greatly, topping one trillion dollars. As we examined this situation reflecting our high cost of funding higher education, we looked for solutions with a preference for a one-time major fix. All kinds of proposals to move student loan financial burdens from one point of time to another (and/or from one group of payers to another), were proposed—all purporting to mitigate the burden and make education beneficial for all. The remarkable aspect is how oblivious proponents of student loan solutions were to high costs, waste in higher education, students enrolling in inefficient programs, potential adverse economic incentives caused by proposed solutions, etc.

America faces gaps in the major sub-sectors of its economy including government financing (or taxes), pensions (including Social Security), health care spending, education and housing. We propose grand, macro "one-time blow out" solutions rather than micro solutions acknowledging tradeoffs and

---

[18] "Nobel Winners Without Much Impact," *Business Week*, Oct. 24, 2004. http://www.bloomberg.com/bw/stories/2004-10-24/nobel-winners-without-much-impact

[19] The "chain-weighted" method of calculating inflation that supposedly does not overstate inflation as much as the non-chained inflation.

losses to some parties. Fixing these large economic systems may simply be impossible. The clichés reveal the impossibility:

- "No person will be excluded." Any health care or education solution is termed this way.
- Benefits for "existing recipients" will not be reduced. Most pension reform proposals say this.
- "Means testing" or "caps" will apply, but only to the rich. This is popular in housing finance reforms.
- Arbitrary numbers, sliding scales, cutoffs and other demarcations are thrown around. For example, new pension schemes will have contributions of at least 3% but no more than 8%, representing reasonable ranges but not based on economic reality.
- Government units, like state and federal, will "collaborate."
- Different household structures will be accommodated in "fair" ways.
- The "appropriate incentives" for virtuous and productive economic behavior will be exploited– indeed, we relish market mechanisms and self-interest bringing out our best.

## I.1.G.a. Solution Clichés

During the 2008 crisis, particularly in the last quarter of 2008, the op-ed pages presented daily solutions: rescue the housing market, nationalize the banks, create a big buyout fund, create a "bad bank" to sop up all the bad debt, cut taxes, open up the borders, engage in big-time fiscal policy, extend consumer protection, end "fair value" pricing, abolish Fannie Mae and Freddie Mac, increase regulation, reduce regulation, and so on. The solution champions broke into two groups: (1) single cause/solution and (2) bunch of causes and cures, which when taken together would provide a general solution. Housing was the most popular and enduring theme, and scolding banks perhaps the second. Solutions-talk was quick to cliché involving terms like better supervision and regulation, stronger financial institutions, shutting down Fannie Mae and Freddie Mac, transparency, frameworks for recovery, stabilize, etc. Many of the solutions had a nativist appeal, like opening up the borders to wealthy immigrants who would bring money, tax rich Americans abroad, repatriate profits, buy American (a major feature of our various government stimulus programs), etc.

Nobody proposed recognizing a marking down of our standard of living and putting it into effect by, e.g., raising taxes to pay for our shortfalls. Nor was the emphasis on long-term improvements to the economy. The prevailing belief is that solutions must be marked by a relatively prompt return to more GDP growth. The same attitude prevailed over the years and when analyzing similar crises abroad. During 2011, ongoing economic problems in Eurozone took a turn for the worse to the point where a crisis (termed the Eurozone Crisis) was deemed. We craved a one-shot, definitive resolution. By early 2012, we seemingly developed a Euro Crisis fatigue and even though the collective economic conditions were not much better, we felt a solution had been secured and breathed a sigh of relief: "Now that the Euro Crisis is contained," was the way it was put by many pundits. By 2014 though, Eurozone faced about the same level of crisis. Again we called on central bankers to rectify it with definitive actions. In this instance, a European quantitative easing program was conceived and initiated in early 2015. Today's Eurozone continues in relative economic weakness.

Even the toughest talking and most earnest analysts of our current problems, such as Laurence Kotlikoff, the Boston University professor renowned for analysis on our dire fiscal position, succumbs to solutions that belie grave tradeoffs. In some of his writings, Kotlikoff proposes economic solutions including building a whole new city, hiring workers by lowering prevailing wages, job-sharing (in the form of a mass hiring of unemployed paid for with pay cuts by the employed) and getting corporate America to pitch in by simply calling a grand meeting of the CEO's of the largest companies and commanding them to hire.[20] His proposals hinge on various debatable ideas including being able to reform taxes with a simpler and more lucrative tax system, the ability to invest in securities markets at high rates of return and the willingness of people to sacrifice and work harder for the same income.

We face a stark, ostensible economic crisis and a longer-term economic dilemma following it, yet we regularly assume neat, comprehensive solutions. We fail to recognize that there is no quick solution and that even long-term solutions will be so costly that they are not true solutions. We crave and ceaselessly hypothesize cheap ways to create growth including broad methods like "lowering the rate" or focused, smaller methods like housing credits or "Cash for Clunkers."

The list below describes some areas that are broached as solutions to our general economic problems along with comment on how realistic they are.

## Education

We have been proposing and implementing fixes for America's schools for my entire lifetime. At this point in time we concede that we spend a vast sum on education, more than any other society. Therefore, for the most part, we do not propose spending more money on education. Rather, we recommend changes that fine tune, perhaps spend more in higher education (which is our strength) or in basic and early education, which supposedly has a disproportionate effect on people's success.

Every politician denounces the poor state of K-12 education and touts some program or another that worked in a certain school at a certain time. President Obama did this routinely.[21] One cliché solution is rewarding teachers with incentive pay. We have done this for 30 years and perhaps it has had some success. We also often related the story of the individual reformer—the outsider brought in to fix a school system. For example, education crusader Michelle Rhee ran the Washington DC schools from 2007 to 2010. She achieved about as excellent a result as any person could in fixing urban school problems and, indeed, she made some improvements. Her efforts did not alter the basic reality that education in many of our school systems has so many fundamental impediments that we cannot position many of our young to become high earning adults.

Our higher education system is not fixable by more resources or by better use of fewer resources. Our higher education is a multi-purpose institution, including consumption and social upbringing as goals—and not simply the training of our labor force. For example, at the higher education level we emphasize a relatively non-practical liberal arts curriculum. Can we convert that to lucrative fields like accounting, computer science, nursing and engineering and be better off? We send many people not motivated for college to college. One of the comical facets of modern day higher education is that many schools spend significant resources disciplining college students like keeping them from consuming alcohol and exhorting them to attend class. Another facet of fixing education prominent today is making education more affordable and efficient at placing students in jobs. Some pundits propose to eliminate law school and make law an undergraduate course; undergrads can do it. Other pundits propose the direct opposite: They advise elimination of undergraduate business education because people at this age have not learned basic skills. These reformers argue that young people should get liberal educations and only do business education in graduate school.

---

[20] "Five Prescriptions to Heal Economy," *Bloomberg.com*, September 28, 2011, and other writings.
[21] For examples, he made such cases with the Bruce Randolph School in Denver, Colorado in his 2011 State of the Union Address and at an appearance at the Worcester, Massachusetts public schools in June 2014.

Given the current high cost of higher education and the great increases in student loans, initiatives to reform education are omnipresent. They are problematic and fraught with contradictions. President Obama supported making colleges and universities demonstrate how a dollar spent on education will translate into more dollars in earnings. This "solution" to the high cost of education would be virtually un-implementable, requiring much information about what and how students study, work, form households and even form their life's aspirations. Higher education today is largely consumption and not investment. College expenditures are largely consumption-related like luxury dormitories, fine dining, sports, activities, health care and psychology services, etc. rather than educational investment. The expensive physical plant, like the comfortable seating and high quality classroom acoustics, might make learning more relaxing but do not increase student productivity.

Another prominent education solution, borne of desperation from the large increase in college costs and borrowing, is forgiving and reducing student debt depending on how much money graduates make after college. Every pundit and his brother jumped on the bandwagon of education debt solutions. Prominent financial journalist David Wessel noted, "one prudent way…linking repayment to income. The more you earn, the faster you pay back. If college really doesn't pay off, you pay less.[22]" Education should be viewed as a microeconomic choice made by individuals, yet it is treated as a macroeconomic quantity. The macro solution involves sweeping initiatives by government dictum applied across the spectrum of a sector. These efforts are absurd.

To examine further, paying student debt depending on the level of future earnings creates a variety of biases toward sub-optimal job and life choices. Those who choose lucrative fields and did so for their monetary rewards will not be happy. They will also be treated unfairly when they bear the full cost of their choices. If salaries in pecuniary fields go down over time, as may likely happen as more and more young people choose high paying fields, you may end up making less and having had your earnings taken as part of a government program. Loan forgiveness would constitute a subsidy of generally richer people's consumption. Since there would have to be some time limit put on the eligibility of loan forgiveness you would get extreme gaming of the system. For example, a married couple with one spouse owing high debt would be incented to delay work effort by that partner while the other spouse supports the household until the student debt is forgiven. Child rearing would also be gamed to the government loan forgiveness program.

## *Immigration*

Both political sides propose bringing in more immigrants (typically with job skills and/or financial capital) as a source of economic growth. This is perhaps the first and most common short answer to a query on fixing the economy. The reality is that the net effects of the immigrants who come to America, regardless of how carefully we select them for their supposed economic contributions, could be minor–or even negative. This also represents an entitlement-based way of thinking, as if we owe our greatness to a constant supply of free talent from outside our borders. We often reference our great history of immigration, citing copious facts and figures of how many enterprises, both past and present, were created by immigrants. We note the high fraction of present-day tech companies that have foreign-born founders.

There are a variety of economics-based immigration programs: immigrants with work skills (the H-1B program), immigrants with special skills (the EB-1, "Extraordinary Ability") and immigrants who provide capital (the EB-5, "Employment Creation"). U.S. businesses apply for the H-1B visas supposedly to get skilled workers not otherwise available in the (American) labor force. Businesses say these skilled

---

[22] *The Wall Street Journal*, "How to Fix the Student-Loan System," November 7, 2013, p. A2.

foreigners are critical and some economists contend that such immigrants create economic spillover. Some politicians want to increase the number of these visas available. In 2015, 85,000 H-1B visas were offered by the U.S. government and promptly snatched up. Critics contend businesses prefer malleable, cheap foreign labor. They cite critical cases like when a company hires under the visa program while simultaneously laying off existing workers.[23]

Formerly the rules pertaining to the EB-5 visas (the capital-bearing immigrant program) were strict. Immigrants were expected or assumed to fund real enterprise like factories or retail outlets. Most investments under EB-5 are financial investments often for real estate ventures. Since most of these ventures would have received other financing in the absence of the immigrant's investment, the only net gain is the difference between the rate that the immigrant loaned the funds for and that of the other lender which might be virtually nothing.

Another facet of immigration as economic solution concerns immigrants as ready purchasers of housing. Such buying supports the housing markets and has spillover effects including wealth effects from higher house prices and spending effects on housing accoutrements. This "immigrant as glorious home buyer" is widely touted. One facet demonstrating how far-fetched it is is that the typical immigrant home buyer is rich buying expensive properties in exclusive markets, like rich Chinese buying properties in California. In order to get economic benefits to average Americans relies on extreme trickle-down effects.

The raw truth about immigrants is that the marginal immigrant is likely a net reduction in standard of living to the existing American citizenry. Our history of our great immigrant past is irrelevant to today. Another potentially adverse development is that the U.S. could experience the emigration of talented and wealthy people: Americans facing higher taxes and greater constraints on their lives will leave.

## Tax System Overhaul and Abundant Sources of Untaxed Income

Tax reform is an eternally favorite source of additional funding for America. This economic reform gets support from both liberal and conservative. We posit getting more revenue for our government without tradeoffs or costs. Two main fixes are proposed: (1) swap our current tax system for whole new systems like a value-added or flat tax or (2) rectify specific flaws in the various taxes. It is dubious that sweeping new systems would have fewer flaws or overall less inefficiency, and collections of minor fixes are unlikely to raise large amounts. For example, we could remove the mortgage interest deduction from income taxes and raise more tax, but that subverts our cherished national policy of supporting housing. We will address taxes in greater detail later.

Taxing unreported income is another magical solution for America's deficit. It is estimated that we could raise about $400 billion in tax on $2 trillion in unreported income. If people had to report that income though they likely would curtail the earning of a large fraction of it. Also, much of the income is simply unreportable. Only if there were an IRS agent standing by when making a drug deal or hiring a hooker could we collect this tax revenue.

## Job Creation

Creating jobs is another perennial refrain, but actually creating net, permanent, desirable jobs is an elusive goal except through long-term investment and sacrifice. We can, of course, temporarily create jobs

---

[23] Southern California Edison laid off hundreds of existing workers and replaced them with H-1B visa holders. "Complaints of IT layoffs at utility continue to stir reaction," by Patrick Thibodeau, *Computerworld*, February 19, 2015. http://www.computerworld.com/article/2886369/so-cal-edisons-it-layoffs-are-abuse-of-h-1b-program-says-us-lawmaker.html

with a government spending program. This will not represent a net employment gain as much as an initial bit of labor substitution. To a liberal, job creation is simple. The government can borrow and spend and then jobs are ostensibly created. To a conservative, job creation is tougher but still achievable. Conservatives' proscription for job creation is cutting taxes on businesses and entrepreneurs, which will incentivize them to expand their enterprises. The latter has a germ of validity but the magnitudes are debatable. Also, it depends upon tax cuts which are problematic in a society already running deficits.

We still indulge old schemes and supposedly new ones. U.S. states create jobs by giving tax and other breaks to businesses. It appeared to work to some extent. Certain states showcase the well-known companies with lofty facilities brought within their state borders. For example, in 2016 General Electric agreed to relocate its headquarters from Connecticut to Massachusetts due largely to government incentives. Studies of these efforts show that one state's gains come at the expense of other states. Also, net gains to a state after tax losses and government expenditures are often small. Another favorite theory or platitude is "job-matching," which posits that there are jobs available and workers willing to take them but that the market does not get the supply to equal demand. Policy recommendations are various, often involving government bureaucracy to facilitate job search. It is not clear that jobs go wanting. Another story is that we chronically lack workers with certain skill sets and we must train more people than ever before. The usual recommendation is increasing education at the community college level, which focuses on vocational training. Again, the failure of markets to work and the opportunity to enhance market outcomes is minimal. Another job creator is bringing in immigrants, which we discussed above.

Creating a job is an age-old endeavor. To demonstrate how extensively we have pondered the labor market, when I was a graduate student, specializing in labor economics, in the 1980s, the wrap on labor improvement schemes was that the only successful and promising program was on-the-job training (or, "OJT"). Other labor schemes simply did not pay off. OJT (which is improving workers skills once they were already employed) could advance existing workers' careers and open up entry-level jobs for newcomers. Even back then, though, OJT was considered pretty played out.

### Rectifying Perverse Economic Behavior (aka Behavioral Economics)

Adjustments to people's economic behavior, a field known as Behavioral Economics and sometimes referred to informally as "nudging," represent a hope to make our people more economically virtuous and, therefore, alleviate economic deprivation. Behavioral Economics is also a new variety of government economic policy that is not macro. Instead, it calls on supervising the economic lives and choices of people individually and in certain groups. Its main proscription is encouraging people to save for their retirements, but it involves a myriad of other methods to ensure that people "make the most of their money," including in education, debt management, investing, etc. This line of policy has another primary goal of encouraging people to live healthier lives (eating right, doing preventative medicine and exercising). This thrust is ostensibly not about the economy except that, supposedly, the high cost of people's poor lifestyles is an economic burden to society and, therefore, a justified focus of government policy.

Behavioral Economics is a popular area today. It is viewed as new and efficacious in results and will likely expand as we face continuing economic problems, but it is a flawed concept both in theory and specific applications. For example, in recent years we have tried to encourage people to save by making the creation and funding of IRA's, 401-k's, etc. available without the people having to perform any task or even assent to the savings. This constitutes forced savings. Advocates say it works, but the evidence is mixed. Typically a forced savings program does result in more people partaking and funding more initially but over time people tend to drop out or borrow against their perceived savings. The long-term effects are hard to pin down too. Perhaps the more we substitute for individual's responsibility in saving, the more people may relinquish responsibility for their well-being in other ways. Also, forced savings is oddly in direct opposition to policies of M&M, which encourage people to spend. For example, in M&M policy we support the housing market by incentivizing people to borrow to buy homes. Once they have bought homes we even hope they will spend more to furnish the homes, thereby stimulating the economy. With Behavioral Economics we compel people to save for retirement. We will talk about Behavioral Economics at great length later.

## Macro Policy Solutions

Examining macro is the main thrust of this book, but I mention macro policy here briefly as a variety of the "quick-and-dirty" grand solutions that commentators employ. They believe policy works and the bigger, the better. For example, policy could take the form of a much larger fiscal policy including either more spending and/or tax cutting. During the post-2008 period economists like Paul Krugman have espoused substantially increasing spending stimulus with some suggesting multiple trillions of dollars— even as much $10 trillion. Another major M&M policy could be relaxing inflation standards by targeting a higher level of inflation, perhaps around 4 to 6%. Kenneth Rogoff and others have suggested this in recent years. On the following pages, we will discuss in detail whether or not M&M works in any case and, if so, at what magnitudes.

## Regulation Reform

We propose reducing regulation, increasing it or even doing both actions. This might seem contradictory but we are ever-sanguine about our ability to rectify and fine tune. Reducing regulation is the refrain of conservatives while liberals harp on an increase. With a reduction, we have to ask why we originally adopted the regulations we are now looking to remove? Surely, some regulation is unnecessary or out-of-date, but how non-optimal should the bulk of our historical regulations be? If we add new regulations, we have to ask something similar. In the 1980s and 1990s, we deregulated extensively, especially in the financial sector and did this with relative conviction. Following 2008, we re-regulated the financial sector much more strictly (notably, with the Dodd-Frank Act of 2010), largely renouncing our prior de-regulation. However, we simultaneously proposed relaxing other existing regulation. For example, under the Jumpstart Our Business Startups Act (JOBS Act) commenced 2012, we allow small companies to sell a wide variety of securities to small investors who are usually considered vulnerable. We will discuss regulation in the section on new central banking policies.

## Housing

We have referred to our excessive support of the housing market. One great symbol of our housing economics is the government sponsored housing apparatus, which consists of many entities, primarily two large government-sponsored mortgage-bundlers: Fannie Mae and Freddie Mac. Throughout the post-2008 period, we heard about eliminating these giants, usually with blustery talk like, "Shut them down!"—as if getting rid of their debts and dropping government support of housing is a short-order task. Specific proposals–and there have been many of them–vary and have gone nowhere. One proposal was to close these companies and create a number of housing entities that would readily be assumed by the private sector. Under one scheme, the private sector would be responsible for the first 10% of losses in the housing market. Again, though, the proposal went nowhere because of the glaring flaw that if the private sector did not step up with the 10%, the federal government would have to. We will discuss housing and its flaws as an economic wealth creator later.

## Conservative and Liberal Proposals

Right-wing solutions proposed by business leaders and conservative economists rely on grand effects of free markets. Leading free markets academic John Taylor recommends adhering to basic principles including rule of law, predictable policy, individual reliance, market determination of consumption and production, lower taxes, etc. Such basic principles are valid as part of a general improvement in economic efficiency, but they do not deliver us from our debt and deficit without higher taxes and spending cuts. Also, right-wing solutions are not palatable to all people. Left-wing solutions—largely raising taxes on rich people or engaging in large, Keynesian spending programs—are unlikely to increase GDP growth and probably likely to weaken U.S. business advantages and not rectify government debt and deficit. Specific liberal proposals such as increases in minimum wages are touted to have copious benefits to incomes and productivity and minor adverse side-effects, but the opposite may be more likely.

## Leadership

We admire certain leaders (especially great business people) and turn to them for solutions as if they could vault the country ahead in the same way they grew their companies. For example, a few years ago General Electric CEO Jeffrey Immelt and other business leaders volunteered for a "jobs council." They presented their recommendations,[24] which were old ideas such as cutting red tape, more community college partnerships to train needed workers, creating construction jobs (the idea of putting construction workers to work is loved by all), helping small business with government programs (as if government help can really make a business), investing in energy projects and easing visa requirements to bring in the free-spending tourists. For another example of asking the great leader, Goldman Sachs head Lloyd Blankfein recommended avoiding recessions while also truing up fiscal deficits, developing resources effectively, tax reform and bringing in the "talented" immigrants.[25] After reading these cliché-ridden proposals, I often wonder if the authors believe their ideas or if, when they speak candidly with friends, they laugh their writings off. The lesson of leadership is that running a company is different from leading the economy.

## Overseas Wealth

American companies supposedly hold substantial money "offshore" and keep it there due to taxes they would have to pay if the money was repatriated. The money abroad exists, but that it would or should return to America is debatable. The money is American in name perhaps, but, if a company earns profit offshore, re-invests in plants and equipment offshore, transfers patents to offshore subsidiaries, etc., then is that money substantially American? Companies will prefer to keep earnings and allocate future capital where markets and growth originate, which is largely abroad for the U.S. companies with money offshore. Even if they want to use their overseas money to invest in America, they can raise funds by borrowing against their cash in the form of swaps contracts. Also, the U.S. corporate tax system and other burdens of reporting and compliance required by the U.S. are compelling factors to keep money abroad and locate future enterprise abroad. Finally, the empirical evidence is not favorable. In 2004 companies were allowed

---

[24] Summarized in an op-ed in *The Wall Street Journal*, June 13, 2011.
[25] *The Wall Street Journal*, "The Business Plan for American Revival," November 14, 2012, p. A17.

to repatriate cash at a lower tax rate and the main effects were stock buybacks and no increase in investment or research and development.

## *Smorgasbord of Solutions*

Of course, there is no constraint of a solitary solution and typically proponents propose multiple initiatives to chip away at a problem. Any op-ed piece on fixing the economy will typically have three or four component solutions. Virtually every presidential State of the Union speech runs through a list that includes some or all of the following buzz words: small business, tax reform, education, jobs mismatch, restoring venerable manufacturing, community colleges, immigrants, exports, cutting red tape, etc.

This invoking of a long list of items is duplicitous. It relieves the policy proposer of the reality that the individual solution components have been analyzed, over-utilized and are up against brick walls. For example, a 2016 *Wall Street Journal* article proposes nine policies to revitalize U.S. manufacturing all of which are clichés including subsidizing exports, switching to a value-added tax, managing the value of the dollar, removing regulation, spending more on R&D, creating regional centers, working with community colleges, reassessing costs of offshoring and counting/valuing jobs differently.[26]

## I.1.H. Defunct Ideas of Economics & Markets

Every day over a million highly-educated professionals ponder the economic lot of America. They analyze, propose theories, collect data (and more data), organize research sessions, collaborate with other experts, inculcate the young, promulgate to the people, survey, apply new methods, implement policies, etc. They have pondered enough already. By dint of our brilliance and dedication, it is safe to assume that we have already squeezed whatever economic output and efficiency we can from our society. At this point in time these efforts and all the intellectual constructs that go with them have one thing in common: They are dead and gone.

- Macroeconomics, monetary economics, central banks, the U.S. Fed, Keynesianism, monetarism, etc.
- Government policies, including both short-term Keynesian "stimulate the economy" type and the long-term "increase the productivity of the economy" type.
- GDP as a measure of our well-being. Growth by demand. Growth by spending. Growth by low rates. Consumer confidence. Wealth effects. Housing as the purchase that pays for itself and drives the economy.
- Unconventional monetary policies like quantitative easing, negative interest rates, forward guidance, etc.
- Behavioral economics and other manipulations of people's choices.
- High rates of return to assets. Diversified portfolios that defy risk. Diversifying over time (aka "stocks for the long run"). Market masters who beat the market.
- Great leaders with a vision and cure for our economic woes. Entrepreneurs with visions beyond their own businesses and proscribe devices for the betterment of the people at large. Ph.D.'s and academic geniuses.
- Science and methods, surveys, forecasting, economic indicators, models, etc.

---

[26] "How to Revitalize U.S. Manufacturing," *The Wall Street Journal*, by Robert Tita, June 7, 2016. http://www.wsj.com/articles/how-to-revitalize-u-s-manufacturing-1465351501

- Glorious economic triumphs of the 1980s, 1990s and early 2000s—the Great Moderations, bond bull markets, etc. and the bold policy following 2008 that saved America from a depression.

Of course, in the real world these concepts and constructs are alive and well. For example, central banks are bigger and more controlling of the economy than ever before; financial service firms that construct securities portfolios that "beat the market" offer a multitude of high-paying jobs; universities and research institutes produce reams of research on behavioral economics; etc. They are dead intellectually, however; so what remains? The answer to that question is microeconomics. We must resort to the parables of micro (tradeoffs, choice, utility, profit, competition, substitution, etc.) both at an intellectual and operational level. A middle-aged person may have a hard time accepting the paradigm shift that is occurring now, but young people should place their bets on the end of M&M and the mighty asset markets.

## I.1.H.a. Paean to Economics

Economics is the premier social science—perhaps even the greatest science in general, if you allow that the study of people in society is a cut harder than physical phenomena. Within economics, microeconomics constitutes the most superb set of parables relevant to human life. When applied modestly, macroeconomics constitutes insight, too. The folly of modern M&M is that its various promoters, including the tweed-coats, central bankers, economists, forecasters, media, etc., purloined the macro parables and made them into stories of control of national fortunes and deliverance of the poor. Even Keynesianism is a compelling parable. Peddlers and over-explainers bend macro with Keynesian assumptions, multipliers, consumer confidence, wealth effects from low rates, spendings, etc.; but that is their folly.[27]

One of the most ridiculous facets of economic discussion is the incessant carping about economists being intransigent in their use of simplifying assumptions. To put it more bluntly, economists fail to recognize the real world around them and, if only they did, they could have much better models. This is ridiculous. When I was a graduate student, I once approached a professor with a proposal to rebuild macroeconomics with "sensible" ideas. He asked, "What do you mean by sensible?" Of course, I had no answer. Every student of economics goes through such trial and error. The economics field is open and competitive. There is no shortage of alternative schools, projects, conferences, etc. If you subscribe to an alternative theory feel free to, "Put your model on the board."

Debates about math in economics are inane. First of all, reasonably advanced math training (like calculus) is requisite to sophisticated training for the study and teaching of economy. It cannot be achieved with raps sessions. Second, the majority of economic research done after graduate training does not require advanced math. Third, the field is generally competitive with a wide variety of forums. If a better way of describing the economy without using math exists, scholars are free to present it. Critics of math's role in economics relate the story that smart non-mathematical economists cannot get academic positions and are excluded from important policy discussions. This is ridiculous. Indeed, a small subset of economists, almost exclusively at universities, does specialize in highly mathematical economics. They do not control empirical research or preclude its discussion. Fourth, math is predominate in many others fields and they

---

[27] The same correctness of ideas but misuse of them by practitioners is valid in the often maligned and scapegoated models of financial economics. These models include the Capital Asset Pricing Model ("CAPM"), the Sharpe Ratio, Black-Scholes, the dividend-discount model, etc.—all of which are great parables and accurate baselines for describing financial markets and investing and even for making decisions. That Wall Street peddlers applied them loosely is a different story.

receive no criticism for it. Theoretical math is pervasive academic mathematics itself. Also, most physics is theoretical. For example, string theory is pure math and has no real-world application.

The debates about wrong-headed economics are almost always demarcated by a blatant partisanship. Critics of economics and its mathematical methods are usually liberals. They accuse the economics profession of being blind to the simple reality that government policy and Keynesianism have been proven effective.

## I.1.H.b. Contending Sciences: Psychology & Physics

Comparing sciences is mostly meaningless. Of all the sciences, including both physical and social sciences, economics is often singled out as a particularly unsuccessful and contrary field. Its intellectual failures, critics contend, have greatly impoverished the people. This is unjust and moronic. Economics is no more flawed than any other discipline.

Economics' main contender among social sciences is psychology.[28] Analysts critical of mainstream economics often cite psychology experts who express shock at the simplistic assumptions of economists. Presumably, psychologists work off of much more realistic formulations of human nature than economists. Psychology has little record of success, however, and many of its prominent areas of research (like multiple personalities or repressed memories) are dubious—if not altogether ridiculous. We may be able to change people's erratic behavior with drugs, perhaps, but the cases of people seeing their psychiatrist and being better off are rare. Critics of economics remark that the science has been unsuccessful at measuring and managing financial market risk thus resulting in booms and busts like 2008. Markets are just as volatile today as they were a hundred years ago. A similar sweeping condemnation can be made of psychology. There is just as much psychological distress in society today as there was in the past.

Among hard sciences, physics is often the field chosen for comparison with economics. Physicists relish mocking economics, characterizing it as senseless science because of its over-reliance on theory and math and its avoidance of obvious ostensible real world applications.[29] There is no shortage of physicists turned armchair economists who mock economic models, yet physics is just as readily derided. Its theories are often abstract ideas based on assumptions demonstrated solely by math, such as string theory and multiple/parallel universes. Other physics concepts, like black holes, wormholes and dark matter, are assumption-based. They are predicted from other theories. For example, we say that black holes exist, but we cannot see them. We assume they exist by the gravitational forces exerted on bodies around them. Supposedly, there is a black hole in our galaxy, the Milky Way, but we are not sure. It is no wonder that physicists dabble outside their field.

Physics is perhaps viewed as the greatest science. It is seen as rigorous and precise, done only by very smart people and with applications to real life, including products and services we use every day like mechanical devices, transportation, communications, etc. Economics also has copious applications that perform well in real world situations. Pricing airline tickets, estimating demand elasticities by power companies, auctioning various goods like wireless spectrum, estimating lost earnings due to injury, setting compensation for executives, etc. are areas where economics works well and with relative precision. When physicists tout their science as having more profound applications, physics becomes just as guess-like and dependent on pure mathematics as anything in economics. For example, applying ideas of quantum

---

[28] Economics and psychology both have methods and models that can be tested consistently. Other social sciences like political science and sociology lack these methods.

[29] For an example of extreme use of theory and math in microeconomics, the model of general equilibrium compresses time and distance (everything happens now and in one place). Everybody can trade with everybody else, e.g., I can trade with Humphrey Bogart, and since there are no other market imperfections we conclude that markets clear and are efficient.

mechanics to everyday life and implying such theories as time going in reverse, parallel universes, simultaneously being in many places at one time, etc. is pure speculation, yet these concepts are presented in lectures and in documentary programs as though they are facts. In the popular physics educational program *The Fabric of the Cosmos: Quantum Leap*[30], we see a shattered glass reassembling itself as it falls back up and, in another scene, a man talking to one person while another manifestation of the man is walking past the man toward another copy of himself. The physicist explaining these scenes does not make it clear if this is reality or theory, and, if theory, how it was determined. Here are just a few more ribs on physics:

- Physics is replete with ad hoc theories that explain various "strange" results. Physicists theorize many ill-defined "forces."
- Physics presents many hyperbolic numbers, like the number of galaxies or the minute period of time within which the Big Bang occurred. The extreme numbers have a faux precision and also present an element of overkill. It is not clear what the relevance of a very big number is compared to an extremely big number.
- Economics gets a bum rap for enabling financial fiascoes like 2008, which was widely blamed on simplistic financial modeling ultimately built and endorsed by economists. Physics has its own share of disasters though and might be underestimating potential disasters. For example, the 2011 Fukushima nuclear power plant accident nearly destroyed the entire country of Japan. For an example of a potential disaster, some analysts speculate that experiments done in super-colliders could create types of matter capable of destroying the entire planet. Scientists say such outcomes are very unlikely but they are not sure exactly how unlikely.
- Economists are often "way off" in routine economic tasks like estimating tax revenues or, for a more specific, failing to estimate how high unemployment would go in the 2008 recession. In contrast, countless applications of physics in engineering, technology, manufacturing, etc. are apparently successful and rarely exhibit failure. These physics-based projects, however, have large margins of error built in, however. For example, engineers build a bridge to support vehicles of a certain weight and indeed the bridge does not collapse, but in actuality they have built the bridge to hold many times that weight. If economists could estimate with such large margins of safety, they would get most every prediction right.

As illustrated above, physicists who criticize economics for either its overly mathematical foundations or ridiculous microeconomic foundations are largely just closet do-gooders, perhaps frustrated that their science has little application in contemporary issues—while economics does. These physicists are gullible for the most simplistic concept of saving people, the liberal/Keynesian construct that governments stimulate economies successfully as if they were the first people ever to notice it. They are amateurish on the subtleties of micro and of the historical debates of M&M.

### I.1.I. Outline of Our New Canon of Economics

This manuscript is sprawling and attempts to muster every aspect of current macroeconomic discussion. It may be hard to follow the general thrust, so I have summarized a few key points below.

- Part I is a general review of our economic world. First, we have overestimated our economic output and its growth rate. It is a broadly-rooted over-confidence but the intellectual lynchpin is the teaching of M&M, which touts the great success of monetary economics and Keynesianism. We

---

[30] Public Broadcasting Service' NOVA series, November 2011, hosted by physicist Brian Greene.

have been instructed to borrow our way to prosperity. We are both gullible and willing to implement M&M solutions. The current adult generation relishes the magic of Keynesian and monetary policies. We learned this in college and take it literally.

- 2008 represents a genuine turning point, a "Conjuncture." Prior to 2008 a variety of favorable circumstances led to high economic growth fortunate in the decades preceding 2008. Now, long-developing and underlying adverse economic trends coupled with certain new extraordinary negative factors are working against us.

- Our people are to blame, both our leaders and populace—and not the banks, the financial system, the market, etc. Our political and business leadership deludes itself about its ability to overcome these problems. Our leadership is not straightforward with the people. We have misallocated our resources and are in debt.

- A rundown of the current state of economic affairs confirms our predicament. The preponderance of factors works against us.

- "Microeconomic" is an attempt be honest about ourselves, ask how much we really deserve and think along microeconomic lines of tradeoffs and choices.

- Part II is the updated Monetary and Macroeconomics canon. First, we broach the character of M&M as a science.

- Next is a review of the pivotal ideas of M&M, focusing on the limits of our knowledge and the effects of monetary policy.

- A rundown of monetary economics follows, highlighting the essential M&M models from before 2008, the diverse new tools and theories and their experimental nature.

- A listing of the standard models of M&M demonstrates that they are merely parables and that they fail to hold up when we need them, like 2008 ff.

- The chains of cause and effect explain how M&M ideas are interpreted by participants in financial markets. This section is somewhat digressional.

- International economics is a sprawling area that can be taught very technically, and largely irrelevantly, in classrooms. Appealing to international factors is a favorite M&M device. Perhaps a quarter of all our economic banter draws on external factors. We address the main points.

- The long list of topics in M&M, mainly like what you see in the financial press, demonstrates how tenuous and cliché-ridden M&M really is.

- Part III covers topics in social and business science in two thrusts. The first relates to specific areas of economics that are seriously flawed and represent faux science yet are used pompously to manipulate people. The second describes selected important, yet hard to understand, methods of social and business science.

# I.2. M&M

## I.2.A. Rates & Spending

A person not well-read in contemporary M&M thinking may find many policy goals counterintuitive. For example, high house prices are one objective of recent M&M policy, yet the average person may perceive high prices as a net undesirable situation. Another example is interest rates. M&M policy has kept rates low for a long time. The average person earns no interest on savings, however, and inflation erodes his wealth. Another example is deficit spending. At a time when our government is running large deficits, he is told that raising taxes and cutting spending will make the economy worse off. A recent example was the public discussion in financial circles circa the latter half of 2012 preceding the Fiscal Cliff. This event was reputed by many to hurt the economy in 2013 and beyond. A final example is M&M policy, like quantitative easing, which is touted as a success because it compelled the purchase of riskier assets by people and institutions. In literally no other government function do we similarly try to get people to make riskier choices.

M&M is the intellectual basis for the above ideas. It consists of two grand parables: interest rate manipulation and aggregate demand ("AD") stimulation. We believe in high AD and in making it grow further by creating cheaper credit by lowering "rates." AD, and really it alone, grants us more economic output. In contrast, thrift does not help—and may even hurt.

## I.2.B. Rate Lowerers and i

Manipulating interest rates or, as we usually say, "Lowering 'THE' Rate," is probably the most central idea in M&M, yet the assumptions underlying a central bank's control of interest rates are one-sided and dogmatic. Supposedly, we prefer low interest rates: Low rates increase economic activity, therefore creating jobs, sales, tax revenues, etc. and ultimately greater prosperity. Few dare to argue with this low rate postulation, but it is fallacious. Borrowers prefer low rates, of course. Also, society might benefit from a general *lowering* of rates for some time (as happened over the 1990s as inflation went down). Low rates, in general, are not superior to high rates, though. A high interest rate indicates a high value for the future, i.e., progress and economic growth. You sometimes sense that people struggle with this "low rates are better rates" story. In a *Wall Street Journal* op-ed,[31] a big money manager opines, "In general, low interest rates are beneficial." Why "In general?" Perhaps his own livelihood of making money on high rates gives him some hesitation, yet he continues his thesis, figuring that his case can be proven by theories and evidence in M&M textbooks.

When we present the low rate case scientifically in an M&M classroom, we unfortunately do little more than blurt out the same chain of cause and effect of economic transactions, with a smattering of jargon and specifics that amount to very little else. If a student dares to ask if there is a tradeoff to lowering the rate, we dismiss it. An instructor might give some color, typically using certain examples of the effects of lower rates, such as people buying more car—"More people can swing a car payment with the lower rates" or businesses borrowing to build new factories—"CFO's run the numbers again and tell the boss that it makes sense to build a new plant." We do not admit that savers would get lower rates on their savings

---

[31] Penner, Ethan, *The Wall Street Journal*, "How Low Interest Rates Contributed to the Credit Crunch," August 18, 2008, p. A15.

and therefore spend less. Nor would we publicize that corporate pension funds see the present value of their liabilities rise and have to put aside more of their net incomes to fund the pensions, and therefore reducing dividend, capex and wages. You might argue that it all comes down to the empirical magnitudes of the countervailing effects, but we do not generally provide any empirical support. I would also guess that a sizable fraction of M&M instructors, perhaps one-third or more, simply do not even suggest the other side of lowering rates and would likely not even understand the idea of low rates raising the cost of pensions.

The copious thoughts below relate to interest rates, low rates, lowering of rates and maintaining low rates (as during the period 2008 to 2015). Orthodoxy is that lower rates means increased economic activity. Secondary effects are, for one, secondary and also minor in magnitude. The secondary effects are not secondary, however. They are just as theoretically valid and their magnitudes may be just as large or even bigger.

## I.2.B.a. All About Interest Rates

Interest rates are the price of financing transactions and transferring economic resources over time. It is impossible to compare how important this price of credit is versus prices of other big aggregates like oil, housing or labor, but interest rates are probably the most important of the economy's prices. Then, the idea that we control this price–that we can lower rates at will to stimulate our economy–is a fantastic and dominating aspect of our economic lives (assuming it is valid, of course, rather than just an article of faith or hope). So we have to understand interest rates and the effects of their changes. There is a plethora of effects in a change in rates and I cannot reconcile the net result.

### *What are the rates?*

There are many interest rates including rates on credit card debt, car loans, student loans, bonds, small business loans, bank savings, etc. Rates vary by markets, nature of contracts, risk, inflation/ expected inflation, national border, time, etc. Rates vary in ways that make sense. Risky borrowings like credit card debt have higher interest rates. Interest rates on riskless savings like checking accounts are low. Short-term borrowings generally have lower rates than long-term. Rates tend to move together, at least over long periods. Households might think that the rates they borrow at (like for car loans or credit cards) are higher and tend to go up more while the interest they get on bank savings and CD's tends to stay low. Over time most rates move together, though.

One fundamental distinction about rates in our theoretical social and business science models is the risk-free rate v. any of the rates of return that investment generates. The spread between the two types of rates is important. The risk-free rate is pervasive in models and investing concepts including the Dividend Discount Model, Black-Scholes option pricing model, the CAPM, put-call parity, the Sharpe Ratio, the Taylor Rule, etc. Before 2008, we would assume risk-free to be anything from about 1 to 5%. Now it is much lower. Investment rates are a wide variety including the Internal Rate of Return as done in business projects, general discount rates for payments and streams, yields of bonds, rates for annuities, money market fund rates, etc. The rates prior to 2008 were in a wide range, generally over 5% and variously up to 15% or even 20%. Since about 2008 we have lowered rates and kept them low for a long time. Such low levels confound many of the teaching stories we tell. For example, if you compound at current bank savings rates it amounts to very, very little.

### Nominal v. Real Rate

The rates we see every day (like a mortgage rate, bank CD rate or the fed funds rate) are nominal, i.e., before adjusting for inflation. We must adjust for inflation to get the after-inflation or "real" rate. Even though we transact strictly in nominal rates, we really decide based on real rates. A rough adjustment to reality can be achieved by simply subtracting current inflation. If the rate is 5% and inflation is 2%, the real rate is 3%. If the rate is 0.02%, like it might be for interest on bank checking accounts these days, and inflation is 1% then your real rate is negative. There are two flaws to this rough adjustment: (1) using current inflation and (2) a (usually) small interaction term in the adjustment formula. Concerning the first flaw, it is "expected inflation" that must be subtracted. For example, if a lender thinks that inflation is 2% and he wants to make 3% real, he will set the nominal rate at 5%. If inflation turns out to be higher, like 4%, he will get only about 1% real and probably would not have made the lending contract. Only after the fact would he realize that he only got 1%. It is critical to remember that expected inflation is the correct quantity for real/nominal adjustment. Also, expected inflation is an estimate and lenders frequently calculate it incorrectly. The second flaw is relatively technical and usually of minor magnitude, so I relegate it to a footnote.[32]

Another key aspect of real and nominal is that in the world of M&M policy, we lower nominal rates—even though the intention of the policy is to lower real rates. We assume that inflation does not change promptly, so lowering a rate from 4 to 3%, if inflation is 1%, will lower the real rate from about 3 to 2% because inflation will stay at 1%. Is this true in the real world? Wouldn't lower rates be tantamount to equivalently lower inflation? It is hard to say. Perhaps inflation moves down as rates are being reduced, rendering the real unchanged. Policy proponents and textbooks maintain that policy affects real rates though. In the post-2008 episode, many real rates were negative when subtracting current inflation. Even mortgage rates, maybe averaging around 4% during a period of a little less than 2% annual inflation, were modest in real terms.

### Why Is the Interest Rate Positive, and Why Do We Fancy Low Rates?

We talked about the two fundamental justifications for positive time value: progress and impatience. Interest rates are positive because people can take resources now and combine them in a productive manner over time to create more goods and services. Sometimes economists use the term "roundaboutness" to characterize this ability to positively transform our economy over time. Thus, higher rates mean greater prospects for economic growth. The impatience rationale for positive interest rates is simply that (some) people crave goods and services now. This case implies no judgment about economic growth. We could have a world with no economic progress but, if people are impatient, there would be positive interest rates.

In either case, in M&M discussion, we do not ponder the fundamental reasons underlying positive interest. In M&M contexts, when we deem the economy to be underperforming, we respond by enacting policy of lower rates. As we have said many times, the lowering stimulates investment by businesses and borrowing and spending by people. That is why we like low interest rates. If an M&M analyst were

---

[32] The precise equation for real rate is $r = i - \pi^e - r\pi^e$ where $r$ is the real rate, $i$ the nominal and $\pi^e$ is expected inflation. If I borrow \$100 from you for a year at a nominal rate of 5% and inflation (equivalently expected inflation in this example) is 3%, at the end of the year I will have \$105 but the average price level will be a factor of 1.03 higher. In real terms I will have a percentage return of 105/103 or about 1.94%. The $r\pi^e$ is significant when inflation is very high.

pressed, he would contend that this M&M low rate story is a short-term argument. He would say that the long-run level of interest rates and of progress in our economy are completely different topics. This bifurcation has become confounded due to the long-term low interest rate regime following 2008. In general, even after years of low rates, M&M diehards will maintain that low rates and additional lowering of rates, even miniscule changes, are beneficial to the economy.

## What is "THE" Rate?

When we "lower 'the' rate," which rate(s) do we change? In classroom recitation and much public commentary we often ignore this detail. We pretend it is unnecessary because we could provide it if we had to. Then, when we do address it, we resort to one of three responses. The rate is: (1) the fed funds rate, (2) all rates or rates in general or (3) something like "any and all of the key rates that contribute to economic activities, and nothing other." The fed funds rate is considered to be the rate that sets the cost of capital, both in the U.S. and largely for the rest of the world. The mechanism is that the price of borrowing in the fed funds market affects other short rates like short-term treasury rates, money market rates, commercial paper market rates, repo market rates, Libor, etc. which in turn affect rates that determine consumption and investment like rates for car loans, mortgages, corporate bonds, bank loans, longer-term government bonds, installment credit, etc. Economists call this "transmission" or the "transmission mechanism." Transmission is, at least, hard to gauge in magnitude and timing. (Economists have many stories of transmission, called channels. They are arbitrary. We will discuss transmission later in detail.) Also of note is that, prior to 2008, we thought we controlled the fed funds rate with relatively small amounts of buying and selling of government bonds, amounts in single digit to low double digit billions of dollars.

Anybody familiar with M&M events in the years following 2008 might argue that the fed funds rate is no longer the main policy rate. It had been set to near zero and the market it cleared became of little importance in financial markets. After 2008 the rate of interest on reserves (aka the deposit rate) became the binding rate for bank reserves, i.e., banks parked their reserves at the Fed at the rate of interest on reserves. The Fed itself referred to that rate as the more important rate in determining policy. Over the years the Fed would also borrow cash in large amounts in the form of reverse repos and the reverse repo rate would become more important than the fed funds in determining interest rates on short-term money instruments. Despite having these two other markets/rates, the fed funds rate is still portrayed as the policy rate in discussion. In December 2015, when the Fed raised "rates" for the first time in about a decade, it was primarily the fed funds rate that the Fed and financial press contended was being raised although its raising did not seem to affect any large amount of borrowings. The same is valid in December 2016 when the Fed again raised rates.

## The Natural Rate

The Natural, or Neutral, Rate of interest is a theoretical concept of a level of a real interest that balances savings and investment when the economy is operating roughly at capacity and with stable prices. The natural rate is not specifically defined in terms of time or risk but usually is considered short-term and risk-free. The fed funds rate represents our best natural rate. The natural rate can only be estimated. Economists have estimated it as much as 5% in the 1960s and as little as 1% in the 1990s. It would have been considered about 2% before 2008 but now many economists view it as closer to 0%.

To steer policy in the right direction it is important to have an estimate of natural rate. Some economists, however, contend that we cannot every really pin down the natural rate since it should fluctuate with economic and market conditions and, indeed, can fluctuate significantly and abruptly in short time frames. In other words, do not pretend, as policy makers do, to be able to determine the natural rate any better than markets do.

## What Is "Lowering the Rate?"

The main government economic policy maneuver to keep the macroeconomy from stagnating is lowering the rate. We already established the fed funds rate as the policy rate. Also, we described the basic mechanism of how it works. The level of fed funds rate affects those of other short rates which affect those of all rates. How lower rates help make our economy grow is, in a way, obvious. You can see it in our national income identity, $Y = C + I + G$, which says that output (Y) equals the sum of consumption, investment and government spending (C + I + G). Lower rates mean more I. In other words, companies can borrow more easily to build factories or refinance debt and avoid default. In theory, this helps companies and saves jobs or even creates new ones. For C, lower rates help borrowers who want to buy a car, get mortgages, put more purchases on a credit card, get a student loan, etc.

What are the effects of a long and pervasive lowering of rates? Since 2008 we have engaged in a large-scale, long lasting government lowering of rates. We really have no idea how much the changes in incentives and investment programs will be affected by such a grand effort. Our theory of lower i was primarily based on small changes and surprises. In this theory, rates would suddenly be lower such that private parties would increase their borrowing and economic activity. Low rates for a protracted time is different, however. We do not know the effects of long-term lower interest rates or the effects of the domination of asset markets by central banks.

Previous episodes of lowering rates are hard to assess. Over the 1980s and 1990s and even into the 2000s, inflation and rates tended downward, which created a one-time benefit to society. Another hard to discern facet of rates is that indeed rates may move together and we can control a policy rate like the fed funds rate, yet there is a question of direction of causation. We assume that long rates change due to our action of purposely changing short rates through policy. The causation could be the other way around. In the economy, real and fundamental economic forces like perceptions of risk, commodities prices, technology changes, consumer preferences, etc. determine rates for corporate bonds, mortgages and other long-term markets. The changing of the short rates simply follows the changing of the long rates.

## Facets of Rates & Policy Effects

Average people assume that the Fed simply lowers nominal rates. In classrooms, M&M teachers are more particular and say that the Fed lowers real rates by lowering nominal rates while inflation sticks. The major interest rate assumption in class recitation is that the only rate that matters is the one at which we borrow. For example, when the Fed lowers rates, people will buy cars now that car loan rates are lower, but they will not be affected by the lower rates on the savings they have in things like bank CD's. In almost all textbook discussions of M&M, we simply do not consider the latter effect, or at most we assume it to be very minimal and/or attenuated by time. People do not challenge this asymmetry and even when they do, they are circumspect about how strongly they make their cases. In a *Wall Street Journal* op-ed, discount brokerage mogul Charles Schwab bemoaned that current low rates are hurting savers.[33] He threw around big numbers ($7.5 trillion in money market savings paying virtually no interest) to demonstrate his case,

---

[33] *The Wall Street Journal*, "Low Interest Rates Are Squeezing Seniors," March 30, 2010, p. A19.

yet he was reticent to question low rate policy overall—believing that it has a net positive effect. Over the following years, you would be hard-pressed to find similar big names criticizing bad effects of low rates. You might counter that certain M&M models weigh both positive and negative interest rate effects, but the vast majority of analysis of interest rate changes, both in class and out, uses a logic that ignores the countervailing effect.

We do not generally even calculate or widely discuss the loss that people suffer from lower rates of return in bank savings, CD's and money market funds. To get a rough estimate of the other effect, plain money savings in our economy is about ten trillion dollars, which before 2008 would earn about 4% interest. In the current low rate environment, that figure would be 1% or less. This low rate has persisted for many years representing well over one trillion dollars in lost interest. Take the case of an American household holding its savings in CD's, as many do. Assume $200,000 in CD's at 5%, circa 2006. If a member of the family needed a car, the family could take a car loan rate at about 6%. Now, in our period of low rates, car loan rates might be about 4%, but CD rates are less than 1%. This family would be less likely to purchase the additional car given the new relative rates. In the textbook, however, lower rates means people buy more cars.

## I.2.B.b. Effects of Low Rates and/or Lowering Rates

The list below represents some additional items related to low or lowered interest rates with commentary relevance to today's environment:

- Lower rates should make companies invest more, but most business expansion is not constrained by interest rate levels. Many companies have the funds to invest or can borrow at prevailing (higher) rates and will invest, or not, based on growth prospects and estimations of future demand. Companies' responses to lower rates are merely refinancing, which adds to their bottom line but probably not to society's. During the period of low rates, we had many cases of cash-rich companies like Apple borrowing at low rates with no intention of building a new plant. Also, lower rates encouraged companies to engage in mergers and acquisitions more readily because the funding was cheaper.
- Low rates made it possible to borrow cheaply. People could get mortgages, car loans and other borrowings at lower rates, and businesses and corporations could get bank loans or issue bonds at lower rates. Perhaps the greatest single beneficiary of the low rates of the post-2008 period was the U.S. government which borrowed great amounts at modest rates.
- Investors search for higher yields by buying riskier assets like high-yield bonds or stocks. Investors may end up with portfolios with bonds of longer maturities creating greater duration risk. (Duration is a measure of the sensitivity of a bond or bond portfolio to a change in interest rates. Bonds with longer maturity have greater duration risk. If interest rates rise bond prices will go down.) Throughout the post-2008 period investors have been recommended to take on riskier and longer-term bonds. To give an example, *Barron's* article "Going With the Flow"[34] instructs people to get out of treasuries for retirement income purposes because of their low rates and instead go to any or some of the following: emerging market debt, foreign government bonds, Build America bonds, high-yield corporate bonds, senior bank loans, master limited partnerships, dividend paying stocks, variable annuities and municipal bonds. A conservative investor who usually holds treasuries, high-grade corporates and mortgage-backed bonds would not normally hold most of these. Whether

---

[34] November 29, 2010, pp. 29-31.

these investments played out favorably or not, they still represent a temporary holding of portfolios with the wrong risk profile.

- Low rates in the post-2008 period steered people toward housing as an investment. Minimal returns in bank savings and bank certificates of deposit, and some trepidation at equity investing, led people to view housing as the place to put their money.

- If interest rates are lower, we assume people borrow more and spend the borrowings. This is a theory, not a fact. Of course, with lower rates savers are compelled to save more to meet savings objectives.

- Due to lower costs, corporations will substitute capital in place of labor. This appears to have happened extensively in the period of low rates following 2008.

- Over our period of low rates, much debt (including a significant portion of sovereign debt) was at real rates and even nominal rates less than zero. Savers actually pay to store their money.

- With lower rates, households can refinance their mortgages and have more money to spend. Of course, the mortgage holder gets less interest. Such holders include banks, pension funds and insurance companies.

- Lower rates impact pension funding negatively. The pension must seek additional funding from the corporation or other entity behind it. Corporations will have less to pay investors or invest in capital, and government pensions will need higher taxes.

- Low rates affect retirees' concepts of how much they can spend in retirement. The rule of thumb that a retiree can spend 4% of his savings without depleting it must be lowered, making the retiree poorer in retirement.

- Lower rates make hitting financial goals in the future harder. Therefore, people have to put aside more funding now and/or increase savings. For example, to provide $150,000 for the future education of a new grandchild in eighteen years would require $62,000 now if the rate of return is 5% but $125,000 if the rate is 1%.

- Lower rates for extended periods could make people feel pessimistic about the economy for a variety of reasons including that people perceive that the central bank knows the state of the economy and chooses to keep rates low, and low rates imply poor conditions.

- The appearance that rates will stay low for a long period is difficult to predict in its effects on people and companies.

- Lower rates reduce the incentive to rectify underlying, chronic indebtedness. This is true for households, companies and governments. Lower interest rates made it cheap for the U.S. federal government to borrow money and national debt has increased greatly.

- Since only a paltry amount of interest income is lost when removing money from interest-bearing accounts, people do not have to wait until a due date approaches to pay bills. This makes paying bills more convenient. It is one distinct, if only minor, advantage of low rates.

- Low rates enable companies to borrow cheaply, which frees up money to continue operations and perhaps expand. Much of the refinancing done in the post-2008 period, however, was debt issuance, typically high-yield issuance used to pay off private equity investors rather than invest in the business. Firms could rollover non-viable loans. Circa 2009 to 2012 a large amount of junk debt was rolled over into lower rates allowing struggling companies like J.C. Penney, Radio Shack and Sears to continue operations. Solvent companies refinanced their debt to lower coupons, which gave them lower interest payments at the expense of bond creditors.

- Low rates translate into reduce profit and various bad incentives for financial firms including insurance companies that issue annuities, money market mutual funds and brokers that perform margin lending.
- Lowering rates presents a myriad of international effects. Many analysts characterized U.S. accommodative monetary policy as contributing to hunger and starvation in poor countries due to raising the prices of basic commodities like food. Commodities prices rose due to the lower dollar and resultant tendency for investors to invest in commodities. The U.S. ignored such claims contending they were minimal in magnitude and that our policy effects primarily impacted us. Another international effect was that countries that pegged their currencies to the dollar had to assume the same monetary policy as the U.S. This is always the case for such countries, but the consequences were more pronounced.
- Lower interest rates lower the value of a currency. That can have many effects including making the people who hold that currency poorer.
- Low rates impact sophisticated investors like hedge funds and commodities' trading advisories that from time to time would consider it advantageous to keep capital out of markets and hold cash. They would be somewhat content with cash returns around 3%.
- Widespread lower rates for prolonged periods distort relative valuations. For example, government debt at 0.10% and corporate debt at 0.60% might represent a high relative valuation on a ratio basis but not on an absolute basis.
- Low rates impact the viability of the financial advising business. Financial advisors typically charge a fee of about 1% on assets. With other fees and charges, the take on assets might be more like 2% or even more for small accounts. Before 2008, when cash generally returned more than 2%, advisors could charge such rates.
- Low rates weaken the appeal of compounding of interest as an exhortation for people to save.

## I.2.C. Spenders and Aggregate Demand & C

The second pillar of M&M is that our economic system is demand driven. Our economic growth and prosperity arise from consuming—rather than producing or saving. You can call it demand-side or Keynesianism, but I like to refer to it as aggregate demand ("AD"), which more closely describes our classroom demonstrations. I refrain from the term Keynesianism because it has many nuances. AD economics has a technical facet, but it also presents one of the oddest ironies of modern intellectual life– AD is so deeply believed in, especially by liberals who prefer a large role for government in our lives, that people who scorn waste, consumerism, gift-giving and most any other type of materialism kowtow to greater AD as a benefit to our economy.

That AD drives GDP is seen in the most basic macroeconomic equation, the national income identity: $Y = C + I + G + NX$ (GDP equals aggregate consumption, investment, government spending and "NX" which is net exports, or exports minus imports). The four items on the right constitute AD.

The AD parable dictates that additional or autonomous spending, like from a government spending program, yields greater output and perhaps even so much more output that tax revenues will rise enough to pay for the additional spending. Also, even if we get into an economic crisis from overspending, we must rectify it, at least initially, with more AD. For the years, even decades, before the 2008 recession, people were over-consuming, largely by borrowing(i.e., too much AD). Once we faced a drop in demand, though, the solution was to keep AD going with government spending until C got back to normal. AD proponents will tell you it makes perfect sense with analogies like the technique to right a skidding automobile by first steering in the direction of the skid.

At a reflective level, the AD parable is opposed to beliefs in moderation or control of waste. As part of a liberal arts education, we are charged with inculcating the young to think critically and to strive for goals like equality and reason, but such ideals are jettisoned when undergrads enter M&M class. Anything that increases AD is desirable. No other course on campus—sociology, history, logic, etc.—has such a parable. The only textbook knock on increasing spending is that it ultimately causes inflation, but as events following 2008 have shown inflation may be relegated to a secondary importance. In any case, on campus most M&M instructors do not spend two minutes on moral implications of AD. This non-questioning of AD permeates society. For example, a social activist might scold rich people about their wealth and individual greed but generally would not argue against salutary effects of economy-wide AD. For another example, people might oppose development in their community (think of a proposed casino) but they would not argue with "improved" economic activity throughout the national economy. The same one-sidedness is evident in the financial press. Strong or improving AD is characterized with positive adjectives and favorable analogies. Experts who are cited or quoted almost uniformly prefer AD. They will usually express dismay and puzzlement at AD shortcomings. If, for example, a monthly Consumption number comes out lower than expected the experts and journalists will typically chastise the consumers for lacking the requisite optimism to keep on buying.

You might say I misrepresent this parable because proponents only advocate AD when the economy is slack, but the belief in AD is never relaxed. When the economy is strong, we strive to get it moving even faster. For example, for many years in Massachusetts when the economy was apparently operating at capacity (2005 to 2007), the state government held sales tax holidays designed to stimulate AD during one weekend in the summer.

AD presents many intellectual oddities. One vacuous aspect of the AD model is the role attributed to consumption: the capital C. C is, as you could probably guess by looking at the national income identity even without having taking one M&M course, the largest component of AD—about 70%. Expert commentators frequently say that GDP will hold up (or fall) if C holds up (or falls). It might sound insightful, but it merely states that GDP will hold up if GDP holds up. I would estimate that more than half of the "expert" comments on the direction of GDP reflect this platitude.[35] The talking heads then attempt to support it with statements about C being determined by "consumer confidence" or by the behavior of the consumer or maybe something more esoteric but still a platitude, like the intentions of the Chinese consumer. Why don't they just say, "I have no idea what is going to happen to GDP?" Their justification is that the book of M&M contains some underlying economic fact or proof that we know more about C than GDP.

C itself is an amalgam of items and does not closely represent what people have decided to buy over any period. For C to reflect people's buying intentions, especially over any short time frame like months or quarters, it should be goods and services people have chosen to buy, i.e., picked off of shelves in stores. A large part of C, however, is health care spending which is not done directly by people but through third parties including the government and insurance companies. Also, health care spending is not chosen. Emergency hospital treatment from a car accident is not chosen by a person. Another large part of C is housing consumption but its aggregate value is not from tallying people's spending on housing. Rather government statisticians estimate about how much they think people spend on housing.

---

[35] I deem the statement, "The economy will be okay if consumption holds up," to be the second greatest cliché of economic discussions in modern times—second only to "They're lowering the rate."

Another glaring AD gimmick is the appeal to NX. We suppose that countries can, and must, pull each other's AD from time to time, keeping us all AD'ing along. The U.S. was so economically magnanimous as to pull the world's economy for decades, even if we were chronically overspending. Today, China and other countries like Germany must oblige: We even scold those countries that they save too much. Of course, if applied to the entire world economy, NX goes to zero and cannot pull anything. Entire courses in international macro depend on NX, usually hypothesizing a changing value of a nation's currency to achieve a change in AD and then generate more GDP. Whereas this might be plausible for a small country willing to devalue its currency (if such a feat can be achieved without offsetting economic costs), it is patently absurd in an ultimately closed system or even in a big country. Analysts highly overstate the value of lowered currency, e.g., Eurozone's currency is going down; but it will not save Eurozone's economy. They also trip over themselves about how many countries can save their nation's economies by selling abroad. We cannot all do it simultaneously, yet currently the U.S., Eurozone, Japan and many others are counting on it.

One day the AD parable will haunt our children as billions of now poor Chinese, Russians, Indians, etc. become richer and richer and damage the planet with consumption. We will have no moral grounds to gainsay them. AD is a wanting basis upon which to theorize society's well-being. It is even worse: Decades of indulging the premise that spending is good for its virtuous spillover has become so ingrained in our thinking that we waste with a smile. We dump the voluminous trash from useless consumption items and say, "This stuff gave me little pleasure and I wasted a lot of it, but, golly, I contributed to GDP. Economics faculty will attest that my waste is virtue."

We do not even have a grip on what constitutes good spending. We relish increases in consumer spending and in consumer credit aggregates and advertise them as signs of a strong economy, without reflecting on what might underlie them. We proclaim that consumer credit has increased recently, yet it is largely borrowing in the form of student loans. Although that could mean spending on additional education that will pay off in the future, it more likely simply translates to the fact that we are broke and have to put tuition on the cuff. We are told that consumer spending in 2011 has gone up by 3.3%, yet inflation was 3.2%. In other words, no real increase in goods was obtained; yet the media describes it as a favorable trend.[36] It does not make sense. Let's say every year you have a July 4 cookout for which you buy a certain amount of food. In 2011, it cost you $200. Then, in 2012 you pay $206 for the same goods, due to inflation. You do not say, "Honey, I did the cookout shopping and paid an extra $6 because I was feeling flush."

AD is a powerful parable. It tells us to worry about now, not the future. It dominates how we talk about consumption and waste, things that repel us in many ways. In an AD world, if you drive by the mall and see its parking lot packed you have to praise the humming economy.

---

[36] There are many others, but here is one article with such analysis: "Consumers Back to Feeling Flush," *The Wall Street Journal*, September 26, 2012, p. A4.

# I.3. Conjuncture & Convergence

Conjuncture is a term for a pervasive and fundamental shift in a social system resulting from a confluence of many factors. When discussing our recent economic fortunes economists often invoke the terms "structural break" or "secular stagnation" when making the case that our economy has changed. Neither convey the gravitas, relative suddenness and potential for a protracted decline in our economy like conjuncture does. 2008 is conjuncture. Popularly, we have deemed the 2008 episode as one of many cyclical recessions. We concede it was a bad recession, designating it the "Great Recession" and described it as a "balance sheet" recession, which meant that it was worse than a regular cycle (whatever that is). However, we still pretended it was merely a cyclical drop from which we would recover to our long-run trend. In reality, 2008 ff reveals multiple fundamental economic changes and inflection points in trends. In addition, the episode has ushered in an enlarged role for government, which will further detract from our overall economic growth.

Convergence refers to the coming together of high standard of living societies, like the U.S., and low standard of living societies, like China. The crisis of 2008 ff did not initiate convergence: It was already happening. Convergence does not mean that we will suddenly end up poor or as poor as the average Chinese. Perhaps both the rich and poor country can grow economically together, but 2008 ff accelerated our convergence. Our M&M economic problems and weaker competitive standing represent significant gradual negative force on GDP growth, as seen in weak job and wage growth for much or our populace and a decline in high-profit sectors that compete on world markets. M&M and all of its related models are dead, gone and useless. Micro is here, and America plays an average micro game.

Why invoke novel and decorative terms? Here is the heft and breadth: GDP growth is significantly below 3%, rates of return to savings are in a negative real level, real wages are stagnant, business formation is stagnant, government finance is perpetually in the red, taxes are higher, returns to riskier assets are significantly lower, we are resorting to government to manage an extended set of our economic decisions, crony capitalism has increased and the costs of basic needs like housing, education and health care are rising. Up until 2008, we seemingly had our economic house in order. Government budget deficits of about 3% of GDP were sustainable with GDP growing close enough to 3% per year. We had two apparent economic holes: Social Security and Medicare/Medicaid. Social Security was viewed as a reasonably manageable problem rectifiable by pushing the retirement age out a few years and raising funding a little in a bunch of ways. The, we figured the big health programs could be handled sufficiently with market forces. 2008 ff exposed deeper problems including pension funding shortfalls and low rates of return to assets, and also revealed that the U.S. was embarking on a greater government-run society.

In the modern national economic history of the U.S. (starting sometime in the early 1900s) the episode of 2008 ff constitutes the third great macro event. The first was the Great Depression, which justified big government for its Keynesian economic role. The second was stagflation of the 1970s, which discredited the simple Phillips Curve (the idea that we could tradeoff between inflation and unemployment). This debunking of the exploitable unemployment/inflation tradeoff put our focus strongly on inflation alone and led us back to markets and away from government intervention. The 2008 ff episode has us returning to government. Did we save the economy from falling hard in 2008 and—if we just wait— we'll soon restore it to smart growth and progress? Or is it a more prosaic story? Did we save nothing but merely temporarily prop up every financial and economic institution—both good and bad—with the support of the Fed by borrowing?

Some have summarily dismissed the idea of conjuncture arguing that there simply could not have been such abrupt change in the underlying potentials of our economy. For example, how could unemployment go from near 4 to 10% in a year? Did our schools degrade by 150% or our capital stock get destroyed? Stanford professor and former head of the Council of Economic Advisers Edward Lazear proclaims, "In 2007, the unemployment rate was 4.4%. Two years later, it reached 10%. The structure of a modern economy does not change that quickly."[37] Many, if not most, other economists maintained something similar, including notable scholars like Boston University professor Laurence Kotlikoff and 2010 Nobel Prize winner Dale Mortensen of Northwestern.

Theirs is a superficial observation. Perhaps the physical layout and labor head counts of our economy did not change; but our perceptions of wealth, debt levels, future wages, opportunities and productivity did. In a short period, U.S. households saw their homes go from being income-generating assets to life-long liabilities, while concurrently witnessing their 401-k's lose so much value that they abandoned stock investing. They witnessed so many nicks in their future net labor income (smaller pay raises, stingier benefits, less pension match, etc.) that the perception of the financial resources they could employ going forward went down.

## I.3.A. The Short Macro Story of How We Got Here

The succinct story of our macro history goes back to about 1980.[38] At that time a most prominent question among macroeconomists concerning the U.S. economy was, "Had the GDP growth trend fallen below 3%?" The informed answer was yes. We were a mature economy facing higher costs in our factor inputs of labor, land and capital. We also faced heightened competition from abroad. Somewhat surprisingly and to the chagrin of many macroeconomists, for the next thirty years we put up high GDP growth (over 3% per year on average). The decades of economic success convinced us that we were on a solid foundation, but they really represented borrowing-based growth and lucky breaks. Trend growth probably had fallen below 3%.

The 1970s had been rocky and left the U.S. in a weak economic situation with high tax rates, lots of regulation and modest prices/valuations of assets. Our main problem was inflation, which topped 10% per year in 1979 and 1980. These were all rectifiable problems, though, and our underlying structure and competitive position relative to the rest of the world was not a grave constraint. In the 1980s we shook things up with many economic initiatives under the mantra of supply-side (including lower taxes and less regulation). The primary M&M initiative, however, was the slaying of inflation, which caused the lowering of interest rates. We had a run of 3+% GDP growth and bull stock, bond and housing markets for almost thirty years.

Along the way we had our doubts and faced challenges that would have destroyed us in weaker M&M times: the stock market crash of 1987; the recession of 1990 to 1991; the first Gulf war; 1994 when inflation appeared at hand and we raised rates; the Mexican peso crisis; the Asian crisis of 1997; the Russian government default of 1998; Y2K; September 11; etc. We seemingly managed them handily with our dynamic free markets complemented by adept and effective policy. We attributed the credit. For example, in 1998 the cover of *Time* featured three economic brains: Lawrence Summers, Alan Greenspan and Robert Rubin—each wearing big grins. The perception of our M&M policy at this time was that it was

---

[37] "There is No 'Structural' Unemployment Problem, *The Wall Street Journal*, September 4, 2012, p. A19.

[38] You might be aware that many economists identify other points in time as pivotal M&M developments, such as 1944 (Bretton Woods conference establishing post-World War II international economic arrangements) and 1971 (U.S. dropping gold convertibility for the dollar). We will discuss such specific events in M&M history later. For now, our history is general and 1980'ish represents when America jumped to an economic track that determined our lifetimes up to 2008.

a parsimonious merely tweaking the successful market system with its iconic businesses (like Goldman, Walmart, FedEx, the tech companies of Silicon Valley, Bloomberg, etc.) and its triumphant practices (like inventory management, securitization, financialization, risk management, computers, etc.)

By the mid-2000s we were either walking on air or running on fumes. We assumed the former. Our economy shrugged off oil price increases, housing bubbles, chronic trade deficits, geo-political events, competition from China, etc. In January 2006, Fed Chairman Alan Greenspan retired, and both liberals and conservatives toasted his sapient monetary policy. The sole criticism of Greenspan was that he supposedly endorsed President George W. Bush's tax cuts. That was a political wrap, though, and not an intellectual flaw of policy.

After thirty years of good GDP growth, we thought we were immune to underlying factors like crime and poor education and short-term shocks like oil price increases and stock market crashes. We laughed them off, assuming that our economy was resilient and our monetary policy prescient and timely. Endless stories regarding our litigious society, decaying infrastructure, bad education system, expensive health care, etc. were no impediment to the Mack truck U.S. economy barreling down the highway.

Today, we look back at a long trend of 3% GDP growth and many analysts think that level of economic growth is still ours to be had, perhaps just a matter of getting 2.5 v. 3%. Also, we can create the jobs and get the rates of return to assets like before. The other take is that our GDP growth was a confluence of many unique happenings: (1) debt facilitated by our central bank; (2) population growth/favorable population pyramid; (3) a one-time upward re-pricing of assets including equity, fixed income and housing; (4) too much deregulation that provided one-time economic benefits; (5) low price of oil; and (6) various cost lowering international factors like the demise of communism and cheap manufacturing from China. The ratio of debt/GDP is much higher now than before. Our population structure is not as favorable. Asset prices are too high. You might argue that we could look at the U.S. around 1980, 1990 or any other year and prospects would have looked iffy at those times too, but, today, the U.S. faces a gross preponderance of adverse economic factors.

One facet of the short story is that from about 1980 to the present we put a price on every resource and idea and bid up the prices of all assets to a maximum. We left nothing of value untouched and we spent most of the "value" we created.

## I.3.B. We *Did* Predict It

From the man in the street to prominent economist Paul Krugman to the Queen of England, we all asked sheepishly, "Why did the 2008 economic calamity take us unawares? Why hadn't we predicted it?" To the contrary, we *did* see "It" clearly, with the It being defined variously as a weak economy as a whole or as any of a variety of markets or sectors including the housing bubble, high leverage of our financial system, high cost of wars, soaring cost of imported oil, government deficits, loose monetary policy, unregulated shadow banking, derivative positions of extreme magnitudes, etc. The analyses and warnings from leading thinkers, the politicians urging restraint and the media coverage copiously described our over-borrowing and other weak links in our economy. That, indeed, is our recurrent problem.[39] We were then and are now completely aware of our economic problems, but we continue to push our luck, both private

---

[39] One reason for pretending nobody noticed excesses in financial markets is that outrageous behavior by the high and mighty makes for stories with more drama and entertainment value. For example, *The Big Short* (2010) by Michael Lewis and the movie based on it (2015) portrayed the housing bubble as foreseen by only a handful of heroic and principled investors making them protagonists in a world of fraud.

parties through self-interest or, as some put it, incessant greed. The government, particularly the U.S. government through its semi-maniacal attempts to expand the consumption set of the people.

For example, the collapse of the housing market bubble is attributed as the most important cause of economic crisis of 2008, yet we were cognizant of the extraordinary increases in housing prices. It was an omnipresent topic in the press in the 2000s. By the mid-2000s, the housing bubble was on the front cover of every major newspaper and magazine. Extreme housing finance was a topic discussed by homemakers and high school newspapers. The notorious *condoflip.com* was operating by 2004 and was the object of jokes at cocktail parties everywhere. By about 2006 we had questioned the bubble so repeatedly and run so many stories that our media, for novelty, had to focus on arguments that it was not a bubble: "Bubble? What Bubble?" is the title of *Barron's* interview with a "savvy real-estate investor.[40]" You could find many more like it. Even in the late 1990s there was copious commentary of housing market indicators getting off trend. We also had many detailed and well-researched estimates of potential effects of drops in house prices. In my college classes, I read excerpts from an extensive and authoritative market research piece entitled *Housing In the New Millennium: A Home Without Equity Is Just a Rental With Debt,* which showcased virtually every major issue of the bubble housing. Then, I ask a student to read the date of the piece: "June 29, 2001.[41]"

We chronically pretend to have neglected the study of important M&M phenomena—if only we did requisite study, we would avoid economic problems. For example, one article profiles a Finnish economist who has discovered a model to detect asset bubbles. Her line of research is characterized as being done almost solely by her.[42] This attitude is specious and self-serving. It makes for great press and justification for academics, portfolio managers, policy makers, etc. to peddle their intellectual distinctions and brands.

Just as we predicted the bubbles and out-of-equilibria macro quantities, we have also thoroughly analyzed all of the other economic relations of our society. We know to the extent knowable what motivates people and to the extent practical or politically acceptable we have given people incentives through spending programs, subsidies and—mainly—tax policies. We have also tried to nudge people to virtuous economic behavior like saving and reducing waste, yet we habitually feign a lack of understanding of our society and implore additional research for new schemes.

You might make the case that we can readily discern bubbles. Indeed, at any point in time it is easy to find assets whose values are well over historical levels. The obvious shortcoming is that we cannot easily rule out that the off-trend levels are justifiable by some underlying economic force or, even if they are not, they can still hold up. Also, we cannot estimate the size of spillover effects of the bursting of any bubble. Therefore, as a science, economics does not predict well now, but with better models and more data we could predict better in the future. One of the major post-2008 crisis projects is the collection of vastly more data to aid in better analysis of asset bubbles. Economics has always been capable of predicting, within plausible ranges; and we could use our predictions to fashion prudent public policy. Our real problem is that we chose to "roll the dice" and hope that the bubble persists. In other words, we do not choose prudent policy. In summary, we have the knowledge; we just do not use it prudently.

## I.3.B.a. Big Bets on Future Economic Output

---

[40] April 10, 2006, p. L10 ff.

[41] What a disappointment it must have been for analysts who correctly called the economic weaknesses but did so far too early. By the time their hypothesis was vindicated many of the specialists were out of the debate or, even more ironically, touting the opposite story, after succumbing to years of apparent economic invincibility.

[42] "Asset Bubbles Found by Finnish Economist Inspired by Grandfather," by Kati Pohjanpalo, September 19, 2013. http://www.bloomberg.com/news/articles/2013-09-19/asset-bubbles-found-by-finnish-economist-inspired-by-grandfather

If something is risky yet we are aware of the risk, it is just a bet with a potentially bearable cost. The American people, government and institutions were willing to push asset values to the limit. Whether it was the U.S. encouraging home ownership, a person flipping a condo for a big profit or a Wall Street investment bank making billions packaging mortgage securities, we tacitly accepted the risk even though we might have been averse to state it publicly. Former Citigroup CEO Chuck Prince was scorned for admitting, "As long as the music is playing, you've got to get up and dance,"[43] in response to why his organization continued leveraged deals, even though signs of excess abounded.

The raw truth is that our macro future is much harder to divine than we pretend. We do not have usable guidelines to bound our macro bets. The causation, linking, recessions, weighty economic indicators (like inflation, unemployment and GDP growth), Keynesianism, multiplier, central banking, stimulation of an economy, international aggregate demand, etc. are ineffective tools in our world of many shifting trends and sudden unexpected developments. Even worse, the tools can be counterproductive by tricking us into policies that cause bad investment and bubbles. They are also pretentious, patronizing and easily refuted.

In macro, we have a dozen or so major indicators: GDP, inflation, unemployment, exchange rates, consumer spending, wage growth, etc. We can explain their movement over time with a variety of models or relationships like the Phillips Curve, the Taylor Rule, yield curves, varieties of exchange rate interactions, the relationship between wage growth and consumption, etc. We throw in sundry social or cultural factors like that the Japanese are thrifty, the baby boom is aging, etc.; and we talk about autonomous changes like tax cuts, exogenous shocks like weather or other major forces like oil prices. Then, we try to start a chain of cause and effect among the quantities. We might say something like the Japanese central bank did not raise Japan's overnight lending rate. This, in turn, will keep interest rates low and keep consumption going. Conversely, we could just as justifiably say: the Japanese central bank did not raise interest rates and this will discourage investment in Japanese businesses and contract the economy.

The acute problem is that, for all our knowledge, we still know little about what changes our macroeconomy—either that of our nation or that of the world. We cannot dissect exploitable effects and new trends. We can make crude statements like, "The U.S. economy grows at about 3% per year, on average" and then assume their continuance. Or we can make highly specific statements like, "A large drop in payrolls data in the month of February 2003 was due to the calling up of military reservists." Between the crude and highly specific statements we do not have much to say. All the policy, models, financial press talk, etc. are just guesses and generalizations. For example, we know that the U.S. economy has been growing substantially but the economies of France and Germany have not. We also know that France and Germany are making certain changes to their economies that economists believe add to greater growth but we have little certainty whether those changes are going to work at all or how much they will affect the economies. We can speculate on trends based on "big if's," for example, if Europe's GDP grows at a much greater rate its unemployment will come down.

Here are three examples from a multitude of potential selections of major ways we pretend to know and control our current economic circumstances, but in reality do not:

- Leading economist Joseph Stiglitz, along with Peter Orszag and Jonathan Orszag (also both notable economists), authored a 2002 piece[44] demonstrating that, in almost no economic scenarios, could the mortgage giants Fannie Mae and Freddie Mac collapse. Soon after, they did. Many other

---

[43] Statement made to *The Financial Times*, July 9, 2007.
[44] "Implications of the New Fannie Mae and Freddie Mac Risk-based Capital Standard," by Joseph E. Stiglitz, Jonathan M. Orszag and Peter R. Orszag. *Fannie Mae Papers*, Volume 1, Issue 2, March 2002.

pundits, including the editorial staff at *The Wall Street Journal*, simultaneously contended that the mortgage giants were broke.

- In the 1990s stock market guru Jeremy Siegel made a strong case that stocks did not go down in value over any long period in "Stocks for the Long Run." Over the next twenty years, indeed, markets racked up minimal return. Many equally-qualified experts warned that stocks could be overvalued and not likely to continue high returns.
- The Asian Crisis of 1997 occurred abruptly and spread rapidly. Many voices in the economics' world were not expecting that part of the world to collapse, yet many others had analyzed Asia and warned of serious flaws.

Which factors make our future so uncertain? Items include large and variably unfunded liabilities, declining and aging population, climate change, long-term low interest rates, underlying value of our housing stock, geo-political problems, etc. Given this, I surmise that people like Janet Yellen, Ben Bernanke and Alan Greenspan know no more about the economy than I do. Even worse they are insiders, so they have a line to toe. For example, in congressional testimony on July 16, 2014, Janet Yellen deemed the stock market not to be overvalued. At that time, I would have disagreed, and I had to wonder if she would have the same opinion if she had no public role. Also, these people are prejudiced by academic and/or political beliefs and suffer great intellectual pride—so they cling to opinions.

We tend to trick ourselves about how well we foresaw events, even in the recent past. For example, circa 2013 and 2014, after years of QE policy by our central bank and a consensus that such extraordinary monetary policy was only natural given the circumstances, we forget about how we perceived the policy as it played out. In the first half of 2010, when the first round of QE had ended, opinion was that we would soon reverse the policy because it was a risky policy and the kind we would only do once. Few saw continuation of QE. If you read analyses of that time period in the following years, like in 2014 or 2015, you do not get that sense of such doubt and trepidation.

## I.3.C. Conjuncture 2008

Has the U.S. come off of its long-term GDP growth trend of about 3% since 2008? Since 2008 many analysts, like bond guru Bill Gross (at the time head of PIMCO), proposed lower growth while others scoffed at the idea. The pessimists became known as the New Normalists and they contended 2% was a better long-run GDP growth number. There is a third more extreme scenario that our growth is even lower, around 1%.

Observe many economic time series spanning the decades before 2008 and the years following it and you will see a break around 2008, followed by a change in the trend of the series. Similarly, inspect the common models of M&M like Okun's Law, the Taylor Rule, the Money Multiplier, the Phillips Curve, etc. and you will see a break. We discuss these models at length in a later section. Will this persist? Perhaps ten years from now social science will be able to do time series with pre- and post-2008 regimes, and we will finally know for sure, but what can we surmise now?

## I.3.C.a. September 15, 2008: Conjuncture Day

During 2008, our economy looked rocky, but for the average person it was hard to discern how extraordinary our national problem was. As people witnessed adverse corporate and financial events and repeated government corrective actions, an attitude formed. On September 15, 2008, Lehman Brothers collapsed. This corporate failure was bigger than anything before it and beyond our government's ability, or at least its will, to backstop. Before September 15, 2008, the average American told himself that his house would one day be worth $1,000,000 and a stock portfolio that would be worth $750,000. He also assumed a reliable flow of labor income representing $100,000 per year. Like a good economic agent, he spread the discounted value of that future payment into his present stream of income and formed a sense of his permanent income, i.e., the amount of income he could rely on for his life. By the end of that fateful day, though, he told himself his house would never be worth $1,000,000 and would instead be a perpetual money pit. The stock market would be a dud, and even his income—or at least good pay raises—was questionable. Over the day September 15, 2008, Conjuncture Day, 100 million people thought something like any of the following assertions:

- "My law degree is a turkey."
- "I am not a real estate salesperson making six figures. I'm a homemaker helping to show homes."
- "I am a day laborer, not a carpenter."
- "My house is not an appreciating asset. It is a money pit draining money from my pocket year after year."
- "I will retire later than I planned."
- "I might not send both kids to college, only the one who does well. I'll steer her toward a state school too. It's cheaper."
- "I won't pay my child's college tuition in cash. Let him borrow and let it be his problem."
- "I will live at home with my parents."
- "I will not get married and have a family."
- "My taxes will be higher for the same, or even reduced, government services."
- "I am an auto worker just like my father but at lower pay and benefits."
- "My 401k is less generous in matches, vesting period, etc. than older workers got."
- "My pension is in my hands, and I don't trust holding my money anywhere except in the bank."
- "The Social Security payments I am will get when I retire will be reduced."
- "I'll keep most of my money in cash and be content with little or no rate of return. I don't believe in the stock market."

At the same time, the average American had another epiphany: My government is there for me, providing, in part or in total, for many of my major expenses like housing, education, retirement savings and health care.

I use hyperbole when I propose that 100 million households woke up on September 16, 2008 with a much lower sense of lifetime earnings and wealth, but over the recent past people have changed their thinking, in many ways, including resigning themselves to high prices for many necessities, higher payments for health care, higher taxes for governments services, higher education costs, lower rates of return to assets, lower or no income growth and diminished returns to educational investments, etc.

### I.3.C.b. A Multitude of Indicators Indicating Structural Break

Conjuncture can be seen in conventional macro series and other data including labor statistics, fertility, population, education, small business, time value of money/rates of return, taxes, government financing, etc. We talked at length about the break in levels of interest rates. Cash savings have been a wealth-losing investment, after inflation, since around 2009. Real rates of return may stay negative in the future since, if rates go up, inflation might go up even more. People and institutions willingly invest in U.S. bonds at near-zero nominal yields (which are negative in real terms) and do so for long periods of time. Stock and housing market returns have been relatively solid from 2009 to 2016 but they may be the product of artificial forces like government largess and may go down in the future. Returns in alternative assets like hedge funds have varied but also have been relatively modest. The list below indicates a variety of indicators reflecting a structural break in our economy:

- **GDP**: The path of GDP itself shows structural break. Per capita and per worker GDP growth are flat.
- **Labor and Wage**: Many job conditions and security including quality of jobs, wages, benefits, etc. have changed for the worse. Structural breaks are evident in employment rate, youth unemployment and long-term unemployment. The real wage and pay levels of jobs have shifted. Much public employment now commences with lower benefits and effectively lower retirement benefits, making the total compensation package distinctly lower. Structural break is evident in areas like salaries of many professionals, summer jobs for kids (fewer and lower paying), two-tiered pay systems (new workers get lower pay) and real wage in general. Income growth levels are stagnant. Labor force participation is going down in general but up for older people, implying that people are delaying retirement. Temporary employment and "gig" employment has increased. Perhaps gig employment is a desirable development affording people choice and flexibility. As of now, however, it appears to be an inferior labor condition. We will talk about many labor indicators like job destructions and job creations later in the section on labor market.
- **Inequality**: Inequality is wealth and income has increased. Many economic indicators might display a positive trend since 2008 but if broken down by rich and poor (e.g., show the indictor separately for the top ten percent of the population and bottom 90%) the indicator will often reveal no progress for the poor.
- **Household Formation**: Households are larger, meaning that fewer households are being formed. Food stamps and welfare claims have increased. Young people living at home with their parents has increased. This is true for young people at all levels of education. There is a big decline in the number of households without formal bank accounts and fewer marriages.
- **Deficit and Debt**: The magnitudes and levels of deficit and debt in government are higher. Households and corporations exhibit changes in trends in debt accumulation. Households built up debt continually until about 2008—at which point they reached a peak level of debt. Some types of household debt tapered off in growth yet debt for student loans and automobile financing rose well beyond historical levels. The character of household debt has changed in that more people are underwater–they owe more than the asset they are paying off is worth–in mortgage, student loan and car loan debt. Corporations, despite holding large amounts of cash, also have loaded up on debt.
- **Taxes**: Taxes are higher since 2008 and may get higher in the future. If there are tax cuts, as advocated by President Trump, they will exacerbate deficits and debt.
- **Education**: There are many trends in education some of which may reflect adverse developments in the economy. A long-running trend that has continued through and beyond 2008 is that the fraction of people aged 18 to 24 enrolled in higher education has risen. College applications and enrollments in cheaper state programs, as opposed to private schools, have risen due to affordable tuition. Financing of higher education requires greater and greater borrowing. The number of applications to law schools and MBA programs is declining. Law school graduates face poorer employment opportunities. Average scores for the law school admission test for students accepted

to law school are lower.[45] We also hear of odd items, like students suing their law schools for restitution that the degrees are not worth as much as advertised. In general, people need more education, it costs more and in many cases it does not bestow greater job opportunities.

- **Small Business**: Business formation, including IPO's, is stagnant. Small business start-ups, or the annual "startup rate," are down; and business failures are also up. Both developments are adverse.
- **Big Business and Corporations**: A wide variety of trends have played out in the corporate sector spanning the pre- and post-2008 recession. Many corporations hold cash in lieu of investing in projects, plant and equipment. Rather, they have refinanced debt at low rates and done significant buying back of stock.
- **Pension**: Pensions for new workers are stingier in many respects.
- **International Trade**: Trade as a percentage of GDP is no longer increasing.
- **Retirement**: Many people figure on later retirements than previously planned.
- **Housing**: A large fraction of the populace owns homes with little or no equity, or even negative equity. Many people have little expectation that their homes will ever have significant value. Mortgage equity withdrawal ("MEW"), which represents the money people extract from their houses from mortgage refinancing, is distinctly lower since 2008. Also, the backing of the mortgage market by the U.S. government is greater today.
- **Monetary Policy**: We will discuss the myriad facets of regime change of M&M, which I call the "Transmogrification," later.
- **Attitudes**: People are abandoning the stock market as a suitable investment. Two major bear markets in fewer than ten years have changed people's faith in equity. It is difficult to quantity people feelings, of course, and surveys are not reliable but people appear to be viewing family raising, retirement, education, etc. more pessimistically. Also people's attitudes toward markets v. government have changed in favor of government. A growing fraction of our populace looks to government to manage the major economic burdens of our lives including education, housing, retirement and health care. The crisis of 2008 has hastened this change.
- **Fertility**: Native U.S. fertility seems to have dropped significantly in the U.S. For decades, we sneered at countries like Italy, Japan and Ukraine in which each woman produced only about 1.4 babies in her lifetime. The comparable number for the U.S. was over two at that time. Now, U.S. fertility is below two at about 1.9 and may be trending lower.
- **Mobility**: People are less likely to move. Seeking jobs away from where a person grew up or was currently living was an important facet of economic efficiency and growth.
- **Sundry Items**: There have always been boom and bust-towns and pockets of America stagnant or in decline, but some parts of America appear terminally poor, e.g., Detroit. A greater number of municipalities and other government districts are struggling. Young people are not driving as much. Car loans have longer terms. We hear of changing attitudes about government employment. More young people, including some of the best coming out of top MBA programs, seek work for the government, choosing a secure income over taking a chance on competitive employment. Jobs in industries that were in recent decades creating many high paying positions (like health care, technology, finance and higher education) are not creating these jobs at the same rate. We hear of various poor person features like the return of layaway in retail. Certain immigration patterns like

---

[45]"Getting Into Law School is Easier Than it Used to Be, and That's Not Good," by Natalie Kitroeff, *Bloomberg Businessweek*, January 6, 2015. http://www.businessweek.com/articles/2015-01-06/getting-into-law-school-is-easier-than-it-used-to-be-and-thats-not-good#r=hp-ls

the flow of undocumented workers from Mexico reflect deteriorating economic conditions in America.

A complement to our story of structural break comes from competitors. Emerging market nations now have decent macroeconomic policies, stronger property laws and other improved business conditions. This development did not happen suddenly around 2008, of course, but heightened international competition represents a tougher challenge in the post-2008 period. In recessions of old, economic quantities went down (or up if the indicators measured negative quantities like poverty or unemployment), and then they recovered to the level they were before. In 2008 ff, many went down and will remain there.

## I.3.D. Economic Growth: The Ultimate Object

For a period in the late 1960s and early 1970s, some bold thinkers got a wide audience for the anti-economic growth case. Around 1970, economist E.F. Schumacher (1911-1977) wrote *Small is Beautiful*[46] minimizing the importance of economic growth. It had a picture of Gandhi on the cover and chapters on topics such as "Buddhist Economics." People like Schumacher soon got laughed out especially with the high inflation and unemployment, and other poor economic conditions, of the 1970s. Even people left of center refrained from disparaging economic growth. Since the 1970s economic growth has gone unquestioned. Republicans love it, Democrats even more. Europeans got switched on to the rightness and value of economic growth and even Chinese communists adopted it. Average people might say NIMBY (not-in-my-back-yard), but they want growth everywhere else. Typically, the only people willing to say economic growth is not priority one are environmental extremists.[47]

Liberals who care about the environment will simply separate issues: (1) Attain as much GDP as possible and (2) Decide how to use it and, presumably, use the output for virtuous purposes. We even crave the other country's economic growth for its contribution to our aggregate demand. We bemoan that GDP growth in China may be tapering off. Anytime it seemed to be dropping, we fretted that it was adverse for our exports and therefore our labor market, housing demand, raw material demand and so on. Whatever costs to the world extensive economic growth may create, they are secondary to the benefits of more AD for our products. As mentioned above, GDP growth for thousands of years was very incremental, so what GDP growth can we expect and what are the underlying models that back it?

## I.3.D.a. The Parables of National Economic Growth

When we ponder the state and future path of our overall economy we invoke one of the following three models/parables:
- The most prominent story is that the American economy is robust and growing, as it always has, perhaps at an annual GDP growth rate of 3% in real terms. The impetus to this growth is Demand, which rises since our incomes and population grow. There is a flaw inherent in this demand system, but through government vigilance and policy we master it. There can be times of insufficient demand due to some pathologies of markets. The recession of 2008 is an example. In these cases,

---

[46] 1973. Harper & Row.

[47] I do not mean to say that since the early 1970s we have not pondered non-economic growth scenarios. At every point in time in the last 50 years, leading thinkers have broached lowered economic growth and its implications. I would say about every two years or so a big name economist or pundit will put out a book questioning everything about economics and economic growth, e.g., Lester Thurow's *The Zero-Sum Society* (1980) or Paul Krugman's *Peddling Prosperity* (1994). In general, 3% per year GDP growth sticks in the heads of most Americans.

our government can step in and stimulate the economy to maintain growth. The model is $Y = C + I + G + NX$ where C is the most important item, and C will continue to grow because people always demand more. Call this AD or Demand-Side or Keynesianism. In this story, productive does not matter since Demand is the key.

- The second story is also one of an American economy that grows, but the key is not Demand. It is production. GDP grows dependent upon real investment including research, education and infrastructure. This is a story of enterprise, technology, hard work, etc. and lower tax rates help. Investment by government in areas like infrastructure and education helps too. The applicable model is Growth Theory where Y is a function of land, labor, capital and entrepreneurship; and America ranks high in all of those factors. You might also call this neo-classical Growth Theory or even supply-side, although the latter is more a short-term and slightly politicized concept.[48]

- A third story is that increasing economic output is not automatic. It depends on fundamental factors as in the second story, but our economy currently faces constant cost pressures, depreciation of its capital (both physical and human), fewer productivity enhancers and other negative domestic and international factors including relentless competition from abroad. America's costs and debt are higher and our historical economic advantages like population growth, a relatively highly-educated labor force and pro-free enterprise policies and conditions are attenuated. We face potentially low GDP growth and perhaps even lower absolute GDP. You might call this Convergence. Indeed, we have always faced competition from abroad, but it is graver now.

Which case best describes our economy today? The third. The first is a silly short-run story about feedback from spending creating a virtuous cycle, with no regard for debt and underlying fundamental micro factors. The second is a little more reasonable reflecting fundamentals about competition and that our economic growth is a long-run story, but it does not guarantee the large increases in economic output on which our future depends.

The first two models have one dubious characteristic in common: They both imply an automatic economic growth including that government can perennially aid growth. Here is a typical statement invoking both models by economic journalist David Wessel: "If the chief problem is one of too many workers and not enough jobs, then today's unemployment is treatable and there is a case for more fiscal and monetary policy….But if the problem is chiefly a mismatch between skills employers need and those jobless have, then more fiscal and monetary medicine won't do much good. That kind of unemployment is treatable only in the long run—with better education and training."[49] There is a third situation for which there is really no "treatment," except, perhaps, to accept lower wages. There are simply too many workers who want wages that are too high given the goods and services we can currently sell. For example, auto workers who formerly earned $35 per hour can work new jobs, but only at $15 per hour. There no demand at $35 per hour for the labor of these workers even with retraining.

## I.3.D.b.i. Demand/Keynesianism

The short-run Keynesian construct is $Y = C + I + G + NX$ where Y is GDP. Y grows if C, I, G and NX are bigger. C is assumed to be a function of disposable income and wealth (or changes in wealth). C will be higher if people's incomes are greater or their wealth increases, of course, but also if interest rates are lower. I is made up of business investment and housing. It can increase if interest rates are lower. G is

---

[48] We will review some rudimentary equations of growth theory in a later section.
[49] *The Wall Street Journal*, May 31, 2012, p. A2.

government spending and it can be increased at will. Government spending can be funded by borrowing. It will add to Y, which will increase wages and profits and then increase C and I. Government spending is an example of fiscal policy. The other main fiscal policy is taxes. If we cut taxes, the incomes of both people and businesses are higher and they can spend more. NX is net exports and NX rises when our exports increase or our imports decrease.

What makes any of these aggregates change? They are usually growing and can just start to grow more from any of a variety of perturbations including, for example, an increase in confidence or a cut in interest rates. We can make them grow with government policy, however. Monetary policy of lowering rates can make people spend more or make the value of their assets go up such that they spend more. NX depends in part on the world economy. If other countries' economies, grow they demand more of our goods. It also depends on domestic policy. By lowering interest rates people abandon assets in that currency and the value of the currency goes down thereby increasing exports. There are other mechanisms. Perhaps active monetary policy simply makes people feel more confident about the future—or less afraid of the future. Once any item–C, I, G or NX–increases, Y increases and all items feed off of the additional Y and the feedback creates a multiplier effect. An initial increase in C feeds into Y and since greater Y means more jobs and higher incomes, we get more C and more Y. This identity and its feedback is the basis of most of our contemporary macro talk.

The whole model may appear to be a circular construct based on an initial increase in some spending, perhaps from borrowing due to lower rates, or, in the case of NX, an injection from abroad. It relates mostly one-sided stories of cause and effect. For example, lower interest rates do not cause people to consume less due to less income on savings. Perhaps Fed policy makes businesses and people feel less confident about the future due to expectations of higher inflation. We do not generally talk about that in our Demand system. Maybe other countries will lower their rates when we lower ours, and we will not export more. The above rundown of Demand theory is rudimentary. We will discuss many of the underlying facets of Demand later in the text.

## I.3.D.b.ii. Growth Theory

The second major macro construct is growth theory.[50] This is a long-run story of economic progress by capital accumulation, investment in human capital, natural endowment and entrepreneurship. It is also a story of saving. In the Demand story saving is either irrelevant or counter-productive. Long-term growth is generally irrelevant to economic prospects at any moment in time as characterized by the business cycle. Countervailing a downturn in the economy is a Demand story. Growth theory is about the long term and the prospects for U.S. in this framework are not as favorable as we tend to think they are.

The long-term growth model is insightful and compelling but it depends on aggregate quantities that may not be favorable for the U.S. Also, we cannot forecast reliably with this model because we have only rough guesses about the factors. Labor is perhaps the key ingredient. Assessing America's labor, for example, is a difficult question. In 1983 a major study of our society, *A Nation at Risk*, informed us that our education was second-rate and it would impact our economic prospects greatly, however, as the years rolled by our economy grew strongly and year after year of similar reports were laughed off. Where are the adverse effects of poor education on our labor force?

The growth theory story is more amenable for analyzing emerging countries like China. China is adding labor and capital, and getting greater capital per worker, which economists call capital deepening.

---

[50] Growth theory is both a general area of economic discussion going back hundreds of years and also specific models notably the growth theory created by economist Robert Solow in the 1950s.

Their education system may be mediocre in many ways but a sufficient number of Chinese put in much longer study hours than Americans do. Its entrepreneurship, which we often dismiss as inferior to ours and ineffective due to corruption, is not that hapless. The country has fundamental factor-enhancing advantages like tolerating the negative spillover effects, like pollution and urbanization, that accompany economic growth.

Growth theory is a bust for the U.S. We have so much labor and capital that additions do not matter as much. We consider our entrepreneurship as the best in the world but our past success is not an indicator of the future. We view entrepreneurship in superficial ways, like seeing it as one and the same as our great stable of business schools, but the benefits of entrepreneurship are not exclusive. An entrepreneur can take his physical and intellectual capital virtually anywhere in the world today. It is also a perception of where we are, what we need to get ahead and what our competitors perceive as tradeoffs. Leaders in emerging markets have learned the lessons the lessons of markets well. For example, they know that grooming an equity market works. It made America grow economically. In America, we are already rich. We are keen to divvy up our economic pie. We call on government, regulate and otherwise fail to make sacrifices for economic growth. It is not a wrong strategy, but it is not a pro-growth strategy. We pretend it is.

There are many misperceptions about growth. In his autobiography, Alan Greenspan avers that since we never lose our knowledge of technology, we will never have lower productivity. We can, however, prohibit the use of technology by regulation or setting a higher social standard. For example, the cheapest way of moving stuff from point A to point B is in a truck with a gas-powered engine. Limit its use and we lose productivity. Another idea is that scientific advances mean greater economic output but a medical advance that makes old people live longer adds costs to our economic equation.

In today's economy our problems are high debt, increasing resource costs and stagnant population, which do not model easily in the growth model. Also, the relationship between capital and labor is not as compelling in a service economy. The growth model characterizes most economic growth as "capital deepening," that labor has more capital to work with. That story applies more readily to manufacturing rather than services.

In public debates the distinction between the Demand model and the Growth model is not belabored. For example, political candidates will propose infrastructure spending (Growth facet) but tout the immediate effects of creating jobs and stimulating demand (Demand facet). There is nothing inaccurate combining the effects but they do confuse two basic economic models.

Both the Keynesian construct and the growth theory story admit weak growth. For example, Keynesianism contends a nation can get stuck in an under-equilibrium and growth theory can be a story of convergence against other countries. Both of these macro parables are favorable for growth and usually assume that a country grows, at least a little. They also imply you are the master of your nation's growth.

## I.3.D.b.iii. Convergence: A Macro Parable for Today

The Demand model describes a world of virgin balance sheets that can take on more debt. That is not we. The Growth model describes a hard slog of sacrifice. That is not we. We should think in terms of a third basic parable of our GDP growth, a model of convergence.[51] This story will dominate our near future. Convergence dictates that if we make $40,000 per year and they make $5,000, and the market clears at $12,000, we should be tending from $40,000 toward $12,000. It is not sensible to compare ourselves to

---

[51] This is a variety of economic theory known as Factor Price Equalization, which states that competition among nations will result in prices of factors, notably wages and returns to capital, converging. I refrain from using this specific model to describe the "macro parable for today" to avoid a technical modeling and make it easier to understand by non-economists.

other rich societies (like Eurozone and Japan) and pronounce that they are worse off than we. We should focus on the many competitors supplanting us.

Why does an American (or Canadian, etc.) make about $50,000 per year while a Chinese (or Indian, etc.) makes much less (maybe about $5,000 for the Chinese and about $2,000 for the Indian)?[52] The answer, related by economics professors to students from Harvard down to Podunk Community College, is that the American has more capital, both physical like machines and human-like education and skills. However, our lead in capital is diminished; and, in some areas we have less. There are more factories in and around Shanghai than New York. We emphasize human capital, our great educated labor force; but human capital is ephemeral. Every day in America, 65-year-old people retire and are replaced by 25 year-olds. The same is true in China. Our older workers possessed better basic skills and a better work ethic, however. Our young have diminished work skills and professional habits in many ways.

Outsourcing of American jobs continues and competition is getting more intense. Virtually every country is gunning to capture the high values added from internationally-traded goods and services, whether it is Singapore growing a biotech industry or Russia building a technology park. Many U.S. executives will assert that they get much more support for business ventures in other countries than they get in the U.S. Convergence is happening and average GDP per American is going down. Under this theory, we may not be able to "turn it on" even if we adopt ideas to increase our long-run productivity. All our macro analysis may not be very good because it is designed for a time when populations and working populations were increasing. They are now decreasing. Analysis of historical episodes of deleveraging and how macro quantities were related to each other during those episodes may not hold now.

In general, economic activities are either local (like many services such as restaurant services, policing, education, landscaping and automotive repair) or traded across borders (like software, manufactured goods, pharmaceuticals and film production). For the former, the jobs cannot generally be exported; for the latter they can. Throughout the last few decades the U.S. has seen a decrease in the traded sector and in the high wage employment that goes with it. Some people argue that most high-paying jobs cannot be outsourced. For example, police, nurses, teachers and accountants are local; yet their standard of living largely depends on economic gains from traded sectors.

Nations of the world are more economically competition today compared the decades following World War II. At that time many countries were incapable of conducting competitive business due to anti-capitalist politics, corruption, chronic strife and incompetence. Another aspect of convergence is that competitor nations can match the U.S. in our attempts to become more competitive. For example, in the U.S. we propose lowering our corporate tax rate, which is one of the highest in the world, to lure companies back to America. We view this strategy as a net gainer to us as if other countries would not alter their rates. Of course, the other countries would match us and could easily achieve this since they are not as broke as we are: They can take the tax loss. The U.S. is not alone in facing convergence. Eurozone, Japan, Canada and any other society with a long-standing high standard of living has its edge to lose. Many developed nations like Sweden, Germany, Singapore and Japan (in some ways) manage their economic houses better.

## I.3.E. Our Economic Output: GDP

---

[52] These are rough numbers for average earnings, and you have to be careful making comparisons. For one, you have to distinguish individual earnings from household earnings. Also, median v. mean matters. The median earnings in the U.S., which I am using, is less than the mean due to the skewed distribution of earnings. Also, when comparing across nations you have to adjust for costs, what economists call purchasing power parity. For example, Indians may have annual earnings of $2,000. A person in the U.S. could not survive on such a small sum whereas in India they can and do.

GDP represents the value of final goods and services we produce, and we want large and growing GDP.[53] The more GDP, the better. GDP is a valid basic measure of economic output but it is an inscrutable concept too. Historically, liberals have criticized GDP for excluding environmental damage, excluding work done at home (a hidden sexism charge), failure to measure happiness, etc. There are other GDP misconceptions. GDP is hard to compare across countries and across time. For example, we often hear that Japan has experienced decades of lost GDP growth, while the U.S. is famous for great GDP growth; however, the standard of living of Japan does not seem relatively diminished compared to that of the U.S. over that time period. Another problem with GDP occurs when you we ponder what really constitutes value in our society. (More on that below.) It is not simply the more GDP, the better. Then, even if deem more GDP as advantageous, what role our government can play in adding value? The answer is certainly not simply building infrastructure and funding education for either their short-term results (Keynesian effects) or long-term additions to our productivity. GDP may be a contentious concept but it also our main measure of economic status and performance.

## I.3.E.a. GDP Growth

A constantly growing GDP is key. The U.S. can "swing its debt" if it attains 3% annual GDP growth, and we assume we can get it. Also, GDP growth underlies the futures of other sectors of our society: Cities and towns assume their tax revenues will grow. Companies assume revenues will grow, Asset managers assume their assets will grow, Average people assume their retirement savings will grow, etc.

Future U.S. GDP growth is almost surely bound to be lower than our historical trend of 3+%. In recent years, many analysts have picked up on this. Over the post-2008, period leading economists, like Robert Gordon and Lawrence Summers, posited lower growth, aka secular stagnation. Bond guru Bill Gross, formerly of PIMCO, was one of the first to broach the "new normal" of something around 2% GDP growth. Prominent investor and market commentator Jeremy Grantham makes a case for something closer to 1%. Yet U.S. government officials maintain growth of 2% or higher. During his tenure as Fed Chairman, Ben Bernanke usually assumed growth of 2.5 to 3%. Of course, there is no perfect way to project GDP growth and anyone's calculation can be pretty arbitrary once he is willing to abandon the long-run number of 3%. Japan hit a brick wall in economic growth starting around 1990 and has posted about 0 to 1% growth per year.

Second, much of our total GDP growth was simply due to population and proportional labor force growth, perhaps as high as 1% of the 3%. Increasing GDP is valuable mainly if it is per capita GDP growth, not just more people created proportionally more GDP. A bigger total GDP may make your country economically richer overall which provides advantages like more clout in international politics and greater ability to wage war. Despite this basic difference between GDP growth and per capita GDP growth, we hardly distinguish between the two kinds of economic growth in public discussions. As the U.S. grew at 3% and Japan grew at 1% we talked about ourselves as if we were three times better economically, even though on a per capita basis we were close to the same.

Third, although we equate spending with growth, spending does not create growth. We have borrowed to get much of our recent GDP growth. Expenditure alone is not value. For example, our GDP in any quarter would go up when we spend more on gasoline just because its price was higher. Many experts would fallaciously relish that increase in GDP.

---

[53] We will do a more detailed review of GDP and its growth later.

Of course, none of the above wraps on GDP precludes its growth and the gradual progress of nations. In the long-running debate between growth pessimists and optimists, like economist Julian Simon (who died 1998), the optimists have prevailed. The world is getting better. Our case for pessimism, as related in this book, is more of a generational story (our GDP is growing less now), al allocative story (we are borrowing against the future), an international story (our GDP is growing less than that of certain competitors) and a story of growth of government managing of the economy (meaning less growth). Perhaps America does not face an absolute decline as much as a relative decline and allocative problem.

## I.3.E.b. Value and Consequence

What is economically valuable in our society? Which specific goods and services provide function and pleasure? It is easy to question the value of many products. For example, I work in investing. My colleagues and I buy and sell existing assets, mostly stocks and bonds, using our investors' financial capital. We increase the value of our portfolio, making money for our investors and, of course, we make our living charging fees. My line of employment is lucrative and is well-respected, but sometimes I doubt its value. We explain the value of our work by claiming that we, first, provide higher rates of return to our investors, and, second, we help allocate capital and help manage risk in the financial system. Both claims are debatable.

Some people question the value of financial services citing its very large fraction, about 10%, of our GDP. Are capital allocation and risk management functions of the existing pool of the economy's assets really that valuable? That is a question popular in movies. In *Margin Call* (2011) and *Wall Street: Money Never Sleeps* (2010) characters renounce their money jobs for meaningful jobs. The Ph.D. risk analyst in *Margin Call* laments that prior to his Wall Street job he was an engineer and built a bridge. He recites in great detail the myriad useful functions of the bridge. In actuality, we have copious bridges and the marginal bridge may not add much. In the latter movie one of the main characters, after her high-paying real estate job disappears in the financial crisis, returns to nursing, another one of the universally-praised occupations. Of course, much of America's health care needs are brought upon ourselves by our bad lifestyles. What is so virtuous about helping obese people with back pain or performing cosmetic surgery?

We need financial intermediaries to make loans to businesses, and we need many financial professionals to service the investing, life planning, insurance, consumer finance, etc. needs of people. How much secondary trading of stocks and bonds does society need? How valuable is all that parsing of risk? It is an impossible question to answer, in a way, and one that we often tackle by finding the most egregious examples of lack of value-added. One sub-category of the greater finance industry is "Funds of Funds" which are money management companies that allocate investments to other money managers like hedge funds and charge an additional layer of fees. Many experts denounce them as especially useless intermediaries and are nonplussed as to their existence.

Earlier in my career I worked for a company that wrote and sold an investment newsletter. Our main marketing tool was mass mailing. We would mail 100,000 brochures at about $0.70 per piece and we hoped for a 1% response rate. At $200 per subscription, we would make a little. Such a business model was profitable and required hiring one or two people. Of course, many of our subscribers came from dropping their subscriptions to other newsletters such that the net benefit to society from our 100,000 piece mailing might have been very minimal. Each year, we would have to continue the mass mailings because many subscribers would not renew. Copious resources were needed for minimal value-added. As a market economist, however, I believed that people's choices prevailed, and better products displaced worse so our newsletter business added value.

Many liberals zero in on the financial services sector, "Wall Street" as they say, as the egregious unjustified sector. They cite cases of extremely high earnings and outrageous investment gains. However, we can find similar excesses in housing, entertainment, health care and education. I teach at the university level. I often wonder why such a multitude of teachers teach the same lectures year after year. Couldn't we develop a more efficient method of instruction involving prerecorded lectures and teaching assistants? Or, what value does research in political science create? What is gained by society when an academic publishes the 20th edition of his textbook? We lament the high cost of college and propose to lower it by, for example, having faculty teach more courses and drop research. That would lower costs and get more people educated. Then, the loss of research would amount to no lost economic output to society. What is the value of another analysis of Stalin or study in sociology? Maybe we want that "output" and view it as an integral part of the price of the consumption of higher education.

You can question any endeavors. What is the social gain of producing an animated film at a cost of $400 million dollars; or what is the value a new shade of lipstick? The answer to what adds economic value is easy if you believe in markets: Whatever gets demanded. About the only qualification is that basic societal laws and standards are adhered to. For example, the 2009 animated movie *Avatar*, which cost $400 million to make, was value-adding even though a movie 95% as good could have been produced for $1 million. In general, products that are demanded, regardless of their social merit (think of guns, pornography, jewelry, etc.) have added value. If a nurse and a tattoo artist each make $70,000 per year, they are of about equal value to society.

If you are peddling government policy, it becomes a much more tantalizing question. For example, do temporary tax breaks to small business create value? Did the government programs in response to the economic crisis of 2008 (like Cash for Clunkers or the quantitative easing programs) add value or just create financial transactions? Over my lifetime our government has heavily promoted and economically subsidized major aspects of our lives including housing, education, health care, retirement and food consumption. The result is copious housing, education, health care, old-age assistance and dietary assistance. Yet our housing system puts millions of households in adverse situations, overpaying and overbuying housing. The same is true of education. A new medical doctor would complete med school with little or no debt. Now he has hundreds of thousands of debt. What made education so expensive? Is it now so expensive that it is not worth it?

GDP, value, standard of living, progress, etc. are difficult to pin down. It is hard enough to figure out what is valuable in general, and it is additionally hard when government comes in and distorts people's choices about spending. As government gets bigger in society we must be all the more sure and conscious of what we mean by value. Either go all the way with government or leave it all to the market.

# I.4. The People

A nation's economic fortune mostly depends on its people. As our populace stands today and as our younger generation replaces the older, our people have material shortcomings and attitude problems. Peoples of other countries have economic handicaps, too. We Americans liberally inform foreigners of their deficiencies: For example, Germans and Chinese save too much; Greeks and Russians are corrupt; Muslims are reactionary, etc. We are forgiving of our economic foibles and almost always conclude that we field the best team.

## I.4.A. The Grand Concordat: Central Bankers & Market Masters

Picture senior Fed officials like current Chair Janet Yellen or head of the New York Fed William Dudley and whichever big name businessperson is currently in the news (like JP Morgan CEO Jamie Dimon or Goldman CEO Lloyd Blankfein) standing together with arms on each other's shoulders. Our government and market leaders comprise a grand intellectual concordant: Our government manages the economy deftly and our entrepreneurs and managers create vast wealth. They differ among themselves, sometimes on which group is more important than the other but they agree that each has excellence, insight and clout. There are other anointed ones: the academics, the media, the money managers and the politicians–people like Lawrence Summers, Michael Bloomberg, Warren Buffett, Barack Obama, etc. If they have one common foundation, it is M&M. It is that they control the macroeconomy.

We like to think that America's leaders are better at getting a job done. Even when facing competitive disadvantages we can prevail. Never mind that the Chinese operate at lower cost, the Swedes have lower crime and Singaporeans have lower taxes. America will always be at the top because our people at the top make the right moves bringing out the best of capitalism and government policy. Some analysts will contend that we must maintain a bravado, even if false, so as not to tip our hand to competitor nations like Russia, China, Mexico and Malaysia; yet, the world sees through our façade and consider us declining.

## I.4.A.a. People of Vision & Action

Some people are great achievers in politics, enterprise, war, art, etc. but mastering the macroeconomy is different. Even Milton Friedman, with his keen insight and outstanding series of M&M discoveries, had a mediocre record of calling economic trends, at least in exploitable time frames. Throughout history, mostly to the plain detriment of the common man, people have stood up and with little more than their own conviction of beliefs attempted to shape society to better the lives of people. Historically, religious and political leaders played this role: Today, central bankers and others who engage in the intellectual management of economies have the preeminent role. The list below provides some sundry comments on characteristics of people who have assumed roles in M&M:

- One of the most steadfast beliefs of leaders in our society is that they should not—in fact must not—level with the people. People are weak, sheep-like and reactionary and therefore must always be guided to their own well-being. In M&M, we think that people will hunker down if they think that the economy is weak thus make the economy even weaker. Therefore, it behooves our M&M leaders to hide certain truths about the economy (like debt). If they hide the truth, GDP will be greater. The unpredictability and inscrutability of M&M plays into the hands of the great heroes. It makes it plausible that our economy must be analyzed with eternal vigilance and it must be protected from downfall with policy. Only then can the masses enjoy their consumption.

- M&M leaders serve both Wall Street and Washington DC. Great capitalists decamp to government for "one more career" and to "give back." Government leaders, like the leaders of the Fed, cultivate close connections to financial firms and senior Fed people frequently end up at big financial firms. After years of public service and modest salaries they feel entitled to take a high-paying job in the private sector.

- They protect their intellectual legacies. Alan Greenspan, for example, is very defensive about his record of performance as head of the Fed from 1987 through 2005. The same is true of Bill Clinton and his team, who ruled over the American economy during the 1990s, a veritable golden economic age. In Clinton's presidential library in Little Rock, Arkansas there is copious listing of the economic numbers for his term in office. In their memoirs, senior government officials like Hank Paulson, Timothy Geithner and Ben Bernanke, are positive about their roles during 2008 and following. They deflect all accusations of failure.

- Luck is critical for most leaders, especially central bankers. The favorable economic events of the 1980s to the early 2000s made many leaders in business, government and elsewhere big heroes. For example, virtually any university president during this time oversaw great success. The Baby Boom generation is full of heroes, many of them just the result of fortune. The great money managers of this era, such as the hedge fund virtuosos like John Paulson, were fortunate to make a few lucky bets. Alan Greenspan was lucky presiding over the economy when most fundamental factors were favorable. His former teacher, Arthur Burns (Fed Chairman during the 1970s), was not. Burns' legacy is one of making mistakes and bad calls resulting in high inflation, yet he merely incorrectly overestimated GDP growth rate. Perhaps Ben Bernanke has made a similar mistake and has office early enough.

- Leaders are always puzzled when events in M&M are sudden and adverse. Conversely, favorable economic developments do not cause puzzlement. Adverse events are deemed, "Once in a hundred-year storms" or caused by irrational markets.

- Journalists are Keynesian-leaning. Almost all believe that the government saved the economy in 2008 and 2009. It is a fact, they will say, and any other way of looking at it is false and subversive. Contradicting facts and figures are also not the thrust. Here is an example from a journalist explaining bad effects of low rates—but who also has to make sure readers do not misunderstand that policy works: "Usually, low interest rates help boost the economy by encouraging consumption rather than saving, raising aggregate demand and boosting risk appetite. Zero rates and unorthodox policy have undoubtedly prevented economies from collapsing."[54]

- Journalists have conviction about their M&M opinions. Occasionally, I write to journalists commenting on their M&M writings, usually simply identifying factual or logical errors that vitiate their arguments. Either the journalist does not respond (half of the time), thanks me cursorily and somewhat derisively, "Thanks for your comment" (maybe 10% of the time) or argues me down (the remainder). Rarely will a journalist concede an intellectual matter. At the most humble, the journalist might partially concede but claim that some greater context made the error tolerable.

- Grandiosity leading to ego is a factor. Leaders have a strong belief in their superior abilities, knowledge and mental fortitude. Their leadership positions reinforce their egos. For example,

---

[54] *The Wall Street Journal*, January 30, 2012, p. c8, "Persistently Low Rate Carry Risk of Negative Side Effects," by Richard Barley.

during the heat of the economic crisis, leading economist and one-time U.S. Treasury Secretary Lawrence Summers, while speaking in front of a group of autoworkers was approached on stage by one of the workers who shook Summers' hand and thanked him profusely for supporting policies that saved auto industry jobs. We hear about William Dudley, head of the New York Fed, and his inhumanly busy schedule of important meeting after important meeting. Their roles as savers of society must go to their heads. Could it be that if William Dudley had never made any of those meetings, we would be any worse off?

- They believe in their role as leader and the success of their actions. My favorite analogy (which I purloin from a *Wall Street Journal* op-ed piece of a few years ago) is to the 1970s movie *Midway*, about the pivotal World War II naval battle in the Pacific. Scene after scene in the movie portrays admirals on ships taking phone calls and promising to do their part to defeat the enemy. The men are brave, determined, willing to do what it takes and know that they can rely on each other. Our economic leaders similarly talk among themselves about moving hundreds of billions of dollars from one balance sheet to another or compelling the rate lower. However, actions in an economy are not like in a battle where you eliminate target after target and end up with net victory. Our macroeconomy suffers severe feedback effects that may confound your actions whether or not you acknowledge them.

- It is doubtful that many of our heroes ever had real conviction about basic beliefs. For example, when the financial crisis hit in 2008, President Bush backed off free market ideas. Liberals, like Paul Krugman, may champion average Americans but may really be quite disdainful of them. Krugman longs for an America in which everyone, both blue and white collar, has about the same standard of living in the same neighborhoods. Perhaps, but I doubt he wants auto workers to share the podium with him at Princeton. Following the crash of 2008, Richard Posner, who usually was a proponent of free markets, promptly authored *A Failure of Capitalism*[55] denouncing markets.

- There is often a circular nature to our knowledge, in which each set of experts assumes the other set knows better. For example, FOMC members look to business people like managers at FedEx and UPS, portfolio and mutual fund managers, company executives and small business contacts for solid economic ideas. These private parties often look to the government for its economic forecasts to formulate their own (i.e., those of the business community) ideas about the economy. Investment and other Wall Street types get their ideas from the academics who are one in the same boat as the government research people.

- They are insiders and have loyalties. For example, prominent industry economist Jan Hatzius of Goldman Sachs is a close associate of William Dudley, the head of the New York Fed.[56] I do not accuse them of intellectual corruption, but they must be respectful of each other's opinions when stating their own. Many leading figureheads in M&M often have careers spanning both industry and government and probably plan their careers and their career actions knowing that they will migrate to the other side. For example, prominent policy economist Peter Orszag (director of the Congressional Budget Office and director of the Office of Management and Budget) left government for a role at Citigroup. A great believer in policy now must put on the gown of a profit maximizer. Due to the increased prominence of government employment since 2008, more and more of today's movers and shakers will perceive an optimal career as requiring both private and public work spells, which will hamper free thinking.

---

[55] 2009, Harvard University Press.
[56] "New Supply of Former Fed Officials Finds High Demand on Wall Street," by Luca Di Leo and Jon Hilsenrath, *The Wall Street Journal*, November 23, 2011. http://www.wsj.com/articles/SB10001424052970204517204577046280907055596

- Political considerations impart timidity. Harvard economist Gregory Mankiw, on leave serving as White House chief economist, made some statements in February 2004 observing that outsourcing of American jobs was beneficial to the economy. He retracted such a belief: "Any loss of jobs is regrettable."[57] My example is from over ten years ago, which may reflect how careful prominent economists are not to make inflammatory statements.
- Never admit failure. Our public leaders deny failure. Fed Chairman Ben Bernanke steadfastly warded off virtually any suggestions that Fed policies did not work.
- As we said before, they crave to be Keynes. They want to be the singular, superior thinker observing the humdrum people and their irrational interactions—and succinctly theorizing economic life in a few equations. Andy Haldane, a senior Bank of England economist and policy activist, quipped, "I'm a great believer in the power of ideas and analysis as a mechanism for getting answers right."[58]

The Grand Concordat is Wall Street asking the Fed, "Can you keep inflation under control?" and, in turn, the Fed asks Wall Street, "Can you produce 8% rates of return?" They both answer in the affirmative but, indeed, neither party is in control.

## I.4.B. Markets v. Government

Modern political economy has undergone a momentous journey. The Western world was leaning left circa 1950. Most Western intellectuals, including many American economists, were socialists, or at least they doubted free markets in substantial ways. For example, in its early editions, Paul Samuelson's omnipresent economics textbook favorably compared the economy of the Soviet Union to ours. Few believed strongly in free markets. As evidence mounted in the 1970s and 1980s that socialist countries were economically deprived and socially backward, those great faculty of social science in America changed their stripes without ever fessing up to their original leanings.

Free markets and the ideas underlying them ultimately prevailed and, over the latter half of the 20th century, we chose freedom. It was largely the failure of the extreme non-market cases, like the Soviet Union and China, that propelled us to free markets. Come about 1984, the name year of George Orwell's iconic book on totalitarian tendency government control was on the run. This was the opposite of society around 1948 when *1984* came out. We chose freedom. Freedom fighters, like Milton Friedman, had triumphed. We now looked poised to go back with our government taking broader control of our macroeconomy and our microeconomic lives. During the 20th century, the U.S. was a society with significantly lower than average government involvement in markets compared to other countries. During the 21st, the U.S. will have more government involvement, in general, and will tend to be more like the progressive European countries. This change is broadly accepted by our people: Surveys of Americans v. Chinese today show that Chinese believe more strongly in capitalism.

Our current knowledge of M&M leaves us with two prejudices: (1) Markets do not work and therefore require constant vigilance, regulation and macroeconomic managing; and (2) Government involvement in economic decisions and markets, with the exception of sundry specialized roles of government, is almost always adverse. I believe the latter, but most Americans support the former or, at least, feel little conviction about the latter. Nobody can answer for sure whether it is the unstable market

---

[57] *The Wall Street Journal*, February 12, 2004, "Some Democratic Economists Echo Mankiw on Outsourcing," p. A4.
[58] "The Subversive Central Banker," by Jennifer Ryan, *Bloomberg Markets*, September 2015, pp. 76-78.

system and the greed of businesses; or a government with terminal adverse tendencies to overpromise, waste and confiscate wealth. We break on prejudices.

We choose government in most public discourse in America. We have deemed the private market, in particular, greedy lenders, as "the" cause of the crisis of 2008,[59] and we present that shakeout as evidence of a fundamental flaw in free markets. That is the opinion of most of the media and most academic and government types, including Fed policy people. For example, in his special series of four college lectures done in 2012, Ben Bernanke, almost without exception, blamed private markets for the economy's failures throughout U.S. history and during the 2000s. When asked relatively benign questions on government culpability he was quick to say, "Don't blame it all on government."

It does not take a great intellectual effort to attribute our economic problems to government. Our financial system was always heavily regulated. The large leveraged bets would not have been made if banks and other financial companies did not perceive the U.S. government as backstop. The housing market bubble and collapse was a government created problem—largely the loosening of housing finance from government mandate to extend housing to the poor. Also, the market likely could have resuscitated itself during the crisis if companies had been allowed to fail. In addition, up to and during the crisis, no government agency (not the Fed, Treasury or SEC) identified the economic and financial problems. Some key elements of the debate include the following:

- Historical analysis is of limited use in answering the question of government v. markets. Many experts point out government assistance in the historical growth of our economy and conclude it was beneficial or even essential. Their favorite example is the Erie Canal, which was government-sponsored and supported vast commerce, yet that is easy to gainsay. The government built many other canals which were of limited value. Private companies have funded similar large projects, including canals. Or you can invoke an Ayn Rand-like argument that everything great in our lives is from the creativity of private parties, and government is nothing more than a moocher. The same can be said of the economic crisis of 2008. Either government saved our system or, indeed, markets could have worked out imbalances just as well and/or it was the government that caused the imbalances in the first place. In the absence of re-running the history of our country without government, we will never know.

- Studying the longer history of the U.S. is similarly futile or prejudicial. A typical bias in many economics textbooks is that the economy was volatile during the 1800s and early 1900s, with constant crises like that of 1907, and this volatility constitutes a proof of market failure. Then, following the formation of our central bank in 1914, our economy became altogether more stable. The 1800s were a century of outsized growth, however, and the alleged crises were not that frequent—nor was their impact on the economy clear.[60] Then, after we formed the Fed we had more volatility, including the Great Depression. During the Great Depression, forays into the management of the economy by the government perhaps created more economic mishaps than they prevented. Following the 1930s, government believers contend that government stabilized the economy against a backdrop of reckless private financial markets exhibiting stock market crashes, housing bubbles and near disasters like 2008. Of course, it looks just as obvious that government created every major economic blunder including the high inflation of the 1970s and the housing bubble that led to the 2008 shakeout.

---

[59] Perhaps the most cited "cause" of the crisis was subprime lending which was motivated by predatory lenders.
[60] The period is inscrutable due to data limitations. We have some data notably on the banking sector and commodities production but do not have an unemployment series that characterizes how many people were involuntarily out of work.

- The media, with some exception, sides with government as beneficial in both macroeconomic matters and most microeconomic markets. The once stalwart market defender *The Economist* pronounces its adherence to principles of free markets vociferously, but it almost always espouses a role for government in matters both microeconomic and macroeconomic. Simply put, *The Economist* believes monetary and fiscal policies work and it has supported virtually every M&M intervention by governments since 2008. *The Wall Street Journal* editorial may advocate free markets, but the regular news pages in the paper, including economics columns, reflect belief in most of the mysteries of successful M&M.

- Both sides in the partisan debate claim their side never got a fair chance. Keynesians often grumble that we did not do sufficient Keynesian spending, or the right kind, or at the right time, etc. They also point out that when Keynesianism was done, like the tax cuts and increased spending of the early 1980s, the policy worked but did not get accredited. The 1980s economic success was attributed to supply-side economics. Free markets people argue that, since government dominates many industries and markets, we are never seeing unfettered competition in action. They also attribute housing bubbles and reckless finance to government subsidies and moral hazard. They contend that if the government were not omnipresent, private parties would have protected their finances appropriately. Anti-Keynesians contend that the entire century was constant Keynesianism. On both sides, these arguments often result in grand contradictions. For example, conservatives relish the great success of the U.S. economy historically but, since government involvement in the economy was so extensive, how much can they despise government?

- Market crashes and/or bubbles are unexplainable by any rational behavior in markets. For example, many cite the stock market crash of 1987 as an example of crazy markets; yet it does not take a lot to see 1987 as a rational reevaluation of markets. Perhaps the reevaluation was sudden, but not outside the operation of efficient markets.[61] Another case is the housing market collapse of 2008. How could this sector, which is so heavily dominated by the government, fail by market forces?

- There is not necessarily anything wrong with choosing more government involvement in our lives, yet we maintain a disingenuous attitude about our stance on government. After World War II, countries like Sweden and Denmark made a decision to pool their resources and economic output; America did not (as much). Now, though, we are converging but we pretend we are not. We contend a desire for the highest average GDP and number one status for America in many economic quantities.

- Americans largely favor additional government involvement in economic affairs. They vote for liberal candidates and in favor of proposals like raising minimum wage. Also in surveys people often indicate they want government to do more, not less.

- Do not doubt the power and heft of government involvement in markets. A prime example is the bond market. Bonds kept rising in value over the period 2010 through early 2014 even though there were many economic reasons that bond markets should not have been so buoyant, Many leading investors (like Bill Gross, Warren Buffett, Jeremy Siegel and Laurence Fink [CEO of BlackRock]) concurred. Government involvement in the bond market dominated, yet we still call it a bond market as if it were run freely. We are often characterized as a markets-based economy in which

---

[61] See "The Efficient Market Hypothesis and Its Critics," by Burton Malkiel, *Journal of Economic Perspectives*, Volume 17, Number 1, Winter 2003, pp. 59-82. Using a standard stock market valuation equation ($r = D/P + g$, where r is the rate of return, D/P is the expected dividend yield and g is the growth rate) and calling on two facts at the time: 1) yields on long-term Treasury bonds had risen from about 9% to 10.5% and 2) risk perceptions had increased due to a variety of current events, Malkiel gets a stock market price dropping from $100 to $66.67.

big business is extremely powerful. However, government wields greater power and recent developments, such as the imposition of very substantial fines on numerous companies and the threatening of U.S. companies about not changing tax residency, reflect diminished open markets.

## I.4.B.a. Sitting at the Kitchen Table with the Government Agent

Present day Americans go through their lives with the government by their sides just as much as or perhaps even more than people of other nations do. Russians, Mexicans, Nigerians, etc. have to rely on themselves more than their American counterparts. This may appear outlandish since America steadfastly boasts its characteristic freedom and individuality, yet many major facets of our economic lives are heavily influenced by the government: the housing market, consumer finance, education, pensions, investment, health care, banking and finance, etc. Our tax system is another major way the economic choices of our lives—like how many children we have, how we choose partners, which products we buy, etc.—are economically supported by the government. Many major industries (including defense, energy and health care) are subsidized directly and indirectly through tax policy. After decades of increasing wealth and income, we have become a people even less able to handle credit, mortgages, retirement planning, etc. than our parents and grandparents were. How did our government come to patronize us so much?

The first theory is that the people cannot handle economic life. They cannot plan retirement, understand the value of higher education (or have the foresight to borrow to increase their human capital), negotiate with big corporations, etc. without government assistance. Many cannot even handle basic aspects of living like feeding themselves, maintaining their health or caring for their children. Of course, it is petty to pass judgment on today's populace since for all of our lives our government has been there for us. For example, no American ever bothered to check the solvency of his bank given FDIC insurance.

Another facet is that certain basic costs of life (including health care, education and housing) are so expensive—in part due to government—that we need government support. A young person today looks at his job prospects and future expected earnings and ponders, "Do I want to take a chance on being very successful and making lots of money in competitive markets, or is it better to attain an average outcome, the kind that extensive government involvement insures?" He ponders major expenses: Housing is very expensive.[62] Health care is simply not affordable without insurance. Funding his retirement requires saving a large fraction of current earnings. Education is very expensive. He concludes that to go it alone is a bad bet. The same is true of any immigrant who arrives in America.

One area in which our government will have a growing presence in our lives, and perhaps a more obvious presence compared to non-Americans, is funding higher education. Our government is entertaining programs to assist people in paying off their student loans including loan forgiveness for people who work in the government or non-profit sector. Such programs may seem helpful, yet they represent a prolonged, significant presence in the economic decisions of Americans well into their middle age. Many forty-year-olds in the future will earn their livelihoods under the aegis and obligation to work closely with the taxman for maximum educational benefits.

Americans resist government in some cases; but in sufficient instances, like raising minimum wages, Americans tend toward government intervention. Will our government make fools of us by pitting us against the rest of the world in a "highest standard of living" contest that compels us to borrow too

---

[62] Sometimes you hear statements about housing "affordability" and that houses are "… the most affordable they have been in decades," but this depends on flawed ways of measuring housing cost. A person buying a house in 1985 got it much more cheaply than his counterpart today.

much? Then, if Americans' economic lives are poorer from government policies will we perversely rally behind more and more government?

## I.4.C. Economic Bluster

Peoples of every country are proud of their lands and predisposed to highlight their nation's successes. Indeed, the U.S. populace may be no more jingoistic in most respects. Recently, though, we have developed a national tin ear to our economic shortcomings and failings, thinking that through some combination of inherent advantages America must always prevail economically.

- Our prime boast is the handling of the Great Recession. While other nations froze or waffled, we singularly took action. We saved our economy with prompt and effective monetary policy following the crisis of 2008. Even before this crisis we skillfully managed our economy with traditional monetary policy through the 1980s into the 2000s. Of course, the final results are not in. Perhaps twenty years hence, scholars will reflect on U.S. policy and say, "They thought they controlled the economy but they were just lucky and ultimately all they did was add debt."

- We fancy ourselves decisive. Our economic and business decisions are determined, born of rigorous analysis, ahead of the pack and sometimes even bold. We compare ourselves to other countries' leadership, like that of Japan, and to those who came before us, like the financial leaders during the Depression. Japanese economic policy, for example, is timid and late. The Japanese call on our great economists to enlighten them. The American leaders from the 1930s, like Fed Chairman Mariner Eccles, were culpable of inaction and narrow-mindedness.

- We do not doubt our economy's ability to provide economic output. More than other countries we possess the essential capitalism, entrepreneurship and market savvy. We talk as if we are the best, with the highest productivity and admired around the world. If we fail to compare favorably with other nations we cite abstract factors. Our President contends the world admires us more and more each year. During the financial crisis, when our economic and budget situation looked grave, many cited Winston Churchill, "You can always count on Americans to do the right thing after they've tried everything else."[63]

- We also believe in our government's ability to conduct efficacious economic policy and reasonably control our economic fate.

- We spurn claims of decline. Our favorite word is "still," as in, "we are still the reserve currency," "still the greatest country," "still have the deepest capital markets," "still have the most entrepreneurial culture," etc. Only in America could you get such a wide variety of innovative companies. One favorite corporate icon is Apple. We are so proud of its creativity and design capability. We point out that its thinking component emanates from Cupertino, CA, while the dreary manufacturing is done elsewhere. We hold up an iPhone as physical demonstration and present a chart showing the value and cost components behind the iPhone, with over 90% going to us.

- We repeatedly propose reforms of seemingly un-reformable problems like our tax system. We ignore repeated failure to streamline our taxes. We lack the fatalism of competitor nations that reforms have been tried before and no more likely to be successful now than they were before.

- We dismiss our economic problems with macro excuses attributing mediocre economic performance European economic inaction, over-saving by Chinese and bad breaks like natural

---

[63] Whether Churchill made quite this statement is disputed, but it is commonly attributed to him.

calamities (like the famous cold winter of 2015). When other nations attribute their economic problems to our economy and our economic policies, however, we admonish them to look at their own economic houses.

- U.S. Fed leaders often assert that we should do policy for our nation and not for others. You find this sentiment in the Fed transcripts. It is as if we are bailing out the world. We cite our self-interested policy as being uniquely advantageous for all nations because a strong U.S. economy will demand goods and services from abroad yet that effect is likely very secondary to adverse international effects of U.S. policy. We are also prone to point out fundamental economic problems in other countries, e.g., we doubt the longevity of Chinese GDP growth, we highlight that Chinese growth comes at the cost of environmental and social disruption, etc.

- We consider ourselves fair, even perhaps magnanimous, in our economic dealings with other nations. During 2010 and 2011 when commodities prices including food prices were soaring accusations were made that our policy was causing poor people all over the world to suffer. We were indifferent both in our press and in public debate. Later in 2013 when we started to scale down our expansionary policy, we were similarly criticized by certain nations, in particular Turkey, facing crises at the time. We scolded these nations noting their economies had fundamental economic problems, and they should not blame us. Simultaneously, we solicited Germany, Japan and China for help, contending that their policies were hurting us.

- We consider ourselves great thinkers and analyzers and assume others think less critically than we, and perhaps perform policy by merely reacting to us. This is patent with how we speak about the Chinese on M&M matters.

- We think we can talk our way out of these very real problems. Among people in charge we deny failure. Ben Bernanke warded off almost any suggestion of mistakes of monetary policy during his tenure as Fed Chairman. In March 2014, as the unemployment rate got near a stated threshold of 6.5% for policy change, Janet Yellen dropped that threshold and admitted no failure.

- We (some of us) interpret our central bank performance very favorably. We stopped inflation handily in the early 1980s and could do it again if we had to. We groomed the economy masterfully during the 1980s, 1990s and into the 2000s. We saved the economy from a depression in 2008. We diminish alternative takes that we caused problems, were sometimes lucky and that our solutions to problems have created many adverse effects.

- Entrepreneurs are part of the debates on the eternal vibrancy of the U.S. economy. Entrepreneurs often point out the folly of too much government, but also marvel at the sheer greatness of the American economic way. They reassure that the underlying system is fine and needs only a little adjustment to keep their kind continuing their contribution to society. Liberals often remark that entrepreneurs are so driven that they will always work their magic regardless of how much tax they must pay. Would Bill Gates, for example, have given up if he only made billions rather than tens of billions, they ask.

## I.4.D. America's Economic Generations

If asked what their greatest concern is, the current "grown-ups" of America would answer their children. They would assert vociferously that the children have been well taken care of and recite a long list of services: fostering education and good diet; encouraging critical thinking; saving them from drugs, hatred, discomfort, cigarettes and pornography; introducing them to culture, sports and other activities; etc.

In reality, how well are America's young prepared for the future? More pointedly, how have the M&M choices of America's grown-ups positioned our children economically?

For our M&M discussion, let's hypothesize three generations.[64] First, the well-known, so-called "Greatest" generation, those who lived through the Depression, World War II, the Korean War and early Cold War. Next, we have our current adults, who I call the "Inflated" (for their perception of themselves) and define as the Baby Boomers plus another fifteen years of births, roughly those born between 1946 and the late 1970s. This time period represents people who participated in strong economies and asset markets, and also those who run the country today. The Inflated were generally "born on third base." Their credits include the fight for civil rights; reigning in of American imperialism (mainly opposition to the Vietnam War) and struggle against old bigotries and systemic corruption such as Watergate. The Inflated are those who have run the country since about 1990 including Bill Clinton, George W. Bush, Barack Obama and Donald Trump.

The final generation, today's young, I peg in time as anyone born so late that he or she would be doing adult tasks after 2008. This roughly translates to anyone born 1980 or later. I call them "BOMP:" Burden of the Monetary & Macro Past, largely for the level and breadth of debt they start out with. This generation will not attain high rates of return on assets and was dealt relatively crummy economic circumstances like an aging and non-growing population, low GDP growth, high cost of essential goods and services, intense competition from abroad, patronizing previous generations, high taxes, flawed intellectual framework for solving problems, etc. The BOMP may or may not be inherently virtuous. They too started out on third base but have a tough economic draw. They have the Inflated managing their economic problems. Getting ahead of the story a little, the Inflated, who make the decisions today, perceive that they inherited a tough lot from the Greatest. The Inflated also believe that they have left the BOMP in a strong position, but both perceptions are invalid.

## I.4.D.a. The Greatest

In his book *The Greatest Generation* [65] television anchorman Tom Brokaw popularized a seemingly hard to contest case that the Americans of the Great Depression and World War II period constituted an usually great set of achievers, exhibiting both personal sacrifice and community service, hard work, adult responsibility and relative thrift. Whether these virtues were a product of an inner greatness of these people or just that they hit a set of extraordinary circumstances in place and time is arguable. The challenges of this generation were, perhaps, easier in many ways to tackle, at least in purely economic terms. Wars are winnable if you have a preponderance of force, palatable if you have common cause and of finite cost. Paying for them is not a struggle, too, if your future economy has the output. As for the deprivation of living through the Great Depression, everyone was in the same situation. My father, born in 1921, would aver that being a kid during the Depression in a household with unemployed parents and six children was arduous in some ways, but not uncomfortable and not characterized by despair.

The Greatest hit the global market after World War II with a near monopoly on capitalism and a domestic market with favorable institutions. They had high marginal products due to their high education levels, work ethic and singular physical capital. They were willing to take losses. The monopoly rents commanded by American companies were great. U.S. entrepreneurs, and the average Americans who

---

[64] These generation delineations are different from the usual Baby Boom (birth years 1946 through 1964, about 76 million people), Generation X (1965 through 1980, about 57 million) and Millennials (1981 through 2000, about 82 million). I include the Generation X'ers with the Baby Boomers because both would have benefitted from the strong economies of the 1990s and early 2000s.

[65] Random House, 1998.

worked for them, did not have to compete against the Chinese, Russians, Indians and hundreds of millions of other people born in societies that stymied free enterprise. The Chinese equivalent of Ray Kroc, the Russian equivalent of Walter Wriston or the Indian equivalent of Sam Walton were born, lived and passed with their great enterprise plans played out only in their heads.

## I.4.D.b. The Inflated

The Inflated inherited ample wealth, efficient factors of production and also the freedom and institutions for commerce and entrepreneurship. They then lived the way they wanted, throwing off many of the constraints on behavior that their parents had. They adopted a 1960s mindset. They could take all good aspects of American life for given and blame adversities on other parties—notably their parents, the system and selected bogeymen from abroad.

The adult lives of the Inflated have been marked by recessions, energy crises, wars and terrorism but overall their economy and asset values have grown significantly, given the Inflated both regular income and the extra income courtesy of unusually high rates of return to assets. Other favorable circumstances, like population structure, cheap natural resources, technology changes, relative peace and favorable political conditions, etc., prevailed for the Inflated. Were the Inflated enhancers of progress, or were they free riders? Did the Inflated do a net negative job, while thinking they created such net prosperity? These are unanswerable questions.

## I.4.D.c. The Burden of the Monetary & Macro Past ("BOMP")

Today's young Americans face mixed signals. They ask, "Are we rich or are we poor?" They start out materially richer than any generation before them. Even today's poor have comfort. For example, can any kid today say "I have to walk miles to school?" They are better protected from hatred, bigotry, bullying, health issues, risks due to motor vehicles, unwanted sexual advances, alcohol abuse, sports issues, etc. Yet, the BOMP faces numerous material growing economic problems; and, even worse, they face attitudinal and mental handicaps. Here are some of the BOMP's challenges:

- No potential price gains to housing because housing is fully valued (i.e., house prices are high). House prices will likely tend down. The days of buying a house, occupying it for its full housing services and then selling at an increased price—such that you made all your money back and lived rent free—are over.
- They will face low rates of return on investments of all kinds (cash, stocks, bonds, etc.). This means lower income in general, especially for retirement.
- Pensions present two other disadvantages (in addition to low rates of return). Pension schemes have largely changed from defined-benefit plans to defined-contribution plans, which means new participants bear the market risk. This could be advantageous if rates or return are high but if rates are low, defined-contribution is tougher for a worker. Also, the reforms of underfunded pensions are mainly being done by reducing benefits for young workers. New hires are required to contribute more, accept lower and later benefits and receive reduced cost of living adjustments.
- A generally lower overall total compensation for work/career will confront the BOMP. This will take the form of inferior job choices, like more gig and temporary work, stingier benefits, diminished retirement options and perhaps even lower wages.
- We now have reverse-Keynesianism. For a century we borrowed; now we must save. If you believe in Keynesianism, that means less GDP.

- The large existing physical capital stock must be maintained.
- They face overpriced education. Consider a decision by a young person to seek an MBA or law degree. Either would cost over $100,000 and, unless the student enrolls in a top program, returns could be negative. Again, perhaps for the first time in history, education in many areas looks fully priced or even overpriced. Another potentially adverse development in education comes from proposals to fund it with claims on future earnings of present-day students. It might appear to be an efficient way for students to fund an education, but it might also result in locking in high prices for education.
- The BOMP will pay higher taxes for obligations already made by governments but not budgeted.
- There have been substantial changes to basic economic rules as a result of current policy. These include the level of inflation, tax rates and the ability of government to debase the currency.
- The potentially high cost of compulsory health insurance will impact this generation.

The BOMP do have advantages. The most obvious is the higher quality of goods and services that exist today. Creature comforts, especially those related to technology and health care, are vastly superior. Older people, like Warren Buffett, who was born in 1930, view this as a prohibitive advantage such that contemporary economic problems pale in comparison. In his 2015 annual letter to shareholders[66] Buffett comments on persistent economic growth over his life and its continuation (if only at a, what he terms, "much-lamented" 2%), "The babies being born in America today are the luckiest crop in history." Of course, you can make the case that the general increase in standard of living over time is irrelevant to generational economic debates. Each generation should be grandfathered in and its economic problems should be viewed for their relative disadvantages. In either case, some other advantages of the BOMP are:
- The BOMP should have longer life expectancy, better health and broader access to health care.
- The BOMP stand to inherit substantial financial wealth. It is hard to quantify if this bequest exceeds the debts the BOMP will inherit, but the debts look more imminent in time and must be borne by the entire populace. Many stand to inherit little or no wealth.
- There are advantages from new sources of energy within America's borders. Perhaps the most important advantage of ample domestic energy is that the U.S. can avoid costly foreign entanglements.
- There could be extraordinary productivity gains from developing technology. We frequently list and speculate about innovation including items like internet, wireless, 3D-printing, biotechnology, space exploration, robotics, nanotechnology, driverless motor vehicles, etc. However, whether such productivity enhancers will equal the average productivity gains during the post-World War II period up until the turn of the century is a guess. Estimating the ultimate economic benefit of new technology is much less certain than merely marveling at new devices and gadgets.
- If, indeed, population growth is slowing and if this persists for a long time, today's young could eventually reap the economic benefits of greater demand for their labor and, therefore, higher wages. A smaller population would mean cheaper housing and an easing of the various burdens of growing populations.

### I.4.D.d. Seeking a Clash of Generations

---

[66] The 2015 letter presented in February 2016. http://www.berkshirehathaway.com/letters/2015ltr.pdf

Comparing generations is a relatively futile task because each rises to its challenges and each pushes its luck, and budgets, to limits. Yet, at this time, we must examine the relatively unique phenomenon of the extraordinary exchange of economic output across generations. The Greatest paid their way and left America to the Inflated in reasonable economic shape—and did not deny them the freedom to handle their own problems. The Inflated have not done similarly. This generation has indulged the M&M story of buying our way out of our economic problems. The Inflated have also met generational legacies with lethargy. For example, generational economic issues get relatively little press. The BOMP are not without flaws. At least they deserve better recognition of U.S. debt problems and respect for intellectual freedom.

Perhaps the Inflated, being the first generation to hold and manage big wealth over time, did a fair job with it and with the economy. Also, perhaps it will be a blessing for the BOMP to have an economic challenge. Unfortunately, I foresee a day of reckoning, perhaps even in dramatic form, with today's young censuring their parents. Maybe they will even drag their parents, screaming and kicking out of their nursing homes, to stand trial for the debt they left.

## I.4.D.d.i. Never Argue With Anyone Over Thirty

The 60's saying was, "Don't trust anyone over thirty." In a wide variety of ways, today's young have less freedom to think and speak their minds than their parents did. Despite mediums like Twitter and Facebook young people must be careful about what they say. I cannot measure how much this condition impacts economic growth and opportunity, but my hunch is that it is adverse. Today's young are reminded regularly that they have had every advantage and consideration handed to them. Criticism of parents and other persons of authority is discouraged. We impute an incompetence to our young. We protect them in school and as they enter the workforce. We protect them from corporations and from adult financial obligations like credit cards. We train them extremely in health and personal safety situations. We even instruct them on how to deal with their peers in personal relationships. Most colleges and universities today, for example, require dating training.

Certainly there is no doubt that parents care about their own children. Today's parents, though, believe that, since they solved their children's problems and provided all creature comforts, they (the children) should be content with average outcomes and not expect greater economic opportunities. In other words, "We gave you a great education and you will inherit the house, so accept the college debt, higher taxes and the cost of my retirement." Even worse is the patronizing attitude and the misinformation that accompanies it. We delude our young that we can make our economic system fair and kind, and have economic growth and prosperity. This misleads them about the reality of competitive markets. We beset our young with M&M notions of governments "lowering the rate" and "increasing aggregate demand."

Today's young have many material advantages notably in available technologies and health care, but that does not offset chronic economic overhang. For example, you cannot tell a young person who has poor job prospects that he should be happier because, e.g., his television reception is better or the pollution emitted from light bulb usage is lessened. Longer life expectancies and better health (or at least potentially better health depending on lifestyle) are natural for today's young even compared to their grandparents. Again, it is tough to say, "Son, 75 is the new 65, so do not take offense that your pension programs require you to work until you're 75."

The Inflated delude young people into believing in the simple solutions that do not involve grave trade-offs. The Inflated have been very generous to themselves in blaming economic failures on surprise and forces beyond their control, most notably the 2008 crisis which they say took us unaware, yet the BOMP will have no such luxury. The Inflated have also liberally used the Keynesian way out–borrowing and spending. The BOMP will face the failure of Keynesian and will have to live within budget constraints. Of course, it is difficult to state with certainty which generation is better off, and what could even be done to rectify intergenerational economic injustices.

Today's youth are desensitized and lackadaisical about many issues. During a decade of active war by the U.S. (roughly from 2001 through 2011), I broached U.S. military expense as detrimental to our economy in my college classes. Students exhibited little or no concern and certainly no passion. I cannot recall anytime a student said to me, "What is the effect of war on the economy?"

America's young are coddled and overly-privileged. They do not challenge. One strange facet is that today's youth are seemingly less agitated about high levels of debt than pre-2008 young people. I recall more student anti-government debt agitation circa 2004 during the run-up in deficits under President Bush than recently. The increases in debt back then were not even as bad. It is as if the gross worsening of debt and deficit prospects has inured young people to the problem. I can speculate about what makes our young apathetic: Perhaps social media has made them introverted or maybe they are overwhelmed by the economic magnitudes of debt. It could even be that they are overly-medicated, especially the hyper-active personalities who normally make up the greatest rabble rousers.

## I.4.D.d.ii. Burdens of the Past

Today's young face tougher competition, relatively scarcer undiscovered areas and have fewer excuses for bad behavior or failure. They are the first generation with an extreme burden of wealth and the idea that they were given all the advantages and protections. For example, students arrive on campus today with every conceivable protection: codes of conduct and speech; strict rules enforcement including surveillance and professional policing; a plethora of specialized deans and counselors; etc. They are often reminded of the extraordinary struggles carried out by their elders, like the fights for civil rights and women's liberation. In addition, today's young have a tougher time of bestowing largess on the unfortunates of the world, including both the poor of America and the indigent and politically handicapped outside the United States. Those people do not look up to the U.S. as much as they used to. Perhaps the most frustrating constraint on today's young is that their parents patronize them, "Sure we did that, but don't you do it."

Finally, they have to work off of modern models of describing the world around them. In this task they face resistance from their mentors, who have dug in the rightness of their thinking, including M&M. It is even worse because today's young Americans face intense intellectual competition from previously non-competitive societies, like China and India. This represents an adverse role reversal. For a century we studied them exclusively, and now they will study us. We analyzed the poor monetary policies of Latin American countries and pronounced on the folly of their hyperinflations. When Asian countries flopped in 1997 (the so-called Asian Crisis), we analyzed their retrograde M&M ad infinitum. Now the tables are turned. Asian and other non-western scholars will have a field day analyzing our current M&M policies. Bit by bit they will pick apart our glorious M&M, ranging from grand condemnations like that Keynesianism never worked to technical items like that what we called consumer confidence never existed. They will recommend policy for Americans to follow to rectify our economy—perhaps that we perform services that we are relatively efficient at like taking the world's trash, as Lawrence Summers once recommended for African economies.

## I.4.D.d.iii. Generational Debating Points

I share a personal observation about my generation (the Inflated) v. my parents' (the Greatest). As I came of age in the 1970s and discovered the world around me, I was amazed at how special the U.S. was compared to most of the rest of the world. The pages of *Time* or *Newsweek* revealed Africa beset by war, the Middle East by incompetence, Latin America by hyperinflation, China and the Soviet Union by ridiculous political systems, etc. I would marvel at pictures of Chinese riding bikes or stories of Russians snitching on each other to get bigger apartments. The world was full of pathetic people created by fanatical governments. I realized I lived in a society with decent and high standards, including economic standard of living. Indeed there were problems in my country like crime and racism, but they did not represent total failure. I believed that my parents, like responsible adults, bequeathed a strong foundation. To me, the perception that my parents were a bunch of Archie Bunker's who left me a world of bigotry was nonsense. The list below touches on a few aspects of the inter-generational economic situation:

- One advantage today's youth have is that the great economic shakeout (2008 ff) indeed happened early on and reasonably revealed flaws in our economy. If by some brilliant M&M policy, we had forestalled the 2008 ff crisis, we might be worse off today. Suppose that, circa 2006 or 2007, we had recognized the gravity of a potential bursting of the housing bubble. Perhaps policies we would have used to support housing and the economy, in general, would have left us with a worse asset-based recession a few years later.

- One of the first assignments I give my students each semester is to find organized projects by young people concerning inter-generational economic problems. Indeed, there are a handful of groups, including The Can Kicks Back, Generation Debt, Americans for Prosperity, It's Up to Us, Fix the Debt, Concord51, Tea Party Students, Young Americans for Liberty, etc. However, many of these are merely right-wing groups, as opposed to efforts focusing on economics; and none are very prominent. I mock, "How many million members?" Many of my students refer to the Occupy Wall Street, yet it faded away quickly. Also, Occupy Wall Street was primarily a left-wing effort asking for government to spend more money, which is probably not in the best interest of a generation facing debt. I admit to my students though that generational economics is a tough cause to rally behind. Why would a talented young person devote his early career to a public issue with little glamor and low compensation? Even if he were willing to try, the Inflated, as we have pointed out, have stymied complaint with the heavy-handed, "America's economic M&M policy has worked for you … you were saved from an even worse outcome."

- Today's young generation is typically born in relative wealth. They might constitute the first to face declining fortunes. Their parents and grandparents rose in standard of living. Perhaps it will be particularly tough on an American generation to face a declining standard of living, but maybe it will be equally fulfilling going down. Human nature is receptive to challenge.

- Cost of providing for dependents is relevant but indelicate to broach. Families in the Greatest Generation sent children off to fight World War II and some died. That was tragic and costly immediately, but not financially costly for years and years. A BOMP with multiple parents in nursing homes will face constant negative annuities.

- The prevailing solutions to future debt problems, such as rectifying public pensions, usually involve a "grandfathering" of existing commitments due the Inflated. Therefore, the solving of these problems might tend to lock in particularly bad terms.

- This current young generation must face up to a regime shift in macroeconomic thinking. Describing macro aggregates with facile theorizing of cause and effect, the "dis causes dis," will sound increasingly trivial. Eventually the economic discussion of issues will focus on microeconomic concepts like choice, tradeoffs, budget constraints, allocation of resources over time and space, jobs and salaries based on marginal products, risk, uncertainty, entrepreneurship, etc.

- The Inflated patronize their children. "We've been through worse." Even hard-liners on generational issues often end with fatherly comments. Big money manager Stanley Druckenmiller, who had been very outspoken on the adverse effects of U.S. debt and deficits, professed that the future was favorable because today's young are the finest cohort of achievers he has ever seen in his 30 years of hiring people.[67]

- The Inflated also overprotect the BOMP by training them how to deal with every life situation and providing psychologists, counselors, deans, chaperones, etc. to aid in every decision.

- I worry that the Inflated will engage in one great "Last Economic Hurrah," like instituting a Value-Added Tax, in a desperate attempt to save our economic world.

- The Greatest had more honor and integrity than either the Inflated or the BOMP. Perhaps, though, being born into material wealth and inculcated that spending, not thrift, makes society prosperous sapped both the Inflated and the BOMP of honor.

- The Inflated impose upon the BOMP the facile macro solutions of large net gains from M&M devices. The Inflated experienced GDP growth, high rates of return in investments, tax reforms that seemingly created more wealth, M&M policies that seemingly saved the economy (notably the post-2008 policy), free trade that benefited all nations, etc. The BOMP will face a world of microeconomic tradeoff. The M&M devices were peculiar to the last century.

- Perhaps the worst aspect about the legacy of the Inflated on the BOMP is that the Inflated sucked the fun out of life for the BOMP by solving all the material problems and leaving the BOMP as constant counters and money grubbers, perpetually seeking the largess of the Inflated.

---

[67] Interview "Stanley Druckenmiller on Strategy…" on *Bloomberg.com* November 22, 2013.

# I.5. Debt, Taxes & Claims on Future Economic Output

The U.S. currently faces debt and deficit problems. Our federal deficit has decreased significantly since it topped a trillion dollars in each year from 2009 through 2012, but it is still very high.

Debt and deficit are not new, of course. We faced a similar debt and deficit crisis not too long ago and became well versed, as a society, in the underlying economic principles. When I was a graduate student in the mid and late-1980s, given the run-up of federal deficits in the early 1980s, research on "public finance" (i.e., government spending, deficits and taxes) was omnipresent. Many of the big names in the economics profession (like Lawrence Summers, Joseph Peckman, Alan Auerbach, James Poterba, etc.) focused on it. Economists at this time were completely conversant with basic ideas like the future insolvency of Social Security, the optimal design of taxation and how large deficits could be relative to economic growth.

As the years rolled by research in public finance simmered down, largely due to the lessening of U.S. deficits over the 1990s. In the late 1990s into about 2001 we actually ran surpluses. Social Security and future health care costs were continuing problems, but they did not appear unmanageable due to the growth of the economy. The acuity of debt and deficit analysis quickly came back to prominence in the Great Recession. As I read current papers in years after 2008, it was déjà vu. I was reading the same analyses, summarizing the same principles of economics and making the same recommendation. They were even authored by the same economists.

Regardless of having hashed through problems before, we are currently running chronic deficits and have a large and growing debt. In addition, we sit on the cusp of what is the greatest transfer scheme ever created by man. Our young generation must fund the retirement and health care of the Baby Boom. How will we pay for our aging population, its Social Security, other government pensions and government sponsored health care? We simply have not funded these items adequately.

## I.5.A. Debt, Deficits & the Fiscal Gap

How much are we in debt? You can get different numbers. As of the end of 2016, the gross U.S. debt is about $20 trillion. Of that, about $5.5 trillion are intra-governmental holdings, including mainly the Social Security Trust Fund and Medicare. That leaves about $14.5 trillion "held by the public," which includes debt held by individuals, corporations, foreigners and the U.S. Fed (which holds about $2.5 trillion). Some experts prefer the $14.5 trillion concept for analyzing burdens of government debt, but the $20 trillion figure is probably a better number since we are obligated to honor Social Security and whatever commitment the Fed has made to hold treasuries. The $20 trillion makes our debt about the size of our annual GDP giving us a debt/GDP ratio of over 1.[68]

---

[68] The way we view the funding of Social Security and Medicare requires clarification. The federal government taxes American citizens and businesses for Social Security and Medicare (together, payroll taxes). One technicality is that, strictly speaking, these payroll taxes are not taxes. They are social insurance contributions. In principle, the funds raised are not for general government expenditure but are dedicated to the person who made the contribution. To the average person and for all practical purposes, however, Social Security and Medicare are simply big federal taxes. Another facet is that each contributor, like me or you, has a record of how much he has contributed and how much he is entitled to in retirement. However, the U.S. does not put individual's payments of Social Security and Medicare taxes aside. The money raised from Social Security and Medicare is used like regular income tax receipts for current expenditures. The U.S. does issue bonds to a Trust funds representing Social Security and Medicare tax proceeds. These Trust bonds (about $5 trillion in total as we mentioned above) have a curious character. Some analysts view them as not part of U.S. debt. In this view, they are seen as money owed from one group of Americans to another

Yet the gross v. public debt numbers are misleading. We are really much more in debt. If we project future spendings and taxes we are in the red going into the future forever. Our projected tax revenues are less than our outlays. Therefore, we should take the present value of our future deficits or the intertemporal budget constraint. We must bring these future deficits into an equivalent amount today by taking the present discounted value of the deficits. We call this the "Fiscal Gap." That gap renders our conventional debt figures bogus. Few analysts focus on the fiscal gap. Most government officials and most supposedly critical analysts (like the media) focus on the conventional concepts of debt. They miss a great point: This present discounted magnitude, of course, depends on future economic quantities that we do not know precisely. We can make projections, however. Key projections are GDP growth, population growth, life expectancies and interest rates on debt. Using relatively optimistic projections about all of these our fiscal gap is about $200 trillion.

My students automatically question the fiscal gap with one common question, "Why do we have to worry about paying expenses way in the future? Won't we have greater economic resources to pay for them then?" Then I laugh out loud, "Sure we have dough coming our way in the future, but we've already figured that in, and we have been overly optimistic!" Some students will retort that we can reduce future expenses, as if budgets will be easier to rectify in the future by some good fortune. The answer is also obvious. No, they are grave commitments that we have to pay.

In other terms, our fiscal gap, defined as the amount of GDP that we are short for our government spending, is about 10% (of annual GDP). To put it simply, we would have to raise our tax take by 10% of GDP or cut our government spending equal to 10% of GDP. This fiscal gap of the U.S. is among the worst of developed nations. Italy, a country considered in bad economic shape, has a fiscal gap of only about 5%, and they have a better lid on their pension and health care expenses. Our fiscal gap grows about $10 trillion per year. To rectify this, we could either cut our current spending by about 30% or raise taxes by about 50% (which would be about 10% of GDP since our taxes are about 25% of GDP).

This fiscal gap is obviously ludicrous, you might say, because it depends on straight-line extrapolation. This criticism is valid, in a technical way: For example, we could never increase our debt into the hundreds of trillions without some offsetting economic effects like being shut out of borrowing in markets. However, the fiscal gap highlights that we are in debt now, getting more in debt almost regardless of the little changes we make in public finance and are in debt as much as most nations. A variety of basic ideas on our public finance are listed below:

- Our federal government spending can be subdivided into discretionary and non-discretionary (sometimes termed "entitlements"). Discretionary spending consists of defense (about $800 billion) and the rest (about $400 billion), which is infrastructure, foreign aid, domestic policing, etc. The mandatory spending includes Social Security, Medicare, Medicaid, federal pensions and interest on the debt. Our Federal government currently raises enough taxes to pay for entitlements like pensions, Social Security and Medicare and interest on the debt and about half of the discretionary spending. We run about $450 billion short.

- To get our budget deficit down, we could either raise taxes or cut spending. We will talk about raising, or otherwise fixing, taxes later. To cut spending without touching entitlements we would have to decrease our discretionary spending drastically. The discretionary spending generally is

at some time in the future. Yet, since future claimants, like me and you, generally need Social Security and Medicare to live when we retire, i.e., we are not going to deem the payments as extra money and give it back to the government, the value of the Trust bonds should be reflected as being debt of the federal government. In a sense, we have already spent this money. Therefore, other analysts view the term "debt held by the public" as misleading since the intragovernmental holdings are ultimately owed to individuals.

more important for future generations. We could cut or alter entitlements, although we demonstrate less will to do that. If we tried to balance our budget by every possible action including cutting discretionary spending (mainly national defense) and decreasing entitlements (like pushing out Social Security retirement age, perhaps linking Social Security increases to a lower cost of living index, raising premiums and co-pays for Medicare, etc.) we would still likely be short depending how much we cut the latter. It would be like in the old Godzilla movies where the Japanese line up everything they have—soldiers, tanks, rockets, etc.—and the leader yells fire; but after the smoke settles, Godzilla keeps coming.

- U.S. budget history is dramatic. After World War II, we were greatly indebted, but we reduced our national debt year after year. In the 1950s, we generally balanced our budget. Then for decades we ran deficits but in many years our debt-to-GDP ratio went down because our GDP grew. That situation reversed in the 1980s. Coming into the 1990s, we got lucky when, due to a confluence of fortunate developments, the U.S. deficit diminished to the point of budget surpluses at the end of the 1990s and 2000. As crazy as it sounds today, at that time we projected the surpluses to continue and our debt to go to zero. As one politician put it, the budget surplus was raging out of control.

- One valid aspect of debt and deficits understood by most intelligent people is that, indeed, a country or other entity can run perpetual deficits and not get deeper in debt, so long as the country's resources are expanding. In the mid and late 1980s and into the 1990s the U.S. was running deficits, but they were not as detrimental as many thought. Top economists at that time, like Robert Eisner (1922-1998), asked, "Should we be saving for our grandchildren?" His answer was no. Given the magnitudes and trends of economic events at that time his answer was correct. The ability to run a deficit depends on (future) GDP growth and also on the interest rate paid on debt, which should be lower than the GDP growth rate (both in real terms). We have discussed prospects for GDP growth and the approximate 3% growth assumed in many government budget forecasts is probably too favorable. Also, the average real interest on U.S. debt is currently lower than real GDP growth but that condition may not persist.

- Economists often explain deficits by invoking a cycle story. Deficits have two components: (1) cyclical, which disappear when the economy recovers; and (2) structural, which persist over time unless underlying economic conditions change. We pegged our structural deficit at about 2% of GDP before the Great Recession and which we believed we could manage since our GDP growth was greater than that. This depiction of deficits was common in economic discussion early in the post-2008 period, like in 2009 and 2010. It petered out as our recovery lagged, and the distinction between temporary and structural deficits became hard to rely on.

- Primary deficit is the deficit excluding interest on the debt. The reason for excluding interest is that it represents an obligation from the past. The primary deficit, therefore, describes the current period's income v. expenditures and can be used to judge the current team in power for whether they are making ends meet or not. On the other hand, since past deficits and the level of debt they have created were integral to our current economic standing, excluding their costs is deceiving.

- Determining the current deficit is difficult due to accounting gimmicks and off-budgets items. For example, we plan budget cuts in the future and record them in the present. We also budget major items like wars and future pension liabilities with accounting tricks to exclude them presently. The way we talk about cutting spending is devious. We cite large numbers for spending cuts, such as over one trillion dollars; yet those cuts are over many (like ten) years. Then, we are not even truly cutting expenditures, we are simply not growing future spending as much. Other tricks include assuming we will be spending less on future wars or that we will save on future other expenses like medical expenses, but this is just under-budgeting and/or not having a rainy day amount. Of course, there is no guarantee future Congresses will agree to any spending curtailment proposals.

- Not all debt is bad, of course: If you borrow for something that pays back, debt is desirable. Even if you borrow for something that does not pay back, like present consumption, it is also perfectly justifiable, if you can reasonably handle the payments. A student loan that pays for having four years of college fun and enhanced future career opportunities is acceptable. A loan that pays for merely four years of college life may be unacceptable.

- Federal debt has grown greatly recently—roughly doubling from about $10 to $20 trillion over the last decade. The increase has received a fair amount of press in some ways, but it is also largely dismissed. There was no public outrage, somewhat confirming the opinion of Vice President Dick Cheney that deficit financing did not affect public opinion. During this time of increasing debt, we claimed we saved our economy with government spending policy which contributed to the debt but was a necessary evil. Was the policy worth it overall? It is impossible to estimate the counter-case with anything but a guess, but big debt hampers other facets of our federal government. For example, our role in humanitarian and military situations like in Syria or Ukraine depends on our fiscal stance.

- International comparisons are somewhat revealing: U.S. conventional debt in terms of debt-to-GDP ratio is high among peers. Only Japan has a much bigger debt burden, yet the Japanese case may not give much comfort to the U.S. since almost all of Japan's debt is held internally and interest cost on Japanese debt is very low due to very low rates on Japanese debt. Looking at the fiscal gap, the U.S. is among the worst. Greece, the U.K. and Japan are close to the U.S. The U.S. is worse largely due to health care and pension spending trends.

- Integral to the debt and deficit debate is understanding how we project our deficit. We assume relatively favorable GDP growth (about 2 to 3%, depending) demographics both in terms of native fertility and immigration (both growing constantly) and life expectancies (not growing much). The Congressional Budget Office also assumes that we will get tax revenue from cash held overseas by U.S. corporations, and we count on getting it even though that will likely never happen. Also, we have exhausted every budget trick and all new revenue sources.

- The U.S. deficit has come down significantly in 2012 through 2015 but has tended back up in 2016. News coverage of debt and deficit has dropped. In 2014 and 2015 most comments on the deficit remarked on its large decrease in magnitude and characterized it as a solved problem. Deficit improvement was largely a variety of favorable temporal factors including: (1) low interest rates on outstanding U.S. debt, about 2% on average; (2) payments from Fannie Mae and Freddie Mac; (3) remittances from the Fed; (4) taxes on capital gains due to extensive stock buybacks and acquisitions done by corporations due to low rates; (5) taxes from extensive IRA conversions; and (6) savings from the termination of various Fed stimulus programs.

### I.5.A.a. Non-Government Debt

Is our government debt offset by solvency in the corporate and household sectors? Corporations today are supposedly flush with cash. Indeed, cash levels have risen following the Great Recession, yet they also hold much debt. Total debt of corporations has gone up at about the same rate or faster than cash, leaving net debt higher than before. Personal or household debt is burdensome, too. There are four main groups: mortgage, auto, credit card and student loan. Credit card and mortgage debt went down or did not continue going up as much at various points during the financial crisis and the period following. They decreased, however, largely because some people defaulted. Initially during the 2008 recession, delinquency rates on all of the major categories of household debt soared. Soon after, around 2010, delinquency rates on mortgages, auto loans and credit card debt began to go down, although much of that was simply a result of the worst debtors defaulting and dropping out of credit. Delinquencies on student loans have continued to rise.

The debate is whether trends in household debt reflects a general greater solvency among most of the populace. Opinions on the decrease in debt were that it was desirable. People were rectifying their balance sheets and would soon start spending more. However, odd developments appeared. For one, student loan debt continued to climb—significantly. There were two takes on this: (1) People were going back to school in large numbers and would attain education adding to the stock of human capital and making America more productive in the future; and ( 2) People were simply having to pay more for the same education, making them altogether poorer. An expense we might have paid out of pocket before now was something for which we had to borrow. A similar negative story can be related concerning auto loan debt. It has grown greatly recently, from about $700 billion outstanding in 2010 to over a trillion outstanding in 2015. Again, there are two takes: (1) The auto industry is strong and people are spending or (2) People are simply poorer and must borrow more for an essential item. Another recent trend in auto finance is longer termed loans, which is a bad sign.

Personal debt levels and their implications for the economy going forward evoke different stories. Traditionally, economists applaud increased debt-taking by Americans, claiming it reflects confidence in the future of the economy and that it represents more current spending that will stimulate the economy. Large increases in debt over the last couple of decades are hard to couch in historical context and are alarming. Student loan debt is the prime example, yet it was simply never a great slug of debt. In the 1960s to 1980s typical student debt was minor and was paid off quickly, leaving the person with only the human capital benefits of his or her education. Now student debt is very large and paid back over decades. Does it represent investment in human capital or spending on overpriced education, a large part of which was pure consumption and not an investment in human capital at all? Recently, federal student debt-forgiveness programs have been instituted and many people have partaken. Debtors can defray some or all of their debt by assuming non-profit and government sector work or showing need. Headlines touted overall student loan default rates decreasing, yet this was in large part due to people opting into the forgiveness programs. Also, young people put themselves on low paying jobs that may impact their lifetime earnings power. The debt does not disappear. Most of it is owed to the U.S. government, so loss of payment by debtors makes our deficit worse.

The student debt also has a fiscal and M&M facet. The federal government has rapidly gone from holding about $100 billion of student debt around 2007 to over $800 billion around 2014. This granting of more student debt constituted a kind of stealth stimulus policy. The government receives about $50 billion in revenue annually from student loans. This is a revenue source that may likely diminish significantly in the next few years due to default.

Economists see changes in debt in two lights. An increase in debt can reflect people being poor and having to borrow, or it can reflect people being confident in the future and willing to take on debt. The latter case is favorable to the rebounding economy story of policy advocates. In the post-2008 period the largest debt increases have been in student debt and auto loan debt. The former is backed by the U.S. government making such debt easy to qualify for. Tatter largely depends on lengthened car loan terms. Both situations reflect poorer households.

## I.5.A.b. Debt Denial

Finalist statements that the debt and deficits do not matter are very common in public discussions in the U.S. Some come from armchair economists, but leading economists like Paul Krugman often shrug off deficit trends and debt magnitudes. One of the most memorable specific statements of debt and deficit pooh-poohing is Vice President Dick Cheney's claim in 2002 that Ronald Reagan proved that deficits do not matter. Cheney was not commenting on the straight economics of debt. He was trying to justify spending for the Iraq and Afghanistan wars. Borrowing for such needed projects would be worthwhile in the long run. He might also have been alluding to the political reality people would not vote against a candidate for a contemporaneous increase in deficits because, in a big economy, the ultimate effects of deficits and increased debt are hard to see.

Generally, though, anyone can spin a story that deficit spending and the debt it creates do not matter by invoking various arguments like a Keynesian story, a supply-side story, a short-run story, a long-run story, an "American is great" story, a relative magnitude story, etc. Some of those are left-wing arguments (like Keynesianism) and some are right-wing (like supply-side), but most are fallacious. In the following pages, I have listed some of the arguments of debt denial. The tone of my listing is a "tongue-in-cheek" mocking of America but, as I have indicated before, we are very liberal in dismissing our economic shortcomings and quick to list the economic mistakes of other nations. For example, we engage in incessant listing of the folly of the Chinese: corruption, low environmental standards, bogus economic data, poor treatment of workers, over-saving, overbuilt infrastructure like the ghost cities, etc.

### We Owe It to Ourselves

Perhaps the most unashamed denial is that our borrowing does not matter: "We owe it to ourselves" because U.S. debt is largely held by Americans (supposedly). You hear this from many analysts, e.g., Paul Krugman. First of all, perhaps 20 years ago most U.S. debt was held by U.S. parties. Today we owe about half of that to foreigners. Regardless, to the extent we do owe U.S. debt to U.S. nationals, we have to pay them. Those of us who are owed the debt, including pension funds and many average people, do not wish—nor can we afford to forfeit that to America at large.

In what way could an individual, borrow and "owe it to himself?" Well, he could borrow from his parents and would not, presumably, have to pay them back if he got "in a pinch." Of course, the parents would surely be worse off unless for some odd reason they always viewed the loan as uncollectable. National borrowing can come from three sources: (1) Foreigners, (2) Americans or (3) The U.S. government itself. Comparing Lenders 1 and 2, are we any better off owing to another American than a foreigner? An American pension fund would expect that the money loaned to the U.S. be paid back with interest just as much as a Chinese would. Lender 3 is when the central bank of a nation buys its country's debt. The central bank must print money or at least stand ready to print money to cover the debt. This is known as monetizing the debt and should result in inflation. Following the crisis of 2008, the U.S. Fed bought large amounts of U.S. debt. Strictly speaking, the U.S. Fed did not buy newly-issued U.S. debt, but only U.S. debt already traded in secondary markets. Also, the Fed granted reserves for the U.S. debt and the reserves were not generally made into cash; therefore, we did not monetize the debt. The buying of existing U.S. debt had the effect of making it easier for the U.S. to sell debt, though; plus, the reserves issued for the U.S. debt could be made into cash with potential adverse effects.

Some analysts invoke the "we owe it to ourselves" case to address future payments of Social Security and Medicare which go from one American (the taxpayer) to another (the recipient), as if the recipient could turn around and hand it back. Medicare recipients cannot hand back the Medicare payments since recipients do not get cash. Instead, their health expenditures are funded. I suppose some rich people can hand back their Social Security payments. Nonetheless, they will realize loss. Indeed, in the future, government will probably nullify much of what it owes in Social Security on the premise that "we owe it to ourselves." Perhaps if debt is too hard to manage, America will even renounce other debt obligations by confiscating wealth from domestic holders, whom we can threaten with punishment, rather than from foreign holders.

Of course, we do owe much of our debt to foreigners. We could default or restructure our debt if we could get away with it. Other nations, like Japan, which by standard measures is more in debt than we are, does owe its debt domestically. About 90% of its government debt is held by Japanese, including large amounts to its central bank, postal savings and insurance company and national sovereign wealth fund. The U.S. owes almost 50% of its debt to foreigners. It is difficult to say whether a large nation with large debt is better off owing it to its citizens or to foreigners. I suppose owing to your own gives a nation more wiggle room to default or restructuring debt. Perhaps a related way of minimizing our debt is encouraging immigration. In principle, immigrants instantly assume a portion of our debt so water down your debt by increasing immigration, yet some have the option to leave and some do. Others may never be able to bear any large portion of the debt simply because they will pay minimal taxes on the low wages they earn. Others will likely eventually become net burdens to the state.

### Offsetting Debt

That we owe it to ourselves leads us to the next idea: Our debt is someone else's asset and vice versa. Therefore, collective changes in debt are meaningless. A debt default or renunciation might make one party worse off, but the system as a whole is not. You hear this argument frequently. For example, a country defaults and we say it is better off to the extent that its creditors are worse off, but the overall system is not worse off. The same is said when a person cannot pay his mortgage and the lending institution takes a loss, but the person records a gain.

This is ridiculous. You have to think of a starting point with an asset that is loaned against. Then, there is a deterioration or quick re-evaluation in which the asset disappears but the debt remains. You have to start before the re-evaluation. For example, I originally borrowed $500,000 from a bank to buy a house. The bank deemed that I had the financial wherewithal to honor the $500,000. At some point, I can no longer afford to honor the $500,000. We re-negotiate my loan lowering it to $300,000 (or you can say lowering it to zero). The bank loses $200,000. I have no gain to offset that loss. Originally, I thought I had the assets, the future income stream or some other financial ability to honor $500,000 of value. Now my financial wherewithal is a mere $300,000. In reality in the world today there is more debt than ever before, and that debt has grown at great rates in the last few decades. The creditors desire all that is due them be paid. Indeed parties constantly mark down, restructure and default on debt but their creditors lose.

### Just a Book Entry

Many analysts contend that U.S. debt is just a book entry or collection of book entries, as though it has no real impact. They make two main supporting cases: One is that all U.S. debt could be paid back with future money that the government could issue. In a sense, the debt could always get pushed to the future. Amateur instructors and armchair economists often state it as ridiculously as that. Light-weight liberals like to make this case too. A similar proposition is that the U.S. Fed could buy out all the U.S. debt and hold it indefinitely with no consequence. Indeed, the Fed would garner interest on the debt and pay it back to the U.S. Another proposal specifically addresses the current Fed holdings of U.S. treasuries, which can be offset against the U.S. Treasury. The Fed could hand back the treasuries it owns, both shrinking the

Fed balance sheet and reducing the U.S. debt outstanding. However, to the Fed the treasuries are an asset that offsets a real liability (reserves held by banks at the Fed).

We also frequently hear this "book entry" story concerning student debt. Students could cease paying their loans and nothing more than an entry in some government books is made. The reality is that student debt is largely owed to the U.S. government and it is treated as an asset on government books (and a secure asset since student loans are not dischargeable in bankruptcy). If students stop paying our government is deeper in debt.

### Governments Live Forever

We believe we can push any government debt into the future since the infinite lifespan of government means an infinite source of funding. The counter cases are households and businesses which we assume do not live forever. Infinite life of a government entity itself is insufficient. Any government is economically viable if it, and the economies they controls and taxes, are growing, or at least not contracting, given deficit spending. Some governments do not live forever, also, including those of states like the Soviet Union and many developing world countries whose governments are overthrown. Of course, if debt levels are growing at too high a rate, government may be insolvent regardless of its horizon or tax revenues.

### Assets Are Greater than Debt

Another dismissal of debt is a comparison with our asset stock and the statement that the value of assets vastly exceeds debt. Assets include business plant and equipment, housing, land, natural resources, financial assets, intellectual assets, etc. We could apply our assets against our debt and supposedly have value left over. This is false. First of all, the assets are needed to generate the cash flows to service our debts. We could not sell assets without then leasing them back. Second, many of our assets, like housing, we cannot sell since they constitute a source of perennial consumption. Third, some assets, like the open lands of America and various natural resources, we may not want to sell in any case. They represent assets that we want to preserve for future generations and not economic goods owned by those of us alive now. Finally, our assets might be overvalued. If we started to sell them in extraordinary ways—think of Baby Boomers selling their big homes and moving into smaller dwellings—the asset values would drop significantly.

An acute contradiction arises when people use these "Assets Are Greater than Debt" and "Governments Live Forever" arguments. If the latter is valid then we can never sell the assets that generate our tax receipts.

If asset values truly increase more than debt does and the asset values hold up and are convertible to cash flows, our relative debt position may not be a burden. If assets can drop in value abruptly and we cannot renegotiate debt down, our debt is grave. We are prone to assume the former rather than the latter.

### It's Cheap, So Borrow & Spend

Currently (circa 2016) the U.S. can borrow for the long term at about 1.5% to 3% (for 10-year and longer debt). Since these rates are so low, we should borrow as much as we can and invest in worthwhile projects primarily infrastructure. Such spendings must, of course, be worth it since we dearly need the goods and services that the projects will provide and the rates are so low. The projects will pay back in immediate spillover spending effects (Keynesian effects) and long-term growth effects. Lawrence

Summers has been outspoken on this one. The flaw is very basic: Regardless of the rate at which we borrow, projects must be affordable and/or must pay back over time. They may meet neither of these hurdles. Infrastructure projects are simply expensive, regardless of how cheaply we finance them. Also, the government has a poor record of selecting projects based on rigorous cost/benefit analysis.

## *We Do Not Borrow; They Save*

We frequently hear arguments like these: "The U.S. does not borrow, other people save" or "The Chinese save too much, and our spending only accommodates their needs." The complementary imbalances will work out over time because, we surmise, these foreigners will eventually have to spend and buy our products and will give us back all we owe them. We are confident that their over-saving behavior is wrong, and they will reverse it. We also make the case that since foreigners, notably the Chinese, need the U.S. market to sell their products, they would never hurt us economically. The odd result is the more indebted we become to people like the Chinese, the more they need us to be economically viable.

## *We Have Been Through Worse*

We reassure our young that we have been through worse debt problems in our history. The most prominent example is the debt level after World War II, which was (using conventional debt statistics; not the fiscal gap measure we talked about above), worse than today's debt. U.S. debt was over 100% of U.S. GDP after the war and was paid down such that it was about 25% of GDP by around 1980. The story is told as if circumstances are the same today, and we could draw down our debt again. Circumstances are different, however. A one-time expense, the Second World War was being paid off and was not chronic deficit spending like we have today. We now run such large deficits it is as though we are fighting a major war in perpetuity. Also, the U.S. stood singularly in economic preeminence and potential GDP growth. There was a different mindset, too. Following World War II, we, collectively, were a thrifty people. At every movie house, public service messages would exhort people to save. We simply do not have any message like that now; instead, we now encourage our people to spend. As previously mentioned, debt has grown greatly in recent years. Neither the U.S. nor the world as a whole has been through this circumstance before.

## *Only a Political Problem*

Today's politicians and the two parties are intransigent and uncooperative and, therefore, cannot agree on economic solutions. In gross contrast is a different past when there was contention, but we were much more cooperative. Analysts usually invoke the story of political arch-rivals President Ronald Reagan and Speaker of the House Thomas ("Tip") O'Neill. These great leaders would jockey against each other but, at the end of the day, they would get together, compromise and agree on a solution. Today, we lament that our current leaders are too doctrinaire to cooperate.

Our debt and deficit problems indeed could be solved but for this mean-spiritedness. The problems are merely political, not economic and—as soon as the intransigent ones listen to reason—we can solve our problems. This is a ridiculous comparison. The economic problems of the 1980s were simply much smaller than current ones, and thus today's politicians have more reason to hold out for their causes. This story is favored by older generation types, including politicians, media and pundits who reminisce about the "good old days" when we were so strong and practical. In my opinion, there is a partisan aspect to this argument:

Liberals, much more than conservatives, hammer the political intransigence story because they attribute the intransigence mainly on the part of conservatives.

### They Buy It

As U.S. budget deficits became very big in the years after 2008, pessimists warned that the U.S. would have trouble selling its debt or that, at least, world investors would demand higher yields. Despite this the U.S. would conduct bond auction after bond auction. Buyers generally took the bonds and yields remained low. Debt deniers rejoiced, interpreting the successful auctioning of U.S. debt as an endorsement of U.S. economic policy and a gross denial of any long-term solvency questions. Many believe that an additional strength of the U.S. as issuer of debt is that, since the U.S. dollar is the world's reserve currency, the U.S. has easier and more long-lasting borrowing privileges. They even go so far as to say that the U.S. can borrow indefinitely because world investors must always accept the debt of the nation whose currency is the world's reserve currency regardless of the fiscal health of the nation. Other countries can issue debt in their own currencies, too, but only to the extent they are perceived as credit worthy. Other countries can issue debt in U.S. dollars, too but would have to pay back in dollars. Therefore, it would be costly if the value of their currency went down ,which would typically happen if they ran up national debt.

The U.S.' ability to issue large amounts of debt in recent years may not be innocuous nor favorable in the long run. First of all, in recent years, the Fed has purchased a large fraction of U.S. debt, making it easy for the U.S. to issue new debt at low rates. This condition cannot continue. Second, foreign buyers may buy our debt and not express reservation publicly, but privately they consider the U.S. gravely indebted and declining. They may just perceive our debt as the best option in a world with a glut of savings. It is not unlikely that the U.S. could face difficulty floating debt at low yields. In fact, as we pointed our earlier, it was not too long ago that the U.S. faced a problem borrowing in its currency. In other words, world investors said no. In 1978, the U.S. issued bonds denominated in Swiss francs because investors were averse to buy U.S. dollar-denominated bonds due to the dollar's value decline.

### Inflate It Away

This is a case often made by sophisticated parties and, in a way, there is some validity to it. Indeed, since the vast majority of U.S. debt is in fixed terms (a small bit is floating rate), inflation would lower the obligation. Some analysts remark that much of the U.S. debt built up during World War II was largely diminished by inflation that occurred in the 1970s. Of course, the parties that held the debt faced large losses. Also, of course, the "Inflate It Away" solution involves bearing the costs of high inflation, which are myriad and grave.

### Grow Our Way Out of It

This is a valid debt management argument in principle but, of course, it depends on relative magnitudes. If debt is increasing but your means to pay is increasing at a greater rate you are no worse off and your debt to income ratio will even decrease. If you are not growing as much as your debt, you are becoming worse off. This argument was the mantra during the increase in debt and deficit in the early 1980s under the Reagan Administration. The tax cuts and increases in defense spending would be paid for by an increase in GDP.

### *Debt Alarmists Made Mistakes, Ergo...*

Leading economists Carmen Reinhart and Kenneth Rogoff analyzed effects of debt and deficits on economic growth of nations and produced a popular and pivotal 2011 book *This Time Is Different: Eight Centuries of Financial Folly*. They concluded that indeed debt was a grave concern and that a debt-to-GDP level of about 90% represented a rough turning point at which economic growth would suffer. U.S. debt was near that point at the time so the Reinhart and Rogoff ("R&R") study constituted a strong anti-debt warning. The work appeared authoritative and got plaudits from conservatives who wanted to reduce deficits. Soon enough though, some errors were discovered in their findings. The mistakes were valid and, although not altogether undermining of the general idea that high debt handicaps societies, they were widely promulgated. As a result, the entire thrust of the R&R warning on bad effects of high government debt was vitiated. The punditry was seemingly very willing to accept minor critiques as complete excuses.

## I.5.B. Taxes

Our tax situation is a "FATCA story." FATCA is the Foreign Account Tax Compliance Act, an attempt by the U.S. government to collect taxes from foreign sources of U.S. income. It was initiated in 2010 to account for taxable sources of income in accounts held by Americans overseas. The belief was that Americans had extensive holdings earning interest, dividend and gains in foreign accounts and these incomes are not getting taxed. Some economists estimated that the U.S. was losing about $100 billion every year in tax revenues from various offshore sources. This was the main motivation for instituting FATCA. Also, to some extent, reasons of fairness and morality played a role.

Despite the large theoretical amount of available tax revenues, however, we also estimate that FATCA will raise about $10 billion over ten years, roughly $1 billion per year. Tax collection proponents do not talk as much about FATCA's costs, neither the direct costs like compliance costs nor indirect like foreigners avoiding doing business with the U.S. due to strict and capricious penalties for minor errors. We are ever optimistic about improving the tax system and constantly propose fixes like FATCA. We think relatively large amounts of net revenues and other tax efficiencies are obtainable, yet here are some of the basic and contrary realities about taxes:

- Economics put forth a number of basic principles about optimal taxation, and our current tax system defies these principles in many gross ways. Unfortunately, even if we rectify our tax system according to these efficiency fundamentals, the fixes will not produce a sufficient amount of extra tax revenue for our fiscal problems.

- On the practical side, reforming our tax system is impossible. Even if we identify and agree on certain tax efficiency reforms according to economic principles, they will be un-implementable for political, social and practical reasons. Our tax systems are embedded in many facets of our lives like housing, family, charity, income redistribution, etc. that we do not wish to alter. When we scheme tax reform, we resort to hopeful assumptions. Oftentimes, proponents invoke the term "well-designed" for a new or reformed tax. This is a euphemism masking endemic problems.

- We have to raise average taxes for most Americans—not just the rich. There is just no getting around this reality. This means we will have a lower standard of living and will pay higher taxes for the same services. This contrasts with a prevailing hope that we can change our tax system by making it more efficient and raise more money without higher taxes.

- There are no significant missing or undiscovered amounts of tax revenue available to us, yet we always pretend there are. For a compelling example, consider the proposals made by President

Obama in the State of the Union on January 20, 2015. The best sources of tax revenue his advisors could come up with were taxes on savings, notably the college savings vessels (the 529's), and taxes on capital gains on housing.

Some economists might cite successful historical tax reforms, in particular, the Tax Reform Act of 1986; but that was a fortuitous case. In 1986: (1) the country was in better fiscal shape; we did not have to plug such big holes; (2) individual's tax rates were lowered but corporate and capital gains rates were raised; and (3) various other tax adjustments came from relatively lucrative pickings (concerning loopholes, depreciation, alternative minimum tax, etc.). Certain of the stronger reforms of 1986 were reversed and relatively soon after, in 1991, tax rates had to be raised again. Perhaps we should not have cut them so much.

Our future in tax reform is probably a "VAT story." First, we will attempt little fixes to our tax system. They will not lead to a significant solution, so we will crack and go for a sweeping change. It could be a national sales or flat tax, but it will probably be a switchover to a VAT.[69] We will embark on it with great fanfare and give it a catchy name like "Very American Tax" to make it more palatable. The switch itself will pose enormous cost, perhaps taking many years and costing hundreds of billions. It will promise to eliminate tax inefficiencies, but as implementation gets closer the benefits will diminish or disappear altogether. As the time approaches to turn on the VAT, we will observe major problems, some foreseen and some unforeseen. Then, we will either bull it through without really solving our fiscal problems or, in a fit, reverse it and return to the old system.

## I.5.B.a. Economic Principles of Tax

I frequently attend sessions with high-level executives and experts from accounting, brokerage, asset management and legal fields. These professionals are well versed in the extremely complicated current tax laws and practices but they are amateurs when it comes to economic welfare analyses of tax policies. They know that our tax system is not optimal and believe fixes can be made and also have belief that the magnitude of revenue to be raised from these fixes is significant. They have faith that economists know these flaws, and that they could design a better tax system—if only we had the political will. Is this belief justified though?

Economists recommend taxes that meet a laundry list of qualifications: simple, low at the margin, non-distorting of choices made by economic agents, unchanging; covering a broad base of taxable activity and/or having few loopholes, not taxing the same item multiple times, taxing spending/consumption rather than saving/investment, encouraging of enterprises to productive activity and not to activities to avoid taxes, easy to collect and hard for tax cheats to dodge. We all agree that our current set of taxes does not achieve these goals, and we want to get closer to these economic ideals. Non-economists indulge the clichés: "close loopholes," "broaden the base," "simplify the system," etc.

### *Simple*

Our tax system is extremely complicated, and to simplify it would be an advantage—at least in terms of tax preparation costs and also in increasing incentives to produce taxable income. The value of tax

---

[69] VAT stands for Value-Added Tax. It is a tax of the value-added at each stage of production and sale of goods and services. It can be done on a large scale. The U.S. currently does not have a VAT, but Eurozone does. It is different from taxing incomes, which is currently our main source of tax. It is like a national sales tax. We will explain all these different tax systems below.

simplification is debatable. Simply put, it would be hard to simplify our tax systems substantially, and a minor simplification might not add much. We usually propose simplification for taxes that are perceived of as particularly complex, like the income tax. Other taxes, like sales taxes, appear much simpler. A simplification of the complicated tax would also probably have to include a general lowering of that tax to make the change palatable to the public, though. In that case, other taxes would have to be raised.

Usually schemes to achieve a less cumbersome system are designed as "revenue neutral" meaning the scheme does not attempt to raise or lower the amount of tax collected presently. The intention is to improve the overall efficiency of taxes overtime or to replace a tax with an adverse impact with one with a better impact. Part of appeal is that the new tax system will be simpler and that alone will engender greater economic growth. Another appeal of revenue neutral is that proponents are not trying to change the amount of government involvement in the economy. That is a political decision. They are trying to improve the economics. One aspect of revenue neutral tax changes is that we have to make assumptions and projections about future behavior of parties being taxed. This science is sketchy and revenue neutral fixes might make tax receipts lower. Projections are difficult to do since revenue neutral tax change proposals often involve so many tax and spending programs and the behavior of so many constituents.

Reducing the number of brackets in the Federal income tax is a common theme of simpler taxation. Sometimes, the case is made for one bracket, but typically three is the most popular number of proposed brackets. We currently have seven. It is not clear why fewer brackets are preferred. Presumably, they are lower on average and not prohibitively high for the highest. Such lower marginal rates should induce more economic output. Also, another potential gain to fewer brackets is the implication that they will not be changed (i.e., we will not add more brackets as we did from time to time following 1986). Therefore, people can plan with assurance that they will have reliable net incomes from their future economic activities. The ultimate benefit, however, is not in the raw number of brackets but their levels and persistence over time.

## *Tax Rate at the Margin*

Some taxes, like income, have rates that vary: The higher your income, the higher the percentage taken as tax. We can calculate an average and a marginal tax rate. For example, assume a person making $100,000 pays $20,000, or 20% on average, in tax. If she makes another $10,000 though, she pays 28% on the $10,000. Income is now $110,000 and average tax about 20.7%, but marginal tax is 28%.[70] The marginal is much greater than average. Since the marginal was higher than the average, the average got pulled up. Eventually, that average will approach the marginal. The rate "at the margin," i.e., the rate we pay on the next step of economic activity and not the average rate is what matters in terms of providing more work effort. We do not want marginal rates to be prohibitive because we want high earners to continue to earn and to expand their businesses. Pundits and politicians emphasize that the people and businesses who face high marginal income taxes are often those who innovate and create jobs for others when they themselves work more.

However, if we are not raising sufficient taxes, i.e., our average is not high enough, then if we lower marginal rates our average will go down. Again, proponents of lowering marginal rates will contend that the economic agents at the high margin will respond with such greater output when their rates are lowered that it can make up for lost tax revenue and actually result in a higher average. That is debatable.

---

[70] These are hypothetical numbers although the 28% tax bracket does currently apply to incomes around $100,000 in the U.S. The U.S. income tax has seven rates as of 2015 going from 10% to 39.6%, which applies to incomes over about $400,000 depending on how a person files (single, married or head of household).

Usually, when people hanker for low marginal rates what they really want is a low marginal rate of their tax or some tax they think is important to economic activity. Unless you believe that the lowering of a marginal rate in one place will create so much more work effort that total taxes will go up, though, you must raise a tax elsewhere.

Regardless of the economic merits of the marginal tax, the concept of the highest rate paid by rich people is extremely potent in debates on fixing the tax system on both sides of the political aisle. It is all about what burden the rich carry in our society. Conservatives worry about stymying the economic contributions of the rich. Liberals dismiss the effects of high marginal rates and believe more taxes on the rich will have little effect on their economic contribution. We simply do not know who is right. Liberals often present hyperbolic cases as evidence. For example, will a hedge fund manager making $100 million per year stop his economic activity if his taxes go up $5 million? Probably not. Focusing on the less extreme but much bigger group of high income households might favor the conservative case. For example, if a person making $750,000 per year is offered an opportunity to work another weekend each month and earn $10,000, will he make that effort? He will face 39.6% federal income tax, state income tax and various other mark-ups on federal tax due to phasing out of deductions, Medicare tax, etc. That will leave him about 50% net. He might likely not care to spend such extra money on current consumption. Rather, he will invest it, possibly to pass it on to his children. In this case, he will face high taxes on the capital income and an estate tax on passing it on. In his head he might perceive that he gets very little from working the extra weekend and prefer to forego it.

## *Distortion*

Taxes should not distort, or at least unduly distort, our economic choices. (Of course, some taxes are specifically designed to distort people's behavior. That is a different dimension of tax policy. We will discuss it later.) There are many obvious distortions in our taxes. For example, our various tax subsidies of housing (including writing mortgage interest of taxable income and having no tax on gains in real estate asset appreciation) cause us to buy more housing. Another tax distortion is how we tax income v. capital gains. In our system, income tax rates for high earners are 39.6% while (long-term) capital gains are taxed at 15% or 20% (depending on your tax bracket for income). In an efficient tax regime you would tax both at the same rate and let people decide how to structure their efforts for making money independent of tax rates.

Of course, we do want to distort people's behavior. We simply never phrase it that way. Rather, we say we want to give "incentives" for good activities or worthwhile expenditures by relieving taxes or that we want to discourage bad activities by taxing them. For example, in our income tax, we have incentives for having children, health care expenditures, education, buying American products, moving expenses (if related to changing a job), retirement saving, low income households and a wide variety of other items all based on assumptions about what constitutes good living. We have so many incentives they often contradict each other. For example, we offer tax credits for having children. On the other hand, the income tax is disadvantageous for poor people to remain married. The higher income of the intact household will cause them to lose benefits like tax credits for children. Another example is getting married. If a high-earning person marries a low-earning person, their joint tax typically goes down. If two high-income people marry, it might go up because they would be in a higher tax bracket. (There are other effects too concerning deductions). Microeconomic theory recommends letting people choose what they do with their resources by not distorting choices. Our tax system, however, is very economically distorting because we have deemed that people do not choose to use resources in their best interest or in the best interest of society. Taxes are perhaps the main way to manipulate people's choices.

## Taxes That Do Not Change

We prefer taxes that remain about the same in character and rate so that people can make optimal decisions on allocating resources over time. In our current system, temporary tax changes are common. For example, in response to 2008 we lowered the Social Security tax as a Keynesian stimulus. Such Keynesian effects are laughed at by many analysts, but Keynesian-leaning economists might think they have a role. We also provide constant temporary tax rebates and credits for specific actions over certain time periods such as incentives for small businesses to hire. These programs are often complicated and have long time lags such that it is dubious they have much of the intended impact. Typically the small business must hire now and realize the tax credit about a year later when the taxes are done. Another maddening facet of our tax policy is that we grant "extensions" of tax programs. Typically these are continuations of an existing benefit. Often it is not decided until late in a year if the extension will be granted making it very difficult for people and businesses to plan.

Another absurd outcome of bad tax policies is the temporary tax change, usually a tax cut to engender a Keynesian effect, becomes a permanent tax policy. For example, Massachusetts grants one weekend in August every year in which no sales tax is charged on certain items. This program was created to stimulate spending and has become a permanent policy and is completely gamed by businesses and consumers alike.[71]

We change taxes frequently and propose tax changes very frequently. Each presidential political race includes some discussion of tax changes. It would be difficult to eliminate frequent changes to taxes. Also, since our tax system is in need of major overhaul and we are running chronic deficits and will probably need to raise taxes, it will be a long time before we have a non-evolving tax system.

## Broad Tax Base

Tax bases should be broad, i.e., we should tax all sources of income or wealth. In practical terms, we want to broaden the tax base by exempting fewer sources and adding sources that we were previously not able or willing to tax. This idea is widely accepted as sensible and capable of significant additional tax revenues, but it presents a major contradiction. First of all, broadening the tax base is raising taxes. The items originally left untaxed were probably not taxed for compelling reasons. For example, incomes of non-profits like universities and hospitals are not taxed. Also, new tax broadenings might be very hard to implement. The main way our income tax is not "broad-based" is that many people simply pay no federal income tax because their incomes are too low. Broadening the tax base by adding the poor would be "regressive" though, meaning that the poor would pay more; and we contend that we do not want regressive taxation.

Another way to broaden our tax base would be to tax illegal activities like drug dealing and prostitution. Since we have made them illegal, however, it is odd to propose their de facto legalization just to achieve the economic goal of revenue generation. Also, this tax would tend to be regressive. Much unreported income is at the small business level. Often this is very small-scale business which involves families and friends. We would need an extensive policing system to get such economic activity to be put on books for taxation. If we tried to tax these economic activities, they would cease or be driven further underground. For example, a plumber does odd jobs on weekends for friends and family under the tax

---

[71] The program commenced in 2005 and ran through 2015. It was suspended in 2016. We will discuss this tax in detail in the section entitled Gaming below.

radar. If somehow the taxing authorities could monitor this work the plumber would try to hide better. Also, as much as we may not like to highlight it, the irregular and illegal business activities create many jobs for people who have hard times getting work and may be unemployable in formal workplaces.

## *Loopholes*

Tax reformers of both the left and right denounce "loopholes." Loopholes are deductions or exemptions from taxable income or credits taken off of the final tax.[72] In micro terms, they are viewed as subsidies of one activity over others, which detracts from efficiency. We mock them, often citing extreme examples including agricultural subsidies and corporate jet plane write-offs. Those two examples are trivial in magnitude and perhaps the only notable outrageous loopholes. The bigger loopholes represent large subsidies we have deliberately selected for some social or economic reason. We probably will continue to maintain them despite how much we wail the cliché loophole. The major tax deductions (in the form of either exemptions, deductions or credits) are medical care, mortgage interest, charitable donations, IRA and other retirement savings, educational credits, home office and municipal bond interest. All of these matter to their constituents, are part of our culture, are part of schemes to compel desirable behavior on people and are schemes for enhancing economic growth. If you denounce a loophole at a cocktail party, make sure it is one everybody has no stake in (like the jet plane write-offs), or be circumspect that the person you are conversing with is not a fund raiser or someone with a big mortgage. Here are some of the common loopholes you hear about (with counterpoint):

- **Donations to Charity (in General)**: People donate to charity knowing that they will get about 35% of the donation back on their taxes. If they lost the deduction they would probably cut back on charitable giving such that, perhaps, the government would have to make up the funding.
- **Oil and Gas Development Tax Credits**: The U.S. has had chronic needs for cheap energy and has had to engage in military conflicts of untold cost to secure overseas sources of oil.
- **Tax Credits for Motor Vehicles**: These are to encourage hybrid vehicles, U.S. made vehicles and vehicles used for business, all of which are considered valuable goals for our society.
- **Excessive use of Educational Savings Accounts (529's)** by rich people: Saving for education is important, and it is hard to establish a cutoff that would not render the entire educational subsidy ineffective.
- **Municipal bonds free of federal tax**: This tax break enables cities, towns and other government entities to finance projects at modest rates. These projects are usually deemed worthwhile if not essential–think of sewage and clean water projects, education, etc. If we did not provide this subsidy, the federal government would probably have to increase funding for important local government projects.
- **Non-Business and Excessive Use of Home Office Deductions**: We should strive to foster small business and must, therefore, expect a fair amount of imprecision.
- **University Donations That Are Really Disguised Purchases**: Tickets to sports events is the main item in this tax dodge. Supposedly the donors are receiving unwarranted charitable deductions for a good they purchase in any case. The donations of these college boosters, however, may not be forthcoming without the tax write-off.

---

[72] Exemptions are amounts of income that are excluded from taxation. Exemptions are mainly the exemptions you get for yourself, spouse and children. Deductions are expenses you paid like charitable donations which you can write of your taxable income. Credits are amounts you take off of your final tax.

- **Corporate Jets**: Companies can write off the expense of flying executives on private jets. Some analysts see it as nothing more than an unneeded perk, i.e., the work performance of executives would not suffer if they lost private jet transportation. That may or may not be valid. Private transportation might be a money saver for companies. Also, the amount of this tax write off is insignificant.
- **Accelerated Depreciation**: Companies are allowed to write off the cost of plant and equipment much more quickly than it typically depreciates. Yet the accelerated depreciation and many other special tax rules about booking depreciation are part of programs to encourage important investment.

Another proposal to make deductions less distorting and less costly to tax revenues is to permit deductions of all types but limit the overall size of deductions as a percentage of income. In this system, a person could take whichever deductions she prefers (charitable, mortgage, health care, etc.) People would presumably allocate deductions efficiently and also more taxes might be raised. It sounds compelling and simple but it might create outcomes like distortion of spending to increase favored deductions. Like any other proposal, however, we could only raise taxes significantly if we greatly curtailed net deductions.

We should dispense with the characterization of outrageous loopholes manipulated by rich people and their accountants.

### Tax Only Once

We want a tax system that eliminates multiple, typically double, taxation. The U.S.'s main case of double taxation is the taxing of incomes of corporations and then the additional taxing of those incomes when people receive them in dividends and gains. The solution would be elimination, or at least reduction, of the corporate income tax, which many economists (including certain liberals) favor.

Another double tax is the estate tax. People earn money over their lifetimes from labor and capital income and pay taxes on it at whatever rates on the particular kind of income at that specific time. Then, to pass the already taxed money to their heirs, the original earners must pay an estate tax. That rate can be very high, very low or zero depending on a wide variety of factors. Here we have the usual bifurcation: Those paying the double tax are outraged; those who want to raise more taxes say these double taxes make perfect sense.

Certain tax reform proposals focus on eliminating double taxation, like most proposals for a flat tax, in which you would add up all your income from whichever source—wages, cap gains, dividends—and pay one rate. Corporations would not pay tax. That one rate has been estimated by proponents at around 17%, which seems reasonable and simple, but as with other tax reform proposals the proof would be in the implementation. The rate would likely be much higher.

### Tax Spending/Consumption; Not Saving/Investment

We should tax people on what they spend or consume rather than what they save or invest. This will encourage savings and investment which will contribute to future economic growth. This sounds eminently sensible, and we often hear it as a justification for replacing taxes on income (both from labor and from investments) with any of the spending-type taxes like sales, consumption or value-added taxes. In reality, it does not make much sense. In theory, since most people eventually spend what they earn, it should not matter whether we tax people on incomes or on spendings. There should only be timing differences. If we abruptly changed taxes from taxes on income to taxes on consumption, we would initially get less spending, and more saving. It should not persist. In microeconomics we say that an optimizing agent like a person or a household should die with zero wealth. In other words, you should spend everything you earn. Re-designing taxes to encourage saving also runs counter to the macroeconomic policies of aggregate demand stimulation. You might argue that stimulative macro policies are only temporary measures until recovery is attained, but our macro policies have almost always, and likely always will characterize our society as in perpetual need of more spending.

### Encourage Productive Activity & Not Tax Avoidance

Individuals and companies devote inordinate effort and engage in elaborate schemes to avoid taxes. For example, certain large corporations such as General Electric are notorious for employing hoards of lawyers and accountants to manage their tax liability. Of course, if we want to raise great tax revenue from a myriad of income sources and use our tax code to encourage a wide variety of social goals, the rules will invariably be complicated. On their part, private parties can only be expected to utilize any means to lower taxes.

### Easy to Collect & Hard to Dodge

We want taxes that are efficiently collected and minimize the ability of income earners to avoid paying their fair share. We often complain about our existing taxes, especially incomes taxes, as being beset by tax avoidance. Sometimes we look to broad sales taxes or VATs as superior in limiting tax avoidance. However, if the magnitudes of taxes were reversed, e.g., some national sales tax was instituted and the income tax was made much lower, incentives to avoid taxes would also shift. We might even have bigger problems maintaining the tax base.

This "hard to avoid" facet is not really derived from basic principles of economics. What economists care about is that people engage in optimal economic behavior first; then, government assesses taxes that do not distort that behavior. For example, some analysts say a tax on gasoline is efficient because gasoline demand is inelastic, meaning we cannot reduce our demand if the price goes up. In this case, indeed you will raise more tax but you will not help economic output. Similarly, other analysts say tax labor income because people cannot avoid tax on this as much as they can avoid tax on capital income. Again, this may not help output.[73]

### I.5.B.b. Sundry Aspects of Current U.S. Taxes

Taxes and tax policy are omnipresent with many subtle facets including the following:
- U.S. corporations pay a corporate income tax. This rate is high (top rate of 35%, although many corporations pay less) compared to that of most of our competitor nations. Corporate income taxes, in particular their level and uncertainty about future levels, are very important to business decisions, according to surveys of corporate CEO's.
- Tax evasion is prevalent in both big and small ways. Some analysts have suggested better collection of taxes of the economic activity in the underground economy (people working off of the books like drug dealers, prostitutes, gypsy cab drivers, moonlighting plumbers, people working without proper licenses, etc.). Some experts estimate the underground economy at $2 trillion, which could generate perhaps $500 billion in tax revenues. They often assume about $100 billion of the

---

[73] "Five Taxes We Should Raise. Really," by Josh Barro, September 28, 2012, *Bloomberg.com.*

$500 billion is a conservative estimate of how much tax could really be raised. This number is debatable. For one, as we pointed out above, we cannot tax much of the alleged $2 trillion. Second, to the extent we collect such taxes, we will garner greater taxes but the people paying the taxes will be worse off. Transferring money from one group to another may not represent net gain except that it is a net gain to government funding. You can also point out that the burden would fall on the people in underground economy most of whom are low income households and perform businesses incapable of being run as normal businesses. Many underground economy businesses would simply be incapable of doing the paperwork to collect taxes.

- Some analysts propose more extensive taxes on wealth. Such taxes would discourage savings, be perceived of as unfair given that existing wealth was already taxed when it was earned and would only be effective if imposed across borders.

- We mentioned loopholes in general. Some analysts highlight certain extreme loopholes and special write-offs for the rich that provide undue relief from fair taxation and create bad economic incentives. Among these gimmicks are special oil & gas partnership structures, the "carry" being taxed at long-term gains rates, Grantor Retained Annuity Trusts ("GRAT's") and farm subsidies. The "carry" is notorious as a way money managers get very low tax rates. GRAT's are a notorious device rich people use to avoid estate taxes. We will explain the carry and GRAT's below. Farm subsidies have a long history as a notorious loophole, but their heft today is minor. Each loophole had an original purpose, which—although possibly defunct today—we specifically chose at one point in time.

- There is debate about how progressive our tax system is, and many contend that it is not progressive at all due to the regressive nature of Social Security and Medicare tax. Some analysts argue that since these two taxes (which are sometimes considered insurance contributions rather than taxes) get paid back to people as much as they contribute the remaining large federal taxes (personal and corporate income taxes) are progressive. Estimating progressivity of all taxes taken together is very difficult to do. Some analysts make the case that U.S. taxes are more progressive than those of many other countries. Their case is that the U.S. relies more on income tax than taxes like VAT. The highest U.S. earners pay more in taxes than high earners elsewhere.[74] Often, to analyze the progressive nature of our taxes we subdivide tax payers by quintiles. The bottom 40% of households pay very little in regular income taxes. They do pay Social Security and Medicare taxes and if you add them in the bottom 40% pay about 5% of the total federal tax. The uppermost 20% pay almost 70% of the total federal tax, yet they also have a lot of income. The same is true in the extreme for the uppermost 1% of households, who pay about 25% of the total federal taxes.

- The most obvious tax to people is the federal income tax. It raises about $1.5 trillion in tax revenue of about $3.3 trillion of total federal taxes as of 2015. Many people do not pay this tax at all since much income is exempted. The other big federal tax is the payroll tax, or what we commonly call Social Security. It raises about $1 trillion, and few are exempted. As we pointed out, strictly speaking, it is not a tax but is a social insurance contribution. It is two parts: Social Security and Medicare, and raises money from two payees: workers and employers. It is like a flat tax except that the Social Security part (the larger segment) is only applied to the first $118,500 of income (as of 2016). The Medicare portion of the payroll tax does not have an income limit and was a true flat tax until recently when the high income earners were required to pay additional Medicare tax. Overall, due to the Social Security income cutoff, it is regressive.

---

[74] "The U.S. Tax System Just Keeps On Getting More And More Progressive," by Tim Worstall, *Forbes*, January 8, 2015. http://www.forbes.com/sites/timworstall/2015/01/08/the-us-tax-system-just-keeps-on-getting-more-and-more-progressive/

- The U.S. taxes its companies for their business by nationality regardless where their commerce is done. This has been a recurrent topic in the press and policy circles due to a number of large U.S. companies moving offshore by having themselves bought by usually smaller foreign concerns, all largely to avoid U.S. taxes. In general, a U.S. corporation can keep it profits abroad and defer corporate income tax. Estimates are that about $2 trillion in profit is held offshore. Other countries offer lower tax rates with some countries' rates being very low. The average for OECD countries is about 25% which is lower than that of the U.S. Some argue that the actual U.S. corporate tax rate paid by companies is much lower due to write-offs but it is not that much lower. The U.S. has made attempts to repatriate the profits held abroad with special deals and sometimes threats. In 2005 a tax break resulted in a significant profit repatriation. In general, U.S. companies will probably continue to keep their profits abroad and in some cases relocate their country of nationality. It is not unscrupulous U.S. companies that keep their profits abroad. Premier corporations like Apple, Microsoft and Google do.
- The basic U.S. corporate tax rate is 35%, which is one of the highest in the world. Adding state taxes can get the corporate tax over 40%. There are many loopholes in corporate taxes which certain analysts contend make the effective corporate tax rate lower. However, the loopholes are largely for desirable purposes, such as energy development or from writing off of past losses (which is important in rehabilitating companies and keeping them operating). Also, the loopholes do not lower the average rate that much. Both liberals and conservatives favor lowering the corporate tax rate to make the U.S. competitive, but they differ on how much. Liberals favor eliminating loopholes first. One facet of our corporate tax is that we apply it to earnings of U.S. companies regardless of where the money is earned, including abroad. Such nationality based taxation means more revenue, in principle, for the U.S. It also means corporations will be less likely to locate in the U.S. The U.S. is virtually alone in that it taxes its companies on income they earn abroad.
- Many people simply do not know how much they are taxed and/or pay very little tax, leading them to underestimate how burdensome taxation is. Some analysts recommend that all people pay some tax just so they understand that tax is a cost. Lower income earners pay little or no federal income taxes but do pay the payroll taxes.
- One facet of the federal income state is its complexity and paperwork requirements. Many people have their taxes done by professionals which can cost hundreds or even thousands of dollars per year.
- One popular tax gimmick is matching a tax on a specific, supposedly bad product or activity with some spending on a supposedly desirable goal. For example, we tax gambling and use the proceeds for government programs to help the victims of gambling. This sounds practical; but it violates a basic principle of economics called Separation, which means we should separate our money raising and spending tasks to avoid misallocation.

### I.5.B.c. Taxes, Tax Schemes & Tax Fallacies

Some taxes and potential taxes that we could institute, change or raise to balance our budgets are detailed below. They are broken into two groups: tax systems and minor taxes/concepts. We have included some comment on feasibility and magnitude.

## Large-Scale Tax Systems

- Fair tax, or national sales tax, is proposed as a replacement to income taxes and Social Security tax. Proponents (of one current variety) envision a 23% rate to start, which would actually be $30 for a $100 purchase; so it can be seen as 30% rate (equal to $30/$100). Proponents believe the tax would be simple, encourage savings and investment and make the U.S. a desirable place to locate business. Opponents contend it would not raise enough revenue, would create great incentives for tax evasion and would be disadvantageous to the poor.

- Flat tax on income with no deductions is another major system to replace income tax and Social Security and Medicare tax. Proponents contend it is easy to calculate, would create great certainty and would not create harmful incentives since the marginal rate would not vary and would not be too high (unlike our current income tax). Opponents argue it is regressive, calculating the appropriate income would be difficult, it would be subject to evasion and it might be prone to adding of deductions.

- Various broad consumption taxes have been proposed. This tax on some form of spending would replace income taxes. The consumption tax is more theoretical since we would have to define an appropriate consumption quantity which presumably would involve calculating income and then subtracting saving. Saving is hard to pinpoint. Taxing consumption, supposedly, would incentivize people to work more and spend less. A sales tax and a value-added tax are varieties of consumption taxes. As we pointed out, in the long run people should spend about what they earn so the tax over time would not have a great effect on work effort. Perhaps initially it would cause a spike in work effort. Taxing consumption also might confound Keynesian effects and the policies we use to engender growth from increasing spending.

- Value-Added Tax or VAT is a tax on each stage of the production of a good or a service. This differs from a sales tax in that it is applied at every step in the production or a good or service including the final sale of the product or service. The producer pays a tax equal to some percent of the difference between the price it sells its product for minus costs. From consumers' points of view the VAT is like a sales tax. It is used in the European Union and in many other countries. The VAT is the main alternative to personal and corporate income taxes in countries. The VAT has many advantages including that it is supposedly very efficient to implement, hard to evade and does not create distortions. One disadvantage is that it is regressive. VAT proponents concede that facet but propose providing tax credits to poor people. Another problem is that it is difficult from the point of view of the public to discern the rate of the VAT so that it might be easy to raise taxes. Another problem is that exceptions to the VAT, like for health care or housing, would be made, perhaps making it as inefficient and distorting as any income tax. To avoid these issues VAT proponents usually invoke the term "well-designed" for the VAT they would institute. This is a grand euphemism. In a large country like the U.S. a VAT would be tough to design. Estimates vary about what rate the VAT in the U.S. would have to be if we switched over. In the U.S., a VAT is usually proposed in addition to a lower income tax.

- The Purple Tax is a comprehensive change to taxes (called purple as a combination of the political colors of red and blue) proposed by economists such as Laurence Kotlikoff. This purportedly tries to break political intransigence on tax reform and would include a sales tax at 17.5%, a FICA (Social Security style) tax and an inheritance tax.

- The Buffett Tax or the Buffett Rule is a proposal that high income taxpayers pay a certain minimum average income tax, something around 30%. It is named after noted investor and billionaire Warren Buffett who often remarks that despite his fortune he pays low taxes. The proposal appeared around 2011 and was adopted in theory by the Obama Administration. It is dubious how much it would actually raise.

- Certain analysts propose taxes from foreign sources as a major revenue source. The two sources are income on assets of American citizens held abroad and foreign profit of American companies held abroad. The former is/was reputed to represent substantial revenue (sometimes in the hundreds of billions of dollars), yet collection of this tax revenue in recent years under primarily voluntary IRS programs has raised taxes in the single digit billion dollars each year. We mentioned the latter before. Some analysts propose a one-time tax break on the approximately $2 trillion of overseas profit. Others propose some kind of requirement that the money be repatriated or companies face penalty. There have been attempts in the past to offer tax breaks for profit repatriation but there has been little response.

- Certain people propose various packages of usually flat tax rates. These are often set to be revenue neutral or "static revenue neutral" in that the total revenues will not change if people's economic behavior does not change due to the new tax system. Politicians running for office often propose these big package-deal changes such as the 9-9-9 Tax Plan proposed by a Republican candidate for president in 2012. In this scheme there would be 9% levies in each of a national sales tax, a business tax and a flat income tax. Such sweeping tax change proposals have appeal for their simplicity but as we have argued they may likely raise no greater revenue, ultimately be no less burdensome on the private sector and distort economic activity just as much the taxes they replace. There is no simple solution.

## Level of U.S. Government Involvement and Tax Levels v. Those of Other Nations

We often hear that our taxes in the U.S. are low on average. Taxes are so low that we could raise them and rectify our budget deficits without greatly impacting our standard of living or growth. This is not valid. The overall total tax take of the government in America is roughly the same as that in comparable nations given certain caveats. In the U.S., our health care and education, although ostensibly outside of government, are largely government administrated. They are pooled activities and payments we make on these expenditures are like taxes. Our government, collectively, controls about 40% of GDP. This is perceived of as a relative economic advantage compared to peers like Sweden or France which the fraction of economic activity done by the government is over 50%.

- In the U.S. the education, health care and retirement industries are heavily affected by government distortions almost to the point where these are provided through the government. They have the same high cost and inefficiency as if they were government run.

- Our government has grown such that original Keynesian hypotheses of a government creating spending when private spending lags are not valid. During the Depression in the 1930s government was small, perhaps less than 5% of the economy. Over years government spending has grown, with some short periods in which it has contracted a bit. Even under Republican administrations government spending increased.

- Our government involvement is more than just what percentage of spending is done directly by government. Government affects other spending areas. The money we spend, for example, in preparing our taxes is ostensibly done among private parties but it is a government expense. Many of our business expenses are similarly-cloaked government expenses.

- We often compare ourselves to Canada and our government involvement in the economy is about as extensive.

## Other Taxes or Tax Aspects

Listed below are several taxes or tax features that are proposed to tackle government debt and deficit, to contribute to government revenue generation in efficient way or to perform other salutary shaping of economic behavior. Every tax scheme broached by experts and amateurs alike, however, represents some sort of acute tradeoff.

- **Estate Tax**: At death, people possessing certain wealth, generally millions of dollars, must pay an estate tax of about 40%. Many people think this is a fair and just way to rectify the fortunes of birth. Others question why people get taxed at death when they already paid tax for earning the money: "How many times do you get taxed on the same income?" is the question they ask. There are ways to avoid estate taxes, such as GRAT's which we mentioned above. GRAT's are complicated and involve substantial administration but can enable rich people to make tax free gifts to relatives. Some people decry GRAT's as devices used by the very wealthy to avoid taxes. In any case, it would difficult to raise a large amount of money from higher estate taxes.
- **Tax Non-Profits**, like universities, cultural institutions and hospitals. This could be a major source of income, especially at the state and local level. Of course, we exempt such institutions for the valuable services and community benefits they provide, and taxing them would hinder their missions.
- **Land Value Tax**: Economist Henry George (1839-1897) promoted taxing land and property as an ideal tax for its general fairness and also as a sufficiently lucrative source of revenue to fund most government expenses. Land produced rents that George believed should be shared by all society. Also, taxing land rather than incomes or business activities would avoid economic disincentives to work and produce. In modern times, the land tax is viewed less optimistically. Qualifications include how much revenue can be raised, how to assess land for tax and the incidence (i.e., who pays) of the tax.
- **Sin Taxes**, like taxes on alcohol, cigarettes, gaming, etc. These are deemed to have desirable distortion under the hypothesis that if people reduce bad behaviors due to higher taxes, these consumers themselves will experience superior lives, usually in terms of health and avoidance of immoral activities. Also, the improved populace will be less burdensome to society from lower health care costs, lower propensity to commit crime, etc. thus benefitting all taxpayers. First of all, to a microeconomist it is not clear that hindering people from choosing what they do with their lives improves them regardless of the laundry list of social problems. Also, we have already raised these taxes about as high as possible. Sometimes the sin tax is combined with some other enticing facet. One prominent and timely sin tax is the taxing gambling done on the internet. Advocates tout it as a new and potentially very lucrative source of tax revenues. Some recent estimates were citing amounts like $44 billion but on closer inspection the estimates depended on favorable assumptions (and, in the case of the $44 billion, it was over ten years). Part of the appeal to advocates is that internet gambling is so easy to do people will do it even more than conventional gambling so it will have a broader tax base. That is, however, a rough and wishful assumption.
- **Voluntary Taxes**, most notably state lotteries. Although lottery ticket purchases are voluntary some analysts consider (state-run) lotteries as a form of taxation for the simple reason that people

forfeit money to the government. States have raised about as much revenue from this source as they reasonably can. Also, it is regressive.

- **Tax Unrealized Gains in Security Portfolios**: Many investments, notably stocks, are not taxed on capital gains until the holder sells, which can be a long time—perhaps indefinitely– for many investments. Some analysts view this as a tax dodge. We could require the periodic recording of unrealized gains or losses and collect taxes on gains. This might change the timing of taxes and provide a one-time revenue source, but it should not create more tax revenue overall. It might create years of lower tax receipts if markets went down and people took losses. It would also be replete with bad incentives.

- **Transfer Tax Burdens to States and Municipalities**: The premise here is that greater efficiency can be attained by getting decisions of what to spend and what to tax closer to the agent performing those tasks, the states and cities.

- **Remove or Limit Tax Advantages** of savings programs like IRA's and 529's (the educational savings accounts that allow people to save for children's education with no tax on gains to the savings). These tax adjustments could raise significant revenue but would be extremely anti-saving and unpopular. For example, in his State of the Union Speech in January 2015 President Obama proposed removing the tax advantage of 529's. The proposal was promptly abandoned.

- **Tax the Internet**: The internet is viewed a source of great and easy tax revenue. People supposedly would not mind paying taxes on various internet functions since the internet is such a transformative technology, i.e., the internet provides so much value that people are willing to share it.

- **Tax Oil/Gas or Carbon**: Taxing these ostensibly dirty products has appeal but such taxation would have costs commensurate with revenues raised.

- **Tax the Rich**, either their incomes or assets. Although this could raise more revenues, it could have adverse effects on economic output.

- **Tax Soft Drinks**: Advocates argue that a mere one cent per ounce levy would raise $20 billion; in other words, hardly any sacrifice would yield great revenue. These calculations involve a simple multiplying of units sold by tax rate. They ignore incentives that would change behavior which might render the $20 billion hard to garner. There are moral issues, too. It is not clear why we want to distort people's choices. The minor levy might represent significant burden to households that consume the taxed product.

- **Tax Facets of Motor Vehicle Transportation**, including gas, miles driven or road use with tolls. There is appeal to putting tax burden on driving and vehicles since this consumption activity is often viewed as excessive. From a microeconomic view there is no special economic efficiency to be had from taxing this industry.

- **Financial-Transactions Tax**, sometimes called the Tobin tax. A (proposed) small tax on buying and selling of various securities including equities, bonds and derivatives, at varying tax rates. This tax was championed by economist James Tobin (1918-2002) as a way of raising revenue and reducing market volatility. According to proponents, it would have little adverse impact on real economic activity since financial transactions do not (again according to proponents) produce valuable output. Also, financial transactions are excessive. Certain countries, including France, Germany and Japan, have instituted limited financial-transaction taxes. In general, unless this tax rate is somewhat high, it will not raise much revenue. If it were high, it is unclear what would happen to the functioning of capital markets. It would have to be applied across borders to be effective. This represents another of myriad tax proposals that supposedly raise significant revenue with only minor burden, or with burden accruing only to rich parties whose behavior and well-being is assumed to be impervious to tax levies.

- **Other Surtaxes on Financial Institutions** and sundry transactions done by financial institutions. These are similar to the Tobin tax in that they will not raise much revenue unless they are substantial, but it they are they will burden parties and it is not clear why such parties should be burdened.
- **Tax the "Carry" or "Carried Interest"**: This proposed tax reform has been recurrent in tax reform proposals for the last decade. It is often broached without much explanation and the assumption it will raise hefty revenue. The carry is best explained with an example: Consider a worker such as a lawyer with high income of around $500,000. If he earns another $100,000 it would be taxed at the federal level as "ordinary income" at a (marginal) rate of (about) 39.6%. In contrast, consider a hedge fund manager who earns his money as part of the change in the value of his investors' investments. He takes a percent of the investments' gain. His earnings are taxable only at the point that the investments are sold and the gain is recognized. If gains are not recognized the earnings get carried forward. If the gains, when recognized, are long-term, then that income is taxable at a capital gains rate of 23.8% (equal to 20% on capital gain plus 3.8% on net investment income) as opposed to being taxed at 39.6%. To "tax the carry" would mean to characterize the money manager's income as ordinary income rather than long-term gain. Although this low rate tax situation is valid for some money managers, it is not for most. During his 2012 run for President, politician and money manager Mitt Romney revealed that his average tax rate was about 16% because his income was mostly in the form of long-term gains, not ordinary income. Many money managers' incomes, however, are short-term gains, dividends or interest, which are taxed at a high rate. Even if we taxed the carry, estimates are that it would raise about $19 billion at the initiation of the tax (due to built-up unrealized gains) and then very little year by year thereafter.
- **Tax Broadening**: This is taxing more commerce or parties. An informal way of putting it would be, "1099'ing everything," since the 1099 form is the one the government requires people and companies to issue to any person or company they have paid over $600 to in any year. In this way fewer taxable transactions can avoid taxes. The offsets are that tax burdens will accrue to many transactions by average people and it is doubtful that a large amount of money could be raised.
- **Taxing Over State Borders**: Currently, many states are requiring tax filings in their states for companies domiciled in other states but with significant operations in the taxing state. The obvious shortcoming is that there no net gain for the nation as a whole.
- **Inflation Tax**: One way for a government to reduce its debt is by decreasing the value of the currency. This assumes that the debt is in nominal terms or not adjusted for inflation. The offset here, of course, is that inflation erodes people's purchasing power.
- **Crack Down on Tax Avoidance**: Sophisticated tax payers use a variety of methods to avoid taxes. Often these involve elaborate accounting tricks and pushing of tax rules to extremes. Some tactics include: (1) collars (a type of option strategy) to avoid capital gains tax, (2) wash sales, (3) derivatives to convert ordinary income to long-term gains, (4) constructing basket options (creating holding periods of longer than twelve months) to convert short-term gains to long-term gains and (5) waiving a management fee (which would be taxed as ordinary income) to get an interest in the firm whose profits would eventually be taxed as long-term gains. For one, the magnitudes of these schemes are not that large. Also, strictly speaking, these techniques are not illegal. Those who use the techniques point out that many rules of taxation themselves are unfair. Many of the maneuvers have to do with avoiding the high taxation of short-term gains and it is not clear why the tax on a

short-term investment is so high. For example, between federal and state income taxes in a state like Massachusetts an investor would pay about 50% of his gains in taxes if the gains are short-term. Another strict rule concerns wash sales. Typically in a wash sale, an investor sells an investment that has a loss, then buys back the same investment. He gets to realize the loss (and apply it against other gains or regular income to lower his overall taxes) and keep his original investment. It is not compelling why investors are prohibited from doing this.

- **Package of Some Combinations of the Above**: Analysts love to make the list of tax increases that would constitute a fair package and presumably raise lots of money. They pretend that the package—a little here, a little there—achieves budget rectification without much pain.

Whether we attempt sweeping reforms or minor tax changes, it is very hard to believe that tax revenues can be increased significantly without higher tax rates that burden parties.

## I.5.C. Inadequately Funded Future Liabilities

We have made certain economic promises that are not fully funded or not funded at all (either "inadequately" funded). Of course, any government has future obligations not explicitly funded at some point. The situation the U.S. faces presently, however, is particularly ponderous. If economic growth is high, like 3% per year, certain government liabilities might be no worse than in the past. For example, FDIC (Federal Deposit Insurance Corporation) insurance of bank deposits has been a government obligation since the 1930s, and it will be no worse in the future than in the past–assuming banks do not fail in great numbers–if the economy stays robust. The same could be said about government backing of mortgages. If property values hold up, which will generally be the case if the GDP grows and household incomes grow, then government housing obligations will be reasonable. Student loans are a new liability facing the government. Again, if GDP grows and new graduates get high paying jobs they will be able to make their loan payments.

Certain government obligations, however, including really weighty items like Social Security, pensions and health care liabilities, will be challenging *even if* the economy is strong. If the economy is weak, we have really big problems.

## I.5.C.a. Social Security

Social Security, America's national retirement program, is broke. Social Security is not funded with assets like stocks and bonds the way corporate or state pensions are. There are no hard assets behind Social Security. It is backed by Social Security Trust bonds. Some people say those bonds are backed by U.S. bonds or by the U.S. This is misleading and pompous, though. These Trust bonds have not yet been issued and sold in the market. People refer to Social Security as being backed by the "full faith and credit" of the U.S., but that is also speculative. People pay their Social Security "taxes" and have paid them all their working lives. We have ledger entries that we arc owed something. The Social Security tax receipts, though, go to pay for current government services.[75] Many of us may not get the money we are due for Social Security. Below are some notable of aspects of Social Security.

---

[75] Many countries have similar pay-as-you-go national pension systems, but other countries maintain sovereign wealth funds for pension funding and other future needs. Oil rich countries, like Norway, the U.A.E. and Kuwait have very large funds with hundreds of billions of dollars. Deeming a need for thrift, certain other countries including Singapore, South Korea, Australia,

- Some rough numbers on Social Security are revealing: For most of its existence, Social Security contributions exceeded spending such that the Trust fund built up. (Of course, keep in mind the Trust fund is bonds not yet issued.) The Trust bonds to be issued are about $2.8 trillion as of the end of 2015 which gives the appearance of a big slug of assets. Indeed this U.S. fund is the biggest public pension reserve fund in the world. The next two are Japan's Government Pension Investment Fund and Norway's Government Pension Fund.[76] Japan's fund holds Japanese bonds but Norway's fund holds mostly other assets like stocks and fixed income that is issued and traded. Since 2010, Social Security is paying out more than it takes in. The Trust fund is roughly stagnant although it does accrue a rate of return. It will be drawn down and exhausted by about 2035.

- Originally, Social Security was intended to supplement other retirement resources. Over time, though, it has become the main source of retirement income for many people and a de facto national pension system. There is nothing wrong with this expansion of the program to a national retirement system, of course; but inadequate funding is a problem.

- Social Security is the main source of retirement income for most people. The average couple can expect to receive about one million dollars from Social Security.

- Social Security can be made more solvent by increasing the retirement age. Perhaps this is sensible given that people live longer, but this is a direct loss to people. Depending upon how much and how soon we change age cutoffs, this could represent a significant change in a contract made with people.

- Similarly, Social Security can enhance its revenue and long-term viability by removing the cap (currently $117,000) on income that is subject to the Social Security tax. Liberals prefer this solution on fairness grounds since the cap makes Social Security a regressive tax, i.e., the poor pay more as a percent of income. Raising the tax makes people worse off, however. It also subverts the character of the original Social Security contract, which is that Social Security is not a general tax but a social insurance contribution to ensure that everyone has some base income in retirement.

- Another way to true up Social Security's finances is to disqualify rich people from receiving their benefits. This change is very popular and usually justified with a glib statement like, "These people already have more than enough...they should not mind sacrificing." One problem is that to recognize significant savings many people will have to be disqualified including many who do not consider themselves rich. Many people perceive that they are not rich enough to have their Social Security curtailed and become indignant at any suggestion that they are the rich ones. Also, bumping people represents an abrogation of a contract which is very un-American.

- Social Security consists of a wide variety of programs. Social Security is mainly for retirees, but survivors of retirees (including children) get benefits. You can be on Social Security starting on the day you are born. There is also a mean-tested supplemental income program called SSI, Supplemental Security Income. It is administered by Social Security but funded by general tax revenues. The biggest additional Social Security program is SSDI: Social Security Disability Insurance. The number of people getting SSDI has soared to about nine million. Various factors are behind this increase: (1) It has become easier to qualify as disabled; (2) Once designated disabled, people tend not to return to the workforce; (3) The poor job market has steered many people toward disability; and (4) The aging of the population increases disability. Disability benefits are not very

---

etc. have built up funds. U.S. states have funds for state pensions but they are not fully funded. Certain U.S. states, like Texas and Alaska, have independent wealth funds.

[76] Norway's Fund is not strictly a pension reserve fund. It is a Sovereign Wealth Fund. Its main function, however, is providing for the well-being of Norway's citizens which is largely pension.

high. The average SSDI payment is about $1,000 per month. The payments, however, are often about as much as a person could make working. SSDI is funded with a portion of the Social Security tax, but it is running short. SSDI will run broke, i.e., exhaust its specific trust fund, in 2016. The program can continue to be funded with transfers from the greater Social Security fund, but such transfers make the greater fund less well-funded.

- In U.S. fiscal accounting we view the Social Security and Medicare taxes as current tax receipts, i.e., general revenues that can be spent presently for government expenses. This is absurd. Since Social Security revenues must be paid out in the future they could just as easily be booked as an expense. This would make our current deficits instantly much greater. The way we do Social Security would be the same as a household spending the money it puts in IRA contributions on current expenses but then still crediting itself as if the IRA contributions were saved.

- The assumptions underlying the future solvency of Social Security are optimistic including assumptions for: (1) revenue growth; (2) the underlying GDP growth that support the revenues; and (3) demographics including high birth rates (which increase the population that will pay into Social Security) and modest increase in life expectancies.

### I.5.C.b. Pensions

I started working full time at about age thirty (a little later than most due to protracted graduate education). Using common assumptions about work and retirement, I figured to work until about 65 and live to about 85 which translated to 35 years of work and 20 years of retirement. My salary in my early 30s averaged around $40,000 annually. A rough recommendation for retirement savings for someone like me was to fund a personal IRA at $2,000 per year. This amount was merely about 5 to 10% of my current pay and it puzzled me that I could provide for so many years of retirement with it. I knew that I would be eligible for Social Security and also that as a retiree I could live off of maybe 75% of working-age income, but I also figured that my generation would live longer and that Social Security might be a reduced benefit by the time I retired.

How could such skimpy savings provide for the large numbers of people retiring and potentially living a long time? I figured that there were a variety of favorable forces making this achievable: high rates of return on investment, the magic of compounding, employer matches of retirement contributions, implicit government backing of the system, increasing values of housing, an increasing population supporting my generation, etc. When I pondered each of those factors, however, I had reservations. My employer was not matching my savings. I did not believe in any magic of compounding. I did somewhat believe in high rates of return to the stock market, but that belief was shattered when the equity market crashed in 2001. The same sobering played out when housing crashed in value around 2008. Now, after twenty years, I think my hunch was right. We underfund our retirement.

Needless to say, the topic of pensions is a vast area. In America there are big groupings of pension income. Most Americans have Social Security[77] which, although not originally intended as a comprehensive pension system, has now become the main source of retirement income for people. Social Security is a pay-as-you-go system where current earners pay retirement income to retirees.

A second big pension group for many Americans is traditional Defined-Benefit ("DB") pensions, in which a certain benefit is paid for as long as the retiree lives. Perhaps 20% of private sector workers have DB. Most government employers do too. DB plans are considered the better retirement plans, but sometimes they are not as reliable or generous as people assume. Companies can go bankrupt and stop

---

[77] Not every worker is covered by Social Security. Some worker groups opted out of the program.

providing the pension. Also, many pension plans are not indexed to inflation. Many are simply not as generous as thought, like certain pensions for public school teachers which might replace about 40% of former salary. The DB pensions are less common in the private sector.

A third large pension type is Defined-Contribution ("DC") pension. This has been growing over time and replacing DB for many people. Under DC people save and invest their savings, and keep their savings and whatever gain or loss they get from their investments. Part of this is through tax free programs like 401(k)'s and IRA's. Approximately 40% of people working in companies have a DC plan. DC has advantages and disadvantages: DC plans are portable (people can take their plans when they change jobs or become self-employed) and people are free to invest their DC funds pretty much as they please. They can select an aggressive portfolio that might provide a high rate of return. They take the investment risk both on the upside and the downside. DC pensions are easy to borrow against. Ultimately if DC pensions are insufficient the pensioners are on their own.

A fourth large set of pensions in the U.S. are government pensions including federal, military, state and local. They are primarily DB. They have relatively generous terms but they are not well-funded. Overall, the U.S. pension system is in poor financial shape. We simply have not funded our pensions fully and may not have the economic output to cover what we are already obligated to pay. A lot of the problem is the hefty time value of money we assume to assess the value of pension funds and obligations. Pensions envision a discount rate of future obligations and a rate of return of investments in the pension fund. Both of these rates are around 7% for most public pensions. Consider a simple example: Assume we have to pay pensioners a lump sum of $1,000,000 in 20 years. How much do we have to put aside? The answer is a much smaller amount if we assume a high rate of return on the investments we are holding to make future pension payments. Indeed, we assume a high rate of return. To give an example of the rate effect, to fund that million assuming 7% growth, you need about $260,000 today. If your rate is 2%, you need $680,000. Pensions assume a rate around 7%.

Pensions invest in a blend of stocks and bonds, and they have somewhat hit the 7% rate of return in the past. That return, however, is probably much higher than can be justified by the typical rates of return going forward. Presently, it looks as though a meld of bonds and stocks might get around 2%. (As we discussed before, investors can reach for return by investing in alternatives, real assets, real estate, etc. but those asset classes are largely just stocks and bonds or have rates of return that could be just as low.)

Another adverse factor is that even given the 7% rate of return embedded in most public pensions they are still not fully funded. Using the example above, the pension that needs $260,000 now to pay the $1,000,000 in twenty years does not have $260,000. The funding level varies: Corporate pensions are pretty well funded. Most of our government pensions, including state and local, are well underfunded. Some large ones, like the State of Illinois, are grossly underfunded. Funding of state pensions averages something around 75% (it varies year by year). Federal government pensions are a multitude of programs some of which are fairly well-funded, some are underfunded or some are not funded at all. It is hard to say how much the underfunding of federal pensions is but it is no doubt significant. There are estimates of unfunded federal pension liabilities of over $100 trillion. Underfunding has been true historically but the problem became more acute in 2008 ff. The historic toleration of underfunding stems from the belief in high rates of return and also that our economies are always growing. Our economic pie in the future, whether it be for the State of Illinois or Beverly Hills, will always be bigger we figure.

Our corporate pensions are more fully funded, typically a little below but close to 100%. Corporate pensions also assume lower discount rates. They use the prevailing corporate-bond yield (currently about 4%). They are required to be nearly fully funded with an allowance for variation year by year depending on economic conditions. Corporations must hit stricter standards because they could go broke, while governments are assumed to live forever and have unlimited revenue in the form of taxes. Certain specific corporate pensions are a little underfunded and others are a little overfunded. There are a few constantly struggling with underfunding, usually because they are companies with chronic operating problems. Strangely, mildly underfunded corporate pensions often get worse press compared to government pension funds that are substantially less well funded.

Going forward, corporate pension funds are looking at chronic adverse circumstances due to increased longevity and low rates of return. We acknowledge the former factor, the latter we typically disregard as temporal. In 2014, new mortality tables were released and adopted by corporate pensions. Life expectancies increased significantly, about two years, since the last update of mortality tables in 2000. Simultaneously in 2014, pension funds were using lower rates to discount future obligations. Those two factors combined to reduce the average corporate pension funding from a level of about 89% at the end of 2013 to about 80% at the end of 2014. Most of the inferior funding was due to lower rates, such that analysis of the overall pension system was seen to face, primarily, the lesser problem of people living longer. Analysts simply dismiss the potential for a continuation of low rates. They argue, "Interest rates will eventually reverse course; ever-longer lifespans won't."[78] But what if rates stay low? Also, if rates do go up, asset values will decrease. Holders of portfolios are in the doubly adverse position of having benefitted from long-running lowering of rates while still being able to assume high expected returns.

Analysts highlight a solution of companies selling their pensions to insurance companies. A number of well-known U.S. corporations, such as JC Penney, Kimberly-Clark, Motorola Solutions and General Motors, have done this in recent years. Insurance companies like MetLife and Prudential have been on the buying end. Since insurance companies make money if people live longer in their insurance business (insurance companies are "long longevity"), acquiring a pension gives them the opposite liability, which they can match and, in principle, create a net gain. This solution is doubly-appealing since it gives the appearance that the pension funding problem is solvable within private markets. Unfortunately, there are limits to the benefits of this merger. These pension restructurings involve substantial one-time costs. The pensions restructured have to be reasonably well-funded. There is generally no going back so whatever advantages there were to the company running its pension are gone. The buying out of pensions may not represent a net gain to insurance companies depending on how events play out. If general interest rates stay low, this particular scheme will not be very successful. Finally, transferring might make sense for a few corporate pensions but if we tried to transfer many of them the advantages to society would diminish.

Another problem area is multiemployer pension plans organized by worker categories and unions. These are pensions for workers who are employed by many different companies in their careers. Multiemployer plans are common in industries like building, construction, entertainment, mining and garment and cover about ten million workers. These pensions are well underfunded yet appear, under conventional government rules, not too badly underfunded.[79] If the industries and companies that contribute to these pensions face economic problems, then either getting out of their pension obligations and or paying everybody off in full would cost much more. This is just another example of our precarious pension system.

There are a number of ways to make pensions more solvent but they all require taking losses or transferring burdens. Proposals include increasing the retirement age, increasing the retirement age for new workers (putting the burden on the young), requiring greater contributions, giving new workers in the pensions lower or further out benefits, capping the salaries on which pensions can be calculated, reducing cost of living formulas for pension increases, converting pensions from DB to DC, etc. One recent trend is

[78] "Bad News: People Are Living Longer; Just Ask AT&T, IBM, GM," *BloombergBusiness,* by David J. Lynch, February 9, 2015. http://www.bloomberg.com/news/articles/2015-02-09/bad-news-people-are-living-longer-just-ask-at-t-ibm-and-gm
[79] *The Wall Street Journal* April 23, 2012, p. C10.

that we typically reform our pension shortfalls by burdening the new workers, one of many demonstrations of how much we care about our children. Presently our society, as a whole, is transferring pensions from DB to DC. This puts the investment risk in the hands of the pensioner at a time when future investment returns look much lower than they were during the lifetimes of Baby Boomers.

Pensions systems in certain other countries are more solvent. Some nations like Singapore put money aside for their federal pensions. Some nations like The Netherlands use much more modest discount factors, around 4%. Many emerging market countries have no major pension systems. This might seem like a disadvantage and, indeed, retirees in those nations are on their own; but the nation itself has not built up large unfunded pension liabilities.

Indeed, the different types of pension (DB, DC and pay-as-you-go) have distinctly different economic characteristics including varying economic obligations and incentives to government, business and people. The pensions are all, however, largely the same in that, ultimately, society as a whole has to fund the retirement of its populace. Many analysts advocate switching from one pension type to another and creating greater solvency, but switching responsibilities in such a big program is minimal. Overall we have simply not saved enough.

The summary and the connection of pensions to M&M is that low rates make pensions even less solvent than they already were making pensions significantly greater liabilities.

## I.5.C.c. Health Care Liabilities

The other large economic liability facing the U.S. is our health care system. The lack of budgeting health expenses across generations is the main factor in our fiscal gap. Of course, health care is a broad topic, so I will only focus on some rough magnitudes and the peculiarities of America's health care economic problem. Health care expenditures and costs have gone up extensively in our lifetimes. I have the hospital receipt for my birth in a hospital in 1960. It totaled $150. In 2015 dollars, that would be about $1,200, which would be a fraction of the cost of having a baby in a hospital today. Expenditures have also gone up as a percent of GDP. There is nothing necessarily wrong with spending more on what is the most important aspect of our lives. Much of the cost relates to better care, more care (whether good or bad), care for an older population, etc. There is still great waste including a lot of what economists call deadweight loss meaning complete waste.

We also spend much more than other nations do, something like twice as much per person compared to spending in similar countries. This additional expense yields health care that is not better on average. U.S. health care is superior for many advanced procedures and is subject to fewer delays. The U.S. spends about 16% of its GDP on health care. Comparable countries generally spend less than 10%. In the U.S., about 5% of spending is government (Medicare and Medicaid) and 11% is private. Our health care spending has grown a lot and at a fast rate year after year. Economists differ about whether this spending will continue to grow. Since our population is getting older, it appears likely to continue to grow. Other factors could offset the trend like technology, bulk buying, competition, preventive medicine, etc. These are hard to estimate.

Medicare and Medicaid were signed into law in 1965. Medicare provides health care for the elderly. At the time it commenced, America's elderly were relatively poor and part of the great policy initiatives of the 1960s to alleviate poverty was subsidizing the health care of the elderly. Medicaid was for poor people, especially poor families with children. Today, Medicare covers about 46 million people (mostly over age 65, but also some younger people with disabilities) and Medicaid covers about 76 million people. Over the years the programs sprawled and increased in cost. One big development was the Medicare Prescription Drug Modernization Act which was signed into law in December 2003 and took effect in January 2006. It included Medicare Part D which is an expensive prescription drug program. President George W. Bush approved this relative budget buster. That a Republican supported such a program demonstrates how unpopular it is to control health care expenses.

The major health care program of recent times is the Affordable Care Act (aka Obamacare) which was signed into law in 2010. This law expanded health coverage for lower income people. It involved a variety of provisions including subsidies, covering people with pre-existing conditions, requiring that coverage be available to everybody at reasonable cost, etc. Also, the insurance was to be provided by private companies. The program has been somewhat successful in adding people to coverage but it has fallen short of projections. Insurance companies have abandoned the program due to the fundamental problem that it misprices health care risk.

# I.6. America's Present Economic Standing: *The Bad News is the Good News is Wrong*

*The Good News is the Bad News is Wrong* is the title of a 1984 book by late demographer Ben Wattenberg demonstrating that, at that time, the economic and social conditions in America were nowhere near as adverse as portrayed in public discussion. That was the 1980s though. Today, our headlines are overly sanguine. Economic output is simply not enough to cover what we want.

Whether we can turn it around depends on our future GDP growth. Which major factors will determine GDP growth? Below I will try to muster and analyze some of the determinants of economic growth and attempt to bucket them in two main groups: adverse and favorable. I emphasize aspects that are evolving and somewhat peculiar to America. Today's America faces many challenges we never faced before. We have few special advantages and are resistant to facing problems; and while many others countries are tending toward more economic freedom, we move toward more government, which is disadvantageous.

One main facet of this analysis is that sometimes an adverse factor may not be altogether negative or unwarranted given society's preferences. For example, we simply may prefer greater regulation, higher minimum wages, etc.

Another facet is that the fact that other countries may face similar adverse factors may be irrelevant because we care about our absolute standard of living. Analysts often compare our problems to those of other countries and contend we are not as bad off. We often cite China's grave economic problems like debt, environmental destruction and lots of poor people, but that is irrelevant. Since our standard of living is high and we are accustomed to that, we will be sensitive to any downward movement.

These factors are not macro "headwinds" or "tailwinds" you hear about in the press—and which I consider faux factors spun out of the AD and "lower the rate" stories. These headline macro factors depend on one macro aggregate causing another but with no hook to fundamental factors (e.g., the "unemployment rate will decrease when people start spending," "GDP growth will improve when the labor market stabilizes," "as soon as confidence is restored," "housing will be the driver in this leg of the recovery," etc.). The factors listed below are fundamental and longer-term economic elements.

Another facet of this analysis is that I do not provide copious facts and figures or attempt to estimate magnitudes of the factors I list below. Therefore, perhaps several bad developments will be overcome by one favorable development. For example, unforeseen productivity from new technologies could swamp many of the adverse items listed below. On the other hand, how many costly burdens can a society add and still be number one? One thinking device to keep in mind when judging any development in our society on the economy is the Aggregate Supply ("AS") curve. Does a factor move our AS out, or in? On the graph below, an outward move of AS yields greater GDP (the Y) and lower prices (the P). For example, the recent trend of labor being less mobile in America today probably moves our AS in (from AS to AS''). It would be somewhat difficult to make the opposite case. Another example would be the more contentious development of the increase in the number of people in America on disability. We can deem that our disabled people are now identified, appropriately treated and potentially more productive as a result; therefore, our aggregate supply curve moves out (from AS to AS'). Or we can deem that treatment is a great cost to business and government, which moves our AS curve in. Perhaps treatment makes people less productive, and this would move the AS in to AS''.

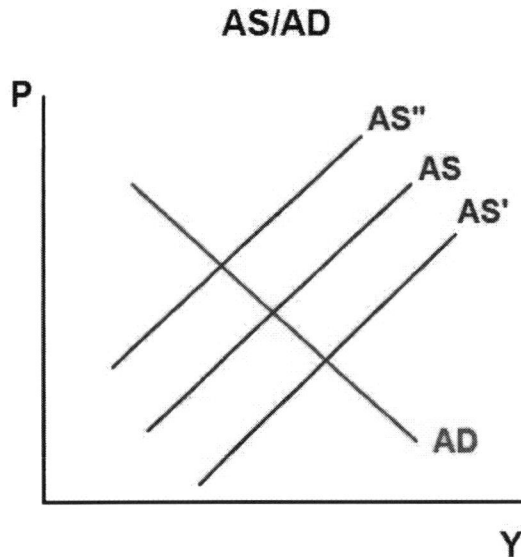

## AS/AD

P

AS"

AS

AS'

AD

Y

## I.6.A. U.S. Pro & Con

## I.6.A.a. Adverse Facets

Set forth below are a wide variety of economic and social factors that are working against our standard of living. They are in no particular order:

- **Attitude of Economic Superiority**: We think that our economy possesses a natural positive growth and always creates jobs. Also, we are the best at business and entrepreneurship with the most productive and independent population. We ignore our general shortcomings like poor secondary schools and specific failures such as our poor responses to crises like hurricane Katrina in 2005 or the large British Petroleum oil spill in the Gulf of Mexico in 2010. We dismiss our economic problems as not true economic shortcomings, just temporary problems from primarily lack of political will.
- **Anti-Business Attitude**: All countries, including America, possess some level of business regulation and persecution, but intensity of anti-business sentiment has increased in America. We contend that we always rank highly in measures of business friendliness, but we are slipping while competitors improve. We often avoid acknowledging this by comparing ourselves to countries like China and Russia with high corruption, yet such comparisons are misleading and irrelevant. Recent examples of U.S. anti-business policies include: the multitude of settlements by banks and financial companies for financial misdeeds following the 2008 crisis; the Boeing union squabble (circa 2013; exemplified a difficulty in selecting optimal location for corporations in the U.S.); and the failure to approve the Keystone XL pipeline. Businesses that can locate in the U.S. or abroad often find other countries more willing to offer favorable business conditions like acquiring land and plant, lower taxes, etc. In the U.S. businesses often face severe and capricious treatment at the hands of government.

- **Increased Regulation** accompanied with a cavalier attitude that regulation has limited negative effect. We place a multitude of little burdens on companies like internet copyright rules and strict worker protection rules. Business advocates are argued down, "This is a small cost in the bottom line of a big company," they are admonished.

- **Labor Immobility**: Americans migrate significantly less due to relatively new economic factors including: being stuck in houses they cannot sell due to lack of equity in the house; health and pension benefits that are part of present employment; unemployment benefits being tied to the state of residence; low in-state tuition for higher education; etc.

- **Attitude of Physical/Mental Infirmness**: We readily characterize our people as weak and incompetent. For example, we revel in the high percentage of returning military who (allegedly) suffer psychological problems. We also have increased the number of young people designated as mentally needy. Whatever the true merits of these changes in the mental health of our populace, the economic impact of characterizing large portions of our human capital as handicapped may be substantial.

- **Increase in Disability**: The Social Security Disability Insurance program, in particular, has grown substantially. The sprawl of the U.S. system may also cause great inefficiencies. Smaller countries, like Sweden, may be better able to manage such programs.

- **Resource Costs**: The 20th century was favorable in costs of basic inputs like oil, metals, agricultural commodities, land, water, etc.; but the future may be less so. The U.S. is not worse off relative to other countries in this respect, and we have some new advantage in the recent increases in domestic supplies of oil and natural gas. Oil is now considered plentiful. The big drop in price in 2014 and 2015 gives the appearance that it will be cheap and plentiful for a long time, but new methods of oil extraction are costly and, over time, will tend more costly.

- **Population Growth Stagnation**: In the U.S., we tout population growth as our ace in the hole. We project our population to grow without interruption, from about 314 million in 2012 to 400 million in 2051. In contrast, Eurozone's projection is for no growth. This U.S. story is accepted by average people and leading population scholars like Ben Wattenberg,[80] yet our population growth to 400 million is merely an extrapolation. Presently, the U.S. population is not growing as much as it did prior to 2008, both in native fertility and immigration. Much of our GDP growth and most of our future budgets for pensions and government depend on population growth.

- **Costly and Mediocre Education**: We consider our education, or at least higher education, to be the best in the world; but the system is costly, compelling our young to spend greatly on education. Other societies produce the similar quality training with fewer labs, books, teachers, deans, recreational facilities, etc. Some propose online education as a potential source of economic efficiency and lower cost, but this is debatable. Time spent with the instructor is integral to educational success. Also, consumers of education may not prefer a cheaper alternative. We generally do not question education's value, yet many levels and types of education are dubious as sources of gain to society as a whole. For example, MBA education may function mainly as an expensive screening device and not add skills.

- **Property Rights**: We are weakening the strictness of our property rights in a variety of ways. During the financial crisis, the U.S. government summarily altered certain basic property rights. For example, secured bondholders of Chrysler had their rights diminished. There are not copious examples, but a precedent was set. The housing market presents questions about property

---

[80] "America's 21st-Century Population Edge," *The Wall Street Journal*, May 23, 2012. (Wattenberg died in 2015.)

ownership. During the financial crisis, it was not clear who owned certain distressed properties: the homeowner, the bank or the government. One potential development may be that if, as years go by, many homeowners will find that they have little or no equity in their houses. They will respond by being stuck where they live, curtailing consumption and, in some cases, abandoning properties. In the U.S., property rights were always extremely enforced and respected by all parties. Rarely did property represent a widespread economic loss but it may in the future.

- **U.S. Credibility in International Financial Matters and the U.S. as a Tax Hound**: Our government is aggressive in suing companies and threatening actions to collect overseas taxable income. The result will be fewer willing to do business in the U.S. and fewer will prefer U.S. citizenship. Under new rules U.S. tax nationals living abroad must file income tax forms even if they have minimal income.

- **Adherence to Free Trade**: Formerly, the U.S. pioneered free trade and promptly entered into free trade pacts, but we are now average among nations in expanding free trade agreements.

- **Moral Hazard**: From banks being bailed out to consumers being protected from credit card companies, our private parties are increasingly insulated from economic responsibility.

- **Free Speech and Dissent Curtailment**: This factor is hard to quantify economically and perhaps a strict adherence to freedom of expression contributes very little to growth of economic output or optimal solutions at companies, schools, government agencies, etc. The U.S. is no longer outstanding among nations for accommodating free speech. We do not challenge authority in our society, and we inculcate our young to be acquiescent. Political freedom is critical to economic freedom, and economic freedom is critical to economic growth.

- **Level and Type of Debt**: We discussed debt elsewhere, but the main point relates to changes in levels and types. Most debt is increasing and is composed of types of debt (such as large student debt and motor vehicle debt with longer maturities) that are relatively burdensome. For example, for the first time in history student debt constitutes a major burden for many younger people.

- **Common Language**: Historically a great economic advantage to the U.S. has been its common language: English. This is less true today[81] and may be a significant economic cost going forward.

- **Acceptance of More Government Involvement**: We are relatively more gullible for both macro solutions and micro solutions emanating from government. Micro solutions would include "behavioral economics," the science of finding flaws in individuals' managing of their lives, and "nudging" them to better choices. It is debatable whether such government grooming truly aids in achieving higher GDP growth or even make us economically better off as individuals and households.

- **Attitude on Future Wealth**, and perception of the rate of return people can obtain. Consumption for the last three decades largely depended on increasing labor income, increases in house values and high stock market returns. Many households now view those three factors as diminished or even stagnant.

- **Entitlement Society**: Currently, over half the households in America receive a significant payment from the government. In 1950, perhaps a quarter of household did. Most trends, like Baby Boomers becoming Social Security recipients, point to an increasing fraction of households receiving money from the government, perhaps as much as two-thirds of households.

---

[81] "Workers' English Skills Wane," by Miriam Jordan, *The Wall Street Journal*, September 24, 2014, p. A2. About one in ten working-age adults does not speak English well. This represents a much greater ratio than before.

- **Diminishing of Great Business Process Improvements** from the last few decades: Innovations like just-in-time inventory, risk management, mass buying, franchising and securitization, which are exemplified by companies like Toyota, Goldman Sachs, Walmart, Federal Express, Amazon, ADP, etc., have made most of their contribution to productivity. Such a set of innovations in business processes may not be as beneficial in the future.
- **Growing Risk Aversion**: We attempt to reduce risks, possibly to zero, in virtually every way. This ranges from our central bank not letting large financial firms fail to strict rules for children's playground activities. This is costly and limits opportunities. Many other societies are more willing to dismiss losses and hardships by their people.
- **Attitude Toward Immigrants** is increasingly mercenary and could backfire: We seek immigrants who have job skills or capital and currently they may add to U.S. product. Effects over time may be costly. We extol immigration and note that newcomers are net contributors. Pundits point out that a large fraction of new companies is started by immigrants. Perhaps, however, immigrants historically came to America to do enterprise because America had other favorable economic features, which, like many of the above items, are now diminished. The best immigrants may stay away or chose to leave.
- **Reserve Currency**: The U.S. dollar is the world's reserve currency. This has many advantages and perhaps some disadvantages. Our reserve currency status could be lost or diminished. This is discussed below at length.
- **Big Data,** in general, and increased government collection of data on people and enterprise: The government collects extensive data which is considered beneficial to model society and determine needs and programs more efficiently. Some argue that government agencies will work closely together and be able to identify and address social and financial problems with greater efficiency. However, efficiency gains in big data may be minor. Also, there is a sinister side.
- **Housing**: The housing market may not create net wealth and may likely come to represent a great inefficient allocation of resources. Houses remain overpriced and our housing finance system is replete with bad incentives to acquire and maintain too much housing. (We talk about housing extensively below.)
- **Manufacturing**: The notion that manufacturing is returning to America to a significant extent is not valid. Certain politicians and economists contend that when all costs (including regulation, law, energy, etc.) and not just labor costs are taken into account, manufacturing in America is competitive. They argue that wages in China have risen so much and productivity in America is so much higher that, by wages and productivity alone, America is cheaper to manufacture in compared to China. These analysts cite well-known companies, like General Electric, that have re-shored jobs. Certain of these manufacturing re-shoring anecdotes are valid, but the general case is not. The labor cost, which is the major cost in most manufacturing, is still higher in America. There are other flaws in the research. For example, they compare high wage areas of China (like the coastal provinces) with wages in low wage U.S. regions (like the South). Also, China is not the only competitor nation. The reality is that manufacturing still tends strongly to go to where the lowest wages are. Finally, productivity is increasing in China and in certain other competitors faster than in the U.S.
- **Prison Population**: A large number of people and large percent of our population is in prison. Some analysts consider this a net negative for our economy and contend we could achieve great savings by releasing non-violent criminals, who constitute the vast majority of prisoners. The effect on the economy may not be very great.

- **Lessening of Consumer Sovereignty and Individual Responsibility**: With increasing frequency in America, we hold producers responsible for economic choices of households including food, medicine, financial services, educational services, etc.
- **National Defense Spending**: We look to our high defense spending as an area to cut our deficit without sacrificing programs that give people goods and services they want. We may be stuck with high defense spending, however, as a result of our prominent legacy in world affairs. As our economic preeminence wanes we might face more, not fewer, military challenges.
- **Crony Capitalism**: This is the protecting and awarding of special economic privileges to big business. It is the kind of perverse economic activity we always mocked other countries for and referred to it as corruption. The U.S. has always had some cronyism. Another prominent example is government sponsored housing entities Fannie Mae and Freddie Mac. Our term for it was corporate welfare. The large U.S. defense industry is often cited as prone to graft. It is hard to quantify cronyism and to discern a change in its severity. Analysts debate how much worse cronyism is today but following 2008, due to the much greater role of government management of the economy (M&M policy, Obamacare, Dodd-Frank, etc.) it appears that many industries like housing, health care and financial services have substantially increased cronyism.
- **Increase in Life Expectancy**: Longer lives may be a singular achievement for humankind but they are costly to society.
- **Increased Inequality**: Inequality is almost universally viewed as a negative economic force. It has been getting worse, at least by many measures. Inequality's raw economic effect, however, is hard to ascertain. The denouncing of inequality by commentators on both the left and the right may be more of a result of each wanting to appear in support of the average person. The economic arguments on inequality's macroeconomic effects are speculative and rely on Keynesian assumptions. Analysts contend that inequality makes it difficult for the middle class to maintain a standard of living without borrowing in excess, and thus the middle class does not spend as much as it would thereby contracting the economy. Another similar argument of inequality dampening spending is that rich people tend to spend less of any additional income and they are receiving more of the additional income.

## I.6.A.b. Favorable Facets

Set forth below are some favorable trends and factors:
- **Various Beneficial Attitudes**: America still has a relatively flexible labor force. People no longer have rigid attitudes about retiring at a certain age or after so many years of work. People are willing to work non-traditional hours and alternative ways like telecommuting. Americans are still somewhat suspicious of Keynesian solutions including stimulative monetary policy.
- **Oil/Energy**: The U.S. has experienced a boom in gas and oil production and, at least for some time, created a new set of oil production companies. U.S. production cost is high, though, and it may represent little value in terms or jobs, exports or tax revenues if the price of oil on the world markets is low. The real advantage to this increased potential supply of domestic energy is that it enables the U.S. to avoid costly foreign entanglements.
- **Efficiency and Cost Gains in High Cost Sectors**: The sectors that have grown in cost recently including health care, disability, education, etc. are potential sources of cost reductions and increased productivity. For example, health care spending in America is very large: by some tallies,

constituting approximately 50% of global health care spending. Obviously, cost reductions are available.

- **Wealth**: We have great wealth to be handed down. It is difficult to say if this wealth will deliver the younger generations from a significant fraction of the public debt they are inheriting or barely make a dent. The wealth to be handed down is unequally distributed.
- **Population Trends**: Aging and non-growing population represents economic cost in many ways, as we have pointed out, but lower costs and efficiency including potentially lower crime, less pollution, less congestion, lower home prices, etc.
- **Tort Reform**: Some analysts believe significant economic gains can be obtained by reducing litigation, but the magnitude is debatable and our legal positioning is deeply ingrained.
- **Revising Inflation Adjustment Calculations for Government Benefits**: In particular, we propose making the cost of living adjustments for Social Security and related programs less generous. This could reduce government expenditures. Of course, it represents losses to beneficiaries as much as gains to government budgets.
- **New Technology**, leading to higher productivity and/or high-profit industries: This is a potentially dominant factor determining our economic future. Notable new technologies and industries include cloud computing, big data, virtual work, 3-D printing, internet, shale energy, space exploration, nanotechnology, self-driving motor vehicles, etc. For example, perhaps the use of big data can drastically improve transportation and commuting, saving a significant amount of time and effort. The effects of new invention are hard to assess but may not be as economically transformative as we hope. New technological improvement may appear remarkable in everyday living but represent very little addition to valuable economic output. New technologies may not create whole new industries with great employment or generate major profit for American companies. Also, these new industries, like the internet, largely lower costs for competitors, eroding job opportunities for Americans. Many advances in technology contribute mainly to extending life expectancy which is desirable for people but creates economic obligations.

In the end, it is difficult to sum up the net economic effects of the factors we listed above. The unfavorable trends seem to dominate the favorable ones, and American also seems to face a greater number of unfavorable factors today than it did in the past.

## I.6.B. Scenario & Some Future Possibilities

We continue hoping for a benign future for our economic lot. We hope GDP growth is high enough to satisfy our consumption and that our business community and labor force continue to be world leaders. We assume central bank policy will be successful enough to keep us from high inflation or recession. We budget some adverse future economic events but take a chance that nothing out of the ordinary will happen. Here are select elements of a future scenario:

- Historical U.S. GDP growth of about 3% as we had in the 1990s turns out to have been largely a confluence of fortunate temporal trends, with extra percentages of growth due to borrowing from the future and a favorable population pyramid. Per capita growth was much lower. Even our GDP growth from the early 2000s, something around 1 to 2%, came from factors that no longer prevail. Today, minimally growing wealth in financial assets and housing leads to lower consumption and, therefore, lower GDP growth. People must save more and manage their debt. This thrifty behavior is not irrational. They do not lack confidence. Instead, they are correctly judging the economic future. Their behavior defies Keynesian nudges.

- Lower wealth, in the U.S. situation at this time, might lead to lower birth rates. Young couples, facing high housing costs, poor wages, low rates of return to savings, high education costs, etc. deem raising children as overly burdensome and families become smaller.
- The U.S. faces increased competition for the production of any goods that trade across borders. New and profitable industries and their economic rents are secured by countries with more favorable business rules, cheaper labor and lower taxes.
- Collectively, these factors put annual U.S. GDP growth at less than 1%, a rate which creates constant government budget deficits.
- Debt, deficits and default grow throughout the economy. Government debt and deficit grow. Companies default on corporate debt. People default on student loan, mortgage and auto loan debt.
- The U.S. persists in macro solutions of stimulation—trying "anything that works" or "doing whatever it takes" by lowering rates, buying assets and stoking demand and causing an ever-growing role of government and distortion of markets. The U.S. utilizes new macro policies like new Fed liabilities (new series of currencies or patriotic bonds), targeting a medium level inflation, managing the balance sheets of financial companies, etc.
- Inflation increases despite poor GDP growth and a constant characterization of being below "full employment." Higher taxes and higher prices on sought after goods and services like health care and education cause expenses by households to grow while incomes stagnate.
- Emerging market economies like those of China, Brazil and India, which are willing to bear the microeconomic trade-offs of development, grow at moderate rates. A convergence of rich and poor countries accompanied with a downward pressure on U.S. wages is a general international economic trend.
- The U.S. adds costs like regulations, higher taxes, environmental rules, uncertainty, threat of confiscation, etc. This pushes aggregate supply in. Many factors that once looked benign or even advantageous to the U.S. (like political correctness and extensive security) now are grave costs. U.S. pension and medical obligations continue to grow as people live longer and longer and demand more.
- The world abandons the dollar as reserve currency. The U.S. fights trade wars. U.S. debt-to-GDP ratio increases, interest expense on U.S. borrowings soars and costly shocks like wars affect the U.S. disproportionately.
- In the 2020s and beyond, intellectual opinion will focus on U.S. economic policy flaws. Analysts ponder why and how the U.S. economy has grown so little in the last two decades. Meticulous research done by international scholars demonstrates the high costs of doing business in the U.S. as a result of crony capitalism, inefficiency of the welfare state, high taxes, pervasive debt, etc.

Such speculations about the future are guesswork and, perhaps, leaning toward on the pessimistic. I believe this is a valid rejoinder to our current naïve assumption of continuation of favorable past economic trends and our perception of America as singular economic entity. Here are a few more realistic potential future trends:

- **Adverse Supply Shocks**: For example, there could be a major terrorist attack, large-scale conflict, oil price increase, nuclear catastrophe, pandemic, sudden climate change event, etc. In the period 1980 to 2010, such supply shocks seemed to have little lasting effect, and thus we became accustomed to writing them off as important. Such shocks at that time were subsumed by greater trends of GDP growth. Today, lower GDP growth will bring out the gravity of supply shocks.

- **Geopolitical Events:** There could be any of variety of actions or reactions by countries to preserve their systems, wealth or sense of importance. Potential disputes could occur in well-known hot spots like the South China Sea and the Middle East, and even in places where conflicts are not expected.
- *Atlas Shrugged* **Event**: Economic capital and talent could flee beyond the borders of nations with high taxation. Entrepreneurs will refuse to commit their lifetimes growing a business for future payoffs that might be subject to confiscation and persecution. Libertarians scheme about autonomous nation-states floating in international waters populated by high achievers who wanted to live outside the laws of conventional nations.
- **Debt**: The U.S. will continue running large budget deficits and increasing its debt.
- **Population**: Immigrants will continue to come to the U.S. but they may or may not bring net economic benefit.
- **Housing**: House prices will stagnate due to fewer households and little income growth. Large swaths of American homeowners will be perpetually underwater on home equity. Instead of perceiving homes as appreciating assets, people will become resentful of the cost of maintaining housing.
- **Work Trends**: People will have to work longer into life, and general labor market conditions will remain adverse for many job seekers.
- **Tax Reform**: The U.S. will engage in minor changes representing little or no net revenue gains nor enhancements to incentives to create higher economic growth. We will raise taxes, at first, on the wealthy. Then, raise taxes on the middle class. Eventually, we will also have to tax corporate America more. Taxes will be higher for the same level of government services.
- **GDP Growth**: Assume GDP growth to be no more than 2% and U.S. total GDP will not get anywhere near as big as conventional projections make it. Various forecasts of our GDP out to about 2030 have it growing to about $35 trillion (from about $18 trillion as of 2015) while China's goes to about $40 trillion. These are both dubious numbers. U.S. GDP will not get to $35 trillion.
- **Investment Returns**: High rates of return will cease to exist in all asset classes. Classes that historically returned double-digits, like hedge funds, high-yield bonds, private equity, small company stocks, etc., will converge on low single digits.
- **Attitude**: A fatalism that our economic lot is static or even declining will settle in among our populace. This attitude will sap our work ethic, invention, household formation, etc.
- **Education**: Higher education will change significantly. College is overpriced and has been oversold as an investment that creates a high rate of return. Interested groups talk about how a college graduate earns much more than a non-college grad over a lifetime, but that amount is easily gainsaid when scrutinized. Student loan debt has become so ponderous and prominent in public discussion that students are becoming averse to take educational debt on. There will be decreases in higher education enrollments. Many colleges operate on tight margins, have significant debt and will not be able to survive drops in enrollment. Many schools will close or merge. Returns to higher education will diminish due to oversupply of educated people. Young people will gravitate to lucrative fields like engineering, computer technology, health related fields and business training creating oversupply in those fields.
- **Climate Change, or Global Warming**: This could result in only mild adverse economic effects or possibly even positive economic effects, but it could also be costly. In that last case, since the U.S.

is already running a large deficit and cannot spend greatly for an anti-global warming project, remedies will involve higher taxation. Developing countries desire to catch us in economic standard of living. They view our historical rampant development as their cue and thus will be resistant to fund action against adverse global warming.

- **Means Testing and Redistribution**: The U.S. government will have difficulty raising revenue and will have to increase taxes. It will collect information on the economic lives and activities of citizens and use the information for "means testing" for programs like Social Security, government pensions, educational programs, etc. People who retire with significant savings will have their Social Security reduced or removed. Perhaps some type standardized financial profile of citizens will have to be created.

- **Government Dependence**: Additional activities of our lives are being performed, funded or assisted by government, further sapping the work ethic, independence and economic decision making of our people.

- **Government Economic Programs**: Evidence of the failure and futility of government programs to enhance economic outcomes (like creating jobs, improving education, creating investment through immigration visa schemes, etc.) will accumulate and add to a general malaise about the economy.

- **Intellectual Basis of Economic Thinking**: Intellectual underpinnings of M&M will change. Either the course will be to abandon the traditional Western textbook of Keynesianism and active monetary policy and reduce government influence in markets, or a greater, international government managed economic philosophy will prevail.

# I.7. Microeconomic

It is time to think microeconomically and dispense with the macro schemes of lowering interest rates, borrowing and pronouncing our destiny of future economic triumph through government policy.

## I.7.A. My Take

Studying economics has made me skeptical of macroeconomics, or at least its policy effects. The parables of M&M are insightful, but implementation of M&M is spurious, faith-based and prejudiced. Like a Catholic who doubts original sin and the resurrection of the flesh, I doubt the effects of monetary policy, stabilizing the unstable economy, Keynesianism and the never-ending growth of GDP from spending. Indeed, competitive economies generally grow but not if the economic system metamorphoses into a regulated, high-tax economy characterized by cronyism in business affairs, bailouts and pervasive government presence in household decisions. Also, I doubt many of attendant intellectual building blocks of our economic thinking like the central bank increasing its balance sheet, causes and effects among macro aggregates, the high rates of return to asset classes and the heroes of economy and market control.

I am a believer in microeconomics. Its parables are singular and relevant to the lives of all of us. Micro reflects a reverence for the rightness of people allocating resources given the constraints they face in life—and for the power of people to bargain through markets and trade at market prices. Here are some of the ways in which I think differently from my peers:

- I am not capable of beating the system neither in macro policy nor financial markets. For decades, I have studied and taught monetary economics and worked as a hedge fund executive but my lesson is that no person can outguess markets. The forces that move markets and economies are factored in by the millions of participants. The next bit of economic growth or stock price change are guesses. For contrast, other people view their careers as singular achievements and are confident they can articulate solutions. They have confidence in their insights and are stupefied by the intransigence of others. For example, a hedge fund executive and economist very similar to me, Eric Lonergan, author of *Money* (Acumen, 2nd edition, 2014) proposed that increasing the supply of money can solve economic problems. A wrongheaded perception that money is debt, which is held by others, is obviously false to Lonergan and glibly demonstrated in many of his life experiences.[82] In any

---

[82] To avoid misrepresenting claims of expertise in multiple fields (investing and monetary economics), let me clarify my background. I graduated in 1990 with a Ph.D. in Economics. I sought an academic appointment but could not get neither a decent teaching job nor other challenging employment in economics. I joined a small investing company specializing in bankrupt and distressed companies, which we called "turnarounds." Initially, I did research on corporate bankruptcy primarily producing a variety of publications for sale. The company also commenced investing services in the form of investment limited partnership (commonly called a "hedge fund"). Employment at the small firm involved working on many tasks, including stock, bond and financial markets research and I devoted a fair amount of time to securities research analysis. Around 2000, as the company grew, I dropped the stock and bond research work and focused on the back-office of the hedge fund side of our business and assumed the title of Chief Financial Officer. The back-office includes accounting, audit, legal, regulatory and client service tasks. Simultaneously I taught economics part-time at a number of colleges and universities including Tufts University since 2000. My most frequently taught course is Monetary Economics. In summary, I can claim expertise in bankruptcy, hedge funds (primarily back-office functions), financial economics, investing and monetary economics. However, as I indicated many times, I am merely one of millions of similar experts, all with about the same education, resources, connections, work ethic, IQ, etc. and watching events in economics and markets unfold day by day.

case, regardless of the ability of other people to beat the system, in the two major intellectual thrusts of my life, investing and economics, I have not.

- Although I deride much of our M&M and doubt our economic preeminence, I recognize that M&M cannot be ignored. Our society has thrown everything we have behind national economic policies, including especially the monetary policy of central banking. M&M is essential to know even if this emperor has no clothes. For example, I believe the next set of outstanding investment managers—those who end up with market-beating portfolios over the next decade–will be those who understood M&M.

- People who address America's economic problems, ranging from Wall Street CEO's to left-wing academics, usually tout deep concern for society. They also contend a perspicacity at discerning economic trends and solving systemic economic problems. I do not care (that much) and cannot discern (at least not in a way to outwit private interests and make improvements in society).

- They are also all deeply concerned about the lot of the poor and denounce inequality. Liberals, of course, maintain this; but conservatives also contend that their proscriptions of free markets and low taxes will lift all boats. Such attitudes are disingenuous, and I am not averse to admit that our economic solutions involve relegating our poor to mediocre standards of living.

- Regardless of orientation, liberal or conservative, virtually everyone roots for more GDP and considers greater spending integral to it. They crave big retail sales, house price increases, low interest rates, high rates of return to bond portfolios, lots of credit, etc. I root against America's spending and hope America's economic problems are indeed so grave that we must endure a significant loss to our standard of living. I do not crave greater economic output for Americans so that they can spend more. I do have some sympathy for the disadvantageous generational transfer that today's young people face and I worry about certain relative hardships like unmanageable student debt. The young generation is not without complicity, however, and if I could find a way to wipe their debt clean, I might not offer it.

- I believe in an unmanaged economy and freedom for people to choose in that economy. This may or may not result in greater GDP, but it will ultimately result in greater welfare. I do not fantasize being Keynes, i.e., discovering the key M&M insight, enlightening the masses and delivering the people to greater and more stable economic output.

- Also, eschewing Keynesianism delivers me from that grotesque hypocrisy of first despising people for their wasteful consumption but then gushing over endless spending and debt financing in the name of stimulating demand. To put it bluntly, "I do not care how much crap morons cart out of Walmart."

- Most social scientists including economists portray average people as virtuous and innocent but also hapless and in need of constant guidance in economic decision-making. People are especially helpless at the hands of powerful corporations and banks. My view is the exact opposite. People are self-interested, clever in taking advantage of the system and competent to manage their lives. To the extent they are not, it is of their own volition and largely due to their laziness and greed. This is not a matter of passing judgment. If a person has lived his life such that he cannot find France on a map of the world, I do not condemn him nor am I puzzled about his ignorance. Why waste time learning geography when there are so many more amusing activities like watching television? If this same person cannot manage his credit, however, it is the same kind of choice and I should not deliver him from whatever problems come from it.

- I will not presume to tell you how to allocate your economic or financial resources, manage your time nor advise on your other choices in life. Leading behavioral economist Cass Sunstein describes how his family gave up gift-giving and was much happier because gift-giving is wasteful and unfulfilling. He advises we emulate him.[83] I might explain a microeconomic principle on a blackboard or tell you which asset classes are good to invest in for tax reasons, and I might mock your lifestyle in debates, but I do not ultimately question what you have chosen as right for you. Like Sunstein, and other people in our upper intellectual and income group, I view gift giving as a sophomoric activity for common people; yet I do not question the pleasure those people get from the choices they make. Similarly, I will not generally mock people for their opinions on issues, and I respect their choice to remain poorly informed and inadequately equipped to deal with their lives and thus live with procrastination, emotion and sloth. For example, Cass Sunstein and copious other analysts scold the public for their overreaction to the disease Ebola. People did not understand the relative risks, according to thought experiments and calculations done by Sunstein and others.[84] I do not believe people overreacted or were hysterical to this threat. They simply do not have nor need sophisticated opinions. In surveys, they merely repeat what they are told by experts and there is nothing un-optimal with that.

- I believe I am no better than any man or woman from China. My peers may feign such belief in equality but most Americans consider themselves more clever and disparage many other nationalities as corrupt and bumbling.

- I do not care how popular I am at cocktail parties. For example, we denounce cigarette smoking, making hyperbolic claims about its cost to society and how one person's smoking is a great burden in taxes or fees to non-smokers. This is dubious. To give another example, we praise our military. While we might not agree with international military escapades we never question the excellence of military efforts of individuals.

- A popular political witticism goes, "Don't blame you, don't blame me, blame that guy behind that tree." I say, "Blame you and blame me, not the Chinese, the banks, bad weather, instability of our capitalist system, irrational markets, etc." I focus on the failure of my own, including my generation, flunky family members and friends, industries with little value-added (like the one in which I work, hedge funds) or extremely inefficient (like higher education, which I also work in), my colleagues like lawyers and accountants who denounce government regulation but are happy to take the extra work the regulations require, my wasteful wife, my uncaring friends, etc. I blame wasteful and retrograde Americans. I also blame macro fools, the millions of do-gooders in the world of M&M and uncaring young people like the students at the outstanding university. In matters of economic discussion, we blame big business and hold government and the people much less to blame. I say blame people and government. Most of all, stop blaming markets, business and banks.

- The people involved in current debates may have excellent records but they are insiders or at least obligated to maintain positive opinions from their histories. For example, Lawrence Summers is indeed a prolific researcher, the nephew of two Nobel-prize-winning economists, a former government executive in multiple senior roles, a senior faculty member at Harvard, etc. but that

---

[83] "Holiday Shopping Tips From Behavioral Economists," by Cass R. Sunstein, November 27, 2012, *Bloomberg.com*. The piece also contains numerous other tips on avoiding gift-giving decision errors born of people's vanity and superficial thinking.

[84] "Why Ebola is Scarier Than It Should Be," by Cass R. Sunstein, October 20, 2014, *Bloomberg.com*. Also, "Stop Fearing the Wrong Things," by Barry Ritholtz, October 22, 2014, *Bloomberg.com*, and numerous others. Pundits relish the finding of panic by people as demonstrative of incorrect judging of probabilities by people. These experts grab any news item to characterize people as foolish. To give another example, the same Bloomberg columnists, a month earlier, mocked people for buying the latest iPhones ("Don't Pick the Wrong iPhone," by Sunstein, September 24, 2014 and "Don't Be a Tech Sucker," by Ritzhold, September 29, 2014.)

compels him to be circumspect about his opinions. It is the same for the investment professionals who can manage money to high rates of return. They have to maintain a belief in an economy that grows sufficiently to justify the continuation of the money management business.

- I believe that people are better off if they are told the truth, regardless. Never hide the truth from people. Whether liberal or conservative, members of the intelligentsia share a belief that average people must be protected from many of life's realities.

- I do not patronize. As pointed out above, outspoken money manager Stanley Druckenmiller was negative on America's economic prospects due to its debt and deficit problems, but, in the end, he felt sanguine because today's crop of young Americans is so talented. This attitude is ubiquitous in policy and commentary but it is condescending.

- Of course, I must point out my own bluster and alert readers to my resentment as motivation for my beliefs. Perhaps I cannot appreciate the rightness and effectiveness of government economic policy due to my own neediness. Maybe I have turned a blind eye to the efforts of many dedicated people whose proactive steps on my behalf have sustained me and my society. Perhaps I resent the help I received from the government throughout my life including the college loans ( without which I surely would not have succeeded in life) and the fast action of our Federal Reserve in response to the crisis of 2008 (which would have bankrupted myself and my family).

## I.7.A.a. As Teacher

Advocating radical change to young people is hazardous. Not too long ago influential Harvard professor Timothy Leary preached, "Turn On, Tune In, Drop Out." Many of the young people of that time took his advice and became bums. On the other hand, I'll be damned before I stand in front of young Americans and pretend that we are in control of our economy and that our models, policies and debates are bringing out the reality of our problems.

As a teacher of M&M who must explain all facets of a current issue scientifically, you develop a sense of the shortcomings of our M&M parables. As I pointed out, we explain with certain teaching devices including models and stories. Reality must match the models. For example, Americans have a much higher standard of living than Chinese. The technical explanation is that we possess greater intellectual capital. You might be nervous telling America's young, who ostensibly have no better education than young people abroad, this story.

I am fatalist about our economic future and am even admittedly rooting against America, as pointed out above; so why do I continue teaching? What good is a teacher who doesn't care about the economic well-being of his students' nation? Whether or not there are great improvements we can make to our society with economic policy, we must think critically and realistically about our economic lives. The main thrust of this recitation is creating a new economic inculcation, both for general matters and specifically a new text in M&M. The macro solutions are faux arguments. We need solutions emphasizing microeconomic tradeoffs. This text is designed for the young, either high school or college age, all of whom will be facing a challenging future if our country continues to "M&M" its way to prosperity. This rewrite includes both a general orientation about our economic life and specific features including a cessation of the teaching of defunct M&M constructs, like the multiplier, IS/LM, the many tools in the monetary toolbox, etc.

## I.7.B. Impossibility of Micro Self-Interest & AD Macro

A *Bloomberg* column relates a triumphant economic story.[85] Once Americans' homes were their piggy banks. People would save by paying down their mortgages and use the accrued house wealth in prudent and moderate ways, like paying for education, starting a small business and retirement. Then, sometime in the last couple of decades this went astray. The unfortunate but virtuous American people were fooled into taking on excessive housing debt, and the housing market collapsed precipitating an economic shakeout. Now, the columnist ponders, how can we collectively get back to this sensible system of accumulating housing wealth? He describes the steps government can take to engender noble economic activity and ensure favorable housing wealth once again.

That's a nice story; but in a society where people are self-interested[86] and government invokes demand-side policies that involve borrowing extremely, it is simply impossible to get such prudent and widespread microeconomic behavior that adds up to macroeconomic success. This is true whether we talk about housing, retirement planning, education, work, public assistance, etc. You might argue that history tells otherwise: We were greatly successful for hundreds of years. However, events from our history before recent decades do not include the comprehensive government managing of people's lifetime economic choices to produce desired macroeconomic ends. If you are born in America today your lifetime economic needs will not jive well enough with those of the collective group.

Our basic story of M&M stimulation starts with an agent (we say person, household or business) that is ready to spend or invest but cannot afford to. For example, a person has an old car and wants a new one but cannot afford it. He can borrow but only at an interest rate that makes the payments too high for him to afford. He constantly ponders the situation, weighing his income and assets, both as of the present and what is expected in the future, against the cost of the purchase. Now, our M&M story is that our central bank "lowers the rate" and our consumer can now "swing the payment" and so he makes the purchase. He only does what makes sense for himself. Of course, the lower rate might make one person borrow more than he planned, but a saver will now be receiving less interest income and will reduce spending. He too only does what is good for himself.

Self-interest also does not mesh well with the science of behavioral economics and its main idea of "nudging" people to be more thrifty and industrious. People will simply take government nudges as replacements for their own efforts, and may even overcompensate. For example, people being forced to save in retirements programs might simply see the forced savings as incentive for less saving on their own. They might even assume that the government managing of their retirement is even deeper than meets the eye and they might actually save less, net. People will always push to the limits of their resources; that is part of self-interest. Health schemes are another example: They are designed to give everyone base coverage while relying on people to maintain good health. Here are several cases of self-interest that show how government economic programs and collective goals of more economic output are confounded in today's economy:

- **Consumers**: At a recent auto show I asked salespersons for the "U.S. content" of their models. Unless the information was on the price sticker (which was not generally the case) the salesperson did not know. "That's a tough question," one replied. Indeed car buyers do not inquire. They simply buy the best car.

---

[85] *Bloomberg.com*, May 22, 2014, "How to Turn Homes Back Into Piggy Banks," by Joshua Rosner.

[86] A major misconception among amateur economists and assorted commentators is that microeconomics assumes people to be selfish. Microeconomics dictates that people are self-interested, not selfish. There is a big difference. I can care about others and still be self-interested. For example, ostensibly non-selfish behavior, like leaving tips, donating blood or voting, are ways that people feel good about themselves and reflect self-interest.

- **Military Service**: Many Americans, including most immigrants, view the military as nothing more than a career choice. Few forfeit other career paths for a stint in the military just for patriotic purposes. They often scorn those who choose the military.
- **Left-Leaning People and Institutions**: We denounce greedy banks freely but even the most admired companies are self-interested. For example, Apple, Google and Microsoft use accounting rules to stash overseas profits from U.S. taxation.
- **Behavioral Economics**: Self-interest will undo the supposedly salutary effects of government policies of engendering better behavior as proscribed by findings of behavioral economics. Devices to make people save, buy fuel efficient automobiles, maintain better health, buy or refinance housing, etc. will have adverse feedback. For example, various tax credits and other assistances for purchasing housing following 2008 caused people to change the timing, but not the overall level of spending.
- **Immigration**: We solicit talented and capital-rich immigrants to create economic output that ripples through to existing citizens. If circumstances change for these immigrants, however, and they determine that they can do better for themselves in their country of origin or in another country, they will abandon the U.S.
- **Excess Savers**: We bemoan that some people over-save. We accuse the Chinese people of not spending as much as they could. Their behavior is unfavorable to us since they do not import as much America products as they should. Americans are also often characterized as not spending as much as they should (which might seem unlikely since they are so in debt, but it is a common M&M refrain). People's thrift behavior is rational, however. People worry about being poor when old. They fear, perhaps disproportionally, for their comfort and health if they should live very long. Then, if these same people perceive that the economy is weak and the central bank tries to stimulate their spending with lowered interest rates, they may tend to save more rather than less.
- **Perceptions of Inequality**: With the exception of the very rich, most well-off people believe their wealth is deserved because they are hard-working and have made tough choices to foster wealth like keeping their household intact (i.e., not getting divorced) and therefore maintaining one high income household.
- **Widespread Government Dependence**: About half the households in America get some substantial payment from the government. To them, losing even a minute amount of their payment (for example, losing $10 on a $400 Social Security check) weighs more heavily than any potential benefits to society at large from smaller government. Also, government support programs are so substantial today that many people simply cannot do better by seeking employment.
- **Shared Sacrifice**: Budget deficit cutting committees talk about "shared sacrifice," which is the idea that disparate groups each give up for the good of the whole. For example, a high income person will agree to pay more taxes if a poor person agrees to a cut in food stamps. Such sacrifices might happen in times of crisis, but not in routine distributing of money.
- **Common Cause**: Americans today have little common experience or goal. The Depression and World War II created a bond and sense of duty among the populace at that time (and they would become known as the "Greatest Generation"). Later generations have no similar bond. In my lifetime perhaps the only common struggle was the Energy Crisis of the 1970s but that is long forgotten. Even the terrorism the U.S. has faced, including September 11, engenders little common cause. Some analysts recommend instilling civic pride by requiring people to learn about American institutions and values and to perform public service. Such efforts have been tried before and hard

to implement resulting in cursory commitment. They also run counter to the economic messages of spending spun out of M&M parables.

- **The Ultimate Test of Self-Interest**: This may come when the Baby Boom generation's demand on U.S. economic output grows sufficiently and really presents a significant detriment to younger generations. How willingly will the Baby Boom take reductions in Social Security, pensions and health care?

One remarkable facet of the study of M&M is that it is devoid of morality. We do not question our consumption (more is always better), how we attain our wealth (if bond portfolios are up 20% in a year, that is great), debt level (some question it, but it is not on the minds of most people), etc. The main simplification is that spending stimulates the economy. The goal of more output is unassailable. Furthermore, we almost always characterize our economy as stuck in a lower level of economic output than deserved. Even in periods of strong economic performance we do not recommend thrift. In the recent past, like the 1990s, when stock and bond markets put up extraordinary returns, no President ever admonished the American people that such returns were too high or that we should put aside the bounty. We also have no qualms about making money on money. If our investments in any year produce extremely high rates of return we simply incorporate that gain into our wealth. We do have some sympathy for the poor within America and we remark at inequality but our empathy for those outside our borders is minimal. If our national monetary policies have had destabilizing effects on the world economy, like raising the price of commodities. People in certain foreign countries may have suffered significantly from our policy but in America there was neither national reflection nor significant emphasis in press coverage. We often boasted our economic policies as beneficial to the world in that our demand would help stimulate other nations' economies.

## I.7.C. Wracking My Brain

I have pondered reforms, policies and other any devices to enlarge our national economy, by whichever metric: more GDP, more efficiency, more jobs, just feeling better about the same amount of output, more equality, more demand, more supply, etc. At this point in time, given what we are and what are capable of, the proposition of substantial improvement in our economic pie is preposterous. Unless we are willing to compel extreme conditions on our populace we have no devices to goose our economic growth and no undervalued sources of wealth. We have some productivity growth, maybe 1% per year, and we can redistribute economic output among ourselves, but that is all.

Below I attempt to look at our economic question broadly, putting everything on the table. I even include items not conventionally considered macroeconomic policy tools like automobiles, video, sports, health care, drugs, children, etc. as well as sensitive areas like sex, race, smoking, environmentalism, homosexuality, etc. I discuss everything. For example, we commonly talk about the hundreds of billions of dollars of extra health care costs due to cigarette smoking, but it is more likely that during the course of their lives smokers require less net economic support than non-smokers.

One general guideline to this analysis is that methods of scheming more economic output can be put into two buckets: (1) Keynesian schemes to "trick" more demand and have it feedback on itself in a multiplied format and (2) fundamental changes in productivity and enterprise. As we discussed earlier, we call the latter growth theory (or long run or even supply-side, if you abstract from the simple supply-side story of cutting taxes). The former set–Keynesian–is ludicrous, but I entertain any of those. Most of the ideas below are of the latter set.

Laugh these musings off or denounce them. They are silly and even ghoulish in some cases. Contrast them, however, with the desperation inherent in our current M&M policies and debates. We are obsessed with stimulating demand even though we run deficits which pile up into voluminous debt. These extreme measures fund our current consumption no matter what it constitutes. Our monetary policy enforces low interest rates such that long-term debt, both government and corporate, yields around zero percent in real terms. We embrace a "New Economic Patriotism" as our President puts it, which basically means selling anything in America that is not nailed down. You can question magnitudes to any of my musings, also, but compare their payoffs to those of any of a variety of economic schemes in which we have recently engaged such as Cash for Clunkers, Operation Twist or imposing zero-percent interest rates on America's thrifty for nearly a decade.[87] Here are the ideas:

- Engage in a massive economic accounting project that puts economic values on activities like leisure activities, sleep, eating, etc. We could tax the activities.
- Sell government assets and privatize government enterprises. The U.S. and its states and municipalities own assets, properties and enterprises. For example, the U.S. owns much of Nevada and Utah. The total value of U.S. land holding is roughly $5 trillion. This includes potential income generating properties like bridges, national parks, roads, prisons, dams, etc. Sale of these assets would raise a fair amount of money but it would be a one-time revenue. Such asset sales represent one of the oldest budgeting-rectifying gimmicks for entities in trouble. A government sells an asset and takes the entire sale proceeds as income for the present period, but then it has to lease back the service incurring ongoing expenses. We are often told that governments face very high costs of maintaining assets such as roads or for operating services like prisons. Then we assume that private companies could operate at lower costs such that there would be a net gain to society. The flaw is that the gains are often not as great as advertised. Also, there is a reason that governments performed certain tasks in the first place. There might be compelling incentive and performance problems. For example, privatizing prisons might give a company incentive to maximize the number of inmates rather than reform criminals. Indeed, in August 2016, the U.S. Department of Justice announced plans to reduce the use of private prisons.
- Value, sell and divvy up the proceeds from any of a variety of scarce resources that we generally have not sold before. These could include water, air, land, citizenship, voting rights, etc.
- Split America up. In America, richer states/areas like Minnesota or Silicon Valley subsidize poorer regions like Mississippi. States and regions have different preferences about the role of government in economic affairs and the degree to which citizens should pool their economic resources. We could create a number of separate nations and allow each to set irs "national" economic policy and cater its policies to its inherent standard of living. We could allow certain states to opt out of the Union, at a price. Some people have enthusiastically expressed interest in Texas leaving the Union.
- Allow people to move freely across national borders. Many economists point out that such a program would create great net gain to the world. It might help the average world citizen, but not the average American. Alternatively, offer countries admission to the Union. Only a country that had less to offer than to gain would apply.

---

[87] Cash for Clunkers was a 2009 federal program that paid people to trade-in certain old motor vehicles. The goal of the program was to stimulate the economy. As part of the program the old vehicles were destroyed. Operation Twist was a Federal Reserve policy of 2011 to 2102 of flattening of the treasury yield curve. Both of these programs had desperate facets. We discuss both of them elsewhere.

- Start a war—real or symbolic—as a Keynesian stimulus. Liberals often claim that only when the U.S. geared up for World War II did we get out of the Depression. Fight a war on poverty. Additionally, this stimulus could be cheap if we could hire workers as low-paid soldiers.
- Instead of stabilizing the economic system, which is the standard objective of our M&M policies, create instability. Perhaps an unstable system engenders supply and growth.
- Remove or greatly restrict patents. They thwart innovation and hinder growth. There may be some validity to this, but it would be difficult to do, and may not yield great gain.
- Mollify the public, especially those with low standards of living. Create diversions that can satisfy a large fraction of our population that cannot attain high quality jobs.
- Put women in charge. According to most research promulgated in our society, women dominate men in prudent decision making and economic outcomes, such as rates of return in investing. "Stocks Perform Better If Women Are On Company Boards,"[88] is the title of one piece demonstrating this omnipresent belief in women's superiority. You could find many others. If such differences were valid, "womanizing" the economy could increase GDP and rates of return greatly.
- Contrarily, we could do the opposite. Reverse the "war on men": the tough and deteriorating conditions in education, crime, health, job opportunities, etc. that many men face today.
- Get more women into the labor force for greater economic output. This economic fix might apply to the U.S. but is mentioned more often as a practical solution for Japan. Of course, this would conflict with another supposedly important goal of increasing fertility.
- Engage in covert political actions to aid our economy. Steal trade secrets or destabilize foreign competitors. Manipulate competitor nations to return to Communism and become weakened competitors.
- Orchestrate household formation. Our poverty and wealth largely depend on the economy of scale of living together. As we got wealthier throughout most of the 20th century, we formed smaller households, perhaps due to the desirability of independence and privacy. To some extent that trend is now reversing. We could manipulate people's living arrangement choices to optimize household size and composition. We could also formalize and standardize marriage and divorce contracts and reduce the many costs of dissolution of marriages.
- Reform financial services. Some analysts consider this industry too large, expensive and employing too much skilled manpower for the ultimate services it delivers. For example, do we need tens of thousands of high level workers analyzing stock valuation? Solutions vary from rules to make financial companies simpler and devoted to single tasks to outfight nationalization.
- Economize on other expensive services that perhaps do not give much value, like social science and other theoretical research.
- Cut waste and encourage thrift. Idling automobiles alone represents significant deadweight loss. It is difficult to instill thrift in the general populace. Getting people to sacrifice comfort is tough. Also, thrift works against our AD and Keynesian view of M&M.
- Institute national service programs. We could instill duty and common purpose with national service programs for American youth or the entire population. This is suggested from time to time by politicians and pundits. One analyst suggest requiring immigrants to visit a variety of historic and cultural sites before earning citizenship. It is dubious that people would maintain any greater sense of public service especially in a society like ours that encourages people to live their economic lives as best they see fit for themselves. Also, compelling people to commit some of their

---

[88] *Bloomberg.com*, July 31, 2012, by Heather Perlberg.

time to someone else's goal would result in inefficient allocation of labor which is another goal we have as part of our quest for highest GDP.

- Encourage job sharing and/or shortened work weeks. Such a program could result in more employment of people but not more total wages. It would also result in a government allocation of people's time which would not likely be better than the myriad ways people already allocate their labor and leisure including working full-time or part-time, having a spouse work, working overtime, etc.

- Implement extreme and perpetual Keynesian policy. Some analysts believe any increase in government spending in our modern world will tend to create more economic output.

- Institute the principles that Milton Friedman espoused, such as negative income tax, monetary policy rules, vouchers for parents to switch kids to private schools, legalization of marijuana, etc. Many of his proscriptions are recommendable but the magnitudes and political feasibility are questionable.

- Institute a libertarian solution. Reduce government to the barest essentials of providing the legal framework and certain other very minor roles. This solution would include paring back national defense and most programs for the poor and indigent.

- Engage in a wide liberalization of activities such as marijuana, prostitution, other illegal drugs, etc. to gain employment and tax revenue from them. This would eliminate some deadweight loss but would not result in a great amount of tax revenue—and it might carry great social costs.

- Manage age and retirement. One of the biggest economic problems many people face is over-saving for retirement. If people knew exactly how long they would live they could plan to retire with zero wealth, an optimal economic goal. To some extent wealthier individuals can already do this planning with insurance products and annuities. If through government we could achieve this goal for all people, perhaps we could gain efficiency.

- Implement a system of fines and taxes for illegal and unpopular activities. People engage in a multitude of activities that are viewed with scorn such as many sexual and interpersonal practices, a wide variety of automobile-related activities like speeding, drug use, telecommunication and software use, various frivolous child-raising activities, firearms use, etc. Many of these have inelastic demand which means people demand them even if their prices go up. We could set up a system of high charges for such activities. The consumers would be worse off, but we might be able to raise revenue and feel good about ourselves.

- Overhaul education. We have been restructuring our education throughout my lifetime. Some improvements have been successful like merit pay, vouchers to attend private schools, charter schools, etc., but we have already used these extensively. More radical solutions might include curtailing high school. We could deem compulsory education finished at age thirteen or fourteen and let young people choose careers earlier in life.

- Propose political solutions and reforms: (1) making the presidency one six-year term rather than (up to) two four-year terms; (2) term limits for senators and representatives; (3) greater executive power; and (4) greater legislative power. Such solutions hinge on transferring power from one branch to another or from one party or another. They might work and result in superior long-term economic planning or simply result in worse economic policies.

- Change the age facets of our economy. Get rid of adolescence, give more votes to the young, raise retirement age, etc. Sometimes population-timing programs can achieve one-time net gains. Nations sometimes solve a shortage of military conscripts by lowering the draft age one year (e.g., from age eighteen to seventeen). Getting rid of adolescence, which would mean mainly closing public high schools and letting people select career paths around age fifteen, might save significant economic resources. Young people would then have to pay for education beyond grade school. Another tactic would be to go the other way and make education compulsory for more years. Giving young people more votes might make for superior long-run economic planning.

- Engage in extensive outreach. As proposed elsewhere, the great multitude of thinkers and do-gooders need not engage in any more research or commentary on social problems. They should roll up their sleeves and help the needy one person at a time. Assume there are about fifty million economically ineffectual people in the U.S. and about one million dedicated do-gooders including academics, journalists, pundits, religious leaders, researchers and others who contend a deep concern for social problems. Each expert could be assigned fifty people or about twenty-five households.

- Penalize the unproductive. Some people are lazy, stingy, wasteful, uncooperative and resentful. Others are just the opposite. Can we transfer from the former to the latter?

- Perhaps we could exchange children between rich and poor households and compel joint optimization problems that make us better off collectively.

- Look at timing and calendar changes. We employ daylight savings supposedly to facilitate work, commerce and transportation (different reasons are proposed). Many school systems have resorted to starting classes later under the assumption that children are not ready to work early in the morning. We could get rid of weekends, change from annual compilations and requirements to some other time period, etc. One popular suggestion for economic efficiency is the elimination of all holidays. People choose their own time off. It is inefficient for someone who does not celebrate specific holidays to alter his economic activities on a forced day off. This might have a minor efficiency gain. On the other hand, removing common holidays might weaken our communitarian leanings, which could decrease aggregate economic potential. In this case, perhaps we could install additional common holidays.

- Assign votes closer to stakes in the economy. We could give more votes to the young, allocate votes by income or deduct votes for being a social burden like being overweight.

- Destroy the economy, and rebuild from scratch. The analogy might be an old house. It is easier to demolish it and build a new house rather than fix the old one.

- Focus on children. Whereas we might be able to ignore unfortunate economic choices and outcomes of adults, society must provide for children. Perhaps we could reduce and phase out government help for adults while directing more extensive support, including health, education, housing, etc. to children up to some generous age, like 21.

- Abolish the concept and data collection of GDP and other economic indicators. Usually, we crave more information to study our failings and address them with policy. Perhaps just the opposite is valid: Our economic failings exist only due to the incessant tabulating and enumeration of our economic lot in life. It creates imaginary economic problems and the attempts to fix them make our economic lot worse.

- Replace GDP as national goal with Gross National Happiness. Certain nations, like Bhutan (a pioneering nation in this project; with efforts going back to about 1972) and the United Kingdom (more recently) are attempting to measure such a quantity and to install it as a goal. Such efforts are fanciful. People's true happiness is an unmeasurable quantity and a goal that cannot be achieved through government.

- Create high inflation to get people to spend. One economist suggested invalidating certain currency by declaring that bills with certain ending serial numbers be worthless. For example, any bill with a serial number ending in 2 would be invalid as of a certain date. People would immediately realize their cash would be 10% less valuable soon and would spend promptly.

- Middle-man our way to prosperity. Groom businesses that act as intermediaries. We are gullible that such enterprises are great sources of jobs and GDP growth. The internet startups that we greatly admire are largely middle-man operations, garnering much of their earnings from advertising. In reality, we have already made about as much money as we can from the middle-man operations. Indeed they represent a cost.
- Draft our most brilliant money managers to manage our nation's wealth. Have them manage the trillions of assets available at our Fed and produce outsized rates of return. Many people in this society seem to believe they have such talent.
- Harness the great power of video. Replace various services that require meeting people with high quality video conferences thereby economizing on the cost of the professional and commuting costs. Many people contend education, especially higher education, can become more efficient this way. Others say there is no substitute for being on campus and having the full attention of an instructor.
- Eliminate or reduce "rent-seeking." This is the practice of businesses securing benefits, contracts and special advantages from government through lobbying, tax provisions, regulation, restraints of competition, etc. Rent-seeking is done primarily by big companies. It can also be called crony capitalism or, more bluntly, corruption. Rent-seeking, compared to profit maximizing behavior, creates welfare loss. Some economists have estimated losses attributable to rent-seeking as anywhere from 5 to 20% of GDP. (We discuss rent-seeking in detail in the section on new M&M theories.)
- Engage good-looking women to be in view in work environments. Then, men will work harder, increasing productivity and adding to GDP.

Parading women around to get more GDP may sound outrageous but is it any more extreme than ZIRP? Why, indeed, are we so obsessed with national income? We have pondered economic schemes enough. Either accept that we cannot improve the economic lives of people or be ready to engage in something that might really work, like outreach.

## I.7.D. Solution Gestures

After we accept the infeasibility of conventional solutions, we have to consider the logical conclusions: marking down our standard of living, reducing wants and admitting failure. This, you might say, is unacceptable since our leaders and populace are so determined and willing to sacrifice to stay on top. We are not that earnest. Before we engage in specific economic and financials actions to solve America's economic problems, we must address what we are and what we deserve. The first step is to level with the people. Tell them the true extent of our debt and our future economic obligations. Make them understand that our economic growth is substantially lower than we have assumed. Then take these steps:

- To show that we are more than just infernal money grubbers, we should start with a gesture. We could blast all of the gold owned by the U.S. to the moon.
- Recognize that our problems are not solvable without some loss and that the recent saving of our country from a depression, i.e., the policy of 2008 ff, was a mirage. It is a microeconomic world. Our economic life is represented by acute trade-offs and not by managing of macroeconomic

swings that attain great GDP growth. In particular, recognize that macro stimulation stories of Keynesian spending and monetary rate lowerings achieve nothing.

- Jettison the M&M banter, in particular the Keynesian-leaning verbiage. Reign in the "this-causes-this" guessing, faux theorizing, silly forecasting, phony budget numbers, vulgar goals of more buying, silly hoping for high rates of return, partisanship of seeing the Keynesian effects, that despicable line of research known as behavioral economics, endless surveying, tedious multi-hundred page summaries of whatever (optimal tax policy, jobs programs, multiplier effects, etc.), curve bending, macro cause and effect, etc. Also, drop the get-togethers: the commissions, Congressional committees, blue ribbon panels, working groups, summits, task forces, roundtables, summoning the CEO's to Washington, university consortiums, etc.
- In money management, instead of the phrase "Assets Under Management" insist on "Liabilities Under Management" to emphasize that invested pools of money are owed to people and must be paid back.
- Cease most, if not all, new economic programs, including Keynesian programs to stimulate the economy and other schemes supposedly designed to foster long-term economic growth.
- Recognize what we are and decide which economic tradeoffs with which we will live. If we are primarily an economic people, rewrite many of our basic doctrines in purely economic terms and remove moral and political terms. For example, how much do we care about the environment? How much do we care about freedom in the world? How much do we care about America's poor?
- Construct a set of national accounts done on an accrual basis (taking into consideration future obligations, primarily entitlement spendings). Disseminate these books prominently displaying our fiscal gap.
- Blame the people or, at least, do not absolve them from their decisions to borrow, over-spend or waste their time and resources.
- Plan to work longer. Expect to retire five to ten years later than your parents did and also prepare for a part-time career after retiring from full-time employment.
- Recognize that we will not fund consumption from asset appreciation. Emphasize that we must live primarily off of labor income.
- Tell the people the truth, with humility. Have leaders like the President, the Secretary of the Treasury and the Chair of the Federal Reserve admit to economic guesswork.
- Name government economic initiatives with realistic names reflecting microeconomic concepts of tradeoff—eschew the pompous, optimistic designations: e.g. replace Jumpstart Our Business Startups Act (with the catchy acronym "JOBS") with Lower Regulation on Business Startups.
- Rewrite M&M texts with emphasis on the macro model of convergence and principles of microeconomics.
- Appreciate markets, including competition from abroad. Dispense with stereotyping of competitors from emerging markets as perpetually backward in business and economic policy.
- Criticize invasive and demeaning social science research. Discourage more forays into government collecting information on people's lives. Assess the science of behavioral economics more critically.
- Curtail or downplay social science research for a time period and observe the results. Perhaps the over-analysis of problems causes them to be worse.
- Curtail and/or terminate data collection of many M&M and related data, including GDP data. The constant counting of our economic lot is useless and even counterproductive to our microeconomic decision making. Provide critical information and/or a listing of potential flaws of economic

indicators promulgated by the government. Perhaps a warning similar to that used for side-effects of medical drugs could be used for economic indicators. For example, pointing out that the Bureau of Labor Statistics monthly jobs count involves jobs that are not full-time, do not represent jobs that can support a household, are subject to revision and seasonal adjustment, etc. might be helpful.

- De-emphasize housing as an investment for average people. Perhaps we should include a statement in mortgage closing papers informing homebuyers that houses do not typically increase in value.
- Guarantee that people can hold assets free from inflation and confiscation.
- Increase age cutoffs for Social Security. Cut back parts of Social Security, including parts of disability.
- Drop the Federal Reserve's dual mandate of unemployment and inflation as policy goals. Target only inflation and set the target to 1.0%.
- In health care, including government programs of Medicare and Medicaid, make various reforms by reducing coverages, increasing eligibility age, having the government buy drugs in bulk, reducing federally sponsored health care spending on psychological ailments, etc.
- Eliminate many licensing requirements.
- Reform defined benefit pensions by limiting cost of living adjustments, raising retirement ages and reducing benefits for current retirees.
- Limit federal bank deposit insurance in incentivize private parties to monitor risk of banks.

This is a long-term project for our nation, that will perhaps take a decade or longer. There is no immediate solution.

## I.7.D.a. The Personal Solution

When I discuss the intractability of our national economic problems with students and friends, they quickly abandon any interest in saving the U.S. economy in general and proceed to broach the topic of their own economic lives. They say, "The heck with stagnant wages, government debt, underfunded public pensions, workers without education….What about me?" It is sobering how quickly some people drop any pretense of worrying about America, and how intensely they focus on their own economic lot. Some consider moving their wealth and talents to a foreign land like Canada or Singapore.

If a person asks me for specific personal financial advice, I mostly defer. I offer recommendations on certain aspects and details, like minimizing costs when investing. I can also make general recommendations about lifetime economic decisions, like do not buy a house as an investment or try to foster a career that you can continue part-time when you retire. When it comes to allocating a person's financial wealth, though, that is tough. For example, experts exhort young people to start retirement saving early in order to amass the greatest amount of money. It is not that clear. If a person is simultaneously borrowing money at a higher rate than he is getting in his investments, he will be worse off. Most young people have substantial installment credit from car loans, student loans and credit cards at rates that might be higher than what the person will get in retirement savings. Even if you include tax breaks and company matches of retirement savings, it still might likely be a bad deal for a young person to save.[89]

It is not that I cannot mix it up with the best of the advice givers. It is easier to give advice once we have made an assumption about a macro trend. For example, if we are assuming that inflation will be high, then taking a big, fixed-rate mortgage and avoiding bonds and bond mutual funds are good advice. Below

---

[89] The company match might seem like a prohibitive factor for choosing to save but sometimes company matches are minimal and also a worker might be able to receive the value of the company match in additional salary.

are a variety of guidelines about your personal solution for economic and financial decisions along with some details about specific asset classes:

- Any personal solution in investing must be feasible, i.e., literally available and achievable. Also, it must be worth any added risk. The tradeoff between risk and return is grave. You may not be able to find stocks that pay hefty dividends and also appreciate in value. It is the same for bonds. High-yield bonds will have high risk. Any other asset categories that are proposed as having a higher rate or return, like emerging market bonds, gold, etc., must be assessed on a risk-adjusted basis. If markets appear overvalued in all asset classes you can take short positions but be wary of any advice to short stocks. For one, shorts will be risky. Some shorts are literally impossible to execute, i.e., you cannot borrow the stock. Shorts also have high carry fees like 10, 20, 30% or even higher for popular shorts. For example, if you short a stock at $36 per share which has a short fee of 20% and a year later it is $30 per share, you have made no money.

- Currently, it is difficult to determine an investment strategy that will get even a small rate of return without risk of loss. Risk-free investments, like interest in banks, CD's or short-term treasuries, return less than inflation, i.e., a negative real return. Looking back over the last few years, it is easy to find successful investments after the fact. Stocks and bonds did pretty well from 2010 through 2014 yet at the start of any of those years it looked as though either asset class was overvalued. Even the most general facet of investing, that there will be inflation or deflation, is impossible to discern. The only advice I can offer is to diversify, including some international diversification, and tend toward holding real assets in case of inflation.

- People have two main economic resources: (1) Labor income and (2) Income from wealth and/or increases in wealth. Wealth income for most households comes from housing and financial assets. Gains from housing appreciation are unlikely. The vast majority of American homeowners will never make money from owning property. For financial wealth you should have a strategy to minimize loss of principal and loss due to inflation. For labor, you should have a strategy for maintaining value of your labor income, perhaps involving constant retraining or diversification of skills with a spouse or within your household. If both spouses are trained as stock analysts and employed in money management, you should be prepared for the potential that your skill becomes commoditized.

- Unless you are rich and mobile across national borders, you are somewhat stuck with your own nationality and the economic burdens or advantages it confers. Americans face high costs for education and health care. They also will likely be facing higher taxes. This can apply to state and local   For example, citizens of Illinois faced much higher property taxes due to pension funding problems.

- People expect some reasonable "out" for their savings, typically hoping for endorsement of one of the following: (1) a second property (a fun and easy way to invest); (2) a stock or mutual fund that is safe and will increase in value at a modest but reliable rate; (3) some secure cash instrument that will outpace inflation; or (4) an annuity. Do not count on any of those options. They all have flaws or risk.

- The personal solution is daunting for upper income types who will live a long time and who have to pay full price for items like education and health care.  Let's say you and your spouse want to retire at age 65 and enjoy a high standard of living. You must assume living to 95. You might have to figure that Social Security and Medicare might be unavailable or reduced for upper income people in the future. Depending on your desired standard of living and assuming minimal rate of return, you need a large sum of money. For example, if you need $100,000 per year that translates to about $3 million at retirement.

- Among the college students I teach most have chosen their personal solution and display little concern about the society around them or public service. The best students get decent jobs and also tend to congregate with similar types, including primarily their spouses or future spouses and also their circle of friends. I think many people already scheme to diversify outside the U.S., e.g., hold dual citizenship, marry abroad, work abroad, speak a foreign language, etc. I rarely meet a student who is greatly worried about the future of America at large, e.g., whether or not auto workers and plumbers are successful. Perhaps the only time I hear a student talk about the poor is when he or she has been assigned a paper or other project on the very topic.

- What are the disaster scenarios and your strategies in response? There are three scenarios: (1) inflation, (2) deflation and (3) stagflation (relatively high inflation and little GDP growth). If there is inflation, you should hold gold and other commodities. Rates would rise with inflation, so invest in floating rate notes (perhaps inflation-protected bonds, although their return may likely be no higher than inflation) and buy puts on treasuries (perhaps some kind of interest rate swap, etc.). If we experience deflation, pay off fixed interest debt, like your mortgage and avoid gold. Bonds would be relatively good holders of value. In the event of stagflation, it is very hard to find a portfolio. You can see that these disaster scenarios, in addition to being hard to discern which will happen, are costly to maintain. Put options must be paid for, and individuals generally cannot do complicated financial transactions like buying put options. ETF's that simulate down market scenarios are available, yet even those are hard to monitor for an amateur.

- Life expectancy for yourself and family members is a major factor. Longevity is costly. You can invest in annuities that pay fixed sums after a certain age and purchase longevity insurance, but those are costly when generous. Annuities are costly, illiquid, not-guaranteed (depending) and have low rates of return. Annuities also depend on the continued financial strength of the company behind them and although that company might have a solid balance sheet today there is no guarantee that it will in the future.

- Hire a financial planner. They are proficient at technical tasks of investing and money matters, but they are amateur economists prone to prejudices. Most are "stocks for the long run" believers. They often justify their services by contending that you yourself will make grave investing mistakes. They cite sundry findings of behavioral economics. For example, they may say that you are an over-believer in your investments and see confirming features, even if the investment is wrong. This is the famous and often-cited "Confirmation Bias." Financial planners, however, will then recommend their investment programs with justifications such as cycles, average rates of return, success and effects of central bank policies, maybe even Monte Carlo analyses capturing risk, etc. Their thinking is Confirmation Bias too. One obvious aspect of using a financial planner is fees. Fees vary but they typically charge 1% of assets and/or some percentage of return. If rates of return to both risk-free and investable assets remain low–a case we have made earlier–the asset-based fees will be especially relevant.

- Be wary of stock returns. Leading markets guru Jeremy Siegel says, "Stocks for the Long Run,"[90] and contends that we can get about 7% return (in real terms, meaning after inflation) by owning

---

[90] *Stocks for the Long Run*, by University of Pennsylvania professor Jeremy Siegel, was first published in 1994. It presented the case that returns to stock investing held up through adverse market and economic times in the U.S. and elsewhere for the 20th and even before. It is now in its 5th edition (2014). Siegel was not the first to discover that the stock market returns over time

stock. This return can be achieved without taking much risk of loss so long as you diversify both over time by holding for long periods and across stocks. Indeed, if you look at a hundred years of annual data, you can get an average return of around 7% in U.S. markets and something similar in other nations' markets. However, we could just as easily look at three points of data subdividing time by century and conclude that the 1800s produced low returns, the 1900s high and the 2000s low. We will analyze potential stock returns later, but I think a better estimate of returns without risk is something around 1 to 3% real. Stock returns depend on earnings, which depend on GDP growth. GDP growth will not be high enough going forward to increase already high stock valuations. Also, stock returns depend on after tax earnings, and taxes will likely go up.

- Specific stock advice often sounds plausible but can be misleading. For example, in recent years people have been told to buy stocks of companies that consistently earn, pay dividends, have good growth prospects, will not be subject to tax confiscation and are impervious to any one nation's fortunes. We hear recommendations like this all the time. Of course, people have been indulging this sensible strategy such that stocks like that are pricey. If you find a cheap dividend-paying company it is probably one that will not grow much and might typically be a company, like a utility, with lots of leverage. Many top analysts and portfolio managers contend that stocks are undervalued on a relative basis. Another piece of advice is look to foreign markets. Yet these experts are often managing portfolios that depend on stocks being a good bet. It is very difficult to find any stock that is undervalued. Holding for the long-term might be a bad bet since all the future profit that can be earned by companies might have to be applied to pay for government expenses. Therefore, look for "real" asset plays and companies that make money internationally. Johnson & Johnson and Cisco are two American companies that make real products with large sales abroad. The opposite of real is financial companies whose margins are squeezed due to low rates and regulation and who depend on government policy. Look for strong, large European firms that make real goods and pay good dividends and are at low valuations such as Siemens and Novartis. Then, look to emerging markets. This advice is risky though. For example, before 2013 many advisors might have steered investors to Russia as an economy where valuations were not too high and that had a growing middle class and improving business practices. It would have been easy to overlook the substantial political risk in Russia which emerged around 2014.

- Consider real assets. Assuming inflation and figuring on low growth and rising taxes in the U.S. and abroad, it might make sense to stick to basics like real estate, land, commodities, infrastructure, natural resources, etc.

- What about fixed income, i.e., bonds? Strangely, bonds, which you might think of as conservative and having low but certain returns, have also had very high rates of return in the last thirty years.[91] Bonds' returns have been high due to a long, general decrease in inflation and interest rates over that period, giving bond portfolios substantial price, or capital gain, increases. Currently, interest rates are low such that: (1) the average of bond coupons is low and (2) since rates cannot go down much more and will probably go up, bond portfolios are likely to decrease in price, i.e., give capital losses. The bottom line is that bond holdings could give very low, or even negative returns.[92] To

---

were high but his book was a particularly nice compilation of facts, figures and arguments. The book became very popular and Siegel became a spokesperson for stock market investing.

[91] Exact returns vary widely by bond types but in general bond returns have been high. We will discuss the bond bull market later.

[92] Some experts contend that you can avoid interest rate risk by holding individual bonds, rather than bond mutual funds. This is spurious. When interest rates increase, the bonds in the bond mutual fund decreases in price and the net asset value of the fund can go down. The value of the bond mutual fund is calculated daily as if the bonds are sold. If you hold an individual bond and

top it off, we could be looking at widespread bond defaults and/or bond restructurings, in which case investors would potentially lose a lot.[93] We could have a protracted bond bear market in which bond mutual funds could lose value year after year. Some financial experts recommend finding quality high-yielding short-term bonds, but they are simply hard to find. Others suggest buying floating rate notes, which will go up with higher rates, but: (1) companies issue them with call provisions; (2) their inflation protection has many conditions and (3) they are relatively rare.

- Should you consider alternative investments? While most opine that plain vanilla stocks and bonds might not give big returns, some experts hypothesize that we can move into "Alternatives" and still attain outsized returns. These alternatives include hedge funds, private equity funds, venture capital and odd asset classes like timber, real estate, farmland, etc. These asset classes have some history of high rates of returns and at times reputable analysts believe such results are reasonable. For example, Blackrock CEO Laurence Fink boasted alternatives as yielding "1000 basis points" (10%) over the stock market and that alternatives should be made available to the general public. That is a tough case to make. Some successful alternative asset investors have done well in era of extraordinary money management (1980s to early 2000s) but the future looks tougher. There is simply too much money chasing a limited amount of undervalued assets. Hedge funds have done poorly for as long as a decade. Assets like timber and farmland are pricy. We have "private-equity'd" everything we can private equity.

- Be cautious with gold? Gold's value could go up or it could go down. Gold is an inflation hedge and if we get a whiff of inflation, gold could surge. Absent this inflation hedge role though, gold should be priced cheaper for its industrial and jewelry demand purposes alone. While gold is often denigrated by finance ministers, nations still buy it. Any individual investor would be wise to put only so much, maybe 10%, of his wealth in gold. Also, gains on gold holdings are taxed at high rates.

- A house is not investment. It is consumption. (We will talk at length about housing as investment and as an M&M policy tool later.) We experienced a period in which house prices rose extremely (1980s to early 2000s), and that will never come again, despite how much we wish it. If you believe that inflation will increase it would be wise to take a (fixed) mortgage or even refinance to a bigger mortgage and invest the proceeds in stock, other real estate or commodities, all of which might hold up against inflation fairly well while the value of your outstanding debt gets diminished.

- Labor income, or what economists call human capital, is the most important source of income for the vast majority of people. Today's young people will likely live much longer than their parents and probably be in superior physical shape at much older ages. They might plan on working much

---

interest rates increase and you do not sell the bond or value it, you do not have to recognize the capital loss. You garner the periodic interest payments and get the face value of the bond at maturity. It seems as though you never face a price reduction but you do theoretically. When rates go up, bonds comparable to yours in quality will have higher coupons. If you want to get those higher yielding bonds you will have to sell your bond at a loss. If you hold your bond you will have a bond with a low yield and may likely be lower than inflation at some point since the main reason that interest rates would have increased would have been higher inflation.

[93] Why should we expect bond defaults, since the default rate has been modest recently? Quite simply, we have been issuing large amounts of poor quality bonds. They are readily purchased due to the reach for yield that has been compelled upon fixed income holders by low rates. We have issued many bonds of dubious quality and security with revealing designations including the following: (1) covenant lite bonds (with few restrictions on the issuer); (2) CoCo bonds (contingent convertible; these are a hybrid debt, typically issued in Europe, that can be converted to equity); (3) PIK toggle bonds (can pay interest in more bonds rather than cash at the choice of the issuer); and (4) dividend recap bonds (designed to pay dividends to private equity investors rather than invest in plant and equipment). We have issued this large amount of poor quality debt on a gamble that the economy is strong.

longer into life. They should attain valuable, marketable skills and be prepared to retrain. Perhaps computer programming is in demand today but twenty years from now that may not be the case. Over the years, as more and more people enter the lucrative professions of today like nursing, engineering, accounting, computer programming, etc. they could suffer gluts of workers and wages could go down. Technology also can erode labor income. Finally, high incomes will be the source for tax revenues. One tip for young people is to maintain basic skills, particularly math. Another smart thing to remember is that, unless you have really extraordinary drive and a good chance to excel, work for the government. You will get relatively good pay (compared to the average American), benefits, vacation and job security.

- Should you retreat to annuities? If you are averse to risk as exists in all of the above, you might consider an annuity, which offers a fixed rate of return or some longevity insurance product. You might have stayed away from annuities in the past due to high fees, strict pre-mature withdrawal rules and generally low returns. The fees and the rules have not diminished much although some companies offer better terms. Also, annuities now have even lower returns and if M&M developments are as we predict annuities will have a hard time offering high rates of return. An additional concern is the strength of the annuity issuer. Purchase annuities backed by companies with strong balance sheets like Fidelity, Northern Trust, BNY Mellon, etc.

## I.7.E. Economic Patriotism

President John Kennedy said, "Ask not what your country can do for you; ask what you can do for your country." Economist Milton Friedman deprecated that attitude. Why give up to a government? What do we owe our nation? Who is right about service to country? Is it simply that we pay our share of taxes and perhaps perform military service? Otherwise, we engage in private contracts that benefit ourselves— and only ourselves? Or do we pitch in economically? For example, if we run a business, do we hire more workers than is economically profitable? If we run a big corporation, do we maintain operations in America even if it is cheaper to locate abroad? Then, what economic obligations do we have to each other? What do we owe our progeny? Do we protest intergenerational transfers of debt? Do we forgive student debt or mortgage debt? What do we owe to business and labor?

## I.7.E.a. Noble America

20th century America was a genuine force for righting the dreadful political misadventures of fascism and totalitarianism. America went beyond self-defense and national interest. A less honorable America could have taken over the world in 1946; instead, we strove to uphold democracy and freedom, a great magnanimous act. America's unscrupulous acts, such as the internment of Japanese-Americans during World War II, were nowhere near as bad as what other countries in similar circumstances might have done. It was a fortunate break that the richest nation in the rapidly industrializing 20th century happened to maintain decent politics. Similar praise can be made for America's achievements in science and commerce. Just a simple trip to a science museum and observation of our great innovation and discovery fills a person with awe.

I wish my progeny could reside in a similarly-outstanding nation, yet future excellence depends on our economic foundations. The 21st century is an economic competition, and the U.S. is at disadvantage in many ways. America is the biggest borrower. We complain and beggar the world about our economic problems. We borrow in our currency and perhaps, due to this circumstance, borrow more than we merit. We tout our economic preeminence but virtually nowhere in the world do people view our economic policies as wise. Throughout 2008 ff you might have read that the U.S. is admired due to its astute and proactive policy which has been more successful than relatively more economically moribund nations like Eurozone, Japan and China, but this is the view of the U.S. policymakers and press. Foreigners, indeed, buy our national debt, but that is no endorsement of our policies despite what financial journalists may say. Investors just consider U.S. bonds to be the best among the alternatives.

## I.7.E.b. Our Fellow Americans

Americans have great patriotism and can rally in times of distress. September 11, for example, demonstrated great sacrifices of time, resources and comfort by many Americans with little complaint and for little direct personal gain in return. In day-to-day economic matters, however, people are self-interested. Even in the face of an economic calamity, as happened in 2008, people pretty much provided for themselves. Also, many Americans take for granted everything that is good in life and are quick to complain when they do not get whatever they want. They have little empathy for the destitute, like poor people in other countries and even those in America. Many Americans do very little hard work. Their entire careers in school and work are marked by passable effort, which is often done grudgingly. A similar minimal concern for the environment also pervades society. Many contribute only in their willingness to throw their copious trash into two separate barrels, one supposedly for recycling. It is a rare American who avoids idling his car.

So what do we owe each other in economic terms? For example, when we buy a car, should we check the American content? Most Americans do not care, and they might have reason. The last 30 years can largely be viewed as a period when the U.S. autoworkers and companies mismanaged their industry. How about our children? People may care about their own children but concern for the next generation in general is debatable. As we reform pensions, the typical fix is in favor of older workers and almost always to the detriment of younger and new workers. We do not hear much public discussion of reducing Social Security or health care for the elderly.

What are we obligated to do for America? You must abide by the law, and do minor services like register for selective service (military draft) and jury duty. Fighting for the country is not required since we have a volunteer military. Our main obligation is paying taxes. For those of us with large incomes we must pay taxes well beyond whatever services we will get back from government. How much redistribution of income should we support? How sorry should we feel for poor(er) Americans? Many Americans try hard, but it is genuinely tough in our expensive society to rise out of relative poverty. These same poor Americans are often callous toward the poor of the world, however, and if they become upper income themselves they have little interest in the poor they left behind.

Giving money to the poor is one thing, but giving money to somebody who is going to spend it on consumption that you yourself think is wasteful is another. We come out of a tradition and belief that a multitude of Americans are needy for basic items like food, but our society now pays for a broad middle-classed lifestyle with many items of dubious importance. Should I pay for health care needs when the average person uses dozens of medicines, most of which I would not use myself?

Another set of fellow citizens is immigrants. Many immigrants have very little interest in American ideals of patriotism, service and freedom. They view living here as purely economic. They do not, for example, join the military. Like the character Sonny Corleone in *The Godfather*, they view anyone who sacrifices for his country a "sap."

## I.7.F. Microeconomic Principles to Replace Macro

Microeconomics gets a bad rap as unrealistic and based on unreasonable assumptions like full information, competitive markets and rational agents. Perhaps, M&M might be sillier with leaps of faith like "banks hold no excess reserves," "the" interest rate, the multiplier and sticky prices. You will have no trouble finding educated people who denounce micro, but non-critically chirp out the macro blabber. Microeconomics is the greatest science known to man. It is the greatest social science. It even compares favorably to esteemed physical sciences if you take into consideration that economics studies people. Smug physicists and chemists deride economics but their fields are just as easy to deride.

At a philosophical level, microeconomic thinking about our aspirations and our problems is better than macroeconomic thinking. For example, for about fifty years the U.S. has perceived oil and its potentially high price as a macroeconomic factor. We have striven to manage the supply of oil with political posturing and military might. If we had viewed oil as just another microeconomic market that would clear at a price, we might have been better off. Consumers would have altered their demand for oil and suppliers would have altered their supplies and we likely would have avoided many of the severe and costly misadventures in the Middle East.

The specific ideas of micro represent our lives wonderfully: Income and substitution effects, public goods, rationality, failure, externalities, choice, diminishing returns, deadweight loss, etc. are all great parables. They can also be modeled and tested in the real world and applied with useful results. Do micro ideas add up to a usable macro? Economists talk about the "aggregation problem" that we cannot combine the actions of micro agents as done in micro formulations and create macroeconomics. That is generally valid but in some cases the micro parable itself may have such insight as a basic idea that it is altogether better than irrelevant and silly macro concepts. For example, one of the fundamental micro models is the Production Possibilities Frontier ("PPF"), which in an x-y plot is a parabolic curve, bowed out with two goods on each axis. It describes economic life as a tradeoff; you can have more of one good by giving up some of the other good. The PPF much better describes our economy today than the macro construct of Y = C + I + G, which dictates that GDP goes up by spending more.

There are a number of ways to utilize microeconomic principles. Micro makes for clear thinking and great coffee table conversation about your life and society. Micro parables are also useful to analyze items usually thought of in macro terms like debt, investing and inflation. How can inflation, which does not even exist in microeconomics, be a micro concept? Conceive of inflation as another constraint on any optimization situation you face. You probably prefer low and stable inflation. Finally, certain micro principles are useful to make life decisions. A microeconomics text is typically hundreds of pages long. In short order though, we can list many of the elements of actionable micro. They constitute nice, although a bit rough, guidelines. For example, you might not want to die with absolutely zero wealth, but your goal should be something close to that. Some with examples and comments of micro guidelines include the following:

- Maximize utility. Allocate resources to achieve your goals and desires. It is not about money. The canonical equation is:

$$\frac{MUx}{Px} = \frac{MUy}{Py}$$

for all goods x and y where marginal utility is denominated in a unit called utils. As you continue to pick consumption, the terms in the equation will tend toward equality across all goods. This is due to the fact that as you consume more of the good with the highest ratio, the marginal utility you get from the next bit of consumption of that good will decrease due to diminishing returns. In other words, the second donut gives you less additional utility, the third even less and so on.[94]

- Price. The importance of price goes without saying and it is hard to recommend the usefulness of prices except to say that prices allocate resources. One of the shortcomings of M&M is that it is a distorter of true price signals.[95]

- Accept failure as a best option. It is the result of taking worthy chances and pushing your resources to the limit. Defaulting on credit card debt, being late for a plane flight, getting divorced, flunking a course, etc. might represent desirable outcomes.

- A most important microeconomic concept is Marginal Product ("MP"). How much output does the hiring of a person add to some production process? Given a worker's MP, I will hire the worker (and/or more of the worker) so long as that additional product is greater than the additional cost of hiring. When MP falls below cost, I stop hiring. You can multiply MP by dollars and talk about value of marginal product if you like but that is a less appealing concept than plain marginal product. Finally, in a competition market, our MP will equal our wage. A corporate lawyer worker makes $250,000 per year; a construction worker makes $25 per hour. These are their MP's. To apply this concept to M&M is tough but the simple truth is that our MPs are not as great as we think they are—whether white or blue collar workers.

- A great micro idea is the Theory of the Second Best. Economists theorize that an economy that is open and competitive results in an optimal outcome, a "First Best." If we constrain the open market in any fashion, the outcome becomes a "Second Best." The Theory of the Second Best says that a little (or one) constraint move you away from optimality as much as big (or multiple) constraints do. Therefore there may be little reward to dropping one constraint on a market, unless you drop them all. An example of this might be our tax system, which is very invasive, distortive of incentives and complicated. If we fix it only part of the way though, we will still have a Second Best, which may be no better than if we did not fix it all.

- The general idea of micro is that we allocate our resources subject to a budget constraint. This is in contrast to the prevailing idea of macro, which is that the budget constraint does not matter. Indeed, adhering to a budget constraint will generally cause your economy to contract.

- Die with zero wealth. This might be hard to achieve in practice and/or or complicated by children and grandchildren but it is a most valid goal. Another way of stating this is do not overwork and save too much.

- Avoid deadweight loss. Strictly speaking, deadweight loss is the loss to consumers in a market that has monopoly power on the part of the sellers. More generally, deadweight loss is any inefficiency and can be the result of taxation, regulation, imperfect competition, etc. We should design all activities, including government programs and taxation, to minimize deadweight loss.

---

[94] For exposition, we can try a numerical example. Suppose I consume two goods: apples and oranges. I have consumed a certain number of apples and a certain number of oranges already such that the MU of consuming the next apple is five utils and the MU of consuming the next orange is ten utils. The price of apples is $1 and the price of oranges is $2.25. By this equation, I will consume another apple: 5/1 > 10/2.25. Then, my next apple consumed, given diminishing returns, will yield less MU. Given a new MU, I will compare ratios again and decide on the next piece of consumption, and so on. The real world is not so simple and it is simplistic to talk about our utility as a function of two goods at one point in time.

[95] Microeconomics is constituted of two major parables: Optimization and Equilibrium. Optimization is the goal of individual agents. It is to get the highest economic outcome given conditions and choices. Optimization is maximizing utility for household or maximizing profit for firms. The former created demands and the latter creates supplies. Demand and supplies meet in market and create equilibrium prices. That is the Equilibrium component of micro. Every problem in micro is either an Optimization problem or an Equilibrium problem.

- Smooth consumption over your lifetime. To a young person, this typically might mean borrowing, which might seem inconsistent with the main theme of this book: that the young generation is facing overwhelming debt. That debt comes from macro policies of government and from the generation that came before though, and is altogether irrelevant to how much debt a person takes on at any point in his life.
- Disregard sunk costs. For example, you have paid the admission for a movie but after ten minutes you realize you are not enjoying the show. Leave, rather than sit through the movie.
- Time your borrowing and earnings correctly. Bring future income into the present by borrowing. Work more when pay is high(er). For example, a mistake made by many young people is to work long hours during college. They will earn a fraction of what they will earn later and their grades suffer.
- Substitute among your major sources of income and wealth. These include labor income, financial wealth, real estate, family, insurance, government services, etc. Envision a broad portfolio of substitutable assets including real estate and financial assets (as everyone does) and human capital and family (view your children as investments).
- Take more risk (perhaps). For example, take more risk in your portfolio investment when you are young by not diversifying. If you are unsuccessful with financial investments then substitute future labor income. In other cases, you must be risk averse. You must purchase certain insurance policies and warranties even though they are over-priced given payouts and probabilities of payouts since the loss would be prohibitively costly to bear.
- Do not overwork, over-invest or get stuck maintaining a capital stock that is too large. For example, think twice about a guest bedroom or overly large house. Own less and rent more.
- Plan on never completely retiring from work. Foster a reduced hour livelihood for middle and old age. The traditional idea or working like a dog in your youth to retire at an early age is no longer optimal.
- Farm out more tasks to specialists. Spend your time on your highest-paying activity (paying either in money or utility), yet do not farm out a task unless you deem it burdensome. For example, if you enjoy mowing the lawn, do not let someone else tell you that you are wasting your time.
- Decrease gift giving and receiving. Make arrangements with friends and family to do the same.
- Minimize inventory. Store paper towels at Wal-Mart and light bulbs at Home Depot.
- Insure against bad outcomes and living long.
- Include both explicit and implicit costs. For example, before you conclude that you are making money on a rental property you own, consider how much time and effort you put in.
- Include psychological costs and benefits. For example, if you really enjoy mowing the lawn, no matter how cheaply you can get someone else to do it, do it yourself.
- Make plans and decisions using expected values. For example, if you figure there is half a chance your child will attend a private college at $40,000 per year and half a chance she will attend a public college at $15,000 per year, plan on spending $27,500. On average over many such decisions your spending will converge on what you budgeted.
- Keep less life and more disability insurance because dying is not as much of an economic burden on your dependents as being disabled.
- Function by your own constraints, not society's conventions or the letter of the law. For example, people may rebuke you for working on a holiday, but if your time is idle on the holiday it may make sense to work.
- Distinguish consumption from investment. View more items as consumption, like schooling.

- Be careful not to invest in items, like education, beyond the value of their returns.
- Separate decisions about consumption and earning. For example, many people link specific incomes to specific expenditures: "We'll take a vacation with the money we get back on our taxes." An optimal strategy, however is to decide how, given all sources of income, to obtain the optimal income, decide which goods and services you want based on their additional benefits (marginal utility) and then apply total income against your entire package of consumption. Similarly separate your investment decisions by deciding (1) the best set of risky assets available and (2) how to allocate your funds between risky assets and riskless assets. (In contrast, a wrong investment decision would be to take an unexpected windfall and decide to invest it all in risky assets since it came out of nowhere.)
- Substitute toward cheaper items. For example, if you prefer to travel to Europe but like travel to Mexico almost as much, go to Mexico now while the value of the Mexican currency is low and visit Europe later.
- Realize that strict constraints are costly. If you will not tolerate leaving your child in the care of any babysitter, your child rearing years will be boring.
- Take advantage of jointness (commonly referred as multi-tasking). For example, fold the laundry while watching television.
- Internalize costs in joint decisions. For example, when managing the household along with your spouse make sure you both realize the costs and gains from every choice.

These micro ideas are copiously scorned by amateur economists and assorted social do-gooders. Their critique is usually nothing more than dreaming of a better model, accompanied by a lot of name-dropping of scholars who challenged orthodox micro like Thorstein Veblen, Herbert Simon, Daniel Kahneman and John K. Galbraith.

We have certainly pondered principles of micro for a long time. For example, in his 1912 *Principles of Economics* economist Frank Taussig says, "An article can have no value unless it has utility. No one will give anything for an article unless it yields him satisfaction. Doubtless people are sometimes foolish, and buy things, as children do, to please a moment's fancy; but at least they think at the moment that there is a wish to be gratified... we must accept the consumer of the final judge." Despite this long academic tradition we have never popularized the use of microeconomic ideas and parables for everyday use.

# Part II: The New M&M Canon

## II.8. The Pretense, Transmogrification & Old "Three Tools" Notes

### II.8.A. The "Pretence of Knowledge"

Friedrich August von Hayek noted in his Nobel lecture of December 11, 1974, "The Pretence of Knowledge" the macroeconomy is too complicated to analyze with sufficient certainty to perform policy. The events of 2008 ff have largely borne it out. Despite all our M&M models and earnest attempts by thousands of analysts to track our economy, as 2007 rolled into 2008 we miscalled virtually every major economic factor, like sub-prime, the bankruptcy of Lehman Brothers, the role of shadow banking, etc. For demonstration, read the transcripts of Federal Reserve Open Market Committee meetings, especially during tumultuous times like 2007 and 2008, and observe our best economists doing little but speculating on current events and resorting to the last data points for their assessment of the state of the economy. Our policy response, although touted to have been effective in saving the country from a depression, might likely have caused as many adverse economic outcomes as beneficial ones–and likely merely draw out our economic loss and relative economic decline. We now have an economy with minimal overall growth and perhaps negative growth for many citizens. We have increased government involvement in economic matters. We potentially have more economic and financial instability, not less, and ostensible large bubbles in many markets.

Over the forty years since von Hayek's speech, advances may have been made in economic science, but macro is even more enigmatic. First, truly fundamental problems of macroeconomic analysis–like aggregation, expectations, feedback effects (more technically the changing of coefficients in macro models), timing of effects, etc.–have not been overcome. Second, greater competitive forces have made the turns and trends of the macroeconomy even more factored in and, therefore, more inscrutable. Third, the convergence of the new competitors like China and the West has a long way to go and, until settled, market and economic trends will be volatile. Fourth, a dominant role for government and the gaming, distortion, uncertainty, moral hazard, etc. that it creates make it almost impossible to predict our economic world. Fifth, magnitudes of assets are suddenly so large now (e.g., think of the nearly trillion dollar Norwegian Sovereign Fund that hardly existed a couple of decades ago), it is unknown how value and economic growth will fluctuate with even little changes in interest rates or even mere perceptions of small changes.

Earnest finance ministers from nations all over the world feign an essential role which is currently very magnified to manage their economies. They all proclaim a willingness to do "whatever it takes," but the world economy moves where it is carried by fundamental micro forces. Although the prices of certain assets and financial transactions may be altered by policy a little for limited periods of time, long-run economic growth is impervious to policy. Even the apparently successful monetary policy of the U.S. from the middle 1980s to the present may likely just have been the absence of bad policy with favorable underlying structural economic forces.

I will not summarize all of M&M, of course: however, I do want to achieve an appreciation of the difficulties of understanding the macroeconomy. Despite the scrutinizing of macro history and the extensive testing of M&M's main models and parables, we are limited in ascertaining economic trends.

## II.8.B. The Transmogrification

In the first problem set of my Monetary Economics class (since about 2008), I assign my students to find historical cases of sudden, fundamental reversals of major, longstanding intellectual ideas (or, you might say, paradigms). They come up with items like Newtonian physics and quantum mechanics, evolution, astronomy discoveries like those of Copernicus and Ptolemy, political changes like the French Revolution or the fall of communism, genetic engineering of food, the birth control pill, germ theory of disease, computer and technology change, etc. All cases (with the possible exception of evolution, in my opinion) fall short, in comparison to what we have recently witnessed in M&M. Sure, the fall of communism was momentous, but not much of an intellectual surprise, except to Soviet hardliners. The discoveries in physics are hefty, but not usually reversals of beliefs and often not tangible in people's lives. For example, the recent (2012) discovery of the elementary particle known as the Higgs boson is unfathomable to average people. Yet, in M&M, since 2008, we have witnessed a complete reversal of the greatest, relatively long-standing social science concept (short-run monetary policy) and a complete U-turn in our ideas of free markets v. government economic management. This has resulted in significant ramifications for life and society—in other words, a true Transmogrification. Below is M&M before and after 2008:

| Pre-2008 M&M | Post-2008 M&M |
| --- | --- |
| Monetary policy facilitated free markets. Markets, we believed, allocated resources efficiently and generally corrected themselves from shocks. We lauded the industries, notably finance, that performed market functions. We talked about a "resilient" economy that adapted to shocks and long-term trends. | Markets fail, in such major and persistent ways that monetary policy must be used to control markets constantly. Major sectors of our economy must be strictly monitored and regulated, ostensibly indefinitely. We suspect Wall Street and capitalism in general. Today, suddenly, government policy and its prestige has grown to the point where massive government intervention is not questioned hardly at all in many capitalist nations (for example, Abenomics in Japan). |
| Monetary policy was parsimonious, boring and effective. We reveled in one simple tool and goal—changing the fed funds target rate through open market operations to control inflation. The tool was potent, concerted and not invasive of the activities of the economy, which were determined by private parties. The story of policy effects through transmission was very simple—little rate changes impacted broad sectors of the economy in significant ways in reasonable time frames. Rate changes worked because banks had a book | Now monetary policy is experimental and sprawling. It boasts myriad tools (the U.S. fed webpage at one point listed twelve monetary policy tools), with magnitudes beyond anything we have ever done before and purposes are ad hoc or even contradictory to what we did before (e.g. flattening the yield curve to stimulate the economy). New policy involves massive buyings of assets with the intention that it will spur purchases by private parties of riskier assets, which then will result in activity in the |

| | |
|---|---|
| of worthy loan applications ready to be commenced. Rates were lowered and the loans got completed, which commenced commerce that multiplied through the economy. We did not need to direct stimulus toward any specific sectors; the market took care of the details. | economy. |
| Monetary policy worked only in the short run. Policy effects were neutral in the long run. The short run was perhaps months, quarters or years, but no more than two years. | Policy works over many years: even decades or indefinitely. We now have a confirmed long-run monetary policy. This changing of the pertinent time frame of effective monetary is a major intellectual change and it gets little critical review in the press. Furthermore, we also often characterize policy's effects as occurring only at the very point of announcement of the policy. This further alters the idea that we have a theory of how variables affect each other over time in the macroeconomy |
| Fed policy involved lending only to banks. Controlling the banking sector was considered sufficient to get broad and potent economic results. Despite that shadow banking (borrowing and lending by non-banks) was prominent and large, we clung to our simple straight banking story, both in policy and in inculcation. | The Fed lends to a wide variety of financial institutions. Formerly, supposedly, the banks were special intermediaries, but, circa 2008, we acknowledged that non-bank financial entities, and shadow banking were just as important to the economy. |
| Effects of policy through lowering rates were thought of as happening through direct effects on borrowing to engender spending (like people buying cars) and investing (like firms building new factories). | Effects are perceived of as happening once-removed by affecting wealth and substitution of financial investments, and then affecting spending and real investment. |
| Policy changes, like lowering rates, were done previously unexpectedly. We assumed that private parties would be taken by surprise and then would react to take advantage of temporarily low borrowing rates. | We now commit to keep rates at a certain level for a certain time. The purpose is to remove surprise and uncertainty for a long time frame. |
| Inflation was the solitary goal of monetary policy. It was to be held strictly at a rate less than 2% and preferably much lower, like near 0%. Getting close to 2% was considered too close for comfort, because inflation could take off easily and rates of even 4% or 5% were too high to manage. Also, we used to view the fight against inflation (as done in the early 1980s under Paul Volcker) as a very difficult and costly struggle never guaranteed to work. | The focus is off of inflation, with many mainstream economists suggesting higher inflation, maybe as much as 4 to 6%, as desirable. That is another drastic change. Remarkably, after decades of talking about hitting our inflation target by not going above it, we now fret about not getting up to it. We now fear deflation and strive to get inflation higher. In fact, virtually every old precept about inflation has turned. We used to worry that inflation, if it started to rise, would take off |

| | |
|---|---|
| | abruptly. Now we seem to think that inflation could only rise slowly. Also, we think controlling inflation is easy. |
| Controlling the money supply was considered critical to keeping inflation moderate. Indeed, expanding the money supply too much would cause inflation. Currency was the principal liability of central banks and reserves were of a small magnitude. | Our central bank balance sheet, the monetary base and monetary aggregates have grown greatly and little inflation has ensued. The result is our renouncement of the once sacrosanct belief of a tight relationship between money supply and inflation. Currency is no longer the largest liability. Reserves are. |
| Unemployment and real output were relegated as secondary goals of M&M policy believing that long-run price stability was the primary goal, and the other goals would follow naturally. | Price stability is a secondary goal. Output growth and full employment are the primary goal. |
| We praised almost without qualification believers in free markets like Milton Friedman and Alan Greenspan. Greenspan was as recently as 2006 a singular hero, perhaps the most outstanding intellectual figure on the planet. Many of the most respected opinions of economic and finance leaders espoused the free market school. | Market champions are diminished or have turned. Greenspan's intellectual standing since 2008 has been greatly diminished. Opinion now acknowledges the fatal flaw of markets. For example, a leading free markets scholar, Richard Posner, wrote *A Failure of Capitalism* (2009), which largely denounced markets for inefficiency and contradicted much of what Posner previously believed in. |
| Fiscal policy was considered unusable. It was hard to implement in a timely fashion and its effects were considered variable. | Now fiscal policy works. Indeed, many contend, we would not have escaped the 2008 recession without the large fiscal policy we did. Perhaps we should have done even greater fiscal policy. As of 2015 and 2016, when money policy has appeared at the end of its usefulness, most analysts recommend fiscal policy with a relative certainty that it will increase economic growth. |
| Our central bank scrupulously avoided meddling in corporations and economic sectors, and relegated regulation to a very minor role. | The Fed now supports certain sectors (housing, notably, by buying mortgage-backed bonds), and the Fed increased its regulatory role significantly–and apparently permanently. |
| The U.S. led the world in capitalism, allowing markets to perform on their own. The U.S. also led in intellectual attitude about economic policy including advocating non-invasive and mostly rules-based monetary policy and also very limited use of active fiscal policy. | The U.S. is now a leader in government involvement. The U.S. has increased its role in the economy in general and in certain sectors in particular including financial services and housing. |
| The Fed was reserved about what it revealed to | Since about 2011, the Fed is voluble and |

| | |
|---|---|
| the public. | provided myriad analyses and guidance including targets for future interest rates, sharing economic projections, press conferences, etc. |
| We previously preferred policy by rules like the Taylor Rule. | Now we use full discretion like the QE's, Operation Twist, etc. and changing or delaying policy waiting on new data. |
| M&M theories described two time frames: the short run, in which the economy could be out-of-equilibrium and a long run, in which the economy was at full employment. We contended that our economy typically operated in long-run equilibrium with occasional short-run dis-equilibria that could be rectified, in quick time (generally less than a year) with policy. | Now we describe policy as performing over a "medium-term" which is so undefined that it can rationalize any unconventional policies that ostensibly do not work in the short run as once advertised. Then, we do policy over the long term. |
| We believed that a zero nominal interest rate bound was an absolute constraint. (A negative real rate was possible. It only required that inflation was higher than interest rates.) | Now, we use negative nominal rates. (Negative policy interest rates are not in effect in the U.S., but are discussed as a policy option and are actually used by the ECB and certain other European countries' central banks.) A remarkable facet of this is how readily we changed our rhetoric from the finalist statement that a negative nominal was impossible to statements like this, "…it is hard to push nominal rates deep into negative territory."[96] |
| The Fed was scrupulously independent of other government branches and aloof from companies and Wall Street. | Now, the Fed works in close collaboration with the U.S. Treasury and various other departments, and the Fed consorts with private parties. |
| The U.S. Fed operated strictly under certain rules, laws and distinctions. We would previously emphasize this is the teaching of Fed policy, contending that such policy would only possess effectiveness if the Fed maintained these distinctions. | Now, any policy can be done under the "unusual and exigent" clause ("Section 13(3)") in the Federal Reserve Act. |
| Fed policy was the liability side of its balance sheet (level of reserves). Previously the assets of the Fed balance sheet were almost exclusively U.S. treasuries. | Now Fed policy involves much greater management of the asset side of the balance sheet. Fed assets consist of risky mortgage-backed and federal agency bonds. In the years 2009 to 2011 Fed assets included claims peculiar to certain industries and companies. |

These abrupt reversals were readily accepted by both the lower-level economic thinkers, like pundits, politicians, business leaders and other amateur economists, and also by leading members of the economics profession including academic, business and policy economists. The rationalizations were that,

---

[96] "Free exchange. Still, not stagnant," *The Economist*, March 7, 2015, p. 80.

"the facts have changed, so we change our theories," or that our business is, "more of an art than a science," or that "circumstances are extreme." Even more importantly, few fessed up to having changed their convictions.

Moreover, we relished the alteration of M&M. The deconstruction represented a renewed need for economists and their research and, especially, a renewed role of saving the world. Once again, M&M economists are more than just teachers of mostly abstract models. They are economy crusaders. Pundits, the media and the big shots of the world are excited. The meetings like Davos and Jackson Hole are more exciting today than they were before 2008.

## II.8.C. Throw Away the Notes

Current times are problematic luck for veteran M&M instructors with great sets of lecture notes used year after year. Teaching is quite challenging now. It is largely salvaging the old models and trying to explain current events in a frenetic method, usually focusing on whichever M&M topic is current in the press or, as I put, the "model du semester." In the years following 2008 we lectured on exit strategy, price-level targeting, quantitative easings, deflation, communication, yield-curve flattening, nominal GDP targeting, negative deposit rates, tapering, reverse repos, helicopter money, banning cash, etc. Of course, many instructors continue teaching the old syllabus with pronouncements of our Fed "lowering rates" and stories of money multipliers and Taylor Rules.

Here are some examples of educational travails of current M&M:

- Although the time value of money and bond price dynamics stories are always valid in theory, today's persistent low rates render many of the formerly finalist statements silly. Even the social science stalwart topic of the time value of money (that a dollar tomorrow is worth less than a dollar today) is hardly compelling. Time value was always one of the most pleasing topics to teach because students knew a little bit about it already and usually had a stake in it in bank accounts, student loans, parents' mortgages and perhaps even investments. Instructors today, to be realistic, have to use low rates for any interests a young person will receive today (no time value) and maybe high rates for many of the items young people are obligated to pay for, like student loans. It can be depressing.

- The Fed balance sheet story and open market operations used to be simple. We used a rarified Fed balance sheet, in a T account demonstration, with typically no more than four items: Securities, Discount Loans, Money and Reserves (in fact, just two, Securities and Reserves, could relate the essential story of monetary policy). This exercise did not use real world magnitudes.[97] We explained policy as a buying (or selling) of a Security from a bank by the Fed with the bank, in turn, getting (or forfeiting) Reserves. Today, to teach correctly, we present the actual Fed balance sheet, which table "H.4.1 Factors Affecting Reserve Balances," from Fed publications. We must examine numerous line items, two or three sub-ledgers and sundry footnotes. Any of a dozen line items imparts as much M&M content/theory as the open market operations story of old.

- For the longest time we taught that an upward sloping yield curve meant economic expansion and a flat or inverted yield curve meant the economy was heading toward recession. In 2011 and 2012, when the yield curve was nicely upward sloping, our Fed engaged in a concerted effort to flatten it, called the Maturity Extension Program or "Operation Twist." An instructor can rationalize the policy by saying that the circumstances at the time dictated that lowering long rates was advantageous. Nonetheless, the policy vitiates one of our most compelling models and the stories we told to rationalize it.

---

[97] Monetary economics instructors at low-level schools where the students cannot handle demanding models might fill lectures with actual data involving the Fed balance sheet and related empirical items like the U.S. budget.

- Our most popular historical teaching examples of effective policy are diminished, if not altogether struck from class notes. Summer and early fall of 1998, when the default on Russian sovereign debt threw markets in a downward spiral, was one of our most compelling examples of successful monetary policy. Markets reacted with a flight to quality and a blowing out of spreads (people bought the best securities, like U.S. bonds, and sold the riskier securities, like Brazilian bonds, and the yields on the U.S. bonds went down while those on the Brazilian bonds went up). The economy teetered (supposedly). Then, we argued that quick, concerted action by the U.S. Fed rescued the economy. Three rates lowerings of 25 basis points each kept markets alive (again supposedly) and saved the world. Looking at 1998 today, though, casts doubt on the effects and necessity of policy. The rate lowerings happened in September, October and November, by which time markets had already adjusted. The Fed policy likely had little or nothing to do with fundamental economic factors that were controlling the economy in the latter half of 1998.
- Longstanding levels and coefficients in many of our models changed to such an extent that an instructor must admit the models do not hold. Examples include the money multiplier, Okun's Law, the Taylor Rule, etc.[98] Concerning the once venerable Taylor Rule, historically its calculation included a constant value of 2% in addition to various variables reflecting the state of the economy. Typically the Rule would produce a level for the fed funds rate of around 4% and the 2% constant would constitute half of that. Now, some Rule users have lowered the constant to 0%, to fit the times, but it represents a fundamental change.
- Instructors formerly made many finalist statements about policy. For example, instructors would say that the Fed could not take certain actions because they were outside its mandate and/or its legal privileges. For example, the Fed could not borrow money. Given the policy following 2008 we see that virtually any rule can change.
- Another longstanding parable of monetary policy teaching was that we could not set negative nominal rates. Many countries have used negative policy rates recently. It may seem like a trivial facet, yet when an instructor has drawn a line on the board and said, "Of course, rates cannot go below here," a thousand times, it is problematic to admit that rates can indeed be in a negative range.

Will the old notes be valid again? Die-hards contend that although we are in an extraordinary M&M period, and must entertain new models and abandon certain old ones, soon we will "normalize policy" and the textbooks will be usable again. This is dubious.

---

[98] We will discuss virtually even M&M model in "Put All the Models on the Board" below.

# II.9. M&M Setting & Major Concepts

## II.9.A. Evolution of Macro Thinking

M&M history comes in two parts: (1) facts and figures and (2) theory. The former is voluminous but digestible for most people while the latter is constituted of subtle M&M distinctions and concepts only eggheads can truly appreciate. I discuss a little of both here.

### Macro Prior To About 1920

M&M is a creature of the 20th century. Only since about the 1930s have we envisioned a significant role for government to manage the economy. Prior to the 20th century, economists wrote about nation building, mercantilism (the main policy of many countries to export more they import) and a little bit about the "trade cycle" and political economy; but they did not ponder stabilizing an unstable economy. For example, inflation was not the chronic and extreme problem it would be in the 20th century. There were bouts of inflation largely during wars or during discoveries of large amounts of gold, yet over the 1800s in the U.S. there was gradual deflation.

As for the real economy ($Y = C + I + G$), we did not have a large government sector (the G). We did not collect data on C and I, generally; and we did not typically measure unemployment. Perhaps the major macro theory from the pre-1900 period is Say's Law, named after French economist Jean-Baptiste Say (1767-1832). Say's Law states, "Supply creates its own demand"—meaning that the macroeconomy takes care of itself. By the way, most M&M economic thinking over the last 80 years has been a denial of Say's Law, especially during 2008 ff. We are AD/Keynesian believers and rally behind the direct opposite of Say's concept that "demand creates its own supply." We crave spending and tax cuts that are spent and we deride saving, all in the belief that spending creates more economic activity. At get-togethers, economists will almost always agree that Say's Law does not hold.

The M&M lessons of the 1800s are inscrutable. A casual look at data on business fluctuations during the 1800s gives the appearance that the business cycle was quite severe, with frequent and protracted recessions. For example, contractions lasting many years (including contraction lasting more than five years in the 1870s and another three-year contraction in the mid-1880s). Economic historians argue on this point, with some contending that the fluctuations were not that severe and, in any case, not comparable with modern times.[99]

Government policy proponents like former Fed Chairman Ben Bernanke[100] often cite these financial panics up to and including the panic of 1907 as evidence that markets did not function well. This thesis is debatable. The banking panics were relatively few and tended to be restricted to certain

---

[99] One pivotal piece of research by economist Christina Romer contended that the fluctuations from the 1800s were an artifact of the data. Romer's analysis was novel and controversial when it was promulgated in the 1980s. Existing business cycle analyses of pre-20th century data showed rampant volatility in the economy, yet macroeconomic data from that earlier period remained incomplete and mostly focused only on commodities. Romer could not make the old business cycle data as complete as more modern data, but she could take the modern data and make it as bad as the old. When doing so, she found that business cycles in modern times were just as volatile as those of the 1800s. This finding shocked many policy economists who considered post-World War II economic policy very successful in controlling the business cycle. Later in her career, Romer would become head of the Council of Economic Advisers from 2009 to 2010 and a strong proponent of policy.
[100] A relatively succinct summary of Ben Bernanke's thinking on M&M is available in his series of four college lectures presented at George Washington University in 2012. These are available on the webpage of the Federal Reserve.

geographic areas. It is hard to tell if they caused economic loss or if this was a case of causation, i.e., some real economic change causing financial problems. Simply put, were these economic changes and failures in a growing and rapidly evolving economic environment like 1800s America unavoidable?

A similar debate exists on the gold standard as it impacted our economy when it was in effect during the 1800s and the first third of the 1900s. Conservatives contend that the gold standard worked well, guaranteeing low inflation and making conditions advantageous for commerce and economic growth. Believers in unstable markets characterize the gold standard as causing either general poor economic growth or instability that created downswings. For example, Ben Bernanke always maintained that the gold standard caused price fluctuations, including bad deflation; however, this is debatable: Prices were pretty stable, and the economy grew under the long period of the gold standard.

Another intellectual battle concerns the role that early central banks played in their economies. Some, like Ben Bernanke, contend that countries that had central banks early in their histories (like England and France) had more stable economies and that the U.S. (which did not have a central bank until well into the 20th century) was volatile and prone to recession.[101] Yet these earlier national banks were not like modern central banks in that they did not try to use policy to manage the macroeconomy. They did not monitor aggregate economic conditions such as unemployment rates and try to do discern business cycles and countervail with economy-wide policies. Central banks from pre-1920 did do some lending in dire times but not a sufficient amount to avoid panics. Also, countries that had central banks did not perform better economically. They suffered the same shakeouts—for example, England suffered a depression during the 1920s. Finally, if the United States had had a central bank throughout its history it might have been a counter-productive economic force. Powerful national banks were opposed by politicians, including notably President Andrew Jackson. His hatred might have stemmed in part from some poor personal financial decisions that he blamed on banks. He also maintained a conviction that concentrated banking could lead to corruption and fraud and is quoted many times with this sentiment: "When you won you divided the profits amongst you; and when you lost you charged it to the (central) bank." Perhaps a strong national bank would have made the U.S. prone to crony-capitalism and also enabled the U.S. government to engage more readily in reckless finance.

## 1920s Through The Great Depression

Coming into the 20th century, national governments grew and assumed pivotal roles in their nations' economies. For example, in the U.S., both the central bank and federal income taxation began in 1913, old-age social insurance and extensive regulation of business and finance commenced in the 1930s. Similar expansions of government in industrial countries occurred, and there were sundry predecessor government initiatives: England began central banking around 1694 and France in 1800. Germany commenced social insurance in 1889 under Otto von Bismarck. Generally speaking, though, it was only in the 20th century that governments had the size and scope to do big spending and manage the financial system.

In the 1920s, Great Britain experienced a protracted economic slowdown; and, in the 1930s, the U.S. suffered the Great Depression. These episodes of recession of the macroeconomy were more severe than those cycles economies experienced during the 1800s and early 1900s. The leading capitalist economies suddenly faced massive unemployment. John Maynard Keynes completed his opus—*The General Theory of Employment, Income and Money*—in February 1936. The basic idea that spending kept an economy moving was not at all unobvious, and many other scholars and practitioners at the time were

---

[101] This sentiment was a main point of Bernanke's 2012 series of four college lectures done at George Washington University.

making the same case. Michal Kalecki (1899-1970), a Polish economist, developed similar Keynesian macro ideas as early as or before Keynes, but did not get wide notoriety for the theory at that time or after. Kalecki published only in Polish and French and got limited circulation. Marriner S. Eccles, a business person from Utah, was Chairman of the Federal Reserve from 1934 to 1948, and he spoke frequently (including testimony before Congress in 1933) about the virtue of stimulative government spending. The economic importance of maintaining spending was not a hidden idea.

The Great Depression is the pivotal event in M&M. During Ben Bernanke's tenure as Fed Chair, he received copious praise as being the right person to handle the 2008 crisis since he was a leading Depression scholar and would be cognizant not to make the same mistakes of policymakers in the late 1920s and 1930s. It is fairly easy to identify certain ostensible economic policy errors: (1) the Fed raising rates in 1928, which precipitated a downturn in 1929; (2) the Fed failing to act in late 1930 when bank runs caused a significant drop in money that persisted for years; and (3) the Fed raising reserve ratios in 1936 because banks were holding increasingly great excess reserves, which action may have led to the 1937 recession. Cause and effect concerning the Depression, however, is facile. Any story can be rationalized. Keynesians say that the economy suffered from an initial drop in demand from some loss of confidence and the economy only got back on track when the U.S. implemented really hefty spending during World War II. Monetarists, like Milton Friedman, contend monetary missteps were the key and monetary policy, including select pro-active monetary policy, is the proscription. Other experts argue with those two basic takes and propose other explanations for the Depression including an agricultural collapse, inequality, productivity shocks, high tax rates, protectionism, etc. The Depression and its lessons for M&M in general, and specifically for today, are a complete muddle.

## After The Great Depression Through The 1970s

The ostensible failure of capitalism during the Great Depression had such an intellectual effect that after World War II most economists and other intellectuals were Keynesians favoring government economic management. Many were outright socialists. Around the late 1940s, the entire world was close to collective planning and the U.S. stood virtually alone in its support of free enterprise. Communist nations, of course, were central planning devotees, but also much of Western Europe and many third world countries were socialist-leaning. They nationalized industries, imposed very high tax rates on business and workers, instituted strict rules protecting labor and more. After the war, the U.S. was determined to avoid going back to the high unemployment rates seen during the Depression. We passed the Employment Act of 1946, which specified goals for economic growth, employment and price levels. Many economists were expecting a return to Depression conditions, but despite a major drop in government spending, the economy grew.

In terms of law and legislation concerning the responsibility for managing the macroeconomy the Employment Act of 1946 put the responsibility for the macroeconomy in the hands of the federal government. At that time the Fed was largely subservient to the federal government and was setting policy to keep U.S. government borrowing rates low. The Fed, in the Treasury-Fed Accord of 1951, retook its independence from the federal government. The explicit statements of national economic goals set forth in the Employment Act of 1946 were revised in the 1978 Full Employment and Balanced Growth Act (known as "Humphrey-Hawkins"). Under Humphrey-Hawkins the Fed become the de facto party charged with maintaining our macroeconomy.

In 1944, the global community orchestrated an international agreement on exchange rates, at the Bretton Woods resort in New Hampshire and referred to as Bretton Woods. The nations of the world were worried that following World War II, struggling countries would end up with weak currencies and have high inflation, even hyperinflation, as had transpired after World War I. Nations yielded to the U.S. as the great economic power and guarantor of value and pegged their currencies to the U.S. dollar. The U.S., in turn, said it would offer gold for its dollars at a rate of $35 per ounce. Bretton Woods held up for a while, but by the end of the 1960s the U.S. was running chronic trade deficits and nations of the world, like France, started demanding gold. The situation became untenable for the U.S.; and on August 15, 1971, President Nixon removed the backing of dollars by gold and let the dollar float. This move allowed the U.S. and other nations to print money as they wanted. Each country's currency would be valued relative to other currencies as markets saw fit. Floating rates seemed to work in the sense that our GDP grew in the following decades, yet the breaking of the link with gold ushered in a period of greatly, continuously increasing debt, high inflation and debasement of currencies at times. Up until about 1970, the total debt-to-GDP ratio for the U.S. was about 150% with some fluctuation. That ratio is now over 350%.

Economics, as a study with policy applications, burgeoned in the 1950s and 1960s. Keynesianism flourished in academia and policy circles. In textbooks and college courses, Keynesian models like the multiplier, IS/LM, the Phillips Curve, aggregate demand, tax cuts and spending as stimulus, etc. were dominant. In policy and business, large-scale macroeconomic models (like the Brookings and Wharton Models) were developed as a result of the confluence of developments in computing power, econometrics and macro modeling. The lynchpin was the Phillips Curve, from a 1958 paper by British economist A.W. Phillips.[102] This model linked unemployment (which reflected the real economy—i.e., jobs and output) and inflation (which reflected the monetary economy of money supply and credit creation).

M&M policy economics of the early 1960s was called the New Economics, and this was the first time Keynesian policies were attempted with intellectual and practical consensus. The policies appeared to work since the economy grew at a strong rate; however, the cause and effect and timing of policy effects are debatable. For example, the Tax Cut of 1964 (formally The Revenue Act of 1964) was cited as an example of successful economic stimulus; yet this tax cut came years after it was conceived for policy. The tax cut was initiated in response to a weak economy from about 1961. It was first proposed in 1963 but not enacted until 1964, by which time the economy was growing satisfactorily. To some, this tax cut is taught as an example of successful demand-side management, i.e., Keynesianism. Others argue that it represents a compelling demonstration of a fundamental problem with policy: lags of implementation and effects. In the 1980s, some economists would say that the 1964 tax cut did affect the economy but only due to supply-side, not Keynesian, effects.

Keynesianism held sway until about the mid-1970s when flaws in its foundation became prominent, first in academia, then the business world, the financial press and among policy makers. Many real world developments, like simultaneous high inflation and unemployment, confirmed the ideas of the critics of Keynesian, and we started to turn away from the idea of active management of the economy— eventually abandoning fiscal policy and any pretense of long-run policy effect, and retreating to our basic M&M device of open market operations impacting the fed funds rate in a (somewhat undefined) short term. Of course, general Keynesian thinking persisted in texts and in the press, even if we did not take it too seriously. Keynesianism has gut appeal: People can easily envision spending out of nowhere initiating a cycle of more spending and can see how a big government can make that happen.

I regret omitting many ideas and debates brought out by economists in the intellectual development of the science, yet concepts like "Neoclassical Synthesis" or "Classical Dichotomy" are abstruse. Also, our theories and models have been analyzed over and over, resulting in debates and clashes among schools of thought to the point where basic ideas became difficult to discern. A Keynesian ends up sounding like a

---

[102]"The Relation Between Unemployment and the Rate of Change of Money Wage Rates in the United Kingdom," 1861-1957, *Economica*, November 1958, pp.283-299.

Classical economist and vice versa. For example, Milton Friedman was perhaps the era's leading anti-government policy economist. He made a career of picking off and articulating critical problems in the management of modern economies, including, for example, that policy was problematic because it had, "long and variable lags." He was not a Keynesian. In the 1960s and 1970s, of course, both in the public eye and the classroom, we couched all of our M&M talk in Keynesian terms. In the introductory economics textbook I used in college in 1978, President Richard Nixon was quoted: "I am a Keynesian now," This proclamation was followed by Milton Friedman's, "We are all Keynesians now." Yet Friedman's actual line was, "In one sense we are all Keynesians now; in another, nobody is any longer a Keynesian." He meant to convey that we all used Keynesian models and rhetoric but did not believe them. Of course, such a distinction was a subtlety beyond the comprehension of average people.

In the 1960s Friedman, along with economist Edmund Phelps, developed one of the most remarkable discoveries in modern social science. Contradicting the omnipresent and authoritative Phillips Curve, they hypothesized no permanent tradeoff between inflation and unemployment. There could be a transitory tradeoff or a tradeoff between unexpected inflation and cyclical unemployment, but there would be no longstanding move away from an underlying rate of unemployment of society's resources. It might seem like an obvious conclusion today, but it took independent thinking to propose that idea in the 1960s. This social science discovery of the flaw of the Phillips Curve was very significant in the affairs of humanity. We tend to think of great scientific discoveries as mostly occurring in physical and life sciences and/or mechanical developments (like DNA, flight, radio, the internet, penicillin, etc.); but Friedman and Phelps' breakthrough may have had more impact on people's lives than any of those.

To round out our discussion on the decline of Keynesianism we have to mention Rational Expectations ("RE"). RE is a theory/model/assumption of macroeconomics of characterizing private agents in the economy (such as businesses, households and labor unions) as using information available to them efficiently (i.e., the rational) and anticipating economic futures (i.e., the expectations). When related to M&M policy, RE implies that private agents will anticipate government economic policy and counteract its effects. For example, agents will assume that a temporary tax cut to stimulate the economy will mean higher taxes later, so they will not spend the tax cut but instead save it to pay for future taxes. For another example, a lowering of interest rates should compel banks to make more loans but they could perceive that lower rates might lead to higher inflation such that they will not want to make more loans. Some try to barbarize RE by claiming that it implies that all people, even average ones like truck drivers, can predict the future with precision. RE only implies that smart people use information and look to the future. If you put RE assumptions into standard M&M models, the Keynesian effects are undone.

### 1980s To The Present

By about 1980, the core constructs of Keynesianism were deeply imbedded in the public mind—even if they were discredited in parts of academia. Government spending was viewed as a stabilizer in general and a stimulant when needed. Economies with large government sectors looked competitive, stable and possessed of an ability to foster innovation and steer a nation to valuable businesses. With its big government presence, Europe looked strong. Japan, with its seemingly successful statist capitalism, looked especially economically robust. Even the socialist countries like the Soviet Union appeared to have economic success in certain ways. Around 1980, the American economy looked relatively weak: Unemployment and inflation were high, economic growth was ragged, productivity was stagnant, the stock market had not performed well in the previous decade, etc. It seemed that the basic capitalist model, and in particular the U.S. version of that model, was flawed.

An amazing turnaround would happen, however. The free market model thrived and its success put government management on the run. Over the decades of the 1980s, 1990s and 2000s, almost every major economic trend changed and the U.S. led the rebirth. Inflation went down, contrary to the beliefs many leading economists had that it was "built in." Unemployment went down to well below what economists asserted to be rock bottom levels, and productivity surged. GDP growth stayed at about the 3% rate. Government budget deficits diminished, and the U.S. even started running surpluses by about 2000. Those surpluses appeared so sizable and growing that we were even forecasting an imminent end of all U.S. government debt. Asset prices (including equity, debt and housing) went up. Profit maximizing firms that were floundering in the 1970s came back with great success.

Developments over these times were often inconsistent with macro doctrine and empirical models. For example, when the stock market crashed in 1987, the economy should have collapsed on the strength of a negative wealth effect; yet it did not.[103] In the 1990s, the unemployment rate kept going down. Top economists, such as Lawrence Summers and Paul Krugman,[104] maintained it could not go below 6% without inflation. This appealed to the concept of NAIRU: the non-accelerating inflation rate of unemployment, which represented a level of unemployment at which labor was fully employed. As the rate went down—to 5.5%, 5%, 4.5%, 4%—and inflation did not take off, they maintained their position. The once rock hard idea that very low unemployment would surely cause inflation proved tenuous. GDP forecasting was also speculative. From 1996 through 1999, GDP grew about 4% per year, much higher than trend. Economists kept predicting it to trend back to 3%. It might not have been obvious at the time, but looking back at the 1990s the economic circumstances were fortunate—including the peace dividend, the run-up in asset prices, low oil prices, ideal population trends, gradually lowering inflation and interest rates, etc. Despite those factors, we had little ability to see how fortunate we were.

Another blow to the canon of cycles happened in and around 2001 when the economy got hit with about every adverse shock imaginable—and successfully shrugged them all off. We faced adverse weather, increases in energy prices, a stock market crash, and, of course, the singular geopolitical calamity: September 11th. Following the minor 2001 recession, many economists predicted a quick return to recession (a so-called double-dip), but that did not materialize. We reversed our thinking and toasted the vibrant private sector that innovated and allocated efficiently, complemented by an astute public sector that could keep the economy on a steady path with mere tweakings of the fed funds target rate.

Then, the financial and economic crisis of 2008 hit. It caught us by surprise. Six months after the recession started most analysts still thought the economy was recession-free; Even after we had locked in a belief of a great moderation of business cycles, an imperviousness to decline and an intellectual framework (M&M) to back it, the economy tanked. History shows that the movements of the economy trick us every time, yet we feign understanding it again and again. In less than one century, the world went from ignoring the macroeconomy (up to about 1930) to conviction about government management of economies and widespread intellectual support of socialism (1930s up to about 1975) and then all the way back (at least in principle) to a relatively laissez-faire attitude (1980 to about 2007). We have now returned to flawed free markets and the need for continuous government intervention (2008 and following).

## II.9.B. The Big Three Macroeconomic Indicators

---

[103] We will discuss the wealth effect in detail later. It can be seen in $Y = C + I + G$, where C is a function of disposable income and wealth as follows: $C = \alpha + \beta Y_d + \gamma W$. The large decrease in wealth due to the 1987 stock market crash should have yielded a substantial large drop in consumption which would have led to some noticeable effect on GDP.

[104] Paul Krugman, *Peddling Prosperity*, W.W. Norton & Co. 1994. P. 46. Summers, various interviews.

Our national economic goals are: (1) GDP growth, (2) maximum employment and (3) steady price level or inflation. The first two we want high or at a "maximum." Historically we wanted inflation low, although recently we have worried about deflation and have vigorously attempted to raise inflation. It is interesting to ponder why those are our goals. Also, our national goals are not agricultural or industrial output, life expectancy, stock market level, health metrics, consumption, education, hedonistic pleasures, copulations, leisure, freedom, happiness, etc. Why is that? For example, leisure is one of the most sought after goals in modern life, yet we do not measure that—nor do we try to maximize or increase it as national policy. Ironically, we strive to maintain the highest level of leisure's opposite: employment. In general, GDP, employment and controlled inflation reflect prosperity and efficiency and give us the greatest set of goods and services with which we can pursue all those other items. They were also the more sensible and measurable goals that economists and policy makers chose when we expanded economic analysis and managing programs in the 1930s.

Over the 20th century in academia and policy circles, concepts, models and data conventions were formed to accommodate these three goals such that GDP, inflation and unemployment have been the major economic quantities during the 20th century and continue to be so today. One key aspect is that since GDP and employment are closely correlated quantities (i.e., you have as much employment as GDP), our operational national policy goal is termed the "dual mandate" including inflation and unemployment/employment/GDP.

What does the future hold for national economic goals? My speculation is that over the next few decades we will go one of two ways: Either we will have reasonably attained our economic goals or at least mellowed about wealth and income, and the obsession and incessant discussion of national economic goals will diminish. GDP, unemployment and inflation; and related economic mantras like stability will be forgotten. We will not perceive our lives as dependent on the macroeconomic fortunes of our nation. The other scenario is increasingly greater scrutiny of our economic lots in life and more infighting over our economic pie and rightful shares thereof. Unfortunately, all kinds of perverse outcomes will manifest themselves in this latter scenario. For example, we will count and re-count our economic output and tout the great successes and strivings the way saps in the Soviet Union and China did in the 1950s. I suppose a third variant could be modification of our goal to some kind of "gross national happiness," like the nation of Bhutan has proposed and certain other nations (like the U.K.) are pondering in intellectual circles. Perhaps in the near future when western nations no longer excel in GDP growth, we might start looking for something like gross national happiness.

## II.9.B.a. Gross Domestic Product

GDP is a well-known acronym. GDP is the dollar value of all the final goods and services (all the "stuff") made in our society over a certain period of time. Working backward in GDP's definition: The period of time is usually one year. Society is generally defined as a country, although we calculate GDP's for any unit including states or metropolitan areas. Stuff includes anything commonly bought and sold in recorded transactions, such as automobiles, clothing, food, dental services, travel services, brokerage services, etc. GDP adds up the value of the final good or service and not the values of the stages of production. In the jargon of economists, GDP is also called output, production, product, income, national income and national product. It is typically designated "Y."

GDP and GDP growth are omnipresent in public discussion. Dozens, if not hundreds, of organizations (both public and private) attempt to forecast GDP growth, which is an important rubric of international comparison. The OECD (Organization for Economic Cooperation and Development) issues standardized forecasts of GDP growth for nations of the world. The absolute level of GDP is not as revealing as GDP's rate of change, or GDP growth. In fact, while many educated people have a sense of GDP growth, far fewer know the level of total GDP. To highlight that condition, in 2000, U.S. GDP surpassed $10 trillion and this milestone received virtually no press. U.S. GDP growth has averaged about 3% per year over the last few decades but closer to 2% over the last two. For a while, during the late 1970s and into the 1980s, the question was whether or not the U.S. had fallen below 3%: its long-run average GDP growth for the last few decades. Later, strangely, the U.S. would grow at about 4% per year from 1996 through 1999 and people upped their guess for growth. Anything short of 3.5% appeared unsatisfactory. For example, during 2002 the economy grew at about 2% and as that year ended some contended we were still in the 2001 recession. Now, since our growth has been about 2% for the last decade, we have begun to question our long-run growth rate, but 3% sticks in the heads of most Americans, most notably the generation currently in charge.

GDP measurement has a number of shortcomings. From time to time, the media will highlight these flaws as if they are fundamental or suddenly timely. They also get coverage in certain textbooks and courses, notably those taught by liberal economics faculty and in related fields like sociology and political science. For example, GDP measures only market activities. Therefore, supposedly valuable services like childrearing performed at home by parents are not in GDP. Another flaw concerns environmental damage: If we are producing more goods but doing so at the cost of pollution, maybe we are not better off. Of course, while such GDP criticisms are valid in the context of certain social issues, they are usually irrelevant to most business and policy issues because what we want is a measure that is consistent over time and across societies. GDP meets those criteria and is, therefore, useful for comparison and judging performance of our national economies. I have listed below sundry and revealing aspects of GDP that are not frequently emphasized by the press and in textbooks.

## GDP & GDP Growth: Selected Salient Aspects

One common mistake with GDP growth is that people neglect to distinguish between GDP growth and GDP growth per capita. Recently, the U.S. has had high GDP growth, but its population grows too—yielding less growth per person. Japan has less growth but the population is not growing. Over the recent past, the U.S. had about 3% growth and about 1.2% population growth. For Japan, GDP growth might have been 1% but its population growth is zero. Suddenly, Japan is not quite the economic underperformer that the Western press often alleges it to be when it comes to GDP growth. The advantages of larger total GDP are primarily political, including a proportionally bigger military. Unless you need that clout, you do not need big GDP. A country like Portugal, for example, should worry primarily about its per capita GDP growth.

Another fundament of GDP data is calculating and comparing GDP with and without purchasing power parity ("PPP") which is a fancy term for adjusting for cost of living. Poorer societies with typically lower incomes also have lower costs. For example, a person making $25,000 per year and living in Washington DC would have a hard time paying his expenses but a person making $25,000 and living in Mexico City would be able to live more opulently. Adjusted for PPP, China's GDP is about the same as that of the U.S. today. Without adjusting, our GDP is roughly twice as big. In other words, if you read one article that maintained that China's economy surpassed ours in GDP and then also read one that maintained that our GDP will be much bigger than China's for another fifteen years the explanation is PPP.[105]

Perhaps the most fundamental question about GDP concerns the persistence of its growth. Is the historical annual trend growth of 3% pretty certain? In these words, must economies like ours recover from recessions to positive GDP growth, eventually getting near 3%? In M&M texts we cling to the 3% because

---

[105] "These Will Be the World's 20 Largest Economies in 2030," by Jeanna Smialek, *BloombergBusiness*, April 10, 2015. http://www.bloomberg.com/news/articles/2015-04-10/the-world-s-20-largest-economies-in-2030

it prevailed over the 20th century, although a lower number around 2% is starting to permeate many discussions. There is nothing sure about constant growth at or near 3%. As we pointed out, about 1% of the 3% is simply population growth. We assume our population will continue to grow since, with the exception of the Depression, it always has. Population growth could change quickly, however. Another weak link in maintaining 3% GDP growth is that some of our recent economic growth was borrowed from the future. We now face an extended period of deleveraging which will detract from our growth. The exact magnitude is hard to pin down, but it is not impossible that a major fraction of our recent annual growth came from borrowing from the future. Most of the rest of our economic growth is productivity-based. How much productivity we will have going forward is hard to say. Although we have invention every year and never lose knowledge, our society is increasingly prone to create "counter-productivity" growth: creating costs, constraints and regulations to every process. My guess for U.S. GDP growth in the 21st century is 2% per year (or less)—about 1% population growth plus maybe 1% productivity growth. The problem with significantly lower growth is that a country with hefty debt and constant deficits must have real GDP growth higher than the real rate of interest it pays on debt (and on the rollover of its debt), or debt will explode. Over the 1990s and into the 2000s, real rates for debt service have been low, but they could quickly become much higher, potentially even higher than our GDP growth.

We have a theoretical concept related to GDP called the "Output Gap," which is the amount GDP is below what its trend growth level indicates. We can estimate the output gap. In 2009, economists of the Obama Administration estimated the size of the output gap at about $2 trillion and then designed fiscal policy of $787 billion (originally) of spending to "AD" our way back to full GDP. The stimulus amount was much less than the gap because the administration assumed a multiplier effect of about 1.5 for the spending and also made political concessions on how much spending it could get past Congress.[106] Like trend growth, the concept of the output gap and its empirical estimation is based on guesses and extrapolations. The output gap is linked to inflation. Many contended that since the Great Recession was severe, the output gap must have been large. Therefore, the threat of inflation must have been minimal. At the time, naysayers pointed out that at first inflation is suppressed because sellers must lower prices to compete, but then if making a buck remains hard to do supply is withdrawn—and prices rise on what is left. The result is that we get inflation while having low growth.

GDP growth depends on the basic factors of production including land, labor, capital and entrepreneurship; but these ultimately depend on a myriad of items. Literally any facet of our society impacts GDP. Of course, we must be careful about how we talk about determinants of GDP growth. For example, standardized tests are widely denounced in our society, yet the ability to sort and match smart people with challenges is crucial to economic progress. Certain tests (like the much maligned SAT) do an excellent job of culling, yet we resist testing: "NYU Exiting National Merit Scholarship,"[107] is a typical piece in the press, which relates, without much rejoinder, how schools are dropping standardized tests that they deem elitist, discriminatory and ultimately useless for selecting students.

It is difficult to see which social and economic forces factor into GDP. America, for example, has always had relatively high crime, yet that seemed not to thwart GDP growth. The same is true for rampant litigation and poor education. Although ostensibly detrimental to our society, we could not see them in the

---

[106] There are many estimates of multipliers used by different branches of government for policy. They change over time, vary by type of policy, are usually given in ranges and are spoken of more or less precisely or loosely depending on circumstances and context. For example, the Congressional Budget Office, in analysis of the American Recovery and Reinvestment Act of 2009, came up with multipliers ranging from 0 to as high as 2.5 for different types of policy including straight federal spending, transfer payments to individuals, transfer payments to state and local government, tax cuts to low-income households, tax cuts to high-income households, corporate tax cuts, etc.

[107] *Bloomberg.com*, October 20, 2011.

GDP. In 1983 a major U.S. government report on poor education entitled *A Nation at Risk* received copious public discussion. We highlighted the link between education and GDP. Decades later, though, we would dismiss continuing findings on weak American education, believing that our economy worked around it. Energy prices represent another GDP paradox. At one time, we worried that relatively small changes in the price of oil would derail our economy; then we hypothesized a great growing economy impervious to anything like rising oil prices. The same is true of technology changes which are inscrutable in GDP data. Borrowing and debt are hard to pick out of GDP trends. During our great period of economic growth of 3%+ per year, we also increased debt about 7% per year. Also, financial services in the 1990s and early 2000s accounted for an inordinate fraction of our GDP growth. What was the true value-added of financial services to our economic output?

GDP grows in small ways, yet we do not appreciate that. In public discussion we prefer to talk in terms of major economic growth impetuses. Vice President Dick Cheney was once derided when he suggested that online retailer eBay added to GDP growth. Surely, critics pointed out, America's growth is more glorious than secondhand goods being peddled by shut-ins. Cheney had insight, though. GDP growth is a game of inches, yet we look for blow-out GDP growth, like from large wealth effects from a rejuvenated housing sector. Then, we often employ similar wishful thinking that anti-growth actions that we institute (like regulation or higher taxes) will not negatively impact our GDP. GDP fluctuations trick us repeatedly. From 1996 to 1999, experts were predicting poor GDP growth and even recession each and every year. Standard theories of business cycles implied contraction was due; however, we neared 4% growth each of those years. Then, as many of the experts reversed their predictions and called for high growth in 2000 and beyond, we got a recession. After the short recession in 2001, many experts were expecting a double-dip recession (another recession soon after), but that contraction did not happen. Then, once again we got fooled in the years from about 2006 to 2008 when most people thought the economy was strong, or at least resilient. Even well into 2008 we could not see a grave recession that was happening. Following the big recession of 2008 many predicted a prompt recovery with high GDP growth. Their evidence was simply that big recoveries had followed earlier big recessions. That recovery did not happen. GDP is erratic and subject to special forces.

The GDP we report is more of a consumption measurement than a production measurement. We spend more by borrowing and obtain higher GDP. We can reduce saving and still be solvent by spending from increases in asset values, like those of stocks and housing. The asset value increases themselves largely derive from monetary policy. Our GDP, therefore, is really spending now and less product later. In contrast, a society that has higher savings might have lower GDP now but higher GDP later. The investment component of GDP, I, is driven largely by spending on housing and not by business investment.

## II.9.B.b. Unemployment & Labor Market

Labor is the pivotal quantity of economic policy. Activist economists like Fed Chair Janet Yellen focus on labor, of course, but even hardliners will concede that the health of the economy is ultimately about the character of the work and the level of the compensation that people can attain. There is a multitude of key ideas concerning unemployment and labor markets today.

### *General Concepts of Labor Economics*

Even a non-economist can envision how the raw unemployment rate might be misleading. The quality of work matters. Also, whether jobs are full-time and permanent positions that pay enough to support a family matters. Also, jobs may or may not be commensurate with people's training and education. The focal debate about the U.S. labor market since 2008 has been the drop in labor force participation. Historical and international comparisons of unemployment are hard to judge. Just to give an example of how the unemployment rate is misleading, many experts contend that the U.S. economy has performed significantly better than Eurozone's in the years following 2008. They cite that, although unemployment in both U.S. and Eurozone initially went up, ours went down while theirs continued to go up. This is a very common case made in the financial press, stated with relative conviction. Labor force participation in Eurozone did not go down, however. Factor that in and the fluxes in our relative unemployment rates look much closer.

For starters, economists often concede that the labor market is not a market like others. You cannot offer your labor for a lower wage and get the job. For example, a college instructor cannot approach a university contending that she can teach and do research as well as a currently-employed faculty, offer to work for $10,000 less in salary and take the job away. When unemployment rose significantly in 2008, we pondered if unemployment is cyclical or structural. If the former, we stimulate; if the latter, we invest in education and infrastructure. Yet what if our current unemployment is neither? Take an auto worker who was making $35 per hour and has lost his job. He could get a job at $10 an hour at Walmart but he will not work at that rate. He cannot easily be retrained in a field in which there is labor demand (for example, computer engineering) so his unemployment is neither cyclical nor structural. Of course, you can characterize anything as structural but this worker is really unemployable and/or voluntarily out of the labor force. We have a micro concept called the "reservation wage," which is the lowest amount it takes to get a person to offer his labor to the market. For this person, it might be $25 per hour, given he can semi-retire and be supported by his wife.

Since the late 1960s, the U.S. has experienced three periods of high unemployment: (1) in the 1970s, especially around the recession of 1973 to 1974; (2) in the early 1980s around the recession of 1982 and (3) recently, following the recession of 2008. During these three episodes, the nation expressed great concern about unemployment, although I think concern was much more urgent in the 1970s and 1980s. The high unemployment of 2008 followed a period of relatively moderate unemployment from the late 1980s up through the early 2000s. The economy had generally grown well and we concluded that our economy employed all of us who wanted a job. We no longer worried acutely about helping the labor market. There were minor recessionary periods, like 1990-91, but they were perceived as requisite to the functioning of capitalism. If anything, we tended to worry that overly tight labor markets would result in inflation. Another irony about trends in unemployment rates in modern times is that around the 1970s, Western Europe had much lower unemployment than the U.S. It made sense: European countries had stronger policies to keep their citizens working. Fortunes shifted, however. The unemployment rate went up a lot in Europe while going down in the U.S. The countries of Europe seemed not to care. They now accepted high unemployment while we relished our open and efficient economy and boasted our superior ability to put people in gainful employment.

### Two Key Labor Indicators: Unemployment Rate & Jobs

The unemployment rate is probably the most prominent labor market indicator. The conventional measure, called U-3, is the usual historical series economists have used although it has come under criticism recently. The unemployment rate is calculated from information gathered in a survey called the Current Population Survey. About 60,000 households are surveyed each month to determine who is in the labor force (children, retired and full-time students, for example, are not) then if the persons are either working or not working. If not, people are asked if they are actively looking for work; specifically, if they have looked within the last four weeks. A key flaw is that this unemployment can go down if people drop out of the labor force. Also, the raw unemployment rate does not take into consideration full v. part-time work or the character of work. For example, you can be working at a job below your station, but still be considered employed. Such facets of employment measurement are not important if they are not trending one way persistently, but since about 2008 (and maybe a little earlier) they are.

Given U-3 shortcomings, economists look to broader unemployment series including U-5 (which includes discouraged and marginally-attached workers) and U-6 (which adds involuntary part-time workers too). U-6 is the more comprehensive and more frequently mentioned series. It is referred to as the "broad" unemployment rate or "underemployment." The U-6 rate is higher than U-3. Also, the ratio of U-6 to U-3 has been high recently, generally as high as it has been since the U-6 series commenced in 1994.

Perhaps the other most intensely watched labor market indicator is the number of jobs created each month. The Bureau of Labor Statistics provides two major countings, each based on a different survey and each showing a different facet of the labor market. "Payrolls" (or the "Payroll Report") comes from a survey called the "Establishment Survey" of establishments (about 144,000 businesses and government agencies) and tallies jobs created as reported by businesses. The "Household Survey" of about 60,000 households is part of the Current Population Survey and reveals the number of jobs created according to surveys of people. There are many differences between the two surveys. One is that the household survey includes the self-employed. There is also a separate jobs tally done with data from the payroll company ADP. This report comes out before the government reports but is considered less reliable. Each number is reported monthly. The net number of jobs created (or lost) is the focal point, and a rough number of 200,000 net new jobs per month is needed to sop up new entrants to the labor force. Jobs created over 200,000 should contribute to decreasing the unemployed. In the 1980s and 1990s, the necessary net number was higher, nearly 300,000. We have downgraded our expectations partly due to demographics but also perhaps as another concession to a poorer economy.

One fundamental aspect of job counts and unemployment calculations that is becoming more prominent in today's economy is that a "job," as we thought of it, has changed. In earlier decades, perhaps from 1950s into the 1980s, jobs were full time, year round and largely unchanging in terms of workload and compensation. Jobs in manufacturing were common. Today, jobs and the labor force are much more variable, in many ways. Many jobs are part-time, gigs or contract work. Many people drop in and out of the labor force due to disability, adult enrollment in education, varied homemaking and family structure factors, public assistance, early retirement, etc. Employment in services rather than manufacturing is more common. Our M&M concepts of full employment and trend GDP depend on counting jobs and that task may be meaningless today. This change in the labor market is not necessarily adverse–perhaps flexible work is advantageous in today's world–but the concept of a job has changed.

## *Other Labor Market Indicators*

As you can see, the unemployment rate and the raw number of new jobs can be misleading. We have a plethora of other labor market data, and economists focus on the following:
- **Labor Force Participation Rate (LFPR)**: LFPR has dropped significantly in the U.S. in the years following 2008. Analysts who contend that the economy is weak despite extensive policy and an ostensible lowering of the unemployment rate cite LFPR as their primary proof. Others counter that the aging of the population is naturally lowering LFPR. Voluntary retirement only accounts for a small amount of the drop in LFPR. People at all ages, including notably age 20 to 24, have lower LFPR.
- **Employment to Population Ratio or Employment Rate**: This is the flip side of the unemployment rate but also can be superior to the unemployment rate since it somewhat avoids the problem of people out of the labor force. The employment rate is down lately, from about 63% to about 59%. Part of the

decrease is demographic. To control for that, look at the employment rate for workers between ages 25 and 54, aka "prime-age" workers. The employment rate for that group is down significantly since before 2008 from about 80% to about 77% in 2016.

- **Unemployment Duration**: This rose dramatically during and after the 2008 recession and still remains elevated in 2016 v. the period before 2008. Analysts contend that duration depends largely on the length of unemployment benefits, which were variously much longer (up to 99 weeks) during the post- 2008 period.
- **Median Weeks Unemployed**: This is similar to duration but being a median it is not as subject to extreme observations.
- **Long-Term Unemployed Share**: This represents the percentage or workers who have been unemployed for 27 weeks or more. It has been elevated compared to pre-2008 and varies inversely with availability of unemployment benefits.
- **Length of Work Week or Weekly Hours**: The shorter the week, the worse off workers are. Work weeks have been getting shorter.
- **Layoffs/Discharges or Layoffs Rate**: The number or rate of laying off of workers obviously reflects the demand for labor. This rose in the recession and has now trended down.
- **Job Openings or Job Openings Rate**: The rate is new jobs divided by the sum of job openings and paid employment. Like layoffs, job openings reflect demand for labor acutely. Openings and its rate decreased significantly during the recession—bottoming out at a very low level around 2009—but have come back circa 2015 to close to previous highs.
- **Hires or Hires Rate**: The difference between hires and openings is that not all job openings result in a hire. Companies often report job openings but do not hire. Hires went down in the recession and have recovered to close to their pre-recession levels.
- **Quits or Quits Rate**: This is workers who quit their jobs divided by paid employees. Quits went down in recession and generally have come back but not all the way. People quitting jobs reflects a strong job market.
- **Temporary Employment**: Temporary work has increased, and this trend appears adverse although some analysts contend it might reflect a strong but changing and flexible labor market. People may actually prefer temporary work. Most economists, though, view temp work as indicative of employers not willing to make commitment to labor and workers being unable to get permanent jobs.
- **Involuntary Part-Time**: This is people who claim to want full-time work but are working part-time for "economic reasons." It is taken as a percentage of total employed and is higher than before 2008.
- **Labor Market Conditions Indexes**: Since there are so many components of labor market conditions an index may reflect the overall situation. There are various indexes, and their usefulness hinges on the weightings of the component parts.
- **Wage Growth**: Nominal wage growth has been about 2% per year lately. Adjusted for inflation, it has been about zero.
- **Hourly Wages**: These also have been flat in real terms for many years. This is a better reflection on workers' compensation than incomes since incomes can go up if people work more hours.
- **Employment Cost Index ("ECI")**: This measures change of employee compensation, including both wages and benefits. This index is seen as a precursor to inflation.
- **Types of Jobs Lost and Gained by Wage**: Generally in the post-2008 period we lost many high wage jobs (over $20 per hour) and gained many low wage jobs (about $9-13 per hour).
- **Companies' Hiring**: We calculate how long it takes a company to fill a vacancy and how intense the recruiting is for each hiring.

- **People Tangentially Attached to Labor Market**: They are perpetual job seekers and are always looking in the help wanted. They are not typically heads of households but are usually without children or divorced with the other spouse taking care of the children.

## NAIRU

NAIRU is the non-accelerating inflation rate of unemployment. It is a very important theoretical labor market concept. NAIRU can be estimated and economists create series of its level, but it is not like other labor market indicators for which data are collected. NAIRU is the unemployment rate the economy would be if we were fully employed and the labor market analog to full employment GDP. NAIRU represents the level of unemployment in the economy at inflationary wage pressure is minimal. Ultimately, it is a guess about the robustness of our GDP and the level of inflationary pressure from labor markets. We attempt to know the level of NAIRU at any time and set policy by its divergence from the actual level of unemployment. Although we approximate a rough NAIRU level, we have been way off many times in the recent past because of the way unemployment changes. Perhaps a better guess of NAIRU may just be the current unemployment rate. For example, at the start of the 1990s unemployment was relatively high—around 7%. As it declined, many economists (like Paul Krugman and Lawrence Summers as we mentioned above) contended that we were below NAIRU and either unemployment could not go lower or we get high inflation. This did not transpire over the 1990s. Instead, the unemployment rate got to about 4%.Then, after unemployment fell to around 4% and stayed near there, we all got on the bandwagon that NAIRU must be around 5%.

Then in the Great Recession, unemployment rose substantially to 10%. Many at that time, contending that NAIRU does not change abruptly, deemed the unemployment of 10% way above NAIRU and thus the economy was operating well under its potential. For example, during the heat of the crisis, *Barron's* chief economics writer Gene Epstein, argued, "…7.5% is so far above the Nairu—which economists once put at 6%, but now put lower."[108] Indeed unemployment would go down over the next few years, again approaching economists' estimate of NAIRU at about 5%. The change in labor force participation though makes the statement debatable. Economists have never measured NAIRU well, and they assume it cannot change abruptly, but this is just a guess.

## II.9.B.c. Inflation & Price Level

Inflation is a semi-inscrutable quantity fraught with insights and misunderstandings about our economic welfare. Almost the entire macroeconomic history of our lifetimes (going from about 1960 to the present) was dominated by two inflation forces: inflation going up and inflation going down. The period of increasing inflation ran from the late 1960s to the early 1980s and decreasing inflation from the early 1980s through the 1990s and into the 2000s. Such fluctuation gave us macroeconomic oddities like stagflation, negative real interest rates, a thirty-year bond bull market and negative nominal interest rates. None of those macroeconomic phenomena should have existed. Therefore, given the two episodes of long-run stretches of meandering inflation—and considering that (1) our economic contracts and the way we model them in M&M depend on "interest rates," (2) real rates are the quantities that matter and (3) real rates depend on inflation or the expectation of inflation, you can see how hard it is to know what transpired in M&M over the last half century. For example, when we ponder if low "i" causes I and C to go up in any short run, we are just guessing. The i might have appeared low, but it could have been high in real terms.

---

[108] *Barron's*, Economic Beat, "Slack Jobs Will Blunt Inflation," May 24, 2010, p. 27.

Another compelling inflation thought experiment is to ponder the counter case. Suppose inflation had been a constant of about 1% for the fifty years, what would our economic life be like? Now, since about 2014 we could be facing a third dominating inflation trend: very low inflation, or even a decrease in overall price level, i.e., deflation.

Inflation is tough to model. In microeconomics (i.e., not macroeconomics–the two branches of economics are distinct), all prices are real. In other words, there is no inflation. In micro prices change, of course; but these are real price changes. They are changes in prices of one good relative to prices of other goods. In contrast, with macro we have the general increase in all prices, or inflation. You might counter that in macro modeling all we have to do is adjust quantities for inflation by using a price index like the Consumer Price Index. That is imprecise at least. For example, if we determine our real GDP to be growing at 2% per year (but think that we are overstating or understating inflation by 1%), we will either be growing by only 1%, which is very poor, or by 3%, which is very good. In theory, in a world of inflation, intelligent agents should be able to see through nominal price changes. If general prices are up 3%, workers should raise their wage demands by 3% and a lender should build in 3% more over the real rate he wants to earn and nobody is worse off. In reality, though, it is not that simple. When inflation is high and variable agents cannot foresee it, they cannot set prices and allocate resources efficiently.

Economists describe the costs of inflation in a number of ways. Inflation distorts price signals. Agents cannot discern if relative prices are changing and therefore they should consume less of a more expensive good; or if general prices are changing, in which case they should not alter their consumption baskets. We also talk about shoe-leather (having to waste time and effort seeking best prices given inflation) and menu costs (having to change pricing schedules excessively). When inflation is high and/or changing, you have to spend more time and effort ascertaining the best transaction, reset contracts more frequently and redo nominal pricing more diligently. Finally, we say that high inflation begets the expectation of higher inflation and that causes inflation to become built in and to spiral.

Inflation is slippery and idiosyncratic and has fooled us all. Milton Friedman made his finalist statement, "Inflation is always and everywhere a monetary phenomenon" and it became M&M dogma. However, that would not hold in the years following 2008 when the Fed increased reserves, which are the raw material for money supplies, and inflation remained very low. At that time many right-wing commentators predicted high inflation, but it never materialized. The lack of inflation though might have been the result of a moribund economy and absence of wage pressure rather than successful policy. Regardless, if Milton Friedman, who died in 2006, came back from the dead today and examined current monetary statistics (like M1, M2, currency, the Monetary Base, etc.[109]), he would be incredulous that inflation was so low.

### Definition & Derivation

There are two main ways to calculate inflation: The better known and more common inflation comes from the Consumer Price Index ("CPI"), which is a price level of a basket of goods and services that people commonly buy. Here is a simplified example of the CPI and calculating inflation: purchase a basket of goods and services, including representative food, clothing, transportation, housing, education, etc. Assume that initial basket costs $100. Then, buy that identical basket again in the next time period, say a year. Assume it now costs $102. Then buy the basket another year later and assume it cost $105. The CPI would be 100, 102, 105 and inflation (for 1st and 2nd time periods in our example) would be: (102-100)/100 = 2/100 = 2% and

---

[109] M1 is a category of money which includes coin, cash and checking account balances. M2 is M1 plus savings deposits and retail money market accounts. We will describe these money quantities and their roles in monetary economy in many topics below.

(105-102)/102 = 3/102 = 2.94%. In practice, of course, the CPI project as conducted by the U.S. Bureau of Labor Statistics is a massive undertaking spanning the nation (as a whole and by regions) and the breadth of goods and services we use. Thousands of goods are bought and priced over various geographic areas and demographic groups, and a wide variety of indices are calculated.

The other method of calculating inflation is called the GDP Deflator or Personal Consumption Expenditure ("PCE") inflation. This inflation calculation simulates the buying of the entire GDP period over period. The term for the PCE is the Implicit Price Deflator for Personal Consumption. PCE inflation typically gives a lower rate of inflation compared to that of CPI mainly because PCE lacks CPI's problems to account for substitution by consumers. CPI-based inflation is more popular in general and also used in many contracts like many labor cost of living adjustments, setting Social Security changes and certain tax levels. Economists prefer PCE as a better reflection of real price change in the economy and, therefore, use it in research and policy.

Then, for both the CPI and PCE inflation we have two main varieties: (1) the full indexes of all goods and services ("Headline" or "All Items" inflation) and (2) the indexes excluding Food and Energy ("Core" inflation). Food and Energy prices are considered volatile and more seasonal, so excluding these might give a less jumpy read of the trend of price changes in the economy. Some economists, like Ben Bernanke, prefer the Core while others prefer Headline. The latter group considers volatility as part of the real world. The difference between core and non-core inflation can sometimes be large enough to be a source of debate. Often Core inflation will be lower and inflation hawks will accuse policymakers, who typically use Core, of ignoring higher inflation. It can work the other way, too. For example, during 2015 Headline inflation was about 0.7% due to the big drop in oil prices, while Core inflation was about 2.1%. Core can be calculated for both CPI and PCE inflation. Of the four varieties, the Fed prefers Core PCE.

There are other inflation series such as those involving prices paid by producers called the Producer Price Index. Economists try to improve on inflation measures with various data or statistical refinements. Specialized inflation measures include Median CPI, Trimmed Mean-PCE and Sticky CPI. Median CPI, associated with the Federal Reserve Bank of Cleveland, uses the middle price change (the median) of the component price changes in the basket rather than a weighted average of all the component price changes. Trimmed Mean PCE (associated with the Dallas Fed) involves sorting the sub-components of the inflation calculation and removing the highest and the lowest of those components. Advocates contend that throwing out the high and low scores leaves a better average. Sticky CPI (associated with the Atlanta Fed) sorts price changes by have quickly they tend to change.

### General Pitfalls in Real v. Nominal

By adjusting for inflation we obtain "real" quantities, i.e., after inflation is accounted for, as opposed to "nominal." Both ideas seem straightforward, but we have to belabor certain fundamental concepts of real and nominal. Real v. nominal manifests itself in two main areas: (1) prices, including wages, and 2) interest rates. Simple examples illustrate the points. Suppose you are earning $10 per hour. Then, over the year prices rise about 5% and you also get a 5% pay increase. In real terms (i.e., in terms of buying goods and services), you are no better or worse off. Concerning interest rates, suppose you have $100 in the bank at 3% interest and prices rise about 3% over a year. You will be no wealthier at the end of the year. Your real rate of return is 0%.

For most of U.S. history, inflation was low and it was easy for workers and lenders to gage how much to adjust for inflation in their contracts. The unexpectedly high inflation of the 1970s brought the importance of real and nominal (and the adjusting for inflation) into mainstream decision making. For example, before the 1970s, lenders made long-term loans such as mortgages at fixed interest rates. For example, 30-year mortgages in the 1960s were between 6% and 8%. By the middle of the 1970s, inflation was higher than many prevailing fixed lending rates, and lenders were earning negative real rates of return. This was the main factor behind the massive failures of saving and loan institutions during the 1980s. In principle, lenders would never have taken a chance on negative real rates of return for money they loaned out. Given the high, unexpected inflation of the 1970s, we had negative reals in the late 1970s and early 1980s. Mortgage rates subsequently shot up to compensate lenders for inflation. Over the 1980s and 1990s inflation went down and inflation expectations eventually went down with it. Lenders again started offering low rates. Then, as the result of extraordinary monetary policy of low rates, many lending rates have gone below inflation and once again lenders are receiving negative real rates in the U.S. Such fluctuations of inflation and the creation of negative returns reflect the maddening facet of real v. nominal. We are never sure of a real return when inflation is changing and can only make assumptions that we can get a positive real rate of return.

One key aspect of real v. nominal is that, very often, when reading an article describing a current release of an economic quantity (like wages or consumption), you simply cannot tell if it is real or nominal. The journalist does not make it clear. For example, wages are reported to be up 2% for a year. Is that 2% real, or is it 2% minus about 2% for inflation or 0% real? Usually, it is the latter. Another key aspect of real v. nominal it that it is very hard to deflate and compare over long periods of time. For example, around 1970, a candy bar would have cost 5 or 10 cents, landscaping for a new house was a few hundred bucks, a visit to the hospital might cost twenty dollars, a cheap new car was about $2,000, etc. Compare to today ($1.25; $5,000; hundreds or thousands; about $25,000, respectively), and there is no easy comparison. It might appear that the items have all increased in price more than inflation but often quality improvements are dominant facets. You can make polar cases. Here is a negative case: A car performed its basic task of getting people from point A to point B about as well in 1970 as today. Since the car costs so many multiples more today, Americans are poorer than their grandparents. On the other side we can make a positive case: A car today is so vastly superior in many ways that it represents a completely different good. For example, in a car accident today you are less likely to cut your face to shreds on the windshield due to a multitude of improvements in safety features. Therefore, Americans are better off than their grandparents. Economists attempt to quantify these quality changes in their price indexes including the CPI and PCE. This process is known as hedonics and it is an imperfect science.

### *History of Inflation*

From about 1970 through 1984 the U.S. experienced unusually high inflation, which was an aberration. Historically in the U.S., inflation occurred in occasional spurts, such as from 1915 to 1920 when prices about doubled. Over the long history, our prices have been pretty stable. The average price level in the U.S. was about the same in 1945 as it was in 1800. In other words, inflation averaged about 0%! Even in the 1950s and early 1960s, inflation was moderate and stable at about 2% per year. During the following 15 years inflation was much higher occasionally over 10% per year, e.g., 13.5% in 1980. Since about 1984, inflation has tended lower and returned to low levels. Given these two distinct inflation regimes since about 1950, average numbers for inflation (which would be in the 3 to 5% range, depending on your beginning and staring date) are almost meaningless. Either a nation controls its monetary policy, in which case it gets inflation between ranging from a slight negative like -1% to maybe as much as 2% or it does not—in which case inflation could be anything, even hundreds or thousands of percent. You would be hard-pressed to find an example of a nation that had inflation levels tightly around 5% for any period.

Inflation was wrested under control in the early 1980s with the concerted contractionary monetary policy engineered by Fed Chairman Paul Volcker accompanied by the Reagan Administration's political support. Many great economists and other pundits scoffed at the attempt to cut inflation abruptly, contending it was "built-in" and could not come down from double digit levels for decades. However, inflation went from about 9% in 1981 to about 4% in 1982. In the post-2008 period of very expansionary money policy, many economists, including Ben Bernanke, and many in the press cited the Volcker episode as demonstrating how easily we can control inflation. The abrupt decrease in inflation was not without grave cost, though. The 1982 recession was severe. Unemployment surged. At the time, liberals denounced the inflation fight as too costly. Although Paul Volcker goes down as a singular champion of our economy now, at the time many people referred derisively to the recession as the "Volcker Recession." Also, the slaying of inflation in the early 1980s occurred when many other factors in the economy were favorable for controlling inflation: Oil prices were coming down; commodity prices were moderate; labor trends like cheap immigrant labor were favorable; and a variety of substantial innovation, productivity and cost cutting opportunities were present.

Following the omnipresent, high inflations of the 1970s, inflation began a downward trend in most countries in the 1980s, including even the nations with hyperinflations. As of the early 2000s, only a handful of countries (like Zimbabwe and Venezuela) had annual inflation over 20%. Many countries had inflation less than 1% (like Switzerland, Taiwan, Japan, Germany, etc.), and the U.S. was in the 2% range. Such low inflation had been the main monetary policy goal and most nations seemed to be able to hit it. They believed fighting inflation was a task requiring constant vigilance. We wanted inflation no higher than 2% but hoped for even lower rates. 2% was considered an advantageous level by many economists because it was both controllable and a rate that would sufficiently grease the wheels of the economy. Some economists, however, believed 0.5% inflation was an optimal goal and some even aspired for slight deflation. Their case was that even slight pay raises would raise the standard of living when consumer prices were generally flat or even decreasing.

Then, in response to the 2008 economic crisis we engaged in expansionary monetary policies of zero rates and quantitative easing. Many economists predicted inflation well over the 2% level would come again. Inflation did not increase though over the years following 2008. We then re-evaluated our M&M thinking and professed that deflation was now the problem. We reversed the direction of price level change concern. Ironically, a thirty-year crusade to maintain inflation below 2% became a fight to get it up to 2%!

In the U.S., Japan and Eurozone from 2012 through 2016 inflation, by conventional measures, was very low. Some economists surmised deflation as the singular macroeconomic malady and one requiring extreme policy measures to avoid. If it ever returned, inflation could easily be controlled. Policy advocates boasted that inflation expectations were "anchored," and any spike in inflation could be readily controlled by policy. They cited the decrease in inflation in the early 1980s. Another favorite intellectual argument was the mocking of right-wing economists who prophesized that loose Fed policy of 2010 ff would cause hyperinflation.[110] Finally, the current moderate level of inflation demonstrated the resounding success of recent government economic policy: Neither basic goal of inflation nor unemployment was getting out of hand. Policy doubters maintained completely opposite ideas, however: Inflation could change quickly; inflation expectations could change quickly; the absence of inflation was simply because the economy was so weak in general and wage increases were particularly non-existent; and deflation was not a severe economic problem. Policy naysayers tout the resounding failure of recent government economic policy.

### *Causes of Inflation*

---

[110] The "Open Letter to Ben Bernanke," November 15, 2010, *The Wall Street Journal*, composed by a number of leading economists, pundits and money managers including John Taylor, Niall Ferguson, Michael Boskin, Seth Klarman, Paul Singer and James Grant.

Many sources describe inflation quite simply: "The cause of inflation is…"—or they may even offer a clear list of multiple causes of inflation. The reality is not that simple. Strange as it may seem for such a prominent indicator, we punt on what its root cause is, variously citing money, money growth, general cost pressure, expectations of future inflation, demand, cost increases in basic commodities, bottlenecks, cost of labor, government deficits, labor cost increases, etc. We distinguish general inflation from relative price increases of one good or another, but we sometimes ascribe certain relative price increases, notably oil's, as a prime cause of general price increases. In the short run, we assume that inflation depends upon demand conditions or aggregate demand but that says little unless the short run and its peculiar demand conditions are specified.

One theory of inflation is the printing of money—i.e., "more money chasing the same amount of goods." Indeed, we often get high inflation in societies that print excessive money. That is not always the case, though. In general, you need more money to get inflation, but more money itself might not cause inflation. Some other economic force like rising labor cost or demand for goods and services must also be present. One compelling example of this is the U.S. today. We have money growth (M1 or M2) at about 10% per year yet little inflation. You can readily explain it by noting that velocity of money has decreased. The velocity of money represents the volume of transactions over a certain time period per unit of money. Then, of course, we need an explanation for why velocity dropped off. A theory of inflation that is commonly taught and simple to remember is the famous Quantity Theory of Money. The equation is $MV=PQ$ where V is the velocity of money and is assumed to be constant or, at least, stable. Q is the output of the economy (the GDP), which is assumed to grow at a very slow pace. Then, for the equality to hold, if M (which represents money supply) increases, P (which represents price or inflation) must go up. (We will have more on the Quantity Theory below.)

Another common inflation theory is that it is caused by costs going up, so-called "cost-push" inflation. Usually commodity price increases, especially those of oil, are the impetus. During 2005, oil prices went up and, sure enough, such a significant price increase of a major component of our spending trickled through to prices of other items. Some economists dismissed this story, contending that the price of any one good may go up but that will not create a general inflation. It simply represents a relative price change and people will substitute away from the more expensive good to other goods. Wage increases can also be the root cause of inflation. Following 2008, inflation was low, even with increases in money supplies. The force holding inflation back may have been an excess of labor keeping labor costs flat.

Another attempt to isolate the singular root cause of inflation is government deficit spending. Inflation will ultimately be the result of money printing by a nation that is running chronic deficits. When a country can no longer tax or borrow in private markets to pay its expenditures, it must print money in some fashion and this causes inflation.

Another story to explain inflation is inflation expectations. If people think inflation will go up, it will. This story is somewhat circular logically. We can make some strong statements about what causes inflation once we assume a certain time frames. In general, in the long run inflation depends on money supply growth. That short-term demand conditions can sustain high inflation is dubious.

### Inflation Expectations

In the investing classic *The Intelligent Investor*,[111] financial markets pioneer Benjamin Graham devotes an up-front chapter to inflation. Commenting as of late 1971 and early 1972, and using all his wisdom and knowledge, he concludes that a current investor should "base his thinking and decisions on a *probable* (far

---

[111] 1973, Harper & Row, 4th Revised Edition.

from certain) rate of future inflation of, say, 3% per annum." (pp. 17 to 19.) Although he does say probable, Graham seems relatively confident that moderate rates of inflation must prevail given the long series of inflation history. History would show Graham to be quite wrong. Of course, given what was known at the time, he was about as right as you could be. Soon after his opinion, inflation would soar, hitting double digits by the end of the decade. Graham's advice would have led to bad investing. If you bought the available bonds at that time expecting inflation of 3%, you would have lost a substantial amount of money over the next decade.

Economic agents, including investors, lender, labor contract negotiators, etc. have a lot riding on their forecasts of inflation. Decisions depend on estimates of expected inflation and expected inflation is determined by people—smart or not—with limited ability to predict how history will play out. Expected inflation is a quantity in the heads of those making financial decisions, especially lenders and other involved with fixed income securities. Before about 1970, forecasting inflation was simple, since inflation had been low and stable for a long period. During the 1970s through 1990s the task became much more treacherous, though. The surge in inflation in the 1970s came by surprise. Lenders suffered significantly and became very circumspect about high inflation eroding their returns. The subsequent decline of inflation over the 1980s and 1990s took a long time for people to believe in. Perhaps by about the late 1990s, financial parties were again pretty sure that expected inflation would be low and stable. U.S. central bank head Alan Greenspan would point out that the greatest achievement of his tenure at the Fed was the anchoring of long-term interest rate levels given the anchoring of inflation expectations.

Like with many other economic facets, inflation expectations pursuant to the events of 2008 and following are hard to ascertain—despite the fact that extreme monetary policy inflation itself never rose greatly. Inflation expectations were also assumed to have remained stable and moderate. During his term as Fed Chairman, Ben Bernanke would contend that inflation expectations were "anchored" and that the U.S. Fed had such credibility as an inflation fighter with private parties and markets that inflation would not increase. If it did, the Fed could easily reassure markets before inflation would ever get high. Bernanke presented as prima facie evidence the attitudes of markets during the period of monetary expansion from around 2009 on. Supposedly market participants had low inflation expectations. Of course, the subdued inflation and apparent expectations of low inflation could just as easily be explained as a weak economy and appearance that the economy would not recover strongly. If it had, private parties could have abruptly reevaluated their inflation expectations. Many economists believe inflation expectations can change rapidly.

The pivotal quantity, inflation expectations, is measured in two ways: (1) market measures (observing market prices of securities with varying inflation protection) and (2) survey measures. Both are tenuous. The main market measures include the TIPS (inflation-protected U.S. treasuries) spreads (or breakeven inflation), the price of gold and observing the stance of monetary policy and money supplies. The survey measures include surveys of bank lending officials, CFO's or other business executives, consumers and economists. Comparing the yield on regular U.S. treasuries (typically 10-year notes) with the yield of TIPS is the most common. This measure has given a moderate expected inflation level of about 2% in recent years. For example, yields on 10-year's over 2010 to early 2012 were about 4%, trending down to about 2%. Yields on TIPS in 2010 and 2011 were about 1% and negative in 2012 (negative since buyers wanted the TIPS so badly they pushed the prices up above par and presumably relied on getting the extra face to compensate for inflation).

Market measures may be distorted when rates are very low. For example, in recent years private parties have held copious debt at negative yields including both real and even nominal. If holders are willing to hold non-inflation protected debt at negative returns, how much wisdom is in the relative pricing of inflation-protected debt by these same parties? Surveys of inflation expectations are scoffed at by many economists. Neither individuals nor businesses—including banks—profess much more than a guess about what inflation will be in the future and people often overstate future inflation. One prominent survey of expected inflation and also of other economic quantities is done by Duke/*CFO Magazine* on high level executives, mainly CFO's. These executives themselves admit they are merely guessing.

Even if inflation expectations measures work they are relatively short-term phenomena. Some sources though, including official reports of the Fed, will cite three- and five-year inflation expectations of consumers and businesses. History shows that inflation can change abruptly and shift expectations along with it just as abruptly. Many central bank leaders boast that inflation expectations are easy to manage and control, but inflation and inflation perceptions can change quickly and be difficult to reverse. At any point in time we extrapolate inflation from a rough feel about what it is like lately, just as Benjamin Graham did around 1970. We crave a concept and measurement of expected inflation, but it is largely guesswork.

### *Deflation*

Deflation is a decrease in the general price level. It was perhaps the most important focal point of M&M following 2008 with a heightened emphasis from about 2013 through 2015. Some analysts contend deflation is an absolute danger to our society, resulting in an economy that substantially under-employs its resources and a tendency toward a downward spiral of deflation that cannot be controlled. The existence of such a problem is stated authoritatively: Deflation can destroy us and its opposite, inflation (which we had seen as the main problem of M&M for decades) is now viewed as easily controllable. Others scoff, contending that deflation is an unreasonable bugaboo and even asserting that a general deflation is desirable. To them, deflation constitutes the general small increase in our standard of living as year after year goods; and services become a little cheaper due to improved methods of production, while incomes generally do not fall.

Deflation, or at least significant persistent deflation, has not been a problem in the U.S. with the exception of the years leading up to and in the early part of the Depression (from about 1927 to 1933). In contemporary times, Japan is the only country among major economies that has experienced deflation. In Japan, price levels went down a little less than one percent per year from 1999 to 2003. Occasionally since the late 1990s, certain economists have spoken about the dangers of deflation and the related problem of negative interest rate, and they cited Japan. Japan's economy had been performing poorly, at least as measured by total GDP growth (generally compared to a benchmark of 3% or more, like Japan had achieved in the decades before 1990). Businesses and consumers were not borrowing. Interest rates had dropped to nearly zero. As of 1999, the bank overnight lending rate in Japan (the Japanese fed funds rate) was about 0.1%. Prices were going down, and Japan was experiencing deflation. In such a situation, banks would have to keep lowering their interest rates until they hit zero. The term for this is "Liquidity Trap." Until recently, Japan was the sole example of the Liquidity Trap. Since about 2013, Eurozone, other European countries not in Eurozone and other advanced economies have come close or even hit zero levels of inflation and nominal interest rates.

Some economists openly deride deflation as an intractable M&M condition case. They joked that low and dropping prices for oil and computers should not be a problem. Deflation talk waned and waxed in public discussion. Alternatively, other people warned about inflation, and deflation discussion came back again in 2002 to 2003. At this time, deflation got significant discussion in the U.S. The Fed itself issued a large report on the topic. A leading authority on deflation was Ben Bernanke. When he was Chairman of the Fed, he was described as a deflation expert and pundits cited recent work of his. The economy picked up in the mid-2000s and deflation waned as a crisis. Worries about inflation reappeared and we raised the fed funds target rate to over 5%. Then, as a product of the Great Recession, deflation returned—this time perhaps more serious than ever before and representing a worldwide (or at least Western) scourge

Economists make a variety of cases about the danger of deflation, and sometimes one or another is emphasized in public discussion. The many problems of deflation include the following:

- Debt becomes more burdensome, at least to those who owe the debt (like a person with a mortgage or a corporation with bonds outstanding). In an economy with deflation, a person might receive pay cuts or—if running a business—lower prices for the products he sells, thus earning less money each year. If his mortgage payment is fixed, debt service becomes more burdensome. The lender, of course, would be better off; but we (or at least those of us who are fearful of deflation) deem society worse off because those who suffer from higher debt are more economically affected and prone to react adversely than those who benefit from deflation. In reality, that is just an assumption. We also ignore that debt can be renegotiated if deflation exists. The U.S. government, which has the largest amount of debt outstanding, stands to lose from this debt increasing aspect of deflation.

- Taxes are lower. If a person has a higher income he pays higher taxes. Assume that, in a deflationary world, people do not get pay raises but because prices have gone down they feel no poorer. Their lower nominal incomes, however, would yield lower tax revenues for the government. A contra case to this is that the government might need lower tax revenues since it would also face lower prices for the goods and services that it buys. Government, though, may not garner the same lower price benefits as people do. Also, taxpayers would go into lower tax brackets in a deflationary world.

- Workers will resist pay cuts resulting in strikes and other slowdowns in employment which will further exacerbate an underperforming economy. For example, a worker will accept a 2% pay raise when inflation is 1% but would supposedly refuse a 1% pay cut—even if deflation were 2%. The workers would react adversely by going on strike or otherwise not participating in their right amount of economic output. This is also another guess or assumption. It really calls on previous history of the U.S. when large, strong union worker groups would go on strike if they did not get big pay increases. One counter argument is that during the years following 2008 many workers accepted compensation reductions in both pay and benefits.

- Banks cannot lend below 0%. Assume that the banks require a return of about 3% in real terms and expected inflation is 1%. They would lend at about 4%. If inflation went down banks would lower their lending rates but if inflation were expected to be around –4%, the banks would not charge negative rates. This is potentially valid; yet if we had such a deflation we could design contracts to compensate for this problem.

- Monetary policy cannot be performed. If rates are so low then the central bank cannot lower rates and, therefore, cannot rectify the economy in its usual efficacious manner. This is a circular argument since we would only have had such low rates if the central bank had lowered rates.

- People will delay purchases if they think prices will go down, causing an unnatural decrease in aggregate demand. Pundits make this case liberally. They cite hypothetical examples. They often mention house or car purchases as those subject to delay. Sometimes they even state that people will delay everyday purchases like food and clothing, but this is unlikely baring a very substantial deflation. Pundits and the press call on the case of Japan for real world evidence but chronic deflation in Japan does not delay purchases. Japanese consumption seems to move along on its long-term trend after adjusting for effects of the aging of the population and real wage changes. If a deflationary economy became a norm, we could design contracts to protect both buyer and seller from deflation. Also, deflation might be a particularly easy condition to protect against with contracts. We do not generally hear discussion of this when analysts describe deflation. They prefer to view the people like "deer frozen in headlights" in the face of deflation. Also, keep in mind the microeconomic case of the changing of prices relative to each other. People typically delay a purchase when they expect a *relative* price to go down, i.e., not the general price level going down, but the price of one good declining to the extent that relative to other current purchases, that one good will be cheaper later. The common example of this phenomenon is an electronic good like a television or telephone that will be cheaper given rapid change in the product and having nothing to do with general price levels. Another counter argument is that when interest rates are low (as would be the case with deflation), credit-constrained households have greater incentive to spend now rather than later.

- Analysts usually list all or some of the above problems to create an overall case against deflation. Any one of the arguments alone may be lacking, but if prices start tending down and (1) some debtors are worse off, (2) some labor unions call for a job action and (3) some young couples delay buying houses, then deficient aggregate demand will start to feed on itself and result in a deflationary spiral.

- Many analysts refer to empirical cases, almost always Japan. They argue that Japan has fared poorly economically for over two decades and attribute it to deflation. From about 1990 to the present Japan was in an intractable spiral of deflation resulting in underperformance of the national economy and a pathology of insufficient aggregate demand. The cause and effect are questionable; even the basic facts are debatable. Japan did not suffer overall deflation in that time period, and the performance of its economy may not have been that bad.

Central bankers all over the world today (including the U.S., Eurozone and Japan) are largely doing extraordinary monetary policy on the view that deflation is the singular destructive economic force. Regardless of the merits of the case, deflation will remain popular as an acute M&M problem. It provides need and purpose to our society for central bankers and the hundreds of thousands of intellectuals supporting government policy. It buttresses the ideas of Keynesianism. Analysts on the other side mock the deflation case. They like to highlight that adverse effects of deflation are largely to the indebted governments since there is less debt inflated away and tax revenues are lower.

The financial press prefers to characterize deflation as a serious problem and has little regard for counter-cases against deflation. For example, that people delay buying due to a perception of deflation is a particularly prevalent and unquestioned assumption. Ironically, many economists and other analysts who make this case also often characterize people with a directly opposite pathology of being incapable of delaying spending. They describe consumers as infernally impatient, e.g., overly willing to buy with credit cards at high interest rates. In economic research the term for this consumer behavior is "hyperbolic discounting." If a consumer is offered $1,000 now, or $1,200 a year from now, people will choose the $1,000 because they dramatically discount the future. Economists have the public both ways: In normal times people discount the future too much. In times of deflation people delay buying because goods will be a smidgen cheaper next year. The people are always incapable of spending correctly.

Deflation discussion in much of the media is also silly: The media relishes demon deflation and reports it with little or no counter-case. A short (supposedly) instructive piece on *Bloomberg.com*[112], quipped "when (prices) actually drop, economic activity screeches to a halt. Households hold off making purchases as they anticipate further price declines; companies postpone investment and hiring as they are forced to cut prices." Evidence of deflation's costs can be found with the Great Depression and Japan. Japan's deflation was "less catastrophic" than the Great Depression's and resulted in "lost decades of almost no economic growth...wages stagnated and consumers reined in spending." Somehow, during

---

[112] "Deflation: The Trouble With Falling Prices," *Bloomberg.com*, by Simon Kennedy, March 19, 2014.

deflation, Japan managed to maintain and even improve on one of the highest standards of living in the world. Finally, the author states with qualification, "Central bankers find it easier to beat inflation than deflation," as if it were uncontestable.

## *Asset Inflation*

Calculating the prices of assets, like stocks, bonds, houses, etc. is omnipresent. Yet asset price changes do not generally enter into inflation calculations. To some extent house price changes are reflected in our standard inflation calculations that compute a rental equivalent price change for the cost of housing. Also, of course, we desire that our assets rise in value. But, should we characterize asset inflation as a problem, either in general, or, perhaps for some subset of the populace? Assume an economy with many low income people and one high income person. The high income person receives a large bonus from his employer and buys a house and stock, thereby raising the prices of assets in those markets. Prices of other goods remain the same. This society has experienced asset inflation. Is this good, bad or of no consequence to the overall society? Whichever the case, our M&M policy following 2008 has generally had the effect of raising asset prices which has aided those who disproportionally own assets. Asset inflation may be an area we have to focus on in the future.

## II.9.C. Business Cycle

The belief that capitalist economies exhibit a recurring and somewhat regular pattern of economic growth and recession called the business cycle ("BC") is integral to M&M. BC is believed to be endemic to capitalism and is presented as capitalism's fundamental flaw—and therefore requiring government manipulation of the economy through M&M policy. Before about 1980, economists explained BC by over-production and the buildup of inventory. More recently, as our economy became decreasingly focused on goods' production, we have attributed BC to overlending or similar excess in finance and banking. Whatever the cause of BC, economists break as follows: (1) Keynesians believe BC represents a fundamental flaw in free markets that must be rectified by government policy (I will call them "Traditional" BC believers); (2) conservatives believe BC is the natural way for factors of production to be reallocated (I will call them Real Business Cycle believers).

The downturns of BC (more of the traditional BC) are supposed to be short in duration (generally less than a year) and to occur every few years. At least that is the way they are described in textbooks, and this is supposedly an observation from literally hundreds of years of capitalist economies. This regular timing and magnitude of BC has not generally transpired in the last 30 years, not even the last 50. BC is more than just the co-movement of macroeconomic quantities like unemployment, industrial production, consumer confidence, etc.: It is that economic shocks cause these quantities to feed on each other's changes such that the economy can collapse well beyond any low point it might merit solely from the economic magnitude of any initial shock. Furthermore, although BC dictates that economies eventually recover, they can potentially get stuck at a lower than warranted equilibrium and stay there for a long time. This justifies countervailing economic actions in the form of economic stimulation by the government.

Economists who question traditional BC theory propose that economic fluctuations are simply reflections of the constant structural changes that society faces—like technology, preferences, weather, climate, geopolitical events, etc. This school of thought is known as Real Business Cycles ("RBC"). Downturns in the economy will be no worse than is merited by the initial changes and the economy will not get stuck in underequilibrium. RBC is roundly dismissed by traditional BC believers as insufficient to explain the perverse economic movements we experience.

A main weakness of traditional BC theory is that, although there may be some general, pro-cyclicity in economic activity the changes in the economy have been minimally cyclical and have lacked regularity in timing, duration and severity. A long series of the pattern of economic growth, like annual percent change in GDP, might convey a somewhat cyclical pattern, but the history of recent fluctuations since 1960 is idiosyncratic. This lack of cyclicity is especially valid during the lifetimes of current college students who were born in the 1990s. They have not seen textbook BC and probably never will. They have experienced only one downswing: the large recession of 2008, which is out of the ordinary for regular BC theory. The only other downswing in their lifetimes is the 2001 recession, which was hardly perceptible and similarly unordinary. The recession preceding that (1990 to 1991) was also minimal and largely precipitated by a shock (the first Gulf War) rather than the result of some inherent tendency of free market economies. Going back another 20 years includes the 1960s, which was almost free of a downturn, and two very big recessions: 1973-74 and 1982, both of which were unique events respectively attributable to the original "Energy Crisis" and a concerted Fed policy initiative. In summary, none of the recessionary events of the last 50 years appear to be the result of any flaw of capitalism spiraling out of control from inventory buildup or bank lending excesses. Earlier data on the BC, especially from the 1800s, is similarly unconvincing. A textbook demonstration of the business cycle and a rough depiction of the business cycle over 1970 to present are shown below.

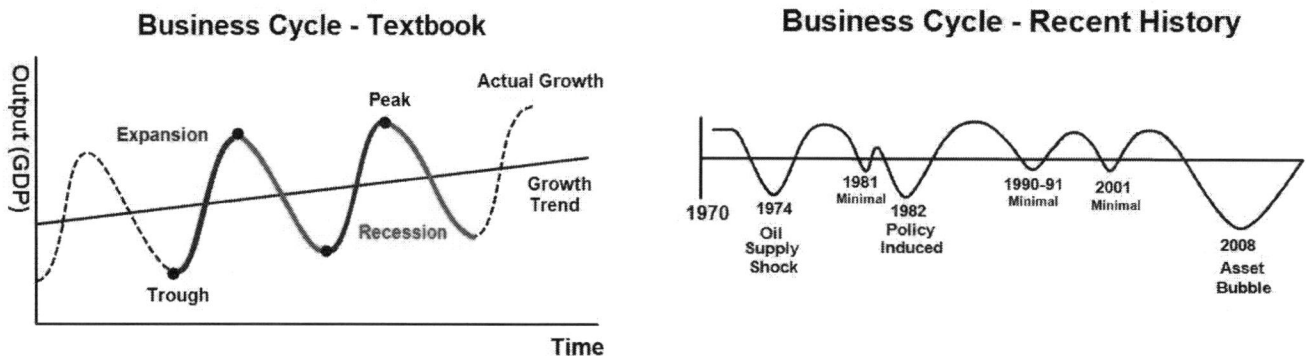

If it is not an interworking of capitalism, then what prompts the up and down movement of the macroeconomy? Why doesn't it grow steadily? Phrasing the question that way somewhat answers it. The economy is buffeted by constant shocks including changes in preferences and technology, prices of basic commodities like oil, weather and climate forces, geo-political forces, government policies both short-term (like the contractionary monetary policy of the early 1980s) and long-term (like our support of the housing market in the 1990s and 2000s), demand –side shocks, etc. Traditional internal build-up factors of the business cycle, inventory and bank lending might contribute too but they are probably dominated by other factors.

One of the distinctive facets of the 2008 ff business cycle as related in popular commentary is that 2008 ff was a financial or balance sheet cycle. It was not an ordinary business cycle precipitated by either of the two main traditional BC causes (inventory build-up due to overproduction and over-lending by financial institutions). As a result, we are told, the recovery can be expected to be more protracted in time and many of the conventional aspects of business cycle theory are absent. According to traditional BC believers, this reconciles the business cycle in general with the odd events of 2008 ff, but this distinction is tenuous. There have been other recessions, like 2001, that were balance sheet recessions but that did not take a long time from which to recover. Also, any downturn—no matter what its cause—can be long in recovery if the fundamental underlying economic conditions and the shocks that subsequently hit the economy are adverse.

Everything we know about historical cycles will not help us discern important turns or trends in today's economy and what the next cycle will be like in duration and severity. Another reality for today's American college students is that if they analyze BC issues with traditional tools while Chinese, Indian and Russian economists are open to non-traditional viewpoints, they will be at an intellectual disadvantage. Our persistence in the belief in traditional BC is remarkable. We routinely describe cyclical forces as if they are much more regular and unexceptional than our history has been. Adherence to such dogma makes sense, though, because it caters to our pretense of being able to discern macroeconomic patterns to justify government policy. Business cycle beliefs are largely prejudices. The day we look at each other and agree that there is very little to business cycle is the day that many egos die. The extensive research and analysis of the Fed staff, other policy researchers, instructors, textbook authors, many business people and pundits, etc. will get knocked down a big notch.

## II.9.D. Policy Effects: (Short-Run) Effects of Monetary Policy & Extensions

Earlier, we talked about whether or not M&M policies and other government economic programs had real effects on the economy. To recap, we have a great muddle, and impacts are largely in the eye of the beholder. Most of today's M&M specialists are more sanguine, however. They think effects exist and that the existence of effects is supported by the gross preponderance of evidence. They also believe that, even if effects do not exist, erring on the side of effects is the better strategy. If policy, indeed, does not have effects then nothing is lost by trying it. If policy has effects and we fail to take advantage, we could lose output and even create a depression. The other take is that it is very difficult to find policy effects but easy to hypothesize adverse, unintended effects. Also, another compelling reason why some people believe in effects is simply that without their existence a million intellectuals in our society lose their very raison d'être. There is nothing that provides such an exulted role to do-gooders than an unstable economy. Here are some additional points germane to policy effects:

- Policy proponents are stubborn about acknowledging failure of favorable effects and the possibility of adverse outcomes. Ben Bernanke, for example, doggedly dismissed counter arguments to Fed policy. Whether it was people being hurt abroad, U.S. savers being hurt, U.S. investors overreaching for yield and taking too much risk, etc., Bernanke dismissed adverse effects of Fed policy.
- Many cite the tenure of Alan Greenspan as Fed Chair (1987 through 2005), a period of economic growth and stability known as the Great Moderation, as proof that economic stewardship works. However, the period was marked by a multitude of favorable underlying economic forces including an extraordinary increase in the values of assets like stocks, bonds and housing.
- I reiterate the great muddle of timing of effects. Historically, in M&M theory to stabilize the economy in face of weakened aggregate demand we hypothesized a short-run monetary policy that had real effects in the short run. The long run would be irrelevant to aggregate demand management and would be determined by factors beyond policy control. The long run could be shaped by structural economic policies done by government but such policies were not perceived of as stabilization policy to manage a business cycle. Presently, we have commenced a long-run monetary policy that guides aggregate demand over a long run. We no longer talk about the short run. Policy effects largely occur immediately in the form of repricing of assets by financial markets. We talk about a Medium Term, which is neither short nor long run. To top it off, we have

seemingly abandoned long-run government structural policies. Either we no longer believe they are helpful or we must postpone them until we escape our current unsatisfactory short-run aggregate demand shortage.

- The vast bulk of media believes that policy works, at least a little if not a critical amount. The popular press will admit that policy does not work precisely or with tight timeframes but eventually it works. If you read 1,000 editorials from the mainstream media you would see mainly confirmations of Fed policy. Journalists cannot say exactly why policy works. The evidence is a gross preponderance, or at least a preponderance, of facts and ostensible results. The popular press excoriates naysayers, especially usurpers. *The Economist*, for example, became indignant with a popular *YouTube* video that mocked policy. Even *The Wall Street Journal*, excluding its editorial page, espouses policy. The economics columns of the *Journal* usually express belief in the success of policy.

- One oddity of effects of policy is that most people, including people from the private sector, will contend that they themselves do not respond to policy the way that it is intended. For example, they are not fooled by a Fed lowering of rates. They anticipate the policy and realize that it will only have temporary effects. These same people believe, however, that others will respond according to the textbook ideas. For example, if the Fed lowered the rate any bond fund manager would say she saw it coming, has already positioned her portfolio for it and may already be setting up for the policy to be reversed. Her peers will respond in the direction and magnitude that the policy figured on.

- Textbooks present various evidence of policy effects. Economic literature has extensive statistical testing of cause and effect of macro policy, but it is not easy to be sure of their conclusions nor easy to convey to a general audience. Many texts omit or minimize empirical proof of policy effects. In its place, many textbooks resort to research using anecdotes or cases. One piece of research often cited is a paper by leading economists Christina Romer and David Romer.[113] They use the "narrative approach," which is analyzing a selection of historical policy initiatives in which the circumstances are relatively clear as to cause and effect. They claim sufficient cases of clear cut success of policy. In higher-level academic work we rely on complicated econometrics to settle the question of validity of policy effects. In any case, evidence for real effects of policy is uncertain.

- Almost all texts present a chart showing the target fed funds rate and the actual feds funds rate over many years (typically from the 1990s to the present). The demonstration is that the two rates are extremely close, indicating that the Fed can set a target and hit it successfully; therefore, we have an effective policy tool. There are questions of causality and magnitudes. The fed funds rate may have been following the movement of short-term rates in markets.

- In the period following 2008, after the fed funds rate approached zero, the Fed engaged in unconventional policies including bond buying and forward guidance. Ultimate cause and effect are impossible to be certain of. Rates did go down and asset class held their value or rose in value. The real economy did recover to some extent, but the mechanism of policy effects was not clear. The traditional mechanism of accommodative policy leading to greater bank lending to businesses and consumers did not frequently occur. Higher asset values and spending due to wealth effects from those higher values did occur. There were other effects including a reduction in interest income by people and distorted asset values in bonds, housing and equities.

---

[113] "Does Monetary Policy Matter? A New Test in the Spirit of Friedman and Schwartz," by Christina D. Romer and David H. Romer in *NBER Macroeconomics Annual 1989*, Volume 4. Pp. 121-184. MIT Press. http://www.nber.org/books/blan89-1

- Magnitude of effects is an issue, and policy effects must be more than a buyout at a dollar for dollar level. For example, during 2011 to 2012 the ECB engaged in extraordinary actions to prop up the European bond market and banking system. Sovereign bonds in troubled countries like Greece and Spain rose in value and declined in yield, enabling those nations to borrow more easily to keep their economies growing. Despite this, the policy seemingly was not more than a buying out with the central bank merely making good for a large slug of bad debt and the underlying economies no better off.

- The effects of the various unconventional monetary policy done following 2008 are a matter of opinion. Some point/counter point would include the following: (1) Does persistent lowering of rates bring out worthwhile new borrowing and lending, or does it merely cause the weakest borrowers (like those taking subprime auto loans), to get in over their heads? Did our policy result in bubbles and subsequent mal-investment like the investment done in the energy extraction business? (2) Do Keynesian effects work at all in our current world of large asset pools that can be changed promptly? Does it not work now but indeed may have worked fifty years ago when people and corporations were more easily fooled by changes in interest rates.

- There are unintended effects. QE contributed to extensive mal-investment like weak companies getting access to capital at very low interest rates. Similarly, financial regulation might have intended to reduce bubbles or stabilize financial markets but might have caused bigger bubbles and more concentration in finance. Side effects like banks losing business from rejecting new customers and exiting markets occur.

- Effects like wealth effects works both ways but policy advocates highlight favorable effects. For example, when the stock market rose we boasted the wealth effect yet when it trended sideways (over 2015, for example) wealth effect analysis got little mention. Similar for the economic effects of oil price increases. When oil rose in price companies borrowed and created jobs. Also, assets whose value depended on high oil price rose in value. Collectively the booming oil sector created wealth effects. When oil dropped from $100 per barrel to $30 in 2014 and 2015 about $100 trillion in wealth disappeared. The wealth of oil companies, countries like Norway and Saudi Arabia and many oil-related assets dropped dramatically.

- Excluding nations whose policy is currency pegging, effects should be general more than just devaluing currency. In particular, low rate policies of Eurozone and Japan in 2015 and 2016 were advertised as policies to stimulate the domestic economies within their own borders by broad credit creation but were ostensibly mainly policies of lowering currencies' values. The low and negative rate policies of Sweden, Switzerland and Denmark, although touted by Keynesians as endorsements of stimulative policy and rejections of austerity policies, were merely attempts to maintain pegs of their currencies against rate lowerings of Eurozone.

## II.9.E. Stability

Another pivotal facet of modern M&M is the goal of stability. Up until the crisis of 2008 any instructor or central banker would have stated that stability, in many forms, was the ultimate goal of economic policy. Like so many other emphases and prejudices, stability quickly got supplanted as the main goal pursuant to the events of 2008. Technically, nations targeted inflation as the M&M goal, but maintaining stable prices was the tool to the greater goal of stability of the economic system as a whole, including GDP growth, financial markets and interest rates. If private parties had economic stability they would make the best decisions in matters of commerce and allocating their resources. Some macro policy proponents contend that stability actually creates greater economic growth. For example, an unstabilized economy might grow at 3%, 5%, -1% and 3%, which would average less than 3%; but a stabilized economy would grow at 3%, 4%, 2% and 3%, which would average 3%. Many economists propound stability as the goal even without assuming that higher average growth. (For example, 2%, 2%, 3%, 2% would be preferred to 3%, 5%, -1% and 3%.) In this case, stability is desirable in and of itself to both people and business. Lack of stability creates disutility.

Stability was pitched very heavily in textbooks and elsewhere. In class, I recite a presentation by former British national budget head Alistair Darling, in which he constantly uses the word stability (or stabilize or stable).[114] We have become so convinced of the virtue of stability that we projected it onto every financial and economic aspect of our society: Oil sellers want stable oil price; the Chinese want stable growth (and cleverly tout the stability of the Renminbi as a great service to the world economy); hedge fund investors want stable returns; the U.S. government wants to stabilize financial markets in a comprehensive manner; etc.[115]

Many readings of economic history show that stability does not give more output. It might even result in less stability. Also, although some people want stability in certain ways, in many other ways they may prefer volatility. The oil peddlers, Chinese, hedge fund investors, etc. may secretly crave instability which they believe puts them on a higher long-run economic path. Whether our central bank has provided stability historically is an unanswerable question. Ben Bernanke and many academics make the positive case citing sundry historical evidence. For example, they note that the U.S. did not have a central bank in the 1800s and experienced more economic instability than European nations of that time that did have central banks. Also, sundry periods of relative success of our economy, like the 1990s or the crisis of 2008 ff, are other pieces of compelling evidence to believers in policy. Naysayers contend that central banks have been sources of greater instability. For example, they argue that the overall economic performance of the U.S. during the 1800s was strong and the alleged wild economic cycles of that time were really minor and regional. We will discuss at length a detailed history of the U.S. Fed and whether its policy has been a success later.

Following 2008 we have engaged in a greater government attempt to provide wider stability, in financial markets and practically in all facets of economic life. This greater role of central banks is worldwide, yet results remain to be seen. Certainly, today's agents must figure in not only market factors but also government policy changes, which are bigger and potentially more variable than ever before.

## II.9.F. Multipliers

Even if you got a D in macro, as I did in Intermediate Macro at Boston College back in Spring 1980, I would bet that the concept of the multiplier (or, actually, two of them: the fiscal or spending multiplier and the money multiplier) is ingrained in your mind. In class we assume that the government

---

[114] Chancellor of the Exchequer's Budget statement, HM Treasury, March 12, 2008. http://webarchive.nationalarchives.gov.uk/20130129110402/http://www.hm-treasury.gov.uk/budget/budget_08/bud_bud08_speech.cfm

[115] Investors in hedge funds may or may not want stable returns. Presumably they want a high rate of return (either absolute or relative to a benchmark). They may desire some other goal like access to certain asset classes or diversification. Another argument for investing in hedge funds is that they, in some cases, promise lower downside risk, which I suppose is a kind of stability. Noted academic Andrew Lo talks about failures in the hedge fund industry and proposes, "for the U.S. Securities and Exchange Commission to play a new role in promoting greater transparency and stability in the hedge-fund industry." "Sifting Through the Wreckage: Lessons from Recent Hedge-Fund Liquidations," *Journal of Investment Management*, Vol. 2, No. 4, 2004, pp. 6-38, authored by Andrew W. Lo, Mila Getmansky and Shauna X. Mei. I cite only Lo as spokesperson because he is the most well-known name of the three.

autonomously engages in a spending project, e.g., government commences a road building project. The autonomous concept itself is hard to explain. The spending comes from nowhere in the text; however, in the real world it generally comes from borrowing. Given the new spending, the building company pays its workers who then spend a large fraction of their wages. In class we might assume 80% is spent. This fraction is known as the marginal propensity to consume ("MPC"). That spending goes into the pocket of other people, who then spend 80% and on and on. The effect on commerce or GDP of the initial dollar is $\frac{1}{(1-MPC)}$ or five times, given our MPC of 0.8. One dollar of spending results in five dollars of GDP. We also hypothesize the effect of a tax cut, which, by the theory, has a lower multiplier because people save a fraction of the first injected dollar before commencing rounds of spending. In our example, the tax cut multiplier would be four.

The spending or tax multiplier is the essence of Keynesianism. In the real world, of course, you will not get the instantaneous churning of spending nor a high multiplier like five (or four for the tax multiplier). It becomes an empirical question about how much additional spending in done from an injection of spending. Naysayers doubt any effects contending that the spending has to come from somewhere and/or that the recipients of the funds do not perceive of them as extra money and do not change their long-run intended spending plans. Those who believe in multiplier effects contend that government spending gets a multiplied effect—especially when the economy is in a recession. During the period of emergency fiscal policy in 2009, the lead economics spokesperson of the Obama Administration, Council of Economic Advisers' head Christina Romer, proposed a multiplier of about 1.5 for government spending, meaning that one dollar of spending leads to about $1.50 of GDP. The media accepted the multiplied effects as if they were fact. Despite extensive research in M&M, we do not have much of a consensus on the multiplier. The press might say that the economics profession agrees on this multiplier greater than one, but many economists believe the multiplier is less than one—which means that government spending comes at the expense of private spending. Some economists attempt to estimate all the effects of government spending, including long-run effects of the government spending and accounting for how the original autonomous spending was funded, but their conclusions break on partisan lines with policy believers saying you get some net positive effects and naysayers doubting any net benefit.

The magnitude of the tax cut multiplier might be a little clearer due to a number of recent tax rebates following 2008. Those tax cuts look like a bust for generating multiples of spending. Various estimates had about 40% of the tax cut going to debt, 30% to savings and 20% to spending (or an MPC of 20% and multiplier of 1.25). Even that magnitude is dubious. One aspect of tax cut policy in practice is that to get significant spending the tax cuts must be directed to those with low incomes because the rich will save the money. We are confident that the poor will spend whatever they get. Although this can be justified theoretically, it weakens the whole appeal of tax cuts for stimulation. Why not just bypass tax cuts altogether and have the government spend the money?

The other great multiplier is the money multiplier, which starts with an initial infusion of money into a bank. We usually talk about the Fed creating money by giving a bank money or reserves in exchange for some of the bank's other holdings (typically U.S. treasury bonds). Another story uses inculcation, for simplicity's sake. Inculcation is an initial deposit of cash taken from under some person's mattress and deposited in the bank. In either case the banks have more money to loan and they loan it out and the money gets circulated through the economy with a multiplier effect. In either case, the initial loanable money has to come from nowhere. In the case of banks getting reserves, we do not view the bonds forfeited by the banks as lessening bank collateral against which other loans were originally applied. That would negate the policy effects.

To round out the story, after the initial infusion, the bank lends its new reserves immediately to someone queued up for a loan. We assume banks have a book of loans ready to be made. The borrower spends the loan proceeds. For example, assume it is a business venture that pays some workers and purchases some supplies. The recipients of those funds deposit into other banks; those banks make loans and so on. Depending on the reserve requirement (use 10%, although in reality in the U.S. reserve requirements are minimal and easy to avoid), then the ultimate effect is ten times the economic activity of the original infusion. It sounds fantastic, or at least like something to be used only for classroom discussions; but some people take it literally. For example, in an April 2009 major economic speech given at Georgetown University, President Barack Obama argued, "The truth is that a dollar of capital in a bank can actually result in eight or ten dollars of loans to families and businesses, a multiplier effect that can ultimately lead to a faster pace of economic growth." The eight to ten comes right out of a typical, theoretical textbook discussion of the money multiplier. I wonder if the President understood what he was saying. The money multiplier is a parable at most, yet it is taken literally by many.

The money multiplier starts with markets out-of-equilibrium. Qualified borrowers are waiting for loans and the banks are waiting for funds to make these loans. This pent up lending is not generally the case in a recession when you need it. In the classroom, we assume banks lend up to the very amount they are required to keep on reserve, and that time transpires instantaneously. In the real world, banks may or may not lend and we don't know much about the timing. They might start lending after the weak period in the economy is over. Another quirky aspect is that for the multiple deposit effect to work, there have to be many different banks in the system. One bank or a consolidated system of bank balance sheets would confound the analysis.

In practice the multiplier is a dud. For example, in the extraordinary monetary expansion of 2008, the money multiplier (which can be measured in a variety of ways) collapsed. The Fed made hundreds of billions of infusions of bank reserves and very little lending and/or money was created. The banks simply held the excess reserves. Proponents of policy will argue that without the monetary expansion there would have been even less bank lending, and this may or may not be valid. Nonetheless, the way it works in the text is not how it will play out in your crisis. By the way, the money multiplier also dropped during the Great Depression. At that time, the story was that currency holdings by people were going up. The money multiplier is a parable of how commerce can grow under special circumstances, yet is taught piously and taken too literally. In the real world credit creation is much more decentralized with a large portion done outside of banks controlled by the central bank. It is harder to pin down where funds come from and where they go. We have notably less control over credit than we think.

## II.9.G. Housing: The New Macro Pretender

Both in our theories of M&M and in the lives of our people, housing has taken on a major role of economic wealth and growth creator. We view housing as a source of net AD and as an asset that generates a positive rate of return. In our economic thinking housing is not an expense: It is an income.

### Stories, Facts & Figures

When my parents bought their first (and only) house in 1975, my father's gruff friend remarked, "Are you f'ing crazy?" Sure, home ownership was a big chunk of The American Dream, but houses were generally more expensive than apartments and remained an economic risk to middle class types who could not afford occasional large unexpected expenses. Very few people at that time viewed a house as an "appreciating asset." By about the 1990s, when I purchased my first house, attitudes toward housing had shifted, and people including myself started scheming about rising property values complementing income, even supplanting income as an integral part of our well-being. My father's generation had it right: Housing is and will continue to be a constant drain on resources—not an asset that that puts up a net positive rate of return. America's housing market will never "recover" as an asset class that pays for itself the way it appeared in the 1990s and early 2000s.

During the 1990s through about 2010, I bought three homes. I also "refied" mortgages many times (five times altogether, in fact). The willingness of my mortgage broker who had negotiated my first mortgage to offer me a refi struck me as curious. Then I discovered that mortgage contracts included no restriction on pre-payment, and that the mortgage was held by some entity that he and I would not have to face personally. The mortgage broker made a commission on each new mortgage so he had incentive to do refis. Like everyone else I witnessed the new housing finance, which was very unlike the impression I had from my parents' strict perspective. In my experiences, I had acquaintances—among them a Russian immigrant with little means—who bought properties for speculation, like mini-real estate moguls. Another impression was how unqualified people turned up with big properties. On one occasion, my wife, on hearing that a poorer friend qualified for a very large mortgage, became angry with me for not having obtained the same borrowing limit. I struggled to explain to her that his loan was unwise but found myself making the opposite case. It was the same story pundits, regular people and even Alan Greenspan made for the jumbo loans, floating rate loans, no-money down loans, etc. We said, "Immigrants are buying," or "Non-conventional households are just getting into the market" or "People will not live in any home for thirty years so why do they need a fixed rate loan."

There are a multitude of facts and figures about the housing market and to discuss even a small fraction of them would take reams. In one way, housing data are inscrutable. The trends evident in pre-1990 data are altogether different from those in data from 1990 to 2006. Trends since 2006 resemble neither period. There is one fact: House prices did not go up in the hundred years before about 1990. From 1990 to about 2006, however, prices did go up. The market collapsed starting around 2007. After years of decline, housing recovered to some extent with some areas experiencing a full recovery. Most levels though, including housing starts, house values, etc., are still below pre-2007 levels and most homeowners either did not partake in the house price recovery or do not perceive that they did/are (even the though the media has people happy that house prices are going up). In certain years following 2008, house prices went up but it was not for average working stiffs buying homes; it was largely hedge funds buying properties as investments. Also, it was bigger, more expensive houses located primarily in hot markets and unreflective of a wide recovery. Today, many homeowners are underwater with their mortgages (about 15% of homeowners as of 2017) and, just as grave, many close to being underwater. If house prices either stay flat or tend down, masses of people will live in houses that never have any value—making them essentially renters with debt. People are holding mortgage debt later into life with bigger amounts of debt. About half of households around age 60 have mortgage debt; which is much higher than before.

A popular theory of the housing market circa 2013 to 2014 was the "shortage of supply" story. Many analysts hypothesized a broadly strong housing market but it did not manifest itself because the market was held back by a shortage of supply. People supposedly had the money and the inclination to buy houses but there were no houses available. This meant that perhaps the market could be helped along with some policy like aiding builders. Indeed, in certain hot markets as soon as a house came on it was sold. We heard copious cases of houses going on the market and immediately getting multiple offers above initial asking prices. This was not a shortage of supply as much as wrong initial pricing. Furthermore, it revealed that buyers wanted to live in certain areas and would not seek housing elsewhere. One central reality about housing today is that it is expensive. House prices and rents in desirable locations are high. Few want to live or move to areas where prices are reasonable. Many households in the U.S. (and more than in previous generations) spend a large fraction of incomes on housing. Housing expenses of greater than 30% of gross income (either mortgage or rent) are considered an affordability cutoff by housing economists, and more households are near that expense level than before.

### Dual Economic Punches: Keynesian Demand Creator & Wealth Incubator

One of the oddest M&M narratives is the way in which housing has come to regarded as a generator of economic greatness—as has been the case over the past ten years in America. This premise receives relatively little intellectual criticism and also reveals the gullibility of the American people and their leaders for economic excuses and pipe dreams. Before the Great Recession, few people staked their lots in life on their housing wealth. Nor did we model our economy as highly dependent on housing wealth. We also did not explain business cycles with housing value fluctuations. For example, the usual explanations/causes of recessions were the build-up of inventories and over-lending in general. Excessive mortgage lending was not seen as a typical cause of recession. All of the economic stories with housing as cause became prominent after the period of the run up and subsequent crash in housing wealth from about 2000 through 2009. Now we have incorporated the "housing as economy driving force" model and we have doubled-down on housing. Following 2008 we have portrayed ourselves as a great housing people in an economy largely depending on the housing sector. Many of the most common recession recovery clichés included statements that "house prices are up confirming a recovering economy."

This emphasis on the role of housing in current economic discussions is notable and reflective of how ad hoc our M&M theories really are. Housing was not previously such a focus of the theories and public discourse on the causes of economic activity. Because housing was the proximate cause of the dramatic events of 2008 ff, we have to characterize it as the main sector and economic stimulation overachiever. Our attempts to save the economy have largely focused on keeping house prices high. In the sense that high house prices make new homebuyers poor, this is completely illogical. We rationalize the housing story by saying that housing creates spillover expenditures and that high house prices create a perception of wealth that causes general consumption. The wealth effect of housing is hardly questioned, yet most people place very little weight on these so-called wealth effects.

Housing has been anointed with two grand M&M facets: (1) spending/Keynesian multiplier and (2) wealth effects. Both cases are dubious yet they are appealing to average people and, apparently, largely endorsed by economists, pundits and financial journalists. Housing is seen as an instant spending stimulator. To go from renter to owner is to increase your life consumption set. We typically hypothesize a young family going from renting to buying a home and starting additional spending because they *must* spend to furnish and/or repair their new purchase. Here is one quote like any of a million you could find in the press, "Few things stimulate the economy as much as a home purchase."[116] Analysts impart a theoretical basis that people feel "wealthier." Simply going from renting to owning gets people to re-evaluate their life earnings and consumption set. You never, or at least rarely, hear an opposite case made like that people buy a home and then drastically cut back on spending because they can no longer afford to go on vacations, eat out, splurge on electronics, etc.

The wealth effect of housing is a relatively new phenomenon, peculiar perhaps to the 1990s and early 2000s. Economists venture various estimates of how much additional spending people will do as their houses increase in value. One rough estimate argued that the housing wealth effect was about a "nickel," or 5%. If your house was worth $500,000 and houses prices in your area were reported to be 10% higher this year compared to last then you would spend 5% of the $50,000 increase, or $2,500. Economists thought of

---

[116] "Healing housing may help lead the economy back," by John Waggoner, *USA Today*, December 28, 2012, p. Money 3B.

the wealth effect as something a sufficient number of people acted on, to varying extents but such that it would have a reliable average of around 5%. One spouse might say to his partner, "Honey, I bet our house is worth $50,000 more so we can take a $3,000 vacation." Some people would borrow the entire value of any perceived price increase through a re-financing while most people merely built house price increases into some overall long-run standard of living they might be able to achieve. Nor did economists dwell on opposite effects. When house prices went down many economists minimized the negative wealth effects. Also, higher house prices constitute big expenses to new households, which typically consist of young people forming new households, and that should curtail overall spending. The reality is that we never knew much about wealth effects from house price changes.

## *Extensive Government Subsidies and Pros & Cons of Promoting Home Ownership*

Housing enjoys a multitude of major subsidies from the government, including the following:
- Mortgage payers can deduct mortgage interest from their taxable income. These write-offs are substantial for many households. Some households may not get a hefty write-off, like people with small mortgages who might do just as well taking the standard deduction on their taxes, but there is a wide perception that having a mortgage provides a big tax break.
- The capital gain from the sale of a house is free of capital gains tax (up to $500,000 gain from the sale of a primary residence; second properties are subject to regular capital gains taxes). This is another substantial factor making housing a preferred investment for many people. In addition to saving money, it is appealing due to the simplicity.
- Mortgage holders can pre-pay their mortgage without penalty, i.e., you can "call" your bond to your lender. This is mandated by law and represents a major financial advantage to borrowers.
- Historically, our government has subsidized mortgages in a variety of ways. This makes mortgage rates lower and longer-term mortgages, like the 30-year mortgage, possible. The U.S. government currently backs a large fraction of mortgages. In fact, about half of new mortgage originations from 2000 to 2008 were backed by the government, while 90% are now government-backed. This is done through the quasi-government agencies Fannie Mae, Freddie Mac and others. These agencies are backed by the U.S. government. Other countries have less backing of housing finance and generally having shorter mortgage terms and variable rates.
- Fannie Mae and Freddie Mac are the large government-sponsored enterprises ("GSE's) that facilitate the mortgage business for the housing industry.[117] Since the 1970s up until to 2008, Fannie Mae and Freddie Mac were perceived of as private companies that made profits and had publicly traded stocks and bonds like any other company. They were seen as related to the federal government at some higher level such that their bonds were viewed as risk-free, but they were not perceived of as backed by the government for their entire operations. When the calamity of 2008

---

[117]Fannie Mae (formally Federal National Mortgage Association) was chartered in 1934. In its first couple of decades it purchased certain federally insured and guaranteed loans like those done through the Federal Housing Administration (FHA) and the Veterans Administration (VA). Fannie became bigger and more involved in the secondary market of mortgage securities. In 1968 it was split up creating Ginnie Mae (Government National Mortgage Association) which took over the role of guaranteeing payment on the FHA and VA loans. Ginnie Mae itself was fully backed by the U.S. Fannie Mae focused on secondary market operations which was a big and growing market. Also, Freddie Mac (Federal Home Mortgage Loan Corporation) was created in 1970 to manage secondary market operations for conventional mortgages. Fannie Mae and Freddie Mac continued to grow substantially up until the crisis of 2008. Another GSE is Sallie Mae (Student Loan Marketing Association) which originates federally insured student loans. Sallie Mae started in 1972 as a GSE but became privatized in 1997.

transpired, however, the U.S. government had to bail them out in total, providing about $187.5 billion. In reality they were never as profitable as they reported because they simply did not hold adequate reserves for losses like any lender would have to do. Over the years, the government, in cahoots with much of the world of finance, sustained this setup with the rationale that only with such large government sponsored entities could a vibrant mortgage market exist including a secondary market for mortgages and the availability of a thirty-year mortgage. Private markets alone could not do it, supposedly. Intelligent parties, like *The Wall Street Journal* which editorialized against Fannie Mae for years, saw through the false façade but the nation as a whole partook in this flawed government backed housing system. We "rolled the dice," as one politician put it, that housing would never face a big price adjustment. We even made a goal of 70% of U.S. households being home owners. Years after the collapse of the housing giants we continue to support them.

- Our government has tacitly indicated that the big banks and other big financial companies supporting the housing market are too big to fail, providing catastrophe insurance to the industry at low or no cost, allowing them to offer lower priced mortgage financing.

- In response to the crisis of 2008, our government created a wide variety of programs to assist distressed homeowners. Millions of mortgage modifications have been done under these programs, which continue today.

We talked about Keynesian spending spillover and wealth effects on spending from home ownership. We tout these for short-run M&M effects, whether they are effective or not. What are some other economic and social aspects of subsidizing housing? Owning housing creates a sense of community, leading homeowners to partake positively in communities, which could have wide positive social benefits. Another specific reason for encouraging housing was that, supposedly, home ownership among immigrants would make them less likely to be sympathetic to anti-social activities like terrorism. Another facet of home buying is that it forces a stealth savings among people, including especially low-income people who otherwise are not inclined to save.

Of course, there are cons to making everyone king of a castle. Home ownership makes people anti-development. In other words, it is harder to locate business—especially any kind of unsavory enterprise—in the neighborhood. Another con is that owning homes makes people less likely to move to improve their lives, primarily by taking better jobs. Migration of labor is a key facet of a strong national economy, and was a substantial net positive in the economic development of America. Perhaps the greatest flaw in housing as beneficial is a simple cause and effect misinterpretation. We observed that neighborhoods with high home ownership also were nice places, with quality schools, strong families and vibrant communities. Therefore, getting people to buy homes would make them superior denizens in nicer towns. It might be that better citizens tend to buy homes and buy them in neighborhoods that already had these superior characteristics.

Another notable economic aspect of house financing is that it is the main way average people can make leveraged bets. If you buy a house and put 20% down (say on a $100,000 condo) and the housing market goes up just 10%, you have made $10,000 on a layout of $20,000, or 50%. Although this may have represented a favorable investment strategy historically it only works if house prices continue to go up.

### Home Ownership as Investment

Consider a typical housing story: A couple buy a house for $200k. They immediately incur various purchase and initial set-up costs, perhaps $20k worth. Maybe also, upon moving in they notice some major repair that has to be done yet was missed in the home inspection. This runs another $5k. They repair the house year after year, maybe laying out $1k in a cheap year and $25k the year they have a big repair like painting the house or re-roofing. After seven years, they hear that a house in their neighborhood sold for $350k, so they decide to sell their house for $350k. Their broker says, "Sure, you can get $350k, but not until you update the kitchen." They spend $25k for the kitchen and put the house on the market for $350k. After a couple of months they end up selling at $310k, paying commissions, taxes, etc. of about $25k. They lost money on the house but at the cocktail party they say, "We sold our house—made $100k!"

In reality, most people are not unrealistic about housing as an investment. Enough, however, are hopeful for their house yielding a positive rate of return or, at least, not losing value against inflation. Also, while the above example might have played out during the 1980s to early 2000s when house prices went up a lot, it will likely be that in the future you will buy a house for $200k and sell it for about $200k. Surveys show that people believe houses will rise about 3% to 4% annually in value, which might not seem like very much.[118]

Do we make money on houses? For one thing, we generally do not consider how much we have to pay to maintain houses. Try searching online for estimation of the annual cost of keeping a house up and you will find very little. The expense is often dismissed and when brought up at all, assumed to be modest. In contrast, search for tips on how to buy a house or get a low mortgage rate and you will find endless resources. Also you will find copious articles on how much housing has changed in price by city and region. If you do not maintain a house, on selling it you will be faced with substantial cost to improve it or have to sell at a reduced price. Cost of carry must be budgeted. For example, a house must be painted perhaps every 25 years. Assuming your house is freshly painted you should put aside some fraction of the cost of that future expense. Rough estimates of the cost of carry of houses range from about 2 to 10% of value. In addition, a homeowner must include real estate tax and insurance. They vary widely but might be about 1 to 3% of the value of the home. The bottom line is that we have been conditioned to see the 4% increase in house prices and not the approximate 5% cost of carry. Also, house prices may fail to go up for long periods of time but cost of carry never goes away. If house prices do not go up, you should assume that the housing "investment" will lose 5% per year. Here are some various aspects of the notion of housing as investment:

- During the housing price bubble people faced expensive repair and improvement and would do it with a smile on the assumption that it would be an accelerant to the increase in house value. For example, it was a popular belief that elaborate landscaping work added more value to the home than the cost of the work. Those attitudes are now more realistic.
- A house is viewed differently than virtually any other purchase because we think houses last forever. The underlying property may last forever, but the house itself is merely a manufactured good, like a car or refrigerator. Specialists estimate that a house lasts about sixty years. Houses can go out of fashion or become technologically obsolete, and new houses can be relatively cheap. If population and household formation trends contain at little or no growth, as is the case now, America is already over-supplied in housing.
- Housing investment does not contribute to the economy as a whole the way other investment does. Buying a house rather than investing it in stocks or bonds adds to consumption and not to a venture that will create new products and, therefore, economic growth.
- Housing represents perverse and facile investing by some. For example, people say, "We were underinvested in housing." Housing has great appeal as part of our desire to put extra money in

---

[118] "2016 SCE Housing Survey Shows Modest Decline in Home Price Expectations," by Andreas Fuster, Basit Zafar and Kevin Morris, *Liberty Street Economics*, June 2, 2016.

assets that make money and are easy to understand. Many buy a second home, add onto existing homes or buy up as an investment. They do so frequently, making a housing transaction every few years. These cost of these transactions (like the 5% sales commission, tax and legal fees) becomes significant (perhaps 0.5 to 1.0% annually). Tax write-offs on financing housing help a little, but not that much.

- It is not that you cannot view a house and house finance as a prudent investment strategy. For example, if you refinance from a 30-year to a 15-year mortgage, the gain of 15 years of rent free housing (in accounting terms, prepaying an expense) may more than offset the higher earlier payments under the 15-year mortgage. Of course, an opposite strategy can work depending upon your perception of market returns. If the longer mortgage is at a modest rate and you believe you can invest funds in a non-housing investment (like a mutual fund) at greater than the mortgage rate, then you should keep a relatively large mortgage.

- During the 1990s and early 2000s average people came to view housing as an appreciating asset but in reality it is a depreciating asset.

- Housing purchased for the purpose of renting obviously constitutes an investment. One current development that may enhance housing as investment and cash flow generator for homeowners is online marketplaces for renting homes like Airbnb.

# II.10. Monetary Theory & Policy: Old & New

Monetary policy is the managing and setting of money supplies and/or interest rates by a central bank mainly to foster stable economic growth. The control of money supplies and interest rates constitute the tools to adjust availability and price of credit. Specific tools and goals of monetary policy are hard to define, though, since they are largely peculiar to prevailing macroeconomic conditions, or the perception of conditions. Monetary policy can be mostly passive, like during the 1950s and the 1990s, or it can be hyperactive, in response to crises or major fluctuations in markets or the economy, like in the early 1980s or in the period 2008 to today.

It is peculiar that we call the field "Monetary Economics" or "Monetary Policy" considering the following: (1) Interest rates (or exchange rates for some countries) are the (much more) focal quantity in monetary policy compared to money supplies and/or (2) What we are really trying to control is the amount of credit in society. Credit levels, which determine spending, commerce, risk taking, asset values, interest rates, etc., are affected by money but also by stocks, bonds and other assets. We should call it "Interest Rate Theory" or even "Credit Theory." To a large extent the Monetary terminology is just tradition and descriptive of how the economy used to be. Historically, money, defined as M1 or M2, was seen as the key determinant of credit and thus economic activity. This was the way the economy was in the 1950s when M&M textbooks were being developed. Then, even as we switched to determining interest rates we still envisioned the task as being dependent on money. We changed rates by changing bank reserves (i.e., money). Finally, credit is a hard quantity to understand. It is hard to measure. Even if we can measure it, it is difficult to control, including both creating more credit or forestalling its creation. Presently, since interest rates have been at very low levels for many years and our monetary policy has hit low interest rate bounds you can take one more step and deem that our M&M policy is largely the maintenance of confidence in our economic future. Perhaps, we could call the course "Credit and Macroeconomic Confidence Theory."

The next major facet of M&M is the policy "tools," which we define loosely and which different analysts talk about in different ways. Also, the nature of the tools has changed dramatically since 2008. Tools can mean specific items, like discount lending or open market operations or broader sets of items and concepts, like wealth effects and forward guidance. We are hard-pressed to state a formal set of tools. In his March 2012 series of college lectures Ben Bernanke defined three tools: (1) traditional monetary policy designed to stabilize the economy, (2) lender of last resort role designed to keep the financial system from collapsing and (3) regulation. A similar lecture given before 2008 would have only mentioned the first two.

In textbooks you will also see M&M policy devices other than tools including instruments, targets, intermediate targets, goals and objectives. The term instruments is similar to tools and includes the target fed funds rate (or you might say, open market operations), discount rate, deposit rate and reserve requirement. Today though, we have new tools like quantitative easing, communication and the repo market interest rate. The goals or objectives are clearer: They are the real economy, including GDP and employment, and also price level/inflation and maybe even interest rates. Inflation is also called a target. Targets are items that we want to achieve or want to control to achieve some goal. For example, we talk about targets like nominal GDP or unemployment. Intermediate targets are also usually items to help achieve a target or goal. Intermediate targets are money supplies, the growth rates of money supplies and interest rates beyond the fed funds rate. Intermediate targets are determined by instruments like the fed funds rate and the Monetary Base, which the central bank directly controls. Intermediate targets are not strictly directly by the central bank though. Items can have very different designations depending on context. For example, in textbooks interest rates are instruments, as if we do not care about them except

**Maximize Utility**
© Christopher M. McHugh

**Page 201**

that they affect something we do care about—like GDP. Some analysts define interest rates as the goals or objectives themselves though. For example, low, long-term interest rates are a goal. In summary, M&M policy and rhetoric involves a variety of different concepts that are spoken of in different ways and this imprecision has become even more unstructured since 2008. For example, we still talk about the fed funds rate as the main tool of the Fed today but it has become nearly defunct. Conversely, we seem to have a goal of maintaining high asset wealth, including high stock market and bonds market valuations. We never phrase it that way.

## II.10.A. Pre-2008 Tools & Parables

M&M thinking was simpler prior to 2008. From about the mid-1980s through 2008 we believed strongly in short-run effects of monetary policy as done through the tool of open market operations to control the fed funds rate. The ultimate goal was to keep inflation low and stable to keep long-term interest rates low. Our monetary policy revolved around minor movements of that single target rate.

The way that our central bank achieved short-run effects was through open market operations to change the fed funds rate. A tyro would say the Fed "sets the interest rate," and an even simpler statement would be that the Fed "prints money." The first statement is more valid; the second is true in principle. In reality, the central bank would change the amount of reserves held by banks by buying and selling bonds of banks. For example, if the central bank bought bonds it would give reserves to banks. The banks would have more reserves to lend and would lend at lower rates. Then, the lower rates would affect the economy. In classrooms we talked about banks' reserves getting passed around in a multiplied fashion through the economy: the so-called money multiplier. This was a parable to describe how low rates worked, but it is not literally true. The lowering of the fed funds rate would result in lower rates in other markets, like bond markets generating more lending there; but lending may or may not have involved any more demand for money. One facet of the inculcation and the real world is that, strictly speaking, the central bank could only control either money or interest rates, not both. Either it sets the interest rate and lets the money supply fluctuate to accommodate that rate, or it sets the money supply and lets the interest rate form around that. We chose to control interest rates and let the amount of money fluctuate.

Money supply itself is a bit of a misnomer. It is not simply coin and cash but rather a set of money used for transactions. Long ago, before innovations in holding money like money market funds and sweep accounts, economists focused on M1. Indeed, up until about 1970, checking accounts, which were the main component of M1, did constitute the way many common transactions were done like any payments made by mail and most big purchases. Starting in the 1960s and playing out in the 1970s, innovations in money and banking made it so that people could move money easily between savings and checking accounts and later between bank accounts and other financial holdings (like stocks and bonds). Economists widened their focus for money to M2, which included M1 and savings accounts (including money market funds). M2 was not very useful though for tracking the amount of credit and commerce because people could increasingly easily move their financial resources in and out of less liquid holdings like stocks. Ultimately the usefulness of both M1 and M2 as monetary aggregates that reflected transactions—and therefore economic activity—weakened. The basic idea that the central bank would watch M1 or M2 and make sure they did not grow too much lest we get inflation became impossible to rely upon. For example, during the 1970s M2 rose but we did not know if it reflected too much money chasing the same goods (and therefore inflation), or if the economy was weak and that people were taking their money out of stocks and putting it into M2.

## II.10.A.a.The Three Tools

For decades, instructors of M&M would recite that the Fed had three tools: (1) changing reserve requirements; (2) discount lending and (3) open market operations. A good instructor would immediately relegate the first two as sideshows generally never utilized in the modern era. Incidentally, we occasionally did significant discount lending, notably in 1987 and in 2001. The third tool was our bread and butter, (supposedly) done with repeated success and relative precision from about the time of Paul Volcker through Alan Greenspan. Fed funds targeting would involve setting a target for the fed funds rate, which would be achieved with sufficient open market operations to maintain the "effective" fed funds (that rate determined in the market) rate at or near the target. Open market operations are the buying and selling of securities by the Fed, historically almost exclusively treasury securities. For example, when the Fed buys securities it gives money to banks in exchange for banks' treasury bonds. Through open market operations, the Fed can move the fed funds rate. The rest of the story is that changes in the fed funds rate trickle through to other rates, at which lending for consumption and investment is done.

The beauty of changing the fed funds rate was that it gave a potent monetary policy effect (again, supposedly)—without meddling in economic contracts and commitments of private parties. The solitary private market we manipulated (the fed funds market) was perceived as a market that, even if distorted by government interference to some extent, represented only short-term lending among banks and not distortion of economic decisions by private agents like consumers and businesses. Our government policy would, therefore, not be in the business of directly setting car loan, mortgage or corporate bond rates or otherwise commanding financial institutions on how to manage their activities. Open market operations were minimal, non-compulsive and non-invasive. This is similar to the notion that you could control all aspects of your teenager's behavior by merely changing his weekly allowance.

Did it ever work as in the textbook? Did the little changes really transmit through to the greater economy? It is impossible to say for sure but magnitude, timing and dominance of other forces make it tough to believe in policy. For one, policy magnitudes were minor. Another odd circumstance is that parties other than the Fed could buy and sell treasuries, ostensibly assuming the role of the Fed, by creating credit outside the reserve system. The "shadow banking community," non-bank financial institutions outside of the Fed system, could lend much larger amounts of money than the Fed ever did. Another leakage was the international sector. For example, the Chinese could take the copious dollars earned from export and buy treasuries from, in part, U.S. banks. Therefore, non-Fed players could have changed as much credit in the economy as the Fed did.

## II.10.A.b. Money

Experts and laymen invoke the term money offhand—for example, "the Fed is putting money out there" or "they're printing money" or "flooding the system with money." You also hear the term in pronouncements made at the highest levels of authority: Economists cite authoritative Milton Friedman's proclamation that inflation is, "always and everywhere a monetary phenomenon." Yet an odd aspect of M&M is that, in a way, money as we think of it is not an important quantity.

Our teaching about money is imprecise and archaic. We theorize money demand and supply. Demand for money depends on need for money for transactions but also on interest rates and returns to other assets. This is the way Keynes talked about it in the 1930s, and we still model money demand that way in textbooks. It is valid in a blunt way, but we cannot determine how much money of whatever definition (cash, M1, M2) will be churning through the economy based on returns to other assets. The money supply story is even simpler: Our money supply is set by the Fed. At any point there is a given quantity of money; then, the Fed can give (or take) reserves to banks by buying (or selling) banks' bonds and increasing (or decreasing) the supply of money. We contend that supply and demand clear the market for money. As you can figure, the clearing of the money market is pretty imprecise. Money enters various M&M models, like IS/LM, where we hypothesize a tradeoff in a portfolio of money and bonds. In all these M&M models though, money is only abstractly defined. Similarly, despite all the data we have on monetary quantities in empirical study, we have always had a tough time simply deciding which money aggregate constitutes the money we want to quantify and control. Back in the 1960s and 1970s, economists focused on M1 as money; but M1 became irrelevant to many transactions and was never successful in modeling the macroeconomy. We shifted to M2 (which adds savings deposits and retail money market accounts to M1), but by the 1990s M2 was not closely related to important quantities like inflation. In the great days of building M&M theories we even hypothesized and collected data on broader aggregates (like M3), but that quantity was so hard to pin and contained little information and the U.S. Fed discontinued the collection of M3 data in 2006. Explaining money to current college students is difficult because they themselves rarely use the economist's type of money. They use debit or credit cards, and many do not even have a checking account.

Defining and measuring essential "money" continues to be difficult. Do we want a money that is used for transactions (i.e., money that "satisfies a final payment") or do we want a money that represents a level of general credit? Historically, economists have attempted to get the right measure of money, with traditionalists sticking with M1, while other analysts include all liquid assets. About the only aspect economists agree on is that demand deposits are part of money. If we define money as a medium that makes for final payments in transactions then a credit card payment is not money in this sense because it does not make the final payment for the purchased good or service. If we define money as anything that enables us to purchase in the form of credit then stocks, bonds and even real estate can be money. For example, if my stocks go up I can sell them in an instant and wire that money, or even use that money as collateral to make a major purchase like a car.

Below is the first page of the Federal Reserve's "Money Stock Measures" (H.6) as of November 3, 2016. It reports monthly levels of M1 and M2. These money aggregates represent amounts from an accumulation of transactions done over time in the economy. M1 and M2 are not the same as the "money" which the central bank initially created. M1 and M2 result from the repeated lending and re-lending of funds, including cash and reserves, originally provided into the banking system by the central bank. The central bank creates cash and reserves. The reserves can be turned into cash. The reserves and cash, taken together, constitute the Monetary Base or High-Powered money. This is the quantity that spending and borrowing are originated from. In H.6 cash is reported on a following page but reserves are found on the Fed balance sheet (we have a Fed balance sheet later). Many amateur economists confuse M1 (or M2), the Monetary Base, cash and reserves, and how those quantities relate to inflation. For example, amateurs say that the Fed is printing money, that inflation tracks very closely with the change in the amount of money, etc. but such statements are imprecise. The Fed creates reserves which can be made into cash. Or, the reserves can remain as reserves. M1 or M2 can increase, or not increase, depending on how much lending and re-lending is done by banks regardless of whether or not the central bank changes reserves. Inflation may or may not occur. For example, from October 2014 through September 2016 M1 went from $2.875 trillion to $3.318 trillion or an increase of about 15%. Inflation rose only about 4% over that period and real GDP growth was only about 4%. The idea that change in money equals inflation applies to hyperinflation economies where, for example, if money supply increased by 1000% the inflation rate would be proportionally close to 1000%. In an economy like that of the U.S. the tracking is not that close.

H.6 (508)   MONEY STOCK MEASURES

Table 1
Money Stock Measures
Billions of dollars

For release at 4:30 p.m. Eastern Time
November 3, 2016

| Date | Seasonally adjusted | | Not seasonally adjusted | |
|------|------|------|------|------|
| | M1[1] | M2[2] | M1[1] | M2[2] |
| 2014-Oct. | 2,874.9 | 11,539.9 | 2,861.2 | 11,506.6 |
| Nov. | 2,886.0 | 11,577.3 | 2,857.3 | 11,582.7 |
| Dec. | 2,930.2 | 11,646.9 | 2,988.2 | 11,728.0 |
| 2015-Jan. | 2,930.7 | 11,706.7 | 2,937.3 | 11,726.9 |
| Feb. | 2,964.8 | 11,803.3 | 2,975.8 | 11,815.4 |
| Mar. | 2,990.7 | 11,839.2 | 3,020.1 | 11,925.4 |
| Apr. | 2,994.6 | 11,890.9 | 3,031.6 | 11,973.6 |
| May | 2,988.6 | 11,927.8 | 2,971.9 | 11,876.9 |
| June | 3,015.0 | 11,975.2 | 3,016.7 | 11,931.4 |
| July | 3,034.2 | 12,036.1 | 3,035.1 | 11,983.0 |
| Aug. | 3,041.2 | 12,100.4 | 3,018.8 | 12,040.5 |
| Sept. | 3,055.5 | 12,157.7 | 3,014.7 | 12,110.3 |
| Oct. | 3,031.8 | 12,180.7 | 3,012.5 | 12,145.5 |
| Nov. | 3,083.4 | 12,266.3 | 3,054.5 | 12,269.8 |
| Dec. | 3,079.7 | 12,313.5 | 3,139.2 | 12,399.8 |
| 2016-Jan. | 3,091.0 | 12,436.5 | 3,093.8 | 12,453.9 |
| Feb. | 3,104.0 | 12,485.2 | 3,098.1 | 12,498.3 |
| Mar. | 3,144.5 | 12,572.7 | 3,177.8 | 12,664.9 |
| Apr. | 3,176.8 | 12,652.4 | 3,213.1 | 12,743.3 |
| May | 3,224.8 | 12,728.8 | 3,209.5 | 12,672.5 |
| June | 3,231.1 | 12,803.6 | 3,232.0 | 12,757.2 |
| July | 3,225.1 | 12,878.0 | 3,223.9 | 12,822.6 |
| Aug. | 3,312.4 | 12,986.9 | 3,292.6 | 12,923.9 |
| Sept. | 3,317.9 | 13,060.9 | 3,272.8 | 13,009.5 |

| Percent change at seasonally adjusted annual rates | M1 | M2 |
|------|------|------|
| 3 Months from June 2016 TO Sept. 2016 | 10.7 | 8.0 |
| 6 Months from Mar. 2016 TO Sept. 2016 | 11.0 | 7.8 |
| 12 Months from Sept. 2015 TO Sept. 2016 | 8.6 | 7.4 |

Components may not add to totals due to rounding.

1. M1 consists of (1) currency outside the U.S. Treasury, Federal Reserve Banks, and the vaults of depository institutions; (2) traveler's checks of nonbank issuers; (3) demand deposits at commercial banks (excluding those amounts held by depository institutions, the U.S. government, and foreign banks and official institutions) less cash items in the process of collection and Federal Reserve float; and (4) other checkable deposits (OCDs), consisting of negotiable order of withdrawal (NOW) and automatic transfer service (ATS) accounts at depository institutions, credit union share draft accounts, and demand deposits at thrift institutions. Seasonally adjusted M1 is constructed by summing currency, traveler's checks, demand deposits, and OCDs, each seasonally adjusted separately.
2. M2 consists of M1 plus (1) savings deposits (including money market deposit accounts); (2) small-denomination time deposits (time deposits in amounts of less than $100,000), less individual retirement account (IRA) and Keogh balances at depository institutions; and (3) balances in retail money market mutual funds, less IRA and Keogh balances at money market mutual funds. Seasonally adjusted M2 is constructed by summing savings deposits, small-denomination time deposits, and retail money funds, each seasonally adjusted separately, and adding this result to seasonally adjusted M1.

## II.10.A.c. Increasing the Size of the Fed Balance Sheet

The source of a central bank's effectiveness, indeed its magic, is that it can write IOU's that will be honored as valuable. The circulation and re-circulation of these IOU's will expand commerce—in theory, many more times than the initial infusion. The Fed's (we'll use this central bank) IOU's are either cash or, more typically, bank reserves. A private party (like a company or a person) cannot create such credit, supposedly. For example, if a company issues more stock, it will face dilution (not including the unlikely case that the company's earnings increase due to the very issuance of the stock). I suppose an individual can issue an IOU. If people accept it, we have increased the money supply and the amount of credit in our world. In practical terms that does not happen—and it is also against the law. Ergo, only the Fed can increase the amount of credit or, as we say, "increase the size of the balance sheet."

Another monetary concept most relevant to M&M theory but also hard to convey in lecture and easily misrepresented is high-powered money or the Monetary Base (the "Base"). The Base is made up of bank reserves (the accounts banks have with the Fed) and cash (paper money and coin). We can measure the Base pretty accurately. For decades up until about 2008, bank reserves were minimal: in the billions to tens of billions of dollars. Cash, through the 1990s into the 2000s has been in the hundreds of billions, more lately in the high hundreds. For example on December 31, 2007, the Base was made up of about $826 billion cash and $6 billion reserves for a total of $832 billion. You can probably surmise that the Base did not change much year over year (until recently), except to the extent cash changes. Although it historically constituted most of the Base, cash, oddly, is mostly unrelated to the essential purpose of the

Base. Cash is mostly used for transactions and, to some extent, in the case of the U.S. dollar, as a store of value in countries with high inflation. Cash is also a liability to the central bank, but one that is never called against the bank because it is used mostly for transactions. The pivotal component is the Base because the changes in the Base, in theory, control the changes in reserves; and changes in reserves can result in changes in lending activity and subsequently economic activity.

For decades in M&M instruction and up until about 2008, we talked about the importance of the Base even though the amount of bank reserves and their changes (about 10 billion on average in any monetary policy maneuver) did not have great heft. Then, within about one year over the latter part of 2008 through 2009, reserves ballooned to a trillion dollars, more than doubling the Base but increasing the reserves portion of the Base about 100-fold.

Such a large increase has confounded many of the pronouncements made by economics teachers for decades. One facet is that many commentators confuse M1 and the Base (or M1 and reserves). M1 is the money aggregate that if increased greatly should create inflation. M1 will not increase simply because the Base has increased; the new bank reserves must be loaned out. M1 is the result of the lending of Base. In the episode of 2008, right-wingers said the increase in the Base would result in inflation, yet it did not. Policy proponents like Ben Bernanke pronounced that no new money was printed. One irony is that the original intention of our monetary policy under Ben Bernanke was that the additions to the Base would be loaned out and contribute to stimulating the economy. That never happened though. In other words, for our monetary policy of 2009 and 2010 to have worked as originally intended, money should have been created, i.e., eventually printed.

Another aspect of money analysis is that the impact of money levels depends on the speed at which money changes hands in transactions. This is called velocity and is represented by the symbol V in economic models, like $MV = PQ$ (which we will discuss later). Some economists say that, although it is hard to know the exact value of V, it is somewhat stable over time. If V is stable a change in money will bring about a change in nominal GDP (the PQ in the equation). V is not stable and changes substantially when the economy is fluctuating. For example, V dropped precipitously in 2008 and following.

### T-Account Analysis

In the classroom we demonstrate expansion of the Fed's balance sheet using T-Accounts, one for the Fed and one or two for the other integral players in the economy (the "banks" and the "public"). The line items in the T-Accounts needed for this exercise are few. In fact, we can demonstrate the essence of monetary policy (perhaps the most powerful economic force on the planet) with T-Accounts having only two line items: (1) "Securities," meaning U.S. treasuries on the asset side and (2) "Reserves," meaning bank reserves (a liability to the Fed) on the liability side:

**Federal Reserve Balance Sheet**

| *Assets* | *Liabilities* |
| --- | --- |
| Securities | Reserves |

Our Fed also has Currency on the liability side, but it is/was an item not critical to the story of increasing the size of the balance sheet. M&M textbook might also have Loans on the asset side, representing the Fed's role in discount lending. This is another of the three traditional tools of monetary policy, but it is very secondary to open market operations. The Fed balance sheet's basic manipulation is represented below. The balance sheet of commercial banks, "Banking System," must be added. The Fed buys a security (usually a treasury security) from a bank and gives the bank reserves, which the bank can then lend. This is the open market operation:

## Case of *Increase* in Size of Balance Sheet

| Federal Reserve Balance Sheet | | | |
|---|---|---|---|
| *Assets* | | *Liabilities* | |
| Securities | +1 | Reserves | +1 |

| Banking System Balance Sheet | | | |
|---|---|---|---|
| *Assets* | | *Liabilities* | |
| Reserves | +1 | | |
| Securities | -1 | | |

Here the Fed has increased reserves and therefore loanable money by expanding its balance sheet. This can result in more economic activity. The key is that the Fed has created a credible IOU. Supposedly, only the Fed can achieve this creation of money/credit. In contrast, for example, if I withdraw money from my bank account to create economic activity, my action will not create credit. I can only alter the composition of what credit was already in the system. I receive cash but my bank has less reserves, so it has to decrease lending. Here is a textbook case to demonstrate that point:

## Case of *No Increase* in Size of Balance Sheet

| Non-Bank Public Balance Sheet | | | |
|---|---|---|---|
| *Assets* | | *Liabilities* | |
| Currency | +1 | | |
| Demand Deposits | -1 | | |

| Banking System Balance Sheet | | | |
|---|---|---|---|
| *Assets* | | *Liabilities* | |
| Reserves | -1 | Demand Deposits | -1 |

| Federal Reserve Balance Sheet | | | |
|---|---|---|---|
| *Assets* | | *Liabilities* | |
| | | Currency | +1 |
| | | Reserves | -1 |

We invoke the money multiplier to complete the expansionary policy narrative of affecting the economy in a magnified way given a change in reserves. We assume that banks are "fully loaned up" and have a book of loans ready to be made when they get the additional reserves. Therefore, they readily lend the money. That money then gets into the pocketbooks of people and businesses who deposit it in their own banks, such that more reserves appear in the banking system. These reserves get loaned out, and so on—and ultimately the economy experiences a multiplied effect of credit and spending. The story is valid as a parable, but hardly describes the real world and the constraints and forces of credit. For one thing, banks view reserves and securities similarly and already lend against their securities. Therefore open market operations do not increase the size of the pool of loanable funds, just the composition. Another flaw in the story is that entities outside the banking system can create credit. Also, for the story to work banks must be fully loaned up and must lend any additional reserves. Another odd aspect of the analysis, at least how it is done in a classroom, is that the multiplier effects require the existence of different banks in the banking system. If there is only one bank and the first borrower deposits his proceeds in that one bank, the multiple effects will not happen.

Referring to the first case of the increase in the Fed balance sheet by an open market operation, I would often tease monetary economics students that we could do the entire course in 15 minutes on the first day of class. We would demonstrate the open market operation using a T-account with the two requisite items. We would utilize the multiplier concept and claim that lower rates from the new credit would "transmit" to other lending and borrowing in the economy, which would result in spending, jobs, investment, etc. We would not describe transmission though, instead taking it on faith. The story of M&M before the year 2008 was a parsimonious theory engendering an effective outcome.[119] In the last few decades, the Fed created reserves pretty much exclusively with open market operations. Initially, in the 2008 crisis, the Fed performed conventional policy until the fed funds rate got to near zero. Then, later in 2008, the Fed engaged in unconventional policy, primarily quantitative easing ("QE"), which is the granting of reserves to banks and other financial services companies by buying those companies' various securities including treasuries, mortgage-backed securities and federal agency debt securities (Fannie Mae and Freddie Mac debt).

Getting a little ahead of our story, with QE reserves grew greatly (to trillions of dollars from amounts that historically hovered around $10 billion). The Fed balance sheet grew dramatically demonstrating that the Fed can increase its balance sheet. Of course, whether or not there was a cost or a tradeoff to such expansion (or whether or not the Fed's action created net economic benefits in credit and lending) is more difficult to ascertain. Policy proponents contend that in 2008 and 2009 Fed balance sheet expansion saved the economy from collapse by keeping the financial system liquid and open for business, without additionally diluting the currency or bankrupting the Fed or the U.S. government. Others argue that the Fed merely transferred assets and gave the appearance of adding credit to the system. Before expanding the balance sheet, the Fed had a balance sheet with about one trillion in assets offset by about one trillion in cash, a liability that would never be called. Now, the Fed has multiple trillions on each side of its balance sheet including trillions of poorer quality bonds on the asset side, offset by over two trillion in reserves (a quantity the Fed owes or must be ready to print money for). Before expansion, the Fed had virtually no credit risk, but now it does. The new large Fed balance sheet is viewed as innocuous by some economists. Others perceive it as holding potentially unsound debt that might have to be monetized. Naysayers contend that the Fed bought U.S. and mortgage-backed debt that might not have had willing buyers without the Fed presence. It cannot sell it back without disrupting financial markets and must wait years for the bond holdings to mature and be paid off, or print currency to honor it. They also like to point out that the mortgage-backed debt is ultimately backed by the U.S.

### II.10.A.d. The Transmission Mechanism & Its Channels

How does monetary policy impact real economic activity, i.e., $Y = C + I + G$? When the Fed does stimulative policy through open market operations it buys bonds from banks and gives banks reserves. The

---

[119] Another version of teasing monetary economics students is that the course could be completed in one class. First, devote about fifteen minutes demonstrating the time value of money and another fifteen minutes showing how the value of bonds, stocks and other financial claims depend on discounting their flows of payments. Then assert (in one minute) that a central bank can change the discount rate for asset valuation by changing its policy rate, the fed funds rate. In another fifteen-minute burst, demonstrate how open market operations (like above) effect the change in the fed funds rate by changing reserves that banks can lend. Then, contend that the lower rates and greater reserves constitute greater credit which gets multiplied through the financial system due to fractional reserve banking. Finally, in about another fifteen minutes develop the Taylor Rule which dictates the target level for the fed funds rate as a function of inflation and employment/GDP.

added reserves directly and initially lower the fed funds rate. Other short rates, like treasury bill rates and LIBOR, move in the same direction. Then, presumably over a longer period, rates like car loan rates, mortgage rates, corporate bond rates, etc. also change. Economists call this monetary transmission. A statement of overall transmission is: (1) Fed makes a policy decision; (2) the fed funds rate is altered; (3) other rates and financial conditions change; (4) consumers and investors act; and (5) employment and price level are changed. Economists sub-divide this general transmission into specific paths of cause and effect. These are referred to as channels and they include the following:

- **Interest Rate Channel**: Lower rates contribute to investment spending and consumption. This is the traditional Keynesian transmission channel. It is theoretically prominent, yet empirically it is considered weak both for investment and household consumption.
- **Balance Sheet (Business) Channel**: Lower rates improve the balance sheets of companies, making them more likely to take on new projects. Also lower rates make interest payments lower increasing the profitability of firms and causing them to expand.
- **Balance Sheet (Household) Channel**: Lower rates make people's assets more valuable so they feel wealthier and spend more. They also have greater collateral to borrow against, and lenders are more willing to lend to wealthier households.
- **Bank Lending Channel**: Lower rates reflect higher bank reserves, resulting in more bank lending. Banks are viewed as important lenders especially to small business.
- **Bank Lending (other variety) Channel**: Lower rates increase net interest margins for banks, which increases banks' lending and profitability; lower rates raise the value of assets (including those held by banks).
- **Asset Values Channel**: Lower rates create higher asset values to securities such as stocks, making portfolio holders feel wealthier.
- **Portfolio Balance Channel**: Lower rates in assets bought by the central bank changes the mix of assets held by private agents.
- **Foreign Exchange or Exchange Rate Channel**: Lower rates mean less demand for assets in your currency, which results in depressing currency value and causing exports to increase.
- **Housing Channel (a New Channel)**: Lower rates mean higher housing prices, leading to wealth effects.
- **Wealth Channel**: Lower rates means a lower discount rate for assets which means assets have higher values. Demand for assets including bonds and equities increases and asset wealth increases and spending increases.
- **Reach for Yield Channel (a New Variety of the Portfolio Balance Channel)**: Lower rates compel private parties to seek higher yields by buying riskier securities like high-yield bonds. In particular, the economic effects of high-yield debt are considered extensive because this debt finances companies that supposedly create numerous jobs, like casinos and energy companies.
- **Expectations or Confidence "Channel"**: Some textbooks or other analyses term these as channels of transmission, as if monetary policy creates effects through them. This may be valid, but they themselves only engender effects through other channels.
- **Signaling "Channels"**: This is not a common channel, but in recent times many analysts contend that extreme monetary policy works through pure signaling effects. Lower rates or other policy maneuvers effect the economy by signaling intentions, economic assessments and possible future policy of the central bank.

Each M&M instructor will emphasize one channel or another—or typically explain current policy in terms of a solitary one. An old-school Keynesian would emphasize interest rate changes as affecting C and I and would lecture students that the Fed lowers rates and people buy more cars and companies open more factories. A proponent of recent Fed policy would talk about general wealth effects or portfolio rebalancing. A believer in the preeminent role of banks would talk about the bank lending channel. However, here are some of the shortcomings of the conventional channels:

- Channels work in opposite directions and causes substantial feedback against each other. For example, accommodative policy will produce more investment in a country due to lower interest rates (interest rate channel) but will incentivize investors to move money to foreign assets to get higher yields. This is part of the foreign exchange channel.

- The channels represent initial effects. For example, accommodative policy might initially cause the net interest margin for bank lending (borrowing in short-term markets and lending in long-term) to increase and result in more lending by banks, but then long-term rates should converge causing the margin to tighten.

- Channels' effects can fail to meet expectations. For example, during 2015 and 2016 certain central banks lowered rates into negative ranges but the ostensible effects were generally the opposite of what theories implied since markets already expected sizable rate lowerings.

- Channels are countered by the actions of other central banks. For example, a rate lowering by one nation is offset by a foreign exchange intervention by another central bank.

- Traditional channels may apply only to earlier times (like the 1950s through the 1970s) when households' and businesses' balance sheets were less accustomed to manipulation.

- Channels are attenuated by time and hard to assess in terms of magnitude. For example, wealth effects are small, vary over time and may take a long while to play out.

- Traditional channels are merely stories of cause and effect and other plausible and more contemporary channels could be proposed. For example, if interest rates goes down a household might feel wealthier but it also receives less interest income. We could hypothesize the following:

  ➤ **Household Interest Income Channel**: Households have less income following an interest rate cut and, therefore, spend less.

  ➤ **Pension Funding Channel**: Rate cuts cause pension funds to use lower discount rates for their liabilities. Therefore, pensions must receive greater funding, which means corporate profits and government tax revenues must be devoted to pensions and not to investment, dividends or spending.

  ➤ **Household Retirement Saving Channel**: Low rates make households realize that they will not get as much return to their savings so they save more (not spend more) to attain retirement goals.

  ➤ **Corporate Refinance Channel**: Low rates make corporations exchange high coupon debt for low coupon debt. This action may give corporations greater net earnings to hire and invest, or it may enable unprofitable corporations that really should shut down to continue inefficient operations.

  ➤ **Labor Substitution Channel**: Low rates incentivize businesses to substitute now-cheaper capital (like robots) in place of labor.

Economists continue to test transmission to isolate either the primary channel or some set of channels that clearly create effects of monetary policy. It is a tough task.

## II.10.B. New M&M Policies & the Expanded Role of the Fed

On a Sunday evening on May 1, 2011, America awaited a special news conference by the President. I was already certain that he would announce some dramatic new M&M policy initiative. Perhaps the Fed would be issuing a new currency, maybe blue, to replace our existing currency. Or maybe our government would announce a new sub-unit of the Fed or U.S. Treasury that would hold select securities or engage in special management of some sector of the financial system. I envisioned President Obama handing the podium over to then-Fed Chairman Ben Bernanke who would say something like, "We worked over the weekend…so that when financial markets opened on Monday we could ensure a smooth transition to a new chapter in the financial history of America." It turned out I was wrong. The announcement was the assassination of arch-terrorist Osama bin Laden, but my hunch was not implausible. Over the period 2008 through today, our central bank in conjunction with other federal government branches, has engaged in a wide variety of economic policy actions, many of which would have been considered fanciful pre-2008. These new tools were termed unconventional policies and went under monikers like quantitative easing, credit easing, policy duration commitment, directed lending and asset purchases. The Fed has assumed control of certain financial markets and companies, loaned large amounts to foreigners, held interest rates at zero for a long time, flattened the yield curve, expanded regulation, embarked on major forays into measuring systemic risk and pronouncing the existence or non-existence of bubbles, etc.

The unconventional policy played out initially in 2008 and 2009. Circa late 2009, after a first wave appeared to have sufficiently put the economy back on track, we talked about another set of new tools intended to undo the expansionary tools and remove money from the system. These include reverse repos, paying interest on reserves, term deposits, asset sales and issuing a new Fed liability. These tools became known as "Exit Strategies," representing the reversing of the original expansionary policy. For a while, in late 2009 and early 2010, the perception was that the Fed was at the point of commencing an Exit Strategy. Since the economy continued to look weak around summer 2010, the Fed abandoned Exit and did more large-scale asset purchases. New policies were broached like Operation Twist (a program of exchanging short- for long-term U.S. debt commenced by the U.S. Fed in 2011) and were continued for years.

As we embarked on these new policies, Fed officials and the press described them as tools, each serving a different function. The different monetary tools could be applied at differing times with varying effects on different sectors and each specially addressing some economic circumstance. Both Fed officials and the media exhibit a belief in the idea of a variety of tools and attendant specific applications. All monetary tools, however, including both old and new, generally effect the level of credit and spending in the economy roughly the same. For example, in early 2016 the ECB commenced the purchase of corporate bonds. Like most other central banks, it had previously only purchased sovereign bonds. The new tool of buying corporates was described as having distinct effects in certain markets yet the overall ultimate economic effects were likely roughly the same. Indeed, a directed policy program can shape some specific end. For example, Operation Twist probably resulted in lower long-term bond yields. The net ultimate effects on the economy of this program, however, might have been no different from a program of similar magnitude utilizing some other tool or policy action.

The toolbox analogy might sound apropos—pick the device for the specific economic task or market–but one fundamental problem with having "many tools" is that it detracts from the original simple and powerful idea that the central bank used a single, non-invasive and small magnitude tool: the fed funds rate. The existence of numerous and large magnitude tools describes a central bank that takes over the system rather than nudges it. Of the New Tools described below, some have actually been implemented by the U.S. Fed. Others have been spoken about as potentially used by the Fed, but not yet applied (like negative interest rates). Some have only been broached by economists and pundits but neither officially engaged in nor even intellectually endorsed by the Fed. Examples of the last group include targeting "higher" inflation and doing a "helicopter drop" of money.

As expected, when there are many schemes they will tend to bump into each other or contradict others. For example, Operation Twist would flatten the yield curve. This subverts the longstanding belief that a highly-sloped yield curve reflects a healthy economy. Now the new tools have become consummate, and they displace the quaint idea of real effects through transmission. Policy becomes a con game: The people must believe in the Fed for the Fed to have effects. Finally, as new tools developed some become defunct before they ever become part of new textbooks. For example, in the years following 2008, topics like (the original) quantitative easing Exit Strategy, draining facilities for excess reserves, term deposits, corridor systems of interest rate management, etc. never transpired as planned in the real world and ultimately became defunct.

## II.10.B.a. Crisis Response & the End of the Fed Funds Target Rate

Pursuant to the crisis of 2007 to 2008, the Fed lowered its main policy rate (the fed funds rate) until by December 2008 the fed funds target rate hit near zero (more technically, in a range between zero and one-quarter of one percent). Virtually nobody at that time would have guessed that the rate would have stayed at near zero for years. During the years following hitting the zero rate, the Fed engaged in a policy of promising to keep the rate low first for a short time and later for a long time. Eventually the basic statement was that the rate would stay low indefinitely. The fed funds rate cleared at various levels, typically around 17 basis points. Since the Fed simultaneously paid 25 basis points on reserves held by banks (the "Deposit Rate"), lending diminished greatly in the fed funds market. This was largely lending done by entities (like Fannie Mae and Freddie Mac) who did not have access to the Deposit Rate.

The Fed embarked on unconventional monetary policy initiatives. The FOMC, which had long focused mainly on the setting of the fed funds rate, now assumed a whole host of different roles, including portfolio manager, business planner, regulator, trouble-shooter, housing policy maker, market psychologist, etc. Long gone were the days when the FOMC[120] would decide to lower (or raise) the target rate by a small amount and instruct the open markets operations desk in New York to buy and sell a few billion dollars of bonds to achieve that goal. In the years before 2008, hundreds of billions of dollars were borrowed and loaned in the interbank market (the fed funds market) and the Fed could change the market clearing rate with small amounts of buying or selling. Interbank lending dropped to about $100 billion in 2010 and has continued to decrease. For years, the Fed planned a prompt return to the interbank market with the old policy method and its effects. Finally, in December 2015 we made a first step into raising the fed funds rate. However, that raising had to be accompanied by other rate changes since the fed funds market still no longer formed the constraint it used to. We may never return to old style fed funds targeting.

Also, as part of the 2008 crisis response the Fed utilized its second textbook method of affecting lending: discount lending. This tool, which for years had only been done in modest amounts generally well under a billion dollars per year, was stepped up greatly to hundreds of billions during late 2008. Straight discount lending to banks was not deemed sufficient so the Fed engaged in a variety of new lending facilities and initiatives directed toward specific markets, such as commercial paper, money markets,

---

[120] The Federal Open Market Committee (FOMC) is the Fed body that decides on interest rate policy. The FOMC meets eight times per year in Washington, DC (there can be added meetings) and is made up of voting members that include the members of the Fed Board of Governors, the President of the New York Fed and four regional Fed bank Presidents chosen on a rotating basis. The Fed Board should have seven members making the FOMC twelve, but in recent years Board seats have been vacant.

mortgages, agency debt, etc. (about ten facilities in all). The new lending policies collectively involved magnitudes unlike anything ever done before—in the trillions.

Extreme central banking policies (as implemented in 2008 and 2009) were things that M&M teachers might only have broached in lectures as thought experiments or actions taken by financially weak nations. I do not know any M&M teacher, myself included, who ever thought such actions would happen in the U.S. You might counter that Ben Bernanke himself had lectured and published on extreme policy. For example, he wrote about deflation, helicopter money drops, etc., but these are more simple tributes to the vast number of scholarly papers that are published on virtually every topic. In fact, the most recent time economists pondered the need for a radical new monetary policy tool was in the early 2000s, when the U.S. was running budget surpluses; and it looked as though the supply of treasuries (which the Fed typically used for open market operations) would dry up. If that happened, the Fed would be incapable of doing monetary policy. Therefore, economists seriously discussed the Fed doing unconventional policy to maintain economic effects like buying corporate bonds, mortgage-backed bonds, reducing the value of the dollar or just sending signals of some sort.

Despite that the fed funds market and the fed funds rate have not been the binding constraint in short term money markets or the transmitting rate to long-term rates, we continue to talk about the fed funds rate when we talk about policy. In December 2015 and December 2016, when the Fed engaged in rate raisings, the vast majority of talk in the financial press, and probably in classrooms, cited the fed funds rate as the rate being raised, even though the deposit rate and the rate in reverse repo markets were the true constraints.

## II.10.B.b. Chronology of Events From 2007

Leading up to, during and following the 2008 economic and financial crisis there was an extraordinary multitude of noteworthy M&M events. To attempt to discuss them or even do a detailed timeline would be tedious and time consuming. On the other hand, we cannot ignore this historic episode of new M&M initiatives and government management of many parts of the private economy that accompanied it. As a compromise I highlight major events below and add commentary, including identification of new M&M policy developments. I try to emphasize uncertainty about events and the complex interconnections in the economy and the financial system. Also, it should be noted that from late 2007 through about mid-2009, the notable M&M events were sudden and specific and required rapid trouble-shooting. After 2009, although events of substantial economic magnitude continued, including both economic and non-economic events (like weather, politics, conflict, etc.), they were relatively routine and unrelated to the original acute M&M crisis of 2008. In the period 2010 to present, the M&M events were mainly follow-up effects of the recession, including continuing debt and deficit, weak economies abroad, the realization of deflation, the increase in house and stock prices, the gradual decrease in the unemployment rate, etc. These events are difficult to peg for starting points and magnitudes but are sometimes included on the list below when appropriate.

### 2007

- Through early 2007, apparent problems in the economy, assets prices and borrowing arose. These were initially viewed as manageable or confined to certain parts of the economy notably the subprime mortgage market.

- In June and July 2007, two Bear Stearns hedge funds invested in mortgage-backed securities, each with about one billion dollars in assets, were liquidated. Relatively suddenly, the funds found that good bid prices (prices that securities could currently be sold at) for fund holdings were unavailable. The economy and financial system seemed to weather these failures handily, and they were perceived of as isolated cases of distress rather than systemic problems.
- By August 2007, Countrywide Financial (the large mortgage company that was at the forefront of recent risky mortgages), reported operating and financial problems. Key at this time was the fact that neither the Fed nor the Treasury deemed it important to take this company over. The problems in the economy at that time were not perceived to be too severe.
- On August 9, 2007, three investment funds of French bank BNP Paribas suspended redemptions from the funds. The funds were experiencing difficulty pricing their assets,
- On August 17, 2007, the Fed lowered the discount rate by 0.5%, to 5.75%. Resorting to the discount rate rather than the more influential fed funds reflected the fact that, at that time, we did not view the general economic situation as grave; instead, we perceived that select financial companies were in distress such that only the lender of last resort function of the Fed was appropriate. As of August 2007 the fed funds target rate was 5.25%. On September 18, 2007, the Fed lowered the fed funds rate to 4.75%. By December 2007 the fed funds rate was 4.25%. As we lowered the fed funds rate, we lowered the discount along with it.
- In late 2007 and early 2008 the vast majority of economists still thought that the economy continued to grow and would continue to do so, yet the U.S. was already in recession as of December 2007.
- On December 12, 2007, the Fed announced the Term Auction Facility, a special discount lending program, as well as swap lines with European central banks.

## 2008

- In January 2008, Bank of America bought Countrywide Financial. The deal was completed in July 2008, and the perception was that Bank of America got a bargain.
- By January 2008, the fed funds rate was down to 3%.
- On March 14, 2008, the Fed (in conjunction with JP Morgan) took over Bear Stearns. This maneuver was significant in that the Fed took over a large company—and a non-bank. Many analysts consider this an important action encouraging moral hazard.
- On March 18, 2008, the fed funds rate was lowered to 2.25%.
- The summer of 2008 through the end of 2008 was the crux of the financial and economic crisis. In the summer of 2008, the general feeling was that we would weather this downturn without great economic dislocation as we had other downturns from the last 20 years. The stock market was down about 12% through the first half of 2008, which was significant but not out of the ordinary.[121]
- On September 7, 2008, the U.S. Treasury placed Fannie Mae and Freddie Mac into receivership.
- On September 15, 2008, Bank of America announced its takeover of Merrill Lynch (a once great investment bank and brokerage that was now broke). This buyout of a distressed financial services

---

[121] Half way through 2008 my money management company was having what looked like a routine year. As of the end of June 2008 we were down only 1% for the year and had not seen any exceptional investor capital outflow or concern. In a meeting with a senior executive from our prime broker he congratulated us on "maintaining capital." We accepted the praise and collectively agreed that the latter half of 2008 would be an improvement. We would be down about 28% over the second half of the year and see substantial capital outflow.

firm by a supposedly stronger one was seen as an important part of the desired private solution to our nations' economic woes. Bank of America's purchase was even viewed as an act of magnanimity. Soon after, though, the bank would be prosecuted for various irregularities it partook in before and during the crisis.

- On September 15, 2008, Lehman Brothers filed for bankruptcy. Key here is that this big company was not taken over by the Fed. Leaders at the time contend they were limited in what they could do. Ben Bernanke said that the Fed lacked the legal authority to take over Lehman. Secretary of the Treasury Timothy Geithner thought the collateral behind this company made it ineligible for government support. A better guess is that our leadership determined that they could not bail out every company, and they had to draw a line.

- On September 16, 2008, the day after Lehman is let go, the Fed authorized up to $85 billion to be loaned to insurance company AIG. AIG's failure was deemed potentially damaging to the financial system due to the role of AIG as major counterparty in many derivatives contracts.

- On the same day (September 16, 2008), the Reserve Primary Money Fund (a money market fund), fell in value below $1 (meaning that a dollar in an account was now worth less than a dollar), causing concern that the public would panic at facing a capital loss in such an instrument. Hundreds of billions of dollars were pulled from money market funds.

- On September 17, 2008, the SEC announced a ban of certain short selling. This was perhaps a minor action but one of many emergency government actions to control markets.

- During September 2008, the Fed and federal government continued various takeovers of financial firms. The Fed continued large currency swap lines, which loaned U.S. dollars to foreign banks.

- During the latter half of 2008, stock markets dropped significantly. For example, on September 29, 2008, the Dow Jones dropped 778 points (about 7%) in one day.

- On October 3, 2008, President Bush signed the $700 billion Troubled Asset Relief Program (TARP) into law. This was a U.S. Treasury and not a Fed action, but at this time the Fed and the Treasury were working together closely.

- On October 7, 2008, the Fed created the Commercial Paper Funding Facility.

- On October 8, 2008, the fed funds rate was set to 1.50%.

- On October 21, 2008, the Fed created the Money Market Investor Funding Facility.

- During November 2008, there was a continuation of programs and buyings by the Fed of interests in financial companies. Also, various financial companies restructured as bank holding companies.

- In November 2008, both the Eurozone and Japan were recognized as being in recession.

- On November 25, 2008, the Fed announced the first quantitative easing program ("QE1") which would include large-scale purchases of mortgage-backed securities.

- On December 16, 2008, the fed funds rate was set to 0 to 0.25%. At that time, nobody would have predicted that the basic policy rate would remain at near zero for seven more years. Also, at this time the interest rate on reserves was 0.25%, and the discount rate was reduced to 0.50%. The Fed had recently obtained the legal right to pay interest on reserves. The discount rate would stay at that level until February 2010 when it was raised to 0.75%, and it has remained there since.

- In November and December 2008, the auto industry received extraordinary support from the U.S. government.

- Adding to the gloom in financial markets, in December 2008, a major fraud/Ponzi scheme by investor Bernard Madoff and his company was discovered. It represented the appearance of widespread foolishness and risk-taking in our financial system.

- Throughout 2008 (technically from December 2007 through June 2009), the U.S. was officially in recession. Few economists, including Fed economists, had discerned that the nation was in recession even as late as mid-2008.
- 2008 was indeed an economic *annus horribilis,* including a large contraction in GDP—a 37% drop in the S&P, the demise of numerous large financial companies and the renouncing of many of the tenants of free market capitalism that had dominated the U.S. and the world for the last two decades.

## 2009

- The actual commencement of QE1 began in January 2009. Over $1 trillion of mortgage-backed, agency and U.S. bonds were eventually bought.
- Also during 2009, with the fed funds rate at nearly zero, the Fed began making statements that it would keep that rate low for long periods of time. This was the start of forward guidance.
- Also beginning in early 2009, the new Fed tool of paying interest on reserves became prominent in intellectual circles and in the press as the policy tool of choice when the Fed would commence the exit from its QE policy.
- On February 17, 2009, the President Obama signed into law the American Recovery and Reinvestment Act of 2009, a fiscal policy stimulus program estimated to be about $787 billion.
- During 2009, many major mortgage relief programs were formulated and put into effect. The prevailing wisdom was that rectifying the housing market was critical to the recovery of the economy.
- The stock market hit bottom in March 2009. The bear market had begun in October 2007 and by March 2009 the S&P had lost about half of its value.
- Chrysler and General Motors filed for bankruptcy protection on April 30 and June 1, 2009, respectively. Despite the Chapter 11 filings of these two large industrial companies, the recession was not characterized by a very significant number of bankruptcy filings by other large companies. Low interest rates allowed struggling companies to refinance operations.
- The official end of the recession occurred both in the U.S. and in Eurozone in June 2009.

## 2010

- The Senate confirmed Ben Bernanke for a second term on January 28, 2010.
- In May 2010, Greece received a significant bailout (approximately $110 billion Euro) from the IMF and Eurozone. For years Greece's budget statistics had masked overspending. Under the terms of the bailout Greece was required to reduce spending significantly. Greece would become the central example of austerity policy which many analysts would decry as counterproductive while others would contend there was no alternative. In the following years Greece would receive further bailouts.
- On July 21, 2010, the Wall Street Reform and Consumer Protection Act, commonly known as Dodd-Frank, was signed into law. This legislation impacted many facets of the financial system and was to be phased in over many years.
- QE2 commenced in November 2010 and would eventually lead to the purchase of $600 billion of U.S. treasuries.

- On December 17, 2010, the President signed into law various tax cuts, including a 2% cut in Social Security taxes, and an extension of unemployment benefits.

# 2011

- On August 5, 2011, the U.S. lost its AAA credit rating from Standard & Poor's. S&P lowered the U.S. to AA+. As of 2016 it has not changed that rating. The two other main ratings agencies never lowered the U.S. credit rating.
- A debt crisis in Eurozone developed throughout 2011. Also during 2011, initially the ECB raised its short-term rate but by the third quarter of 2011 Eurozone was in a second recession. In response, in December 2011, the ECB cut rates.
- In September 2011, the Occupy Wall Street demonstrations become prominent, but this movement soon faded away. On November 15, protestors were removed from New York City's Zuccotti Park, the main locus of the protest.
- In September 2011, the Fed commenced a program to buy longer-term and sell shorter-term U.S. debt. It was commonly called Operation Twist (more formally, the Maturity Extension Program) and was intended to reduce long-term interest rates. It continued through 2012.
- In November 2011, the major central banks of the world collaborated on providing global liquidity.
- In December 2011, the U.S. extended payroll tax cuts, which was one of many fiscal stimulus policies from before.

# 2012

- In February 2012, the U.S. further extended payroll tax cuts and continued extended unemployment benefits.
- On August 1, 2012, the City of San Bernardino, California filed for bankruptcy. This was notable because rarely had cities, towns or other government entities sought U.S. Bankruptcy Court protection.
- Throughout this year (and leading up in 2011), state and federal governments prosecuted banks and other financial companies for mortgage abuses.
- QE3 began in September 2012. It was initially $40 billion per month of bond buying and increased to $85 billion per month in December 2012. Purchases were comprised of mortgage-backed and U.S. government bonds.

# 2013

- In January 2013, both higher federal taxes and cuts in federal spending were instituted. As these policy changes approached in the months before January 2013 they were referred to as the Fiscal Cliff. Many analysts predicted that this double dose of contractionary policy would adversely affect GDP growth.
- In March 2013, a financial crisis occurred in Cyprus, a member of Eurozone. Eventually Cyprus' problems were rectified without contagion, but for a while it appeared that the greater Eurozone could be thrown into a crisis by the events of a minute country.
- Eurozone's second recession ended in the second quarter of 2013.

- In early 2013, Japan commenced major stimulative economic policies known as Abenomics, which included fiscal spending which commenced in February 2013 and monetary stimulus initially in the form of quantitative easing. Abenomics also including a third intended component of structural reforms but these were never significantly implemented.
- In May 2013, Ben Bernanke broached the possibility of the Fed reducing QE3 bond buying levels; and in June 2013 the Fed indicated it would start to "Taper" its asset purchases. It began a gradual reduction in the monthly amount of QE3.
- The City of Detroit filed for bankruptcy on In July 18, 2013.
- Stock markets rallied, surpassing pre-crisis levels, during 2013.

# 2014

- Janet Yellen became Chair of the U.S. Fed in January 2014.
- In March 2014, as unemployment dropped to 6.7% Janet Yellen announced that the Fed would not stick to a strict numerical target of 6.5% for unemployment that it had set in 2012. The Fed would refrain from altering its low interest rate policy until additional labor market indicators showed improvement.
- Over the year 2014 the U.S. budget deficit shrank substantially.
- In June 2014, the ECB set its Deposit Rate for bank deposits to a negative rate. The rates was set to -0.10%. The ECB's basic refinancing rate was lowered to 0.15%, which was low but still positive.
- In October 2014, the ECB commenced buying sovereign bonds, a form of QE.
- QE3 ended in the U.S. in October 2014
- Starting in the latter half of 2014 crude oil prices suddenly decreased substantially, from over $100 per barrel in July to about $50 per barrel by the end of the year.

# 2015

- On January 15, 2015, the Swiss National Bank dropped its peg of the Swiss franc to the Euro. The Swiss franc soared in value. Loose monetary policy of the ECB and other nations put constant buying pressure on the franc as a currency safer from potential inflation. The Swiss had tried to keep the value of their currency low, but extreme demand for the franc required the Swiss to expand their central bank balance sheet too much. The action was viewed by certain analysts as a capitulation of the Swiss and a failure to cooperate with monetary policy of other nations. Others contended that the Swiss government had no other choice and faced losing control of its economy in face of monetary policy being done abroad.
- In January 2015, the ECB announced its intention to do a major quantitative easing of over $1 trillion Euros of bonds. This commenced in March 2015.
- By early 2015, various countries including Sweden, Denmark and Switzerland utilized negative policy interest rates.
- In early 2015, most countries were stimulating their economies with lower rates, quantitative easings and other policy devices.
- Throughout 2015, the U.S. Fed anticipated raising rates at some point during the year. There was great expectation that the Fed would raise in September 2015, but it did not. The Fed raised the fed

funds rate to the range of 0.25 to 0.50% in December 2015. It set the deposit rate at 0.50% and also committed to enter the overnight reverse repo market at a rate of at least 0.25%.

- The price of oil started 2015 at low price and went up and down but ended lower, below $40 per barrel. This continuation of the downward price trend caused substantial unemployment in the energy business, many business failures and default on energy company credits.

# 2016

- In early 2016 world equity markets declined, the price of oil declined and the Chinese economy struggled. World GDP growth was weak.
- Energy companies and their high-yield debt faced bankruptcy and losses. Oil prices hit lows in the mid-$20 per barrel range.
- Negative interest rates prevailed in policy of many nations (including both overnight lending rates and deposit rates) and a large amount of negative yielding sovereign debt existed including long-term debt like twenty-year Japanese government bonds.
- In June 2016 the ECB began buying corporate bonds as part of its QE.
- On June 23, 2016 the UK voted for Brexit, to leave the EU.
- Through November 2016 the U.S. Fed left interest rates unchanged.
- On November 8, 2016 Donald Trump was elected President.
- On December 14, 2016 the Fed raised rates including raising the fed funds rate by 25 basis points to a range of 0.50% to 0.75%. It also raised the deposit rate to 0.75% and the discount rate to 1.25%.

It is impossible to know what would have happened had the Fed not taken the emergency actions during 2008. The same can be said about unconventional policies after 2008. Concerning the Fed crisis actions of 2008, almost all analysts, including many conservative thinkers, assume the economy could not have withstood the financial shocks of 2008 without Fed support. Private parties would not have stepped up and bought the distressed financial companies. There would have been some kind of elemental shutdown of our financial system. It has come down in history as cliché, "…we avoided a complete shutdown of our financial system."

It is not debatable, however. Perhaps the banks and other big financial companies could have taken losses and continued to operate. Perhaps the parties in the money market and commercial paper market, for example, that got Fed support, could have borne losses without runs on funds or payrolls not being met. The same can be conjectured for AIG, General Motors, the banks, etc. that received bailouts by the Fed and/or the U.S. Treasury. Concerning General Motors and Chrysler, proponents maintain that special government help saved the iconic companies and historic auto industry. By about 2013, it appeared that the Fed takeovers were all paid back in full, demonstrating that Fed policy represented no cost to the public. Again, hardliners argue that the government did not have to take over those companies. Indeed, some analysts believe the government got these assets cheap. They point out that strict "mark-to-market" pricing mandates made financial companies insolvent during 2008 and that when these pricing rules were relaxed in early 2009 the markets were no longer in dire shape.

## II.10.B.c. Unconventional Policies

The following pages discuss the major new policy initiatives undertaken in response to and following the 2008 recession. Although many years have transpired, we cannot make any finalist statements about the success and and/or effects of policy. For example, the three quantitative easing programs engaged in by the Fed seem to have affected the stock market consistently. The stock market went up with each QE round and ceased going up when QE ceased at the end of 2014. The market's movement over the approximate five-year period of QE tracks closely with QE in time and magnitude. Of course, an increase in the stock market was not necessarily the original intent of QE. The original purpose of stimulative policy was to increase business lending and consumer spending through lower rates. Even specific numerical estimates of effects of QE on interest rates are guesses and estimates vary, with a range of 40 to 120 basis points of lowering of general interest rates.

We can only speculate on other effects of QE. For example, the price of commodities like oil and gas rose in correlation with the QE's, which potentially offset beneficial effects. Some consequences have not yet played out.

## II.10.B.c.i. Zero Interest Rate Policy ("ZIRP")

We set the fed funds rate near zero and kept it there. Other short rates clustered near or at zero. When the Fed first lowered the rate to near zero, few analysts thought it would stay that low for a long time, yet ZIRP became a longstanding policy. It is important to emphasize that it is the nominal rate that is set to zero. Subtracting any amount of either current or expected inflation from many short-term rates gives negative real rates. Even rates on longer-term bonds, like U.S. treasuries that have yielded about 2%, hover around zero after inflation is subtracted. We have discussed the effects of low, or lower, interest rates at great length. We do not know the long range consequences of very low rates.

## II.10.B.c.ii. Negative Interest Rate Policy ("NIRP")

Negative real interest rates are not uncommon. Simply, when inflation is higher than expected and higher than nominal rates, we get negative real rates. This has happened frequently in history. For example, in the 1970s banks made numerous 30-year mortgages at rates around 6%. When inflation rose above 6% the banks were receiving negative real rates of interest. The existence of negative reals is in every M&M textbook. Negative nominal rates do not make sense, however, and would have been categorically dismissed in M&M instruction and models. Today, extraordinary monetary policy has created such low rates that certain interest rates, like those controlled by central banks, and certain types of debt have embarked on the next step of negative nominal yields. The negative nominals have become common enough in certain nations and among certain types of debt that this development cannot be dismissed as a short-term oddity.

The negative interest rate, or "NIRP," has become accepted and talked about as a sensible policy tool. It is interesting to see how it developed both intellectually and in the real world. It is too early to determine the effects of negative rates. Listed below are some of the facets of negative interest rates:

- **Negative interest rates are new**: People sometimes pay fees to have their money held (like in Swiss bank accounts) but the world has never seen large amounts of credit with borrowers paying lenders. It is a truly remarkable event because, theoretically, a negative nominal rate should represent a bound beyond which lenders would not go. They would simply hold cash which pays a zero rate of return. It is additionally remarkable in the sense that virtually every economist and instructor of economics would have spent his career pronouncing that nominal rates could not be negative: Negative (nominal) rates are not generally in most textbooks unless they are very up to date.

- **Negative rates exist in both main central bank policy rates**, including the deposit rate and the overnight lending rate. Negative yields are more common for sovereign debt. Parties like pension funds demanded so much sovereign debt that they pushed the price of debt up to the point where the yield was negative. Almost every western country has had some sovereign debt priced at negative yields with the total amount in trillions. In U.S. government debt negative, negative yields have existed but only occasionally for very short-term bills. In Germany and Switzerland, negative yields are common for debt up to about the ten-year maturities. As of 2016 approximately $8 trillion of sovereign debt trades at negative yields including about $5.6 trillion Japanese and almost $1 trillion German. Some corporate debt has also been priced at negative yields.

- **In terms of M&M theory certain economists began to explain and tout the benefits of negative rates**: Their theory was simple–negative rates would induce a further encouragement of bank lending and consumer spending, and thus economic activity. The policy rate that would be lowered into the negative range would be the deposit rate for reserves held at central banks. Later some counties would resort to a negative overnight lending rate. If the deposit rate were negative banks would be compelled to lend reserves out rather than hold them. The way some economists justified the negative rate was as a penalty fee for lenders for not lending.

- **With negative nominal rates many common practices are turned on their heads**: Bond holders pay interest rather than receive it. Interesting questions arose concerning factors like whether or not the interest payment would be deductible on taxes. There were practical considerations too like whether financial software could accommodate negative rates. With negative rates, businesses and individuals would pay bills sooner rather than delaying. In particular, agents would pay their tax bills as soon as possible and delay their tax refunds as long as possible.

- **There is not much theory behind negative rates** (at least as of the first few years of using them) other than that we believed that lowering rates in general has stimulative effects and going into the negative range would be a continuation of lowering: When central banks started using negative rates they apparently did so on the theory of trying it and seeing if it worked.

- **Certain European countries were the first to use negative policy rates** (like Sweden, Switzerland and Denmark): To a large extent these smaller nations lowered their rates in response to the ECB's low rates. For example, one early mover was Denmark, which in July 2012 made its deposit rate negative. The idea was to compel Danish banks to hold less cash at Denmark's central bank with the ultimate goal to put downward pressure on the value of the Danish Krone.

- **Among large central banks the ECB has a negative deposit rate and the Bank of Japan has both a negative deposit rate and overnight lending rate**: The U.S. has neither and has no official plans to use negative rates. Senior Fed officials in 2015 and 2016 have said negative rates are worth studying.

- **The measured effects of negative interest rates on lending are hard to determine**, but apparently not large. Proponents would contend that the rates have only been of a small negative magnitude so effects may also not be too large. A case can be made that negative rates impede lending. Banks cannot easily pass the costs of the negative rates along to their depositors, so the banks pay the costs and face a lower spread to lending and stay away from lending in general. Regardless of such counter arguments, central banks that have used negative rates have maintained that they have had desirable effects.

- **Negative rates can have contractionary effects** if they cause people and businesses to flock to cash and sit on it.

- **The central banks that imposed negative rates did so mainly for deposit rates of reserves held by banks**: The ECB has a negative deposit rate but left the refinancing rate (their overnight lending rate) at 0%. Also, the negative rate setting was done at small increments like ten basis points rather than a customary 25 basis point changes. Also, the negative rates have not gone very low. For example, as of June 2016 the ECB has a -0.4% deposit rate. Some experts estimate that banks would balk at converting to cash until the negative rate got to about -1.0%. Commercial banks have not passed negative rates onto accounts held by households. In odd cases like Denmark some variable rate mortgages ended up with negative interest.
- **A negative nominal rate can be seen as a tax on cash or the cash kept at a bank or financial institution**: Private parties, of course, could convert bank holdings to real cash. This would be limited by practical considerations and would require bills with large denominations like $100 bills of €500 notes. During 2015 and 2016, some economists such as Lawrence Summers and certain central bank officials began to propose removing high denomination bills from circulation. They claimed the reason was to curb illegal activity yet many analysts thought it was part of a move to get physical cash out of the system such that a future negative interest rates policy would have more hold.
- **A negative deposit rate on reserves held by banks at the Fed has been recommended by some analysts**, like Princeton professor Alan Blinder: At the time reserves were getting 0.25%, enough that banks could hold them and make a little money, rather than lend and stimulate the economy. The U.S. never took that action and has since raised the deposit rate to 0.50%.
- **ECB policy of late 2015 is among the notable latest developments in M&M related to negative rates**: The ECB has a negative deposit rate of -0.3% as of December 2015.
- **There are numerous potential and hard to measure problems with negative rates**: People might lose confidence in the entire idea of saving money at a gain. Bank profits are impacted negatively. Negative rates distort the price of capital. Negative rates may alter basic business practices. If rates remain negative for a long time corporations could make profit simply by issuing debt, rather than producing products and services.

### II.10.B.c.iii. Large-Scale Asset Purchases & Large Market Support

Large-scale asset purchases ("LSAP's") have been the main new tool of monetary policy. LSAP's is a broader category and includes the more commonly termed quantitative easing, which is increasing the size of the Fed balance sheet and credit easing (changing the composition of the fed balance sheet). LSAP's effects are various but mainly impacting yields (lowering rates), thereby causing increased economic activity and/or substitution of investment into other asset classes. The details on these are voluminous, so I shall try to focus only prominent features in the sections below.

LSAP's can be designed as targeted buyings and temporary in nature or as broad new M&M policy possibly to be done in perpetuity and ad hoc, meaning that the central bank may buy whatever has to be bought at the time or whatever is available to keep the economy afloat. There may not be compelling economic theory underpinning the buyings. For example, Japan's central bank has purchased large amounts of the Japanese equity markets and the ECB, commencing in June 2016, has purchased corporate bonds.

### II.10.B.c.iii.1. Quantitative Easing ("QE")

QE is the buying of assets in the financial system by the central bank for the purpose of putting reserves into the system and keeping interest rates low. It is similar to regular open market operations except that open market operations apply strictly to short-term rates and involve the buying of U.S. debt while QE attempts to control long-term rates and buys longer-term debt of many kinds. Before 2008, QE was rarely broached in M&M lectures and might have been brought up as last-gasp policy that could be used in extreme circumstances. QE might have applied to struggling nations but not our economy. Some instructors might have mentioned QE monetary policy done in Japan but would probably have relegated this case as a special situation of a country with grave economic deficiencies. Specific facets, like which assets would be bought and how much QE would be done, would only be answered with speculation.

The diagram below shows Point A, which represents the fed funds rate clearing the fed funds market for Reserves. Supply is vertical because it is set by the Fed. Demand is downward sloping and represents the demand for funds in the fed funds market. Think of demand as determined by banks that need Reserves thus, at lower rates, they would demand more Reserves. The Fed can increase the amount of Reserves by doing open market operations. That moves the supply curve out, thereby lowering the fed funds rate. If it gets to Point B, the rate is zero. Up until 2008 instructors would rarely have addressed what happens at Point B (or even close to Point B) and certainly not beyond. Now, under QE, we continue increasing the supply of Reserves. This is supply curve S''. The range of C minus B represents the amount of QE.

QE policy in T accounts would look like the example of open market operations we did above. The only difference with QE is that we have already reached zero interest rate.

## Quantitative Easing

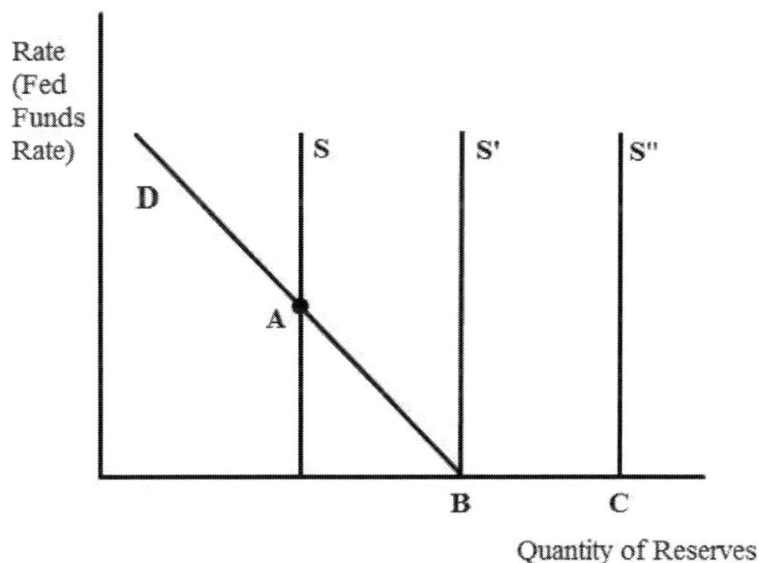

Quantity of Reserves

QE would look similar to open market operations using t-accounts.

| Federal Reserve Balance Sheet | | | Banking System Balance Sheet | | |
|---|---|---|---|---|---|
| *Assets* | | *Liabilities* | *Assets* | | *Liabilities* |
| Securities | +1 | Reserves +1 | Reserves | +1 | |
| | | | Securities | -1 | |

In practice, certain assets were purchased in QE. The U.S. Fed chose primarily mortgage-backed securities and U.S. government bonds as the QE assets of choice. It could have bought other assets such as auto loans, corporate bonds, student loans, small business loans, etc. or, presumably, even public equities or individuals' homes. Mortgage-backed securities were preferable because they were a large, liquid market held by many important financial institutions. The goal was to support the financial sector and also believed that buying mortgage-backed would exert downward pressure on long-term rates in other markets. The Fed also wanted to directly support the housing market under the idea that housing was critical to overall economic health. Prominent facets of QE's of the United States and other nations are listed below:

- QE1 commenced in November 2008 and ran through March 2010 and was constituted of about $1.25 trillion of mortgage-backed securities, $175 billion of agency debt (i.e., Fannie Mae and Freddie Mac bonds) and $300 billion of U.S. treasuries.
- QE2 ran from about November 2010 through June 2011 and was about $600 billion in treasuries. QE3, the monthly program, began in September 2012 and was a commitment to buy until the economy went above 2% inflation and/or under 6.5% unemployment.
- QE3 would be $85 billion per month, split as $40 billion in mortgage-backed and $45 billion in treasuries. We began to decrease QE3 in late 2013. We first talked about decreasing QE3 earlier in the year. Markets reacted adversely to that move, which was known as the famous "taper."
- Eurozone commenced a QE in 2015.
- Japan had done QE policies earlier in the 1990s and 2000s, but they received minor academic or press coverage in the U.S. and the West.
- When we embarked on the first QE we did not envision the multiple rounds of QE, their magnitudes and their durations for many years. After the first round of QE around March and April 2010, the talk both by Fed officials (including Ben Bernanke) and the press was that we would start reversing QE by selling the bonds back to the market. At that time, we wanted to remove the extra cash to be able to control the fed funds rate again. We were not, generally, anticipating more QE.
- Around January 2012 there were murmurs of a new round of QE (a QE3) to be done with mortgage debt, and people bought bonds in anticipation making us wonder what remained of the policy effects. Perhaps the Fed purchases after the front running just gave profits to those initial speculators rather than having true effects like lowering rates and making people take more risk by forcing them to riskier asset classes from raising the price of bonds. All of the big bond buyings by the Fed (including Operation Twist) seemed gamed by private parties. Speculators seemed to be buy the long-dated treasuries along with the Fed, which was not the intention.
- The QE's (including Operation Twist, described below) all "worked" according to consensus financial press. QE's rallied stocks, bonds and saved the housing market by lowering rates in general and, as proponents put it, "the economy would have been worse," with QE. QE gave consumers in particular a sense of more wealth, helping consumption, which in turn kept the struggling recovery going. Costs were believed to be non-existent or minor.

- The first two QE's created favorable effects on the stock market as they ran, but the market pulled back as they ended. QE3 followed a similar pattern. At its end, which can be dated at late 2014 (when markets were anticipating it) or early 2015 (when it was actually implemented), the market slowed. Proponents of QE policy mocked QE disbelievers at the termination of QE when the great disruptions in the economy and in financial markets that naysayers had forecast did not occur. Naysayers pointed out that the economy was growing no more strongly at the end of any QE (especially QE3) than before. Naysayers also contend that we will not know the true effects until the actual exiting of the large bond positions built up in the QE's.
- The magnitude of QE's effects is difficult to determine, and the answer involves two levels, both of which are guesses: First, how much did interest rates go down? Second, how much did lower rates impact the economy? We have sundry estimates of the former. Ben Bernanke once attributed a decrease in long-term treasury yields of between 40-110 basis points due to QE2. Most analysts and academic research came in with similar salutary and acceptable numbers, reflecting a significant, but not really big, effect. Others analysts made polar claims, both on the no-effects and the substantial effects sides. Academic analysis is not reliable here because we cannot hold other factors constant. For example during the time period in question, the economy was generally weak, which might explain the lower rates attributed to QE. Also, other central banks were simultaneously lowering rates. The latter question (how much did lower rates affect the economy?) is anyone's guess.
- What were monetary policy theories of the effects of QE? They varied and developed as circumstances and events changed. QE was initially viewed as a traditional way to get reserves to banks and other financial companies that would be loaned out and thereby stimulate the economy. That lending did not materialize. Subsequent rounds of QE were viewed as lowering interest rates in general; it was perceived that the main goal of QE was maintaining low long-term interest rates. Some analysts emphasized that QE was a support for the housing market and for U.S. treasury debt. Others maintained that QE was primarily to save the balance sheets of banks and other financial institutions. As the years passed and QE policies continued, the two main monetary policy stories for QE effects were wealth effects and reaching for yield. The latter meant that, since QE caused a lowering of the yields of higher quality debt, market participants would be encouraged to buy higher yielding assets like high-yield bonds and stocks. This reach for yield would enhance employment since companies that got funding from high yielding securities tended to create jobs. For example, one common story is that yields for casino and gaming bonds were lowered and support of those industries was desirable because they create so many jobs.
- QE was criticized in many ways, some of which were specific to the times and seem to have faded in importance, and are, therefore, deemed invalid criticisms. For example, QE's effects of lowering rates meant that money had to be invested elsewhere. Many analysts contended it was parked in non-productive assets like commodities, real estate and foreign assets. This caused bubbles and distortions, and leaders of emerging market nations complained. At the end of U.S. QE, we forgot about any of these adverse effects and focused on the success of our economy, but we could just as easily have tallied up the losses and deemed our economy not so successful. Some QE criticisms have to do with grander, longer-term effect and still remain uncertain. QE has created high valuations in many markets. We do not know what will happen. Also, since we have now used QE any policy short of that (like traditional fed funds rate changes) may be deemed irrelevant.
- Did QE's work, both in terms of affecting targets like interest rates and affecting the ultimate economy. Many conclusions are plausible. Nearby in time to each QE there was some increase in

related financial or economic quantities (like the stock market going up), but the increases faded, reversed or changed over time. Some say there were significant effects, primarily through stock market and home value increases, which made people feel wealthier and kept consumption going. Naysayers contend that effects were only in financial assets, with no spillover to real economic decisions. The prevailing assessment is that QE did work initially but petered out. We may not know the full effect until we exit the strategy.

- QE raised other questions: If the mechanism was to make private parties buy riskier assets like junk bonds which supposedly supported industries in which many jobs were created, why not just buy the riskier assets directly or even subsidize those sectors that were deemed bountiful in terms of creating jobs and spending? The answer to that is that the Fed is supposed to give the appearance of working through markets in general, as opposed to directly controlling specific markets.

- The U.S. and U.K. did QE following the 2008 crisis. Japan had implemented QE-like increasing of its reserves before the crisis, including a major increase from 2001 to 2006 by buying government bonds, asset-backed securities and equity. This was not considered highly successful. Japan has also done QE post-2008, including the very large economic stimulation knows as Abenomics that commenced in 2013. Japanese QE was extensive and dubbed QQE for quantitative and qualitative easing. Japanese policy bought bonds to lower rates in general (the quantitative part) and also bought assets like certain real estate assets, government bonds and certain exchange-traded funds in their stock market to affect certain sectors (the qualitative part). The ECB committed to a program of QE in January 2015 and commenced in March 2015. This program had been anticipated for much of the previous year. The ECB's program is large. As of April 2016 the amount is €80 billion per month. In June 2016 the ECB added corporate bonds. The main take is that QE "done right," as done by the U.S. and U.K. starting around 2009, worked and Japan and the ECB learned and have been following suit. Some countries did not engage in QE, including Canada and Australia as well as developing countries like Russia, China, Brazil and India.

## II.10.B.c.iii.2. Credit Easing

Credit easing is a variety of QE in which the central bank buys bonds other than just government bonds. Under basic QE, the goal of the central bank may be only to get money out there. Under credit easing the goal may be to affect the demand for assets in certain sectors. Much of the original QE done by the U.S. could be considered credit easing: for example, the buying of mortgage-backed bonds. Ben Bernanke contended that we were doing a form of credit easing. In contrast, after their interest rate hit about the zero bound in the 1990s, the Japanese engaged in a basic QE that did not purport to affect certain asset groups more than others. In t-account analysis credit easing would be a change in holdings of central bank securities, like selling a short-term U.S. security for a long-term U.S. security:

| Federal Reserve Balance Sheet | | |
|---|---|---|
| *Assets* | | *Liabilities* |
| U.S. treasury bill | -1 | |
| U.S. treasury bond | +1 | |

With credit easing as with QE, we increase the size of the Fed balance sheet, but since credit easing involves other markets we more directly impact those markets. To demonstrate how murky or subtle these distinctions are, however, credit easing is also akin to fiscal policy in that we are targeting a sector.

Similarly, Operation Twist, which involved only government debt, can also be viewed as a kind of credit easing.

### II.10.B.c.iii.3. Operation Twist

Operation Twist, formally called the Maturity Extension Program, commenced in late 2011 and was the swapping of about $400 billion of shorter-term U.S. debt (maturities under three years) with longer-term U.S. debt (six to 30-year maturities). The goal was to achieve a QE-like stimulation without increasing the size of the balance sheet. We termed it "extending maturities," and the intention was to bring down long-term rates of related debt (perhaps mortgage rates). Twist would flatten the yield curve. Of course, this action ran counter to our normal preference for an upward sloping yield curve. Flattening the spread would be adverse to banks, which supposedly borrow at the short end and lend at the long, but an overriding goal was to get lower long-term rates. Whether or not Twist worked, in the sense that it reduced the spread between long and short-term maturities is hard to say since the program did not last very long—nor did it prove to be of great magnitude. The original Operation Twist was done in 1961 and is a similar policy under which we bought long-term U.S. debt for short-term debt and indeed lowered spreads. Whether it worked or not is still debated. Some analysts say it did not go on long enough to have substantial effects.

### II.10.B.c.iii.4. Tapering

While QE3 was in progress in May 2013, Ben Bernanke told a Congressional panel that the Fed, "could in the next few meetings…take a step down in our pace of purchases." Markets picked this up a drastic future policy change. The term "taper" was popularized in the financial press and came to mean a potential policy action of reducing QE3 bond buying amounts. At the time, it was neither a firm policy commitment, specific magnitude nor date for changing or stopping QE. It would become a big signal. During June 2013 and the rest of the summer, markets reacted with the bond market selling off to the point of an approximate 0.75% increase in yields in treasuries and a similar rise in mortgage rates. In September 2013, the Fed and Bernanke seemed on the verge of commencing a buying cut, but they did not. In December 2013, a $10 billion per month reduction in the monthly $85 billion Fed bond buying program was announced.

Tapering–both the actual action of reducing bond buying in terms of amounts, timetable, etc. and just the plain jargon of Tapering as a signal of intent and hint of future policies– had become, de facto, a new tool of the Fed. Tapering highlights monetary policy effects in anticipation rather than actualization. When the Fed actually commenced reducing the bond buying in late 2013 and through 2014, interest rate fluctuations were not as great as at the time of Bernanke's original broaching. Some analysts contended that during the period of Fed tapering it was buying longer-dated bonds, which weakened the effects of tapering. In other words, buying a smaller amount of bonds, but buying longer dated ones was like buying more.

### II.10.B.c.iii.5. Continuing Large Fed Balance Sheet and Normalization

QE3 terminated at the end of 2014 and the Fed balance sheet has not changed much in size since then. The Fed balance sheet, however, does not decrease due to maturation of bonds because the Fed reinvests the proceeds of matured bonds into more bonds. The Fed balance sheet has been about $4.5 trillion since December 2014.

The elevated balance sheet is considered advantageous for various reasons primarily that it provides financial stability and continued accommodation. The downsides are various: (1) the big balance sheet has interest-rate risk; (2) great size makes it hard to set and control policy rates including the fed funds rate, the deposit rate and the overnight reverse repo rate; (3) great excess reserves could lead to inflation; and (4) the elevated Fed balance sheet leads to uncertainty in markets about what size and form the central bank will have in the long run.

Some analysts recommend reducing the size of the Fed balance sheet by discontinuing reinvestment of matured principal. Others recommend actively selling a stated amount of Fed asset holding each month.

## II.10.B.d. Forward Guidance, Communication &Transparency

The level of explanation of central bank policy has changed greatly in the last twenty years. Before 2008 we spoke sparingly about policy and made little projection or estimation of its effects. The Fed was aloof and presented the appearance that its policy worked as advertised and that it could engage in more powerful policy if necessary. It generally did not need to clear this with markets. Now, we engage in multi-faceted policies and talk frequently and confidently about their effects. Is the increased talk truly effective, or is it merely resorting to attempting to explain the unexplainable and defend the effects of policy that ostensibly has little or no effects? The extensive developments in Fed communications' policies and related concepts represent a wide variety of ideas and come under headings like forward guidance, communication, transparency, triggers, guidelines, thresholds, contingency planning, etc. Prominent aspects of this include the following:

- Much of the new policy is mere talk, essentially statements by the authorities to maintain a policy (or stand ready to implement a policy) to achieve an economic goal. There is even sometimes talk about more talk. We consider our central bank to be among the most transparent in the world, which exemplifies the belief that our intellectual basis for economic policy is the best and most genuine. However, this transparency is primarily the additional explanation of facets about which we know little.

- Before the crisis, senior Fed people (including the Chairman, members of the Fed Board of Governors and Regional Fed Bank Presidents) were generally not too outspoken. Before 1994 the Fed did not even indicate what the basic policy rate was. Over the 1990s and into the 2000s, however, the Fed and its leaders became more outspoken in the form of official FOMC statements of policy rate and speeches and presentations by certain Fed people, but they generally spoke as one and seemingly agreed that standard Fed policy worked well and did not require much reinforcement of future policies and effects. This agreement made sense: since over the 1990s and early 2000s economic crises were not as controversial. For example, the economic crisis following September 11, 2001 or the Asian Crisis of 1997 did not involve as much fundamental intellectual questioning of our ideas as the 2008 episode did.

- Before 2008, Fed communication included basic research, various data releases and general economic reports including: (1) the Beige Book (a short summary of economic conditions and anecdotes released at each FOMC meeting); (2) the minutes of FOMC meetings released three weeks after each meeting; (3) full transcripts of FOMC meetings released only after five years; (4) periodic reports by the Chairman to Congress; and (5) sundry speeches by Fed Governors and regional Reserve Bank Presidents. Collectively, the Fed did not reveal future intentions much except that it wanted low inflation and high growth. Initially in the post-2008 period, forward guidance was a verbal commitment by the Fed to keep rates low by keeping the fed funds rate low.

The verbal commitment we hypothesized would create real M&M effects. For example, a Fed promise to keep rates low will cause people to do more borrowing presumably because they know that future rates will be favorable too and that their business will benefit both now and in the future.

- There are a multitude of problems about talking so much. The various regional Reserve Bank Presidents have differing opinions. Some are hawks and others are doves, and they become well-known in the press for their comments. How much apparent influence should the Fed system tolerate for any one official? Also, much of our transparency talk is steadfast denial of making mistakes or of reneging on policy promises. The Fed will lose credibility after a sufficient number of major episodes of backtracking become ingrained in the press. For example, the targeting of an unemployment rate of 6.5% as the point for tighter policy (and then subsequently backing off when we got near that rate in early 2014) is fairly well-known in the press. The Fed set a point level of 6.5% for the unemployment rate, yet as we got near it we hedged. In March 2014 under newly-installed Fed Chair Janet Yellen, we simply dropped the point threshold. In its place we put a vague set of other labor and other market conditions. This abrupt change is policy whose entire purpose depended on commitment, and it was extremely predictable. All along the period of Forward Guidance, combatants of policy said the Fed would waver. Another example is that at the end of QE1 the Fed planned to exit the loose money policy; however, that plan was promptly dropped.

- Communication (as opposed to policy action) is the primary tool of today's Fed policy. Before recently, we acted and did not talk; now we talk and may not act. Whatever the effects of our standard monetary policies, communication is a promise that in the future we will continue certain policies. I can enforce a rate now that does not seem to do what I want, but I will achieve that rate in the future when conditions are normal and it will then represent real transmission.

- Communication can be persistent and direct or ad hoc and indirect. For a long time the Fed has committed to low rates at a relatively specific level. However, when the Fed came out with a report in January of 2012 exhorting the U.S. government to support the housing market, it was not viewed as a finalist policy statement by our central bank; nor was it scientific or clear about the tradeoffs of the goal. It did constitute a kind of communication, however.

- The main element of communication is that the Fed will continue policy that will support the public's and business community's needs. In other words, we will "be there for you."

- The Fed can communicate policy. It can also engage in expanded regulation. Commanding markets through regulation or the threat of regulation is potentially more potent than any either conventional or unconventional tools.

- Transparency is not frankness. For example, Ben Bernanke never remarked that America was broke, that the Fed's mortgage-backed holdings were of dubious value, that he miscalled many of the major economic trends of recent decades, etc. Despite claiming to reveal all, the Fed maintains a pretense of knowing and of being in control. In general, no senior Fed people admit to any kind of failure, lack of control or understanding, possibility that we might face a really adverse economic future, etc.

- The Fed now holds quarterly press conferences and releases economic projections. One problem is that the public will learn that Fed projections are no better than those of other economists. Also, if the Fed commits to one policy, it might cause people to game that strategy. Then if the Fed has to suddenly change to another strategy (like fighting inflation), it will have to break its commitment. Big private parties (like hedge funds) would game the Fed relentlessly.

- Fed policy today is to urge strongly but promise not to do. This is the direct opposite of what Paul Volcker did in the early 1980s when he spoke little about his tools to slow the economy but indeed implemented them.

- Another even more fundamental problem with the long-term commitment is that it runs entirely counter to old policy process to act preemptively to inflation. Now, the Fed will somewhat have to get the blessing of the bond market before it "pulls the punch bowl."

- Fed officials are obsessed with the idea that they must be believed and trusted. They must project that they are right and will prevail. This leadership must never appear indecisive.

- Commenting on Fed transparency on the Fed web, Ben Bernanke boasts that they released 21,000 pages of loan transactions on December 1, 2010. What he fails to say is that the Fed had no intention of releasing these data and did so only under duress from press lawsuits.[122]

- The biggest flaw is that the policy maker can simply renege on policy. Economists refer to the changing of policy as time inconsistency.

- There is a commitment to keep rates low. At first blush, this does not make sense. Formerly, we lowered rates to get private parties to invest and consume given the suddenly better borrowing cost. Now with a commitment, why would a consumer, for example, accelerate economic activity if he or she knew rates would be low for a long time? Presumably, the logic behind the duration commitment is that private parties will think the economy, in general, will have favorable borrowing terms for a long time and will continue to expand economic activity. Or it could be something like even if a private party fears inflation and thinks rates will go up, they will still be held down. These are both weak cases. Perhaps you can make a case that longer-planning entities like businesses will start an investment program now knowing that rates will stay low, since they will have to borrow more as time goes by, but that is a weak case too.

- We analyze the pros and cons of forward guidance and that very process gives it the appearance of absurdity. We say a commitment ties the Fed's hands, yet, if it really has to the Fed can renege on its commitment. The tradeoff is that the Fed will lose future credibility. That may not matter if we have survived the crisis and the economy has recovered.

- Fed officials will contend that communication is designed, at least to some extent, for the general public. John Williams, President and CEO of the San Francisco Fed states, "It is essential that the public have a solid base of knowledge about economics and monetary policy that will allow people to make informed judgments about the Federal Reserve."[123] Average people, though, are not capable of understanding the Fed and its policies. Financial companies and sophisticated businesses have this ability, and they can, perhaps, act sufficiently on the behavior average people. Yet the idea that the Fed is explaining its control of the economy to the people (and thus the people are endorsing it as a team effort) is elitist and arrogant.

- After the Fed lowered the basic rate to near zero it began a policy of describing what it would do in the future concerning, primarily, when it would raise rates. Initially the Fed stated it would hold rates low for a short time, then when the short time passed, for a longer time. Then it started to refer to points in time: first 2013, then 2014, then 2015. The Fed set specific thresholds that would trigger policy changes, like the unemployment rate at 6.5%, but changed those.

---

[122] Ben Bernanke on February 3, 2011 in comments to the National Press Club, Washington, DC.

[123] "Economics Instruction and the Brave New World of Monetary Policy," presentation to the AEA National Conference on Teaching Economics and Research in Economic Education, by San Francisco Fed President and CEO John C. Williams, June 1, 2011.

- Forward guidance can backfire in the sense that if the Fed's actions are predictable they result in a complacency by market participants, causing excess risk taking and bubbles. During the period 2004 through 2006 when the Fed was raising rates, Fed actions were so consistent market participants became convinced they could rely on certain actions of the Fed.
- One grave problem with forward guidance is lengthening time. When we first gave forward guidance in the form of the fed funds rate being kept low, "for a considerable time," markets expected that the Fed has some command of a time frame and relative control or knowledge of the economy, yet as the commitment continued over many years it gave the appearance that the Fed was subject to improvement so unpredictable in terms of time frame that, indeed, when the Fed found that it had to change its forward guidance, it might likely do so abruptly. In other words, it would not offer much forward guidance at all.
- As the Fed continued its policy commitments, advocates recommended formal Fed guidelines to convey more information and assurance to the private economy. Two typical statements were made: (1) The Fed would continue low rates until inflation rose above a certain level, say 3% or (2) The Fed would continue whatever stimulative policy it was doing until unemployment got below a certain level (for a long time a level of 6.5% or 7% was the trigger).
- The Fed intends the triggers to add stability and remove uncertainty, but the result could be just the opposite. Private parties like big money managers incorporate these triggers in their models, both formal and informal, and act in self-interested ways. For example, perhaps some short-term favorable unemployment data could make a bond house start to sell its bonds prematurely on the idea that the Fed is about to raise rates.
- More extensive contingency planning for policy given different economic scenarios and its promulgation to the public has been proposed.

### II.10.B.e. The Fed as Central Planning Agency

When the Fed was founded, its role was to lend to financial companies against good collateral in times of need, usually when they faced seasonal crises and short-term cyclical crises. This straight role of the Fed persisted until the Great Depression, at which time the Fed expanded in scope to include monetary policy to shape the overall level of demand in the economy. The Fed grew in size over the post-World War II period as the economy grew but its role remained relatively restricted to a specific and non-meddlesome role in the economy. Since 2008, the Fed has expanded extensively. The Fed, in its current role does the following:
- **Controls interest rates, or the price of money**: The Fed always had this role, of course, but now it controls rates with more force, multiple policy initiatives and for longer periods of time.
- **Controls the time profile of credit (the yield curve)**: The Fed historically controlled the short end of the curve but now it controls the long end and it controls the yield curve for longer periods of time.
- **Supports specific industries notably housing and banking/finance**.
- **Has a greatly-increased role as regulator**, including regulating banks and financial companies and also an expanded role in consumer regulation: The Fed is like a debt counselor and financial planner to people.
- **Conducts what could be considered fiscal policy**, such as subsidizing the housing markets.

- **Manages a large portfolio of securities of many types**. The Fed's balance sheet, as of 2016, includes mortgage-backed securities, agency debt, and longer-term treasuries. (The ECB manages corporate bonds and the Japanese central bank owns equities.)
- **Engages in "macroprudential" supervision**: In this role, the Fed collects copious data and does extensive research to serve as economy-wide risk aggregator and detector of financial bubbles.
- **Aids the U.S. government in its issuance of debt**: The Fed buys U.S. debt in large quantities and in certain ways to ensure the smooth issuance of debt by the U.S.

Other central banks have increased their roles, too: The Japanese central bank, for example, is a major investor in the Japanese equity market. The Chinese central bank meddles in China's economy in myriad ways. The main point to note is that the U.S. central bank has metamorphosed from being a player in the general background of the economy to being an active participant in many facets of the economy.

## II.10.B.e.i. Engaging in Fiscal Policy & Fed Independence

Fiscal policy is U.S. government spending or taxation, e.g., the U.S. government spending money on a highway project or giving a tax rebate. Monetary policy normally does not change government spending or tax levels, nor does it subsidize economic sectors; rather it sets interest rates (or money supplies) and controls the monetary base with its main goal of keeping inflation stable. During the unconventional monetary policy following 2008 many analysts contended that the Fed engaged in fiscal policy. Other analysts, like Fed Chairman Ben Bernanke, contended that Fed policies had implication like fiscal policy but were still primarily monetary policy.

The Fed does not engage in direct spending or tax. It does, however, buy the U.S. bonds that are used to pay for spending. It also buys large amounts of bonds, like mortgage-backed bonds, which alter economic conditions in specific markets (like the housing market and related credit markets). Whether this is still monetary policy (just ultimately attempts to change general interest rates) or fiscal policy (actually attempting to change demands and economic tradeoffs in certain sectors) is debatable. Other perceptions of the Fed as doing fiscal policy include the following:
- Fed policy has lowered yields on risky securities and thereby favored borrowers over spenders. This can be seen as a type of fiscal policy in the form of a tax on investors and a subsidy to borrowers.
- Another way the Fed has a heightened fiscal impact–even if it is not intentional fiscal policy–is that since it holds a much larger amount of interest paying debt, it makes much more money than it used to, which it remits to the U.S. government. This has a significant impact on the federal budget. The nature of Fed holdings therefore impact fiscal policy. Then, if the Fed's net interest income were to go down (which could happen if interest rates rose), the Fed would remit less or even be funded by the federal government.
- Bank reserves could be viewed as debt of the U.S. government. They are obligations of the Fed and the Fed is ultimately backed by the U.S.
- Problems with a central bank doing policies that have fiscal policy effects include distorting of markets, distributional effects on society and political and independence issues.
- Fed's independence is called into question. During the crisis of 2008 various Fed-Treasury initiatives were done. Many major Fed policies, like Operation Twist, appeared more like a helping to the Fed to buy long-term U.S. bonds rather than true monetary policy.

- Our central bank must be seen as consolidated with our federal government. When the U.S. Treasury borrows it issues a government obligation. That obligation could be long term or short term. When the Fed buys bonds it issues cash which is simply a short-term government obligation. If the Fed buys U.S. bonds, like in QE, it merely replaces longer-term U.S. debt with shorter-term debt. Given the consolidation of the books of the central bank and fiscal authority, any economic policies must explain any of the problems of the federal government.
- The national housing finance system including the entities Fannie Mae and Freddie Mac should be consolidated in greater U.S. government books. The bonds issued by Fannie Mae and Freddie Mac are really just another form of U.S. debt.

## II.10.B.e.ii. Expanded Lending & Support of Institutions and Markets

In 2008 and 2009 the U.S., mainly through the Fed, engaged in a variety of special market support programs. Reflecting on those years, we often break on opinions: The programs can be deemed great successes that protected markets from collapse and contagion. Also, the facilities were mostly wound down in a timely fashion. On the opposite side of the spectrum, they can be deemed as unnecessary, causing moral hazard and subsidizing of the financial sector at the expense of the greater economy. Many more analysts subscribe to the former opinion rather than the latter. The list below details some specific cases and related comments (see also the timeline of events in the crisis period discussed above):

- Term Auction Facility (TAF): discount lending to banks.
- Commercial Paper Funding Facility: a support of the commercial paper market that represented an expansion of collateral acceptable by the Fed.
- Asset-Backed Commercial Paper Money Market Mutual Fund Liquidity Facility.
- Term Asset-Backed Securities Loan Facility (TALF): involved asset-backed securities.
- Primary Dealer Credit Facility: provided loans to primary dealers for collateral and is another example of the Fed widening its counterparties.
- Troubled Asset Relief Program (TARP): run by the U.S. Treasury, not the Fed.
- Bear Stearns bailout through the supported acquisition by JP Morgan.
- Lending commitments to large banks including Bank of America and Citigroup.
- AIG bailout: multiple programs were provided by the Fed for this multinational insurance company that had expanded into credit default insurance.
- Currency swap lines: programs under which the Fed provided dollars to foreign banks, primarily European banks, in exchange for foreign currency. The magnitudes were very large, yet risks were dismissed by the Fed as minimal due to the swaps counterparty, Eurozone, being a solvent economic entity. Indeed, there were not defaults on the currency swap lines, but there was risk.

One problem with the new lending and market support facilities is that they can change and grow and it may not be clear who is really backing our lending. For example in December 2011, the Fed commenced policy to aid European banks. We did not lend directly to these banks, which we had done before, giving the appearance of risk. Rather, we loaned dollars for Euros backed by the ECB. We charged interest rates higher than market rate, which gave the appearance of prudent lending and belief that both the Fed and ECB were protected from the fate of the banks. Ultimately, however, the Fed backed the European banks and if some of these banks failed either the Fed or the ECB would have had to take a loss or continue to lend.

## II.10.B.e.iii. Bank Stress Tests

Starting in 2011, the Fed required banks and other large financial institutions to report on how they would handle extreme economic situations, like real GDP going down by 8%. These stress tests became formalized and were to be done annually. They attempt to judge entities' solvency against historical episodes like 2008 and 2001, and the goal is to ensure that companies have enough capital to withstand shocks and, therefore, avoid the need for government bailout. Stress tests have been done; results are released to the public. In general, with some exceptions, the banks have met the stress tests. Counter arguments include that the tests actually test little, in fact adding to systemic risk by giving private parties and regulators the appearance of control. Stress tests compel banks and other financial institutions to do business to meet the testing requirements. Some banks curtail valid lending and other profitable practices. Stress tests are also potentially flawed in that future crises will not resemble past ones, instead likely representing different initial causes and systemic factors. It is impossible to conclude if the stress tests are highly successful, better than nothing or perhaps even making the overall system less safe.

## II.10.B.e.iv. Macroprudential Supervision

Macroprudential supervision or regulation ("Macropru") describes a variety of regulations and other supervisions of the financial sector, including stricter capital requirements for financial companies, trading rules and curbs for financial companies, monitoring of size and scope of financial firms, consumer protection and analyses of markets to assess financial markets for bubbles, contagion, liquidity, etc. In contrast, microprudential regulation (which the Fed and other government agencies have always done extensively) involves individual financial institutions. A tenet of Macropru is that even if individual companies are in good shape the system as a whole can still be unstable. Macropru could mean breaking up of big financial firms, prohibiting issuing of dividends, prohibiting mergers or takeovers, requiring mergers or takeovers, setting interest rate levels for transactions, requiring companies' living wills that detail how they would wind themselves down in a crisis, etc. It also is intended to examine cross-border stability considerations and potentially utilize internationally coordinated policies. About the only big limit on Macropru is that it focuses mostly on the financial industry. It is not an industrial policy intended to pick winners or manage sectors like retail, transportation, energy, etc.

In conjunction with other branches of the government, the Fed identifies the industries and the particular firms within those industries that should be supervised. Then, those firms would be required to hold assets that are liquid, can be valued accurately and have stable funding and strong counterparties. Various government entities have engaged in certain of these Macropru tasks in the past but today's innovation is the re-organizing of supervision, greater data collection and analysis, more intense and frequent checking and presumably greater willingness and authority to take action. The end goal is to enable the Fed to measure and control systemic risk, not just save financial institution separately.

Controlling bubbles is as yet an unproven science. The mantra is that we cannot discern a bubble until it has burst. Operationally, countervailing bubbles is difficult. For example, to cool off the housing market by raising mortgage rates would involve raising related rates in other markets, which might affect those markets adversely. Similarly, encouraging markets to provide capital to markets in need of liquidity would be hard to achieve in time, magnitude and even direction. The government would perhaps end up with either trivial effects or effects that are too great.

Another idea sprung out of Macropru is a return to narrow banking, which means a variety of ways to keep banking functions separate (like separating the savings and lending parts of banking). Certain government policy makers believe Macropru can be very successful. They contend that 2008 itself was caused by a lack of such supervision. For example, in his series of special lectures done at George Washington University in 2012, Ben Bernanke focused heavily on lack of regulation and contended no flaws in monetary policy. Macropru is scorned by market-leaning types who think that it is simply impossible for government analysts to improve markets. Macropru ultimately assumes government planners can pick investments and business opportunities better than markets can. They also point out that the efforts so far have resulted in a larger "too big to fail" problem today than it did before the extensive government regulation.

## II.10.B.e.v. Housing as Monetary Policy Tool

Housing is a monetary policy tool. We discussed housing at length above for its new role as a major macro formation quantity. Housing is perceived of as a prime macro manipulator and not solely a micro decision by households. We do not rely on people to spend on housing depending on how much they want, relative to the other goods and services on which they can spend their money. Through promulgation of research on housing and buying of housing-based securities, the Fed now resembles a housing promotion department. Housing will forever be a market targeted by the Fed, but it is slippery. Raising the price of housing may engender wealth effects for those who currently own but it also makes housing prices so high that newcomers are locked out of the housing market or forced to overspend.

## II.10.B.e.vi. Currency Manipulation & Currency Wars

Economically struggling countries can devalue their currencies in an attempt to rectify economic problems. Typically a country is running a trade deficit, a government budget deficit or both. Lowering the value of currency causes exports to rise and adds to economic growth. The nation's populace will be poorer given the devalued currency for whatever good and services they import, but this is considered a secondary factor. The devalued currency should increase GDP and therefore tax revenue such that the nation can rectify its deficits. Another factor is that trading partner countries could retaliate against one nation's devaluation, negating the policy effects in part or in whole.

A nation can lower its currency by lowering rates. Investors abandon assets in the low rate currency, causing selling of the currency. QE achieves the same result. When you lower your currency, you export deflation to other countries by providing your goods and services cheaply. There are various ways a country can keep its currency low. One is to print money and sell it for other currencies. Another is to lower rates, or circa 2015, to set interest rates negative. A third method is to use capital controls, like tax and regulatory rules. Notable cases in recent history of countries devaluing their currencies and restoring their economic growth to some extent are Sweden in the early 1990s, Argentina in the early 2000s and South Korea around 1997.

A primary question and area of contention concerns to what extent stimulative monetary policies (like QE's and lowering of rates) are merely attempts to lower currencies. For example, the ECB's QE announced in January 2015 and commenced in March 2015, appears to have the lowering of the euro as its main mechanism for improving the economy. Similarly, earlier in the post-2008 period, QE done by the U.S. worked in part through a lower dollar value. This was not a stated policy initiative of the U.S., but many foreign countries perceived that we were doing this. Abenomics, commenced in 2013, had its greatest effects through the currency level. The yen went down and Japanese exports surged. Politically, it is impolite to let on that your stimulation, QE or other policy is designed to lower currencies. Rather, policy people obscure the thrust by talking about enhancing lending through lower rates, instilling confidence in the future, creating wealth effects, etc. In 2015 and 2016 most nations including Eurozone, Japan, Canada, Australia, India, etc. were lowering rates and ostensibly devaluing their currencies.

Some analysts are altogether dismissive of and contend that stimulative policies benefit all countries and the world as a whole. This is something like a super Keynesian outcome: The favorable effects of my cheaper currency are much greater than the negative effects on my trading partners. Other analysts contend currency changes represent a zero-sum outcome and that history has no cases of countries that gained prosperity by devaluing. Currency devaluations hurt the standard of living of a nation's own people and can even result in net negative effects for all nations in that a "race to the bottom" has all the bad effects of lower currency, little of the good and creates great distortions and incentives for countries that had no intention of devaluing their currencies to commence to do so.

Concerning the U.S. situation since about 2008, initially (in the post -2008 period) with the accommodative monetary policy, the U.S. dollar went down in value. Investors sought currencies that would hold value against the dollar like the Swiss franc, the Australian dollar, the New Zealand dollar, etc. To some extent those countries accommodated their higher currency values. At other times, however, they engaged in policy to counter rising currencies. Culminating around 2010, the U.S. was accused by countries like Brazil and India of using a currency devaluation strategy. The U.S. dismissed these complaints. Later around 2014, as the U.S. ceased its QE, the dollar got stronger. At this point other countries were lowering the values of their currencies through various monetary policies. Around 2016 it is yet to be determined if the high U.S. dollar will crimp exports so much that the U.S. will have to rethink its policy.

## II.10.B.f. Exit Strategy & Raising Rates

Exit Strategy refers to the removal of the large reserves injected into the banking system by QE. After the first QE we optimistically assumed a prompt exit strategy would be the next policy. It did not transpire. At the end of QE2 we were contemplating an exit strategy. We deemed the economy still weak, however, and continued putting liquidity into the banks. At the end of QE3 in late 2014, we did not even talk about an exit strategy, or at least not with the same vigor that we did at the end of QE1 and QE2.

The primary methods or tools of any future exit strategy would be: (1) sell the securities; (2) raise the interest rate on reserves; (3) use draining tools (removing reserves by giving the counterparty some kind of security); (4) allow the securities to run off themselves as they come due and pay back their principal; and (5) some combination of the preceding.

Discussion of complete QE exit is very infrequent since 2014. Rather we talk about gradual drawdown of the Fed balance sheet by not reinvesting all, or some, of the proceeds of the matured bonds. As of early 2017, though, the Fed is still reinvesting in new bonds.

## II.10.B.f.i. Paying Interest on Reserves: the Fourth–and Highly Touted–Tool

Paying of interest on reserves ("IOR") is the prominent new Fed tool, which goes by the designations, Interest on Balances, Deposit Rate and Interest on Excess Reserves ("IOER"). It is now in my textbooks listed as the fourth basic tool of monetary policy and is an administered rate so it can be dictated by the Fed. It is very tractable for classroom discussion because the rate can be added to a supply and demand diagram of loanable funds formerly to demonstrate the fed funds rate and, even though the fed funds rate can appear to be nonbinding, the Deposit Rate will be binding. At least for now it is the dominating policy target rate.

On October 1, 2008, the Fed initiated the authority to pay interest on reserves (although the actual act for this authority goes back to 2006). Formerly, banks received no interest for the reserves they held at the Fed. IOR gives the Fed three tools/rates for manipulating reserves: (1) the fed funds rate, which the Fed sets a target for but leaves to banks to set amongst themselves; (2) the discount rate at which the Fed lends to banks directly and (3) IOR. The rate of interest on reverse repos will represent a fourth rate used as a tool of monetary policy. Using IOR to remove large amount of reserves from the system is simple in theory. To do so, the Fed merely raises IOR to the point where banks will find it profitable to lend reserves back to the Fed.

The IOR tool sounds simple and potentially powerful; but it proved problematic when teaching monetary policy in the period following 2009. Before IOR, teachers presented a supply and demand for reserves with interest rate on the vertical axis and reserves on the horizontal. The demand curve was downward sloping because banks would demand more reserves at lower rates. The supply curve for reserves was vertical and set by the Fed with open market operations. The intersection was the fed funds rate. That would constitute the basic story and then we would talk about the Fed increasing or decreasing the supply curve for reserves and thereby manipulating the fed funds target rate. To demonstrate potential policy in a crisis, we also hypothesized a horizontal portion of the supply curve at the level of the discount rate, which we typically kept above the fed funds rate. Supposedly, if there were increased demand for money for reserves, the fed funds rate would go up to the discount rate, at which point banks would drop out of the fed funds market and borrow directly from the Fed. This supply and demand model showed two ways the fed could control rates. It was also a pointless demonstration, in a sense, because it really only showed the superfluous nature of discount lending.

Now with IOR, the Fed can also set a floor. Assume the market for reserves initially clears at a fed funds rate of 3% while the discount rate is 4% and the IOR is 2%. If demand for reserves went down making the fed funds rate drop below 2%, banks that held reserves and were lending them out would now just lend them back to the Fed at 2%. Similarly, on the high end, the discount rate is a ceiling. Now, at least at the blackboard, the three rates can create a "corridor" where the highest rate could serve to limit upward spikes of the fed funds rate and the lowest rate could serve to limit downward movements. To demonstrate another scenario, suppose again that the market is clearing at 3%, and the Fed wanted to remove reserves from the system. It could raise the IOR to 3.5% and banks would give their reserves to the Fed.

It sounds clear but students ask obvious questions: "Aren't we lending the same quantity at three different rates?"; "Why don't we just remove the reserves with regular open market operations?"; "Why doesn't the Fed remove reserves by raising reserve requirements, instead of creating a new tool?" The Fed prefers IOR to reserve requirements perhaps because IOR avoids giving the appearance of dictating prices and quantities to private parties. Like setting the fed funds target rate with open market operations, IOR is only a nudging action that still relies on rates being set similarly in private markets.

Getting back to the real world, the Fed put hundreds of billions of dollars in reserves into the system with the intention that those reserves would be loaned with a multiplier effect, and the economy would be stimulated. The reserves seemingly were not loaned and sat dormant on banks' balance sheets. Analysts focused on the potential inflation from those large reserves. These inflation hawks were calling on one of the most fundamental theories of modern macroeconomics–that increasing the money supply results in inflation. Around the end of QE1, intellectual discussion was around the Exit Strategy of bringing those reserves back. In late 2009 and early 2010, officials (including Ben Bernanke) touted IOR as the key to removing reserves from the banking system. Neither inflation nor an Exit Strategy happened, but we did additional rounds of QE. Talk of using IOR to drain reserves died down, as did talk of inflation. For many years, up until December 2015, IOR remained at 0.25% and the fed funds rate sat somewhere around 0.20%. The below diagrams illustrate the theoretical concept of the corridor and the actual level of Fed policy rates up until December 2015:

**Supply & Demand for Bank Reserves**

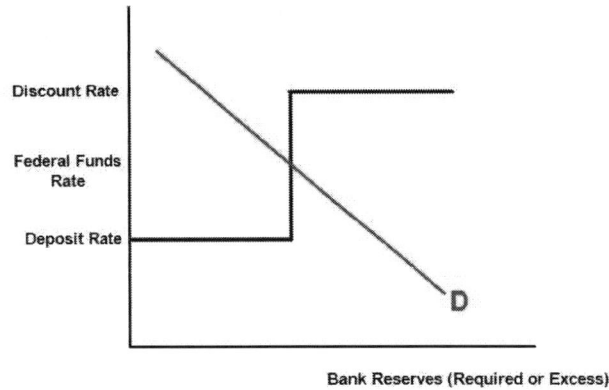

Discount Rate

Federal Funds Rate

Deposit Rate

D

Bank Reserves (Required or Excess)

**Supply & Demand for Bank Reserves - Actual**

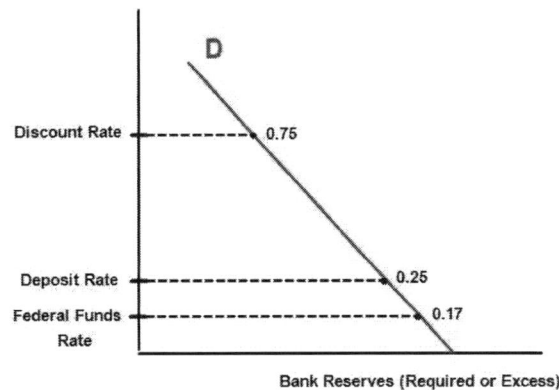

D

Discount Rate — — — — — — — — 0.75

Deposit Rate — — — — — — — — — — — — — 0.25

Federal Funds — — — — — — — — — — — — — 0.17
Rate

Bank Reserves (Required or Excess)

For a while, roughly during the years 2009 through 2012, many instructors of monetary economics presented the above diagram and corridor, or channel, theory of policy as if they were imminently implementable. Since the fed funds rate remained outside the corridor the model lost its appeal.

### II.10.B.f.ii. Reverse Repos

Repurchase Agreements ("Repos") and Reverse Repurchase Agreements ("Reverse Repos") are loans of securities for cash (Repos) or cash for securities (Reverse Repos). The loans are to be reversed in s short period, typically over one day, and are collateralized. These transactions and the markets for them are large and important, and also difficult to understand and assess for their importance to the economy.

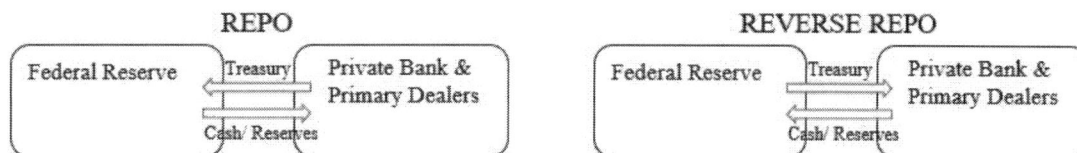

Normally, the Fed would use Repos to put or remove Reserves into the system. The Fed would buy bonds from banks and in return give banks reserves. Before ZIRP the Fed would do Repos every day typically in amounts in the single digit billions of dollars with bigger amounts when changing rates. It would do the Repos with the primary dealers and the collateral would typically be U.S. treasuries.

Now that the Fed has greatly increased reserves (i.e., cash) in the system its faces removing the cash in order to raise rates and Reverse Repos are the tool. The Fed had done Reverse Repos in the past but not in the amount and persistence it faces doing them today. The Fed will lend to banks and other eligible financial companies like investment management companies in return for their reserves. Reverse Repos are typically short term but would presumably be renewed. For a while the Fed did not refer to these trades as Reverse Repos because it gave the appearance that the Fed was borrowing money. In a Reverse Repo the Fed gets money from a counterparty in exchange for securities. Reverse Repos have become prominent as a tool that the Fed can use to take money out of the banking system. Some salient aspects of Reverse Repos used by the U.S. Fed to raise interest rates include the following:

- The Reverse Repo tactic has become known as ON RRP (overnight reverse repurchase agreements).
- ON RRP goes back to September 2013. Since then, the Fed tested the facility at various magnitudes and time durations. The intent is to set and enforce an interest rate floor on money rates. Reverse Repos are not intended to be permanent. The Fed intends to use treasuries as the collateral rather than the agencies or mortgage-backed's.
- The size of Reverse Repos that the Fed would be allowed to perform rose from about $300 billion to a daily cap of about $2 trillion. In 2015 and 2016 the Fed has maintained about $300 billion in Reverse Repos.
- One odd but important legal facet is that a Reverse Repo stays on the balance sheet on the Fed.
- The Fed increased the number of eligible Reverse Repo counterparties in early 2015. Formerly there were 22 primary dealers, mainly big name financial institutions like Band of America and Goldman Sachs. Now, more than 100 financial companies are partaking, including mutual funds that do money market funds and Fannie Mae and Freddie Mac. Reverse Repos allow the Fed to deal with anyone; not just banks.
- The Reverse Repos facility began in earnest in December 2015 when the Fed commenced raising rates. The amount of Reverse Repos has been in the few hundred billion, and the facility will probably end up very large and permanent.

## II.10.B.f.iii. Term Deposits

Term Deposits are another facility designed to remove the large bank reserves created pursuant to Fed policies of 2008 and following. The Fed began planning Term Deposits in 2009 as loans by the Fed to banks for banks' cash. They would have various terms, like 30 or seven-day. Although the banks, perhaps, would not view Term Deposits much differently from the overnight money held with the Fed, at least in theory the Term Deposits could not be loaned so the cash would be out of the system. In late 2014, the Fed engaged in hundreds of billions of these Term Deposits. Circa 2015 though, Term Deposits fell from prominence as the main device for removing reserves.

## II.10.B.f.iv. The December 2015 and December 2016 Rate Raisings

When the Fed appeared ready to raise rates in late 2015 analysts were speculating on how it would be done. At that time, five rates were talked about: Term Deposit Facility rate, Reverse Repo rate, Discount rate, Fed Funds rate and Interest Rate on Excess Reserves. Economists speculated that the Fed would raise them all about 25 basis. The raising of rates meant that the Fed–unlike in the policies following the crisis of 2008 when it bought bonds in exchange for reserves–would now be a seller. Some economists speculated that the Fed might do mini-hikes, like 1/8 of a percent. Others speculated that the Fed would raise and do the hundreds of billions or even trillions of Reverse Repos (in other words, whatever it takes) to drain money from the system and get short rates up. Other economists, however, speculated that the Fed would do raise in December but no again for a long time, and the effort to enforce the rate raises would be minimal.

Indeed, in December 2015, for the first time since 2006, the Fed raised rates. The fed funds rate target was raised to a range of 0.25% to 0.5% from 0% to 0.25%. The interest rate on reserves was raised to 0.5% and the discount rate was raised to 1%. The Fed indicated it would perform sufficient Reverse Repos to make the rate in that market rise about 25 basis points too. As of December 2015 the Fed indicated multiple rate raises would happen over 2016 and that the fed funds rate would be over 1% and then keep rising to around 2 to 3% in couple of years. That did not happen. The Fed raised rates another 25 basis points in December 2016. Market rates, such as mortgage rates and corporate bond rates, did not following the December 2015 rate increase. The December 2015 rate raising was a prominent event in financial markets but the December 2016 rate raising was anti-climactic.

## II.10.B.g. Wealth Effects

Traditionally, the Fed and most economists viewed monetary policy as working through interest rates both in theory and in practice. This created actual lending and economic activity, like investment and consumption. Since 2008, the focus of how policy effects the economy has changed to wealth effects. This is a fundamentally different way of viewing policy. Another difficulty of wealth effects as policy is that they are virtually impossible to measure; most wealth effect estimates are mere guesswork. For example, in 2013 both the stock and housing markets (the two main sources of household wealth) rose in value significantly: The stock market was up about 30% and the housing market was up about 10%, yielding trillions in each market. Analysts liberally related increased wealth to GDP growth, typically using ostensible and plausible stories of cause and effect such as numerous homeowners buying cars due to their homes suddenly being worth much more. With GDP growth of only 2% in that year though, any rough fraction of spending on wealth should have overwhelmed every other aspect of economic growth. Over the period 2009 to 2013, wealth increased by about $25 trillion. How much that impacted consumption is anyone's guess.

People consume out of disposable income, but also out of wealth, or more precisely, change in wealth. A person might spend most of his after tax income (his MPC on income might be 90%), but only a small fraction of his flux in wealth: For example, if he thinks he is worth $10,000 more this year, maybe he will spend 5% of that. That percentage is the wealth effect, and it applies to all categories of wealth, including bank savings, stock and bond holdings and real estate. Estimates of this wealth effect vary. It was once said to be a nickel out of each dollar increase in wealth (or 5%), with some economists going as much as nine cents. Following 2008 many economists believed the wealth effect dropped to about three cents or as little as zero. It is such a tough number to really know. In $Y = C + I + G$, the C is a function of disposable income and wealth, $C = \alpha + \beta Y_d + \gamma W$. The coefficient on the change in wealth, say 0.03, is the wealth effect.

All such numbers are guesses: For one thing, they are averages. Most households do not change their spending much on changes in wealth. Other households might crave spending and actively measure and re-measure their wealth and spend as much as they can against its increase. Typically, in the housing price run-up, some people actively refinanced their mortgages and spent 100% of the refied amount. Others ignored any increase in housing wealth, steadfastly believing that their house was just a place to live in. Perhaps during the heady days of house price increases many people did review the value of their houses periodically, perhaps year by year, and decided to spend along with the home value; but in general the idea that you turn to your spouse and say, "Our house is worth $25,000 more than it was last year, let's take that extra vacation" is a stretch. Big changes in wealth are inscrutable. For example, the 1987 stock market crash was such a large wealth drop that C should have gone way down and plunged the economy into a recession. The economy did not collapse, though. Similarly, the drop in stock market wealth in the period 2000 to 2002 should have made that most tepid recession of 2001 much worse.

Housing wealth effects are pivotal today. It is curious how they became predominant in our economic policy. For one, history may demarcate the period of about 1990 to 2007 of the great age of wealth effects. Before that, most people never thought of their houses as increasing in value so much each year that they would spend more on an annual basis. Nor were most households big stock holders at that time. Also in the period before 1990, wealth effects were not prominent on the lips of economists. Wealth effects are in certain macro models, but the magnitudes and overall effects are minimal. When house prices started to increase noticeably in the 1990s, guesses by economists about wealth effects (like the nickel we talked about above) became more prevalent. Going forward, perhaps a long-term realization that house prices changes only slowly will set it rendering the wealth effect minor. I have listed some miscellaneous aspects of the wealth effect here:

- The wealth effect, previously a side-show to Fed policy, is now the main thrust of Fed policy.
- Wealth effects are more relevant to wealthier households. Average people simply possess too little net wealth to perceive of changes in it. A rich person might think his million dollar home is worth more so he moves up to a $1.5 million home and buys additional home furnishings.
- The Fed wealth effects rational of 2012 to 2013 was that the Fed would buy bonds (like treasuries and mortgage-backed bonds), raising their prices and lowering their yields. Holders of these securities, including big holders like pension funds, would then have to buy higher yielding bonds and stocks to be able to attain sufficiently high average returns in their portfolios. As a result, everyone generally would feel wealthier. Also, an additional salutary effect on the economy may have been that the high-yield bond and stock investments funding companies that were likely to create jobs.
- It is reckless to assume the existence of a large wealth effect over a protracted time, i.e., that we flourish by constant increases in our wealth.

## II.10.B.h. Targetings

M&M instructors and practitioners, even including central bank heads, often talk about targets and goals interchangeably. The policy "target" refers to the macroeconomic quantity used to attain certain economic goals. The target is typically itself also a goal. The usual economic goals are inflation, employment (unemployment), GDP growth and any of a variety of related economic items like labor force participation, interest rate levels, levels of the stock or bond market, etc. Our most common target has been inflation. The device to attain that target, however, is interest rates and in particular the fed funds rate. You might call the fed funds rate an instrument, but we also refer to it as a target. The fed funds rate was our target from around 1982 up until about 2009. From 1979 to 1982, the Fed targeted money supply, but since 2009 our target has been a level and rate of large-scale asset purchases, or quantitative easing.

The "targetings" we are describing in this section are the various newly-proposed economic items that would make for superior economic policy compared to an inflation target. Until this recent crisis, low and stable inflation was the universal and singular target. We did not want inflation higher than 2%, and preferred it even lower. The method was to watch inflation and it appeared to be heading higher: Do policy to contract the economy. By controlling inflation we could rely on competitive markets to get us our highest GDP growth and employment. If a nation did not control inflation, it would face costs and distortions in markets and other anti-growth circumstances (like flight of capital). Since the 2008 recession though, we have dropped the strict and sole targeting of inflation. To some extent we still focus on an inflation target, but we are trying to get inflation up to 2%. Our efforts to get inflation higher have, according to some analysts, been unsuccessful; so we must override it as a policy goal with something more efficacious.

We could target virtually any quantity, and it is largely practical aspects that determine choices. Also, we are subject to certain conventions and restrictions. For example, income inequality is considered a grave economic problem today but we do not target it. Some economists would say we cannot measure it with precision or sufficient frequency. That is a technical issue, though. We could probably find an inequality measure. Others would argue that such a quantity is too far removed from what we control (like money supplies and interest rates); yet given the extremity of our central banking policies in recent years it is not impossible to attempt to target economic quantities outside inflation, interest rates, GDP levels, etc.

Below, I discuss items popularly mentioned as targets, and the distinctions are subtle. Our Fed has a formal target for inflation and has a less precise one for unemployment as part of our dual mandate. Targets can vary in the frequency of adjustments of policy with some, like inflation, engendering frequent policy changes and others, like unemployment, being longer-term targets. Some of the ideas discussed below are bandied about in discussion yet are not part of any formal Fed policy.

## II.10.B.h.i. Inflation Targeting

Inflation targeting (IT) is, or was, one of the greatest social science theories of modern times put into practice with relative conviction. IT represented a response to policy difficulties in the 1970s and 1980s that resulted in high inflation and volatile growth. IT was a nominal anchor that superseded theories of managing money supplies, exchange rates and the real economy. IT was most common monetary policy strategy up until the crisis of 2008 and, until 2008, IT was a one-directional and simple strategy. We wanted inflation no higher than a certain level, typically 2%; If anything, we hoped inflation was a lot lower, like 0.5%. Despite having the dual mandate for a long time, we let the unemployment situation resolve itself. If private parties could count on low inflation they could optimize creating the greatest output for our economy and the lowest unemployment. Under strict IT, intermediate targets (such as money supplies and certain interest rates) were secondary. In other words, the central bank would not try to maintain levels for those quantities. Rather, the bank would simply watch the level of inflation. If it got too high it would raise the fed funds rate; and vice versa.

Like other M&M ideas of minimal government intervention and simple rules like the Taylor Rule, IT came of age intellectually in the late 1980s and early 1990s and to prominence in policymaking in the 1990s. In formal central bank implementation, IT was pioneered by the central bank of New Zealand, but soon many other national banks embraced it. By the early 2000s many countries (including the U.K., Sweden, Chile, Canada, Australia, South Korea and Eurozone [to some extent]), were inflation targeters. Even the U.S. was a "closet" targeter. When Ben Bernanke became Fed Chairman, he was pretty much ready to adopt inflation as our sole goal. Also, by this time IT was incorporated in M&M textbooks as the prime goal with compelling empirical support and the evidence was pervasive: Countries with high and variable inflation performed poorly.

The events of 2008 and following abruptly relegated traditional IT to a minor role. The slow growing, low inflation economy of the post-2008 period even made IT appear to be the problem. Strict adherence to a set inflation rate would render central banks incapable of responding to endemic crises of markets, perhaps resulting in deflation and a chronically underperforming economy. Ironically, in January 2012 the Fed adopted an inflation target. The thinking was that we must strive to get inflation up to (i.e., not down to) 2%. This represents an odd adoption of a goal from original IT but for virtually the opposite reason.

## II.10.B.h.ii. Targeting Higher Inflation

Given the low inflation and low growth (both in real and in nominal terms) of the post-2008 period, many economists have proposed targeting higher inflation. Considering our history of fearing that inflation can get out of control, this is viewed as a risky proposition and, indeed, the policy was never endorsed or even proposed by the U.S. Fed or other senior government officials. Certain leading economists (like Olivier Blanchard, Kenneth Rogoff and Paul Krugman) have recommended shooting for higher inflation as being worth the risk. The risk of the economy falling into very low growth takes precedence. The specific levels of this higher inflation target vary but are something around 3 to 5%. The main idea is that only by aiming for higher inflation can we assure that we will not get stuck in deflation. Another benefit is that higher inflation will cause nominal interest rates to be higher which re-enables stimulative monetary policy. The potential for inflation to get out of control is considered low due to the Fed's supposedly-strong ability to control inflation. The counter cases to higher inflation targeting are that we could never reliably hit such a high level without running a risk of getting even higher, and possibly very variable, inflation. Also, higher inflation would create great economic distortion, and attaining the higher inflation level would quickly make it built into higher prices, wages and nominal interest rates. This would render its effects null after perhaps only a short period of effects. Higher inflation targeting is similar to, or virtually the same as, "overshooting" inflation, but the latter term sounds worse.

It is not really clear how we would attain higher inflation except by utilizing the usual methods of lowering rates, quantitative easings and communication by the central bank to private parties to expect higher inflation. The main theory behind wanting higher inflation is that, according certain economists, private parties perceive higher inflation as a signal for a strong economy and this in turn makes people spend, borrow, hire and work. Deflation, on the other hand, makes people hunker down. Economists scheme ways of engendering higher inflation. Some believe that higher oil and gas prices would make people spend more and create inflation and that people would take the high prices as a signal. Other analysts hope for higher housing prices, contending that people will rush to buy property and accoutrements if they think housing prices are rising. Some economists proposed charging fees, or negative interest, on savings. Others proposed giving people credit cards that they must spend immediately or lose.

One idea[124] that was popular, at least as a discussion tool, was to increase inflation expectations by having the government announce arbitrary invalidation of certain currency. For example, currency with serial numbers ending in a specified digit would be invalid after some time period. This would create an instant inflation (for example, 10% if currency ending in one certain digit were made invalid). Although this idea was never seriously proposed as policy, it reflects how extensively we ponder contemporary economic issues and how agreeable we are to manipulation of the macroeconomy.

## II.10.B.h.iii. Price Level Targeting

Price level targeting is a modification of IT to correct a potential flaw. With IT, "bygones are bygones," meaning that if we miss the inflation target in one period, we do not adjust in the next period to make it up. For example, if we wanted to hit 2% inflation per year and in a first year inflation is 0%, our inflation target in the next year would remain at 2% and not 4%. Price level targeting requires us to make up a shortcoming (or compensate for overshooting if that is the case). Our price level targets might be 100, 102, 104, 106, etc. If after the first year we are not at 102, we still shoot for 104. Price level targeting was not a popular topic in M&M until around late 2010 when it got picked up as a way of fighting apparent deflation tendencies prevalent in the economy.

## II.10.B.i.iv. Nominal GDP Targeting

Nominal GDP ("NGDP") targeting is another attempt to avoid falling into a trap of falling prices brought on by unintentionally overly tight policy. NGDP targeting supposedly creates a tendency towards greater confidence and, therefore, greater spending. NGDP is usually justified by comparing it to inflation targeting, which supposedly can result in overly rigid policy, typically in cases of adverse supply shocks. Shocks would create temporary high inflation that would, in an inflation targeting policy, be required to be countered with excessively tight policy. Inflation targeting also engenders problems with sticky wages. Workers are resistant to pay cuts and therefore inflation targeting can result in additional downward pressure on wages. Unlike inflation targeting, NGDP targeting would include a make-up feature similar to price level targeting. For example, if you do not hit your nominal GDP target in one year, you have to make it up in the next year. Many economists consider this a desirable policy feature to avoid deflation. Some elements of the debate on NGDP targeting are listed below:

- NGDP targeting is based on the idea that GDP grows about 5 to 6% nominally, with about half real growth and half inflation. Such a level has persisted over long periods of time. In practice policymakers would watch NGDP and enact policy to get near 5 or 6%. Under NGDP targeting, either prices or output would rise, but either way businesses perceive that revenues are increasing so they are not averse to expand and hire workers. Workers on their part would always get pay raises. Perhaps in any year the pay raise would be entirely nominal; that is, inflation would be the same as the wage increase. Regardless workers would feel confident and continue to spend.
- NGDP targeting proponents believe something like 6% nominal GDP growth will yield about 3% inflation and 3% real growth, but lower nominal GDP growth, like 4%, will yield a worse combination, perhaps 2% inflation and 2% real growth.

---

[124] The origin of this is not clear. I am sure it was conceived long ago by some teacher and brought up from time in time in lectures as a thought experiment or a clever point to titillate students.

- NGDP targeting is relatively new to M&M debates. It has come in response to the slow recovery from the recession of 2008. It goes far back in academic and policy circles. NGDP targeting was proposed in the late 1970s and early 1980s by economists such as James Meade and James Tobin.
- NGDP targeting is also known as market monetarism. This school views low interest rates as a sign of a weak economy and fears that the economy can hover too close to zero rates and deflation under regular monetary policy. Market monetarism is a relatively activist policy style that could be viewed as Keynesian leaning idea.
- NGDP targeting is based on general economic tendencies that may be flimsy: (1) If GDP is growing nominally, wages will grow too and workers will be hired without hitches; (2) If GDP is growing nominally, both a real GDP growth and inflation target will be hit; (3) If GDP is growing nominally, expectations of a continually growing economy will prevail.
- Targeting NGDP involves judging the looseness or tightness of monetary policy based on nominal GDP growth. Economists cite the case of Japan whose NGDP stagnated for long periods. They view this as evidence of tight policy, yet economists have little conviction of the true underlying path of real output growth in Japan. Perhaps if Japan had attained higher nominal growth it would not have been accompanied by any higher real growth.
- NGDP targeting might be perceived of as simply allowing higher inflation. Nominal GDP is hard to calculate. Existing calculations of it lack precision. Nominal GDP may become a simplistic goal, not reflecting unemployment or income inequality, which may be important facets of the economy.

## II.10.B.h.v. Unemployment Targeting

The Fed has a dual mandate to direct both inflation and unemployment. This commences with the passage of the Full Employment and Balanced Growth Act, or Humphrey-Hawkins, which passed in 1978 and set an unemployment target of 4%. This was well below the actual rate during that time: Unemployment was 8.5% in 1975, 7.7% in 1976, 7.1% in 1977 and 6.1% in 1978. Over the following decades, unemployment would decrease to the point that we did not focus too much on the unemployment component of our dual mandate. We believed that if we targeted inflation solely, the economy would perform optimally and attain minimal unemployment. Either our economy was efficient and strong or we were just lucky, but our unemployment rate tended close to the 4% target of Humphrey-Hawkins.

Like so many other economic quantities, everything changed with 2008. Unemployment soared to nearly 10%. Over the following years we recalibrated our estimate of full employment. The correct estimation of what unemployment should be was very contentious, yet we set targets. At one point 6.5% unemployment seemed like a reasonable target and certain Fed communications indicated that would be threshold to commence reversal of stimulative policy. As we approached that level in early 2014, however, the Fed hedged and dropped the numerical target in the March 2014 FOMC meeting. It would be almost two years later (when the unemployment rate was around 5%) before the Fed would raise. Ultimately, our monetary policy, especially under a labor-focused economist like Fed Chair Janet Yellen, rests heavily on an unemployment target as both an immediate and longer-term goal. We do not adjust our unemployment target frequently, but every FOMC meeting is largely focused on unemployment and related labor market indicators.

## II.10.B.h.vi. Equity Market Targeting

Maintaining a stock market level has been proposed as a valid and even preferred policy. One such proponent is UCLA economics professor Roger Farmer.[125] His idea is that our corporate sector is, indeed, perennially profitable, but people often underestimate the future profitability. Thus, they tend to undervalue stocks, causing a negative wealth effect and unwillingness to spend and invest both in the short and long term. Targeting the stock market has not been adopted yet as a formal monetary policy, although certain countries regularly engage in rhetoric about the importance of equity prices. Some countries have bought into the stock market, notably Japan, which has purchased about 10% of the Japanese stock market as of early 2016. The Chinese have also extended credit with the stated purpose that it finance stock trading. The Chinese embarked on this policy in July 2015 when their market was crashing.

Equity market targeting plays to our belief that we are the great entrepreneurs, that our corporate sector is very profitable and that people should partake in this wealth and must be goaded along through the process. Targeting the stock market is similar to what we called the central bank "put": the willingness of the Fed to hold up the value of asset markets, especially the stock market. We used to refer to the "Greenspan put." Under Greenspan, the Fed ostensibly did stimulative monetary policy anytime the stock market looked gummy, and many analysts think this is indeed a tacit Fed policy and the Greenspan put became the Bernanke put and is now the Yellen put.

## II.10.B.h.vii. Goodhart's Law

As pointed out above, we could target virtually any quantity. We stick to quantities like interest rates, inflation and nominal GDP growth that are integral to level of real economic activity. If such conventional targets appear less and less effective over time, we could shift to something bolder. We could target wealth quantities, notably the stock market, housing and bond market and be ready to support those when they hit certain levels.

Perhaps further in the future we could attempt even more basic manipulations. For example, one very prominent economic issue in America today is inequality, the gulf between the poor and the rich is vast and trending worse. In fact, most experts agree that a major effect of our government policies since 2008 has been to significantly exacerbate inequality. Policy insiders counter that the policy was needed since America would have suffered a great calamity without it, and surely the poor would have suffered even more than from the inequality that was the by-product of the policy. Could the Fed make inequality its target? One problem is that the measures of inequality that we have (like the Gini Coefficient) are crude and not easily updated promptly. A bigger problem might be designing monetary policies to offset adverse changes in inequality. Presumably if we saw the trend in inequality going up we would engage in looser monetary policy, but that may not work as intended.

Regardless of which target we choose, some economists theorize that once a quantity becomes a target and the focal point of substantial efforts by the central bank (and simultaneously by substantial efforts by private parties such as investors), it no longer functions as it did before. Therefore, it is no longer a genuine and exploitable target. Historical relationships that the target previously maintained with the economy become distorted in value and timing. This is known as Goodhart's Law, named after English economist Charles Goodhart. Lucas Critique, named for American economist Robert Lucas, is the more general statement that historical behavior of economic series changes once becoming part of policy goals. Both the Law and Critique go back to the 1970s, yet such critiques may not shape attempts by central banks to seek new goals.

---

[125] *How the Economy Works*, Oxford University Press. 2010.

Central banks could adopt other targets such as levels for equity markets, aggregate consumption levels and labor market levels (like labor force participation, consumption, etc.). Ultimately, the final goal should be utility: the microeconomic concept of what optimizing agents seek. If you believe that we can never measure what makes people happy (i.e., gives them utility), we may never have the best goal for our government policy.

## II.10.B.i. The Fed Balance Sheet & Its Transformation Since 2008

Before 2008, analysis of a central bank's balance sheet was done in the abstract, with T-accounts typically having two to four items (Securities and Discount Loans on the asset side, and Currency and Reserves on the liabilities side). The real Fed Balance Sheet ("FBS") would not have been examined. It had little else of interest on it. Today, the FBS, and balance sheets of other central banks too, have a multitude of line items representing unconventional monetary policy tools and special facilities. Many of these new items appeared on the FBS in the period 2009 to 2011 and have since been removed. Others remain. In general, any up-to-date M&M instruction must review the major items and changes of the central bank balance sheets. It is an easy lecture since the Fed balance sheet is updated weekly and posted on the Fed website as table H.4.1. with the technical name, "Factors Affecting Reserve Balances of Depository Institutions."

Up until 2008, the FBS grew in size year after year but its growth was slow and gradual. At the start of 2008 the FBS' bottom line was about $940 billion. On the asset side was roughly $800 billion in U.S. securities which was offset by about $800 billion in cash on the liability side. The asset side also held gold (of a small fixed magnitude; described in detail below), discount lending facilities (of magnitudes usually in the hundreds of millions) and Repurchase Agreements ("Repos"), which fluctuated a little and represented the facility in which open market operations were carried out. The liability side included items not integral to monetary policy including the U.S. treasury account and branch federal reserve banks' accounts. The liability side also held currency, Reverse Repurchase Agreements and Reserves. Reserves constitute the lifeblood of theoretical monetary policy. Increasing reserves leads the banking system to create credit out of thin air. Generally, before 2008, Reserves fluctuated a modest amount, usually in single digit billions of dollars.

The following three pages are excerpts of the FBS of November 9, 2016 including the first two pages showing the asset and liabilities sides and one page of sub-ledgers including a maturity distribution of the major Fed assets.

# FEDERAL RESERVE statistical release

H.4.1

**Factors Affecting Reserve Balances of Depository Institutions and
Condition Statement of Federal Reserve Banks**

November 10, 2016

## 1. Factors Affecting Reserve Balances of Depository Institutions

Millions of dollars

| Reserve Bank credit, related items, and reserve balances of depository institutions at Federal Reserve Banks | Averages of daily figures | | | | | Wednesday Nov 9, 2016 |
|---|---|---|---|---|---|---|
| | Week ended Nov 9, 2016 | Change from week ended | | | | |
| | | Nov 2, 2016 | | Nov 11, 2015 | | |
| Reserve Bank credit | 4,414,728 | + | 1,971 | − | 38,546 | 4,415,454 |
| Securities held outright[1] | 4,217,970 | + | 71 | − | 22,011 | 4,217,995 |
| U.S. Treasury securities | 2,463,629 | + | 65 | + | 1,897 | 2,463,654 |
| Bills[2] | 0 | | 0 | | 0 | 0 |
| Notes and bonds, nominal[2] | 2,340,674 | − | 173 | − | 5,965 | 2,340,674 |
| Notes and bonds, inflation-indexed[2] | 105,526 | + | 173 | + | 6,992 | 105,526 |
| Inflation compensation[3] | 17,429 | + | 65 | + | 870 | 17,454 |
| Federal agency debt securities[2] | 18,493 | | 0 | − | 15,653 | 18,493 |
| Mortgage-backed securities[4] | 1,735,848 | + | 5 | − | 8,255 | 1,735,848 |
| Unamortized premiums on securities held outright[5] | 175,503 | − | 333 | − | 16,349 | 175,402 |
| Unamortized discounts on securities held outright[5] | −15,274 | + | 41 | + | 1,546 | −15,263 |
| Repurchase agreements[6] | 0 | | 0 | | 0 | 0 |
| Loans | 28 | − | 30 | − | 93 | 32 |
| Primary credit | 1 | − | 3 | | 0 | 0 |
| Secondary credit | 0 | | 0 | | 0 | 0 |
| Seasonal credit | 27 | − | 26 | − | 92 | 32 |
| Other credit extensions | 0 | | 0 | | 0 | 0 |
| Net portfolio holdings of Maiden Lane LLC[7] | 1,708 | + | 2 | − | 5 | 1,708 |
| Float | −356 | + | 479 | − | 502 | −538 |
| Central bank liquidity swaps[8] | 1,000 | − | 15 | + | 859 | 1,000 |
| Other Federal Reserve assets[9] | 34,149 | + | 1,756 | − | 1,990 | 35,118 |
| Foreign currency denominated assets[10] | 21,092 | + | 176 | + | 1,749 | 20,875 |
| Gold stock | 11,041 | | 0 | | 0 | 11,041 |
| Special drawing rights certificate account | 5,200 | | 0 | | 0 | 5,200 |
| Treasury currency outstanding[11] | 48,295 | + | 14 | + | 818 | 48,295 |
| **Total factors supplying reserve funds** | 4,500,356 | + | 2,161 | − | 35,979 | 4,500,864 |

Note: Components may not sum to totals because of rounding. Footnotes appear at the end of the table.

## 1. Factors Affecting Reserve Balances of Depository Institutions (continued)

Millions of dollars

| Reserve Bank credit, related items, and reserve balances of depository institutions at Federal Reserve Banks | Averages of daily figures | | | | | Wednesday Nov 9, 2016 |
|---|---|---|---|---|---|---|
| | Week ended Nov 9, 2016 | Change from week ended | | | | |
| | | Nov 2, 2016 | | Nov 11, 2015 | | |
| Currency in circulation[11] | 1,486,273 | + | 7,061 | + | 82,890 | 1,489,610 |
| Reverse repurchase agreements[12] | 370,188 | − | 24,943 | + | 97,218 | 363,349 |
|   Foreign official and international accounts | 235,190 | − | 4,515 | + | 40,237 | 232,356 |
|   Others | 134,998 | − | 20,428 | + | 56,980 | 130,993 |
| Treasury cash holdings | 186 | + | 4 | − | 55 | 195 |
| Deposits with F.R. Banks, other than reserve balances | 419,824 | − | 49,266 | + | 282,333 | 410,637 |
|   Term deposits held by depository institutions | 0 | | 0 | | 0 | 0 |
|   U.S. Treasury, General Account | 376,217 | − | 41,448 | + | 269,092 | 365,454 |
|   Foreign official | 5,234 | + | 61 | − | 273 | 5,517 |
|   Other[13] | 38,372 | − | 7,881 | + | 13,513 | 39,666 |
| Other liabilities and capital[14] | 48,215 | + | 1,622 | − | 18,059 | 46,992 |
| **Total factors, other than reserve balances, absorbing reserve funds** | 2,324,685 | − | 65,523 | + | 444,326 | 2,310,782 |
| **Reserve balances with Federal Reserve Banks** | 2,175,670 | + | 67,683 | − | 480,306 | 2,190,082 |

Note: Components may not sum to totals because of rounding.

1. Includes securities lent to dealers under the overnight securities lending facility; refer to table 1A.
2. Face value of the securities.
3. Compensation that adjusts for the effect of inflation on the original face value of inflation-indexed securities.
4. Guaranteed by Fannie Mae, Freddie Mac, and Ginnie Mae. The current face value shown is the remaining principal balance of the securities.
5. Reflects the premium or discount, which is the difference between the purchase price and the face value of the securities that has not been amortized. For U.S. Treasury and Federal agency debt securities, amortization is on a straight-line basis. For mortgage-backed securities, amortization is on an effective-interest basis.
6. Cash value of agreements.
7. Refer to table 4 and the note on consolidation accompanying table 6.
8. Dollar value of foreign currency held under these agreements valued at the exchange rate to be used when the foreign currency is returned to the foreign central bank. This exchange rate equals the market exchange rate used when the foreign currency was acquired from the foreign central bank.
9. Includes accrued interest, which represents the daily accumulation of interest earned, and other accounts receivable. Also, includes Reserve Bank premises and equipment net of allowances for depreciation.
10. Revalued daily at current foreign currency exchange rates.
11. Estimated.
12. Cash value of agreements, which are collateralized by U.S. Treasury securities, federal agency debt securities, and mortgage-backed securities.
13. Includes deposits held at the Reserve Banks by international and multilateral organizations, government-sponsored enterprises, and designated financial market utilities. Also includes certain deposit accounts other than the U.S. Treasury, General Account, for services provided by the Reserve Banks as fiscal agents of the United States.
14. Includes the liability for earnings remittances due to the U.S. Treasury.

Sources: Federal Reserve Banks and the U.S. Department of the Treasury.

H.4.1

## 1A. Memorandum Items
Millions of dollars

| Memorandum item | Averages of daily figures | | | Wednesday Nov 9, 2016 |
| --- | --- | --- | --- | --- |
| | Week ended Nov 9, 2016 | Change from week ended | | |
| | | Nov 2, 2016 | Nov 11, 2015 | |
| Securities held in custody for foreign official and international accounts | 3,111,376 | − 8,965 | − 191,956 | 3,114,260 |
| Marketable U.S. Treasury securities[1] | 2,790,985 | − 9,652 | − 191,390 | 2,793,815 |
| Federal agency debt and mortgage-backed securities[2] | 259,861 | + 444 | − 14,985 | 259,750 |
| Other securities[3] | 60,530 | + 244 | + 14,418 | 60,695 |
| Securities lent to dealers | 20,462 | − 919 | + 3,295 | 18,326 |
| Overnight facility[4] | 20,462 | − 919 | + 3,295 | 18,326 |
| U.S. Treasury securities | 20,436 | − 920 | + 3,316 | 18,295 |
| Federal agency debt securities | 26 | + 1 | − 21 | 31 |

Note: Components may not sum to totals because of rounding.

1. Includes securities and U.S. Treasury STRIPS at face value, and inflation compensation on TIPS. Does not include securities pledged as collateral to foreign official and international account holders against reverse repurchase agreements with the Federal Reserve presented in tables 1, 5, and 6.
2. Face value of federal agency securities and current face value of mortgage-backed securities, which is the remaining principal balance of the securities.
3. Includes non-marketable U.S. Treasury securities, supranationals, corporate bonds, asset-backed securities, and commercial paper at face value.
4. Face value. Fully collateralized by U.S. Treasury securities.

## 2. Maturity Distribution of Securities, Loans, and Selected Other Assets and Liabilities, November 9, 2016
Millions of dollars

| Remaining Maturity | Within 15 days | 16 days to 90 days | 91 days to 1 year | Over 1 year to 5 years | Over 5 year to 10 years | Over 10 years | All |
| --- | --- | --- | --- | --- | --- | --- | --- |
| Loans | 7 | 26 | 0 | 0 | 0 | ... | 32 |
| U.S. Treasury securities[1] | | | | | | | |
| Holdings | 13,573 | 32,691 | 148,239 | 1,198,574 | 435,177 | 635,400 | 2,463,654 |
| Weekly changes | 0 | + 2 | + 1 | + 12 | + 12 | + 42 | + 68 |
| Federal agency debt securities[2] | | | | | | | |
| Holdings | 0 | 2,313 | 9,423 | 4,410 | 0 | 2,347 | 18,493 |
| Weekly changes | 0 | 0 | 0 | 0 | 0 | 0 | 0 |
| Mortgage-backed securities[3] | | | | | | | |
| Holdings | 0 | 0 | 0 | 1,582 | 11,198 | 1,723,068 | 1,735,848 |
| Weekly changes | 0 | 0 | 0 | 0 | + 290 | − 289 | + 1 |
| Repurchase agreements[4] | 0 | 0 | ... | ... | ... | ... | 0 |
| Central bank liquidity swaps[5] | 1,000 | 0 | 0 | 0 | 0 | 0 | 1,000 |
| Reverse repurchase agreements[4] | 363,349 | 0 | ... | ... | ... | ... | 363,349 |
| Term deposits | 0 | 0 | 0 | ... | ... | ... | 0 |

Note: Components may not sum to totals because of rounding.
...Not applicable.

1. Face value. For inflation-indexed securities, includes the original face value and compensation that adjusts for the effect of inflation on the original face value of such securities.
2. Face value.
3. Guaranteed by Fannie Mae, Freddie Mac, and Ginnie Mae. The current face value shown is the remaining principal balance of the securities.
4. Cash value of agreements.
5. Dollar value of foreign currency held under these agreements valued at the exchange rate to be used when the foreign currency is returned to the foreign central bank. This exchange rate equals the market exchange rate used when the foreign currency was acquired from the foreign central bank.

**Maximize Utility**
© Christopher M. McHugh

**Page 250**

The FBS is posted weekly and available on the Fed website going back to the mid-1990s. Listed below are aspects of the FBS that should be broached in an advanced M&M class today. To relate the story of unconventional monetary policy and other changes in central banking brought on by the 2008 financial crisis start with pre-crisis FBS's, perhaps a version from 2007 or early 2008. For advanced treatments, examine select FBS's from points during the crisis especially 2008 and 2009, when many of the extraordinary Fed facilities were initiated.

- The FBS from before the crisis (for example, anytime in 2007 or early 2008) would show a large holding of treasury bills (the short-term U.S. debt). The Fed no longer holds short-term debt.
- Reserves, called "Reserve balances with Federal Reserve banks," is perhaps the most important item on the FBS according to traditional monetary theory. Changes in Reserves determines credit, in a potentially multiplied way due to fractional reserve banking. The magnitude of Reserves before the crisis was moderate, in the single billion to tens of billions of dollars. For example, in May 2008 Reserves were about $11 billion. November 2016 Reserves were about $2.2 trillion.
- The total assets of the FBS were $921 billion in March 2008. Assets peaked around $4.5 trillion at the end of 2014, when QE3 was finished and have remained there since.
- On July 3, 2008, a line item of about $30 billion entitled "Net portfolio holdings of Maiden Lane LLC" appeared on the FBS. This represented the 2008 Bear Stearns takeover. It was the first major extraordinary item of the 2008 crisis to appear on the FBS.
- Before 2008, the predominant Fed liability was currency, constituting roughly 90% of liabilities. Currency is a liability that is never called. Cash simply stays in the economy for transactions purposes. If a central bank does not issue too much cash and has minimal other liabilities (like the Fed prior to 2008), its liabilities are minimal.
- Beginning in 2008 and playing out during 2009 and into 2010, the Fed opened a variety of facilities that appeared as assets. (We mentioned them above in *Expanded Lending…*and *Chronology…*). They include Term Auction Credit, Primary dealer credit facility, Foreign currency swaps called "Central Bank Liquidity Swaps," the acquisition of insurance company AIG (seen in line items such as "Credit extended to American International Group, Inc., net," Commercial Paper Funding Facility, Asset-Backed Commercial Paper Money Market Mutual Fund Liquidity Facility, Term Asset-Backed Securities Loan Facility and lending commitments to large banks such as Bank of America and Citigroup.
- Bonds of Fannie Mae and Freddie Mac are "Federal agency debt securities," and these Fed holdings were over $100 billion at times. The Fed continues to hold some of these today.
- Repurchase Agreements, or Repos, are, to the Fed, the buying of a security from a financial institution in exchange for reserves. This action adds reserves to the system. Repos used to be the main Fed device to perform open market operations. Before 2008, Repos would often be in the tens of billions on the asset side of the FBS. In recent years, however, Repos have been equal to zero.
- Reverse Repurchase Agreements, or Reverse Repos, are the opposite of a Repo. In this case, the Fed provides a security in exchange for cash. On the FSB Reverse Repos are liabilities. As of November 2016, they were about $370 billion. In the past Fed Reverse Repos were done with foreign counterparties (e.g., the Fed takes cash from a European financial company and gives a security as collateral). Lately, the Fed has been doing extensive Reverse Repos with domestic counterparties. The purpose is to remove money from the financial system to effect the raising of interest rates. The Fed tested this procedure throughout 2015 and implemented it in 2016.
- Gold is an asset on the FBS but its $11 billion value does not adjusted for market value. The approximately 262 million troy ounces are recorded at a book value of $42.22 per the Gold Reserve

Act of 1934. Given the current price (about $1,228 per ounce as of November 11, 2016) the market value would be about $322 billion. The gold is held by the Fed yet owned by the U.S. Treasury.

- Maturity of FBS holdings is very important since longer maturity bonds have more price risk. The "Maturity Distribution" demonstration shows the Fed's holdings' time to maturity. Up through 2008, most maturities were under three years. Now, as of November 2016, the vast majority of Fed holdings are relatively long-term. Almost all of the approximate $1.7 trillion of mortgage-backed holdings are over ten years and about 40% of the total $2.5 trillion of U.S. Treasury holdings are over five years in maturity.

- There is a noteworthy footnote on the mortgage-backed holdings. They are, "Guaranteed by Fannie Mae, Freddie Mac, and Ginnie Mae." These companies are, of course, backed by the U.S. government and the Fed itself is a quasi-government agency. Furthermore, the Fed backs the U.S. government with its monetary policy including its QE. One government arm is backing the other, and vice versa.

- Certain information on the FBS helps reveal how the Fed makes money. The Fed receives interest from its holdings, of which it has multiple trillion with an average coupon interest rate of something around 3%. For the year 2015, Fed gross earnings were about $114 billion and net earnings were about $103 billion. The Fed pays its operating expenses and also interest on reserves. Since that rate is low the expense is low. Currently, at interest rate of 0.5% interest expense on the $2.2 trillion in Reserves is a modest $11 billion. If the Fed raised rates, of course, its interest expense would increase. Fed earnings are remitted to the U.S. Treasury. The detailed earnings information are complicated and the amount ultimately transmitted to the U.S. Treasury can include various adjusting items. Details can be found in Fed Annual Reports.[126]

- The major asset side items are U.S. debt, mortgage-backed securities and agency debt (bonds of Fannie Mae and Freddie Mac). The Fed values its securities at par, i.e., at 100 cents on the dollar, regardless of the market price. The Fed adjusts for the market values in the items "Unamortized premiums on securities held outright" for bonds above par and "Unamortized discounts." At November 2016, those amounts were $175 billion and -$15 billion, respectively.

- Liability side items are fewer. As of November 2016 there was about $1.49 trillion in Currency in Circulation, $370 billion in Reverse Repos, $376 billion in the U.S. Treasury, General Account and $2.18 trillion in reserves.

- The "U.S. Treasury, General Account" represents the bank account for the U.S. government. This is merely a convention and our federal government could utilize a commercial bank for its banking. The balance goes up and down with tax revenues and expenditures and has nothing to do with monetary policy.

- A case for insolvency of the Fed is not without possibility. Many analysts contend a central bank cannot be insolvent since it can always print money. Also, it does not have to adhere to regular rules of accounting. For example, it does not have to mark its assets to market value. Under certain circumstances, though, financial markets could look past these conventions. If interest rates rose and the Fed had to pay significantly more interest on reserves and simultaneously the Fed was compelled to mark it assets at market prices, the Fed could struggle with attaining policy goals and could at least appear un-operational. Perhaps it would require an enormous loss of confidence in the greater U.S. government for the Fed to actually be deemed insolvent, but it could result in high inflation.

---

[126] http://www.federalreserve.gov/publications/annual-report/files/2015-annual-report.pdf. See p. 103 Table 4, "Income, expenses, and distribution of net earnings of the Federal Reserve Banks, 2015 and 2014.

- The monetary base (Currency plus Reserves) is visible on the liability side of the FBS. Under conventional monetary theory changes in the monetary base enter the banking system and result in lending which is magnified by a multiplier effect. As this happens, M1 and M2 increase in value. M1, M2, etc. are not visible on the FBS; rather, they are found on Fed table H.6 Money Stock Measures. H.6 itself does not show the monetary base. Many experts in monetary economics and copious students never understand the theoretical and computational differences between monetary base and monetary aggregates like M1 and M2.

### II.10.B.i.i. Depiction of Central Bank Assets & Liabilities Over Time: The Magma Diagram

Another popular and revealing demonstration of recent Fed policy is a time series of the magnitudes of the items of the Fed (or other central bank) balance sheet. It can be done with either the asset or liability side quantities but is more commonly done for the asset side. This is informally known as the Magma Diagram and has been prominent since the balance sheet expanded greatly in 2009. Prior to 2008, the Magma Diagram could have been depicted, of course, but would have offered minimal insight since the components of central bank balance sheets changed very little over time in character or magnitude.[127]

The Magma Diagram's asset side shows the institution, growth and discontinuation, in some cases, of various special programs to support the financial system in 2008 and 2009. In other instances, Magma reflects the continuation of these programs. The Magma Diagram highlights the LSAPs that played out over the period 2010 to 2014. Viewing the picture over the shorter historical range of about 2008 to 2010 gives more insight about the variety of programs engaged in by the Fed. The liability side typically has currency (Federal Reserve notes) moving along at a steady amount (around $1 trillion), with Reserve Balances increasing starting in about mid-2008 from levels of tens of billions until they become multiple trillions. On the liability side starting in 2015 Reverse Repos have also become a hefty amount.

Similar depictions are available for other central banks and make it easy to compare the various balance sheet expansion programs and their timings and components. The Bank of Canada and Royal Bank of Australia balance sheets grew in 2009 but then contracted to about what they were before 2008, in contrast to the Fed and the Bank of England. The Swiss National Bank's assets grew greatly in the form of currency purchases. The ECB showed gradual increase with a spike in 2012, but then a contraction to a level not much more than before the crisis. As of 2015, the ECB is increasing assets.

A diagram of combined assets of the major central banks of the world including the Fed, the ECB, the Bank of Japan, the Bank of England, the Swiss National Bank and the People's Bank of China would have total assets at about $6 trillion in 2008 and over $17 trillion in 2016, a very large increase.

---

[127] A Magma diagram, entitled, "Federal Reserve assets and liabilities," is in the Annual Report of the Federal Reserve. For 2015, see http://www.federalreserve.gov/publications/annual-report/files/2015-annual-report.pdf, Figure 19, p. 20.

## Magma Diagram of the U.S. Federal Reserve: Asset Side

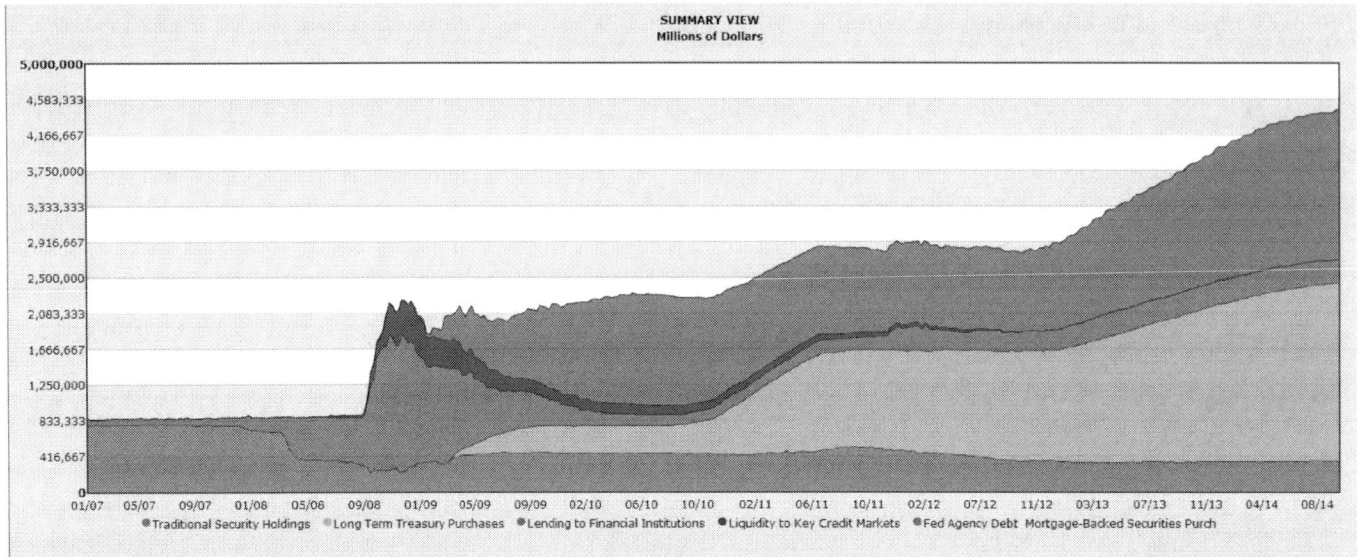

SUMMARY VIEW
Millions of Dollars

● Traditional Security Holdings  ● Long Term Treasury Purchases  ● Lending to Financial Institutions  ● Liquidity to Key Credit Markets  ● Fed Agency Debt  Mortgage-Backed Securities Purch

## Magma Diagram of the U.S. Federal Reserve: Liability Side

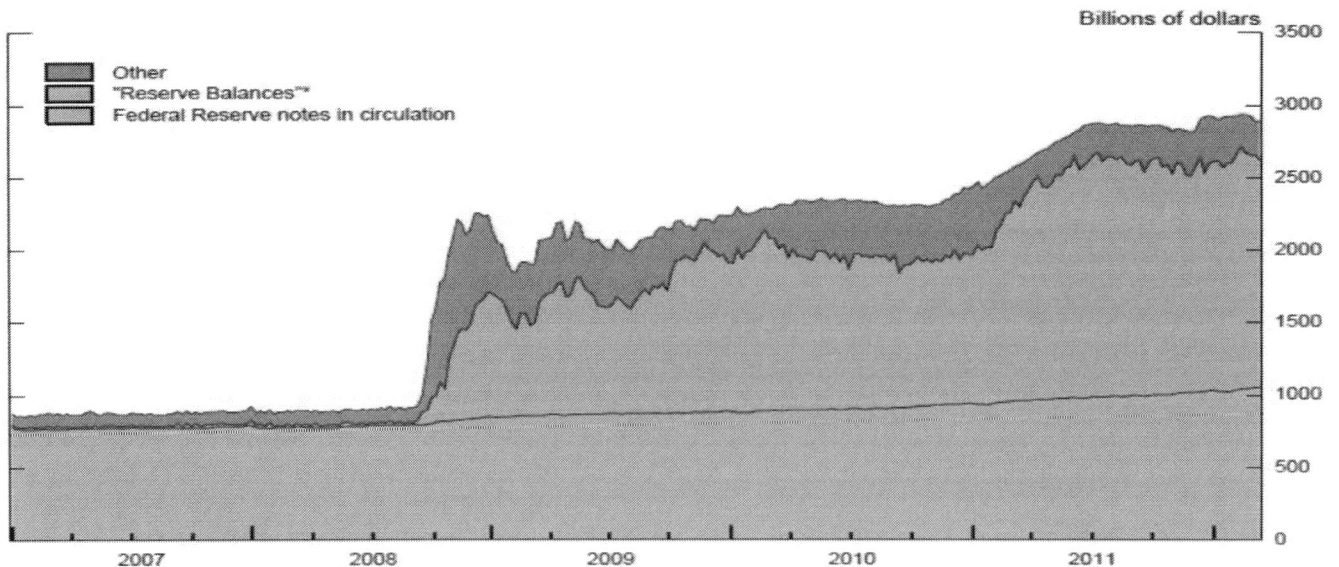

**Federal Reserve Balance Sheet, Liabilities and Capital**

Billions of dollars

- Other
- "Reserve Balances"*
- Federal Reserve notes in circulation

* Term deposits and other deposits held by depository institutions.
Source: Federal Reserve Board.

## II.10.B.i.ii. The Fed Balance Sheet: Summary

The above discussion demonstrates that the Fed Balance Sheet is different from those of banks or other companies: Currency is a liability that may never have to be paid down in any way, and bonds are marked at par not market price. The central bank's net equity does not represent a value the owners can take away. An abrupt increase in the size of the balance sheet can be engineered. Since the central bank is so different, many analysts contend that it can defy valuation constraints indefinitely. In the extreme, some analysts argue that a central bank can issue liabilities, including currency, forever and that this will not result in collapse of the bank or great detriment to the economy. A sophisticated financial columnist opines, "Does it matter that the central bank's equity is reduced? No. Standard accounting terms lose their usual meanings when applied to central banks. Money isn't a liability in the ordinary sense…a central bank needn't worry about losses…an entity that can create money can't ever go bust."[128]

The flaw is that if a central bank issues too much money there is a point when people doubt its value. They may sell assets denominated in that currency and/or demand more of that currency in exchange for real goods. These actions would lead to inflation and a decrease in the foreign exchange value of the currency. Ultimately, this could lead to a fiscal crisis and a funding crisis for the government. The government would have to pay higher interest on its debt or perhaps be unable to float debt in its own currency. In a severe enough crisis the central bank, which technically speaking cannot become insolvent since it can issue currency, would become unable to function. Such collapse has happened in many countries that issue too much currency. Sometimes markets continue to accept a currency and sovereign bonds even with chronic high inflation but there is a tipping point in which the monetary system fails to function

## II.10.B.j. Central Banks of the World

In M&M there is a perception, at least in the West, that the U.S. central bank is the leader, certainly in size and force of policy. This is also true and perhaps even more importantly in sophistication and application of policy by genuine economic goals for inflation and output (i.e., not policy to manager political, regional, exchange rate or other specialized circumstances). The ECB, the Bank of England and central banks in countries like Canada and Australia are our intellectual peers in most respects. We, however, relegate the policy actions of most other central banks as being dependent on local and specific national factors and/or to exchange rate maintenance. For example, Russian monetary policy reacts to local geopolitical factors, like the Ukraine crisis of 2014 and the price of oil. For another example, Denmark, from about 2012 to the present, set its basic policy rate to below zero: a negative rate to keep the value of its currency (the krone) down in response to preponderant policies of the ECB. This perception that we alone perform theoretical monetary policy while other countries react to local factors has some validity, but it is waning. Today, the U.S. competes intellectually with many other major central banks that have sophisticated research departments and often engage in policies that are arguably no less theoretically insightful, and often more rigorous and less arbitrary, than our own. To put it more colloquially, we are overrated as monetary policy experts.

Therefore, another requisite lecture for M&M classes is a review of the world's central banks, including those of the major developed nation/states like the ECB, Bank of England, Reserve Bank of Australia, Bank of Japan and, more importantly, banks from developing nations including the People's Bank of China, Central Bank of Russia, Central Bank of Brazil and the Reserve Bank of India. This is a

---

[128] "Monetary Policy for the Next Recession," by Clive Crook, *BloombergView*, May 31, 2015.

straightforward task because they each have webpages in English. There are several features to look for and discuss, including the following:

- **Basic Statement of Policy**: Most banks have a single mandate of inflation control or, as it is often termed, price stability. Despite the prominence of deflation today and the desire to get inflation up to a certain level, most banks describe their inflation target as a level to stay below. The U.S. Fed is almost unique in that it has an explicit dual mandate of inflation and unemployment. A few central banks (like the Reserve Bank of Australia) mention full employment as a goal but have historically targeted inflation. Of course, even though other central banks do not have an explicit goal of unemployment level, they often set policy with unemployment as a de facto target. Indeed, many banks have various official statements of which quantities they target and the best description for most banks might be that inflation targeting is a hierarchical mandate, which means inflation first and then other goals.

- **Level of the Inflation Target**: Central banks in developed economies have inflation rate targets at or around 2%. The rate is higher for emerging market countries like Russia and Brazil. Russia, for example, sets a target of 4% (for 2017) and explains that is target inflation is higher than that of developed countries due to ingrained recent experiences of high inflation. Since inflation is hard to measure another interesting distinction is the choice of inflation measurement. The U.S. Fed focuses on core inflation while the ECB focuses on headline inflation.

- **Policy Tool**: As is typical since 2008 the simplicity of a solitary basic policy tool has changed. Prior to 2008, most central banks controlled an overnight lending rate. This goes by different names: For the Fed it is the fed funds rate; for the ECB, the marginal lending rate; for the Bank of Japan, the uncollateralized overnight call rate; etc. Some banks (like China's) manage reserve ratios. A country like China, however, also sets its currency exchange rate and other rates. Many nations' banks manage their currency levels, and therefore largely set levels of interest rates to accommodate monetary policy of nations, like the U.S., since our policy affects currency exchange rates significantly.

- **Other Policy and Institutional Facets**: The ECB has a role in member nations' fiscal policy, setting levels for deficit and debt. The U.S. Fed does not. Again, since 2008, many policies and practices are changing. Before recently, the ECB was not supposed to buy the sovereign debt of nations, and this restriction was designed to keep the ECB from funding governments and arose ass an issue in 2014 and 2015 when the ECB planned and then commenced QE. Another impediment to performing QE in Eurozone is smaller pools of liquid assets compared to the U.S. Also, certain ECB members (notably Germany) oppose QE for many reasons, including that it simply would not create lending or reduce broad borrowing costs in a way to create desirable economic activity. It would also involve buying highly-priced assets, thus making the ECB balance sheet weak and jeopardizing central bank independence if it had to turn to national governments for funding.

- **Leadership**: The leaders of emerging market central banks, like those of China, Russia, India or Brazil, usually have educational backgrounds with Western exposure. They are also not too old, typically in their 50s. We often derided national competitors, like the old Soviet Union and Communist China, for their parochial and geriatric leadership. Another leadership facet of central banks is that decision making is done by committee.

- **Sophistication of Research**: Twenty or thirty years ago banks like Brazil's and Russia's would not have had sophisticated research departments. Each bank now has research including scholarly papers and official guidebooks for policy models and tools. Some banks' research displays relatively activist policy leanings and certitude of efficacy of policy. Others are more fatalist concerning the efficacy of central bank policy in the greater economy. In the latter case, the central bank stabilizes prices but underlying economic forces determine overall economic growth.

- **Public Commentary by Bank Senior Officials Concerning Purpose of Policies**: Are they invoking Keynesian assumptions? Are they attributing their problems to policies from abroad? Do they express more concern about inflation or unemployment? Do they attribute problems to structural forces or cyclical forces? Do they blame fiscal authorities for not doing their part in stimulating the economy?
- **Transparency**: Which reports, meeting transcripts, meeting minutes, etc. are released to the public, and with what frequency? The ECB does not release transcripts of its meetings.
- **Independence**: Is the central bank independent from the national government? Some nations historically have more independent central banks. Poorer nations tend to have central banks that are more under the control of national governments. Also, in general, since the unconventional monetary policies of the post-2008 period, central bank decision making has ostensibly been accompanied by greater pressure from national governments. Japan is a good example of this.
- **Balance Sheet Size Compared to Nation/States' GDP's**: For the U.S., this is a little over 22% (as of 2016) from about 6% (as of 2007). The Bank of England's is similar, and Japan's is higher. Switzerland's figure is very high. How selected balance sheets changed post-2008 should also be noted. The Fed's grew almost constantly from about $1 trillion to more than $4 trillion. The ECB's started at about 1.4 trillion euros in 2008 and increased, peaking at about 3.1 trillion euros in 2012 as it engaged in emergency lending. It then contracted to about 2 trillion euros at the end of 2014 and now is about 3 trillion euros in 2016.
- **Levels of the Basic Short Rates Managed by Banks**: The banks' main rates are the rate of interest for deposits and the overnight lending rate. The overnight lending rates are low for the U.S., Eurozone, U.K. and Japan. The U.S. recently raised the fed funds rate in December 2015 to a range of 0.25 to 0.50%. Central banks in Brazil, China, Russia and India have higher rates: 14.25%, 4.35%, 10% and 6.5%, respectively, as of September 2016.

Certain central banks have undertaken extreme policy intervention in recent years. Other do policy differently from that of the United States. The list below details some contemporary facets:

- China does a variety of monetary policies, some of which are peculiar to its type of state-run capitalism and its position of constantly having to control (or sterilize) the large amount of foreign currency earned from trade. In much of the recent past, China has fixed its currency exchange level. Such policy largely relinquishes domestic monetary policy to maintain the peg. China also uses reserve requirements as an active policy tool. They are typically high for most banks in China, about 20% in recent years. The high rate is designed to keep capital in the country. China raised its reserve requirements frequently around 2010 and 2011 to control the money that was flowing into China at the time, largely a result of U.S. expansionary policy. In February 2015, China lowered its reserve requirements by a half a percent (to 19.5%) to encourage lending. The lowering varied by region and type of lending that banks performed, with even lower reserve requirements extended to banks that loaned to small business and rural projects. This demonstrates the specific and targeted nature of Chinese monetary policy. China also buys bonds in its interbank market and sets an overnight lending rate. In summary, China does whatever policy it believes will achieve national goals. Does this constitute a reactive and unprincipled M&M, or is it an altogether more effective system than that of Western nations?

- Early in the financial crisis, around 2010 to 2011, the ECB bought sovereign bonds of weaker member nations like Greece, Ireland, Portugal, Italy and Spain. By about 2012 though, the economy in Europe weakened and the ECB had to ponder additional action. Almost everyone in M&M remembers the July 26, 2012 "whatever it takes" pronouncement of ECB head Mario Draghi when the ECB offered various bank financing and credit market support facilities. It also set the deposit rate on bank reserves to zero in June 2014 and then to a slight negative in attempts to get banks to lend. The ECB also commenced a major monthly QE program in 2015 including in 2016 the purchasing of corporate bonds.

- Recent monetary policy of the Swiss National Bank (SNB) is an interesting case study for its extremes of circumstances, policy initiatives and resultant market behavior. It also culminated in a dramatic policy reversal in January 2015. Following 2008, as the major nations of the world performed expansionary policies that weakened their currencies (like U.S. QE's), people flocked to the Swiss franc as a safe-haven currency due to its reputation as a currency that holds value in a nation with a perennially strong economy. This demand raised the value of the franc though, making Swiss exports uncompetitive. The Swiss responded with a currency cap by engaging in the buying of foreign currencies and a zero interest rate policy. This resulted in a massive expansion of the bank's balance sheet. Inflation, as might be expected, did not transpire. Rather, inflation tended toward zero. Swiss government bond yields also went to near zero, yet people continued to buy them. Throughout 2014, the Swiss faced increased pressure on their currency from murmurs of loose monetary policy in the form of a QE from the ECB. Suddenly, just before the ECB was expected to announce the QE, the Swiss dropped the currency peg; and the franc soared in value. Consequences were extreme for many parties, including Swiss exporters who would lose business and investors in the Swiss franc who immediately made or lost fortunes. Liberal economists denounced the Swiss for failing to partake in coordinated monetary loosening policies. The Swiss defended their action contending that their entire financial system was at risk.

- Another case of extreme central banking is that of Russia in response to sanctions and lower oil prices. Starting in late 2014 the central bank raised rates and dropped the peg of the Russian currency to the dollar to thwart inflation and forestall capital flight. These relatively austere and market driven actions belie typical policies of central banks in emerging market countries.

- Japan's monetary policy is, and has been even prior to 2008, experimental and extreme. Japan performed quantitative easing as early as the 1990s. It has had low and negative rates. The central bank has purchased assets including extensive equity. Recently, in September 2016, it commenced a pegging of the yield curve by promising to keep 10-year government bond yields at 0%. In an odd irony, although Japan implements experimental policies ahead of the West, it is perceived that Japan looks to the West to endorse their policies. Japan's monetary authorities invite a constant stream of western intellectuals like Paul Krugman and Ben Bernanke and, at least in the eyes of the press, there is the appearance that the Japanese seek the go-ahead from these figureheads.

- Currently the central banks of the advanced economies with the most sophisticated monetary policies (like the U.S., ECB, Japan and the U.K.) have inflation targets around 2%, and they are trying to get inflation up to that level while the banks of many emerging market countries (like Brazil, Russia, China and India) are trying to keep inflation low. Circa 2016 China's inflation target is 4%, Russia's 4%, Brazil's 4.5% plus or minus 2% and India's 8%.

- In addition to the central banks already mentioned, others with notable monetary policy include the banks of Israel, New Zealand, South Africa and Sweden. Their policies are often cutting edge and mentioned in the financial press as examples for other nations' banks.

- In recent years, 2014 through 2016, most countries are lowering rates and/or engaging in QE's to lower the value of their currencies and presumably aid their economies by increasing exports, among other goals.
- Central banks, given low yields, have had to seek higher-yielding securities. This has been done by the big banks like the ECB and the Fed but is also done by smaller central banks that previously invested mostly in government bonds typically U.S. bonds. Buy equities, corporate debt and other risky assets alters the function of central banks from managing liquidity to seeking yield.

## II.10.B.k. Reserve Currency

The U.S. dollar is the world's leading currency and it functions as the world's reserve currency. Many countries hold the dollar as their official reserve currency. Also, international transactions are financed in dollars, including trade in commodities like oil and gold. When global businesses have to buy certain items they must get dollars, which results in an extra demand. Having the reserve currency means that we can issue debt in our own currency largely without a hitch.[129] There are many demands for our currency to meet dollar holding needs of nations. Since we have a larger base of buyers of our debt, our funding cost is low (in general), and seemingly without interruption. Therefore, having the reserve currency means that we can, to some extent, print dollars and buy things. No other country can quite do that. Also, we control our own monetary policy. We cannot be subject, generally, to exchange rate manipulations directed against us. In 1965, French finance minister Valery Giscard D'Estaing famously termed this special status of reserve currency an "exorbitant privilege."

If the economic importance of the U.S. declines, perhaps the world will drop the dollar as reserve currency. Maybe the U.S. will never lose its reserve currency status, at least not for a long time since the U.S. is such a powerful economic unit and there is no contender. On the other hand, fortunes of nations can change very quickly. In any case, economists argue about the net effect on the U.S. of losing the reserve currency status. Some people argue that to lose this role would mean great economic loss. Their main case is that U.S. borrowing cost is lower since it has such a big pool of debt buyers. Cheaper credit is good for U.S. borrowers (including primarily the U.S. government) but is disadvantageous for U.S. savers. Other economists think the advantages of reserve currency are minor. Paul Krugman, for example, contends that the advantage is mostly just "seigniorage," which is the value a nation gets from printing currency that is accepted and held by people for transactions. That factor might be worth about $10 billion per year to the U.S. Being the reserve currency generally implies a higher value of the currency that has both positive and negative effects for the nation's citizens.

When and to whom might the U.S. lose this status? To be sure, it may never transpire. Or, it could happen soon and could be precipitated by a routine economic event like a recession. If the U.S. deficit soared, nations might sell off the dollar. There are not many historical cases of transition of reserve currency to make comparisons, however. In the last 200 years only the U.S. dollar and the British pound (up until 1914) have served as reserve currencies. It is a little easier to speculate on which currency could supplant the U.S. dollar as reserve currency. After the advent of the Euro (in 1999) and during its early life when it rising in value analysts listed many facets of the Euro that could make it replace the dollar. Lately, though, emphasis have been on the Chinese yuan.

---

[129] Of course, we could face being unable to issue debt if our ability to pay back our debt without loss was in question. Indeed, in 1978, when U.S. inflation was very high our government found it had to issue debt denominated in Swiss francs since lenders were afraid of losing value if they took U.S. dollar denominated debt.

In conventional analyses we list the economic facets needed to replace the U.S. dollar. A currency would have to represent a national economy with all or most of the following:

- Large GDP like that of the U.S. (which China has).
- Large holding of gold (which China has).
- Broad trade among nations and durable trade agreements (which China has).
- Free trade and a floating market value of its currency (which China is close to having).
- Deep capital markets including a large and liquid bond market (which China is short of; China would have to offer to supply a large quantity of short-term debt for other nations to hold its currency as reserve).
- An amount of wealth roughly as great as that of the U.S. (which China is short of).
- Political stability and strict adherence to law and rules of contracts. (China may not be a democratic nation, but it is stable. On the other hand, it is perceived as not being fully reliable for contracts).

Listing the facets may be misleading. Perhaps any switchover process would be partial and gradual, involving certain countries making contracts among themselves without using the dollar. Exclusive oil and gas deals come to mind here. We already see greater-sized currency swap agreements being made among BRIC (Brazil, Russia, India and China) nations, Japan, etc. and avoiding the U.S. dollar. If there were an abrupt drop of the U.S. dollar, dollars would come back to the U.S. and cause inflation. Another possibility is that the International Monetary Fund (IMF) could assume the role of reserve currency issuer. The organization is solvent. It can borrow and lend large amounts of funds and already has Special Drawing Rights (SDR's): a type of currency, which it can issue to nations. Currently, SDR's are not issued in large quantities, but they could be.

Perhaps the U.S. has little to lose and perhaps, indeed, losing reserve currency status might represent advantages. On the other hand, the ostensible main economic impact for the U.S. concerning a change in its position as reserve currency is negative. We know that other countries (including China and Russia) view this status as important and have devoted significant study to a potential change of the present system. It is also difficult to tell if other countries of the world would welcome any change in reserve currency from the U.S. dollar to a currency from a country like China or entity like the IMF. Most countries consider the U.S. dollar advantageous. The U.S. is benign or at least the "devil you know." However, since the recent episode of very loose monetary policy in the U.S., which many emerging market nations perceived of as to their detriment, there may be more sentiment to displace the U.S. There is much animosity in the world toward the U.S. Iran, for example, would relish removal of the dollar as the oil pricing currency. Perhaps the greatest advantage of being the reserve currency is really its biggest con: It draws the U.S. into borrowing too much.

## II.10.B.I. Monetizing the Debt

Monetizing the debt occurs when a central bank buys government debt directly from the government and pays by printing money, which the government uses to pay its bills. We have not done that exactly. Instead, our Fed buys all U.S. debt on a secondary market from the primary dealers, and all U.S. debt remains current and actively traded by private parties. Yet our Fed bought a large amount of this U.S. debt on the secondary market and without such buying by the Fed, newly-issued U.S. debt might not have sold successfully. Our Fed buying, therefore, has the similar effect as direct monetizing which is allowing the U.S. to borrow to spend. Our Fed also buys other securities on private markets, largely mortgage-backed bonds that ostensibly have nothing to do with U.S. government financing. These securities are part of the greater housing finance system though, which is ultimately backed by the U.S. The Fed may not sell its large holdings of U.S. bonds and mortgage-backed's into the private market for fear that this would cause bond price drops and yield increases that would perturb the economy. In other words, the Fed has to continue holding U.S. debt which it backs only with ready-to-be-printed money.

Whether we monetize or not in the future depends on many circumstances: If federal deficits are at a level that debt does not explode there will be no need to do so. If deficits increase and our federal government encounters difficulty borrowing money, our Fed could step in and buy swathes of U.S. debt for newly-printed money, constituting a kind of de facto monetization of our debt. The ECB faces issues of debt monetization as well. For example, in 2015 the ECB bought Greek debt, therefore, holding its value up. Greece was able to issue more debt and finance its government operations. Ultimately, the ECB may pay back the Greek debt with newly-issued money, which would constitute a kind of monetization of government debt.

Fed officials steadfastly deny we are doing anything like monetization. Our QE is non-monetizing for the following reasons: (1) We do not buy the debt directly; (2) Our objective with QE is not government finance; it is stimulating the economy; (3) We intend to reverse the QE; (4) We have not seen a run on U.S. debt, crash in the dollar or inflation, which are the typical results of debt monetization; (5) All U.S. debt issued has been honored or, for the debt that remains outstanding, appears it will be honored for payment in full. The question of monetization will be settled in the future.

## II.10.B.m. Helicopter Money

When rates are zero, QE appears undesirable and standard fiscal policy of tax cuts is also deemed unworkable, a potential policy to stimulate spending and avoid deflation would be to distribute money directly to people. This is sometimes referred to as dropping money from helicopters or helicopter money.

Milton Friedman and Ben Bernanke are associated with this term and concept, but every teacher of M&M has talked about dropping money out of helicopters or planes, and the economic effects such a move would have. In class, the back and forth goes something like this: Money is distributed. So long as some people perceive of it as new wealth, the money is spent. Whether it affects the economy depends on whether: (1) increased production and employment of unemployed resources occurs; or (2) if the additional money simply chases the same goods and services (i.e., no new production is done) and causes inflation. In old days, economists used to broach helicopter money to explain the idea of the neutrality of money, i.e., that changes in money do not effect changes in the real economy. If money distributed by the helicopter drop falls in exact proportion onto the holdings of existing wealth in society, and recipients spend simultaneously and at the same marginal rate, the result should be only increases in the prices of existing goods and services (including labor), and the effects of the money will be neutral.

Such a policy has been broached by many analysts in recent times and received copious discussion in the last few months of 2015 and early 2016. This would not take the form of literally throwing money out into the streets, but it could be done by mailing a check or pre-loaded credit card to households. The funds would come directly from the central bank, not from the fiscal entity of the government. The belief is that this policy would engender some stimulative effects and possibly minimal adverse effects of higher prices. Helicopter money would have one advantage over bond buying or lowering rates in that the money would get right into the hands of people and if they were prone to spend, the spending would occur. Other monetary stimulations rely on a second action.

It could just as easily create inflation, a run on the dollar and economic collapse. If sellers of goods thought they were receiving money that dropped from the sky they might not give up their goods, or ask for more dollars.

How does helicopter money compare to fiscal policy and traditional monetary policy? Under fiscal policy, the government sells bonds in markets and uses the money for spending or for cutting taxes. The bonds the government offers must be purchased by private parties. In traditional monetary policy, the Fed buys U.S. bonds in secondary market from dealers who hold the bonds. Those government bonds themselves had been sold to the public and their prices were determined by markets. In the Fed maneuver the money reaches people through the banking system. With helicopter money the Fed would issue bonds to itself or the government (technically they would issue some special bond, like a zero coupon infinite maturity bond) and issue money to the public. This creation of money would not involve markets. The money would be distributed to the people in some fashion, perhaps a check sent in the mail. There would be no price discipline on the helicopter drop, at least initially and depending on volume. Historically countries that had their central banks issue new money this way experienced high or hyper-inflation. In recent years, Argentina, starting in 2007, printed money this way and indeed got inflation.

Like many other ideas of M&M, helicopter money was very, very prominent in intellectual circles and in the press for a period of time and then it died out. The buzz about this device began in 2015 and culminated in the first half of 2016, then it abruptly dropped.

## II.10.B.n. Other Noteworthy Facets of Contemporary M&M

Which other tools, goals, targets, ideas, etc. are in consideration for monetary policy? Which asset class can we buy? How else can we get banks to lend more and people to spend more? How can we prevent excesses in the financial system? Also, how can we achieve such goals without being ham-handed? If we are willing to step out of the mold of traditional central bank policy and use unconventional tools, we have a wide variety of tools and policies available. Below, I have listed various ideas, somewhat out of the mainstream, that include actions already enacted by central banks and some just pondered:

- A program called Funding for Lending was commenced by the Bank of England in July 2012. No version of this particular scheme has been done by the U.S. Instead of lending to banks in distress, this program provides funds to the strongest banks. The central bank lends to good banks at below market rates and asks those banks to funnel the money to good customers especially those that will borrow and create jobs (e.g., small businesses). It is difficult to identify the ultimate effects of Funding for Lending, but it appeared that lending in general did not increase, and the beneficiaries might largely have been people refinancing mortgages. The effort demonstrates the difficulty of engendering financing of real economic activity. This also brings up other questions like why central banks work through banks at all: Why not just lend directly to people? In this case, the central bank loses the appearance that it is the market that is allocating resources. To recap, "lending to the best" is the exact opposite of our original purpose of central bank lending. We (for example, Ben Bernanke and others), often refer to English businessman and pundit Walter Bagehot (1826-1877), who recommended that in financial panics central banks lend freely to financial institutions in need but against good collateral and at an interest rate to exclude parties not in need.

- Another major innovation for our central bank and others is a change in international coordination of policies. There could be two roads: (1) each nation takes care of its own (like Japan's three-pronged initiative of fiscal, monetary and structural policies known as Abenomics commencing in 2013) and therefore having less international coordination; or (2) nations coordinate policies even more than they do now, including allowing a supranational entity like the IMF run monetary policy. It is difficult to assess which road the world is taking. For example, during the financial crisis of 2008, nations worked together. The U.S. arranged for large dollar swaps for European banks. Nations also take care of their own: Eurozone's weak euro policies have compelled nearby nations like Sweden, Denmark and Switzerland to lower rates even to negative ranges to counter rises in their currencies. If the future holds more coordination the formalizing of rules of nations backstopping each other could have great benefits or it could increase moral hazard and systemic risk.

- Another possible important Fed tool is the already existing setting of reserve requirements. This is one of the original three tools as related in textbooks. It receives little discussion, but the tool could be effective and is legally at the Fed's disposal.

- There are proposals, primarily from right-wing members of Congress, to "Audit the Fed." This would be different from conventional audits that are already done. The standard audit involves the counting of Fed holdings, their valuation and their listing, with copious technical notes and explanations. That this audit of Fed books is done is prominently displayed on the Fed webpage (a box with large lettering is on the front page of the Fed Board homepage, positioned right in center top). Rather, the new proposed audits would attempt to judge monetary policy, with possible intent to subject it to control by Congress. Pros and cons break (mostly) on partisan lines: Advocates contend that the Fed has become a sprawling, very powerful entity that is above U.S. law. All they are seeking is transparency and accountability. Opponents contend that this audit is a masked attempt to control many of the policy decisions and other powers of the Fed and will result in political meddling and, ultimately, poorer monetary policy.

- We could engage in more extensive QE programs, buying various asset classes depending on which we deemed would have the most effect. Perhaps we could increase the size of the Fed balance sheet by many trillions of dollars more. In this case our Fed is like the U.S.'s hedge fund, investing in big asset classes and being able to garner a high rate of return due to its size and time horizon.

- One flaw of giving people money is that they might be resistant to spend it, instead choosing to save (in the form of money in the bank) or apply it to debt resulting in no increase in spending. Economists have pondered this problem and have proposed eliminating paper money and replacing it with electronic currency, the value of which could be summarily reduced by the government thereby compelling people to spend now. This policy is not being implemented by any nation currently, yet it is being discussed as a possibility by leaders like English government economist Andrew Haldane.

- Another policy to increase spending is giving people credit cards at low or zero interest. Tapped out households are reluctant to spend with their own high interest rate credit cards. They are savvy that interest is costly; and, they suddenly received a credit card at zero or perhaps 1% or 2%, they might likely spend. This would stimulate the economy. Credit cards could be funded by the U.S. government by borrowing at its rate, which is about 1%. The U.S. would be lending money to these households but, presumably, the households would be able to pay the borrowing back, especially since Keynesian effects of the spending would raise the economy in general.

- Policy is described (by the U.S. Fed, e.g.) as "data dependent." Decisions await current levels of key economic indicators. This is at once a sensible and unavoidable way to proceed, yet relying on the latest data implies little conviction about the trends and models used to analyze the economy.

- Another suggestion to rectify financial instability is full reserve banking. Rather than allowing banks to create money out of thin air, which is the result of fractional reserve banking, under full reserve banking banks could only lend against time deposits. Banks would have to keep all demand deposit accounts fully backed by funds. Banks would generally be more solvent against drains on funds. On the other hand, less lending would be done. Since banks would earn nothing by lending their demand deposit funds the banks would probably have to charge fees which would discourage the public from holding money in that form. No nation has full reserve banking and it speculative about what would happen if the policy were adopted.

- Blockchain ledgers including Bitcoin represent payment systems and/or currencies outside, as of now, the control of central banks. They may revolutionize M&M or have minimal impact. There are many facets that we can only list at this point: (1) much depends on the computer technology, including the network of people running the system, of maintaining safe public ledgers; (2) in theory blockchain payments systems eliminate banking which can result in more efficient and lower cost transacting and commerce; (3) the systems may be created by central banks or beyond the control of central banks; and (4) they may indeed manifest themselves soon or be decades before having a great impact.

## II.10.C. History of the Fed

The history of the Fed is complicated, and to review it comprehensively would require a great volume. There is one main issue to determine: Has policy worked historically? More specifically, has policy created more output or a more stable economic path and has it prevented protracted recessions and high inflation? There are two takes: (1) Fed policy made some mistakes mainly in the 1930s, but mostly since then it has performed very well, including success in normal times and outstanding success in saving the economic system in 2008. (2) Policy never enhanced economic growth and likely has been the source of major adverse swings in the economy. Policy has typically been late, often not counter-cyclical contrary to what theory proscribes and has created moral hazard, which perhaps created more instability.

My reading of Fed history is that the Fed frequently did not anticipate economic problems, that it learned and reacted as it went along and that Fed policy was typically overwhelmed by circumstances or, if not, then the policy was not needed. It is not that people at the Fed were incompetent or partisan, but underlying the task of the Fed was, and is, an economy whose real changes are too rapid and momentous to capture or counter with policy. In my assessment, it is impossible to discern if policy ever worked sufficiently well to deem it a success. Fed policy has some effects, but whether they are significant or work toward the intended goals is dubious.

One concerted lesson of history is that, today, we sit in judgment of the monetary policy decision makers of the past. This is especially true of the policy done during the Depression. We aver that they did poor policy and were ignorant of economic facts that we now know. The Fed was not created until well into the 20th century, specifically in December 1913 when the Federal Reserve Act passed. Why was the U.S. so late, and you might say resistant, to a central bank? England's central bank was founded in 1694. American history was largely shaped by "states' rights." America had an aversion to centralized power as well as a distrust of big business and big banking. Therefore, big national banks were doomed from the start. Prior to formation of the Fed, the U.S. established the First Bank of the United States (1791 to 1811) and Second Bank of the United States (1816 to 1832), but their scopes were limited and charters were not renewed by Congress, predominantly for political reasons. Also, even when the Fed system was set up it was relatively decentralized with a central office in Washington but also 12 regional banks.

Some economists, like Ben Bernanke and the authors of many M&M textbooks, contend that the absence of a "lender of last resort" resulted in chronic banking panics, which created extreme business cycles. The lack of a central banking authority demonstrates a fundamental flaw in private markets and a propensity for economies to have protracted recessions. In a banking panic, people would draw money out of banks to the point that banks would run out of money, shut down, create a ripple effect and cause credit to dry up. The 1907 panic caused the U.S. to seriously consider a central bank and, without getting into details, we established a relatively restricted central bank. In my opinion, this common analysis of the 1800s as financially and economically volatile is dubious. The financial shakeouts were not that bad. They appear notable in conventional data but the data from the 1800s reflect little about the underlying economy. In reality, the economy grew robustly during the 1800s. The proposition that a strong central bank would have contributed to greater economic growth is a guess. Business cycles of the 1800s are difficult to judge. The 1907 panic gets plenty of coverage today as quintessential proof that markets fail but other analyses show that is was nowhere near as bad as touted and that the period preceding the Fed (from 1900-1914) was characterized by a strong banking private system. Another contrary piece of evidence is that the economic downturn in 1920-21 (which was post-Fed but in which no significant government policy was conducted) was characterized by a prompt recovery, ostensibly by market forces.

## II.10.C.a. Decade by Decade

Let's examine central banking history by focusing on several specific facets like the effectiveness of policy, choice of policy tool, whether policy is counter-cyclical or not (it should be counter-cyclical), whether or not private parties ignore or offset policy initiatives, whether or not policy was swamped by outside economic factors, whether or not policy worked within its intended time frame, policy in response to crises, etc.

# 1910s

The Federal Reserve System started in December 1913 with the enactment of the Federal Reserve Act. Initially the Fed enacted a form of discount lending to banks primarily to manage seasonal cycles related to agricultural production and occasional crises. At this time, inflationary effects resulting from central bank actions were not considered important. The gold standard prevailed and history displayed little inflation except for specific incidents of inflation related to wars and large discoveries of gold. Open market operations ("OMOs") were not mentioned as a policy tool when the Fed was originally set up, nor was there much discussion or intent on goosing the entire national economy with more money.

The two main monetary policy objectives at the time the Fed was established were the gold standard and the Real Bills Doctrine. Both would fade from prominence soon but they dominated attitudes in the 1920s. The world was on a gold standard up until World War I, and at times following the war and before World War II. Paper currency was backed by gold. As more gold was discovered, or otherwise turned up in a country, there would be greater money and inflation. In general, though, the gold standard kept inflation moderate. In certain periods, like in the 1870s and 1880s, very little gold was produced and the supply of money could not keep pace with the growing economy causing deflation. Oftentimes, populists opposed the gold standard because low inflation or deflation would make borrowing tough for debtors (such as farmers whose debt service would remain constant while the prices of the goods they sold would go down). In his "Cross of Gold" speech[130] Democratic presidential candidate William Jennings Bryan denounced the effects of a gold standard. He proposed creating a bimetallic standard by adding silver, which would presumably cause inflation and help debtors. In general, gold flows had big effects on prices and credit. Gold flowed into the U.S. during the early stages of World War I–at least before the U.S. entered the war–and caused inflation. The Fed had little mechanism to deal with this already existing macro condition.

The Real Bills Doctrine dictated that the Fed should encourage real commerce and not speculation. If a bank showed up at the discount window looking to borrow, the Fed would comply if the bank were lending

---

[130] On July 9, 1896 at the Democratic National Convention in Chicago.

for a real venture. In terms of policy and business cycles, Real Bills could be pro-cyclical (i.e., reinforcing swings in the economy). When the economy was strong there would be more demand for credit, and the Fed would/should accommodate.

## 1920s

The 1920s began with a substantial recession from January 1920 through July 1921, which was marked by deflation. It is challenging to ascertain exactly how severe these pre-Depression recessions were. Leading scholars have the 1921 unemployment rate anywhere from 8% to 12%, but Fed policy included raising rates, which was probably counter-productive. In any case, Fed policy at this time was not very influential and the economy recovered relatively quickly from this recession on its own.

Into the 1920s the Fed's main task was discount lending and, during this time, OMOs were discovered. Supposedly in the early 1920s, the amount of discount lending was so minimal due to a weak economy that the Fed, which made all its money from discount lending, started to park its money in other securities and noticed that this had an effect on private bank reserves and short-term interest rates. By the late 1920s, OMOs were the main tool.[131]

The lead up to the Great Depression and the episode itself are hard to pin down in terms of cause and effect. Some analysts believe that the Fed did not perform well, but was certainly not the main cause of economic problems. Others contend that poor Fed policy even before President Hoover took office in 1929 caused the episode. Other analysts focus on non-monetary policy factors as the causes of the Depression, including a decline in productivity, international and trade policy events and financial market imbalances. Every school of thought–Keynesianism, monetarism, Marxist, Austrian economics, etc.–has its own story for the cause of the Great Depression.

The stock market crash did precede the Depression, so determining the root cause of the stock market crash might reveal the cause of the Depression. One of the contributing factors was loose margin lending rules. Investors could borrow from brokers almost unlimitedly, and an investor with $10,000 could borrow $90,000, which meant that gains (and losses) would be magnified many times. The Fed allowed the loose margin lending, and some analysts therefore blame the Fed for the stock market crash. After the crash, the Fed limited margin to 50% of an account value.

## 1930s

Coming up to the 1930s, there was little consensus on requisite Fed policy, either pro- or counter-cyclical. At the time of the stock market crash, the Fed did act as lender of last resort and loaned money to banks who passed it on to brokers and other financial companies in need. However, the economy was deteriorating and, starting around the end of 1930, banks started to fail in large numbers. People withdrew money and banks were short of funds. At this point the Fed failed to lend to banks. In fact, in October 1931, the Fed raised the discount rate. Later, it lowered that discount rate, but by this time, the lowering had no effect because the discount rate was typically higher than market rates in short-term lending markets. As a result, the Depression continued. Later in the 1930s, the Fed received the authority to change reserve requirements. In late 1936 and early 1937, the Fed increased reserve requirements, incenting banks to want to hold too much excess reserves. Banks preferred to hold excess reserves because the banks feared runs.

---

[131] The Open Market Investment Committee (OMIC) was created in 1923. It was replaced by the Open Market Policy Conference in 1930, which was replaced by the Federal Open Market Committee in 1935 as part of the Banking Act of 1935. Today's FOMC is substantially like this.

From 1937 to 1938 there was some economic growth and it looked as though the country was coming out of the Depression, but then another recession occurred and kept the Depression going. Almost all analysts agree that the Fed increasing reserve requirements was bad monetary policy. Perhaps this adverse use of the reserve requirement made the Fed averse to use this tool in the future. In general, contractionary Fed monetary policy around 1937 is held up by many analysts as compelling proof that the Fed should err well on the side of keeping stimulus going. During the post-2008 period, policy advocates would cite it as reason not to reverse accommodative policy.

The situation in the 1930s was grave but a multitude of federal government agencies were actively pondering government solutions. The Banking Act of 1935 reorganized the Fed, including the creation of the Federal Open Market Committee (the "FOMC"). In April 1933 the U.S. went off the gold standard, and some analysts believe gold flows contributed to the Depression. The U.S. was running a trade surplus and bringing in gold. This should have increased the money supply and stimulated the economy but, wary of this typical inflationary effect of gold, the Fed worked to offset the increases in money. This was a typical central bank response to increase of gold, but not appropriate for the times. Also during the early 1930s, the country engaged in other legislation that affected banking and the greater financial system. We cannot dissect if changes in reserves at banks were due to monetary policy, regulation (like deposit insurance and Regulation Q [which limited interest on deposits]), flows of gold, international trade policies, etc.

## 1940s

In September 1939 World War II started in Europe. The U.S. entered the war in December 1941. Special central bank policies were requisite to finance the war. From 1942 through 1951, the Fed "pegged" interest rates and committed to buy treasury bills at 0.375% and longer-term U.S. bonds at 2% to facilitate war finance. This peg started in April 1942 and held until 1947. The Fed achieved the peg by doing sufficient OMOs, typically buying bonds. Of course, to maintain the peg the Fed now could not control its monetary policy. The money supply would be expanded causing inflation. This possibility incented the Fed to wish to switch to managing the money supply. A power struggle ensued between the Fed and the Treasury, which liked the peg policy because it kept borrowing rates low. In the early 1950s, the Fed prevailed and regained its monetary policy in an agreement known as the Fed-Treasury Accord of 1951.

## 1950s

Free reserves (excess reserves minus discount loans) were the intermediate target. They were viewed as reflecting the available credit in the system. If there was an increase in free reserves, the Fed would sell bonds and reduce reserves in the system. This policy generally engendered a pro-cyclical monetary policy though, and a strong economy would result in an increase in lending causing excess reserves to go down. The Fed would then make open market purchases raising the reserves and monetary base, and ultimately the money supply and inflation. At this time, the Fed generally did not target interest rates. That's what it had done in the 1940s, and it was trying to get away from that. However, throughout the 1950s and 1960s the Fed was monitoring both monetary aggregates and interest rates. Policy between 1953 and 1960 was known as "bills only" because the Fed operated in short-term U.S. debts and left longer-term debt to be settled in markets. By the end of the 1950s, OMOs were the policy tool and the use of discount lending and reserve requirement changes as tools was minimal. In textbooks, though, all three tools are always presented as if they had about equal weight in the real world. I have often wondered why these three tools remained so intact in the pedagogy.

# 1960s

The policy tool was OMOs and it seemed to work yet was generally pro-cyclical. The economy came out of a recession early in the decade and grew with low inflation, at least for the first half of the decade. The Fed was still primarily targeting free reserves. Perhaps because the underlying economy was experiencing various favorable economic growth trends whatever policy the Fed did appeared to work. In the latter half of the 1960s, inflation rose. It was attributed to the strong economy–unemployment got to about 4%–and to the large government spending programs including the Great Society[132] and spending for the Vietnam War. Other analysts were making a monetary story for inflation and researching money aggregates like M1 and M2.

# 1970s

The 1970s commenced in tough economic circumstances, which persisted throughout the decade. Inflation was high and interest rates rose with it. For example, in 1972 and 1973 the fed funds rate rose from 4.5% to 8.5%. Arthur Burns (1904-1987) became Fed Chairman in 1970. He formally adopted monetary aggregate targets like M1 and M2, but the Fed was also trying to target the fed funds rate and could not do both. Policy tended to be pro-cyclical, the opposite of what it is intended to be. For example, in 1974 the economy was in a bad recession and the fed funds rate fell greatly: from about 12% to 5%. The latter amount was at too low a level for the Fed's target, so the Fed did contractionary monetary policy, for example, selling bonds to get the rate up. However, that took money out of the economic system at a time when the economy was in need of credit. When the economy recovered, income and interest rates went up, and the Fed would buy bonds to get the interest rate down, but that would increase the money supply. Many questions remain from the 1970s. How precise were the money aggregate and rate targets, and which target had precedence? Why did Burns ostensibly tolerate inflation? The most accepted explanation of the period is that Burns overestimated GDP growth by looking back to the 1960s. Perhaps a contrast was the term of Alan Greenspan, which ostensibly had better than expected underlying economic growth and thus policy appeared successful.

Many other notable M&M happenings played out in the 1970s: In this first half of the 1970s, the Bretton Woods exchange rate system broke down. The U.S. was running trade deficit and had been beset by demands for its gold in exchange for dollars, as was promised under Bretton Woods. The U.S. ceased conversion of dollars into gold and let the U.S. dollar float. This was the effective end of the gold standard for the U.S. and the rest of the world. Also in the 1970s, stagflation (i.e., high inflation and unemployment at the same time), existed, in contrast to what most economists (at least in classroom discussions) believed was a tradeoff between the two. The tradeoff was the hallmark of the great Phillips Curve. Facing inflation in August 1971, the U.S. (under President Nixon) instituted wage and price controls. This was an episode that goes down in the lore of economic infamy. Reserve requirements became a problem. Banks could choose either to be members of the Fed system or just state-chartered. The state-chartered did not have to keep such high reserves, so many banks decided to leave the Fed system. In the 1980s, the Fed lowered reserve requirements. All along through that time there was financial innovation, such as NOW accounts (checking with interest), money market deposit accounts (also had no interest rate ceilings), ATMs, sweep accounts, etc. Inflation was high and people strove to maintain the value of their dollars and put their cash

---

[132] The term for the extensive federal programs to fight poverty, improve health care and conduct various other social programs commenced in the mid-1960s.

wherever it got the highest yield, like money market funds. Monetary aggregates like M1 and M2 had little consistency over time. In general, the multitude of challenging 1970s M&M events contrasts with the relatively less difficult circumstances of the late 1980s, 1990s and early 2000s. Alan Greenspan would characterize (to some extent, witness the title of his autobiography: *The Age of Turbulence*). The 1970s appear to be the tougher draw.

The poor economy of the 1970s resulted in passage of Humphrey-Hawkins which made the Fed accountable to set and hit certain monetary targets as well as a goal of 4% unemployment. We attained this level in the late 1960s but by the 1970s, it looked problematic to attain.

## Summary of 1950s through 1970s

The 1950s through the 1970s might represent a period in which monetary policy could work as in textbooks. For one, the U.S. economy was not as subject to international leakages, especially large movements of assets across borders. Also, banks in the Fed system handled most of the credit creation, and the fractional reserve banking system was probably more potent. Corporations and households were likely more prone to react to interest rate changes. We targeted monetary aggregates or the fed funds rate. Policy was often pro-cyclical, primarily because more money was created when the economy was strong. This contributed to inflation. The Fed sought to change this pro-cyclical policy in the 1970s but was not successful.

## 1980s

In October 1979, just after Paul Volcker became Chairman, the Fed started targeting reserves (the quantity of money) and deemphasized the fed funds rate (the price of money). Interest rates rose and inflation fell. This was the famous anti-inflation strategy of October 1979 to October 1982. It is not altogether clear which policy Volcker was following. He said he would target monetary aggregates but might really have been trying to raise the fed funds rate. Volcker essentially admitted that getting rid of inflation would be costly. Before him Fed officials thought they dodged an economic contraction: The fed funds rate, which was below 10% in the 1980s, hit a high of 22.4% in 1981. The economy went into a recession and inflation, which had been a little over 10% for about three years, dropped. This played out from 1982 through 1984. Keynesian economists doubted Volcker would be successful contending that inflation would not come down because it was "built-in" and also said the U.S. economy would not return to great growth. Many economists believed the long-term trend had fallen below 3%. After unemployment hit 10% in 1982, however, the economy grew including an extraordinary year in 1984 of real GDP growth at 7.2%.

To some, Volcker was a singular hero, but to others (probably more at that time), he was perceived as villain for causing a deep recession that many would call the "Volcker recession." Over time, history would be kind to Volcker. The memory of unemployment faded and the following generally strong performance of the economy was attributed to his drastic action. Over the years (including during the 2008 crisis) we looked to Volcker for right ideas. Nobody characterized Volcker's efforts by referring to a Volcker recession anymore. Now they only recall and reference a heroic monetary achievement of Volcker from the 1980s. As of October 1982, Fed policy was formally back to targeting interest rates. In February 1987 the Fed stopped targeting M1 altogether: The quantity had become irrelevant. Policymakers then focused on M2, the greater basic money category; but soon after that became irrelevant to what we thought were important and effective tools for managing the economy. Targeting of money quantities subsequently ceased. Our target would be the fed funds rate. Alan Greenspan became Fed Chairman in August 1987.

The stock market crashed soon after (specifically on October 19, 1987) and the Fed announced that it would stand ready to make loans to financial institutions in need. No economic crisis ensued.

## 1990s

In the late 1980s (through June 1989) the Fed raised the fed funds rate. In early 1990s, in response to the 1990-91 recession, the Fed cut short-term interest rates substantially from a little over 8% in 1990 to about 3% by the end of 1992. Concurrently, the U.S. was facing the "S&L Crisis," which was the failure of thousands of banks and savings & loans. This crisis traces back to high inflation from the 1970s and the subsequent deregulation of banking. From late 1992 until spring of 1994, the fed funds rate was kept at 3%. In the infamous spring of 1994, the Fed jacked up rates (eventually to 6% by early 1995) to forestall inflation. Mortgage brokers will relate stories of people who planned to buy houses but had not locked the rates. Over a couple of months, rates went up so much they could no longer swing the payments, but whether or not the abrupt raising of rates was correct policy is debated.

In July 1997, a financial crisis occurred in Asia profoundly affecting certain Asian countries' economies and requiring many years for recovery. This Asian Crisis came by surprise, like other crises supposedly. Of course, as we have pointed out before, many analysts had noted weaknesses and bubbles in the area. The Asian Crisis appeared serious from its start: The Fed kept the rate stable during this time, and as that Crisis played out the U.S. economy held up. In summer and early fall of 1998, Russia defaulted on its sovereign debt and a prominent and large hedge fund, Long-Term Capital Management, collapsed. Bond markets experienced an extreme flight to quality in August of that year. The Fed responded with three small rate cuts that came somewhat after the crises has already worked their way through, and the economy prospered for the remainder of 1998. For a long time, this 1998 case of Fed policy was the most cited textbook story of effective monetary policy. Policy naysayers contend that the underlying economy was strong and the Russian default and hedge fund collapse were minor items and, therefore, the Fed policy was probably meaningless.

As history would play out the Fed's role in assisting the failed hedge fund would be debated again and again. The Fed's role was, in a way, minor: It organized a meeting of Long-Term Capital Management creditors and encouraged them to agree on a private solution. For this minor action, the Fed received ample criticism. The Fed had put up no taxpayer money and merely encouraged private parties to work together. At that time however, our central bank was deemed to be more pure and above company-specific problems. In 2008 the Fed would become involved in a multitude of companies. Therefore, many analysts look back at 1998 and the Fed's stepping up to save the hedge fund as the cardinal sin of moral hazard. The Fed at that time signaled that any big private concern would be prevented from spreading its losses to the greater financial community.

In hindsight, the late 1990s would be deemed the era of Alan Greenspan's sapience. Supposedly he kept rates low because he saw productivity growth that would keep the economy growing with low inflation. This is debatable though: In 1994, for example, he raised rates drastically apparently because he feared an overheated economy. At other points in the decade, he kept rates low apparently because he thought the economy was not growing greatly. Both behaviors belie a belief that productivity growth was strong. The last four years of the 1990s were characterized by strong GDP growth and surging stock and bond markets. Fed policy was stable, and it began raising rates in 1999.

## 2000s (up to 2008)

Facing Y2K (the turn of the century computer dating problem), the Fed engaged in a number of behind-the-scenes actions to maintain extra liquidity in the system. It did not lower rates. In January 2001, the Fed started to lower rates in response to the recession or, at the time, the appearance of recession. The fed funds rate went from 6.5% in late-2000 to less than 2% by the end of 2001. This period includes the September 11, 2001 terrorist attack. In response to the crisis, the Fed lowered and made strong commitments to lend freely to markets, and it continued to lower rates over the next two years, eventually going down to 1% in 2003.

Circa 2003 rates in the economy were low (by recent historical comparisons) and inflation was low. The fed funds rate was near 1% for about two years. The intellectual justification for keeping rates low was deflation. As with many issues of social science, experts break on prejudices as to the effects of these low rates. The conventional take, by policy people and believers in government, is that the Fed pulled it off, maintaining a growing economy without inflation and not falling into a downward deflationary spiral. The other take, generally that of policy and central banking adversaries, is that the Fed pumped too much liquidity into the economy causing a housing bubble and too much spending. A sensible third take to be considered is that Fed policy really did not matter. Attitudes about growth v. inflation reversed in the summer of 2004, when the Fed started raising rates. This concerted policy action had little effect on the long bond market though. This contrariness to policy was termed the "Conundrum" by Alan Greenspan. In his opinion, it represented a contrary and rare case in which policy did not work as proscribed. He attributed it to a global savings glut, swamping the effects of policy. Of course, similarly large global trends existed in other periods of policy changes.

## Post 2008

Following 2008 the intellectual basis, policy applications and empirical events in the world of M&M have so drastically changed that comparisons with conditions and policy from earlier times are shaky. We have referred to this development with terms like Conjuncture and Transmogrification and indeed the post-2008 period requires a different M&M. For demonstration, empirical macroeconomists will face difficulties reconciling relationships among data series from before and after 2008 due to their extreme levels like the fed funds rate remaining terminal for seven years or the quantity of reserves increasing so greatly.

## Summary of the Decade by Decade Analysis

Drawing definitive conclusions about the effects of monetary policy is not quite possible. Does policy shape economic events or simply respond to them? It does seem that when the underlying economy is strong, policy appears to work. Do the small maneuvers of policy matter? Did the Fed fight off inflation in 1994, guide the economy to great growth in the rest of the 1990s, fight off crises and save the economy from a deep recession in 2001? Contrarily, could it have left the fed funds target rate at 3% and had just as good results? Before the 1970s the performance of monetary policy is uninspiring and contains plenty of mistakes, like in the Depression. During the 1970s it was not much better. Since then, we have three episodes: (1) Paul Volcker's change of the system, (2) Alan Greenspan's run and (3) Ben Bernanke's crisis management. Volcker's policy worked but there was a grave cost. Greenspan's term was characterized by relatively favorable events, but the success of Bernanke's policy is yet to be decided.

## II.10.C.b. Alan Greenspan

When Alan Greenspan retired they wailed Hosannas. He was the greatest central banker of all time. Even liberal economist Alan Blinder, a Greenspan opponent in basic economic leanings and a rival when they both served on the Fed Board from 1994 to 1996, fawned, "There is no doubt that Greenspan has been an amazingly successful chairman of the Federal Reserve System." Blinder also conceded that Greenspan's success was not just luck. The few criticisms Blinder had involved Greenspan's occasional political stances and his own elevation of his persona as the bank head.[133] I always considered Greenspan a stalwart conservative economist but also maintained that he was a guesser and that the underlying economy he managed was benign. In other words, he got a good draw for GDP growth. He would characterize his tenure as facing constant tough circumstances but, in retrospect, the crises (like the Mexican peso crisis of 1994), seem quite moderate. Favorable factors (like crude oil being around $30 per barrel for most of his run) were prevalent. Most analysts during Greenspan's time bought the success story and assumed he succeeded with superior M&M thinking. Greenspan was generally deferent to the power of markets but he also demonstrated the belief that he could truly forecast and control the economy.

When his autobiography, *The Age of Turbulence*, came out in late 2007, I put it on my syllabus as required reading. The book was a competent economic history of the 20th century right up to the then current time. My main impetus for class use though was to review, case by case, Greenspan's record on major policy initiatives and see if policy worked as advertised. My contention was that it did not, and that the underlying economy just happened to be robust. My evidence included counter cases, wrong timing, inconsistencies with intellectual beliefs, etc. After a few semesters, I had to drop the book from class assignment because events of 2008 ff in M&M changed so fundamentally and rapidly.

Under Greenspan, did the Fed prevent recession, moderate the business cycle, achieve soft landings (cooling a strong economy without causing a slowdown), forestall inflation, anchor inflation expectations, permanently lower long-term bond rates, etc.? Some of the actions during Greenspan's tenure were pure crisis management (like the 1987 stock market crash and September 11) but most of his monetary policy forays (such as 1990-91, spring 1994, fall 1998, post-2001 recession, etc.) were done under relatively unexceptional economic circumstances and represented textbook business cycle management. Greenspan contends his policies succeeded (or had the effects the Fed intended within reasonable time frames), and that they were necessary given the tough conditions. He attributes the success to the Fed possessing superior knowledge of economic matters and performing prudent policy. Greenspan concedes rare exceptions (such as the "Conundrum" of 2005), when repeated fed funds rate raises seemingly had no effect on other rates. Even for this case, though, he provides an excuse–or at least an explanation–that the policy in 2005 was overwhelmed by a global savings glut yet was otherwise appropriate. Here are some milestones of Greenspan's tenure along with related commentary:

- **Stock Market Crash of 1987**: The Fed provided liquidity and the economy did not collapse or even slow down its growth. The market crash, though, probably would not have derailed the economy even if the Fed had not acted.
- **1990-91 Recession**: This was one of two recessions during Greenspan's term and 1990-91 was probably the only relatively typical economic downturn. The other, in 2001, was characterized by more special events. Concerning 1990-91 it is impossible to judge as to whether central banking action truly made a difference.
- **1994**: In an apparent pre-emptive strike to keep the economy from overheating, Greenspan raised interest rates substantially during the first half of 1994. It is, of course, impossible to know what would

---

[133] "Understanding the Greenspan Standard," by Alan S. Blinder and Ricardo Reis, CEPS Working Paper No. 114, September 2005 presented at the Federal Reserve Bank of Kansas City symposium, "The Greenspan Era: Lessons for the Future," at Jackson Hole, Wyoming, August 25-27, 2005.

have happened without such drastic interest rate increases. The action conflicts with Greenspan's claim of discerning higher productivity in the U.S. economy around that time. Such a belief would have indicated little need to raise rates to forestall inflation. Productivity growth would have been sufficient.

- **1997 Response to the Asian Crisis**: The U.S. stood ready to take action but ultimately initiated no domestic response. This would turn out to be successful and central bankers believed their calm was the right policy, but it also demonstrates that the workings of free markets may not need assistance.
- **1998 Default of Russian Sovereign Debt and Collapse of Long-Term Capital Management**: The Fed lowered interest rates to keep the world economy from stalling in light of the tumultuous shocks to international financial markets. This was apparently successful yet the rate changes came after the economy and financial markets seemingly had already rectified themselves. (We discuss the policy action of 1998 later.)
- **1999**: The Fed commenced a reversal of loose policy to keep the overly-hot U.S. economy and stock market from causing inflation. Once again, Greenspan apparently succeeded although it is hard to tell what would have happened otherwise.
- **2000 Y2K Problem**: The Fed stood ready to provide liquidity. This reflects the lender of last resort role of a central bank more than intellectual monetary policy of stimulating demand.
- **September 11, 2001**: The Fed stood ready to provide liquidity and was successful in terms of its lender of last resort function.
- **2001 Recession, Lowered Rates**: The recession itself was minimal. A double-dip recession, as many economists predicted, did not follow.
- **2003 & 2004 Lowering of Rates to Very Low Levels**: This was done to fight deflation, and the effects of the policy are hard to divine. Indeed, the U.S. did not fall into a deflationary period or a recession. On the other hand, there may have been no need to fight deflation. As many analysts remark given 2008, the low rates contributed to asset price bubbles (including in the housing market), and these bubble led to the great crisis of 2008.
- **2004 Raising of Rates to Cool the Economy & Forestall Inflation**: This was not effective in raising markets rates of long-term debt. This is the Conundrum, which we referenced above. The ultimate effect on the economy is difficult to determine.

The question remains: Would the world economy have been any worse off in instances like 1994, 1998, 1999, 2001, etc. if the Greenspan Fed had taken no actions? Another observation is that the major M&M challenges over the nearly twenty year Greenspan period were relatively few and not too severe.

Greenspan was a worthy and relatively non-meddlesome central banker, but he fell prey to the vanity that we could control the economy and thereby better it. His autobiography and FOMC transcripts contain multiple examples of his confidence in his ability to comprehend the macroeconomy: In FOMC meetings, he frequently states, or alludes to, the ability of Fed policymakers as understanding the economy better than private parties do. In his autobiography, Greenspan is somewhat forthright, but he reflects favorably on his success as a forecaster of economic trends. This is a cardinal sin to economists who believe that economies are highly complicated and markets are so quick and efficient that a person or group of people cannot discern economic movements better than markets can. Greenspan's career as an economist was with a forecasting consultancy firm whose relatively mediocre record of calling trends should have convinced Greenspan that out-guessing markets is futile. His recollection is different though: He characterizes himself as an economic data "ferret" and refers to a prescient call made early in his career: In 1957, he detected a build-up of inventories and called the 1958 recession.[134] You also find passages like this in his descriptions of his collaboration with other leaders. For example, he described his special relationship with Larry Summers, who was perhaps considered the world's most brilliant economic mind: "He and I are a lot alike: we both like to argue from basic principles and from evidence. I'm sorry we did not have a tape recorder running, because this was a textbook case of policymaking by rational compromise. We sat and argued point by point." The agreement that they calmly and brilliantly came to, in this case, was the 1999 Financial Services Modernization Act, which (at the time and at the time of Greenspan writing his book) might have resembled a correct new law but later would look more like one of the culprits in the 2008 crisis.[135]

As abundantly as people praised Greenspan through his term right up until retirement, they turned on him after the 2008 crisis. It is difficult to pass final judgment on Greenspan. You can list his achievements: He attempted to rectify Social Security; Identified problems with Fannie Mae and Freddie Mac; Detected increases in productivity: Highlighted froth in asset markets; Did not let his success go to his head excessively; Refrained from being political; etc. It is just as easy to find flubs, however: He failed to act on bubbles; Failed to discern the danger of deregulation and the importance of regulation; Failed to raise margin requirements when given the chance in the late 1990s: Facilitated the tax cut of 2001 (which resulted in large deficits); Did let his success go to his head sufficiently to provoke certain economists; etc.

## II.10.C.c. Ben Bernanke

When resigning from the Fed, Ben Bernanke hoped he would live long enough to see the textbooks of his tenure as leader of the Fed. Ten years should do it. Bernanke is/was a top academic but, indeed, he was a consummate tweed coat professor and never a manager, entrepreneur or executive. He would be credited as especially knowledgeable about current M&M maladies (including deflation and Depression economics), but he studied these areas no more than other major areas of M&M (such as transmission of monetary policy and inflation targeting). Many other economists had similar research heft in the areas of deflation and Depression analysis. Bernanke was appointed by President Bush. It was often remarked that Bernanke was a Republican, giving an impression that Bernanke was a policy conservative. Indeed when Bernanke commenced as Fed Chairman in 2006, he looked like any other markets-oriented economist who was mostly wary of inflation. As late as early 2008 he considered the economy strong and not in need of special government support. However, Bernanke then did a prompt turnaround and became a fervent stimulator. If you read many of his writings, you could discern a belief in Keynesian ideas and dislike of conservative doctrines, such as an extreme intellectual opposition to the gold standard.

As of yet, Bernanke monetary policy actions cannot be deemed successful. The media has pronounced success due to the absence of a bigger calamity befalling the U.S. economy following 2008. Analysts predictably break on partisan lines and very general beliefs. It is easy to scrutinize and poke fun at various mistakes of Bernanke's, like his often-cited inaccurate assessment of the sub-prime housing market in a speech in June 2007: "…the troubles in the subprime sector seem unlikely to seriously spill over to the broader economy or the financial system." Bernanke generally received widespread support, especially from the media, some of which credit him with nothing less than saving the country. He did face vituperation, but only from cranks, assorted pundits and analysts. His critics made legitimate critiques of Fed policy supported with evidence and data, but Bernanke dismissed these. For example, Bernanke dismissed any suggestion that the Fed's low rate policy of the early 2000s contributed to the housing bubble. His manner was less like that of a

---

[134] *The Age of Turbulence*, 2007, p. 47.
[135] *The Age of Turbulence*, 2007, p. 199.

scholar who would "bias the case out of his favor" to prove a point and more like an executive who is coached to deny any wrongdoing.

The media often characterized Bernanke as being widely persecuted and would frequently label anyone who disagreed with him (and with America's active monetary policy) as subversive. Bernanke was routinely characterized as a mild-mannered person who wanted nothing to do with hardball politics and public debate. He was also cast as a victim of a lack of complementary support for the Fed's policies from U.S. government fiscal policy. When Bernanke left the Fed in January 2014 he was roundly praised as extremely successful in his monetary policy. Bernanke, in turn, was extremely defensive of his tenure and prone to feel sorry for himself, however. Any person assuming a public office must be able to field criticism, yet he repeatedly remarked on how harshly he was treated and how thankless the job as head of the Fed was. Promptly after leaving office Bernanke accepted roles at major money firms, including a big hedge fund dedicated to "beating the market" in investing. Like other leaders from the 2008 crisis, including Timothy Geithner and Henry (Hank) Paulsen, he authored a book with a stout defense of his case. Bernanke, I believe, exhibits classic "grandiosity": the characteristic of believing himself to be smarter and, in a way, stronger than the vast mass of people in society.

## II.10.C.d. Janet Yellen

Janet Yellen assumed the Fed Chair on February 1, 2014. She is a Keynesian and takes pride in her lifelong devotion to policy all the way from her youth through her economics training under great Keynesian economist James Tobin. She is believer in the Phillips Curve, NAIRU, output gaps, sticky wages, etc. She also believes in the dual mandate of inflation and unemployment and that keeping unemployment low is as important as or more important than price stability. During the 2000s she was reasonably vocal about the dangers of the housing bubble as it developed. Before, during and after the recession of 2008 Yellen was generally more keen to the depth of the recession than many other economists including her compatriots on the FOMC.

Her tenure so far has been relatively uneventful. Perhaps the most momentous event of her time was the rate raise of December 2015, which she had promised for a long period. Yellen is supremely careful about what she says and tries to give the appearance of precision in data, effectiveness of monetary policy and the power of the Fed to act.

## II.10.C.e. FOMC Transcripts

What can we learn from the ideas of the best economists and financial specialists, like members of the FOMC? What are their models and sources of information? The actual FOMC transcripts are available, with a five-year lag, e.g., the transcripts and supporting papers for 2010 became available to the public in January 2016. Normally, there are eight FOMC meetings in any year with some exceptions (such as 2008 when there were an extraordinary 14, including six by conference call). First, there is the issue of releasing FOMC transcripts. Before 1995, they were not released. The Fed resisted and even at one time denied their existence. Pressure from Congress got the Fed to release them with a five-year lag. Even with that lag, many analysts contend that, since FOMC participants know their meeting contents will be revealed, their discussion is scripted and less frank, to the detriment of monetary policy. Transcripts are notable for the absence of controversy, and FOMC participants are highly circumspect.

Other analysts question why FOMC proceedings are not immediately public, or at least why the transcripts are not released sooner. This is another contradiction of open Fed policy that is done only with delay and control over what the public hears. The release delay of five years is intellectually stultifying:

When a new set of transcripts is released, specialists (including the financial press) comb through, looking for clues; however, the "how they were thinking five years ago" facet removes urgency and relevance. Since events in M&M are always voluminous, people are hard-pressed to remember details of debates so far back. It is difficult to judge whether the FOMC was more on top of events than the markets. Indeed, the release of a new set is usually good for a few stories in the press, primarily by commentary writers who tried to find FOMC member's ideas that proved prescient or wrong. They look for doubt, controversy, hyperbole, etc. but it all appears to be old news. Here are a few specific facets of the FOMC meetings as revealed in transcripts:

- The topics and ideas brought up by the FOMC members and support staff are mostly current economic trends and events. They scrutinize long-term trends in important series but usually focus on the last data point, i.e., the most recent data. They also focus on the current crises much more than long-term trends. This demonstrates an elemental flaw about forecasting or even simply comprehending the current state of the economy. The last data point may provide the best estimate of what will happen next but, indeed, that very condition implies that the historical data and models are relatively useless. Also, the latest data point is largely just a random blip and the economic indicators they discuss are the same ones that economists and everyone else in our society study. They have certain models maintained by the Fed, yet still speak only about well-known indicators.

- They belabor surveys of businesses in their districts, and they refer to briefings with business executives. Depending on the district, the emphasis may be on local economic conditions, although some Fed bank Presidents also opine on prospects for exports from leading companies in their districts with global operations.

- They often refer to articles, series or editorials from prominent financial publications like *The Economist* and comment on how to use it or jockey against it. They seem highly conscious and very defensive about the multitude of intelligent thinkers pondering the economy.

- They frequently tout and restate the Fed's independence.

- They rarely use, or even cite casually, typical textbook models, like Okun's Law, the Phillips Curve, the money multiplier, etc. This is understandable since such models are often too rudimentary for discussion in a FOMC meeting and more suitable for long-run analysis. It also reveals that the models are of limited use. They do not talk about specifics of transmission of policy (for example, how an interest rate change will reverberate through the economy to create real effects of spending and investment). Effects are taken on faith.

- Participants relate anecdotes from their districts. The stories are collected from various sources at the Regional bank, its branches and major companies in the district.

- Participants appear very conscious of what they are saying, as if to protect their legacies as sapient. They do not take strong stands or go out on limbs. Debate is altogether polite, which compares to economics discussions, such as on blogs, which is often vituperative. The process is democratic, with each FOMC member getting equal time and a requisite amount of extra time for the Chair.

- They spend an inordinate amount of timing talking about how they will communicate to the world, sometimes literally going on for five to ten minutes, or even longer, over one word or phrase. For example, in the December 2005 meeting they spoke at great length about the word "measured" (used at the time as in "measured pace") to describe that rate of policy changes. Approximately pages 60 through 90 of the 90-page transcript are devoted exclusively to discussing that phrase. FOMC members and staff try to justify their fulsome effort as only a precaution to fanatic scrutiny of Fed statements by the financial press and the investment community, but it still comes off as a group of people utterly convinced that they are so important that their choice of words matters so much. This reflects a contempt for the public.

- A recurring theme in meetings is that they (both the FOMC members relative to their policy tools and the central bank itself relative to the economy) are truly in control. Or, at least, they know they must pretend to be in control. In the December 15 to 16, 2008 meeting, FOMC members discussed at length the fact that, even though the policy interest rate was now near zero, they (the FOMC) were still in control of the economy and financial system. You will never hear them saying that events are out of control. They might admit that a specific event was unexpected and/or of a magnitude beyond usual parameters, but they will never say, "I don't know what to make of the economy" or "I don't know what we can do."

- They are not oracles. The transcripts from 2008, a very tumultuous year, show that the Fed personnel were unaware of key magnitudes and trends in the economy at that time. Even after Lehman Brothers failed, Fed experts thought the economy would soon recover. Some even thought that inflation was the main problem.

## II.10.D. Alternative Ideas on M&M & Central Banking

Unintended consequences, moral hazard, distortion, uncertainty, gaming, etc. are some of the concepts analysts invoke today to describe the effects (usually adverse or perverse) of government economic policy. They are not distinct M&M models, nor are they easily demonstrated with equations. Rather, they are buzzwords that represent economic behaviors created from changing circumstances and situations. They are also largely redundant. For example, financial aid for college largely depends on government programs and grants and is distributed by universities using an application that assesses applicant's income and wealth (typically, the poorer you are the more you get). Financial aid programs could create the following:

- **Unintended Consequences**: Divorced people do not remarry to keep their income low on the college aid application.
- **Moral Hazard**: Knowing that your child is more eligible for financial aid if your earnings are lower or if you accumulate less wealth you have incentives to avoid earning and accumulating money.
- **Distortion**: You earn less income by supplying less labor when your child is applying for college aid.
- **Uncertainty**: Not knowing how your child's financial aid eligibility will change if you make big decisions like remarrying or buying a house makes those decisions more tenuous.
- **Gaming**: Have your teenager reside with a relative for a year in a state with an excellent university system so she can establish residence and qualify for the in-state tuition rate.

The section below further details major areas of discussion for non-standard M&M.

## II.10.D.a. Unintended Consequences

The term Unintended Consequences is a catch-all for any unexpected–and typically contradictory and adverse–economic effect of an economic policy. Unintended consequences could be major items (like financial services firms abandoning the money market funds business or the central bank losing its independence) or minor (like software not being able to handle negative interest rates or people remaining unemployed longer due to some new assistance program). Critics of active policy broach unintended consequences usually as bad or offsetting economic outcomes. First, we have to muster and measure the intended consequences and accepted tradeoffs that result from policy. When we do fiscal or monetary policy (think of stimulative policy for this discussion), we hope to increase economic output (or its growth) and thereby reduce unemployment. We expect adverse economic outcomes in the form of higher deficits, in the case of fiscal policy and higher inflation in the case of monetary policy. Yet we assume that the debt or inflation will represent less loss than the gains in output and employment. In other words, policy pays off. We do not–at least in textbooks and much public discussion–focus on other substantial adverse economic effects. Here are some aspects of unintended consequences:

- Perhaps the most curious unintended consequence of unconventional monetary policy is the loss of conventional monetary policy, mainly the controlling of the fed funds rate.

- Some argue that unintended consequences may exist but are unavoidable, of small magnitude and not permanent. They peter out or can be legislated away. Even if unintended consequences cannot be completely predicted, we still have to implement needed policies. Others argue that the unintended effects are often so big and long-lasting that those are more impactful than any of the positive, intended effects of monetary and/or fiscal policy. Doing a cost/benefit analysis of unintended consequences in modern M&M is difficult.

- Any change in laws will have unintended consequences. The sprawling Dodd-Frank Act of 2010, which is the largest piece of financial regulation since the Great Depression, has had and will continue to have many unintended consequences. Even a much more pared down and targeted program may have odd outcomes. For example, the JOBS Act (Jumpstart Our Business Startups Act of 2012) is intended to help small businesses get started. One provision allowed hedge funds to advertise to small investors, so that the hedge funds could raise more money. If the Act works and small investors invest in risky ventures, we cannot estimate the magnitude and negative effects of unsuitable or downright reckless investments.

- Another unintended consequence of current Fed policy is that banks and other financial institutions become so fearful of getting caught and penalized for any infraction that they curtail many lending or productive economic activities.

### II.10.D.b. Moral Hazard

Moral hazard is the main model/concept of "Information Economics": the study of information asymmetries in microeconomic decisions. Information Economics analyzes market failures brought on by wrong incentives and choices due to information differences of parties.[136] Information Economics goes back to about the 1970s and is a mainstay of economics texts and courses. One of the original models of this field is the 1970 piece by University of California, Berkeley professor George Akerlof concerning information asymmetries. Akerlof used the example of the used car market in which the buyer would not know the quality of the product he was buying. The paper is known as the model of lemons and plums.[137]

---

[136] There are two other major categories in information economics: (1) "adverse selection," which is parties choosing a program or action because they will use it extensively (e.g., the sickest seek health insurance) and (2) "principal-agent," which is a separation of an owner's interest from the economic decision maker's interest (e.g., you own the firm and I manage it; my incentives as agent may not be in your best interest).

[137] "The Market for 'Lemons': Quality Uncertainty and the Market Mechanism," by George Akerlof, *Quarterly Journal of Economics*, 84 (3), 1970, pp. 488-500. When you buy a used car you impute an average quality to the inventory on used car lots, yet people selling cars may be more likely to bring cars with problems (lemons) to market than quality ones (plums) such that the average car may be of lower than average quality. People therefore work off of biased information. This is supposed to

This has become one of the most frequently-lectured models and it is often picked up in the press. It supposedly demonstrates how micro decision makers can go astray and come to non-optimal outcomes.

When we talk about moral hazard in contemporary M&M we are usually referring to the effect of the government standing behind our economic choices and incenting us to take greater risk. Like other economic phenomena, moral hazard has become heightened perhaps since the broad government bailouts pursuant to 2008. Moral hazard occurs at the household level. For example following 2008, the government aided homeowners extensively, giving the appearance that if you bought too big of a house without much of a down payment, you could expect some bailout. Also, if you stayed within your means you got nothing, so the incentive is to buy beyond your means. Other examples of moral hazard currently pertinent to average people are increased consumer and investment products regulation. People recognize that the government is holding credit card companies more responsible for credit card mistakes or requiring financial services firms to be "fiduciaries" for individual's investment choices. That, in turn, might make them more reckless or careless with financial decisions.

Moral hazard also applies to the bigger parties in society, including large financial companies and even nations. For example, throughout the financial crisis it appeared that risk borne by the financial giants (with Goldman Sachs as probably the most common example) was backed by the government and therefore companies could take big risk. The housing market also would likely never have become so overpriced if it were not implicitly backed by government. In Eurozone the prominent example is countries such as Greece and Portugal that come to view bailouts from the ECB as optimal strategies. The needier you are, the more support you might get if someone perceives you as worthy of being supported when insolvent. The difficult question is what is the extent of moral hazard? Do major parties in the economy take excess risk and assume that the government (including agencies like the FDIC, the Pension Benefit Guaranty Corporation, etc. and now also the Fed) will back them? Or is it the opposite: That despite extensive bailout actions by Treasury and the Fed the kinds of bailouts done in 2008 through 2010 will not happen again? The best way to tackle this question is to relate a narrative of events:

- Historically, during the post-World War II period, the U.S. government had a fairly strict record of not bailing out companies. Over the 1970s and 1980s the entire list of bailouts included only a handful of odd names (like Lockheed, Conrail, Franklin National Bank, Chrysler and Continental Illinois National Bank); and they were only partially bailed out with loan guarantees and tax relief. Hard-liners like to remember those old days by citing President Nixon who supposedly, on being briefed that a big American company was too big to fail, remarked, "Tell it to get smaller."[138]
- Bailouts in the years prior to the 1990s were for banks facing runs and companies or industries that represented great job losses. In the 1990s our support shifted intellectually to entities that reflected systemic risk within the financial system or some other asset valuation situation.
- Many analysts propose that during the late 1980s through the 1990s the Fed created a moral hazard for stock markets. One term was the "Greenspan put," which implied that the Fed would take action to offset certain significant drops in the stock market. We know for sure that the Fed responded to any, and generally all, shakeouts in markets like the 1987 stock market crash or the 1994 Mexican

---

demonstrate how asymmetric information results in bad choices. It may be valid in theory, yet in the real world people are clever enough to avoid simple mistakes and seek more information like, in the case of used cars, testing the car, getting a warranty, bringing a friend knowledgeable about cars with you when you buy, etc. Many economics teachers oversell Akerlof's model and remark that, "You cannot buy a good used car," yet the used car market remains very efficient.

[138] It is not altogether clear which company he was referring to but it might have been Penn Central Railroad, which filed for bankruptcy in 1970.

peso crisis; yet, of course, it is impossible to judge whether the Fed responded so automatically such that market participants came to believe the Fed would always be there.

- The most pivotal moral hazard sway may have played out in the summer and fall of 1998 when the Fed lowered rates three times in response to the Russian bond default and failure of hedge fund Long-Term Capital Management. These Fed actions are viewed by some analysts as the moral hazard cardinal sin. In reality, the Fed had not performed any specific bailout action concerning Long-Term Capital Management. The Fed merely organized a meeting of the company's creditors, held at the New York Fed's headquarters in New York City. The Fed did not provide funding; however, there was the sense that the Fed desired that the hedge fund be wound up without affecting markets. Over time, even though the Fed did not spend one penny of money to prop up the failure, the Fed would be criticized for giving the appearance that the Fed stood ready to at least step in and referee capitalism.
- The events of 2008 and following profoundly changed the level of government support. The seizure of Bear Stearns in March 2008 was the initial bailout, followed by takeovers or extraordinary support for housing agencies Fannie Mae and Freddie Mac, many large financial companies (including AIG) and many big banks, markets (including the commercial paper market and money market), etc. Later in 2008, Lehman Brothers' executives expressed dismay when the Fed did not support their company after it had bailed out so many more.
- Those who believe that moral hazard is a problem contend that it is endemic in our policy and ingrained in our economic system. Others point out that the takeover policies during and following 2008 included harsh terms to failures (like AIG and Fannie Mae and Freddie Mac) and will thus limit moral hazard. Such ultimate penalties against a company may not affect decision makers, though, especially if competitors are also pushing limits.

### II.10.D.c. Distortion

Distortion is also a relative catch-all term. It refers to the warping of values or economic decisions given an economic policy or other event and it is best described with examples:
- The major distortion of QE policy is investors like pension funds flocking to riskier assets due to a need to reach for yield. The distortion is that prices of poor quality stocks and bonds are too high.
- The fed funds rate near 0% and many other rates closely related to it remaining very low for very long. The price of credit is distorted.
- QE's have distorted asset values. For example, government bond purchases by the ECB commencing in 2015 and continuing through 2016 have pushed large amounts of sovereign bonds into negative yields. ECB QE has also distorted the corporate debt market. Companies issue debt to sell to the ECB rather than for business development and investment. In Japan, the stock market has been so heavily bought by the central bank that stock analysis focuses on central bank buying and not company fundamentals.
- Programs, both government and other, create dominating and perverse incentives and shape the major decisions of people's lives (including housing choice, education, marriage and remarriage and how to raise children). Due to low mortgage rates and the ability to write mortgage interest off on taxes, people are compelled to own more housing and constantly refinance housing debt.
- Programs affecting life decisions by the young and the old suffer distorting effects. For example, college savings accounts (the 529's) are exempt from taxes. That gives an incentive for parents and grandparents to put other savings (i.e., not savings designed for education) into them. Over time

though, people become savvy to how much less financial aid their kids will get due to having college savings. For example, the additional $5,000 a grandparent saves for a grandchild's education might mean $2,500 less financial aid, so people save less and never save money in a child's own account. Also, divorced people do not remarry into a rich household. Finally, young people perceive that their children's educations might be financed by parents' tax free savings, distorting the price that these young people perceive they will pay for a large future obligation and shaping decisions for current consumption.

- Our higher education system is replete with incentives that change people's behavior in mostly non-optimal ways. For example, state colleges are cheap for in-state residents and some states have better schools than others. A young person living in one state might find it in his interest to take a year or more off to establish residency in a state with good schools, just to get the in-state tuition. In that time he might work a sub-standard job and do other costly actions like renting his own place and registering a car just to establish residency. It will pay off for him if he gets four years' discounted tuition. Another example of distortion concerns incomes reported on financial aid forms. Since the forms require all parents' incomes it is in people's interest to avoid getting remarried, or even to get divorced before the child nears college age.

## II.10.D.d. Uncertainty

Uncertainty is yet another catch-all term for a very general economic factor. The list below names prominent aspects of uncertainty as an M&M model and topic of discussion:

- Our central bank policies are intended to be credible forces to remove uncertainty, e.g., guaranteeing that interest rates stay low for a long time. Yet private parties rely on market forces to set rates and perceive of Fed promises as prolonging and exacerbating future uncertainty.
- Economists estimate uncertainty due to changing policy and changing government involvement in the economy. Economists measure (policy) uncertainty variously including: frequency of terms related to uncertainty found in news sources; dispersion of economic forecasts by professional forecasters; and frequency of law and regulation changes. A common finding is that uncertainty has increased. It is a tough measurement, though. For example, uncertainty indexes find that uncertainty surged following the 2016 Brexit vote yet, of course, a great frequency of press stories on the tumult of Brexit naturally followed the event.
- Uncertainty is omnipresent and easy to find yet effects are hard to discern. For example, over the year 2012 there was building uncertainty about the Fiscal Cliff. Would the U.S. indeed raise taxes and lower spending or, at the last moment, would the policies be overruled? Over the period of the cliff apparently businesses continued to invest. Many analysts concluded that uncertainty as an economic problem was overrated. Of course, their case was just a rough impression.
- Uncertainty is big and small. People question whether or not they will get their Social Security. They worry about inflation. Tax policy and its constant changing are great sources of uncertainty. For example, every year our federal government rules on "Tax Extenders" which are temporary tax breaks that must renewed or they will terminate. Usually they are renewed but people cannot be sure of that until very late in the year making decisions of households and businesses difficult. For example, a small business might only want to purchase a big piece of equipment if it gets a tax write-off. If it is not sure, the business might drop the investment. Since we are running chronic deficits we will likely have to continually change our tax rules.

## II.10.D.e. Gaming

The idea that people use every trick in the book to move ahead is not new. Any economic program can be taken advantage of in some way. Therefore, obviously, we cannot cease all programs due to gaming: It is just part of the cost. Yet today we have increased economic gaming of government programs and much of it is related to recent M&M policies. Many M&M programs are also short-lived, which renders them even more prone to be manipulated. Also, we Americans usually attributed "mooching" behavior as a pathology of people in other countries, like Greece. We believed we did not exhibit it as much, but perhaps that difference is no longer valid. Gaming is a topic that defies a simple model or quantification. Two specific examples of gaming government economic policies and a list of general gaming facets are discussed below:

- **Massachusetts Tax Holiday**: In Massachusetts, we have a tax-free weekend every August, during which state sales tax on purchases are dropped for two days. This tax break is, or was, designed to stimulate spending. Ironically, this policy was actually started in 2005, well before the Great Recession, which demonstrates the never-ending appeal of schemes to get people to spend. Whether consumers spend more or not due to this policy is dubious. Perhaps they did on the first incarnation. Since that time, however, the program has become a tradition and both consumers and retailers respond to it in a variety of ways that make economic sense to them as optimizers but are perverse to the purpose of the program. People plan around the tax holiday dates by pushing up or delaying a purchase. People come from other states into Massachusetts to make a purchase, thereby detrimentally impacting neighboring states. Some retailers are savvy to gradually reduce regular discounts as the tax break weekend comes up. Others run ads weeks before the weekend telling people to "come in today" and make a purchase, which the retailer will then process on the tax-free weekend. One retailer offers twice the state tax rebate. People and the media mock it, "Why don't we have a tax-free weekend every weekend?" A handful of politicians questioned the value, yet the policy persisted through 2015. In 2016, due to budget shortfalls, the policy was cancelled for the year. Subsequently numerous retailers offered to replace the tax, even two, three or more time its value. This reflected how extensively such government programs are gamed and how much they can distort economic incentives and decisions. Over the ten years of running this program, what did it eventually accomplish?

- **Cash for Clunkers**: This was a component of the large federal stimulus of 2009 that attempted to get people to swap large, fuel-inefficient vehicles for new, energy-efficient ones. The program therefore would both stimulate the economy by getting people to buy vehicles ahead of their schedules and also get people out of gas-guzzling vehicles that supposedly would have advantageous social and environmental effects and perhaps even long-run positive on the general economy. It is impossible to pick apart the net effects with great certainty but much anecdotal evidence pointed to various odd deals among related people and swaps of consumption in time. For example, a father wanted a new pickup truck and his son wanted a new car. The father traded his old pickup for a car, and the son bought a pickup, then they swapped vehicles. Or possibly a husband tells his wife, "Let's skip the Florida vacation and buy a new car now, while we get this government kickback." The increase in auto sales might be easy to see in the data, but the drop off in other consumption is not.

- **Household Formation and Labor Supply**: Almost every household can relate a story here. For many years my son received unemployment, Food Stamps and subsidized rent and education. Another young male relative of mine was on disability. I kept proposing employment for which he could apply when suddenly his guardian (my cousin) finally blurted out, "We're not trying to get him a job. If we did that he won't qualify for disability." Unemployment is a highly gamed government program. In recent years with the greatly expanded benefits it was even more manipulated.

- **Education**: New federal programs to relieve college debt for certain debtors (low income graduates and those who work in non-profits or government) will incentivize young people to scheme to choose too much education and then avoid certain types of employment to reap the savings on education costs. If you save for college tuition for your child, you stand to be eligible for less financial aid since you will have extensive financial resources. Households might invest their money in additional housing and be cash poor when their child applies to college. As we pointed out before, the tax-free education savings accounts, 529's, may be used as intended to save legitimately for college, but they are also overused by rich people and grandparents to delay taxes and shift assets. Similarly, we hear that many young people are borrowing in student loan programs to fund their regular lives (housing, automobiles, travel, etc.), rather than devoting loan proceeds to education. These people are simply broke and are gravitating toward more easily available credit.
- **Taxation**: We mentioned gaming of the Massachusetts tax-free weekend, which is a very minor tax program. Virtually all taxes, however, are manipulated in myriad and substantial ways. Corporations game taxes, of course; but individuals do, too. For example, people structure their tax-free savings vessels, like IRA's and 529's, to pass money across generations. The results are inefficient in many ways, including that lost tax revenues must be made up by taxing other sources. Also, private parties spend inordinate resources and change their optimal behavior to avoid taxes. People game pension and other tax advantaged programs. They borrow against their pensions and use those proceeds to spend or invest in housing and subverting the pension purpose of the savings.
- **Companies & Employees**: Companies encourage workers to synch work with government programs. How many times has a boss said, "Go on unemployment and we'll take you back when it runs out." This has been going on for years, but the magnitude and expanse of collusion is greater today as a result of more extensive government programs in health benefits, tuition reimbursements, retirement funding, etc. Short-term tax incentives to hire and spend, as were common in the post-2008 period, incentivize businesses (especially small ones) to manipulate programs.
- **Banking**: Banks game the new Fed stress tests, trying to meet the tests rather than meet better goals.
- **Investing**: When the Fed was rumored to commence more QE or specific programs like Operation Twist, investors bought in to take advantage of government buying. The same played out in other nations with their programs. When Japan announced its major stimulation initiatives, Abenomics, hedge funds bought ahead figuring to hold positions for a few months. Such actions result in private parties holding wrong-sized and incorrectly priced portfolios. Keeping rates low for long periods and under the control of the government subverts the usual business purposes of financial companies and makes them interest rate gamers.
- **System**: Our government watches markets intensely, attempting to manage them in a wide variety of ways. In turn, markets focus on government as gamer, manipulating government policies. The true roles of government and markets–for government to provide certain services and for markets to produce and allocate goods and services–become secondary. In financial markets, parties formerly viewed government as small and non-active. They valued companies and assets for their economic

values as determined by market forces. Now, leading investors and capital allocators watch government actions as the main determinant of value, and relegate markets to a secondary role.

- **Health**: Of course, health programs present myriad situations for gaming. For example under Obamacare, people get credits for health care depending on earnings to the point where less work is advantageous.
- **Immigration**: Immigration is gamed extensively for availability of government services including health care, Social Security, educational benefits and housing subsidies. One gaming method for U.S. immigration is visiting America at the time of giving birth so that a child will qualify for citizenship. Many immigrants seem willing to expend more effort obtaining a government handout than obtaining the same benefit by working, just to get it "free."[139]

## II.10.D.f. Rent-Seeking & Crony Capitalism

Rent-seeking or crony capitalism (which is a less formal and more derogatory term) are devices to increase the wealth of a business or organization without contributing to, and often detracting from, the economic output of society. They are from gaining special treatment by government. Economists estimate the cost to the economy as high as 20% of GDP. America may consider itself less prone to crony capitalism. We like to believe that our companies and other institutions take advantage of the basic rules but do not unduly curry favor from the government or at least nowhere near as much as in most other countries. However, we are just as likely to seek strict rules from government to thwart competition and to get subsidies and special help. We often characterize our businesses as arch opponents of regulation and inviting of open competition. They are, however, willing to accept a legislative role in their businesses if it helps them hold onto profit and market share.

The defense industry in America is one that is often characterized by cronyism. Politicians support the defense industry in their districts and, in turn, shelter these companies from international competition and cost-benefit analysis that might imply their services are not worth it. Other American industries are in deep with the government including health care, financial services, education, housing and telecommunications. One facet of America's cronyism is that the states often jockey against each other by providing tax breaks and other subsidies to companies to locate or remain in a state. Even the very finest names in American business like Boeing, General Electric, Ford and Google succumb to this cutting of special deals with the government.

Crony capitalism is in the eye of the beholder. For example, those who think cronyism is rampant cite Fannie Mae and Freddie Mac and the entire housing industry in America. They also see the bailouts of financial firms following 2008 and many years of low interest rates as nothing more than welfare for Wall Street. Other analysts might contend that such policies as necessary to manage inherent flaws of capitalism and ultimately benefit every citizen.

## II.10.E.a. M&M Inculcation Modifications

The existing M&M canon is defunct. Perhaps I am mistaken and, indeed, we will get back to the old monetary economics of minor intervention in the fed funds market but it is doubtful. Within ten or twenty years we will recite a new text, possibly authored by someone outside the Anglo-American M&M tradition. Here are some sundry improvements we could make to M&M teaching:

---

[139] This is based on personal experiences with in-laws and friends.

- We should rename the basic course from *Monetary Economics* to something that better describes the greater expanse of central bank policy, including potential reference to credit, confidence, asset prices and regulation. Of course, *Macroeconomic Credit, Asset Pricing, Confidence and Regulation Theory* is too verbose, so perhaps we could say *Macroeconomics of Central Bank Financial System Planning*. Depending how much you retain of the old story and how much you indulge our system as correct you could highlight our western variety of thinking with the following course title: *Macroeconomics of Central Bank Financial System Planning: West.*

- We must make a variety of adjustments to the theory and magnitudes of time value of money. We must emphasize that the actual magnitude of time value is the key and that it is not a high, like 7%. For any inculcation using a risk-free rate, use 1%. For any non-risk-free rate of return highlight the tradeoff between risk and (high) rates of return. Also, be circumspect about invoking long time frames. A section on the wide variety of rates (yield, IRR, discount rate, risk-free rate, etc.) and how they relate to each other is important. Demonstrate the nonsense of the magic of compounding. Do as many examples of drawing down savings and negative rates of return on investments to show the other side of compounding. Be circumspect using examples in which you assume you borrow at a lower rate than you invest at, without an explicit statement of risk.(For example, assuming a mortgage of $500,000 at 4% and then invest $300,000 at 8% to pay off the former with the latter would be incomplete without a description of the risk of the 8% investment. For charts and graphs demonstrating time value principles (which in most texts use rates ranging from 1% to maybe 20% with 5%-10% being the typical discussion points), use lower rates (including fractions of 1% like 0.01%, 0.1% and 0.5% and even negative rates like -1%). Use modest rates like 1% to 3% for discussions unless explicitly assuming risk.

- We should explain the relationship between bond prices and interest rates with circumspection. That bond prices rise when interest rates decrease is valid but the magnitude and direction of bond price increases depends on historical circumstances and those circumstances may be so different today that the relationship might not be as omnipotent as before.

- Add a section highlighting that macro manipulations hinge on tricking the private parties. In other words, it is a con game.

- Qualify statements or models that assume Keynesian effects like that lower interest rates or autonomous government borrowing creates more output. Of course, without Keynesian effects, M&M instructors lose much of their authority on economic issues.

- Teach that the Fed balance sheet is important and also describe it in relation to the U.S. fiscal authority to demonstrate that our nation's finances should be viewed as a consolidated balance sheet, including the Fed and the U.S. Treasury. Specific Federal Reserve releases (including tables H.4.1., "Factors Affecting Reserve Balances of Depository Institutions" and H.6., "Money Stock Measures") should be scrutinized. H.6 reveals M1, M2 and currency and along with Reserves from H.4.1 instructors can calculate the Monetary Base and relate the changes in M1, etc. to inflation, perhaps using $MV = PQ$.

- There should be a focus on debt and deficit, including the Fiscal Gap (the calculation of an accrual set of government books). Describe future liabilities of retirement and health care cost.

- Efficient financial market is a compelling and relevant parable that should be taught and presented as a baseline and case to beat. Also, the basic models of financial economics (such as dividend-discount model, CAPM, option pricing, risk measures) are rigorous and applicable models.

- Models of M&M including the money multiplier, IS/LM, yield curve, etc. should be taught as parables. They reveal how the world may work in general or under special circumstances.

- Instructors should create a perspective on whether the central bank has many tools or to what extent the tools all represent the same effects.
- We should emphasize the distinction between Fed policy to lower rates (to stimulate investment and consumption and create incomes) as opposed to lowering rates (to increase the level of wealth and engender wealth effects).
- We should study a variety of world central banks in addition to the Fed and the ECB.
- Field trips and guest lecturers are not very common in M&M courses. Typical field trips might be a visit to a Fed branch bank or the downtown business district. Guest lecturers are usually professional economists or business executives. A more insightful economics field trip–although hard to do in practice–might be a visit to a middle income neighborhood, going street by street and seeing what people do, or do not do, for a living. A better guest lecture would be members of households that have no savings and live paycheck to paycheck.

## II.10.E.b. Teaching by Skit

The macroeconomy is so vast and with such extreme feedback effects that we cannot trace effects, including the effects of M&M policies, with any precision. Our models are only parables. Reciting the chains of cause and effect (for example, a country lowers its rate and its currency goes down in value, then it exports more and GDP goes up…) become speculative after the first cause and effect (in our example, the people in the country are poorer due to the devalued currency and investors invest less in the lower rate environment and thus the GDP contracts…). Often a better way to convey effects of changes in the economy given a policy is feigning a conversation, in particular between two people embarking on a contract or other economic choice. Also, since the policies often involve getting people to take economic actions they were not intending to take, it is important to see what new force had makes them act. I often invoke a married couple facing some change in the economic environment. I usually portray the man as the active character and the woman as more hesitant which might appear sexist but the latter character is usually the more critical thinker.

Below is an example of a skit to broach and analyze the effects of an economic policy. It analyzes a low interest credit card distributed to low income households by the federal government with the intention of stimulating the economy. (This, by the way, is a policy that has been proposed by certain economists but not actually implemented):

- **The Low Interest Credit Card**: Setting - many households spend their entire incomes and still wish to buy additional goods and services. They are averse to purchase with their own credit cards due to high interest rates. Assume a young couple with modest incomes. After paying their bills they have no money left over. Each can earn extra income working weekends or second jobs but both defer because it is too much work. They covet a new purchase like a television.
  *He, "Why don't we buy it today on the credit card."*
  *She, "Yeh, like last time? It was a nightmare. Payments never ended!"*
  One day they get a credit card in the mail. It is not a usual credit card or credit card offer. Rather it is a government issued credit card with a certain maximum borrowing amount and a negligible low rate of interest.
  *She, "I heard about this. My girlfriend got one. We can borrow with hardly any interest."*
  *He, "You know what I'm thinking."*

They buy the television. Analysis: Indeed they have made a purchase they were not intending to make. That should increase AD with some multiplied effect. In our television set example, however, the spending might leak outside the U.S. since it is an import. The store orders a new television from abroad. The people make payments of their borrowing month by month which they would not have made otherwise. That lowers other discretionary spending. The U.S. government has borrowed for the people increasing debt and deficit. The government (various levels) potentially receive additional taxes due to the purchase. Etc.

These mock conversations can elucidate a variety of M&M topics:

- **The Housing Market**: Setting–after the couple has purchased an over-sized house due to low rates: *"Steve, we've cleaned out our savings. What are we going to put in all those rooms?"* she asks. *Steve replies, "Don't worry, honey, now that we own a house we're so much better off. We'll just put everything on the credit card."*
- **Fed Commitment**: Setting–a small business comprised of a husband and wife are contemplating opening a third donut shop. *He argues, "Rates are going to be long for a long time, so we should borrow more now. Even if we have a problem, we can borrow more later." "Why don't we just wait?"* she replies.
- **Lower Rates**: Setting–young couple sitting around on Sunday with nothing to do. *He tells his wife: "Honey, hey, rates are so low on car loans these days. What do you say we buy the new car now?" She replies, "But we're not making anything on our bank CD's. Doesn't that bother you?"*
- **Wealth Effect**: Setting–couple reading the mail after work. *He asks, "Honey, did you check out the 401-k statement that just came in the mail? We should spend a chunk of that. We got means now." She quips, "Can't say I've paid much attention to that account in years."*
- **Perceiving a Hot Economy**: Setting–couple driving down the road, and the husband states, *"The price of gas is really high. The economy is humming. Everybody's hitting the roads. They ain't staying at home. Hey, maybe we should buy that time-share."*
- **Deferring Spending due to Perception that Prices are Declining**: Setting–couple shopping in the mall. *He says, "Honey, you know, I've been watching prices go down. Maybe we should come back next year and buy. Everything will be cheaper by 2%."*
- **Nominal GDP Targeting**: Setting–a young couple comes home after eating out. *He comments, "Whew! Honey, we paid $100 for a steak dinner. That's a first. Everything is humming." She adds, "Prices are higher at the supermarket too."*

## II.10.E.c. M&M Video Resources

I fondly recall the first class of my first college economics course back in 1978. The instructor had lugged a record player the size of a suitcase to class and played a recording of FDR's First Inaugural speech to instill some passion for economics. I was impressed with both the motivation for economics and the effort of the teacher. The instructor of today has just the opposite problem concerning audio/visual teaching aids: There is a plethora of material available at the click of a mouse. Of course, some M&M concepts are difficult to dramatize. For example, I cannot find a dramatic demonstration of the dual mandate. The list of videos and other visual displays below names resources available online (*YouTube* or elsewhere) that I find insightful for teaching M&M courses. It is selective and notable by their absence are recitations by John Maynard Keynes, Milton Friedman and other historical and contemporary figures:

- William Jennings Bryan's "Cross of Gold" speech. Done at the Democratic National Convention in Chicago in 1896, this is a well-known speech in general. Most American college students know it from their high school U.S. history. Also, it broaches deflation: a timely M&M topic. Bryan advocated moving the U.S. from a gold to a bi-metallic standard that would include silver. That action would increase the supply of money and create inflation, or at least forestall deflation. Many Americans, such as farmers, had fixed debt and year after year the prices they received for their products were going down due to a gradual deflation, making their debts more burdensome. The video is part of the speech and a rereading and not the actual voice of Bryan. https://www.youtube.com/watch?v=9SafTrjVY9o

- The March 4, 1933 Inaugural speech by Franklin Delano Roosevelt includes the famous, "We have nothing to fear than fear itself." Roosevelt also describes at length the economic circumstances at the time, the prevailing attitude of which institutions were responsible for the economic collapse and the solutions he proposed. https://www.youtube.com/watch?v=WpEdYp1Nn-k
- *Any Bonds Today?* This is a patriotic song composed by Irving Berlin (Barry Wood sings the version below) exhorting people during World War II to buy U.S. bonds to fund the U.S. government for its war efforts. https://www.youtube.com/watch?v=kkNLZfQi_M4. Also, *Post War Victory Bonds Ad Campaign* is a promotional piece circulated circa 1946 that Americans to buy US savings bonds so that the country could rebuild after World War II. https://www.youtube.com/watch?v=Gau9STTX-bQ. Both of these bond buying videos make a compelling contrast with our current AD emphasis in M&M. Today, we simply do not ask people to save for national projects. We somewhat encourage people to save for their own retirements. In fact, national spending is recommended for the very borrowing it requires. Similarly, many government programs attempt to get people to spend profusely. The intellectual support for spending comes from M&M.
- President Nixon's August 15, 1971 announcement that the U.S. would drop the gold standard underlying Bretton Woods. This reflects the end of an era of sound money and the commencement of our modern floating rate and debt financing era of M&M policies. https://www.youtube.com/watch?v=rcnhF09QN78
- *Fight of the Century: Keynes vs. Hayek Round Two.* (Produced by EconStories.) This ten-minute wrap battle summarizes many of the facets of the debate between activism and free market. It is set following 2008 and is, therefore, Round Two, following the initial intellectual debate of the Great Depression. https://www.youtube.com/watch?v=GTQnarzmTOc
- The U.S. National Debt Clock, www.usdebtclock.org. Demonstrates the major economic quantities relevant to M&M and their interconnections.
- The Dynamic Yield Curve on StockCharts.com is an animated U.S. treasury yield curve from 1999 to the present. http://stockcharts.com/freecharts/yieldcurve.php
- *The State Pension Actuary,* produced by Stanford professor and economics Nobel Prize winner William Sharpe demonstrates the underfunding and risky holdings of pension systems. https://www.youtube.com/watch?v=Mk87_qg4ObA
- Senator Jim Bunning's statement to the Senate Banking Committee in December 2009 reviewing monetary policy as done by Ben Bernanke and the Fed is notable for various items. It reflects the tone of the debate early in the 2008 financial crisis. It is remarkable for the ex-baseball player as spokesperson for conservative M&M and for his matching wits with a tweed coat professor. It is notable for references to M&M items like the Taylor Rule and moral hazard. http://www.youtube.com/watch?v=rka9VbPPMys
- There is also a series of four college lectures delivered by Ben Bernanke in March 2012 at George Washington University School of Business. These are suitable for their history and for Ben Bernanke's take on the beneficial role of government in M&M matters. http://www.federalreserve.gov/newsevents/lectures/about.htm

# II.11. Put All the Models on the Board

M&M courses have about two dozen major models/equations/parables/empirical relationships. I say we should "put all the models on the board." Before we list the models, however, some general comments are in order. One acute flaw in M&M models is that they work right up until they are really needed and then they break down, like a seat belt that holds tight in a five mile-per-hour fender bender, but disconnects in a crash at sixty. The models veer—or de-couple, as some say—in that the quantities they relate no longer behave in the same way relative to each other, or they might even exhibit outright reverse results. The main explanation is that models work around means (averages) of macro quantities, and under extreme circumstances (like 2008 ff) means change.

In 2008 and following every model and construct—the business cycle, the timing of policy, the yield curve, the Taylor Rule, MV = PQ, Okun's Law, etc.—were, and to some extent continue to be, off in magnitudes and/or timing. The knowledge of the past that any model shows does not explain what is happening in the present. At first, analysts feign puzzlement: Why aren't the models holding? Then, they either explain the de-coupling with a confluence of factors, a structural break or special circumstances. As for economics teachers, some bull the old models through, lecture by lecture. Others admit they are mere parables. Others overly denounce the models.

A second curious general facet of M&M models and theories is their broaching and life-spans in the financial press. Typically, a piece of research using some M&M model, usually from some academic source, will get discovered by the press. The research will be picked up because some empirical analysis of the model presents a compelling statement pertinent to current events. The research and model will subsequently get a flurry of press, be omnipresent for months and then drop from prominence. It is kind of like prospectors searching for gold. Graduate students, journalists, portfolio managers, professors, pundits, etc. scour for justifications and clues to explain current events. Somebody strikes a clever combo of model and data. Everybody then works on it until the mine gets picked through and everyone abandons it.

Set forth below are the main models encountered in the classroom, press and professional circles. For example, these are found in the transcripts of FOMC meetings, *The Wall Street Journal,* stock analysts' research reports, academic working papers, etc. For each model, I will identify if it is theoretical, empirical or both. Even a simple aspect like this can often get lost on the public because the science of M&M can be arcane. Also, I will describe models' Keynesian leanings, in particular, if the model assumes that stimulating the economy produces more output without an offsetting tradeoff.

## II.11.A. Aggregate Supply/Aggregate Demand

Aggregate supply and aggregate demand (AS/AD) is a plot of supply and demand curves for the entire economy in a field of price level on the y-axis and GDP on the x-axis. The aggregate demand curve has a downward slope like any demand curve from microeconomics but not for the same fundamental microeconomic reason of lower prices bringing forth more demand for a product. Rather, AD is downward sloping because lower interest rates are associated with higher GDP: a kind of built-in conclusion. The AD curve is a hokey story, and I think many instructors simply do not understand it.

The AS curve can represent key insight, as I pointed out earlier. The shifting of the AS curve, either in (or to the left) for some adverse development in the economy or out (or to the right) for a favorable development can demonstrate important economic changes in our society. Of course, movements of an economy-wide AS curve can only be quantified crudely. Also, AS is a supply-side story and, therefore, less emphasized by analysts who prefer Keynesian ideas. Usually we move the AS curve out due to technological advances and in from increased costs resulting from some external source, like a calamity.

AS/AD is theoretical: Depending on the shape of the AS curve it tells a Keynesian or a non-Keynesian story. If the AS curve is vertical at a full-employment level (like the long-run supply curve labelled LRAS below) moving the AD curve will result only in higher price level, a non-Keynesian story. We assume a slope to the AS curve (the SRAS below) to relate a Keynesian story of the beneficial effects of increasing demand. We typically depict AS/AD model with both a long-run vertical AS curve at the full employment level of the economy (Y*) and an upward sloping short-run AS curve, as if in the short run we could get more output from increasing demand.

## AS/AD

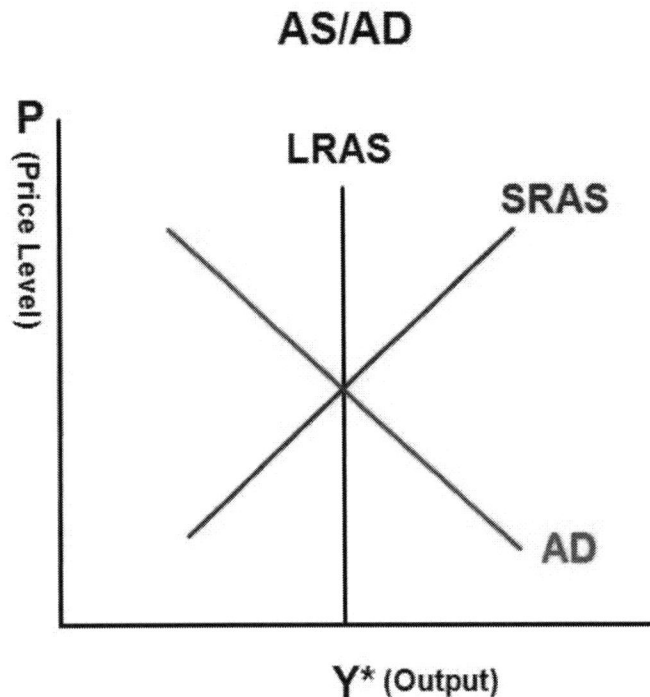

When you wax philosophical about the macroeconomy and the myriad factors that affect it, at least check that thesis with the AS half of AS/AD. It provides the best "first approximation" of an economic event or action. There is a key question though: How does the development affect our general ability to supply or create economic output—enhancing our ability to create output (move the curve out), diminishing our economy (move the curve in) or having an indeterminate effect? For example, if the Fed does more QE, does it affect how much our economy can produce? If you are a Keynesian believer, yes.

Of course, the supply curve is merely a parable and impossible to quantify. Every day the AS moves out in little ways due to constant improvements in technology and procedures, like removing a business regulation. However, it also moves in everyday due to constant adding of costs and constraints, like perhaps a minor new business regulation that appears so inconsequential. Then, envision occasional big favorable movements, like a technological breakthrough and large adverse movements like a terrorist attack.

This introductory discussion brings us to some specific cases. A common lesson in the classroom is the moving in of the AS curve with an adverse supply shock, typically either bad weather or a surge in the price of imported oil. Perhaps over the next few decades we reach peak oil, global warming causes calamity after calamity and our AS moves in (like going from AS to AS″ below). In classroom recitations to move the AS out (like going from AS to AS′ below) we hypothesize a breakthrough in technology. Perhaps we are entering an era of great innovation. For example, driverless motor vehicles could free up time and resources. Regulation normally moves the curve in but the question is magnitude. A conservative will say regulation has a grave effect on our ability to supply and a liberal will pooh-pooh any effects. Earlier in this book, we talked about many trends affecting America today, like labor immobility. Most of those move AS in.

## AS/AD

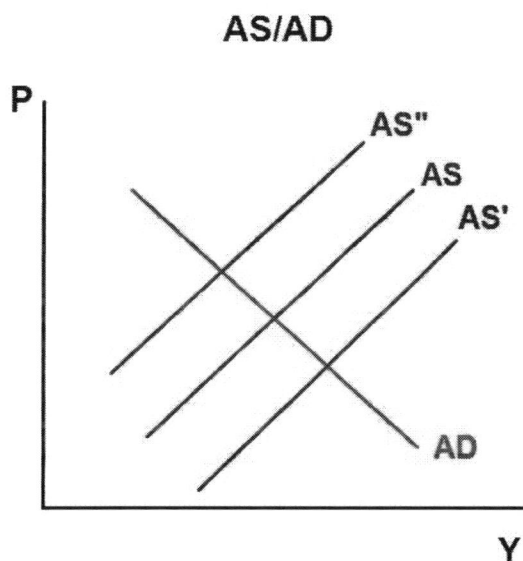

Shifting the AS curve out is not simply a matter of technological advances or other ostensibly favorable economic events. For example, a health care breakthrough that increases life expectancy might move the economy-wide AS curve in because it is costly (harder to supply) given that old people are costly to care for. For another timely AS example, recent extensive government policy to keep people from defaulting on mortgages might move AS in because it keeps people stuck to their homes and incapable of migrating to a part of the country where labor could be better used.

It is hard to pick out or quantify the main determinants of economic progress in recent times. Major technology innovations—like cell phones, the internet and GPS,—add substantial efficiency and productivity to our economy. The cell phone may have been a major shifter of the AS curve. For example, think of every time someone dialed his friend and said, "Don't bother coming. There's no work for you here"; thereby saving unnecessary effort and resources.

### II.11.B. MV=PQ

MV=PQ, known as the Quantity Theory, is another classic M&M construct. It is at once (1) a very simple statement that increasing the supply of money results in higher prices for an economy at full employment and (2) also a very subtle story about inflation depending on minute distinctions about the stability of velocity and full employment. The equation says that PQ, which is nominal GDP, equals some money supply quantity multiplied by the number of times that money supply is churned in transactions: the V. The usual direction of explanation starts with a change in the supply of money and an assumption that V is stable, followed by price level and nominal GDP changing. For example, a 10% increase in the money supply should cause a rough 10% increase in prices assuming that real production does not increase much in any short period. Few economists take this literal use of the equation as reflective of the real world, especially since the V is not stable and any of the money aggregates—including the Monetary Base, M1, M2 or MZM[140]—are crude concepts of what is used for transactions that have themselves fluctuated substantially given financial innovations in payment methods.        Prior to 2008, MV=PQ seemingly revealed a constraint on the economy and certain M&M experts, such as former Dallas Fed president Robert McTeer (a plain speaking and prominent economist in public discussion during his term from 1991 to 2005), regularly invoked it to attempt finalist statements about contemporary macro conditions. MV=PQ fails to demonstrate its usual story, however, since about 2009. As we increased our Monetary Base greatly (currency plus reserves rose from about $1 trillion to multiple trillions), M should have risen substantially. In theory M should have increased many multiples of the increase in the Monetary Base. Assuming Q, which is real GDP, to be growing only a little, MV=PQ implied high inflation (the P would have gone up). Inflation did not go up much. We now know that V dropped dramatically, unlike any other change in V during recent history, which renders the usual assumption of stable V invalid.

Analysts explain the failure of MV=PQ to hold pointing out that the Monetary Base does not constitute credit in today's economy. Another argument is that the sheer size and nature of QE rendered the model useless. MV = PQ is primarily theoretical although you can put data to it, with the caveats above about money supplies being crude measures. It is not a Keynesian story because the focal thrust of the equation is that increasing M increases P and not real output.

## II.11.C. Money Supplies & Demands

There are a variety of models and ideas involving monetary aggregates and their relationships with the economy and inflation. To recap, economists define M1 as the sum of coin, currency, demand deposits and travelers checks and M2 as M1 plus savings deposits. Originally, in M&M theory, M1 was the key theoretical money quantity. People would use M1 for transactions. If economists found that the M1 aggregate was increasing too rapidly we would conclude that too much money was chasing about the same amount of goods, and inflation would rise. Economists studied the rate of change of M1 very closely. Although M1 as medium might have described the 1950s and 1960s well, over the 1960s and 1970s it became less useful due to the changing of financial institutions and financial securities—what economists call "financial innovation." People could move money between bank accounts (e.g., sweeping funds from checking accounts into savings accounts) much more quickly. They could also move funds into other assets like mutual funds and equities much more readily.

Economists resorted to M2 and its the rate of change. We compared it with M1, and we could theorize that (1) either the monetary aggregates moved together (e.g., the economy was strong and both M1 and M2 were increasing); or (2) that they moved opposite to each other (e.g., people were substituting between the quantities). In the latter case, people would be putting money into M2 savings vessels and reducing their M1 holdings, primarily checking accounts. By the 1980s, the rates of growth of monetary aggregates moved in unpredictable ways, both compared among themselves and with inflation and GDP growth. Economists had great conviction that very high rates of money growth implied similarly high inflation, and in every textbook there was a plot of inflation rate v. money growth rate. The points clustered along a 45 degree line.

Economists would model money demand and money supply. Money would be demanded for transactions and as part of a portfolio of assets. Money demand would also depend on income, interest rates and returns on alternative assets. For example, as the return on other assets decreased, demand for money

---

[140] MZM is money of zero maturity which is M2 excluding mainly CD's. MZM is money that people can readily use for transactions, and some economists think it is the best money aggregate.

would be assumed to rise. In the modern economy, however, we never really had a strong sense of the demand for money. Sometimes the teaching would be way out of date. For example, during the time of Keynes, economists said people held money for speculative reasons, as if people would hold lots of money waiting for a big investment opportunity. Such a motivation does not make sense now. Modeling money supply was easier. Simply put, the central bank set the money supply. Given money demand by private parties and money supply by the central bank we would assume they would meet at a certain equilibrium price of money, an interest rate, and that we could lower that rate by increasing money supply.

For a time, during the 1970s and early 1980s, economists and markets watched monetary aggregates very closely. In the early 1980s, however, the Fed de-emphasized monetary aggregates as a goal and focused on interest rates. People still checked data on monetary aggregates but over the 1980s, interest in the quantities waned. In 2000, the Fed stopped publishing target ranges contending that money did not matter too much to federal funds target rate policy. Models of money can be either theoretical or empirical. Depending how you relate these models, they may or may not relate an effective activist policy—i.e., Keynesian effects.

## II.11.D. Yield Curve

The Yield Curve was held up as the consummate M&M model for perhaps twenty years. The yield curve, however, is not a construct developed by macroeconomists. It is not found in M&M textbooks from even twenty years ago. It was a tool used on Wall Street starting around the 1970s for bond investing purposes. It was subsequently discovered to possess, supposedly, a long-standing record as precursor to turns in the economy. Now the yield curve is in M&M texts with various theories invoking fundamental behavior of economic agents to explain—or rationalize—why it is a strong leading indicator. As for its record of prediction, it is easy to find flaws in it.

The yield curve is the plot of the interest rate (or "yield") on the vertical axis and time to maturity (aka the term) of a certain class of bonds, usually U.S. government bonds, on the horizontal axis. The curve should slope upward (supposedly) because normally bonds with longer maturities command higher yields because holders must be compensated for committing their money for a longer time. The term/yield relationship can flatten, flip or invert, producing a flat or inverted yield curve. (See pictures below.) Both of these diagrams show the yield curve at one point in time. You can also exhibit a yield curve over time by taking the difference between the yields of one of the longer-term bonds (usually a 30 or 10-year) and one of the shorter-term bonds (either a three-month or one-year treasury. Some analysts use the fed funds rate itself, which is a rate on short-term funds similar to U.S. debt. Then, you plot these differences day by day. The number should normally be positive. When negative, the point in time yield curve will be inverted. (See Yield Curve Time Series below.) Both the point in time and time series demonstrations of yield curves are important to teach students, and with animation you can exhibit both. The Dynamic Yield Curve shows a snapshot of the daily curve day-by-day for about the last ten years.[141]

---

[141] http://stockcharts.com/freecharts/yieldcurve.php

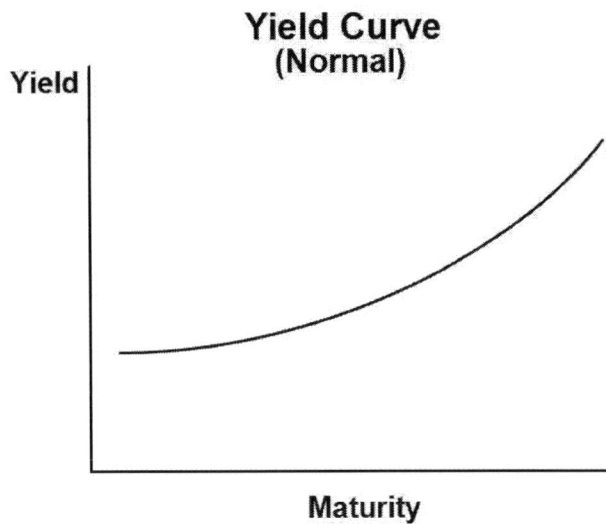
**Yield Curve (Normal)**

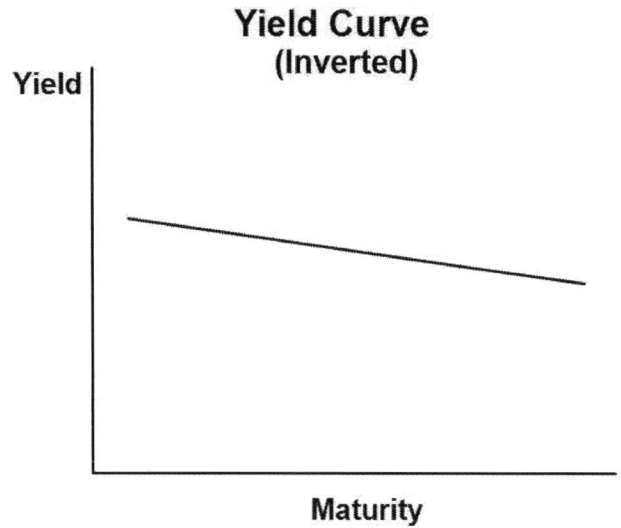
**Yield Curve (Inverted)**

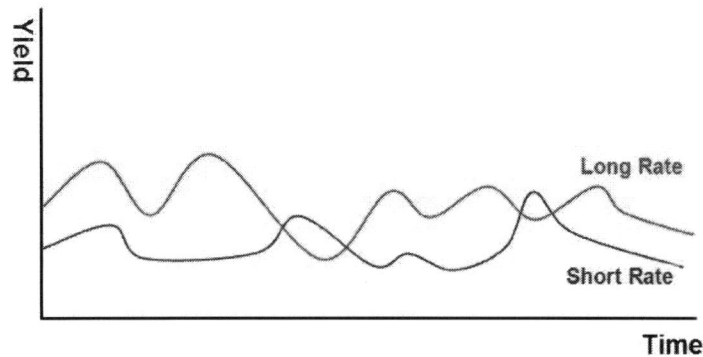
**Yield Curve Time Series**

When the yield curve is inverted (which, depending on whom you ask, included a downward slope or even just a flat range) it is considered, by some analysts, as a precursor to recession—or at least a relative slowdown in the economy. There are various rationales for this predictive power: The most common story is that when investors expect the economy to sour, they assume company earnings will be lower. That will result in lower stock prices. Therefore, they sell equities and buy long-term bonds. The bonds should have relatively high returns because in bad economic times inflation will be low and interest rates will go down, pushing bond prices up. This buying lowers long-term yields and causes the curve to flatten. This is the most elegant "theoretical" story for the relationship between yield curve and economy. A second story is that an inverted curve reflects that the central bank has been tightening (i.e., raising rates at the short-end). Simultaneously, tightening will lead to economic contraction. A third story is that banks lend on the spread: They borrow short and lend long and that spread is bigger when the yield curve is taller and is reflective of a strong economy in which lending is in demand.

Yield curve believers contend that "for forty years" the inverted yield curve has called recessions with only one false alarm. They contend that the curve inverted in 1966 with no recession, but since then it has inverted before each of the subsequent seven recessions. The yield curve/recession relationship, however, exhibits the usual magnitude and timing problems of M&M models. It also seems to vary along with the idiosyncratic patterns of our modern macroeconomic history, i.e., case by case it is hardly consistent. For example, over a period that included the recessions of 1980 and 1982, which was also marked by very high inflation, the pattern of yield curve inversion was extreme and volatile with at least one major reversal. After history played out, analysts could somewhat demarcate a before and after of yield curve inversion and recession, but the relationship at the time was inscrutable. There are other flaws or arbitrary aspects:

- The selecting of maturities that define inversion is arbitrary. Proponents usually use the ten-year v. three-month maturities but often use others.
- There are close calls and false signals. The curve was inverted or flat on many occasions (e.g., 1995 and 1997) and, because favorable underlying economic factors dominated, the economy did not tank.
- The relationship does not hold as well in other countries.
- When interest rates are low in general, the theory does not follow. When interest rates are controlled by extraordinary government policy, effects are less pronounced. For example, after 2008 the yield curve became upward sloping but the typical recovery from recession was lacking.
- The relationship holds much more tightly from about 1970 through the early 1990s than it does after the early 1990s.
- The yield curve is not unique as a major series related to recessions. Oil prices, the housing market and other items (like consumer durables) have the same co-movement with roughly as much lead.

People cling to the yield curve precursor story by naysaying timing and magnitude problems and arguing that something resembling an inversion will be followed by something like a recession within a reasonable time frame. How did the yield curve perform during our most recent recession of 2008? The yield curve inverted as early as very late 2005 or early 2006, and the event got copious press; but the recession would prove to be so far off that the yield curve forecasters suffered prediction fatigue and gave up calling a recession.

Earlier in 2005[142] yield curve proponents were picking up on the impending inversion and yield curve doubters were saying recession would not follow.[143] Yield curve defenders will ultimately say the curve did not flatten until around July 2006 and that the recession started in December 2007. This is within their usual three to 18-month window; however, it looked flat in 2005. When recession was not obvious in early 2008—consensus opinion still doubted recession through much of 2008—and the yield curve was now already sloping upward again, it would have great resolve to stick to the proscription of the model. Proponents explained that the yield curve was very upward sloping by early 2008 and the economy did not

---

[142] "My concern is the yield curve. It is flattening, which suggests a recession," says money manager Warren Isabelle in *Barron's* interview: "Pairing Back, Shifting Focus," May 23, 2005, p. 28.

[143] Inverted yield curve analysis was omnipresent in late 2005 and early 2006, including these four examples, among countless others: "The 0.004 Percentage Point That Shook the World," by Caroline Baum, *Bloomberg.com*, December 30, 2005; "Economists Ask If Bonds Have Lost Predictive Power," by Mark Whitehouse, *The Wall Street Journal*, December 29, 2005, pp. C1, C3; "Don't Be Thrown by the Yield Curve," by Roben Farzad and Justin Hibbard, *BusinessWeek*, January 16, 2006m, p. 40; and "Is Iran the Cause of That Inverted Yield Curve?," by Kevin Hassett, *Bloomberg.com*, January 3, 2006.

grow greatly in the following years as a result of extraordinary Fed policy that changed the relationship. From 2009 through about 2013, the steep yield curve was interpreted by some as reflecting stagflation (the complete opposite of its usual story). The stagflation story was that the long end was high because the market was expecting higher inflation so bond buyers demanded high yields (the inflation part). The short end was low, however, because the Fed had to keep rates low because the economy was weak (the stagnation part).

There are two more notable aspects of the yield curve:

- Many analysts think the yield curve should not have much of a slope—regardless of the state of the economy. A large, liquid, risk-free debt market like that of U.S. treasuries should require minimal additional yield to get parties to hold longer maturities. Why has the curve been distinctly upward sloping for most of its history? Perhaps constant government policy of first raising inflation and then lowering inflation has made it that way.

- Another droll aspect of the yield curve as precursor to recession is that we usually assume that the public (meaning private parties including macroeconomists, investors, banks, companies, pundits, etc.) cannot predict turns in the economy. That is why we need a central bank. The Fed and other policy makers know more about the economy; At least, we believe that private parties look to every decision of the Fed for clues on the economy. The yield curve as precursor, however, assumes that the private parties (i.e., the "market") are able to discern turns in the economy. It is private parties' buying of bonds in anticipation of a recession that flattens the curve. This is egg on the face for both the Fed and the market. Fed officials such as FOMC members resort to prescience of the market when the Fed officials use the yield curve for policy support. The market watches the Fed closely and reacts to Fed actions, yet it is the market that originally provided the Fed with the clue to the state of the economy.

The yield curve is primarily an empirical item, with a rationalizing theory put to it. It is not Keynesian, although it does make for a story of a business cycle that can be predicted and successfully managed with policy.

## II.11.E. Phillips Curve

Perhaps the most famous macroeconomic relationship is the Phillips Curve, which relates inflation (on the y-axis) and unemployment (on the x-axis). When first promulgated in the early 1960s, a tradeoff between the two quantities, seen as a downward sloping curve, was evident in very long historical data series. It should be noted that the original analysis was done by economist A.W. Phillips using data for the United Kingdom from 1861 through 1957. Phillips' inflation measure was wage rate changes. This relationship was supremely useful in M&M modeling because it made a link between the real economy (unemployment) and the money economy (inflation). Since we could control inflation through the control of money, we could alter unemployment—in other words, control the real economy. The relationship ostensibly held in the 1960s and the main thrust of our macro policy was that we could move along the curve as we pleased. However, this was a grand illusion that broke down in the 1970s when the curve "blew out." In other words the curve moved up and to the right with the tradeoff between unemployment and inflation happening at higher and higher inflation.

Milton Friedman predicted the demise of this idea during the period (the 1960s) when it appeared to hold very well. He hypothesized a short-run Phillips Curve that would not persist, but a long-run Phillips Curve that put unemployment at its long-run natural rate (or NAIRU) regardless of the level of inflation. He said there were numerous short-run curves at different levels of inflation. This constituted another debate about short v. long run with conservatives saying assume we are always in the long run and liberals saying the opposite. The traditional Phillips Curve and a long-run or Expectations Augmented Phillips Curve, which has many short-run tradeoffs but unemployment revolving around a long-run rate, are pictured below:

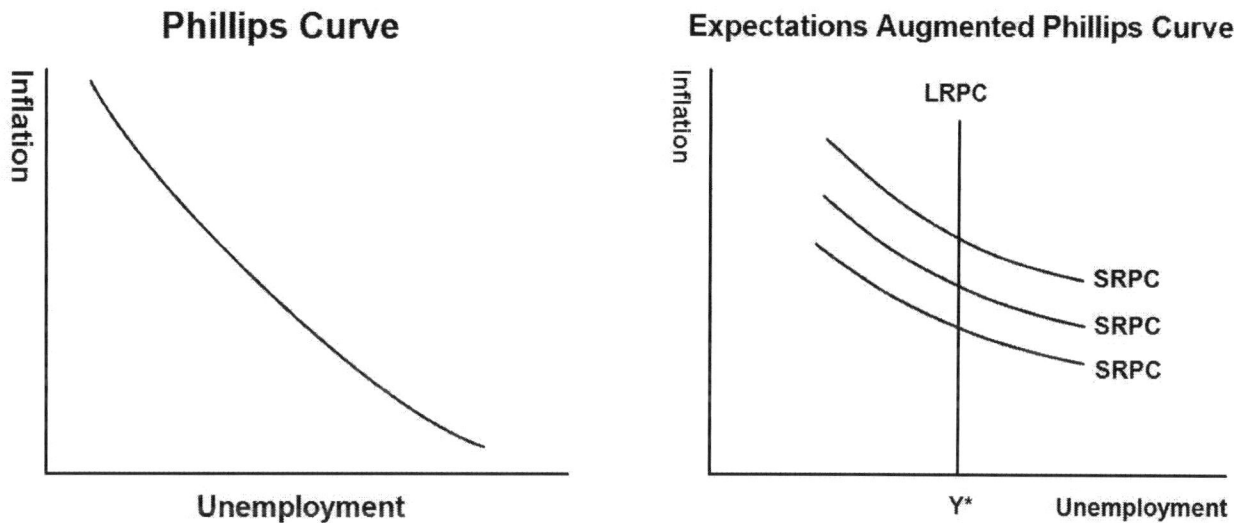

## Phillips Curve

## Expectations Augmented Phillips Curve

The Expectations Augmented Phillips Curve can be explained like this: The economy starts out at some level of Y and on the lowest of the three SRPC curves in the diagram. We decide to lower unemployment by simulating our economy with monetary or fiscal policy. The policy causes the economy to move left along the SRPC to a level of lower unemployment and higher inflation. The policy also might cause us to overshoot full employment (Y*) and/or overstimulate the economy with too much money and/or credit. Thus, the economy tends back toward Y* but also jumps to a higher SRPC (in our example, the one in the middle). Higher inflation gets built into wage raises, price increases and interest rate changes. If, at some future point, we decide to stimulate the economy again we can move left now along the middle SRPC. Also, again, the economy tends back toward Y* and onto another SRPC at an altogether higher level of inflation (the top one).

The Phillips Curve remains popular in texts and in the press and almost always appears compelling as a story for the economy at any point in time. Fed Board economists frequently cite this in their deliberations at FOMC meetings. At some level the tradeoff between inflation and unemployment is considered the operational model of Fed policy. Janet Yellen has professed belief in the tradeoff. The Phillips Curve is often taught by many instructors in its simplest form, as if the premise had not been invalidated nearly 40 years ago. M&M instruction at the lower echelons of college and community college often culminates in a Phillips Curve. You might think that the Phillips Curve has been rectified with the Expectations Augmented Phillips Curve, but that is just an appeal to the distinction between short and long-run.

In another compelling irony and theoretical reversal, in the post 2008 period policy seemingly abandoned our beliefs against long-run tradeoffs between unemployment and inflation. Our long-term stimulative monetary policy attempted to reduce unemployment in the long run. This is another example of how the basic tenets of M&M have changed. For decades copious teachers said, "There is no long-run tradeoff between unemployment and inflation, but there is a short-run tradeoff." Now apparently there is and only a long run.

A plot of the Phillips Curve from about 2009 through 2016 is a horizontal line with a slight positive slope as inflation tended down with unemployment going down. Such shape is at odds with either the traditional short or long-run cases, demonstrating how the models become confounded. The Phillips Curve is both theoretical and empirical. In lecture we begin with theoretical diagrams like above then put data to it by showing scatterplots of unemployment and inflation for many years, demonstrating the hold that relationship maintained in the through the 1960s before blowing out. The traditional Phillips Curve is Keynesian while the Expectations Augmented is not—at least not in the long run.

## II.11.F. Taylor Rule

One of the most reputable M&M models is the Taylor Rule ("TR"), which is an equation solving for the fed funds target rate as a function of major economic inputs (including inflation and GDP growth). The TR goes back to "Discretion versus Rules in Practice," a 1993 paper by Stanford professor John Taylor.[144] The TR was our main model up until 2008. It was not an official rule, necessarily, but most of the big central bankers were TR'ers. For example, in his preface to a review of his career at the Fed Laurence Meyer, who was on the Fed Board from 1996 to 2002, referred to two monetary policy devices: NAIRU and the TR: "I will refer on occasion to a specific set of principles—summarized by the Taylor Rule—that identifies how monetary policy should be set to promote full employment and price stability."[145]

The TR is considered exceptional for several reasons: (1) It is rich in economic content, yet simple. (2) It is a rule as opposed to a model/policy involving judgment. (3) Supposedly, it fits (or fit) history well, i.e., its proscription and the actual fed funds target tracked well. In the financial press, you probably see (or saw at least before 2008) more references to the TR than any other M&M model, and no matter who invoked it, the TR was accorded respect—unlike other M&M models. Of course, since about 2009 with the fed funds target rate so low the TR appears much less perfect. Both Alan Greenspan and Ben Bernanke were reputed to prefer the TR, and politicians invoke it. For example, U.S. Senator Jim Bunning, the former baseball player turned arch-conservative politician, excoriated the Fed and Ben Bernanke in 2009 while citing, with authority, the TR. It is also a major element of Federal Reserve audit and reform acts that have been proposed in recent years.[146]

The TR states:

Fed funds target rate $= 2\% + \pi + 0.5(\pi - \pi^T) + 0.5(g - g^T)$

Where:

2% is a constant reflecting the true long-run real return to safe assets (like the neutral (or natural rate); this constant was 2.5% a few years ago)

$\pi$ is current inflation

$\pi^T$ is the inflation target (considered to be 2%)

g is the actual growth rate of GDP

$g^T$ is trend GDP growth (some economists say 3%; some say less)

---

[144] Carnegie-Rochester Conference Series on Public Policy, 39, 1993, pp. 195-214.

[145] *A Term at the Fed*, HarperCollins, 2004, p. xvii.

[146] For example, H.R.5018 – Federal Reserve Accountability and Transparency Act of 2014, has a formal implementation of the TR as its main reform.

$\pi - \pi^{T}$ is known as the inflation gap

$g - g^{T}$ is known as the output gap

To give a quick example, using annual data for 2014 for the U.S., inflation was 1.6% and GDP growth was 2.4%. Our inflation target is 2.0% and trend GDP growth is about 2.5% (using a rough average of Fed projections; similar to views of trend growth). Fed funds should equal 2% + 1.6% - 0.2% - 0.05 = 3.35%. The actual fed funds was about 0.12%, which is far off. We explain this below.

The TR varies a little in different texts. The constant is usually 2% although it is 2.5% in some versions; inflation is the previous 12 months inflation; the inflation gap is current inflation minus the 2%; and the output gap is current GDP minus potential GDP. Since rates have become very low, the constant term becomes the dominant item. If you use a constant of 2% rather than 2.5% that 50 basis point change could dominate in certain policy situations like in recent years (with the fed funds rate at 0 to 25 basis points up through 2015 and about 37.5 basis points circa early 2016). Many TR specialists today have recommended lowering the constant, sometimes to zero, to true-up the TR to contemporary times. This demonstrates two major M&M points we have discussed: (1) When rates are low, different economic rules apply. (2) M&M models break down when extreme circumstances prevail.

The TR is a rich macro equation in that it has both our monetary (the inflation items) and real economy (the output item). Altogether the TR consists of two parameters, three estimates and three pieces of data. The parameters are somewhat arbitrarily both set to 0.5, which weighs the price deviation and output deviation the same. The three estimates—the constant, the inflation target and trend GDP growth—each represent weighty areas of economic theory: respectively, the risk-free return, optimal inflation level and long-run trend of the economy. Proponents say the TR fits history well, and textbooks typically display a times series of the fed funds rate predicted by the TR v. the actual fed funds rate; and the two track closely. The fit of the TR was "striking," as the text I used puts it.[147] If you look more skeptically, though, the model output may track well when the economy is growing close to its average rate but not during extraordinary times such as during and after the three recessions since 1990. Since the TR has only been around since the early 1990s, its record is simply not that great. In fact, the tight fit is largely a result of retroactive fitting of the rule with actual data as it becomes available, which tends to reset the series being forecasted to the trend that is shaping it. This causes it to look like a good fit.

Every semester in my class we examine the TR with current data and compare our calculations to the current fed funds target. The two are usually significantly off. Simply put, the Fed is, or was, ostensibly not using the TR for current policy. Initially in classroom demonstrations we use data for the last year. Then I put in reasonable estimates about the TR looking six months to the future since, optimally, we would want to set the target to reflect present and slightly future values. Then, the class and I propose changing inputs based on current perspectives: "Using GDP and inflation estimates from a recent speech by Ben Bernanke." Without making extreme assumptions, we can get target rates with great ranges. In general, doing the TR anytime from about 2011 to 2016 would produce a result much higher than the actual policy rate.

Another problem with the TR is that it may recommend a rate below zero, which renders it somewhat useless. When the proscription comes out negative you can set the fed funds rate at zero and solve the TR in reverse—in particular, solve for the output gap. If inflation is positive, the output gap will come out negative implying that the economy needs additional stimulus. Depending on details during the years 2012 to about 2015 this exercise will give a current GDP growth rate in a range of -2 to -5%,

[147] Cecchetti, Stephen, 2008, *Money, Banking, and Financial Markets*, p. 447, 2nd edition.

implying hundreds of billions of lost GDP. Then, using estimates of QE effects on the economy, you can assess the correct level of QE.

Another attempt at dealing with the zero bound is the "Shadow Rate" or the Wu-Xia[148] Taylor Rule calculation. By relating the fed funds level to other rates in the market, and employing sophisticated econometrics, the Shadow Rate calculates a fed funds rate based on economy conditions. The shadow rate fell below zero in 2009, continued to trend down getting as low as about -3% in 2014. Then it trends up breaking into a positive range by late 2015. The shadow rate can demonstrate that the stance of monetary policy was tight in years like 2014 and 2015 even if the fed funds rate was very. Of course, it applies to the fed funds market and rates in other markets like were low, due ostensibly to policy of quantitative easing, and therefore policy was accommodative.

Perhaps a leaner TR might be to remove the guesses about the state of the economy and simply set the fed funds target equal to some long-run rate for short-term risk-free lending, like 2%. Suppose during the 1990s the U.S. Fed used this simplified TR and set the fed funds target to 2% and left it there; would the economy have been worse off?

Despite that the conventional TR has not produced a fed funds rate recommendation consistent with our current policy rate, the TR is nonetheless recommended by many economists and politicians. It is integral to the various bills in Congress in recent years asking for an audit of the Fed.

The TR is empirical, although it does have theoretical grounding in output gap, optimal level of inflation and long-run real rate of return facets. It is not Keynesian.

## II.11.G. IS/LM

IS/LM is perhaps the most popular advanced undergraduate M&M model and often the culminating model of introductory macro and the focal model of intermediate macro. IS/LM, which goes back to the 1930s, constituted a demonstration of the economy Keynes described in *The General Theory*.[149] IS/LM is two equations: (1) the investment/saving ("IS") curve for the goods market and the liquidity/money ("LM") curve for the money or asset market. They are plotted in a field of GDP and "The" interest rate and purport to show where real output and interest rates are in equilibrium.

Most instructors teach IS/LM as if it were rigorously derived from basic principles and also applicable to contemporary macro issues, including government policy in particular. Many instructors do not really belabor its theoretical building blocks though, and merely use IS/LM because it gives short-run Keynesian effects for both monetary and fiscal policy. This is especially true in M&M classes taught in tangential departments like International Studies and Public Policy. In International curricula they copiously use exchange rate changes to shift IS and LM curves as if the combination of an autonomous change in exchange rates and the IS/LM model elucidate the success or failure of modern national economies. Furthermore, IS/LM requires plenty of time, maybe four or five classes: "We will spend the next few classes deriving and developing the IS and LM curves then work with them in a variety of situations, including some open economy analysis."

Below are two typical IS/LM presentations. The first diagram demonstrates a monetary expansion in which we increase money supply, shown by the moving out of the LM curve. This yields lower interest rates and more GDP. The fact that inflation might also increase in this money expansion policy is not analyzable in the IS/LM framework since prices are held constant. The second diagram represents a contraction in the economy due to some cut in aggregate spending, typically a policy action of a cut in

---

[148] Named after University of Chicago professors Cynthia Wu and Fan Dora Xia.
[149] *The General Theory of Employment, Interest and Money*, by John Maynard Keynes, originally published in 1936.

government spending or increase in taxes, or an autonomous development in the economy such as a reduction in consumer spending. The drop is detrimental to the economy in the sense that output goes down.

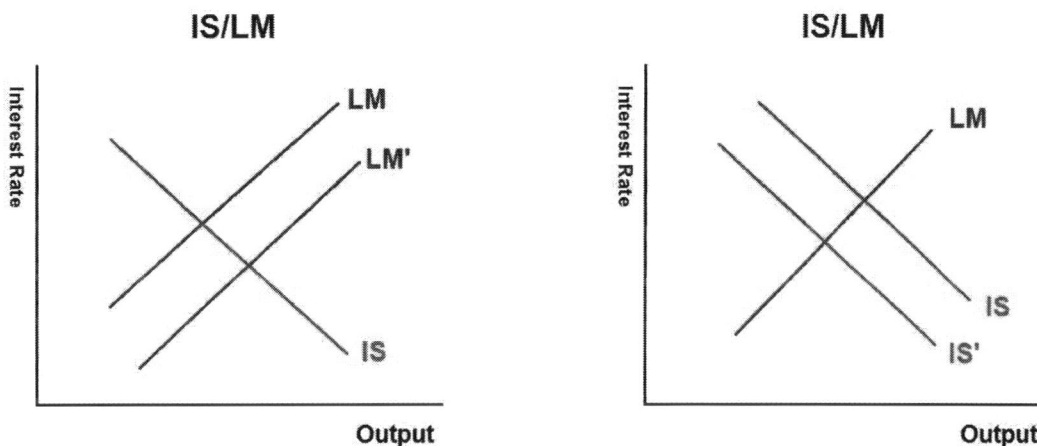

IS/LM

IS/LM

IS/LM is simplistic. It has varieties but most versions are fixed price, meaning there is no inflation. The model works off of a solitary interest rate. That limits what it can model about an economy with assets with differing rates of return and risk profiles. The LM curve posits the asset market as a tradeoff between bonds and money, but it is not clear what money is—except that it earns no interest. As for magnitudes, the model mostly depends on what is assumed about the slopes of the two curves. Therefore, IS/LM is mainly a theoretical story. In empirical models economists can construct IS and LM-like curves with data and estimated parameters, but in class it is just a theoretical exercise.

Some instructors and texts use simple IS/LM constructs. In some textbooks though, the IS/LM model is modified to reflect that interest rates are the Fed's tool and not money supplies. They assume the Fed can control real interest rates and utilize a curve that is horizontal at any level of real interest rate that the Fed chooses. Other variants of IS/LM have an explicit role for banks. Other IS/LM models peg a point on the x-axis to represent full employment. They draw a vertical line at that point that forms a boundary past which stimulation only yields higher interest rates, not more output. Even in these cases though instructors typically assume a short-run situation in which the economy does not hit the full employment boundary or the boundary does not hold. The IS/LM construct is often used in conjunction with AS/AD where policy changes in the IS/LM plane mark to combinations of price level and GDP. IS/LM is mainly theoretical. As a result of the shape of the curves, it is almost always presented as producing favorable Keynesian results.

## II.11.H. Enhanced "New Keynesian" Models With IS Curves

Many use IS/LM but then drop the LM curve and use the Taylor Rule to specify how monetary policy sets the interest rate. They then also add unemployment by invoking the Phillips Curve. There are various other New Keynesian models that are popular in classroom instructive and research. These are

Keynesian models in which monetary policy impacts the economy. They are better than simpler Keynesian models for certain demonstrations but they are not much better in prediction of the macroeconomy. For example, the New Keynesian models did not predict the crisis of 2008, and there are other shortcomings. They do not, generally, model the financial sector (which is ignored in simpler constructs). Economists continue to work on these, and the goal is to have a model that (1) is based on fundamental principles, (2) can predict swings in the economy and (3) shows Keynesian effects. New Keynesian models are mainly theoretical and produce Keynesian results.

## II.11.I. Okun's Law

Okun's Law is a numerical relationship between GDP growth and unemployment. Despite the term "law" economists always refer to it as a "rule-of-thumb." The equation for Okun's Law is as follows:

$$\frac{\Delta Y}{Y} = c\Delta u$$

$\Delta Y$ is the change in output and Y is output, so the left side is GDP growth. c is the coefficient relating output and unemployment, and $\Delta u$ is the change in the unemployment rate. A scatter plot would have change in GDP on the y-axis and change in unemployment on the x-axis. The points would cluster in a line with a negative slope. The c is measured to be about 2; so if Okun's Law held a 1% decrease in unemployment would cause GDP to go up about 2%. Alternatively, a 2% rise in GDP growth should get unemployment down by 1%.

One weakness is that the coefficient changes over time, sometimes without proponents highlighting the change. When teaching, I noticed that without explanation the coefficients in Okun's Law changed. It was 2.5 in the 4th edition (published 2001) of the popular macro textbook authored by Andrew Abel and Ben Bernanke but only 2 in the 5th edition (published 2005). Okun's holds up well except when we want it to work. Early in the initial apparent recovery from the 2008 crisis, GDP started to grow, but unemployment did not come down. For example, *The Economist* (May 1, 2010) notes, "This is at odds with what economists refer to as Okun's law." Okun's Law is mainly an empirical rule and is not Keynesian.

## II.11.J. Sacrifice Ratio

Naturally, if we can relate inflation and unemployment with the Phillips Curve and GDP and unemployment with Okun's, we can relate GDP and inflation. The Sacrifice Ratio tells how much GDP must change to get inflation down 1%. In terms of popularity in public discourse, it ranks behind the Phillips Curve or Okun's Law, but it does turn up in the press from time to time. Estimates of the Sacrifice Ratio vary. For the 1980s, perhaps a 1 to 2% drop in GDP would yield a 1% drop in inflation. That amount of drop in GDP would equate to about a 2 to 3% drop in employment (i.e., a 2 to 3% rise in unemployment). In other words, we had to sacrifice much economic output to get inflation down just a little, but we considered lowering inflation our main objective. The coefficient of sacrifice went up, according to economists. Circa 2006, perhaps we needed 4% more unemployment to get 1% less inflation.[150] However, like the other M&M models and relationships following 2008, the relationship is

---

[150] "Bernanke, Trichet have to Sacrifice More Jobs to Curb Inflation," *Bloomberg.com*, August 21, 2006 and *The Economist*, August 19, 2006, p. 64.

topsy-turvy. Since our inflation is low and we are not attempting to get it lower, we have dropped the discussion of sacrificing output to get lower inflation. The Sacrifice Ratio is empirical and is not Keynesian.

## II.11.K. Tobin's Q

From time to time, Tobin's Q (aka, Q-Theory or the Q Ratio) gets resurrected in the financial press. James Tobin, a Nobel prize-winning economist affiliated with Yale University, developed a theory in the 1960s for the replacement cost of capital. The model is a ratio of the market value of assets of all the companies in the economy divided by the cost of replacing all the capital of those companies. Tobin's Q was primarily an academic concept due to the difficulty of estimating the denominator, but in the mid- to late-1990s analysts (including notably stock market guru Andrew Smithers) rediscovered it as a counter-argument to the stock market bulls at the time. Smithers contended that Tobin's Q showed the market well overvalued, and his case received copious business press. Tobin's Q flew under the radar for years but gets occasional mention and is presented as one of alternative ways of measuring the stock market compared to move conventional measures notably the price-earnings ratio.

One obvious aspect of Tobin's Q concerns measuring capital, which is one of the most difficult tasks of economic research. Capital is one of the four traditional major input categories for production and GDP analysis (the others are labor, land and materials); but it is virtually impossible to define and aggregate society's capital. For example, what are the values of the software of an insurance firm, machines at a General Motors factory or the plant and equipment in the Chicago public schools? Tobin's Q is both theoretical and empirical and not Keynesian.

## II.11.L. Beveridge Curve

The Beveridge Curve (named after British economist William Beveridge [1879 to 1963]) plots unemployment on the x-axis against the rate of job vacancy (jobs available over labor force) on the y. High unemployment usually means low vacancy and vice versa, and the relationship is a curve (i.e., not linear) convex facing the origin. In the diagram below the curve closer to the origin represents the Beveridge Curve for the U.S. from 2000 to 2009.

## Beveridge Curve

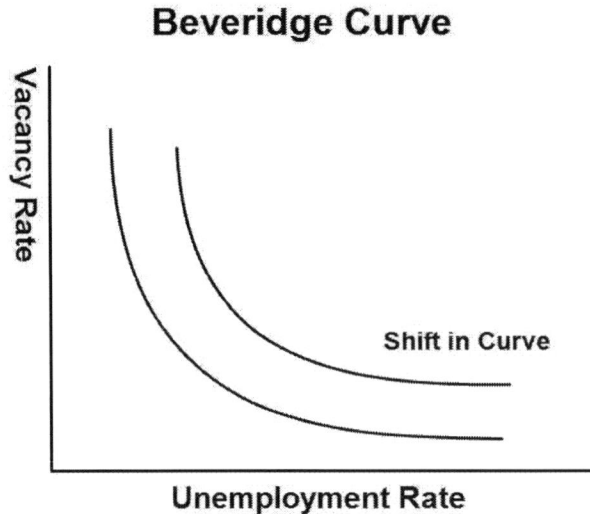

The curve blew out during 2010 to 2014. When the curve is further out it reflects a decrease in the efficiency of matching job openings with workers. This can be interpreted as an adverse structural development in labor markets. Another way of viewing it is that in the new curve as unemployment goes down, vacancy rates indeed go down, but they are at an altogether higher level—as though it is altogether harder to fill jobs. Like other models, the Beveridge Curve broke down when fundamental underlying changes happened to the economy. The Beveridge Curve is empirical and not designed to make a Keynesian or non-Keynesian story.

### II.11.M. Laffer Curve

The Laffer Curve, named after economist Arthur Laffer, is the consummate supply-side parable. It is a simple story that as a government raises tax rates (think primarily of taxes on earned income), tax revenues rise—but only up until a point. At some higher tax rate work effort is reduced so much that tax receipts decrease. It is better thought of the other way, which is the way proponents describe it: Cut taxes and greater work effort will actually yield higher tax revenues. In the diagram below, this effect is exhibited on the right half side of the curve. The Laffer Curve is a politically charged model and is often derided in the press and excluded from textbooks as if it relates a prejudicial, non-scientific story. It was popularized in the early 1980s as one of the building blocks of Reaganomics/supply-side economics. Some people consider the Laffer Curve as the only facet of supply-side economics but supply-side is a broader area including low regulation, free trade, low tax rates in general, property laws, etc.

## Laffer Curve

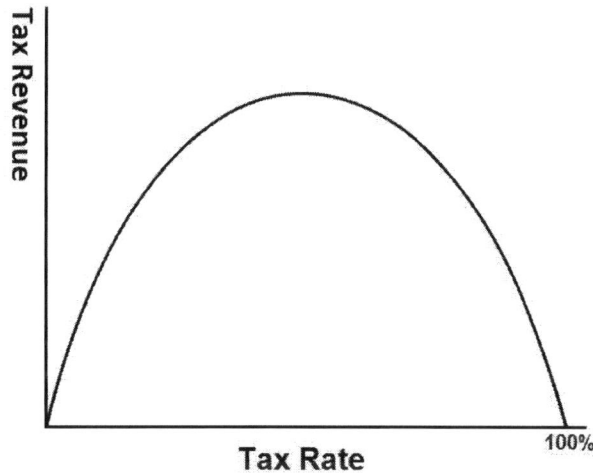

The Laffer Curve as theory is pretty simple; so its validation is an empirical question: What does the Curve look like? Which rate is the tipping point? Economists have estimated it empirically in certain ways, although since the curve reflects broad sources of taxes on income, estimates are rough. We do not have a specific definitive answer but the tax rate at which government maximizes revenue is likely greater than 50%. This is a negative fact for proponents of the curve who wish to reduce current overall tax rates which are something short of 50%.

In public debates, liberals highlight the above estimate and similar findings. They also claim (mostly with anecdotes) that tax increases do not seem to thwart the efforts of high income people. They invoke stories that great entrepreneurs relish enterprise and also rely on marginal incomes very little. Anti-Laffer proponents also make the case that if you tax income at a higher rate people actually have to work more to attain a certain standard of living. On the other hand, the Laffer Curve is compelling as a basic parable. It is difficult to discern the myriad of economic burdens that people face and how they impact their work, entrepreneurship and savings efforts. High-earning people view higher taxes as follows: (1) the initial higher taxes on income; (2) higher taxes on the income from the investing of their savings from income; and (3) higher estate taxes when passing accumulated wealth to the next generation. Viewed this way it does not does take a lot for a high-earner to conclude, "It just isn't worth it!" about a new work opportunity. The Laffer Curve is a supply-side story and is not Keynesian.

## II.11.N. Fed Model

The Fed Model compares the "earnings yield" on stocks and "interest yield" on bonds. The relative values of these two major asset classes is deemed to assess which is overvalued and which is undervalued. The earnings yield is the inverse of the aggregate stock market P/E ratio; and the interest yield is the yield on some government bond, formerly the 30-year bond and more recently the 10-year note. For example, if the P/E ratio is about 20 (as it was around 2001), the earnings yield is 5%. The long-term treasury rate was about 5% at this time, too. It should be noted that I use 2001 data to demonstrate the Fed Model because today's low yields render the Fed Model a less compelling story. Around 2001, the two big asset classes were about correctly valued relative to each other. If the earnings yield on stocks (preferably the forward earnings yield) is greater than the interest yield, then stocks are undervalued.

The two series supposedly tracked pretty closely and when one became higher than the other, they would converge. The underlying theory is that stocks and bonds are substitutes and that when one is "cheap" relative to the other, people buy it. Indeed, the two series did track together pretty well from about 1970 through 1998. Since the late 1990s, they have tended to diverge as much as converge. Come 2004, the model implied that the market was grossly undervalued.[151] Even in its great day, the Fed Model presented many false signals—like showing stocks undervalued just before the market crashed in the late 1990s—and overvalued in the early 1980s just as the market rallied. The model did not become prominent until about 1997, when Alan Greenspan was said to be using it. Soon after it received wide coverage among press and economists. Noted stock market expert Jeremy Siegel, of *Stocks for the Long Run* fame, mentioned the model in his 2002 third edition (although not in the 1994 first edition or 1998 second edition).

The Fed Model depends on the behavior of portfolio managers and the notion that they move money from one asset class to another depending on relative valuation. This investment strategy is valid at some times and in some markets but, over longer periods of time, fundamental valuation, valuing securities on discounted real earnings, should overrule relative valuation. The Fed Model is a comparison of a nominal (bond yield) and a real (earnings yield), so varying inflation should affect it. The model does not hold well when inflation is low, and it also ignores the basic character of equities: that earnings grow and equity commands a risk premium.

The relative valuation concept of the Fed Model can be applied more broadly. For example, if both stocks and bonds are highly valued then perhaps real assets like real estate and commodities are relatively undervalued. Of course, all assets can be overvalued and investors at any time can flee to cash rendering any such relative valuation strategy risky.

The Fed Model got picked up in discussions of market valuation during the initial low bond yield days commencing about 2010. As the years went by and bond yields remained low (around 2% for 10-year treasuries) and stocks continued to have higher earnings yields (around 5%), it implied a constant signal to buy stocks, even though stocks appeared highly valued.

The Fed Model is empirical. Its theory is not much more than that a change in the return to one class of asset makes people invest more or less in a substitute class. It is not Keynesian.

## II.11.O. Circular Flow

One or even a few circular flow diagrams of the economy in general and, in some cases, of the financial system are prominent in any macro textbook. They demonstrate the flowing of funds from different parties including households, corporation, intermediaries (like banks and brokerages) and the government in different markets including a factor market, labor market and goods market. The circular flow is often designed to show financial intermediation, i.e., how banks and other financial companies take funds from savers and allocate them to borrowers. Circular flow diagrams are some of the original attempts to model the macroeconomy and go back hundreds of years.

Each aggregate sector's inputs and outputs depend on other sectors: This exhibits dependency on the continuous exchange of resources and also shows the potential effects of feedback effects. The circular flow picture is simplistic and assumes no flow stoppage. Nor does it show leakages, although you can add an international, or other, sector and hypothesize flows going out or coming in. The diagram below is

---

[151] "Fed Model May Distort Stock View," *The Wall Street Journal*, by Justin Lahart, p. C2, March 22, 2004.

rudimentary. You can easily add modules, like for taxes going to government and transfers coming from government.

# Circular Flow

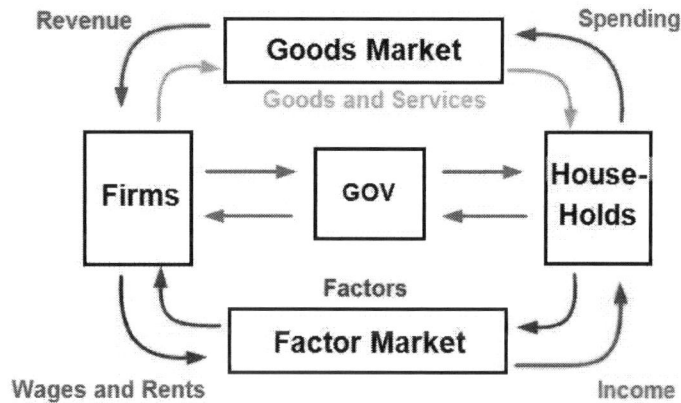

The models typically have ultimate savers and ultimate lenders. The savers are usually modeled as households, although in the real world households are both savers and borrowers—and probably net borrowers. In most circular flow models, companies are exclusively borrowers, yet in the real world today many companies are net savers. Governments are mainly borrowers. Circular flow models are primarily theoretical. They are not explicitly Keynesian, although the flow model highlights that flow must be maintained; and that is a very constituent idea of Keynesianism. There is not much emphasis on production, supply, or the original sources of flows.

## II.11.P. Macro Systems & Statistical Macro Forecasting

You might have taken an M&M course in which the instructor developed a system of equations that would have appeared highly scientific and precise, with each equation based on a M&M model—such as the AD curve, the IS curve, a Phillips Curve, the national income identity $Y = C + I + G$, some kind of monetary rule, a money supply equation, etc. The instructor would have described policy and economic events by tracing through the system. As we have shown, however, each underlying model in the system is itself an approximation; and any system is generally only as good as its weakest link. One component/equation in most macro systems is that money supply equals money demand. This is an extremely rough concept. You might have noticed that in commentaries, current M&M issues analysts (even leading experts like Paul Krugman) prefer "back-of-the-envelope" estimates to make points rather than estimates from elaborate systems. Elaborate systems do not add much insight.

Economists developed many large-scale macro models, some with hundreds of equations. The models grew out of Keynesian economics from the 1930s and 1940s and came to prominence in the 1960s. Some of well-known names in the history of macro modelling include the Wharton and Brookings Models. At one time, every large bank had a big macroeconomics department running its own model. The models were designed to show how any of a variety of quantities (like GDP, unemployment, the level of the stock market, etc.) would respond to trends in the economy (like productivity) or to shocks, including both policy changes (like a tax cut) and shocks from without (like adverse weather). The models were unsuccessful especially during the high inflation of the 1970s. Academics simultaneously found theoretical flaws in these Keynesian-based macro systems. Economists attempted to incorporate ideas from Keynesian critiques mainly focused on incorporating sophisticated expectations of private parties (aka rational expectations) but they were never able to fix the big systems. Macro modeling declined in prevalence and authority in the 1980s, although some are still maintained today. The Fed has a large-scale macro model called FRB/US. Proponents of macro modeling might contend that the devices are useful and cite supposedly scientific analyses of the models demonstrating success. Another problem today is that the macro models must model policy through wealth effects rather than through direct investment effects. The history of these large-scale macro models is extensive and colorful with many great names and grand concepts, including the following: the Cowles Commission, structural Keynesianism, macroeconometrician, the Rational Expectations revolution, New Classicalism, New Keynesianism, ad hoc formulations, etc.

Vector autoregressions ("VARs") are econometric tests of causality used frequently to analyze M&M issues. They purport to show that monetary policy changes lead to changes in the economy. Some economists, like Ben Bernanke, apparently view VARs seriously or at least have researched them extensively. They are pure time series analysis: The equations relate variables without invoking theoretical cause and effect assumptions. Of course, the models can be augmented with certain structural or theoretical facets. You see occasional references to VARs in the financial press as if they represent a vein of M&M that is a harder science, but this kind of time series analysis is easy to question on direction of cause and effect, magnitude and timing. VARs are too complicated to describe here: They model variables like GDP growth, money supply changes, interest rates, inflation rates, various real economy indicators (i.e., industrial production) by regressing them on themselves and other variables—and by lagging a certain number of time periods. VARs sometimes show little or no causation or varying causation—like stimulative monetary policy resulting in much more economic output, or virtually none. VARs do not forecast well and suffer from data problems, especially with data revisions.

The U.S. Fed is perhaps the biggest user of a large-scale macro system. Fed economists offer this succinct description of the FRB/US model[152]:

> The FRB/US model is a large-scale model of the U.S. economy featuring optimizing behavior by households and firms as well as detailed descriptions of monetary policy and the fiscal sector. The model's large number of endogenous variables permits the study of the effects of a broad range of macroeconomic policies and exogenous shocks on real GDP and its major spending components; the unemployment rate and other key labor market indicators; several measures of inflation and relative prices; the main categories of national income; a detailed treatment of the government's account; and various interest rates, asset prices, and components of wealth. FRB/US has a neoclassical core that combines a production function with endogenous and exogenous supplies of production factors and key aspects of household preferences such as impatience. To account for cyclical fluctuations, the model features rigidities that apply to many decisions made by households and firms; these rigidities enable the model to generate gradual responses of macroeconomic variables to a wide range of exogenous shocks that are consistent with the economic data.

As you can see, this contains virtually every M&M facets economists could ever reasonably model. The construct is still mainly a traditional system of macro equations but also includes elements of microeconomics, like the production function and the preferences of households. Advocates of large systems will admit the shortcomings of such sprawling models, but their defense is that the model can

---

[152] "The FRB/US Model: A Tool for Macroeconomic Policy Analysis," April 2014, Fed Notes, www.federalreserve.gov, by Flint Brayton, Thomas Laubach and David Reifschneider.

provide insight in some cases. To put it more plainly, the macro systems users know everything everybody else knows about the economy, and they also can run their large-scale models for whatever insights the models might add.

This section describes a wide variety of models. They are generally primarily empirical with sub-components based on other macro models, each of which has various assumptions. Depending on how you set up the equations and select estimated parameters, they can be Keynesian or non-Keynesian. In general, however, macro models assume Keynesian feedback: An injection of spending through policy will have multiplied effects.

## II.11.Q. Growth Theory

You might have noticed that all of our macro constructs, no matter how many or esoteric the symbols in their equations, mark to GDP, or better stated, its future growth. Each individual M&M concept is largely a restatement of GDP, and so individually and collectively they are dependent on GDP growth rate estimates. Here are some examples: The Taylor Rule equation is explicitly half dependent on GDP growth, and the other half is indirectly dependent. MV=PQ simply says that if M is up then prices go up, unless your GDP goes up. NAIRU and the Output Gap are just GDP estimates. Moving AD and AS is all about GDP. The Keynesian multiplier only works if there is a GDP gap and GDP is poised to go up. Even the Fed's increasing of its balance sheet or money multiplier only really work if there is GDP growth underlying the economy.

Then what does GDP depend upon? The answer is a multitude of factors, obviously. Economists might term these factors fundamental or structural factors. I prefer to refer to them as underlying microeconomics and would list them to include preferences, technology, risk, marginal products, innovation, entrepreneurship, rules, law, regulation, respect for contracts, trust, certainty, education, capital, factor mobility, tax rates, etc. Economics' single best model for these factors is growth theory. Growth theory, which we mentioned briefly earlier, is a long-run macro that posits an aggregate production function to estimate the material prosperity of our economy. It is GDP as a function of the basic inputs of the economy, typically these four: GDP = F (land, labor, capital and entrepreneurship).

Looking at the four individually, economists often contend that land is not important. Some economic historians even contend that great natural resources can be a curse to overall economic development. The usual example is an oil rich nation living off exports of that single resource and failing to develop other industries. The oil wealth typically causes the value of the nation's currency to rise, making its other factors even harder to employ competitively. This is often called the Dutch Disease after the discovery of great natural gas resources in The Netherlands around 1960, which lead to export of gas, rise of the Dutch currency and a decline in Dutch manufacturing. This belief of minimizing land as an important factor is somewhat defunct in the modern world. We now tend to think of natural resource wealth as very important in economic growth once again. Ironically, even the United States has touted its future prospects due to recent developments in energy production while earlier we boasted our capital, labor and entrepreneurship advantages.

To an average person capital might seem like the key factor of economic growth. In the basic growth theory model, capital is usually physical (like machines and plant) and not human. The reality is that physical capital can be retooled relatively quickly. Therefore, many growth theory economists have come to emphasize the importance of labor and entrepreneurship. America was successful because it had those two items. Perhaps today, we can claim to be competitive but not dominant in labor and entrepreneurship. Competitors like the Chinese are equally smart, work as hard, and are more willing to take greater losses. This is a triple whammy that we may not be able to beat. In popular discussion we often retreat to entrepreneurship as the great factor input that we singularly excel in, yet that is dubious at best. It is a difficult empirical question to answer because it is difficult to quantity entrepreneurship.

What economists call growth theory goes back to the work of Robert Solow during the 1950s. He set up a model with an economy-wide production function with two inputs (labor and capital) and squeezed some basic economic parables out of it. Either a country could add to these factor inputs or enhance their efficient use by productivity increases. A nation should seek total factor productivity. Growth theory lay dormant for a while in the 1960s and 1970s, when the profession focused on the short-run Keynesian world of Y=C+I+G, and experienced a rebirth during the 1980s. The new insights were complicated: In the original Solow model growth was exogenous, i.e., it came from without. The new growth theory made growth endogenous, meaning it could be enhanced by a nation's policies like low taxes, less regulation and protecting property rights. In a well-circulated 1992 paper, economist Alwyn Young used growth theory to compare two similar city-states: Hong Kong and Singapore. He found that Hong Kong performed better because it grew by higher productivity, while Singapore grew by adding factor inputs. Another major focus concerned how long it would take for economic convergence among nations. One of the findings was that convergence would take a long time. For example, India would be poorer than the U.S. for a considerable period of time.

We know some things about the growth of nations' economies. Piling up capital yields more output, but at a diminishing rate of increase and great ongoing replacement cost. Nations like South Korea experienced the problem of maintaining a gigantic capital stock.[153] We also know that intangibles, like entrepreneurship, matter. We do not know much about how to cultivate a spirit of entrepreneurship. We believe that standards of living and growth rates of economies converge, but we do not know how quickly. It might be that convergence among nations, or among certain ones like the U.S. and China, is happening faster than growth theory models imply. The factors in growth theory are highly aggregated and we cannot easily pick apart the effects of specific factors on the economy. For example, the economic effects of parent laws, cigarette smoking, standardized testing, racism, etc. are virtually impossible to model. Growth theory is theoretical and empirical. In classroom instruction we discuss the theory. Some instruction might comment on empirical findings but with the caveats that measurement of the factors is rough. Growth theory is not Keynesian.

## II.11.R. Production Possibilities Frontier

The Production Possibilities Frontier ("PPF") demonstrates the greatest amount of total output for an economy (or it could be for a household/person), given certain existing factor inputs. It is not a macro model, although it is usually done for a nation and thus can demonstrate macro stories. It is a micro model demonstrating the most fundamental reality of economies, tradeoff, i.e., if you want more of one good you must sacrifice some of another. The PPF is (usually) plotted in two-space with different outputs or products on each axis. The frontier shows combinations of the two goods. To get more of one good, you have to sacrifice some of the other. The curve is bowed out (or concave to the origin) because the tradeoff varies due to diminishing returns as you go from producing one good to another. If you are producing mostly one good and then transfer some resources to producing the other, you will get a relatively large amount of the other good; but if you keep transferring production each movement will yield less and less of the second good.

---

[153] An analogy to a household would be a second full-size refrigerator in the basement. It is useful for storing certain food and enables you to hold big parties efficiently but it is costly to maintain and replace when broken.

The PPF can be assumed to move out reflecting economic growth, or productivity. Of course, that is the goal of society, but the PPF typically is not presented to demonstrate growth (moving the PPF out); rather, it indicates scarcity and that our economic existence is only tradeoffs (moving along the PPF).

## Production Possibilities Frontier

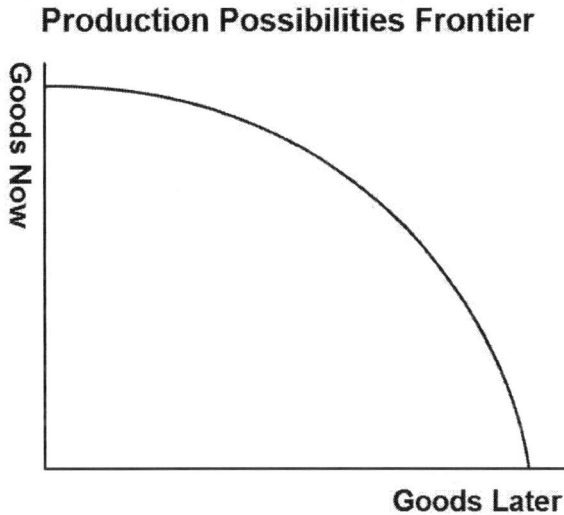

The PPF is great to demonstrate sacrifice made by society and what the instructor chooses as the goods on the axes can make a point. Some teachers use guns or butter, which supposedly Adolph Hitler couched his nation's choices as. For a contemporary analysis involving generational economics, you could label one axis "Goods Now" and the other axis "Goods Later," which tells us that to have more now we will have less later. The PPF is theoretical and not Keynesian.

## II.11.S. Real Business Cycles

Real Business Cycles ("RBC") is another major model/framework of M&M used in some classes and discussion. We mentioned RBC before. RBC explains economic fluctuations as culminations of various and constant structural changes, both big and small, to the economy. RBC implies minimal effects of policy and is usually presented with simulations of shocks to the economy and how they can form a cyclical pattern of overall activity like GDP, or employment. The structural factors include shocks like weather, climate, geopolitical forces, changes in technology and changed in preferences, In the 1990s for example, the U.S. economy benefited from cheap oil, favorable immigration (copious cheap labor), the abrupt end of the Cold War, a multitude of favorable technological developments (like computers and cell phones), a multitude of efficient business practices (like improved inventory management and securitization), etc. The decade had high GDP growth and relative stability, which became known as the Great Moderation. A believer in RBC would attribute the strong economy to the real factors while a naysayer would cite skillful monetary policy.

Liberals mock RBC. They point out obvious effects on the economy of monetary policy and note that business cycles seem to occur with a regularity and intensity beyond what any real shocks would imply. A favorite jocular RBC counter case is that according to RBC the 25% unemployment during the Depression must have been caused by a mass tendency of people to take vacation. RBC is not Keynesian. In fact, it is the main rejoinder to Keynesian ideas of stoking aggregate demand. In most presentations, RBC is more theoretical than empirical, although various empirical RBC models can be done.

## II.11.T. Other Models & Rethinkings

You might allege that I omitted more sophisticated M&M models, maybe something you encountered in grad school or read about in *The Economist*. Likely candidates would include Dynamic Stochastic General Equilibrium (DSGE) models, models of bubbles and self-fulfilling prophesies, and overlapping generations models. Or you might say that I have neglected alternative macro models, including ideas proposed by other, sometimes more current, schools of thought.

DSGE models are relatively new (going back to the 1980s) and attempt M&M with microeconomic foundations. They include micro concepts like a utility function, budget constraints, technology changes, etc. Copious new research is being done with DSGE models, including much by Fed economists; and proponents will say DSGE is in its incipient stage and might not possess useful proscriptions now but in the future DSGE will be useful. DSGE models may never be capable of revealing much about the real economic world, though. For example, DSGE uses a representative character, so you cannot really model financial intermediation. DSGE models can be cooked up Keynesian by assuming multiple price rigidities or Classical by focusing on budget constraints. In the aftermath of the economic crisis of 2008, our leaders searched for explanations—and better models—as to why our existing macro models had not anticipated the economic shakeout. In 2011 Congress called leading academics, including Nobel prize winning economist Robert Solow, to explain DSGE.[154] Solow and most of the others highly doubted DSGE models. These great academics dismissed DSGE and focused on denouncing the folly of macroeconomists and their failure to look at the "real world." Some proposed solutions, but they were suggestions or statements of the obvious and not any other tractable M&M model.

Bubbles are timely in economic research, and economists (including many Fed economists) are working on modeling and understanding bubbles. We do not have useful models, just a belief that markets can get out-of-equilibrium—as the stock market did in the late 1990s or the housing market did in the 2000s. We can set some levels of how far a series must be from its average to be a bubble, but it is easy to deny any bubble you preside over as Alan Greenspan, Ben Bernanke and now Janet Yellen do. For example, in congressional testimony on July 16, 2014 Janet Yellen concluded that the stock market was not a bubble.

Specifying or setting the level for what constitutes a bubble is arbitrary. Any of the following markets in recent years could be viewed as far enough out-of-equilibrium to be bubbles: U.S. treasury market, Japanese government finances, Chinese property, various real estate markets in the U.S., the U.S. stock market, technology stocks, etc. Even if you can identify bubbles it is difficult to take policy action to mitigate them. For example, some countries have deemed their housing markets too frothy and have tried to regulate housing finance and raise rates, but the markets have not responded. It is also for investors to bet against bubbles. It is easy to find a market seemingly out-of-equilibrium but the timing of its return to norms is impossible. For a long time, an investment strategy very popular with hedge funds is shorting Japanese government debt due to the country's unsustainable debt ratio. So far, however, that crash has not happened. I tease my students on bubbles: "What's the next big bubble to burst? Could it be college tuition? Is $50,000 a year for this education way off trend?"

When I was a graduate student in the mid-1980s, the Overlapping Generations ("OG") model was a popular M&M one with microeconomic foundations. Young Turks in the field (economists, then in their 30s and 40s who followed the great Keynesian generation of economists like James Tobin, Franco Modigliani, Lawrence Klein, etc.) were hoping to develop OG into an insightful macro model. OG was a

---

[154] The testimony was given on July 20, 2011. The other scholars were Scott Page, V.V. Chari, Sidney Winter, and David Colander. Chari made some favorable assessment of DSGE.

micro construct assuming agents who lived finite lives, which overlapped with other agents' lives. As simple as that sounds, that finite life and overlap created the need to save and to exchange. Then, we added money into the model to try to get M&M results. OG seems to have gone nowhere. It had a little fanfare in the economics' profession a few years ago because of its 50th anniversary but dates back to a 1958 paper by Paul Samuelson that every grad student reads.

When you hear agitation for new M&M ideas today it usually involves left-wing criticism of capitalism and speculation that controlling big business will make the masses better off. They habitually relate historical examples of market excesses and denounce the way mainstream economics has supposedly abetted instability, but they come up short on new models. Another source of constant criticism of mainstream M&M is outsiders, often physicists or other scientists, who blithely contend that economists' assumptions are simplistic and tyrannical. They aver that obvious superior assumptions, tools and methods could easily build better economic models and believe that intransigence among economists precludes their use. These critiques are as useless as they are commonplace. Other new attempts to model M&M that you might encounter in the media or at conferences are primarily schools of thought who are not able to "put a model on the board," as we say:

- Post-Keynesian economics is a rejection of many of the ideas of conventional Keynesian economics and an attempt to get closer to true and extreme Keynesian principles. For example, Post-Keynesian economics views the economy as being prone to lack aggregate demand not only in the short run but also in the long run. Post-Keynesian economics is associated with certain economists and they themselves espouse varying ideas.
- Austrian economics contends that markets work well if left alone and that policy distorts markets.
- Marxist economics are various historical and political musings.
- Applications from physical sciences and mathematics to economic research and contemporary problems are broached frequently in debates and in the press but are usually nothing more than incessant, simplistic characterizations that mainstream economists are ignorant of the real world with some pronouncement that other sciences have applicable tools.
- Complexity and chaos theories focus on tendencies of complex systems like the macroeconomy to tend away from equilibrium, sometimes abruptly and extremely. Complexity theories have been applied to areas like meteorology and movements of bodies of water in the past and are being applied to economic and financial markets more and more. They draw on mathematics, statistics, physics and sundry social sciences and are difficult to describe in comparison to standard M&M models. Complexity largely represents that little changes can result in large repercussions.
- Biological models attempt to model social systems and markets based on behavior of swarming insects (like bees, ants, or locusts) or to model based on various organisms and human bodies.
- Manifestos/treatises by sundry economists and other intellectuals purport to explain the unexplainable macroeconomy and financial system. Perhaps the most notable of these is Hyman Minsky (1919 to 1996), an American economist and author of *Stabilizing an Unstable Economy* (1986). Early in the aftermath of the financial crisis of 2008, Minsky and his theories of uncontrollable boom and bust got copious press. Minsky's models were difficult to present except as general descriptions of market excess and the press coverage dropped.
- Another foray is "Cross-Disciplinary." Scientists get stuck in silos, supposedly, and the pooling of ideas and models from different fields would be the innovation that would find a new economics model. This approach, however, is also picked-through. Every leading university has cross-disciplinary departments. Dedicated research institutes, like the famous Santa Fe Institute (founded 1984), have been around for decades.

- Behavioral economics is a relatively new field that has become popular in academia and in the press. (We discuss it at length later.) It is more of a microeconomic discipline trying to improve economic decision-making by households and businesses but it gets broached as a tool helpful to address macroeconomic problems like savings, funding education and investment returns.

The same applies to attempts by big-shots to reject orthodox economics and re-explain the economic system. They endeavor to start from scratch, without the intellectual baggage of mainstream economics. For example, Reflexivity (the philosophy of investor George Soros) denies equilibrium and focuses on feedback of prices on themselves. Reflexivity, however, is inscrutable. What is comical is the frequency that such new economics projects get proposed. They are funded with money from some rich person like George Soros or a foundation. The new school or institute will be well-funded and charged with figuring it all out. The end product will be a recitation of the flaws of economics and of capitalism. Yet, for all the flaws and denouncing of capitalism, nobody would prefer to live in North Korea over South Korea. Another example of a big investor turned economic philosopher is Ray Dalio, the founder of Bridgewater Associates, one of the biggest and most successful hedge funds. His promulgates a theory of a credit-driven economy very prone to cycles of varying lengths. Dalio's models are unconvincing and patronizing, however—as if economists had not already recognized the same principles Dalio describes. There are many other thinkers who try to rewrite economics from some other or new perspective. George Gilder, for example, has described technology and its changes as the key determinant of the fortunes of nations, but the development of technology does not constitute a general science of macroeconomic behavior.

One common theme of most of the above schools is denouncement of a supposed de facto orthodoxy in the field of economics. Supposedly better ideas are prohibited from getting a fair hearing. For example, leading Post-Keynesian economist Paul Davidson has always maintained that research outside mainstream economics gets excluded from serious journals. In reality, the field is replete with examination. There are copious think tanks, conferences, experts, counter-journals, financial supports, blogs, etc. Indeed, "rethinking economics" may be one of the most popular academic pursuits.[155] My condemnation of conventional M&M is different. I do not believe we can find a new theory. We know the essential nature of our macroeconomy. It has endemic problems that we can neither predict nor manage with monetary or fiscal policy. We must tolerate volatility and adverse economic outcomes. We continue M&M policies but they represent redistributions of the economy's output and bad budgeting by governments. We simply prefer to pretend that new policies will bring new solutions.

---

[155] Almost every large university has some formal research group or at least some cluster of faculty devoted to new ideas in economics. Some attempt theories but since that is a picked-through area they often emphasize economics teaching or social advocacy. The small, liberal arts school I work at, Tufts University, houses a branch of an international network called Rethinking Economics. It was founded in 1999.

## II.12. Links From M&M to Markets

Even if M&M lacks reliable and deterministic models, a wide variety of people and institutions in our society crave macro information, primarily to create plausible stories of cause and effect for their undertakings. They call on either entire models or just snippets from M&M. For example, the myriad of professionals managing those trillions of dollars of assets need justifications for asset allocation decisions, so they utilize M&M models like the Phillips Curve, exchange rate adjustments, the yield curve, etc. The following pages discuss the most common ways markets, economists and the financial press interpret and track macroeconomic effects, which I call "Links."

The economic impetus for these Links is primarily announcements or the anticipation of announcements of economic indicators. Also, statements or actions by the central bank and its spokespersons affect markets greatly. Indeed, since about 2008 the central bank has become the predominant factor in financial market action and reaction. Before 2008 the central bank was important, of course, but since 2008 the gravitas and frequency has been much greater. Before 2008 most of the commentary on central bank maneuvers hovered around the eight annual FOMC meetings. Finally, real events including economic developments and sundry items like weather, major social or political events and even remarks by important people can instigate a Link.

There are four introductory, round-up comments: First, these Links are not, strictly speaking, M&M models; nor are they the same as the channels of monetary policy transmission. Instead, Links are related in general ways but are quite different in lines of cause and effect—and in timing. Also, Links are largely expectations-driven, meaning that the market actions happen in anticipation of real economic effects, which themselves may play out over months or years (or may not even play out at all). Monetary transmission, as in textbooks, describes how changing interest rates by policy affects the real economy through chains of effects, including the bank lending channel, asset price channel, investment channel, portfolio balance channel, foreign exchange channel, etc. Unlike Links, these channels, at least in textbooks, are supposed to play out over months or years and do not depend on expectations.

Second, these Links often demonstrate a "bad news is good news" aspect. That can be explained with expectations, which makes true effects in M&M hard to ascertain. In other words, bad news should be bad news. For example, positive economic news should mean our incomes and assets are worth more, but markets often view positive economic news as giving the Fed reason to raise rates. This causes the bond market, and maybe the stock market, to sell off. There is a more current example that was really prominent throughout the third stage of QE during 2012 and 2013: Chronic bad news on the economy (supposedly) helped raise the stock market because market people believed that the bad news would increase the likelihood the Fed would continue QE. This "bad news is good news" mentality is not irrational on the part of the private parties because their objectives depend on planning ahead.

Third, relating and explaining stock market movements with economic news and theories as seen in these Links (e.g., "The stock market was up this morning due to…") must surely be one of the most ridiculous and futile facets of modern markets. Journalists and other commentators crave and remark on causes and effects that are deeply tenuous and easily turned on their heads. Every stock market movement, no matter how small, will receive commentary with some theory or explanation. There will never be a day with a headline like, "Market up today; no particular reason can be attributed."

Fourth, Links have come and gone in popularity over the years. The Fed Link predominates today but others have been relegated to marginal roles. The days when a market guru could comment and start a sell-off in markets are long gone. Even a big geopolitical event now has minor effect. Only the all-powerful Fed can make markets move.

## II.12.A. Phillips Curve Link

The most prominent historical Link is a product of the Phillips Curve. Although scorned by many analysts—including, notably, the editorial staff of *The Wall Street Journal* who have railed against it for decades, the Link has maintained popularity and influence. I list this Phillips Curve Link first even though it is secondary in potency to the Fed Link(s) (listed second below) simply because it came first. When the Fed was not making such frequent pronouncements as it does now, our markets looked to changing labor market conditions to make estimations about what inflation would be and then to position portfolios and engage in consumption and investment decisions.

Typically, through the Phillips Curve Link stock and bond markets would react adversely when employment-related data (like the unemployment rate, employment cost index, jobs counts, etc.) came out and reflected a strong economy. For example, if the unemployment rate came out unexpectedly *low* markets would go down. This seems counterintuitive since markets should respond positively to improvement in the economy. After all, if unemployment is low then more people are working and have more money to spend. That means higher profits for companies, which means companies would be better able to pay the bond interest and would have higher earnings and dividends—and thus higher stock prices.

A recap of the Phillips Curve Link historically looks like this: Labor markets (e.g., tight with unemployment down, wages up, initial claims for unemployment down, etc.) imply a state of the economy (growing, in our examples). This implies a level of inflation (rising primarily due to rising wages) and potential action by the Federal Reserve to raise target interest rates. This suggests actions by markets to, for example, sell bonds. Markets will sell bonds because their prices will go down with higher rates. The market response for stocks, however, can go either way. Some investors will buy stocks because they are now a better asset than bonds, or they will sell stocks because corporate earnings will be lower in a higher interest rate regime.

Relationships among inflation, interest rates and bond prices almost explain this Link. However, the final building block is the inverse relationship between unemployment and inflation: the Phillips Curve. Other evidence of a strong economy can also imply higher inflation. High(er) industrial production, consumer confidence and retail sales are certain indicators market participants watched. For a while during primarily the 1990s, the U.S. Department of Labor's Employment Cost Index (a measure of changes in employee compensation, including both wages and benefits) was watched very closely as the best precursor to labor market conditions and therefore inflation. With all of these Links, the key was expectations. Only unexpected economic developments will have a big effect. If the unemployment rate comes out lower than before markets may not move if that lower rate was anticipated.

## II.12.B.a. Fed Link(s): Pre-2008–Inflation & Interest Rate Focus

Market reactions to either actual Fed policies or Fed intentions are Fed Links. Since the heightened Fed policy of 2008 ff the most minor Fed murmurs, and even merely experts' interpretations of Fed developments, have been important. Before 2008, the perception of the Fed's resolve to control inflation was the dominant concept. Since 2008 the containing of inflation as a sole goal has diminished, and the Fed's willingness and resolve to continue stimulating the economy is now the predominant focal concept.

For a long time and up until about 2008, on the decision day of Fed FOMC meetings (which typically occurred eight times annually), financial markets would start the day with some expectation of what the Fed would do with the fed funds target rate. The stock market would usually be calm during the morning before the meeting announcement. However, when the policy decision was announced a little after 2 PM, the market would typically rally then pull back, almost regardless of what happened—provided that the policy was not outside what was expected. Perhaps the overriding market philosophy was that the Fed indeed knew more about the economy than everyone else and would prudently maintain its long-run determination to control inflation. Given this, markets could count on another month or two of smooth sailing. For most portfolio managers this meant moderate buying into the market.

This simple story played out for about for about 20 years. Since 2008 it is different though because the Fed no longer enacts incremental changes in the fed funds target rate. With the Fed doing unconventional policy involving increasingly sprawling purchase amounts and more concerted communication, the market watch on FOMC meeting days is somewhat muted. Greater attention is now paid to sundry Fed comments on non-FOMC days. Markets still seem to trust in the wisdom and power of the Fed, but scrutiny is heightened.

Occasionally, when something relatively unexpected emanates from the Fed, the simple story becomes a dramatic and large-scale news event. For example, on May 21, 2013 Ben Bernanke broached the intention that the Fed might begin gradually reducing its monthly buying of bonds going on under QE3. This became known as the "taper." It would significantly impact markets that month and for the following months (bonds sold off and yields went up). Markets were moving on expected policy outcomes (a real taper) even though that actual action would be months away. Fed Links are important. Commentary on how the Fed's actions, hints of actions, justifications for actions, lack of actions, etc. is so voluminous that it may well constitute the single greatest topic of the financial press in the last couple of decades.

## II.12.B.b. Fed Link(s): Post-2008–Asset Price & Wealth Effects Focus

Unconventional and protracted low-rate Fed policies have made changing asset values and their reverberations throughout the financial system the new Fed Link. The Fed either buys bonds (typically mortgage-backed securities or U.S. debt), announces the intention of buying bonds—or, at least, is rumored to commence buying bonds. Then the prices of the targeted bonds rise and their yields decline. Private parties then strive to find relatively high-yielding bonds so they buy riskier bonds, including high-yield bonds and other risky assets such as stocks. That raises the prices of stocks subsequently making a wide swath of people feel wealthier, so they increase consumption causing GDP to increase.

For one example of this Link, consider Ben Bernanke in addressing Congress on May 21, 2013. He mentioned a potential reducing of the level of bond purchasing engaged in under QE3. The briefing was not an action taken by the Fed, nor was it even a promise of action. It also did not represent a major reversal of policy, just a gradual change. Despite these facts, this Fed murmur got picked up by markets, and bond markets crashed.

## II.12.C. International Link

One textbook story is the relationship of international trade balances and currency values (or exchange rates), which we could call the International Link. One odd reality is that this most basic theoretical idea simply never seems to hold, or at least not in a reasonable time frame. This theory is that a nation's trade deficit,[156] or changes in the trade deficit, determines the exchange rate of that nation's currency. An

---

[156] The same applies to a nation's surplus, but since the U.S. runs a chronic deficit we usually talk in terms of deficits and currency dropping in value. The trade deficit is also called the trade balance, but it is different from the balance of payments. A more thorough definition of trade concepts follows.

increase in a nation's trade deficit means that the nation's currency should decrease in value since the growing trade deficit means the nation has bought more from abroad and its currency is in oversupply abroad. However, the real world confounds.

The U.S. ran large deficits for long periods, but its currency remained strong. Data on trade balance are reported monthly. In theory, an announcement of a larger than expected trade deficit should lower a nation's currency but that outcome is neither certain nor of any magnitude. This chain of events is chronically overpowered by bigger forces (such as demands for currency for investing in a nation's bonds and/or stocks) or simply the relative economic growths of countries. If a country runs constant trade deficits in the long run, on the other hand, its currency should go down. The other basic international link is simply that one country's GDP growth affects other countries'. For many years including the years following 2008, the buzz was that only the U.S. economy was growing. Other nation/states including Eurozone and Japan were either in or close to recession or, in the case of emerging markets like China and India, not growing as much. Their poor growth was to our economic detriment. Such interconnectedness provides ever-ready explanations for your nation's fortunes. While each trading nation affects others and unexpected changes in growth rates can have real effects, there is something trivial about invoking and delineating economic fortunes by national boundaries.

## II.12.D. Gold Link

When there are signs of (higher) inflation, or perhaps a major calamity, you may expect the price of gold to shoot up. This is known as the Gold Link. Historically, gold is an inflation hedge. Gold prices rose dramatically during the high inflation times of the 1970s and early 1980s,. When the high inflation finally seemed to be well under control perhaps around the late 1980s, gold dropped in price and lost its role as an important component in portfolios. At this time, individual investors might have continued to make gold a part of their investment strategies, yet it was shunned and even derided by professionals. Gold as an investment hit its low point during the 1990s when it plummeted in price, and since it also provided no yield it appeared a doubly-foolish investment. People made a fortune shorting gold at that time, but it has come back in price in the 2000s. Gold is also linked to calamity historically: People buy gold when disaster strikes. This effect though is attenuated today. People might cite the long running increase in the price of gold following September 11, 2001 as an example of this facet of gold, but movements in gold following dramatic news of anything short of a September 11 magnitude event are minimal and have been ignored both in the press and by investors. If you study any of the top dozen calamities of late you will see gold prices merely blip. Before about 1990 any terrorist attack would cause gold to move up significantly. Today gold markets do not react to anything that is not out of the ordinary.

Historically, gold seems to move in the opposite direction of the U.S. dollar; but, like other relationships, the correlation breaks down with sufficient frequency. What will become of the value of gold in these times of great expansionary monetary policy? The price of gold is determined by a relatively discrete and quantifiable set of factors of demand (industrial use, jewelry especially in China and India, and demand by speculators and central banks) and of supply (primarily mining capacity and exploration and old gold scrap volumes). Copious data for all of these factors are available; however, the path of gold prices will still come down to guesses about people's attitudes on inflation, which depend largely on their guesses about the future of M&M. We have shown this is very uncertain. For example, if merely a few hedge funds raised their bets on a rising price of gold, its price could surge significantly. A simple whiff of inflation might cause a quick scurrying to gold. What if a major gold-holding nation decided to sell abruptly (nations are loosely in agreement not to sell their gold), and a couple more followed suit? This could cause a gold price crash. If inflation stays low, which is possible if the economy remains weak; then regardless of how much the money supply is increasing, gold could go down in price.

## II.12.E. Force Majeure Link

Geopolitical events and natural disasters can move markets but, like gold price dynamics, it takes an extraordinarily momentous event to move markets nowadays. The mechanism is basic: A bad event implies economic and financial losses, perhaps lower GDP growth and lower profits for companies. Therefore, markets should go down. September 11, 2001 is the most obvious recent example. Otherwise, you would be hard-pressed to discern major effects from the other big events in the world arena during the 2000s.

For example, during 2006 terrorist attacks occurred in England and market movements were minimal. In the 1980s and 1990s similar attacks would likely have caused heftier market movements. The Kobe earthquake of 1995 moved markets more than the Japanese tsunami and tidal wave in 2011 did. Also, there is a one-sidedness to this Link since a good shock will hardly have enough heft. For example, in 2006 a large oil find in the Gulf of Mexico was touted in the press, but related market movements were minimal. In fact, I cannot think of a sudden and consequential geopolitical or natural shock that really made markets move significantly. A series of adverse geopolitical events in 2014 (including conflicts in Ukraine, Israel, Syria and Iraq) seemed to have little impact on markets, another confirming case of the lack of effect of such events. Of course, the Force Majeure Link might be the true tail risk story and when a real off event occurs—perhaps a pandemic, nuclear accident, war or asteroid—it will take us by surprise and markets will suffer greater than any Fed Link or Phillips Curve Link ever instigated.

## II.12.F. Big Shots' Comments Link

The leading central bankers, notably the Chair of the U.S. Fed and the President of the ECB, move the markets. If central bank heads speak confidently or with a concerted policy and plan, the stock, bond and currency markets will be impacted. Also, surprise statements can have even larger market effects. U.S. Presidents have little effect on markets. They speak on economic issues and reference key facets like economic growth, inflation, taxation, income inequality, etc.; but their comments are so scripted and at a level far removed from what markets practitioners act on. Big shots in markets and the economy (like Warren Buffett, George Soros, Bill Gross, Jeremy Siegel, Ray Dalio, etc.) frequently speak or write—or are simply attributed by the media with some opinion. Their opinions might appear to move markets yet this may only be coincidental. Typically, the effect attributed to the important thinker reverses so quickly that his comments may not have been a factor at all. For example, the person spoke and the stock market was up in the morning but by noon the market had lost all of its gains. If you are leaked the contents of an imminent presentation by Warren Buffett, do not try to time the market with it. Just for the record, there are some famous cases of big names speaking and moving markets. Most notably, investment newsletter author Joe Granville made a number of bearish calls during the 1970s and 1980s. Henry Kaufman, once chief economist for Salomon Brothers, made some calls during the 1980s; but such events seem quaint today.

At times, I have hypothesized that certain truly credible people could/would move markets if they spoke infrequently but with great authority from having a specific message based on a lifetime of achievement. This is contrary to the frequently quoted pundits who opine on many issues often with broad and sometimes partisan commentary. One compelling example was evidenced by a March 14, 2000 *Wall Street Journal* op-ed piece by academic Jeremy Siegel labeling technology stocks a sucker bet. Following this writing, stock markets (especially technology sectors) commenced a long, large drop. This gave the appearance that this well respected and disinterested scholar's opinion really mattered. Over the years, however, similar statements by comparable authorities, including an equally well written op-ed by Jeremy Siegel on an overvalued bond market (*Wall Street Journal* August 18, 2010), amounted to nothing.

# II.13. International Economics

In formal terms, international economics is the study of how differing productive resources and consumer preferences among nations affect the economic activities of those nations and how they engage in commerce among each other. "International" is a popular undergraduate course that as well is presented as if it has scientific veracity with rigorous models and consistent empirical findings. I offer a more informal discussion of certain theoretical and empirical aspects of international. I focus on prominent debates about our economic competitive position versus that of other nations, how international economics impacts our M&M policy and certain other factors related to economic forces from outside America.

When I lecture on international economics topics, I point out the following seemingly contradictory case: (1) international economic and financial interconnections among nations are extremely important for the fortunes of nations. (2) Yet for M&M they are a dodge. Young Americans must know international economics since, obviously, more and more commerce is done across borders and capital markets are more and more interconnected. However, basic M&M phenomena—like recession, inflation expectations, policy effects, etc.—must be explained in a closed economic system. We cannot simply say, "The world market sets the level"; yet we often do. For example, if you explain the level of interest rates in a certain country because the world's interest rates dictate such levels, you must then explain the world's interest rates. You can appeal to an outside level for a small country whose fortunes depend on much bigger economies around it (like Sweden relative to Eurozone) or perhaps in a short run for any nation, but you cannot explain the U.S. Many instructors of M&M courses make a chronic mistake of couching fundamental issues as dependent primarily on external economic forces.

International models and their connections of causes and effects hold a fair amount of mystery for most business and finance professionals. A few years ago a local bond portfolio manager contacted me to lecture him on international economics. I suggested that I could explain some of the basic ideas of international over a couple of lunches, but he did not believe it was that simple. I then recommended he sit in my international economics course, but he did not want to devote that much time. He sensed that international was more than the former but less than the latter and became indignant when I explained it was not easily mastered. In the end it is a sprawling, imprecise study calling on much estimation, rough models, history, culture, etc. To wit, there are a number of major areas in international that need elucidation. For example, why do we believe so strongly in free trade? Perhaps a more timely question is, can the U.S. "immigrant" its way to prosperity forever? Can bringing in a steady stream of the right kind of immigrants to America ensure, or at least buttress, our leading economic status? This is a widely-held belief and one that is tough to argue against.

## II.13.A. Basic International M&M Connections & Beggaring Thy Neighbor

We discussed some basic mechanisms by which changes in one country's economy affect other countries' economies. They can be theories, parables or empirical cases. To spin these macro/international stories you usually have to commence with an important economic quantity of some country being out of balance. Some of the more common narratives are listed below:
- A country runs constant trade deficits, and its currency goes down.
- A country's currency rises in value (for whatever reason, strong economy, e.g.), thus the country exports less and imports more—causing its GDP to go down. Of note, one important "export" of many countries is tourism within its borders. If its currency goes up it is more expensive for foreigners to

visit the country so it exports less.

- A country's economy is strong (i.e., its GDP is growing), which causes it to demand for goods made in other countries (i.e., other countries benefit). (Of note to this story is that the U.S. economy due to its size and continued growth has provided this benefit to the world.)
- A country's interest rates go down (by policy or by market forces), which causes parties to abandon assets in that country's currency with now lower yields and buy assets from abroad.
- A country devalues its currency, perhaps abruptly (we will discuss this below).
- A country pegs its currency to that of another country and possibly drops the peg.

There is often a circular nature with the international M&M interconnections and sometimes even a convoluted rationale. Generally, a nation prefers a strong economy and usually that is accompanied by a strong currency. A strong currency reflects a robust economy and growing national wealth. A nation, though, also desires a weaker currency to enable growth by export. A country cannot have it both ways. Beginning about July 2014 and continuing into 2015 the value of the U.S. dollar rose significantly and its high value probably detracted from GDP growth. Analysts wanted to maintain a favorable opinion on U.S. economic prospects though, so they made the case that the strong U.S. dollar could help the U.S. economy. A strong dollar would mean weaker currencies for Eurozone and/or Japan, which would mean growth in their economies and subsequently more demand for U.S. goods, ultimately increasing U.S. GDP. The appeal is to a secondary effect but it made some logical sense and appeared plausible as an answer to the question: "What are good effects of a high dollar?"

Finance ministers spend much time attributing their national economic situations to other nations' economies and M&M policies. For example, circa January to February 2014, Turkey and certain other emerging markets nations bemoaned the effects of U.S. tapering of QE on its (Turkey's) currency. Specifically Turkey argued that it had to raise interest rates to get people to buy Turkish debt because the Turkish currency was crashing due to U.S. policy changes, which would tend to cause the buying of U.S. debt and the selling of emerging market debt. The U.S. retorted unsympathetically, contending that emerging countries created their own currency problems by poor domestic economic policies. In testimony in February 2014 Janet Yellen showed a relationship between exchange rate problems and an index of vulnerability (how poor your country was). We contended that the emerging nations were hypocritical since they also complained when the U.S. originally did QE. We mocked that they "had us both ways"—but perhaps our policy did confound them in both cases.

The U.S. also complains vociferously in the international economic community though, harping on two main villains: (1) Germany for thrift and productivity and (2) China for thrift, currency manipulation and general contrary behavior in international matters. We generally blame the world for not stimulating the global economy as much as we do and lament our (American) economic lot, contending that Europe was diminishing our economic growth because it was not growing quickly. Of course, for decades we (including both right and left-wing American analysts) derided Europe for having grave fundamental economic problems that kept their economies from growing. Also, the whole idea of a nation helping the economy of another nation can be reversed. We help China by buying their goods and lament that they do not buy ours, but you can just as easily say that they help our economy by lending to us and we in turn do not lend to them.

To a Keynesian who believes in deficit spending, the U.S. intellectual position might make sense. To anyone else, however, the idea that a country like the U.S.—which runs both big budget and trade deficits—blames thriftier countries for its economic problems must seem curious. Overall, the U.S. is not magnanimous in economic matters.

## II.13.B. Why Do Economists Believe in Free Trade?

We believe that free trade benefits both trading partners economically. If one country begins selling a product to your country that your nation was already producing, then your country will be better off even if jobs were lost for your populace. Not all individuals will be better off: Perhaps, the person who lost his job due to imports will be poorer, but on net the nation will be. Here is a typical statement by an authoritative voice in a prominent source: "Trade is not a zero-sum game where one nation's success is another's failure. Trade makes the cake bigger so everyone can benefit."[157] We are also told that economists who disagree vociferously on most economic issues uniformly and strongly support free trade. Economists who dissent, like economist and journalist Lou Dobbs, often get disparaged. Certainly, from time to time, we question free trade in the public forum. The opponents though are interested parties, like labor unions, or demagogue politicians. In the presidential primaries of 2015 and 2016 major candidates doubted free trade; however, calmer minds remind these weaker economic thinkers that free trade remains valid.[158]

Following economists' cue, most intelligent people support free trade. Perhaps average people cannot articulate why they believe in free trade but, if pressed, they would say that any professor at any university could demonstrate both the theory and evidence that free trade is superior. An analogy might be to our belief in democracy. We think democracy is best and are confident that if we researched political systems, democracy would prove its advantage every time. We also use various arguments and parables to prove free trade's rightness. Many cite 19th century French economist Frédéric Bastiat's faux petition by candle makers to outlaw the sun. Sometimes we use other simple arguments; for example, I choose to buy a foreign-made automobile: Would I be better off if I bought an American made car already deemed inferior?

I do not doubt the general benefit of open competition, i.e., free trade. The most important impetus to the progress of humanity has been free trade and open exchange. Societies open to trade flourished, and those that were closed (like China for centuries) fell behind. Free trade is not that clear-cut today. We must be careful of how much additional benefit maintaining or adding to "free trade" adds and exactly how it is backed or not backed by the theories and empirical findings of "international economics." What we think of as free trade and the implementation thereof may not generally make our economic pie bigger. In fact, our economics text has only one model unequivocally supporting free trade, and what it describes is not what you would think of as international trade.

Regardless of the above discussion, every nation must maintain free trade. Even though it does not guarantee a growing economy, thwarting free trade would cause decline. The superiority of free trade rests on the theory of Comparative Advantage ("CA"), which is a relatively simple model going all the way back to English economist David Ricardo (1772 to 1823). CA is perhaps the most longstanding basic model in economics. In the early 1800s, CA represented a counter-intuitive but insightful extension on the prevailing idea of trade's advantage existing only in the case of Absolute Advantage. This states that countries should trade goods they produced absolutely better, not just relatively or comparatively better. Ricardo's CA shows that even if a country produces nothing better, it should still partake in trade.

CA is a microeconomic story, describing individual agents, and it is demonstrated with the agents being countries. Assume two countries (U.S. and China) and two goods (Software and Televisions). The U.S.

---

[157] Op-ed piece in *The Wall Street Journal* by the Prime Minister of the U.K., David Cameron, May 13, 2013, p. A15.

[158] In March 2016 the issue came to the forefront and the top editorialists from sources like *The Economist* and *Bloomberg* made the free market case. See, for example, *Bloomberg.com*, senior executive editor David Shipley: "The Case for Free Trade Is as Strong as Ever: View," March 31, 2016, http://www.bloomberg.com/news/audio/2016-03-28/the-case-for-free-trade-is-as-strong-as-ever-view-audio

is more productive than China in producing both goods. The U.S. can produce ten Software in one day and seven Televisions, while China can produce only two Software and three Televisions. The U.S. has Absolute Advantage in each, but nonetheless the countries should trade with each performing what it is "comparatively" good at doing. China should produce Televisions even though America is more productive in that. The world as a whole will get more output if countries specialize and exchange. Trade yields greater total output. All we have to do is divvy it up. Here is the demonstration that is put on the board in the first few classes of any International Economics course:

<u>2000</u>                                                    <u>2014</u>

| | Manufacture | Services | | | Manufacture | Services |
|---|---|---|---|---|---|---|
| China | 3 | 2 | | China | 6 | 6 |
| U.S. | 7 | 10 | | U.S. | 7 | 11 |

Above, we have two points in time. At 2000, the nations should trade (i.e., exchange), and they will both be better off. That tells the story of CA and is the main reason we support free trade. It is a point in time story and not a dynamic one. As of 2014, the nations should also trade to make both better off. The way we set the numbers, the world is better off in terms of productivity. The fallacy though is that we interpret these two static states to mean that over time or dynamically, each nation will never be worse off since they trade. What is happening today though is that the productivity of China is going up relative to ours, displacing production in our country. Suppose that come 2014, relative productivities have changed such that the Chinese are more productive in both activities. (In this case set China to eight in Manufacture and twelve in Services and the U.S. to seven and ten). The two nations should still trade, but China, due to its higher productivity, will have displaced some of our workers. The net result is that we will not be getting as much as before.

The doctrine of CA gets overplayed in a way. Generally it is taken to mean that free trade guarantees a nation a lock on its absolute standard of living or its standard of living relative to that of other nations. That is not the case, however: CA is an exercise in comparative statics at two points in time. If our competitors become more economically productive, we will still benefit from trade but be absolutely poorer. Our competitors come back every period with higher productivity and thus our terms of trade have deteriorated. Leading economists, like Paul Samuelson (in the early 2000s before he died) and Princeton professor and former Fed Vice Chairman Alan Blinder,[159] point this out from time to time. They do not support protectionism or even oppose free trade, but they do warn that a simplistic belief in free trade ignores many real world realities, like changing productivities. They also bring up the issue of unemployment, which is not a part of the model. CA assumes full employment. If our competitors become more productive, they will produce more and we will generally produce less. We will have additional unemployment. We will be worse off—unless average productivities for the world as a whole go up sufficiently enough to offset unemployment.

In the real world free trade does lower the cost of goods and services as CA implies and makes the world economic pie bigger. It also results in unemployment for certain workers in certain nations. In public debates most economists will conclude that we should support free trade but then have other policies to aid those who suffer concentrated losses from losing a job or profitability of their industry. For example, workers should be retrained. It is very difficult, however, to identify the losers and to design programs to help them.

This real world convergence of productivities is not the fault of free exchange nor is it a statement that

---

[159] "Alan Blinder on Trade," *The Wall Street Journal*, March 28, 2007. For Samuelson, "Paul Samuelson: Rethinking Free Trade," OnPoint with Tom Ashbrook, http://onpoint.wbur.org/2004/09/27/paul-samuelson-rethinking-free-trade.

we should curtail trade today. The problem of CA is that by ignoring the changing productivities it clouds the debate about free trade. It biases us against savings and investment and in favor of AD. It supports Keynesian policies of current demand.

There are a variety of other models and empirical findings put forth by economists on international economics. Perhaps the most important model is Heckscher-Ohlin, which states that trade does depend on comparative costs, like Ricardo's CA, but further explains those factors.[160] These textbook items are important and insightful, but do not say much about how to achieve the kind of economic patriotism we crave. Many economics teachers in both top schools and community colleges conclude that free trade works. They display the CA model as proof and do not emphasize the changes in productivities and dynamic aspects. The CA construct is especially tractable for classroom. It can be shown with the two-by-two matrix and accompanying graph. It, makes for great test questions. It is great irony that the basic model that provides our conviction about the value of free trade really demonstrates why we are declining.

## II.13.C. What Makes a Nation Rich?

Scholars have long pondered what makes countries economically successful: "Why do some nations succeed and others fail in international competition? This question is perhaps the most frequently asked economic question of our time," said renowned competition expert Michael E. Porter on page one of his 800-page 1990 volume, *The Competitive Advantage of Nations*. In conjunction with other experts and research organizations, Porter mustered and empirically tested every known answer including macroeconomics, labor supplies, natural resources, government policy and management policy. He concluded that the above question was not to the point. A better question was why and how specific industries or industry segments succeed: "Why does a nation become the home base for successful international competitors in an industry?" His empirical analysis came up with "threads of a new explanation" centering on four factors: (1) economies of scale, (2) technology, (3) having a home market and (4) having multinational corporations.

Strictly speaking, Porter's analysis is not about short-term attempts to increase GDP, so it may not tie in perfectly with much of our discussion of M&M policy. It does contribute to the debate about our maintaining our world-leading economic position though, and the U.S. advantage in the four factors has shrunk since Porter published. This begs an even more basic question: Does it matter which nation your economic fortunes are tied to? Of course, in pure material terms it is better to be born in a rich country than a poor one. Additionally, it is better to be born in a solvent country with a manageable debt for long into the future. A citizen of Norway, for example, with its outsized oil wealth, is guaranteed a high standard of living. Greece is a comparable European society to Norway in many ways, but it is poorer and facing constant relative economic deprivation. Of course, excluding migration, we do not choose the country we will be citizens of but at least we should be aware of changing fortunes of a society. U.S. citizenship may present a constantly growing tax burden to its citizens due to chronic fiscal deficits accompanied by years of overly-accommodative monetary policy.

Sometimes the very idea that standard of living depends so critically on capability to sell abroad seems difficult to accept. For example, a person from Indiana might wonder why his fortune depends upon Indiana having companies that export to remote places like Asia or Europe. Isn't a large enough society capable of providing the vast majority of its basic goods and services? Also, in its history, wasn't the U.S. very wealthy without significant import and export? At this point in time, the U.S. faces a gradual, relative decline: With increasing international mobility of finance and commerce, more and more products and services that were

---

[160] Heckscher-Ohlin is a mathematical, general equilibrium model of trade. It was developed by Swedish economists Eli Heckscher and Bertil Ohlin and publicized in the 1930s.

produced in the U.S., and from which high profits were distributed to U.S. citizens, are now produced abroad.

## II.13.D. The Trade Deficit, Balance of Payments & International Flows

We discussed theoretical international links of trade positions and currency values. To understand these and related international economics in the real world, a primer on trade statistics is helpful. The various quantities that represent a nation's international position can be confusing and are discussed below:

- **Trade Balance**: This is calculated using exports of goods and services minus imports of goods and services, and financial transactions are not included. A country that exports more than it imports will run a trade surplus—China has a trade surplus. The U.S. has run trade deficits since about 1976. Subdividing the trade balance down by goods and services shows the U.S. typically running a surplus in services but a big deficit in goods, although the categories are strictly defined. The trade balance is the quantity most frequently reported. It is often referred to as the trade gap. A deficit in this gives the appearance that a country is declining. It is the NX component of the national income accounting identity.
- **Current Account**: This is calculated as trade balance plus net investment income plus net cash transfers. Net investment income is what one country earns on its foreign investments minus payments made to foreign investors from their holdings of the country's investments. Net cash transfers are primarily monies remitted abroad from foreign workers in a country. For example, Filipinos working in Kuwait remit much of what they earn to families at home.
- **Capital Account**: This reflects net ownership in assets: These are borrowings, not incomes. Net investment income from the current account reflects an income. Chinese buying U.S. treasuries is a capital account item.
- **Balance of Payments**: This is current account plus capital account. The balance of payments must be zero, although statistical discrepancy allows it to veer from zero a bit. If we in the U.S. run a current account deficit (which we typically do) we must run a capital account surplus.

Statistics concerning the U.S. position in the world economy have represented political fodder ever since the 1970s, when U.S. dominance was challenged by countries like Japan and West Germany; and as the years passed by countries like South Korea, Taiwan and China. Such countries represented infinite supplies of cheap labor. The mantra of political candidates, union heads, executives and other U.S. advocates was to limit imports and encourage exports to save U.S. jobs and keep commerce from leaking outside our nation. Others, typically economists, would dismiss the problem. Their position was that free trade benefited all. Often they would make impressionistic arguments like, "What is the trade deficit between Texas and Minnesota?' or "Would the American people be better off if they could not buy automobiles like Toyotas and BMW's that they have freely chosen?" Ominous rhetoric concerning the U.S. financial position in the world has been omnipresent but waxes and wanes. A major focal point occurred during the mid-1980s when the U.S. became a net debtor nation, meaning that the U.S. apparently owed more to foreigners than foreigners owed to the U.S. When the economy was strong during the 1990s, the American people and politicians were less conscious of the trade gap.

## II.13.E. Can a Nation Devalue Its Currency and Attain Higher GDP?

Devaluing a currency is perhaps the easiest demonstration of effective macro policy, yet it can be presented to trumpet the success of policy—or it can be broached to demonstrate the futility and desperation, of policy. Recall our national GDP equation: $Y = C + I + G + NX$, where NX represents E (exports) minus I (imports), or net exports. The basic manipulation of international economics is devaluing your currency. Through policy, primarily lowering interest rates, or by QE, a country lowers the value of its currency. This enables it to export more and increase growth, or perhaps forestall growth from decreasing, and ultimately, supposedly, maintain jobs, wages and standard of living. Also, perhaps companies, including foreign ones, will locate production in the country. Whatever ill effects of a lower currency occur are assumed to be small or to happen later when the economy is altogether richer and can absorb the costs. This is the great success story.

What are the tradeoffs? For one thing, other countries may want to achieve the same goal and attempt to lower their currencies against yours. If a country does devalue, it will face higher prices on imports yielding higher inflation. Then, the higher inflation will require that rates be raised, which should contract the economy. Also, a lower currency will cause flight from holding assets denominated in a country's currency. This is the futility story: Part of this narrative is a currency war, in which two or many more countries devalue—each hoping to gain. It is difficult to determine the typical result of currency devaluations in our world. Some countries have temporarily forestalled crisis with devaluation, but over time it is tough to discern if the effects persisted or did not result in worse outcomes largely accrued to average citizens in lower standards of living. To sum up, a devaluation might get a national government out of a crisis and aid certain industries and businesses, but it does not make the populace richer.

Many countries do manipulate interest rates under the hope that, if done adeptly and in the right amounts, a country can, indeed, stimulate economic growth to a net gain. Oftentimes though, policy is only done in reaction because other countries' currencies are declining. During the post-2008 period those European countries that did not use the euro (like Switzerland, Denmark and Sweden) had to engage in reactive policy. As people sought the Swiss franc as a safe currency Switzerland had to engage in an extreme increase in its central bank balance sheet. Denmark and Sweden had to set negative rates to get people to sell their currencies.

Another situation is that if a country is running a trade deficit due to failure to export enough but the country is part of a monetary union the country cannot devalue to rectify the deficit. A nation must have its own currency to engage in devaluation. For example, Greece, a member of Eurozone, faced recession but could not devalue because its currency was the euro. In more formal modeling we take $Y = C + I + G + E - I$ and make theories and empirical estimates of trade. We model $E = \text{constant} + \gamma*\text{Foreign Income} + \delta*\text{Foreign Wealth}$ where $\gamma$ and $\delta$ are propensities to import. Estimating those propensities precisely is difficult.

Another variety of improving a trade deficit is the blatant encouragement of citizens to spend on domestic products. This is routinely done by some nations although in today's world it is considered to be in poor spirit of international economic cooperation. In 2008 ff certain of the U.S. stimulus initiatives were "Buy American" schemes that rewarded people for choosing a domestic product. Another facet of devaluing is what happens if many nations attempt to devalue their currencies. Following 2008, most countries of the world did monetary easing, a large result of which was the lowering of the value of currencies. Some nations perceived this as competitive devaluation and responded by policy to lower their currencies— primarily lowering their main central bank policy rates. Some analysts described this as a tacit currency war, although officially nations refrained from admitting that. Following a large drop in the value of the euro in October 2014, Sweden, which had refrained from expansionary monetary policy, lowered its rate to zero. Some analysts described this as an acknowledgement by Sweden that expansionary policy, rather than austerity, was the more successful policy. Others maintained that Sweden simply had to counter currency declines in trading partners' currencies.[161] Switzerland and Denmark also faced similar situations and

[161] "Central Banker Hero Becomes Face of Failure in Swedish Tale," *Bloomberg.com*, October 31, 2014, by John Carlstrom.

employed negative rates. As you can conclude from the above, it is not at all clear that a country can confound the odds and save its economy with forced currency movements.

## II.13.F. Do Immigrants Create Net Wealth?

The opinions of people who contend that immigrants are net economic burdens on our society are seemingly easy to falsify and often appear vulgar. Contrarily, those who argue that immigrants add more than they cost, especially 2008 ff, are equally easy to argue down—and just as vulgar. Proponents contend immigrants are great entrepreneurs citing stats that many great high companies were founded by immigrants, but that is history. They also point out that immigrants do the low-paying work that native Americans will not do. The "net" is important: Immigrants probably result in more total GDP, which may be good for certain purposes; but do immigrants add economic output to the average existing American? That is a much more difficult question to answer affirmatively. In reality, the answer may likely be no.

Regardless, the "bring in the immigrants—no matter how or what" philosophy is an idea loved by almost all of the intelligentsia. The idea may constitute the leading "solution" to America's economic woes. A large number of favorable spillovers from immigration is assumed, and sometimes specific economic goals are addressed. Big money manager Andy Kessler recommends bringing in a million immigrants to buy housing with their external wealth.[162] At that time, housing was seen as the key to our economic salvation, and Kessler was sure that immigrants coveted property.

Historically, immigrants have been great contributors to overall American economic wealth by creating enterprises. Of course, since the country's entire historical population was largely immigrants and since America (due to its high standard of living) drew the best and brightest, it is meaningless to list the great enterprises started by immigrants. Proponents of immigrants creating net wealth will cite history and statistics involving hyperbolic tallies. One executive turned economist remarks, "Immigrants or their children founded 40% of today's Fortune 500 companies."[163] Again though, since so many Americans were immigrants or children of immigrants it is a meaningless statement. This history of the 1800s and early 1990s is completely irrelevant unless you believe that the future of the world outside of America is potato famines, pogroms and Nazis. About more current trends the same economists say, "One quarter of U.S. high-technology firms established since 1995 have had at least one foreign-born founder. These new companies today employ 450,000 people." While it is plausible some enterprise would go undone within America without these entrepreneurs, it may not be the entire amount—or even close.[164] Analysts tally companies by founder and find that immigrants run a disproportionate share of businesses, including high value-added businesses that become large public companies. Yet, that immigrant-owned and operated convenience stores and gas stations appear ubiquitous does not mean that those businesses would not exist without immigration.

Proponents will also cite stories and cases, mostly of large American corporations claiming they need skilled foreign workers to operate. They imply American labor cannot qualify and also might reference academic research that models and estimates the many effects of immigrants. This is tough to assess, and the models are simply not that robust. Another facet of immigration is how we sell U.S. citizenship. We purport to offer the visas to entrepreneurs and skilled workers and maintain that we are not selling citizenship. The effect is the same though, and many wish to increase citizenship selling visa

---

[162] *The Wall Street Journal*, September 2, 2010.
[163] AOL executive Steve Case, 2013, Partnership for a New American Economy.
[164] "How America Loses a Job Every 43 Seconds," *The Wall Street Journal* Op-ed, Matthew J. Slaughter, former Council of Economic Advisers economist, March 26, 2014, p. A15.

programs. If indeed there is great value to U.S. citizenship then, like any other scarce resource, we should ration it.

One U.S. immigration program is called EB-5, which requires that an immigrant bring so much money and create so many jobs (exact amounts vary, but they are relatively modest and easy to massage). The net economic effects of the program are dubious. Often EB-5 money replaces standard lending. For example, a real estate developer already may have a bank loan for a project. Some of the funding is replaced with EB-5 money though. No new jobs are created, and this merely puts a little more profit in the hands of the developer. Proponents argue that the program has effects in some cases—perhaps tipping some entrepreneurial people to set up shop here rather than elsewhere, but that is debatable. The program is heavily gamed by immigrants. Those with needs, like dependent children, might partake of the program eventually creating more cost than benefit. There is also the lack of morality and principle of this immigration policy, which is based simply on how much money an immigrant brings. What true loyalty would such economic immigrants to America have? You might argue that America's history proves the success of such immigration. For example, a famous Boston-area immigrant was An Wang, who immigrated to America from China in 1945. He founded a company called Wang Laboratories that at one time had approximately 30,000 employees. The profits of his life's endeavors included great philanthropy. An Wang, though, in his time and circumstances, came to America with a belief that America was singular among nations for opportunity and decency. He also had no intention of abandoning America. Today's immigrants see America as one nation among any of dozens, and perceive that they can back and forth.

A final answer of the success or lack of success of such economic immigration programs requires valuing numerous factors about which we know little. Immigrants run businesses, are highly educated, contribute to the community, etc.; but they also sponge off of public assistance, leave America when circumstances change, etc. I frequently converse with Tufts undergraduates that are foreigners or who have dual citizenship. They express the belief that America is stable economically. They believe this to be important, yet they also disparage America relative to many other competitor countries. America is not the all-around best society. They profess to seek career wherever the economic conditions are best and rarely choose America for its traditional non-economic sources of greatness like freedom and democracy.

Our leaders should at least be blunt with our populace. We may have an open immigration policy with special economic incentives and it may, perhaps, result in greater total GDP. This may mean no higher and possibly even lower per capita GDP for current Americans, however. Greater total GDP could be to your advantage in that the U.S. can raise more taxes and pay for more government services, some of which may go to you. Yet the costs of new immigrants ultimately may more than exhaust those additional tax revenues. Our best estimates on this are insufficient to give a definitive answer.

## II.13.G. Economic Advantages To Size of Nations

Around 2012, when it appeared that certain countries in the Eurozone (like Greece) might have to abandon the currency and drop out of the union, there was much commentary that the U.S. was fortunate and impervious to such a regional breakup because our union had fundamental economic advantages. We would not, for example, get a circumstance where a rich region (like Germany) would have to support a poor region (like Greece). To the contrary, we do have that circumstance. Some U.S. states support others: Minnesota and New Jersey, for example, support Mississippi.

Since the U.S. has a federal fiscal union, unlike Eurozone, we can tax and transfer to aid poorer areas. Greece could not receive similar subsidy from Eurozone. Many economists boasted that the U.S. was a much stronger entity due to that aspect and argued that we could not get a situation like Greece. The U.S., though, has poorer states and territories (like Puerto Rico) and other struggling regions (like Detroit and the Illinois pension system). Another advantage our union has is that our labor moves freely. In the U.S. a person with either poor or excellent work opportunities in another state can readily move. This is a valid economic advantage, but it does not forestall that poor regions are poor. A poor U.S. state cannot devalue the dollar to stimulate business. Also, although any American is free to move across state borders legally U.S. labor mobility has been decreasing for other reasons. In particular, many people are averse to change jobs due to health care benefits that they perceive will be worse if they move. Also, many people are stuck due to housing commitments like underwater mortgages.

Within the U.S., states jockey against each other to attract businesses by giving tax breaks and other incentives. Since one state's gain is another's loss and there are substantial tax distortions and other bad economic incentives it is not an advantage to the nation as a whole. Many economists consider small entities to have inherent economic advantage. They cite successful city-states like Singapore and Hong Kong. Small units are efficient for recognition and supervision of government services. Also, small units can often benefit from advantageous migration to or from them. Silicon Valley may be an example of a successful economic area—and if it were a separate nation it would be very rich. On the other hand, some government services (like defense, basic research, and large infrastructure) may be done much more efficiently in a large nation.

One distinct facet of a large, unified nation is that its central bank could be minimally influenced by parts of the nation. The U.S. Fed does not do monetary policy subject to needs of states. The monetary policy of the ECB must cater to specific needs and constraints of the independent Eurozone nations such as Germany and Greece.

## II.13.H. Germany: Keynesian Killjoy or Scapegoat for Dysfunctional States?

Germany deserves special mention as the anti-Keynesian bugaboo. Keynesians like Paul Krugman rail at Germany for failing to spend enough. The U.S. government has also singled out Germany as not pulling its weight. Even a more tempered erudite analyst, perhaps like that of former Governor of the Bank of England Mervyn King in his memoirs after leaving office, portrays Germany as not spending enough.[165] According to critics, Germany creates a great deflationary force by its large trade surplus. Germany saves too much. It has relatively high taxes and its citizens are not altogether big spenders. This imbalance allegedly draws down the economies of the European Union which in turn draw down the entire world economy. It is an extremely odd argument really dependent on pure Keynesian belief. Below is a list of the debating points of Germany as M&M party pooper:

- The Germany government does spend a lot and run fiscal deficits. Its deficits may not average as large as those of other nations but it carries national debt. Germany believes that it must control budgets to provide for its aging population. Germany does spend significantly on infrastructure. Critics contend that Germany could increase its infrastructure spending to the benefit of Eurozone and the world.
- Germany's domestic unemployment and inflation levels do not necessarily recommend stimulation.
- Germany possesses certain fundamental economic factors like an emphasis on practical, technical education, excellence in production of exportable products and thrifty household behavior. Germans do not use credit the way Americans do. It is not clear that German behavior should be rectified. Germans, perhaps, simply prefer fewer goods and services and more leisure. To make them more like American who are willing to buy on credit from Walmart may not be in their well-being.

---

[165] This case is made in many passages of his book *The End of Alchemy*, W.W. Norton, 2016.

- There is an element of an intellectual vendetta. Germany and its economists reject Keynesianism. Germany believes in balancing budgets and minimizing inflation. It views managing unemployment as a structural problem involving long-term policies and not a short-run demand management problem. Germany believes that it manages its employment correctly. For example, following the adoption of the euro in 1999 Germany believed each nation would have to make structural reforms. Germany made those reforms while other nations did not.
- Countries that usually run trade deficits as policy do so by intervening in markets to keep their currency low in value. Germany does not have its own currency or central bank. In fact, before the creation of the Euro, when Germany had its own currency, it ran smaller trade surpluses.
- Supposedly, within Eurozone, Germany benefits from the low value of the euro which lowers German wages and allows Germany to export. The stimulative ECB policy, however, that creates the lower currency value was generally opposed by Germany. Also lower wages mean lower standard of living.
- The issue of Eurozone having no fiscal union such that resources can be transferred from a rich nation to a poor nation is another condition that Germany believes was part of the agreement creating the common currency.
- For its exports Germany accepts paper claims that yield very low rates of return. This can be seen as largesse to other nations of the world that run deficits. If Germany saves less it is not clear what it would import with its surplus. Also debtor nations would have to find other sources to borrow from. The idea that added German spending would create so much more GDP growth that it would pay for itself is an extreme Keynesian leap of faith. In an odd way Keynesians mock Germany for accepting IOU's that might not be honored in the future and admonish Germany to spend those IOU's now before they lose value.
- In addition to not spending Germany also forces austerity on countries by requiring indebted countries, notably Greece, to pay their debt. Yet Germany has supported multiple mark downs of Greek debt. It has also agreed to unrealistic future goals that Greece has to hit which is tacit agreement to additional debt forbearance in the future.
- The magnitudes are questionable. Germany is held responsible for lack of demand in Eurozone, which cause insufficient growth there which impacts America and the rest of the world. Its surplus is simply not that large.

## II.13.I. Other Concepts of International Economics

The saving of the American economy by international forces has many important facets, including these additional contemporary issues in M&M and international:
- Popular in M&M discussion is how nations' economic policies and developments affect other nations' economies and how they can pull together as a team for the greater good. For example, in early 2016, world economic growth was looking weak due to a variety of shocks and long-term trends. At that time pundits were calling on the U.S. to discontinue its rate raising plans, China to spend more, the U.K. to cease certain spending cuts, Germany to reverse certain tight fiscal policies, and nations not to devalue currencies against each other. Then, presumably through these coordinated actions, the world would get through a tough period. Of course though, then it would be left with getting to original desired policies of raising rates, cutting spending, etc.
- Is your nation's international position cash flow positive? Do you make more from your nationals' holdings of foreign securities than foreigners make from their holding of your securities? This story

was popular around 2006 with some research contending that the U.S. earned significantly higher profits from its foreign investments. This constituted a strong statement of economic superiority. We have a large pool of wealth in our name. Our "net investment income," the amount Americans make on foreign investments minus the amount foreigners make on our investments, is positive. We get much higher rates of return. One facet is the holdings of U.S. companies. Indeed U.S. corporations do have valuable foreign subsidiaries which earn great profits that apparently are "ours"; but this value cannot be taken without losing it.

- A major topic in economic issues for decades is offshoring, or outsourcing abroad, of jobs. In the years following the crisis of 2008, politicians, economists and the media claimed that many manufacturing jobs were returning to America. This is called "reshoring." It is said to be due to low energy costs, proximity to customers, higher costs in places like China, quality control, etc. Believers in reshoring typically cited cases of famous companies/brands that have brought certain production back to the U.S. including Duracell, Master Lock and Whirlpool. Yet manufacturing offshoring continues on net and the offshoring of services has also grown greatly. In the 1970s to 1990s, we acknowledged that jobs went abroad but consoled ourselves that they were mostly lower mark-up or downright dirty jobs like low level manufacturing, e.g., shoes, textiles, etc. We argued that the U.S. maintained a great edge in high mark-up service work like finance, marketing, legal services, design, creative arts, branding, etc. and would continue to do so. The U.S. edge in high mark-up services has been declining. As the manufacturing went abroad, it became advantageous to also have the design, legal, marketing, etc. work done abroad.

- Comparing economic strength by national border is misleading. A country may rank poorly in overall economic standing due to weaknesses like corruption, crime, inequality, education, etc. but may be competitive in certain industries. For example, Russia as a whole may be a weak economic power but certain regions (like Moscow) or industries (like oil & gas) are highly developed and dedicated to enterprise.

- Following the financial crisis, the U.S. has stepped up attempts to collect taxes from overseas. These efforts include significant requirements on foreign nations, businesses and citizens to provide information to the U.S. or face penalty and persecution (notably FATCA and other initiatives). It is difficult to judge the net effects of these efforts but they may have significant unintended consequences. Foreign businesses and consumers may avoid doing commerce with the U.S. and other countries are also adopting similar tax collection schemes.

- Another prominent economic facet that we discussed before is how a nation's corporations are taxed for their overseas operations. Virtually alone among nations, the U.S. taxes its corporations for operations abroad. U.S. companies pay local taxes to the country their operations are in but then must also pay corporate taxes to the U.S. unless they do repatriate their profits. A case can be made that a company should only pay tax on its operations to the nation in which operations are located because that nation bears the costs of providing services like roads, legal structure, policing and security, health care for workers, etc. The U.S. sees it differently. Although there is some ability to write off foreign taxes against domestic in general (since the U.S. corporate tax is high and must be paid for with income earned at home or abroad), U.S. nationality can be a significant handicap.

- How much is our economic struggle an international contest? Are we really in an economic war, for example, with China?

- Some pundits dismiss any notion that trade imbalances and national economic positions matter. They contend that trade stats are mainly accounting conventions, and do not reflect economic strength. They employ certain arguments that make sense in some contexts. What it the trade deficit between Minnesota and Mississippi, they ask? The answer is we do not care, and rely on the free movement of resources between U.S. states to get us to an optimal result for the whole. Why not apply that across nations? They also focus on the consumption side of import/export saying that we are economically better from the benefits of what we import. Would Americans be better off if they ceased purchasing quality foreign products, like cars, and substituted inferior U.S. products? They have a point, but they miss the dynamic changes in wealth and product that are transpiring.

- Also in previous decades like the 1980s, the U.S. partook in free trade agreements as a matter of course. We did not boast our openness to free trade agreements; nothing less was acceptable. Other nations lagged and resisted free trade. Now other nations engage in bilateral free trade agreements as readily as we do and without fanfare.

## II.14. M&M for Skeptics

Concepts of M&M interconnections are omnipresent in the financial press and even in the regular news. Although they have some information and consistency, most M&M stories are "ad hoc"—meaning that they relate facts or developments to whichever theory they appear to be consistent with and ignore equally plausible alternative ideas. Such facile pronouncements of M&M are also virtually impossible for the lay person to gainsay due to a pretense of science (econ talk sounds scientific) and the perpetuation of knowledge and authority by economists and other economy commentators.

Listed below are a variety of facets of modern M&M. Modern can mean various time frames, including (1) 2008 ff; (2) the period from about 1980 to present, which constitutes a time when our nation engaged in mainly economic goals (i.e., we were not preoccupied with war); or (3) the last hundred years, which is the time of national economies with large government sectors. The topics focus on how we think and talk about M&M as opposed to textbook M&M models and facts. Also, I have focused on topics that are challenging for an average person to understand but still relevant. These are not arcane academic debates like, "Did Keynes believe in Keynesian economics?" Finally, of course, the fact that we spin stories about macro connections that lack scientific rigor is neither new nor peculiar to Americans. For example, the Nixon Administration and current day Chinese employed/employ fallacious economics, which were/are embellished by the financial press. However, my case is that in America today we are resorting to increasingly-bogus macro rationalizing because we are struggling economically, making the faux science altogether more expedient. More pointedly, we baffle our children with M&M nonsense.

### II.14.A. General Inanity & Guesswork

Public discussion in M&M is cavalier. For example, "Sandy Seen Boosting U.S. With as Much as $240 Billion Rebuilding,"[166] proposes that a calamity (like hurricane Sandy in late October 2012) actually more than pays for itself by stimulating economic demand. Over a half dozen expert economists and their prestigious companies are cited, almost all contending the disaster results in an increase in GDP: "It's certainly a form of stimulus, no doubt, and the ripple effects of the spending could leave you further ahead than where you were at the start before the storm," says one economist from a firm that "oversees about $331 billion." Mark Zandi, a frequently-quoted economist, vacillates, "Whether construction gets GDP back above where it would have been otherwise depends on the insurance money and government aid and how people use it." Funding is assumed to come from nowhere, citing government and insurance payments as if they represent no offsetting cost. There is also a fair amount of high precision, such as economic effects continuing for 18 to 36 months. There is not one reference to a microeconomic tradeoff, e.g., that a homeowner rebuilding after the storm does so only with funds taken from other consumption. This article exemplifies how we crave M&M stories, prefer Keynesian ones, and pretend there is a science and expertise underlying our M&M prejudices.

Other examples of inanity in M&M abound, and we will only list a sample. We almost always confuse spending due to high cost as desirable because it creates demand. For example, a favorite is the comment that the economy is strong due simply and solely to people spending more because the price of gas went up. Another common yet ludicrous concept is that the economy is strong when people's borrowing has gone up, even though the borrowing was exclusively to pay for necessities like education.

---

[166] *Bloomberg.com*, by Jeff Kearns, Susanna Pak and Noah Buhayar, November 23, 2012.

Another silly story, omnipresent circa 2012 to 2013, was that the housing market, which at the time was seen as the key to macroeconomic success, was held back by a lack of supply. People were ready and wealthy enough to buy but there weren't houses for sale. The evidence was various tallies of housing market data, combined with anecdotes of people not being able to buy properties in hot housing markets. That people want to live in Silicon Valley or Manhattan but cannot find properties they can afford and/or those they do find are unacceptable to them does not imply a shortage of supply. Simply offer a higher price and supply will be forthcoming.

Perhaps the single greatest lucky break for economic output and standard of living in a society is the decrease in the cost of a basic input. In the fall of 2014 the price of oil dropped substantially. This seemingly-favorable development, however, was called into question as a detractor to GDP and its future growth. For years, as oil prices were high and oil production in the U.S. was ramping up due to new technologies for extracting oil, many media outlets touted the great positive economic effects of the rejuvenated U.S. oil industry. Some even made the additional and perverse case that high gas prices made consumers feel that the economy was strong and encouraged them to spend. Then, when prices went down the same parties described a great economic boon to the U.S., this time focusing on the extra money consumers would have to spend and how it represented a stimulus. Other analysts pointed out that recent U.S. GDP growth had been largely the result of high oil prices creating great business development in oil production.[167]

We often demonstrate a simplistic one-sidedness. During the crisis of 2008 we strove for lower interest rates, largely hoping for lower mortgage rates so that people could refinance ("refi") their mortgages and have lower payments, thus spending more on other goods. It never mattered that the refi counterparty, either a bank or other ultimate holder of mortgage debt, got less. The idea of refi's impacting aggregate consumption sounds plausible. Although some mortgage refi'ers do nothing with their windfall, some spend a little of their savings from reduced payments, and some spend a lot, yielding in total some effects. Again, the counter-party is not generally considered. The fact that mortgage holders now hold lower yielding bonds is not even considered. You might argue that it is an empirical question and researchers in the following years will analyze the data to answer the question of whether the refi's affected aggregate consumption. Even if they come to a consensus, on the next round of stimulation we will ignore it and think in terms of one-sidedness.

The episode of 2008 and following demonstrates how tough it is to discern macro. We doubted the depth of the recession. After we realized how bad it was we projected a strong recovery. We expected high inflation due to the extensive monetary accommodation. We expected low rates to foster real investment and to work primarily through the labor market, not asset markets. As events surprised we rationalized our partisan M&M leanings. Liberals mocked conservatives when inflation never turned up. Conservatives mocked liberals when the economic recovery benefited mainly only the rich. The bottom line is a M&M that is largely speculation and prejudices, which—when it comes to policy decisions—implies guesswork and hoping for the best.

Does our guessing make us engage in bad policy or just make random mistakes? For example, around 2007 to 2008 the bubble that was our housing market burst, causing grave loss and hardship. Our Fed did not foresee it, generally having analyzed housing market economics incorrectly. Suppose, though, that the Fed had recognized the bubble. Suppose Fed economists had discerned that house prices were too high in the years before 2007. What would the Fed have done? Presumably the Fed would have attempted to lower home prices gradually and given people and markets time to adjust. Or perhaps it would have tried to keep prices high, assuming that over time economic growth would catch up with and support the high

---

[167] "The Big Chill," by Randall W. Forsyth, *Barron's*, November 17, 2014, pp. 9-10.

house prices. In the first case, it would have contracted the economy. In the second, I suppose, it would have exacerbated a bubble. Who knows where we would be now if the Fed had been more perspicacious. Play those counter histories out in your head: I play them out in mine, and I always come to absurd conclusions. Here are a few examples of M&M causation, tracings of effects and other circular stories:

- A case for certain sectors having disproportional effects is common. For example, manufacturing is described, "But manufacturing's role in the economy extends beyond the factory floor. After a car rolls off the line, it gets hauled by a trucker and then sold by a dealer, each of whom gets a cut of the sale. It can begin to add up."[168] Of course, you could just as easily say, "After a consumer decides to buy a car…a car dealer has to restock his inventory…the manufacturer and trucker are hired." The initial cause is demand.

- One common circular story is GDP to jobs or jobs to GDP. Economists often bluntly state that unemployment would go down if there were greater GDP and that GDP would be greater if more people were employed.

- Another circular story is borrowing less in order to spend more later on. In recent years we commended people for deleveraging. A main result of having less debt would be that these people could then spend more and generate spending and economic growth.

- Another example where we get tongue-tied is inflation, interest rate and monetary policy. We lower rates to stimulate the economy but we worry about getting inflation, which we then will counteract by raising rates.

- We also crave high house prices and hope people buy more and more housing. Existing owners will be wealthier but new buyers will face higher prices.

- We confuse wealth and spending and their causes and effects. After years (circa 2012 through 2014) of maintaining that consumption would hold up because the stock market was rising we reversed our thinking. When the stock market started to stall, we deemed it could continue to rise due to our consumption.[169]

- In academic research we try to be more scientific. For example, we take macroeconomic macro series, such as imports and GDP, detrend the series (which means remove the average long-run trend that each series exhibits) and then regress them against each other to see which causes the other. Macroeconometricians have a variety of methods with names like ARIMA, vector autoregression, Granger Causality, etc. What if you decide the GDP causes imports and to forecast imports you solicit a forecast of GDP, only to find that GDP forecasts were made given forecasts of things like imports because some other analyst had found that imports cause GDP?

- Expenditure on education is analyzed glibly. Recently people have been borrowing greatly for college tuition. Pundits rationalize it saying that that borrowing to pay for schooling is a good investment in the future, although a much more plausible story is that education is just getting more costly.

- We love stories of big units like nations and industries, including China, Germany, housing, autos, small business, stock market, banking, import/export, currency, etc. Germany in one such big unit amenable to macro theorizing. Countless analyses in recent years[170] implore the Germans to grant largesse (through government spending presumably) and stimulate the European economy. Making

[168] *The Wall Street Journal* column by Justin Lahart, January 18, 2012, p. C1.
[169] For example, Shobhana Chandra, "The $11 Trillion Advantage That Shields U.S. From Turmoil," *Bloomberg.com*, October 14, 2014.
[170] For example, the cover of *The Economist* June 11, 2012 portrays Germany as a sinking super tanker that refuses to start its engines.

Europe stronger would in turn aid the U.S. economy, which just needed a little help. Of course, AD from the U.S. economy would carry the world as it has done for decades. The auto industry is described as having wide effect on the economy, including positively affecting home values. The housing market itself, of course (we have talked about it at length) affects other sectors—including autos. Why don't we talk about the potato chip industry? It is not a big enough economic slug.

- There is also the favorite and perverse case of the natural disaster or other major calamity as stimulative to the economy. Spending comes out of nowhere such that a disaster can increase GDP without detrimental effects. The tsunami in Japan in 2011 was described that way by many analysts. They even pegged it in time, hypothesizing that positive effects would happen in the following quarter or two.

You will argue that much of the above merely reflects journalists and pundits trying to fill daily quotas and should not be taken too seriously. You can easily find wiser M&M commentary. For example, "Storm Exacts Toll On the Economy, "[171] relates the loss of valuable output due to a calamity. Nonetheless, we are obsessive with counting amorphous GDP and with pegging timings and attributing causes and effects. Our weak thinking is not unlike historical witch hunts to which we look back with scorn.

## II.14.B. Experiencing and Comprehending the Macroeconomy

A business executive colleague was convinced the economy was strong based on his observation that the places he frequented (mainly downtown restaurants, airports, vacation destinations, major league sports events ,and other venues typically patronized by him and his business clientele) were always busy. I asked him about the cities and towns outside of the downtown area and the wealthy suburb he lived in. He confessed he had not been to such places lately, if at all—ultimately admitting that he knew little of places or situations except for wealthy towns and urban areas. People think they see the economy, but no matter how observant and well-travelled you are, this knowledge is limited and/or biased. In my own experiences, I myself am routinely surprised when I visit a new place and find it radically different economically— either boom or bust—from what I pictured. That people do not see much of the wide economic world we live in is true in the extreme for economic leaders, including policy makers, academics, Wall Street pundits, Davos attendees, etc. It is rare for them to go to the poor areas unless it is part of some orchestrated event.

I suppose the most common experience of seeing the economy is the packed mall parking lot followed by the thought, "What recession?" Another common way of "seeing the economy" is buying a house or condo and encountering high prices. People are suddenly impressed, probably falsely, that everybody is rich since real estate is so expensive. Also, it is easier to see a recovering economy than a failing one. My colleague would see the crowded restaurants and the handful of downtown construction projects, but would not see street after street of people sitting at home with mediocre jobs and bills they can keep up with less and less.

This "seeing the economy" premise complements Keynesianism. Policy advocates will almost always be able to cherry-pick facets of the economy that give the appearance of spillover of spending. An improvement in the study of M&M would be a recognition of the inability of any person to truly comprehend the state of the economy by observation. You might argue that this seeing the economy is just a natural tendency of people craving to spin stories and also a facet of media zeal to attempt to explain

---

[171] *The Wall Street Journal*, October 31, 2012.

everything. The very extremity of media stories sometimes renders them laughable. For example, "U.S. Stocks Fall After German Comments on Banking License," started, "U.S. stocks were little changed as better-than-expected earnings tempered a statement from the German finance ministry that it sees no need to give Europe's bailout fund a banking license, "[172] The articles went on to link these various factors, including explaining that the source of the German message was an email response to an inquiry.

## II.14.C. Indulging Multipliers

We talked about the two most prominent multipliers in M&M theory (the Keynesian multiplier and the money multiplier), but you also encounter multipliers on any of a variety of spending projects or endeavors—often involving a role by government. The examples are typically infrastructure projects, big events in sports and entertainment and construction of convention centers and sports stadiums.

A good example of multiplier hype due in part to the glitzy character is the funding and granting of tax exemptions by U.S. states and cities for film production. Virtually every state or city covets being a locus of movie production. The economic story is that one dollar spent by a movie maker will result in numerous multiples of other spending, typically about five times. In reality, this multiplied spending for movie making is dubious. For one, the movie production displaces other economic activity. A movie production team hires a restaurant or hair salon for the duration of its project, but the regular customers stay away subsequently reducing or skipping their spending. Second, businesses are adept at absorbing temporary increased demand for services by simple inventory adjustments, reworking of employee time off and overtime and hiring of temporary workers. Then, of course, the government often has to fund the special project and/or forfeit tax revenue.

It is easy to question significant, like five-fold, multiplier effects from spending projects. Similarly, the multiplier we use in textbooks, which is typically five to ten, is easy to doubt. Therefore, in public policy studies we talk about more modest multipliers. We rely on economists' estimates from models, ranging from a vast system of equations to back-of-the-envelope calculation. Different government agencies use different multipliers to describe their spending programs. A multiplier of 1.79 is assumed for Food Stamps by the USDA's Economic Research Service.[173] Such estimates are generally the product of models that assume feedback effects based on historical correlations among variables. They ignore other factors, like adjustments in people's behavior that change the very coefficients of the correlations and the offsetting effects of the higher taxes or debt needed to fund the spending. Such multipliers are ultimately guesses and biases.

Another aspect of spending multipliers is being one-sided. We usually assume an unexpected or unscheduled occasion, like a big event held in a city. Tourists attend with their families and spend large sums, which are assumed beyond regular spendings that happen in that area; so that they create a multiplied effect. There is no mention that the money spent gets removed from somewhere else. Similarly, we broach multipliers for new projects and initiatives, but do not generally mention reverse multipliers when the projects are halted or curtailed—nor do we bring up multipliers when we curtail projects that are unpopular or distasteful to certain people. For example, nobody talks about the anti-stimulative economic effects of gun control initiatives involving curtailing gun shows. For a specific example, in 2010 in a suburb of Boston, a dog racing track that represented a significant amount of commerce in that area was shut down by the government through a public referendum. People who complained that the closing would hurt the economy were argued down with statements like, "The laid off workers will find jobs elsewhere;"

---

[172] *Bloomberg.com* on July 31, 2012.
[173] *Wall Street Journal*, "Food Stamp Nation," September 5, 2012, p. A16.

"Other businesses will spring up;" and "The facility will be put to other use." Also, we assume a public multiplier is greater than a private one. Government spending is more prone to be described for its multiplier effects than spending done privately on some rationalization that government spending defies budget constraints over time. Perhaps America's current most fanciful multiplier is housing. Upon buying a house, people make additional home ownership-related expenditures beyond the house purchase causing ripples through the economy.

Among all the peoples of the world, Americans—at least in public discourse on economic matters—are the greatest believers in multipliers. For example, President Obama saw multipliers everywhere and at high rates, typically in high single digits. References to multipliers are omnipresent in his speeches: for example, "Every dollar we invest in high-quality early education can save more than seven dollars later on."[174]

Belief in multipliers is strong among analysts of all sorts (politicians, journalists, etc.), yet average people are not as gullible. For example, we have occasional large snowstorms that, all of a sudden, have people cleaning up and spending beyond their budgets, both government and individual. Clean up can be extensive and viewed as an employment of unused resources. Thousands of men spring to work plowing and cleaning. Yet average people are clever enough to characterize this burden as representing only costs. I have never heard a person characterize a snowstorm as a Keynesian stimulus. Rather, such events are condemned as causing loss, due to government spending that has to detract from other spending and/or requiring higher taxes. You might make counter-arguments: One, the efforts are by state and local government, not the federal government. Therefore, the spending (including borrowing for spending) cannot come out of thin air as federal spending is seen to do. A second counter-argument would be that the local calamities are too small to stimulate spending. Yet why would size matter? Also, in reality, some of the local one-time spendings are not that small. In any case, people are not fooled. Telling a guy who just bought a snow blower and pays for it by canceling some other equivalent purchase that he has increased spending and that will have substantial spillover effects will sound preposterous to him.

We see a multiplier anytime we like in any movement of money. In an article about companies buying back stock an expert (a business school dean) opines that such a transfer of cash from company to shareholders is "a good thing…probably...They're liberating capital and putting it back out into capital markets, and letting that multiplier effect kick in."[175] The company had cash and now has less, while shareholders have more cash. Presumably the latter group will use their cash in a way that creates a multiplier. The multiplier is indeed a queer concept. The premise that my spending of $1 represents more than $1 of economic output to society is misguided.

## II.14.D. Always Equally Plausible Stories

Here are some economic stories with two takes. Bolster whichever prejudice you prefer:

| Economic Event | Optimistic Interpretation | Pessimistic Interpretation |
| --- | --- | --- |
| People have increased borrowing | People are confident about the future | People are strapped for cash and must borrow to pay for necessities like higher education |
| An increase in car loans | The auto industry is thriving | People cannot afford to pay cash |

---

[174] Speech on education in Decatur, GA on February 14, 2013, http://www.whitehouse.gov/the-press-office/2013/02/14/remarks-president-early-childhood-education-decatur-ga
[175] "Firms Send Record Cash Back to Investors," *The Wall Street Journal*, March 8, 2013, p. A1, A2.

| | | for cars |
|---|---|---|
| Temporary employment is up | Improvement in the economy | Companies avoid hiring full-time |
| Debt is down | People are less levered and better able to make purchases | People are so poor their debt has been written off by lenders and no longer appears in the statistics |
| Gas prices rise | The economy is strong and people are spending more | An increase in the cost of a basic input is hurting our standard of living |
| Fewer houses are for sale | Houses are selling robustly | House prices are so unsatisfactory that people do not attempt to sell |
| Unemployment is down | More people are working | People are leaving the labor force and/or settling for sub-standard jobs |
| Increase in student loans | People have found it desirable to invest more in human capital | Basic needs like education are more costly |
| Inflation is low | Price pressure and inflation expectations are under control | Wages are stagnant |
| Dollar has risen in value | Investors are flocking to dollar denominated assets | American companies will find it harder to export |
| Increase in credit card debt | People are confident and consuming | People are broke and have to put expenses on the cuff |
| GDP growth is lower than expected | households spent less on heating cost due to mild weather | Economic growth is stalling |

In financial journalism, both sides of a macroeconomic story are usually presented, but often the story will focus on either the optimistic or pessimistic case—and the counter case is only mentioned with occasional comments or frequently just a line or two in the last paragraph.

## II.14.E. Market Movements Confirming Policy

There are so many big financial markets including stock, bond, currency and oil and many ostensible events like economic data, statements by notable people, political developments, weather, etc. The media and punditry link changes between markets and events in self-serving ways. Typically, a market rises or falls just following some news and the media wish to describe the market as confirming basic ideas of M&M, particularly that policy works. Sometimes, the market movement may reverse even though the policy or other force had not disappeared. Sometimes the market turns within a few hours or sometimes in a few days. This is true for daily market movements and for longer trends, e.g., longer-term market movements confirming long-term policy like QE's. Almost everybody is guilty of knee-jerk theorizing using the market for proof. Even business executives see what they like and crave to regale clever stories of macro cause and effect. Everybody has selective memories for failures.

Even if the market seems to move with some specific economic force we still have to be circumspect about the relationship to the economy. For example, in July 2012 after a down period for financial markets on generally weak economic news, securities markets rallied up a couple of percent. The impetus was the possibility of another round of Fed QE. Rumors of more QE had been circulating. Policy advocates interpreted the news as confirmation of the real effects of policy, i.e., that QE affected the economy since it affected the financial markets. Soon after, when the Fed announced QE3 on September 13, 2012, the market was up about 1.5% and policy advocates again praised the cause and effect. Over time QE's did track fairly closely with stock market movements, but whether that was beneficial to the economy or not is debatable.

Particularly egregious are the attitudes of political liberals, who regularly scorn and question the wisdom of Wall Street yet cite market movements as confirming the effectiveness of government economic policy. Typically, if markets rally on the day, or near in time, of an announcement of a new government policy initiative, the liberal will cite the markets. A similarly misplaced idea about confirmation of policy from market behavior concerns the willingness of private parties to buy U.S. debt. As the U.S. ran extraordinary deficits around 2009 to 2013, private parties continued to buy U.S. bonds. Yet the motivations of these buyers involved no general endorsement of the U.S. budget; instead, U.S. was simply the most suitable investment available. Also, without the large concurrent Fed buying of U.S. debt, the situation could have been different.

## II.14.F. Special Spendings: Education, Infrastructure & Defense

If you are a true Keynesian, war spending should be just as useful as any other kind for stimulating the economy, at least in the short run. War spending, however, is never touted for short-run Keynesian spillover effects. It is denounced as supplanting desirable economic spending both now and also in the long run: If we are borrowing for this spending we will have to pay for the borrowing plus interest. This contrasts with the usual Keynesian mindset that deficit spending pays for itself somehow including interest. During 2008 ff my local paper, *The Boston Globe*, which is usually a Keynesianism stalwart, mocked defense spending, pointing out leakages of such spending as stimulus and making statements like that spending on Filipino contractors in Iraq did not help our economy. The prejudice of hating war and war-mongers trumps the prejudice of Keynesian effects from government spending.

Another half-baked argument in favor of spending as stimulus concerns certain government spending as having a dual purpose of both stimulus and real social usefulness. "Infrastructure" is the perennial GDP enhancer with this dual purpose. People are naturally amenable to the idea of beneficial effects of infrastructure spending. For one, they contrast it with government spending that ostensibly is used immediately and has no lasting effects like welfare or Social Security. Also, another appeal of infrastructure is that since Americans drive motor vehicles copiously they appreciate better roads, bridges and other transportation enhancers. Also, we have a soft spot for the unemployed construction workers. They are the prototypical workers who appear ready to work, deserving of work and like heads of households. It is revealing how readily people, including highly-educated ones, see the virtuous economic contribution of a construction worker but would never perceive an equivalent contribution for work performed by a pornographer or insurance salesman as creating economic output. In reality, infrastructure projects are extraordinarily expensive. They are subject to extensive regulation, high wages (public projects are often done under rules of "prevailing wages" which stipulate high wages) and resistance from local communities. Infrastructure projects do not necessarily create many jobs, either. The experience of certain nations with large infrastructure spending, like Japan, does not support net economic benefit. Education is the other prominent type of spending with popular appeal that is it always valuable. No matter how much we already spend on education, we are averse to oppose more spending. Ultimately, infrastructure and education may have beneficial long-run economic effects but those effects might be small and far in the future.

Similarly, in state and local initiatives we will regale spending projects as having desirable economic spillover (like any construction project) yet refrain from negative spillover from projects like a crackdown on online prostitution. In 2010, internet service Craigslist dropped ads for escorts and massage services, which were deemed prostitution. No consideration was given to the contraction of spending and ensuing negative multiples of spending. In reality, in this particular market we prohibited a large group of sellers with limited ability to sell their labor from meeting a large group of buyers with discretionary income and who may not have otherwise spent their money.

## II.14.G. GDP Decomposition

GDP is our ultimate goal and our success or lack of success as a nation will surely, at least in the minds of many, hinge on how much it grows economically. There are about a dozen analyses you can make on any period's GDP growth, including mainly decomposing it into sub-components and also speculating on timing and effects of shocks. When a quarterly GDP number hits, these dozen facets can be combined and juxtaposed into just sufficient specific storylines that your commentary will not seem redundant and/or contradictory. Analysts will always sound as if they know what is happening to the economy but the raw reality is that fluctuations of GDP are largely unpredictable.

First, analysts love to sub-divide GDP into its big components. It is a tricky business and even the basic distinctions between C and I are questionable. We know that tennis balls or dining out are C and building a factory is I, but what about when a person buys a house or car? Is that C or I? What about when a company provides health club services for its workers. Is that I? Another big question is C itself. We always note that it is predominant, roughly 70% of GDP. If it comes out low we bemoan that it implies a weak economy. We look to other sectors (like trade, business spending, residential investment (housing), etc.) to see if they have held up and offset a weak C. The sub-divisions are fundamental in some important economic aspects, like timing, propensities to change, persistence or intentions and expectations. For example, an increase in housing expenditure implies a revival of a very important part of our economy according to some analysts. Given the sector theories, we can analyze further and hypothesize useful policy by taking advantage of a sector's temporary strength or weakness with policies that are, "targeted, temporary and timely." Of course, by the time we could set up an appropriate policy the relative performance of sector might likely have changed. Ultimately, if we try to explain GDP changes by looking at components, we have to admit that we do not know much more about the subcomponents of GDP than total GDP, and that reality renders many analyses useless. Here are the decompositions and their standard commentary:

- **Inventory**: Inventory is one of the most discussed components of GDP. Every economist or journalist knows that GDP growth due to the buildup of inventories by companies in any quarter may mean less GDP growth in the following quarter since the companies can draw out of inventory. Of course, maybe companies are building up inventory because demand is expanding and then the inventory buildup will not be a drag on next quarter's GDP. That inventories shape the business cycle is something we have been aware of this for a long time. It was a focal area for business cycle research since at least the 1980s. Vicissitudes of inventory quarter by quarter are no more predictive than the guesses about the general movement of GDP quarter by quarter.
- **Trade Sector Stories**: The net exports ("NX") component is exports minus imports. First, the interpretation of trade's effect on GDP is somewhat counterintuitive. That an increase in exports reflects greater domestic product makes sense but that greater imports detract from growth does not necessarily. We could be importing more due to a strong economy. Greater imports can be interpreted favorably as your consumers having great buying power due to strong value of their currency or other strength. Another confounding aspect of the NX component is that if your currency decreases in value you will export more but a lower currency means you are poorer.

- **Business Investment**: This is spending on assets like structures, equipment and software by businesses and non-profits. At one level it reflects the productive capacity of the economy so a big or increasing number is favorable. Yet, in any quarter it could reflect a mere rebuilding of depreciated assets and little net addition to productive assets. It is about 10% of GDP and is volatile. Its measurement is tough too.
- **Housing**: Housing is part of I if in the form of private residential fixed investment. Some analysts include spending on housing services when the talk about housing's contribution to GDP.
- **Durable Goods**: Economists state that a large and/or rising GDP contribution from durable goods reflects both a continuing strong GDP growth and more growth in the long term. Durable goods, is a very volatile category, however; and it is often revised significantly. Many analysts ignore it for those reasons.
- **State and Local Government Expenditure**: This can be a large contributor to GDP flux.
- **Federal Government Spending**: Federal spending is about 20% of GDP. It includes government spending on goods and services, certain forms of government investment and transfer payments. Government spending is one of the two main tools of fiscal policy. Taxation is the other.
- **Defense Spending**: Defense spending is large and can be lumpy in the sense that a lot of defense spending gets recorded in one quarter.
- **Timing Stories**: Many analysts will primarily characterize a strong or weak quarter to be followed by a weak or strong quarter simply on the speculation that a make-up for some unidentifiable anomaly is likely. This is just a guess.
- **Proximate or Dominant Events**: Single events like weather, transportation disruptions, labor actions, major new product releases, major political events, etc. can have a big impact on any one quarter's GDP. Commentators call on these to explain and rationalize the data. For example, in certain quarters in the recent past the release of new Apple iPhone versions was alleged to add significantly to GDP. One moronic commentary is that an adverse event, like a destructive storm, will add to GDP in a later quarter or explain a surge in GDP this quarter from an event in a previous quarter. We have talked about this, and in general adverse economic events do not create more output. They might cause a shifting in time of output. For example, in anticipation of a big storm people buy generators from Home Depot's and Lowe's, many of which get returned.

Perhaps the most overwhelming characterization of GDP decomposition is the absolute glory of consumer spending. For example, the 4Q 2014 GDP growth "advance" came out on January 30, 2015 at 2.6%, a little lower than experts were expecting (following a 5% GDP growth in 3Q 2014 and extreme press that the U.S. economy was very strong). *Bloomberg.com* ran a headline, "The American Consumer Is the Economy's Big Hero," with subheadings (that kept varying), "Open Those Checkbooks," "Start Spending," and "Fire Up that Credit Card," and intro lines like, "But there was one piece of great news. The U.S. consumer is really starting to show some strength. Personal Consumption Expenditures grew at 4.3 percent, the fastest pace since 2006."[176] Is it that deterministic? Our product is our consumption: What we can consume, we must equivalently be producing. To spend, therefore, is to increase our GDP. Our GDP tallying is more of a "GDC" quantity, gross domestic consumption. If GDP is consumption rather than product and its going up is just the using up of current wealth, then a growing GDP is nothing to boast.

---

[176] Author was Joseph Weisenthal.

## II.14.H. Sticky Prices & Wages

The Keynesian story hinges on the idea that as the economy contracts, prices (including wages) do not go down to clear the market, which leaves unemployed resources. If markets cleared continuously wasteful unemployment would not occur. Lower (or higher) wages would simply reflect real, structural changes constantly occurring in the economy. Short-run monetary policy in particular supposedly works because market prices exhibit frictions and markets do not continuously clear. Another term for the circumstance of sticky prices is "rigidity" or "nominal wage rigidity."

Academics claim to find pervasive and extensive price stickiness, confirming this lynchpin for Keynesian models. They cite price stickiness in sundry market pricings including the pricing of newspapers on newsstands and in mail order houses, like L.L. Bean. Yet this research is easy to counter: The markets studied are odd and minor markets where prices indeed might not move that much. Prices of various fuels (for cars and home heating), foodstuffs, electronics, automobiles, houses (for the most part), clothing, commodities, many services, tickets to events, lodging, air travel, etc. change frequently— belying stickiness. The same is true with wage stickiness. It is a subtle academic debate and economists come to different conclusions, with some analysts claiming to find extensive wage stickiness during 2008 ff.[177] The research hinges on magnitudes and on aspects of the data and measurement. Initially in the M&M debates following 2008 ff both in academia and in the press, little reference was made to sticky wages, ostensibly because wages were not sticky. In virtually every sector of the labor market some wages, and also benefits and job categories, were adjusted down in total compensation pursuant to the weakened economic conditions. Proponents claimed the theory held.

Many analysts contend that the entire idea of wage stickiness is defunct today. It is very hard to quantify a true average wage and its fluctuation due to factors like: (1) new workers hired at lower pay scales like in the auto industry; (2) temporary employment, which has increased in recent years and is often at lower wage and lower benefit; (3) people changing jobs which might actually represent disguised pay cuts; (4) increased gig employment which might represent hidden lowering of wages; and (5) migration of jobs to lower wage regions of the country. Many people maintain a job not for the wages as much as for the benefits and even for compensation as seemingly trivial as employee discounts for their employers' products (popular in retail employments). They might leave jobs because of decreases in these benefits, even if the wages appear to stick. Stickiness was more applicable when the labor market was increasingly unionized and the outsourcing of jobs less prevalent. Naysayers cite cases of pay cuts in the nations of Eurozone in recent years as evidence and also cite the drop in U.S. unemployment due to the acceptance of an extraordinary number of low paid jobs.

## II.14.I. Teeming Unfilled Jobs

Another macro story relished by business people, certain economists and many journalists is the idea of copious jobs going unfilled despite the economy being weak. It is supposed to demonstrate another grave market failure requiring government solution. Economists couch it as "coordination failures," meaning a mismatching of labor and jobs in time and place. Of course, there is some coordination failure in the economy. Some sectors of the economy and areas of the country are growing quickly and face some

---

[177] See "Cutting Wages Is hard to Do: Why That's Bad for Unemployment," by Brendan Greeley, September 18, 2014, *Bloomberg Businessweek*, www.businessweek.com/articles/2014-09-18/cutting-wages-is-hard-to-do-why-thats-bad-for-unemployment.

labor shortages. However, markets solve labor allocation efficiently, belying the need for government-sponsored crusades of immigration, education, matching, etc.

Business big-wigs love to relate the difficulty of getting sufficient qualified workers and to bemoan that "if only the government would help out with subsidies, etc." significant social improvements could be attained. They argue that their goal is not cheap labor for their companies but rather the fostering of enterprise making America better off. Brad Smith, Executive Vice President and General Counsel of Microsoft, had his chance to pronounce magnanimously, "At Microsoft, we have more than 6,000 open jobs."[178] He provides hyperbolic statistics and recommends broad government initiatives in education and sponsoring of visas for immigrants. He neglects to mention that Microsoft has billions of dollars in free cash and could probably fill its 6,000 open positions if it raised salaries a little. Nor does he solicit resumes—and don't bother to forward yours, especially if you are American and your grade point average is below 3.0. Top companies do not want most of America's talent: It is not as tractable and, ultimately, not as cheap as foreigners. Also, older workers need not apply: Retraining old workers is simply not worth it.

Stories about numerous unfilled jobs smell funny and can be offensive to people looking for work. For example, analysts talk about numerous public sector jobs like teacher's aides, but they are at wages below what most anyone will accept. Also, companies want to hire but do not want to train workers. Sometimes jobs require people that have good "interpersonal skills," which might translate to being able to do a job and deal with a difficult environment—ultimately doing a job and a half. Oftentimes jobs are advertised that simply do not exist. Companies must go through a protocol of posting open positions even though the position is already filled. When you read a story about copious jobs you have to be circumspect. For example, "There Are Plenty of Jobs Out There, America," describes an employer hard-pressed to find workers. All he is looking for is honest and friendly people, according to the journalist. The journalist writes, "…pay starts at $12 an hour and goes to $70,000 a year including overtime and bonuses." Yet, twelve dollars per hour is only about $25,000 per year so there must be lots of overtime or bonus.[179]

Teeming unfilled job stories are offensive to earnest Americans who are qualified workers and who have sent their resumes to companies (like Microsoft) only to get summarily rejected. One comical aspect is that in surveys, employers will often state that the main reason workers turn down openings is that the candidates refuse the offered wage. To a microeconomist, either the buyer should pay a higher price or the seller should admit that he does not want the product. In other cases, the jobs that go unfilled have not had pay increases for years. This issue highlights a general fallacy of macro takes on our economy. We love to feign macro stories and solutions even if the micro decisions belie the problem.

## II.14.J. Search for High MPC

For stimulative policy to do its job, the money put into the economy must get into the hands of those with the tendency to spend it: those with high MPC's. We relate a variety of standard stories of search for high MPC. Getting money to the spendthrift of course might seem like a stupid idea in an economy with too much debt already. If you are a Keynesian, however, it is valid. Monetary policy also presents a basic play on relative MPC's. If we "lower the rates" then it should hurt creditors (i.e, savers) and help debtors (i.e., spenders), resulting in a higher overall MPC.

We believe poor people will spend newly-acquired money more than the rich, so we direct tax cuts and tax rebates to the poor. Following 2008 our tax cuts (like the Social Security tax cut) favored the low

---

[178] Op-ed in *The Wall Street Journal*, October 19, 2012, p. A13, "How to Reduce America's Talent Deficit."
[179] "There Are Plenty of Jobs Out There, America," by Peter Coy and Matthew Philips, *Bloomberg.com*, December 15, 2016. https://www.bloomberg.com/news/articles/2016-12-15/there-are-plenty-of-jobs-out-there-america

income population. Simultaneously though, we heard that luxury spending was holding up. There were endless stories circa 2010 to 2011 about high-end retailers flourishing so we theorized that rich people were spending. Journalists are creative in describing a wide variety of household spending group that vary by income or sometimes type of household. Journalists hopped onto the concept of the "aspirational" consumer who was a lower income person or household becoming wealthy. This type would buy a lot. Sometimes we reverse the idea to make a positive case for saving. A beneficial aspect of increased income inequality is that the rich have a lower MPC, which means that more money in their hands means more savings. In reality, varying average MPC's across groups may be valid statistically but the link between MPC's and beneficial effects of either spending or saving is capricious. Certainly, varying marginal propensities exist: If you give a dollar to a poor person he or she will spend it (MPC = 1); and for a rich person, save it (MPC =0); and in-between people might exist but we cannot play them with policy for greater output. In the U.S. we have over 100 million households, each with its own MPC which is a product of the great multitude of microeconomic forces households face.

That poor people have a high MPC is a pillar of AD economics. Although economists will contend it is a scientific fact to be used solely for requisite policy there is something very condescending and immoral about using poor people as a vessel to increase spending in society.

MPC stories related to housing abound. The main line is that people buying a house and/or getting a new or refinanced mortgage simply spend more. Various extensions of housing related propensities were prominent in the post-2008 period. Young people were not buying homes at the same rate as before, which translated to a disproportionate effect on housing spending in the future because today's young buyers would be the ones who would later buy bigger houses and furnishings to go with them. Therefore, house prices would remain low—which was adverse for the economy because current homeowners would not feel wealthier. There were a multitude of musings about households defaulting on mortgage payments and whether it added or subtracted from the economy as a whole. Either these households would not spend on home-related goods and services or being free of big mortgages they would spend more on other goods. We also speculated about the MPC of the Chinese consumer, mainly bemoaning that Chinese save too much. We also talked about the shares of our national income shifting greatly from workers (through wages) to businesses (through profits) and we pondered the varying MPC's of workers versus the Marginal Propensity to Invest of business. Which would result in more output?

## II.14.K. New Industries & Demand from Emerging Economies

People frequently argue that our GDP must continue to grow for two incontrovertible reasons: (1) New industries and (2) increased demand at the global level since emerging markets are growing. Both big sources of demand seem plausible. Indeed, if you look at America's prosperity over the last 30 years, it was largely driven by transformational industries, including high tech, health care, real estate, education and finance. If you are currently middle-aged and upper middle class, most likely the majority of your friends found employment in those industries and became America's economically successful group. They were not completely new industries, of course; but they did surge in size and job opportunities as if they were whole new industries. Today these industries have peaked and are even declining in some respects. Analysts deduce that there must be similar new industry movers. They cite environmentally-related sectors, new types of power generation, biotech, 3-D printing, nanotechnology, big data, cloud computing, space exploration/tourism and internet-driven companies like Uber. The assumption is that these new industries will have copious, high-wage employment.

A tenuous case can be made. A new breed of companies and industries will not capture the large monopoly rents the way companies like Microsoft, Oracle, Apple, Merck, Cisco, Goldman Sachs, Federal

Express, JP Morgan, EMC, Intel, etc. did in the 1980s and following. The other lynchpin of never-ending demand for our economy's output is a growing world economy. High costs and stagnant demand in America do not matter because companies like McDonald's, Johnson & Johnson and IBM can sell to the big growing economies like those of China, Brazil, India, Mexico, South Africa, etc. This is also dubious. First of all, world economic growth may not be that strong. Second, the profits from enterprise abroad will not accrue to Americans since the production will be done abroad. Finally, high world economic growth is already factored into our valuations of companies (for example, we assume revenues grow greatly) such that stock values of those companies are elevated.

## II.14.L. Household Budget Analogy As Invalid to National Economies

In every textbook and on the lips of many—both expert and amateur—is the conviction that a national economy does not have to balance a budget the way a household must; nay, balancing a budget for a nation is detrimental. This basic budget reality of your life does not apply to a country. Some analysts view a country's economy as prone to underemployment of resources. Therefore, deficits create increased demand which enhances output. This is the Keynesian story: If a person were spending $100,000 a year but only bringing in $90,000 of income, reducing spending to $90,000 would create no adverse feedback to earnings. The person would be solvent going forward. If we are spending $100 billion in a national economy but only taxing $90 billion and then cut our spending to $90 billion, we assume a drop in national income causing taxes to go down to, say, $88 billion; so we still running a deficit. Depending how much of a believer in Keynesianism you are, the counter-productive effects of trying to balance the national budget might be severe. Therefore, the national budget constraint does not matter. Another argument that governments can run deficits year after year is that as long as the economy grows, debt can grow along with it. People, including many economics' instructors, will out of hand accept the idea that the government need not balance a budget based on these growing economy stories.

Of course a country, like a household, can run a deficit year after year and become less in debt as a percentage of national income, or household income if incomes are growing. Furthermore, in a long period of growing economies and populations like the last hundred years, there can be the appearance that deficit spending does not matter. Most countries are already and have for a long time been running deficits at rates equal to or greater than their growth rates, however. Their debts have risen. As for Keynesian effects, these may have been minimal over time. In the last few decades many nations have given the appearance of being impervious to debt and, therefore, budget constraints; but at some point the budget constraint must be met. The household analogy looked valid as the economic crisis in Greece played out over the years following about 2010.

## II.14.M. Non-Distinctions We Love to Regale

For a while we grumbled that America was no longer a great manufacturer of the classic industrial goods like steel, autos, tires, televisions, etc. We got over manufacturing perhaps in the 1980s when we tuned in to being a producer of many and superior services—including software, film, financial services, design services, consulting, etc.—and theorized about which type of output was more valuable or more fruitful to create jobs. Most recently, we have talked up our need for more manufacturing, with government assistant in the form of tax relief for manufacturers.

Does it really matter which goods a nation produces? Manufactured goods give the appearance of being exportable. Services appear more reflective of brain power though, and we relish the idea that we are producers of services. Part of the distinction is merely definitional, however, since certain items (like defense hardware) are classified as services. Some industries seem to have extensive spillover effects too, like technology. During the Reagan Administration some countered that it did not matter whether we made computer chips, wood chips, or potato chips.[180] Competitive markets would determine the mix of goods produced and any good could have as much spillover as any other. Many analysts disagreed, assuming that high tech (computer chips) is superior to low tech (potato chips) and most politicians would side with high tech. Government economic policies are not concerted in which areas we support though. For example, our recent M&M efforts have largely involved aiding the housing market, which is low tech.

## II.14.N. Timing

We talked about the desperation and silliness of the Medium Term concept in M&M and will describe it at length below. Also we described how policy effects happen instantly through financial market reactions that involve large repricing of large asset values. These immediate effects of policy timing undermine the entire textbook and way leading economists view and describe the economy. In general, timing will confound the M&M armchair economist every time. Talking heads relate copious stories of M&M cause and effect. They play out logically but more often than not specified time frames do not hold. Even more extreme, the forces reverse within the specified time frame. This is grotesquely demonstrated with commentary on daily or weekly stock market movements. For example, a big increase in the stock market is attributed with a certain macro cause, yet the market reverses and the macro cause is still present. For a real example, circa May and June 2012 there were expectations of new stimulus by the U.S. Fed and markets soared. Markets turned though, but the stimulus talk and hope continued. Simply put, we cannot discern the effects of day-to-day news on markets and economies. Also, of course, we can foresee the longer future or even be sure of where the economy will be in a month. Large changes in GDP, inflation, etc. happen abruptly. Even the most privy economists—including central bank heads—await the last data point to decide what to think about the economy and which policy steps to take.

To reiterate a point we have made before, the gravest folly is our vacillation about the idea of short run and long run. Policy is supposed to have effects in the short run, but in the long run the demand-induced effects of policy will not matter. In the jargon we say, "policy does not affect long-run supply" or "money is neutral in the long run." According to traditional theoretical and empirical ideas of M&M the short run could be months or quarters, maybe a year or two, but should not persist more than a couple of years. In textbooks and popular discussion, this timing story is altogether facile. Some policy initiatives seemingly take much too long, like those following the 1990 to 1991 recession, yet they are still touted as effective. Others seem to have an immediate effect. Typically, for example, the Fed lower interest rates and the stock and bond markets rally over the next few days or weeks and analysts conclude policy had effects. These cases could not represent normal monetary policy transmission but only psychological effects and expectations. The convenient aspect of policy timing is that no matter how long policy seems to take, policy believers characterize that amount of time as consistent with what they call the short run. For journalists, the rule for the timing of policy is most glib. If you write a column touting policy's effects and they seem to be happening presently, then the short run is immediate. If you wrote a column six months ago yet the expected economic effects have not transpired, then you say policy's effects should take more than six months. If it looks as though policy is taking years, then policy, "…sometimes takes years."

Since policy frequently does not seem to work in the short run and we are reluctant to say that it works in the long run—and given the craving by some to believe in the relevance of policy, proponents have improvised the Medium Term. This concept is a canard, yet experts rationalize as follows: "I doubt

---

[180] Reagan's economic advisor Stanford professor Michael Boskin made this case.

the policy we are doing will work in the short run. I cannot contend it will work in the long run, or else I will be at odds with consensus opinion about markets. But gosh darn it, I have been explaining policy effects to so many people for such a long time, and the existence of effects constitute my very reason for being. Ergo, 'Policy effects should turn up in the Medium Term.'" Some of those who pretend to be so rigorous and sage, like economist Nouriel Roubini and the editors of *The Economist*, adore the Medium Term.[181]

## II.14.O. All You Need Is Demand

We have been trained to believe that demand dominates economic processes and trends, and that ultimately our standard of living depends on our desire to have goods and services. Such demand thinking permeates our press and the opinions of many business leaders. For example, a big money manager is confident about our economic future, "In your life, you do four things that cause everyone else around you to do better economically, that are more impactful on the economy than anything else: you get married, have children, you buy bigger cars to accommodate the children and you buy a house. We're about to have 86 million people do those things constantly for the next 10 years, and that's why the U.S. economy will do extremely well."[182] Just that people exist and want goods and services does not mean they can afford them and/or will put forth the economic effort to attain them. As a counter case there are already many more than 86 million households in Africa that have the same cravings as Americans yet whether they create any economic output depends on their underlying productivity and enterprise.

We are pathological in our persistence in viewing any expense as demand and not cost. There are countless examples:

- A most grotesque demand story is that a disaster stimulates the economy. Following a calamity, people must replace their losses including houses, cars, public facilities, etc. The funding is assumed to come out of thin air, including from insurance, which is perceived of as free. In reality, the spending displaces other spending.
- People will always need housing so the housing market and related sectors (like furniture, home repair supplies, etc.) must flourish. High house prices reflect more demand and future demand.
- The buying of a house also creates more demand because once you have purchased a home you must furnish and repair it.
- We will bring outsourced jobs home, the business economist says, because Americans will not tolerate phone people with imperfect English. Customers demand better service and business must supply it regardless of cost.
- Stocks must go up because the world economy is growing—especially the emerging societies like Brazil and China, and their demand must be met by companies. Those companies must, therefore, make more profit.
- Another "demand dominates" rationalization invokes new inventions of goods and services. Our future will be replete with new products that people will crave, like virtual goggles, space travel or home 3D printing. The argument goes that their very existence will compel people to work to buy them. That argument should apply to the present, however. Any non-rich household desires any of

---

[181] I recognize that economists do have specific definitions of Medium Term both in academic work and in empirical models but commentators who invoke the Medium Term in public discussion are not referring to any specific concept. They are merely being vague about timing effects.

[182] "Fund Manager Has Faith in Millennials," Q&A with money manager William Smead, *Wall Street Journal*, April 4, 2016.

a wide variety of already existing products like the latest smartphone, a luxury automobile or a high-end range. Most any household could attain more goods and services if they worked sufficiently to get them but the household have already precluded making that sacrifice.

- Media renditions of economic impacts of any phenomenon focus on demand effects. For example, an article about the drop in U.S. fertility is seen mainly as a factor decreasing demand and, therefore, reducing national income. Simply put, people buy less of myriad items (including diapers and pregnancy test kits) if they have fewer children. There is really no mention that these outlays are costs. It even contains estimates of how much GDP will decrease due to less spending. Of course, causality may likely be the other way: We have less real output/income and, therefore, cannot afford children.

- Another droll aspect of the macro talk is how we call on each nation to pull the other with demand. U.S. demand carries other countries' economies, and we scold nations that are not spending as much as we think they should to reciprocate. Economists and laypersons cite this cross-national stimulation constantly as if it represents some net gain for the world as a whole or some policy tool that can be taken advantage of by savvy finance ministers of nations.[183] At any point in time, of course, if one nation starts spending more it will affect its trading partners but over time each nation must attend only to its own economy.

- The concept of pent-up demand is another mysterious force. A drop in consumption must lead to more demand later in time to make up for delayed consumption. For example, we are told that average age of a car has increased; therefore, people must buy new cars. Analysts compare aggregate motor vehicles from a prior period (like before 2008) to a later period (like now) and assume sales must tend back to that level. Microeconomic factors—like fewer young people getting drivers licenses, people moving back to cities, older people choosing one car per household, etc.— paint a different story.

## II.14.P. Say's Law

Say's Law is named after French economist Jean-Baptiste Say (1767 to 1832). It is the observation that production will be consumed, i.e., that economic activity comes from production rather than from demand. This is similar to supply-side economics and suits the ideology of conservatives, those who advocate thrift and production and who doubt Keynesian effects. Under Say's, the act of people saving is desirable. Under Keynesianism, it generally is not.

Most M&M instruction and the majority of economists and other commentators like journalists relegate Say's Law to odd and impractical situations. They often broach it only to claim it is invalid. Then they readily explain that the economy is demand-driven and that we must encourage people to borrow and spend. We do not have to worry about accumulating savings because spending will create more income in the future from which we can save. Some economists will couch the issue in terms of timing, contending that in a short run or medium term it is indeed demand, but in the long run or course, savings to create enterprise to increase production matters the most. They will contend, though, that we are generally not in that long run.

Initially, in the policy responses to the crisis of 2008, Eurozone took more of a Say's Law approach while the U.S. was more Keynesian. This represents a strange reversal of roles since at one time the U.S. was more supply-side oriented. Eurozone seems to have tended more toward Keynesianism in the years 2014 and following.

---

[183] "With Fiscal Policy, Canada Does Global Economy a Favor," by Greg Ip, *The Wall Street Journal*, April 21, 2016, p. A2.

## II.14.Q. Paucity of M&M Observations

If you wax philosophical about current M&M issues with the intent to foresee where we are going, how many historical cases can confirm your ideas? In social science-speak, we could say how many "obs" are in the dataset? The answer might be very few. You might protest: We have hundreds of years of macro data, which include ten or more business cycle episodes. We also have a list of crisis events and policy responses that is quite lengthy, especially if you include foreign cases. Alas, the historical cases are very hard to draw conclusions from. As we have pointed out before, the level of debt and the number of large nations that have mortgaged their futures on great economic growth and high assets returns is unlike any situation the world has ever seen.

The way we analyze the past in economic debates is often facile and breaks on partisan lines. For example, we know that our central bank did not perform well during the Great Depression. In particular, we agree on certain big blunders, like raising the reserve requirement in 1937 just after obtaining legal authority for that tool. There were myriad events during that ten-year period, however, and the causations and magnitudes are hard to judge and ultimately any story can be told. Keynesians will say that Hoover contracted spending and Roosevelt increased it. Indeed the economy responded but not enough—until World War II spending provided the requisite stimulus. Conservatives will argue that Hoover spent more than Roosevelt and that the economy was rectifying itself except that continued poor Fed policy prolonged the Depression.

If you ask egghead economists, we have three major M&M episodes: (1) the Great Depression, (2) stagflation of the 1970s and (3) (the new one) the financial crisis of 2008. The main lesson(s) of 2008 are still undetermined and could be hyperbolic. Either government policy works and the unregulated economy fails or governments destroy capitalism and economies with printing of money. M&M economists also invoke a wider variety of case studies. Here is a list of major M&M events, some are so well-known that any armchair economist would broach them while others are more academic:

- **Crisis of 1907**: 1907 was one of a series of economic collapses that the U.S. had been facing over the 1800s and early 1900s but it was severe and finally (supposedly) demonstrated the necessity of a central bank. Like the Great Depression, the lessons are subject to interpretation. Some analysts contend that banker J.P. Morgan (the man), by his sheer financial reputation, acted like a central bank and, indeed, without his forceful role the economy would have floundered for years. Other analysts make the case that 1907 was not unlike any other downtown from that era. Its affects were not nationwide and markets would have rectified themselves with the usual wringing out of inefficient businesses but probably nothing more severe. It was followed by a prompt economic recovery which would have happened sans Mr. Morgan.

- **The Great Depression**: This is used as the justification for today's monetary policy: In 2008 government policy makers did not make the same mistakes as were made in the 1930s, supposedly, and therefore we avoided another depression. This is a dubious contrast. The episodes are not easily comparable. Also, the premise that Ben Bernanke was an outstanding scholar of the Depression and therefore the right person at the right time making the perfect moves is also dubious. Thousands of economists are equally versed in the Depression, which has a number of sub-episodes—perhaps the most concerted of which is 1937 when the government cut back its deficit and doubled reserve requirements. These were both contractionary policies that some analysts contend aborted recovery from the initial recession (from 1929 to 1932) that started the Great Depression. Other scholars explain the Depression with other factors including international forces, real shocks like drought, a build-up of excess credit from the 1920s (partly from bad central bank policy), etc. The Depression is inscrutable.

- **High Government Debt-to-GDP Ratio at Conclusion of World War II**: The adverse debt situation after the big was is broached by government debt deniers as an example of how a society can flourish with high debt and how it can bring debt down promptly. These analysts compare that time to today. Our debt-to-GDP ratio is about the same now as it was in 1945, but circumstances are very different today. Following the War we set on a program to pay down government debt given a one-time expense. We followed our debt reduction diligently. We saved to pay down debt. Our economy was uniquely strong and well-positioned in the world at that time. Our ethic was different too. People during and following World War II bought U.S. bonds as a patriotic duty; we have nothing like that today. Today, we revel in spending that we contend actually saves us money through stimulative effects. Our budget shortfalls today represent the near equivalent of continual war.

- **Large Drop in Government Spending Post-World War II**: This spending contraction seemingly did not affect the economy adversely as a Keynesian AD and multiplier story would imply. People who do not believe in the effects of spending policy enjoy citing this example.

- **1970s Stagflation**: Active policy in a low growth economy resulted in inflation concurrent with stagnation (hence the term stagflation). The economy experienced a major supply shock in the form of increased oil prices and also accommodation monetary policy. Policy makers at the time overestimated GDP growth rates. Although the recession of the mid-1970s was as severe or worse than that of 2008 in many respects (including big rises in unemployment and inflation, a drop in aggregate consumption and a drop in the stock market), parallels between the two are rarely made.

- **Reduction of Inflation Engineered by Fed Chairman Paul Volcker from 1981 to 1984**: This is widely-touted as an example of the ready capability of our central bank to control inflation. Again, though, circumstances were different. Many economic factors like oil prices, the value of the stock market and population dynamics were favorable in the early 1980s. Also, the inflation fight of the early 1980s did not succeed without a severe recession, i.e., great cost. Indeed, we have merely a single observation of vanquishing inflation in America in modern times, yet we cite it today without reservation as proof we can control inflation. Another facet of this episode in monetary policy is the length of time of monetary policy effects. Rates were raised significantly (about 10% from September 1980 to January 1981) and the economy contracted promptly (July 1981 to November 1982). Then rates were lowered significantly (about 10% from July 1981 to November 1982) and the economy expanded promptly (1983 and following). This contrasts with the protracted policy effects surrounding the recession of 2008.

- **Japan Post-1990:** The bursting of stock and real estate bubbles in Japan was followed by a long period of low GDP growth. This is used as a great example of failure to do right policy, and this case is cited to the point of cliché. We talk about lost decade(s) of Japan's economy and will discuss Japan in more detail below.

- **Fed Raising of Rates in 1994**: After five years of no action by the Fed, it raised rates, supposedly to rein in a potentially overly-hot economy. Coming into 1994, the effective fed funds rate had been around 3% for a number of years. By the end of 1994, it was about 5.5%. The bond market sold off, and the stock market was flat for the year. People who qualified for a certain level of a mortgage in early 1994, found that a few months later, given the rise in rates, they no longer qualified. Was this prudent policy to halt incipient inflation or completely unneeded policy because the underlying economy was not "overheated" but simply strong?

- **The Asian Crisis 1997**: Due to poor national economic policies Asian economies over expanded—then crashed. The West, including the major nations and organizations like the International Monetary Fund, compelled the Asian nations to an austerity solution of balancing budgets and restructuring their economies in fundamental ways, including writing down their assets. Reforms started about 1998 and did result in sounder fiscal houses for the Asian countries, e.g., low debt-to-GDP rations; yet the Asian nations themselves believed they were treated with undue harshness. When the Western nations faced a similar crisis in 2008 they mostly, including the IMF, did not call for austerity among themselves. To some extent Eurozone engaged in some degree of austerity but generally Western nations chose accommodation when facing their problems.
- **Market turmoil of 1998**: During the summer of 1998 the Russian government defaulted on its sovereign debt. Later this summer large hedge fund Long-Term Capital Management collapsed. Later in the year the Fed lowered rates. At one time, this 1998 episode was the most compelling example of successful crisis monetary policy, but it did not stand up to scrutiny in many ways. The Fed policy came after the two major crises had played out in markets. The 1998 story is now obsolete.
- **The Conundrum**: Over the period 2004 to 2006, the Fed raised the fed funds rate by 4.25%, but long-term yields did not go up. There are multiple interpretations. Mainly it demonstrated that policy did not work. Policy proponents, however, turned this policy failure to their side by contending it was a solitary failure in a long history of policy successes. Other analysts offered explanations like a global savings glut and more predictable markets and policy. The Conundrum, which was relatively prominent as a focal point of monetary theory, has been mostly been forgotten. Like many other M&M facets, it was overwhelmed by the events following 2008.

There are other contemporary examples of M&M crisis and resolution, but they lack heft and staying power in intellectual discussions. The Swedish banking crisis of the early 1990s was a favorite frequently cited as proving some point or another early in the 2008 recession. It was then dropped as too minor and too specialized for the current events.

Collectively, what do these historical cases tell us about today? You can interpret them to suit your belief—either Keynesian/government or free market/policy doubter. A Keynesian would compare our concerted policy actions in 2008 ff to the blunders of the Depression, describe the chronic low growth of Japan and tout the easy control of inflation by citing the actions of Paul Volcker. The policy doubter would cite the stagnation of the 1970s, claim that J.P. Morgan was only saving his and his friends' money and that the real economy was fine in 1907, say that the policy of 1998 was irrelevant to the success of the economy that year and characterize the policies pursuant to 2008 as creating a poor recovery. Here are a few more comments about our history of M&M:

- Beware the major blustery pronouncements concerning our ability to rectify contemporary economic problems like inflation and debt. We contend we can easily control inflation by raising rates like we did in the early 1980s. Some of us also contend that we can easily manage our debt just as we drew down debt after World War II.
- The multitude of observations from long ago are not too compelling, including especially the data from the 1800s. As time goes by we have to weight old cases less and less. For example, the recessions of the 1950s are of minimal instructive value. Our post-World War II business cycle history has numerous little business cycles, as you might see in any time series picture in a textbook, and three whoppers: 1973 to 74, 1982 and 2008.

- We bemoan that macro analysts use data only going back to about 1980, or 1950 at the earliest. Some economists make this case and analyze longer history but episodes from before modern times are less compelling. For one thing, government was much smaller in the economy; for another, asset wealth was a much more minor aspect of economic activity.

- Parallels of the Great Depression to today are tenuous. The. U.S. had small government, a growing industrial economy and altogether different labor and retirement dynamics. Monetary policy was different too. Ben Bernanke would typically compare 2008 and the Great Depression without much reservation, basically contending that our policy did not leave our economy as bad as it was in the Depression and therefore current policy worked. This is simplistic.

- As we pointed out in the section on inflation, the U.S. macro history since about 1960 breaks into two major episodes demarcated by inflation: (1) rising inflation from the later 1960s until the early 1980s; and (2) declining inflation for the next thirty years. Essentially, we have two observations. For example, asset prices went up over the 1980s through the 2000s largely because inflation went down.

- There are a sufficient number of major unique economic factors that exist now and going forward such that that past cases are not very helpful to judge modern times. We have billions engaging in capitalism, populations declining, capital and labor moving easily across borders, major nations in debt, resource constraints, etc. We have zero historical observations of a large country with a large government sector and a large level of debt that is experiencing a decline in population.

- In general, countries that manage their debt are more successful economically than countries with growing debt. There are few examples of countries running big deb and prevailing. It is difficult to make finalist statements, of course. The last third of the 20$^{th}$ century was largely marked by constant increase of debt for many countries including the U.S. and Great Britain and they seemingly prevailed. As we have pointed out before, the world is suddenly a more highly and pervasively indebted place than ever before.

## II.14.R. Aspiring M&M: Japan, China and Most of the Rest of the World

After World War II many analysts predicted that Japan would be an economic basket case, but the nation was extremely successful economically in total GDP, GDP growth rates, per capita GDP, assets prices of housing and stocks, industrialization, corporate growth, international trade, consumption, etc. It dominated many industries and, at one point in the 1980s, was projected by many pundits to overtake the U.S. as the leading economic power. Come around 1990 though, its economic growth slowed dramatically. Japan's economy had ostensibly matured. It stood as a country with a stagnant and aging population and lacking basic natural resources but with a high standard of living and excellent in many industries, education and health care. It continued to grow a little each year on a per capita basis. Due to the lack of raw economic growth, however, analysts for the next 20 years would describe the nation, including its M&M policy, as a constant failure. To say "Japan in the 1990s" and "lost decade" was unquestioned, and even to say Japan continued to struggle in the 2000s was generally not argued with. In policy circles the conclusion has been simple: Japan did poor M&M policy and lost substantial economic output. We, meaning the U.S. and other western countries, did policy right—or at least better; and we use Japan as proof of ineffective policy. The irony is that taking into consideration Japan's declining population, aversion to immigration and certain cultural preferences to protect industries, they have not done that poorly compared to the U.S. or Eurozone.

Policy advocates maintained that Japan could have had greater growth if it had had active policy. Simply put, the nation did not do enough government spending or monetary accommodation and therefore lost much GDP. Opponents counter that the Japanese economy faced structural and not cyclical forces; therefore, policy would not have helped. It is difficult to say for sure. First, the Japanese did do extensive fiscal and monetary policy, and they have increased their government debt to one of the greatest levels in the world. Second, as noted above, their economy did not perform that poorly. For example, the nation has always maintained low unemployment and low inflation. Today, we do not know what to make of Japan's permanent low growth except to assert that our growth is higher and that our economy will not follow the path of Japan's.

You will find virtually no defense of Japanese economic policies. Japan utilizes a variety of economic statism in which the government supervises the economy favoring certain industries and economic relationships between companies, government and workers. We criticize their inefficiency and anti-competitive ways in various industries like agriculture, but we also have a bloated state with waste and bad incentives in housing, defense and finance. We have always derided Japan's anti-immigrant policy, yet we never ponder that it may have been a relatively successful policy. Japan ranks high on wealth measures, generally higher than the U.S. Japan's real per capita GDP growth over the recent past tracks closely with that of the U.S., belying Japan's stagnation. There is a period in the 1990s where Japan performed less well than the U.S. but in the late 1980s it did better, yielding a rough equivalence for the period 1980 to the present. Japan's asset valuations, both stock and housing values, performed poorly. To a large extent we view that as the evidence of Japanese failure, but apparently it has not detracted from Japanese ability to generate high incomes.

The current issue with Japan is its debt, which is among the highest in the world. Yet the Japanese have one advantage over us in terms of indebtedness: Indeed they "owe it to themselves." Japanese people and companies buy the bonds. They need the large yen-denominated pool of savings. Therefore, the Japanese government can rely on holders to stay put even in the face of low returns and possible write-downs. Also, the Japanese may have room to raise their taxes, which are low by some measures, to pay their debt down. Another irony of us v. them in M&M policy is our perception of policy superiority. For example, when we embarked on QE policies, we looked to the experience of Japan, who preceded us in such unconventional policies. In the final FOMC meeting of 2008 (December 15-16), when the basic policy rate had been lowered to near zero and the FOMC was discussing the start of QE, references to Japan's recent policy history were perhaps the most common theme of that meeting. FOMC members were seemingly chagrined at the comparison of America with the nation widely deemed to have failed in monetary policy. Americans were confident our policy would prevail, however. In general, we contend that they did a weak kind of QE and ours was better designed and directed toward sectors that would produce efficacious policy.

Starting in early 2013, Japan embarked on a major multi-trillion dollar economic policy known as Abenomics. It involved three thrusts (they were referred to as arrows in the press): (1) monetary, (2) fiscal, and (3) structural policies. This was widely-touted as the right action to take (i.e., for the government to be pro-active) and was also viewed as vindication of western policies—in other words, the Japanese finally got wise and did sensible policy as we had done. Japan was previously pathologically conservative. Abenomics had sundry effects, and evaluations broke on partisan lines. The Japanese stock market surged, confirming the policy but then pulled back. Naysayers contended that the initial surge was just investors trying to make a buck off of the policy. Japanese exporters did better given the reduced value of the yen, but domestic and small companies apparently did not do any better. Japan saw some higher inflation, which was one of the goals; but naysayers racked it up to higher costs of imported energy and other imported commodities from the reduction in the yen. The policy did not engender any great internal investment nor did it raise real wages. Some supporters blamed the overall effects on failure to perform the structural changes prong.

Our attitude toward policy by Asian countries is part of a general belief that, in any open competition, we beat "them." We are more clever and protective of our long-run well-being, reaffirming our role as the entrepreneurs and able policy makers. One thing is certainly true, we (meaning the U.S.) scold them (meaning China, Japan and others like Germany) for doing wrong policy more than they scold us. We in the West often characterize their policy decisions as reactionary and blatantly political, unlike our own—which are intelligent and deliberate. For example, in August 2015 when Chinese markets were falling, opinion was that the Chinese were doing quick policy action to save face for an upcoming 70th World War II parade and celebration.[184]

Chinese monetary and economic policy is inscrutable. It is not clear what their overriding economic goals are, and their economic challenges are vast. They have succeeded in raising the standard of living of many people greatly. How much they trade off the economic well-being of their entire populace versus the success of certain areas and sectors is unclear—as is their willingness to sacrifice economic growth for geopolitical goals. In monetary policy, they use every conceivable device, including managing their currency, reserve requirements, overnight lending rate, directed lending programs, market support including stock market support, both public and tacit jawboning, etc. They engage in extensive government spending throughout their economic system, some of which is designed as fiscal stimulation but other of which is cronyism.

## II.14.S. Partisan Economics & Austrian v. Keynesian

One major partisan story that comes out of the 2008 crisis and post-crisis policy is the failure of inflation to appear despite the accommodative monetary policies. Rights-wingers of all stripes prophesized rampant inflation which never materialized, and they have been mocked by liberals for such an inaccurate call.[185] A greater partisanship embarrassment of the post-2008 economic debate can be leveled at liberals. The liberal side got stuck defending America's economic performance, which—despite extensive fiscal and monetary policy—ostensibly resulted in mainly a massive transfer of wealth to the rich from the poor. Stimulative policy produced minimal economic investment that benefitted the average working person. There was little wage growth. House prices went up but mainly in wealthier locations. The stock market rose, yet that also disproportionally benefitted the rich. Policy effects of lower rates caused businesses to substitute capital in favor of labor and labor's fraction of national income dropped significantly. Commodities prices went up—also largely due to policy, and the rising costs of items like food and oil hurt average people. Liberals defended it all claiming that asset price increases had favorable spillover effects. This rationale was similar to the rationale of supply-side economics of the 1980s that a rising tide lifts all ships. In the early 1980s it was termed "trickle down" and that term has been derided by liberals for decades up until about 2012 when the current recovery hinged on trickle-down.

Liberals had to defend the policy because it occurred under a Democratic administration. If John McCain had become President in 2009 (and was subsequently re-elected) and had done roughly the same M&M policy, the judgment would have been different. Indeed, a Republican administration would probably have enacted similar policies of spending programs, tax cuts, support of Fed actions, support of

---

[184] "China Intervened Today to Shore Up Stocks Ahead of Military Parade," *Bloomberg News*, August 27, 2015. The article cites two "authorities" who are not identified as confirming that, indeed, the government did monetary policy to look good for the parade.

[185] For example, we mentioned the "Open Letter to Ben Bernanke" (November 15, 2010, *The Wall Street Journal*) written by leading conservatives and prophesizing big inflation.

regulation (in some form, probably not as extensive as Dodd-Frank yet still substantial), etc. Prominent policy advocates and the media, however, who generally maintained positive reviews of the economy's response to government M&M policy, would have denounced a Republican Administration for the deficits, largess granted to Wall Street, inferior jobs created, etc. They would have made constant comparisons of the poor recovery relative to previous recoveries. The media would likely have created numerous new indicators of economic misery of the populace and outlets like *The New York Times* and CNN would have had regular presentations of new economic misery measurements like "The Labor Force Degeneration Index" and "The Housing Negative Equity Level."

One popular partisan economic demonstration is the contemporaneous comparison of economic performance with the party in power (usually as determined by the sitting President). Analysts tally GDP growth, unemployment, inflation, stock market performance, etc. and compare terms. For example, using averages over 1993 to 2000 to judge performance of Democrats since President Clinton was in office then President Carter comes out a big underperformer. President Reagan, despite the usual claim of economic success during his times, does fairly well; but not as well as President Clinton. Clinton is the best data point showing that Democrats do a better job with the economy.[186] This exercise is a favorite of Lawrence Summers, Paul Krugman and Alan Blinder. Of course, it is semi-ridiculous: If anything, the analysis should be lagged by either a short period like two years or even a longer period like two decades. Any President's policies would take at least a couple of years to implement and take effect and would also persist for some many years after leaving office. For example, assigning Clinton 1995 to 2002 would detract from his performance averages. Moreover, though, we can easily make the case that spurred growth in one period can be taken from the future ten or more years away. During Clinton's terms loose monetary policy marked up asset values and added to GDP growth then by taking from future economic growth in the 2000s and 2010s.

Reading most press reports on the economy in the years following 2008 was largely an exercise in the press justifying policy. It was always accentuating the positive and doubting the negative. Bad economic news, like a drop in consumer confidence or negative GDP growth number, was "unexpected." Good news confirmed recovery and vindicated the success of active M&M policy. This slant that policy worked is even present in most of economics articles in *The Wall Street Journal*. Macroeconomic philosophies roughly break into two schools: (1) Austrians (or conservatives), who believe markets work and they work from the bottom up, meaning that households and businesses create valuable economic output; and (2) Keynesians believe markets do not always work, mainly that aggregate demand can be lacking for no fundamental reason. This justifies government action in the form of spending policy. I say Keynesian, which sometimes implies only fiscal policy; but I mean a more general belief in government policy effects and include active monetary policy as part of Keynesianism.

The Austrians are derided more frequently in most public forums. Often their basic arguments are associated with cranks, conspiracy theorists, or armchair economists making irrational claims like that inflation was underreported. They are made to look like sore losers. Some media outlets are anti-Keynesian but they are much fewer. In America, the majority of the press and other public opinion is supportive of Keynesianism: We are Keynesian-leaning society. All textbooks and most instruction revolves around Keynesianism. Even if an instructor does not believe Keynesianism, he must teach it. It is in standardized tests such as the Chartered Financial Analyst exams. Austrian Economics is not widely taught.

The Keynesians' position may be more absurd, however, in one major way. Many Keynesians are political liberals and contemptuous of American over-consumption, yet their AD M&M relegates them to

---

[186] At the Clinton Presidential library in Little Rock, Arkansas a large prominent display boasts the economic achievements during his terms.

believing in rampant consumption and debt. Their singular goal is greater GDP, and they usually perceive of the economy as below full employment. Keynesians are doomed to always perceive of the system as lacking demand and a true Keynesian must respect any person no matter how vulgar his consumption.

Just to show how convoluted the partisan debates can be, here is one historic case. In the early 1980s, President Reagan led a supply-side economics revolution, including the strict monetary policy designed to eliminate inflation. Liberals maintained that the policy would fail because inflation was "built-in" and would not come down no matter how contractionary the policy. At first, as we experienced a major recession in 1982 unemployment rose greatly to over 10% and liberals wailed. They termed the recession the Volcker recession to disparage Volcker and the people who supported him. The policy ostensibly succeeded with strong growth in the economy over the next few years. The liberals argued that the policy only succeeded because it was nothing more than a Keynesian stimulus. Thirty years later, the way we view the 1980s episode is reversed. Liberals no longer talk about the grave unemployment of the time. Rather, they cite the Fed policy as proof that we can control inflation easily such that we do not have to worry about the possibility of runaway inflation today.

One aspect of policy debates between liberals and conservatives is that the opponents may not even disagree about the ultimate economic effects of any policy. Rather, they care primarily about distributional effects. For example, a liberal might argue that he supports new government spending for the Keynesian multiplier effects, but really all he prefers is that the government spend more in times of crisis since the spending tends to help poor people at the expense of the rich. A conservative might not believe that stimulative policy by the central bank will result in rampant inflation. Rather, he simply does not want the central bank expanding in size or scope.

Another aspect of partisan debates concerns the accusation that orthodoxy in the economics profession thwarts discovery of better models that will make society. This is primarily a complaint of the left. Policy economists rail against bad M&M ideas and models. In particular, they denounce DSGE[187] models as if they are so dominant they preclude sensible alternatives. The economics field, however, is wide open and constituted of hundreds of thousands of specialists who are free to propose new models and have a multitude of forums in which they can be heard. DSGE itself is only a minor topic in teaching and research in M&M. I rarely invoke DSGE in my recitations. This vein of partisanship is even weirder. The economists who despise orthodoxy usually cite the numerous great minds in economics who concur with them. They lament that their intellectual opponents fail to hear their protest and, indeed, if only the hardliners would provide moral support for the liberals, the next great Keynesian model could be discovered.[188]

Partisan debaters will appeal to empirical magnitudes. Each side focuses on its stronger arguments. For example, liberals will mock the Laffer Curve copiously, saying that tax cuts will generate nowhere near enough new tax revenue to supplement for taxes lost due to tax rate cut. They will not comment, however, on evidence of small or non-existent Keynesian multipliers.

There is a wide variety of other elements of the partisan debates in economics. One prominent form of partisanship is not a left or right bias but intellectual. People take their economic opinions very seriously and, when confounded by real world events, become reactionary and resentful. For example, following the Brexit vote of June 2016, experts who opposed the U.K. leaving the European Union, were sure that the Brexit decision was folly. They characterized the action as clearly not in the best interests of the people

---

[187] Dynamic Stochastic General Equilibrium models (mentioned above).
[188] For example, economist and Bloomberg columnist Noah Smith routinely lectures on this supposed orthodoxy of economics. See, for one of many examples, "Economics Struggles to Cope With Reality," by Noah Smith, *Bloomberg.com*, June 10, 2016. http://www.bloomberg.com/view/articles/2016-06-10/economics-struggles-to-cope-with-reality

who voted for it and denigrated it as mob rule motivated by xenophobia. They believed that the choice was the wrong economic choice based on their estimation of future GDP. They also characterized the action as unexpected even though polls for months had the vote very close.

## II.14.T. Lags in Policy & Seeing Contemporaneous Cause & Effect

Perhaps the oldest and most cited critique of M&M policy is that policy is subject to lags. Almost anyone interested in economics can recite the famous comment by Milton Friedman that policy has "long and variable lags." Pre-2008 we focused on one main lag story that concerned fiscal policy: Recessions were short-lived. By the time you recognized the recession, settled on a policy and implemented it, the recession would be over and your policy would work against your now-defunct goal. Therefore, we resorted to monetary policy in the period from about 1980 to the early 2000s. Monetary policy was quicker. Once we recognized our macro problem, we could act and implement monetary policy promptly—generally by the time of the next FOMC meeting.

That historical belief about lags aside, the way policy believers talk about lags is interesting: It is simple and rationalizing. For people who believe in policy, lags are exactly as long as apparently happen. If policy effects happen right away, the lags are not too long. If effects happen in a few months, lags are a few months. If it takes years, policy lags are about years. In news clips on comments on lags in policy you typically find the policy advocate customizing lag time with exactly the events that are playing out. One of the most misleading facets of lagged effects is judging right v. left-wing macro policies. As we pointed out above, economic data arranged by U.S. president's tenures is misleading because economic performance should be lagged a couple of years.

## II.14.U. Oil: The Omnipresent Multi-Purpose Macro Factor

During the mid-1970s and then again in the late 1970s and early 1980s, oil prices spiked affecting our economy adversely. Oil was the major input to the economy and its price increase was a true and substantial shock from without. In M&M, we always modeled it as a supply shock shifting our economic capacity (picture the AD/AS diagram with AS moving left) and making us poorer. This unambiguous and hefty macro "story" of oil price spike has been with us ever since. For example, thousands and thousands of macro exams start with something like, "Assume a large increase oil prices….use Aggregate Supply and Demand." You could fill a super tanker with all the blue books written on this one.

Over the remainder of the 1980s oil prices went down and stayed flat through the 1990s, hovering around $20 per barrel. Then, in the 2000s oil prices began rising. At first, price increases were viewed as deleterious to the economy. Experts projected recessionary effects similar to those of the 1970s. Despite large price increases, the economy seemed to move along unaffected. As oil prices passed $40, $50, $60, $70, etc. per barrel, the media and analysts warned of dire consequences. After a while though, macroeconomists suffered "oil price croaking the economy" fatigue and commented about how our "resilient" economy was impervious to oil price changes. As the price of a barrel hit $80 and $90 we shrugged it off: Our economy was so efficient and profitable in other sectors and oil was a limited fraction of our knowledge economy. Most importantly, we could "buy it on a free market" with profit earned from other sources.

As the 2008 recession hit, we re-recognized the deleterious economic effects of expensive oil. At first, following 2008, oil prices went down with the drop global economy, but then went up again. Pessimists highlighted the high expense of this scarce quantity and invoked the age-old arguments about peak oil. Then, in another extreme reversal of opinions, circa 2011 to 2014, America discovered great oil and other energy resources within its borders. With high oil prices and new extraction technologies, this could form a whole new industry. The U.S. reveled in this new business. We could become rich both as a net exporting energy nation and also due to the advantage of having low energy prices for our domestic economy.

Then, the world of oil took another turn and we embarked on one more story of confounding oil price changes on our macroeconomy. In 2014 the price of oil dropped continually, starting from about $100 per barrel and getting close to $20 per barrel by the end of 2015. What should have been a boon to the world economy first appeared as the demise of large swathes of the oil and gas industry. Companies failed and their stocks and—even moreover their high-yield bonds—dropped in value. We discovered that a large fraction of our debt market, new enterprise and job creation was in the energy sector and depended on high energy prices. Additionally the drop in oil price constituted a massive drop in the value of oil reserves as they appeared on balance sheets. Multiplying the amount of reserves by the price flux could yield paper losses of over $100 trillion. A multitude of entities rely on oil wealth and oil revenues, both current and those of the future discounted to today, for their estimation of their economic well-being and therefore their spending and enterprise.

Economists and laypeople alike saw a positive side. They did back-of-the-envelope calculations: The average household drives 20,000 miles per year in a vehicle that gets about 20 miles to the gallon. The price of a gallon of gas has dropped by a dollar. Therefore, households have $1,000 more, plus maybe another few hundred for home heating fuel, etc. We surmised that spending on other goods and services would increase. Economists were nonplussed when the spending seemingly did not turn up. They speculated that people, being prudent, were saving the largesse. It was a great irony that when the price of oil dropped precipitously we could find just as many adverse M&M effects as positive effects. Then, in an irony within an irony, as the price of oil rebounded significantly (by later 2015 the price per barrel was in the high $20s but rose steadily in 2016 to about $50 per barrel in May) we seemingly breathed a sigh of relief and scarcely anyone, even politicians, bemoaned that oil price was up.

Our waffling on our conviction about economic cause and effect of oil price demonstrates how little we really know about our economy. There are a few other ways we theorize oil in M&M:

- Oil is seen as a signal to people about the state of the economy. In our automobile-oriented society people can perhaps uniquely grasp their economic standing and sense of society's economic standing from the price of gas for cars. After 2008 as the price of oil rose and prices of gas at the pump went up, analysts pondered if price rises were signs that the economy was strong. The theories were circular and silly. Either the economy was strong and people were flush and could afford the expensive gas, or gas was expensive and people would take it as a cue that the economy around them was strong and their expenditures would stimulate the economy. In the latter case, people would have to be thinking, "Gas is expensive. I'm not doing too well now but this economy is humming so I think I'll go out and spend since my future is bright."
- Oil was seen as moving in lockstep with Fed policy. As the Fed continued quantitative easing, the money went into financial markets, which largely funneled it to commodities like oil, driving up their prices.
- Another oil story is that oil price is a precursor to recession, just like the (inverted) yield curve, and perhaps just as reliable. Indeed, a plot of oil price and the business cycle shows that high prices usually make the economy contract. Of course, high prices over the years 2009 through 2013 did not cause a recession.
- Another oil-based economics story is that an oil price change is "like a tax." Economists are quick to describe a price change as coming from without and with no offsetting good side, so it represents

a taxing of household's income. It is odd, for one thing, since we do not talk about other price changes that way. When house prices or college tuition prices go up, economists do not interpret them "like taxes."

- Also, oil is an automatic stabilizer in that when the economy is poor, the price of oil goes down and makes us richer.
- We also like to invoke oil as a quick budget deficit fix. The pundit or politician will propose adding a dollar, or whatever tax per gallon and then doing some quick math—arguing we could raise so many tens of billions.
- Oil is also a great shaper or explanation for unexpected consumer confidence shifts. If there is no ostensible reason, relate confidence to any shift in gas prices—no matter how big or small.

Of course, there is nothing wrong with applying M&M causes and effects to a product so homogeneous and large in our budgets as oil. The history of relating M&M with oil, however, is guesswork.

## II.14.V. By Definition & Macro by Accounting Identities

Frequently, analysts (including some professional economists) will state that one macro quantity must change, either be higher or lower in relation to another quantity—"by definition." Invoking the definitional condition, the analyst will then impute either a causality, or at least a link, between the quantities. This is a favorite of amateur economists and analysts who are looking for simple, finalist statements to unwieldy questions. People state "by definition" in different terms but with the same finality. For example, "A mathematical identity governs the relationship between government budget deficits and corporate profits, known as the profit equation." This analyst makes a case that lower decreasing government deficits will mean lower earnings. The author goes on to claim that nobody pays attention to this law despite its great relevance to current events. He points out that it goes way back to 1930s economist Michal Kalecki and contends that it must hold. Indeed, he claims, it has held over time.[189] This demonstration is flawed, however. Profits depend on certain variables and government deficits depend on certain other factors. Over time the two series might track together or against each other but for any single time period or even a longer collection of periods the quantities can be unrelated.

To give another example, around 2004 to 2006 when the U.S. current account deficit was large and was receiving copious press, it was common to read that the trade deficit "by definition" represented how much the U.S. was undersaving, "The U.S. now is running a current-account deficit of 7% of GDP....That gap, by definition, represents how much less America saves than it invests.[190]" Let's do a rudimentary rundown of the main identity of M&M: the national income identity. We will apply it to issues like if the government runs a budget surplus then the private sector cannot save and see if they are true—or if it is an empirical issue of magnitudes and timings. Of course if you define a quantity as constituted of other quantities and those increase, then the original quantity increases too. So if $Y = C + I + G$ and G goes up, then Y should go up; but then if you conclude that G increases our economy you have more to explain.

The use of macroeconomic identities is commonplace and found in textbooks to demonstrate basic concepts. For example, we often contend that Investment is important and to show how it relates to Savings we do the following (in this case, we are considering a closed economy):
Start with $Y = C + I + G$ and solve for Investment, $I = Y - C - G$

[189] *Advisor Perspectives*, "Why a Shrinking Deficit Means Lower Earnings," by Robert Huebscher, November 26, 2013.
[190] "Bull Market in Bull," by Randall W. Forsyth, *Barron's* Up & Down Wall Street, April 24, 2006, p. 6.

State that Savings equals Private Savings ($S_{private}$) plus Public Savings ($S_{public}$), $S = S_{private} + S_{public}$

$S_{private} = Y + TR - C - T$

$S_{public} = T - G - TR$

Where TR is Transfers and T is Tax

Therefore $S = Y + TR - C - T + T - G - TR$, or $S = Y - C - G$

Finally, $I = S$

The exercise shows that Savings equals Investment therefore we must save.

Another exercise is to add exports and imports, $Y = C + I + G + X - M$. Then breaking out taxes, T, we isolate $I = (Y - C - T) + (T - G) + (M - X)$. Then we relate stories about how I could be higher if Private Savings ($Y - C - T$) were higher, if Public Savings ($T - G$) were higher or if we import more ($M - X$). In the last case, foreigners are providing credit. Our Y will be lower if we do not save or if neither our government nor foreigners finance us.

These manipulations are truisms. The distinction between the private and public sectors is irrelevant. If the government does not save the private sector must save more. Since capital flows across borders the international distinction can also become irrelevant. Another way of showing the same truism is: $I + C + G = S - X + M$. In this case, Y, or all the GDP we can have must have come from savings and net foreign.

Such equational defining is necessary to set up a system of equations to describe the economy. Of course, these identities do not necessarily have any economic meaning or underlying theory of cause and effect. There must be some hook relating these macroeconomic aggregates to each other but there is none. Jumbling around these aggregates around is a dubious exercise at best.

## II.14.W. Just a Book Entry

We referred to this concept in the debt and deficit debates. In big-time M&M debates analysts often claim various debts—like U.S. debt, Social Security trust fund obligations, reserves on the Fed balance sheet, etc.—are merely book entries that may represent no significant value, real obligation or other economic constraint. (In contrast, presumably, these analysts would not doubt the real value represented by book entries such as the accounts receivable on a company's balance sheet or the balance in a person's checking account.) Frequently, a debate in M&M is settled in a finalist way: "It is just a book entry," "They don't understand accounting," or "It is just a convention." In some minor and special context an analyst may be correct when he makes this case but for the most part the book entries are real items, and every one represents an asset to some party. For example, if I have lots of holdings of U.S. treasuries to use for my retirement (a very common case for millions of Americans) they cannot be cancelled by the U.S. government without destroying my retirement. We typically play this "just a book entry" card when we are debating and must diminish debt levels. It has some appeal since financial debt and assets indeed resemble nothing more than book entries. Your stock portfolio or bank account balance are book entries. Of course, you would not think about them as summarily being able to be set to zero just because they are book items. You hear this in various contexts (like mortgage debt being a book entry), as if the financial company would lose nothing if a person was relieved from his mortgage.

Here is a specific example: *Bloomberg* columnist and economist Noah Smith[191] describes Japan's severe public debt problem. He cites one solution: a government default on the debt. However, he concludes, "But I'm not worried. In the end, a sovereign default is just an accounting exercise—marking down the assets of some Japanese people and marking up the assets of others. It would redistribute wealth

---

[191] "Japan's Debt Trap," *Bloomberg.com*, September 24, 2014, www.bloomberg.com/articles/2014-09-24/japan-s-debt-trap).

from the old to the young. And after a default, Japan would still have all the same factories, all the same land, all the same people with all the same education." In simple terms, Smith is assuming that a Japanese retiree gets less value but his son gets relieved of the similar amount that he owes. Yet the default would represent a mark-down of the retiree's value. Before default, however, the young man does not realize that he is incapable of paying the debt at its current level. He thinks his taxes cover his government's obligations sufficiently and default would not represent greater wealth to him.

People might be gullible for "book entry" rationalizations from their experiences at work or in another, typically large, organization. One department in a big organization might get a service from another. Indeed, the original department might be charged and some receipt might be signed. For example, a worker from maintenance does some task in your department which gets charged. No money changes hands. Nor does the maintenance worker or his department receive any more real salary or goods in-kind. Personnel in organizations are savvy about this, "Don't worry. It's all 'funny money.' We don't really get charged," the boss assures the junior worker who thinks he has incurred an expense for his department. In this kind of case, since resources are not constantly occupied, you can move them around at no cost. If you asked a worker to come in on a weekend and do some task for your department he would ask you to send real money from your department's budget or from your pocket.[192]

## II.14.X. Ricardian Equivalence & Effects of Policy

If a government borrows, can the public realize that this borrowing must be paid back later in the form of higher taxes and then save an amount equal to the borrowing—thus undoing the stimulative effect of the government borrowing? It sounds unlikely but could be roughly true. Let's put the question another way: Are people unaware that government debt is their debt? Most probably are aware and perhaps average people have little idea about what specific future tax burdens might be following changes in government fiscal position; however, high income tax payers and businesses attempt to anticipate future tax burdens. This is known as Ricardian Equivalence. It goes back to a 1974 paper by Harvard economist Robert Barro entitled "Are Government Bonds Net Wealth?"[193] The general concept can also be traced to writings of late 18th/early 19th century English economist David Ricardo. Economists have wrangled over the validity of Ricardian Equivalence with liberals laughing it off as preposterous and conservatives saying it is both plausible and supported by empirical findings in some broad ways. Anti-Ricardian economists doubt people's ability to calculate future tax liabilities and consider the doctrine completely irrelevant for people who are liquidity constrained, i.e., people who spend any income they get their hands on. Pro-Ricardians contend that wealthy people and institutional investors are clever about maintaining their wealth.

Since Ricardian theory is ultimately an empirical question it should be settled with research. Copious research has been done but it is not conclusive. Economists cite cases. Doubters, for example,

---

[192] In accounting and bookkeeping many procedures can involve arbitrary adjustments that make value seem to appear or disappear. Here are two common cases: If you have a security in a portfolio and its value differs from its cost, it will have an unrealized gain or loss (for example, if you have a share of stock that cost $25 and it is now worth $40 you have an unrealized gain of $15). If that security is altered pursuant to a corporate action then, under booking rules, you might have to pretend to realize the unrealized gain. You would not have receive any cash but you would remark the cost at market value and take a tax gain of $15. Your accountant would say, "It's just a flip between unrealized and realized." This particular flip would have tax implications. Another case is when you encounter some unexpected loss of value in a portfolio of holdings. For example, a security you had been marking as having a value of $1,000 turns out to be valueless. The accountant might instruct, "Run it through P&L," where P&L stands for profit and loss statement. It sounds as if there is no loss to be had but, indeed, the bottom line will be lower.

[193] *Journal of Political Economy*, 82(6), pp. 1095-1117.

refer to the run up in deficits following the tax cuts of the George W. Bush Administration. People ostensibly did not increase their private saving.

Ricardian theory is equivalent to asking whether or not policy has effects. Again, we break on partisan lines and see what we want to see. For example, the policy pursuant to 2008 is seen as a success by policy defenders who contend that stimulative policies worked and that we would have gone into a depression without them. They note that the recession ended and cite sundry positive economic quantities that improved following 2008. Deniers compare other historical recession cases with 2008 and then cite the small magnitudes and seemingly contradictory facets of the 2008 recovery—and also contend that future effects are unknown and probably adverse.

## II.14.Y. Out-of-Equilibrium

One insightful method of economic analysis is determining economic quantities, markets or any other social quantity that appear "out-of-equilibrium" and estimating how they will return to equilibrium. Historical cases abound. For example, the housing market took off in the 1990s and early 2000s, became out-of-equilibrium and then crashed. And there are many others. Think of any item called a bubble, either in the past or currently, or anything "way high": the internet stock bubble in the 1990s; oil prices over the last four decades; the shifting of the P/E ratio; etc. Of course, the prevalence of so many apparent bubbles is problematic. For example, currently any of the following could be perceived of as out-of-equilibrium: the Chinese economy, Chinese real estate, the bond market, interest rates, the trade deficit and U.S. treasuries. Then there are more sweeping examples, like the education, pension, research and U.S. government debt bubbles

Of course, perhaps the largest out-of-equilibrium situation is that the average American makes around $40,000 and the average Chinese less than $10,000. This disequilibrium may swamp all others and, also, is not polite to broach among Americans because it implies they should be making about $15,000. Most economists would prefer to emphasize that both the U.S. and China can grow (China perhaps a little faster) and at some point in the future will converge at an amount much higher than $40,000. In reality, we have no more reason to believe that outcome than the one in which we decline.

The main problem with out-of-equilibrium quantities is not finding them but timing their movement back to equilibrium. An out-of-equilibrium situation may remain that way longer than you can hold an investment position against it or do policy to offset it. For example, when the fed funds rate hit just a little above zero in late 2008 it seemed out-of-equilibrium but it has remained very low for very long.

We bemoan our trade deficit and fiscal deficit and urge others, like the Chinese, to right those imbalances; but those most out-of-equilibrium items make sense: We have a never-ending need for credit and they are looking for safe assets to hold their savings. There is no shortage of this kind of grand matching and resetting of imbalances as the economic elixir. "A Case For Optimism"[194] matches up imbalance (for example, between the U.S. and China and Germany and Spain) and contends that we all come out ahead if they rectify themselves. It is replete with ideas that an imbalance rectifying itself gets rid of the imbalance but may not help your economy. The grand matching is also often the thinking of Keynesian leaning types whose policy advocacies are typically for expanding an imbalance.

## II.14.Z. Hysteresis & Eurosclerosis

---

[194] *Bloomberg Markets*, January 2012, pp. 34-40 by Simon Kennedy and Rich Miller.

From about the mid-1980s through the early 2000s the U.S. had lower unemployment than comparable economies in Europe, yet conversely in the 1960s and 1970s Europe had lower unemployment. This made sense though since public policy in European nations was designed to provide employment opportunity for all citizens. European nations had programs and rules to maintain jobs and deter layoffs. Given the tough economic times of the 1970s and early 1980s, unemployment rose in Europe. Surprisingly, however, unemployment remained high in Europe. In the U.S. unemployment came down. The European trend ran counter to business cycle theories and European social policies and economists looked for explanations.

A concept/analogy called hysteresis was purloined from chemistry. The idea was that if unemployment rose, workers would lose their skills and become unemployable. Unless they were promptly retrained, they would remain permanently unemployable and the base rate of unemployment would go up and stay up. The chemistry analogy is that a certain substance will maintain a certain equilibrium, but if perturbed by some factor the substance will reach a different equilibrium and stay there. This was discussed in a well-known paper at the time (1986) by Lawrence Summers and Olivier Blanchard entitled "Hysteresis and the European Unemployment Problem."

Eurosclerosis was another term and parable used to describe the less competitive European economy due to a variety of anti-market facets like regulation, less labor mobility and extensive welfare programs. Like so many ideas in economics, hysteresis was broached, circulated and studied extensively in the 1980s and 1990s. It lay dormant but was picked up again—this time to explain the rise in unemployment in the U.S. 2008 ff. Analysts resorted to hysteresis to advocate the urgent need for more stimulus. Notably, a March 2012 paper by Lawrence Summers and Bradford DeLong entitled Fiscal Policy in a Depressed Economy (Brookings series) made the case that government fiscal policy (i.e., spending) could pay for itself by having such a strong effect on keeping the economy's potential economic output from falling due to obsolescence of skills, resulting in a counter-hysteresis effect.

Hysteresis is of interest to me because it is one of the prominent pop theories that I got to see from its start around the mid-1980s (when I was a graduate student in economics) through its dormancy and re-birth. Hysteresis was always a weak concept and did not support the case for jobs creation though. For one thing, the masses of unemployed usually include numerous construction workers, real estate workers, factory workers, government workers doing basic services, etc. whose skill sets do not really degrade much. As the economic recovery following 2008 dragged, both experts and amateurs brought up hysteresis, sometimes not invoking the term hysteresis but simply talking about the idea that long-term unemployed were losing their skills. Their comments were rarely put in any context or applied to the broad labor market. For example, was it that workers at Walmart and McDonald's who were out of work for six months could retain their skills, but if they were out of work for 18 months they would forget how to stack shelves or grill burgers? Advocates of the theory speculated that, indeed, when people are out of work for a long time they get depressed, develop bad diet habits (like overeating), and otherwise tend to become unemployable. Of course, an opposite case might be that too many people were employed before 2008. Perhaps employers had to hire mediocre workers when the economy was overly-strong due to borrowing and bubbles in industries like housing.

## II.14.AA. Exogenous v. Endogenous & Exogenous Events Hype and Excuse

A key concept in macroeconomic modeling and forecasting is the idea of whether or not an event comes from without (which we call exogenous) or is determined within the economic system we are analyzing (which we call endogenous). At any point in time there are exogenous shocks to our economy. They seemingly come as a surprise or clearly from outside the norms we were expecting. Examples are weather events, geo-political events, abrupt large changes in preferences, unexpected insolvency in large companies or organizations, labor strikes, etc. Of course, some events may be occasional, like bad weather and terrorism, but they may not qualify as exogenous in the macroeconomic sense unless they are really big, like the terrorist attack on September 11, 2001. Routine bad weather should not qualify yet in recent years the weather has received inordinate attention as a reason for poor GDP growth. A low GDP growth number in the first quarter of 2015 was blamed almost entirely on alleged extreme weather. Perhaps the only truly exogenous weather factor is El Niño. An exogenous event will often appear hefty or even dominating at the very time it occurs. Also it may affect certain monthly and maybe even quarterly data, but it should not matter much for long-term trends. For example, in late November and early December 2006 a large storm hit the U.S. Midwest. At the time, it got major play as causing big economic effects but even a few months later it was forgotten.

A change in the price of oil can be viewed as either exogenous or endogenous. Usually, for the U.S. economy, we would view oil price changes as coming from without—from a non-U.S. economy force like a geopolitical event. In this case, oil is an exogenous shock. If the price of oil goes down in a recession though, you might view that price change as endogenous. Now that the U.S. is a bigger oil producer, oil's role as exogenous shock is diminished. Economic boom and bust in other nations and unions are often termed exogenous but since the world economy is pretty well integrated they should be seen an endogenous. A slowdown in growth in China, Eurozone, Japan, etc. should not be used as an excuse for the failure of the domestic economy. Exogenous events exist and are important but they count for more rationalizing of prejudices on the economy than real effects on the economy.

## II.14.AB. Fed Watchers & "Worked for the Fed"

M&M is very subtle and making finalists statements about the macroeconomy is treacherous and simply too unpredictable. One group of macroeconomists has found a way around this: They refrain from explaining the economy, instead just explaining the actions and words of the Fed and its spokespersons as they will be interpreted by the "market" and how they will then subsequently affect the economy. These are the famous and omnipresent Fed Watchers—macroeconomists or similar strategists working for a big bank, consultancy, think tank, the press, etc. The Fed Watcher's role is not to explain the real economy or commit to a model or state a conviction like "I believe NAIRU to be 6%." Rather, he explains what the Fed does, under the façade that the Fed is doing something purposeful and/or that the Fed believes in some economic model or fact like, "The Fed is assuming that the economy is above NAIRU." This greatly simplifies the job of the economist and completely relinquishes him from responsibility. Being a Fed Watcher is carte blanche for indulging in loose talk.

Another related expert is the economist who "worked for the Fed," in either a senior or research role. His inside knowledge supposedly makes for greater insight on issues. Yet aside from stories that the former Fed worker can tell about events that happened in his role at the Fed, his commentary seems as guess-like as anyone else's. The number of ex-Fed and current Fed economists is very large. Perhaps more economics Ph.D.'s have been affiliated with the Fed than any other entity and many senior academics consult for the Fed. Many commentators consider such interlocking careers among many of our leading economic spokespersons a negative force for criticism of policy.

Many young people I encounter desire to work for the Fed for a few years before they move into more lucrative fields, like money management or investment banking. They seem to think that there is an advantage to having a Fed credential including both that the Fed represents top economic discussion but also that the credential is respected.

## II.14.AC. Rigged Keynesian

To an average person, Keynesian insight has much appeal. That a dose of autonomous spending must reverberate through the economy to some extent makes sense. The only question is how great the multiplier is. It is difficult to envision the offsetting effects and how the spending arose out of nowhere. Non-economists, like politicians, are gullible for Keynesian effects. When they are presented with estimates of the spending that will follow a new public project some politicians do not question where the multiplied effect comes from. It is just an assumed number produced by a government statistics office or consulting firm.

Keynesian effects are assumed in models. In theoretical constructs like IS/LM and AS/AD the curves are sloped to give Keynesian results. IS/LM leaves prices fixed so expansionary policy does not get offset by higher prices. Multipliers in models are assumed to exist and be larger than one.

Keynesian models assume various sticky prices such that prices will not adjust to make markets clear. They also assume effective demand which means that households spend income that is currently available to them rather than income that they would have if the economy were at full employment. When economists, including the leading names in the business, say they have found favorable effects of expansionary policy what they do state is that their findings come from models rigged with Keynesian assumptions. The subtitle of an op-ed piece by leading economists Alan Blinder and Mark Zandi states with certainty, "Without the emergency measures of 2008-09, the U.S. economy would be far worse off today."[195] They give copious statistics and prove that GDP and jobs are greater. In reality, all are just guesses sprung out of rigged models and constitute nothing more than a prejudice.

## II.14.AD. Income & Wealth

When we think of our macroeconomy, we envision a complicated mechanism that changes in myriad ways. The interactions defy any simple depictions but we assume that the internal dynamism of capitalism accompanied by purposeful M&M policy ensure reasonable economic growth. It is useful to ponder what truly underlies our economic standing. We, as individuals or as a society as a whole, have income (which is the period by period amount we earn or create), and we have wealth (which is the asset amount we have built up over time). Historically, our income and its growth was the greater contributor to our standard of living. Most people worked the bulk of their lives and paid for their goods and services with labor income. They had little wealth. For example, they did not live many years in retirement using wealth. Today, a large fraction of our populace lives off of wealth, not income. Indeed, much of the growth of GDP in recent decades came from upward re-evaluations of wealth and not earned incomes.

To explain the difference of income and wealth, assume a person can choose one of two spouses: The first spouse has $1,000,000 in wealth (some set of assets). The other has the ability to earn $100,000 per year for 20 years. If our person will live for 20 years, which partner will provide him with more consumption? Only if the person with the wealth can garner high rates of return on his assets is he more economically desirable than the person with the earnings.

## II.14.AE. Economic Output From Abroad or From the Future

---

[195] "Don't Look Back in Anger at Bailouts and Stimulus," by Alan S. Blinder and Mark Zandi, *The Wall Street Journal*, October 15, 2015. http://www.wsj.com/articles/dont-look-back-in-anger-at-bailouts-and-stimulus-1444948370

Another blunt reality of our economic lot is our assumption that stimulative policies can increase economic output. We can envision increasing our economic growth by two ways—we either get economic output from abroad or from the future. To get output from abroad, we typically lower the value of our currency. As we have discussed before though, that action is not generally successful in improving the long-run wealth of any nation. The other method is to borrow or take from the future. In this case, we have to pay it back. A Keynesian, of course, would deny this tradeoff contending that under certain circumstances, a net increase in total output can be achieved such that we do not have to pay it all back. Whether this is valid or not, of course, is the fundamental debate of Keynesianism, but regardless when you view policy as taking from other countries or from our children it appears less glorious.

## II.14.AF. At the Margin

This is more of a micro concept and term but it applies to macro. How much does a little change affect economic activity? We already talked about the marginal tax rate. The concept of marginal, though, applies to all markets and prices. When the Fed was engaging in QE's, interest rates came down but ostensibly only a little. Policy proponents hypothesized that those little changes had effects by claiming that significant economic activity occurs "at the margin." Naysayers would make dismissive statements like, "Such a small drop in rates will not make people buy a house," but they missed the concept; and advocates of policy derided such naysayers. Then when rates went up a little in 2013, due to Fed tapering, people said it would hurt the mortgage and therefore housing markets. He argued that such changes would "kill the market, at the margin." Policy advocates reversed their roles and contended that people would not stop buying houses because rates, even with little increases, were still low.

## II.14.AG. Entrepreneurship

Entrepreneurship is one of the four basic factors of production of growth theory (the others are land, labor and capital), but it is difficult to measure and groom. We know that good laws, good education, competitive institutions, a culture of achievement, etc. contribute to growth but those items are hard to pin down and other more subtle motivations that create outstanding entrepreneurship are even harder to capture. Many nations try to foster entrepreneurship with subsidies, special trade zones, tax incentives, contests, etc. Some nations have limited success in this but most entrepreneurship still seems to spring from odd sources. Growth theory scholars attribute much economic growth to entrepreneurship.

We relish characterizing America as the singular land of entrepreneurship. We even contend our entrepreneurship is impervious to higher tax rates, greater regulation and other added burdens like labor rules and health care burdens. Our business pioneers would work their magic regardless of how much of the profit would be confiscated. We are told that taxes were high when Bill Gates founded Microsoft in 1975, proving he would do it again today regardless of how much tax and paperwork he faced.

Attempts to create entrepreneurship with government programs like small business loans, science parks or tax breaks may create few establishments and jobs, if any. Also, creation of new small business or industry may represent jobs purloined from businesses and industries displaced by the new ones. When pundits talk about entrepreneurship they mainly mention giants and super-achievers like Bill Gates, Steve Jobs, Ray Kroc, Andrew Carnegie, etc. Pundits less frequently refer to the multitude of small entrepreneurs, many of whom work very hard for very long periods and make relatively little. When we talk about adverse effects of government policy, we flippantly remark that Bill Gates would not have stopped due to tax on his next million of income. Small businesspeople are in a different situation. Small increases in taxes can affect them significantly. Another facet of a small business owner is that his final goal is usually selling his business. The entrepreneur sacrifices his time and effort for thirty years, maybe netting a modest income of $100,000 or less per year. After a certain age he wants to realize that net annual $100,000 for the remaining life of the company and attempts to sell the concern for maybe eight or ten times earnings. If taxes are higher, that amount is less. Another facet to remember when attempting to characterize businesspeople as so rich that they are impervious to tax is the time profile of business profits. Many people run a business for a long time, during which it nets them very little, often amounts like $25,000 per year or just enough to pay the bills. Then, it abruptly becomes a success and for a few years the person is making a million a year. There may be very few of these high paying years and during these the business owner will pay very high taxes. These realities of small business are important to keep in mind before setting policies that add burdens to business.

If there is one common characteristic about the great entrepreneurs it is that they worked hard and long and made great sacrifice before they produced profitable products. In contrast, today we rally behind accelerated entrepreneurship from our myriad business schools, venture capital firms and government come-ons for business. Entrepreneurs are stars on television shows. There are services that solicit new business ideas by email. The entire world of entrepreneurship is seemingly picked-through. Comparisons with Andrew Carnegie or even Bill Gates are inappropriate.

## II.14.AH. Inequality

Perhaps the economic debate of the future will be inequality. As the U.S. and other developed nations realize their GDP's do not grow enough to support a broad rise up in economic standing by all people, more emphasis will be placed on distributing from the wealthy to the poor. Inequality already gets copious press, yet there remains a belief that through our entrepreneurship and earnest public policy we will grow our way out of poverty. The economic analysis of inequality in general, and how policy can change it, is an expansive area. Here is some point/counter point:

- One of the remarkable developments concerning inequality is the extreme extent that our allegedly successful economic policies, including monetary policies like QE, were largely transfers from poor to rich. The prominent results of our recent policy included stock market increase; housing price increase with much greater effect on high-priced properties; support of the financial sector; low rates for corporations that enabled them to refinance debt and to substitute capital for labor; etc. All of these favored the rich more than the poor. You have to be a true believer in trickle-down economics to support recent policy. Similar effects of policy occurred in other countries such as Japan where the favorable effects of Abenomics largely accrued to the wealthier like owners of expensive properties, stock investors, large Japanese companies, etc. while the average person saw higher prices and no increase in real wages.
- Fostering inequality in our economic policies is apparent in our housing policy. We deemed support of the housing market as key to causing direct spending and spending through wealth; and the intention was to affect housing, in general, with a large fraction of benefit accruing to average Americans.
- In general, the link between general Keynesianism (i.e., active policy) and inequality is dubious and prejudicial. Advocates say the spending gets to Main Street; Opponents say the general public is left holding the debt. There is some consensus that inequality creates economic growth in that incentives cause growth but also typically lead to outsized payoffs for some. Others argue that equality, including programs to create equality (like progressive taxation), creates more economic growth. Their argument is just a guess and a hope.

- We talk about great and growing inequality, but the main metrics of inequality measurement are income and wealth. Some conservatives like to point out that facets closer to quality of life, like life expectancy, access to education, leisure time, consumption of basic items like food, etc., are vastly more equal among people today—both over time and across countries. For example, the average Chinese citizen's standard of living has moved much closer to that of an American. A liberal would argue that such other measures of inequality are irrelevant. Those facets should be very equal of course. The same liberal would argue that what remains is getting income levels, wealth and consumption of luxuries less unequal. A poor person might live as long as a rich, but he is still poor. A conservative might retort that what remains is a problem of poverty and that otherwise the level of inequality does not matter.
- There are concerns about inequality hurting people's motivation to work and to establish small business, and thereby affecting potential GDP adversely.

# Part III: Use of Knowledge

## III.15. Misconstructions Underlying M&M

The late science educator Carl Sagan[196]was a stickler for scientific method and fact. He disapproved of the television program *Star Trek* for its silly scientific innovations like the transporter and time travel—not to mention the fact that English was spoken by most of the universe's inhabitants. Sagan made sport of the episode in which Captain Kirk and Mr. Spock encounter, on a certain planet, two warring factions called the Yangs and the Comms. Kirk realizes that the two sects are Yankees and Communists, just like in Earth's history.

Economist Sherwin Rosen disliked the use of the Irish potato famine as an example, omnipresent in texts and lectures, of a Giffen Good, which is a good whose demand rises when its price goes up.[197] He contends it is a false case: "Fictions have no place in the teaching of economics."[198] There is a place for fantasy in science entertainment, but in any true scientific work we have to be sticklers for fact. For M&M and the rest of social science we must emulate Sagan and Rosen no matter how many cool lecture items we forfeit.

In this section we discuss a multitude of grand fallacies of social science. If such research is useless how do I explain its continued existence and the high monetary value and prestige that is often placed on it? Like any other good or service, "knowledge," no matter how rigorous, may be needed or wanted for any of a variety of peculiar reasons. This is true in every aspect of modern life. For example, in nutrition and diet we have known most of what we needed to know for a long time. We are aware that eating salads is good, while eating Twinkies is bad. Eating too much makes us overweight. These facts are widely-accepted, yet we keep rehashing nutrition knowledge as if breakthrough concepts are being uncovered constantly. The reason for this obvious: We just like to talk about our diets.

### III.15.A. The Mystical & Fallacious

Below are models, methods, concepts, aspects, projects, etc. that I believe do not substantially exist. Either they do not exist at all, or they exist, in some dimension, but represent nowhere near the magnitude, importance or cause and effect attributed to them. They are, therefore, meaningless to track or quantify and for economic policy foundation. They are also dubious to teach. To put it in a colloquial way, they are

---

[196] Known for the television documentary series *Cosmos* (Public Broadcasting Service, 1980) and many books and appearances as spokesperson for science.

[197] The Giffen Good is a theoretical oddity of microeconomics. It is the case of the price of a good increasing and causing the buying of more of the good, not less as a price increase would usually result in. The usual explanation for a Giffen Good is that it is so necessary in a person's consumption package that if its price goes up, the person must buy more because he becomes so much poorer by its price increase that he cannot buy other, less necessary goods. Supposedly, in Ireland around the 1840s, Scottish economist Robert Giffen observed that Irish people were so dependent on potatoes for survival that, when potato prices went up, they would actually have to buy more, i.e., buy less meat, just to survive. In micro parlance, this demonstrates the domination of an income effect from a price change over the substitution effect.

[198] "Potato Paradoxes," *Journal of Political Economy*, 1999: 107(6), pp. S294-S313.

highly overrated. To put it in a narrow social scientific way, they are not significant. To put it in a way for repartee, "They are silly superstitions for gullible fools and for people with lots to prove."

To give an example, if I told you that varying marginal propensities to consume do not exist you would counter that certainly poor people would spend more of a $1,000 gift than rich would. Then you would also contend that economists and other intelligent people talk about MPC's and have elaborate and confirmed models and empirical findings proving varying MPC's. While I do not doubt that different classes of people indeed have varying MPC's, it is doubtful that we can identify and exploit them with policy to get more multiplied spending. It is equally unlikely that the media can discern consumers by low, middle and upper class and that they may be spending more or less due to being at this or that stage in the business cycle. Finally, that investors can use varying MPC's to zero in on profitable stocks picks given economic developments (e.g., buy stocks of luxury retailers v. discount retailers because the rich are benefitting more from low rate monetary policy) is dubious.

You may successfully peddle services or consultancy for questionable social science models or concepts, but that people pay money for goods or services does not prove any inherent rightness: It only demonstrates a demand given whichever possibly ulterior purpose. For example, an investment manager may have to regularly prove the value of his services to his investors. Utilizing a macro advisory service to support his investment program in his presentations and letters to investors suffices. He might write, "We continue to hold General Motors stock because pent-up demand for automobiles and a strong wealth effect from increases in house prices will keep people buying cars."

This craving to find distinctions and have rich and exploitable methods to better ourselves and our society is not peculiar to M&M. Modern man discovers copious patterns and accompanying theories where none exist in analyses of diets, childrearing, politics, culture, relations between men and women—just to name a few. We are naturally gullible for ready cause and effect and love to regale others with presumed wisdom. As usual, it behooves young people to think more critically and recognize certain ideas from the world of M&M as defunct for real life application. Even the common rationalization that an idea or model exists because other people believe they exist (and subsequently act on that belief) will not prevail. To demonstrate the point here are a few modern-day superstitions:

- **Business cycles and recoveries**: nowhere near as much and as regular trending as is needed to deem historical GDP movement cyclical as much as we do.
- **Cycles in general**: that a time series plot shows some up and down movement with occasional cuing up in one direction does not constitute a cycle.
- **Keynesianism**: In general, that economies can spend their way out of under-equilibria and, specifically, that $1 spent gives more than $1 of output.
- **Effects of monetary policy**, including both the former concept of monetary policy (parsimonious fed funds rate targeting exemplified during the term of Alan Greenspan) and the current unconventional tools (large-scale asset purchases, verbal guidance, negative interest rates, etc. used since 2008).
- **Multipliers**, including the Keynesian multiplier and the money multiplier.
- **NAIRU** or, at least, we cannot discern when conventional unemployment is a movement off of a true NAIRU or just a new NAIRU).
- **U.S. trend GDP growth of 3%**: peculiar only to the 20th century.
- **Models of M&M as anything more than parables.**
- **GDP**: We discussed GDP at great length, so how could we now maintain it does not exist? Of course we can add up the pieces produced or consumed and multiply them by some prices and get some total value of our economy. Yet, our economy is a collection of households, firms and other

entities. What they value and what makes them valuable has little to do with an aggregate confined to national borders. The GDP we hear about is an artificial construct representing current spending largely due to borrowing and has limited relationship with the real creation of valuable goods and services.

- **The "confidences:" consumer, business, home builder, investor, etc.** and any of the other surveys of people and companies about their economic beliefs and intentions.
- **Behavioral economics as an entire field** is unscientific, demeaning to people and counterproductive to the commonweal.
- **Behavioral economics' constituent parts** like the confirmation bias, anchoring, framing, representativeness, etc. These buzz-phrases represent general vagaries of human behavior coupled with uncertainty in life, and not categories of sub-optimal behavior.
- **Prediction and forecasting**, including macroeconomic forecasting. Our ability to forecast the future beyond simple extrapolations of rates and levels is nil.
- **Enhancing net wealth by transferring assets and liabilities from one balance sheet to another** which is something like what the U.S. did with QE.
- **The wealth effect**, which is an integral part of our current monetary policy and omnipresent in current discussion of M&M. That agents (primarily people and businesses) spend more or less as their wealth changes in valid to some extent yet the time frames, agents involved, level of the effect, persistence over time, feedback effects, etc. are so hard to ascertain that we cannot utilize the wealth effect for policy nor even for explanation of current events.
- **Inflation expectations** and the idea of anchored inflation expectations: Measuring inflation expectations by surveying people or by using devices like TIPS spreads is dubious.
- **Varying marginal propensities to consume** and their exploitation by policy.
- **Leading economic indicators**, including formal indexes of leading indicators and constructs like the yield curve.
- **Offbeat leading indicators**, like corrugated boxes, Federal Express or UPS volume, hemlines of women's dresses, tone of Billboard No. 1. songs, property crime, death rates, lipstick sales[199], etc.
- **Individual economic indicators** as useful for prediction, in general, and calling of business cycle turning points, in particular. For example, the ISM index is useless.
- **Investment methods that beat the market**, including general strategies like value investing or momentum and specific programs and projects like alpha generators, multitudes of hedge funds beating the market, books on techniques to beat the market[200], dollar-cost averaging, the magic of compounding, technical analysis, buying stocks of products that you know, covered calls, inefficient niches, etc.
- **The medium term in popular M&M theories**: Elsewhere we discussed short v. long-run, and the invocation of the medium term as a rationalization for intellectual failures of both the short and long-run M&M tenets.
- **Protracted effects of routine weather events** like the Japanese tsunami of 2011or unusually harsh winters.

---

[199] The cause and effect for some of those indicators is easy to guess. Death rates supposedly decrease in a recession because people drive less, eat food at home which is healthier and cut back on smoking and drinking. When the economy is poor, women buy more lipstick as a cheap way of looking good because they cannot afford more expensive beauty enhancements like clothing or cosmetic surgery.

[200] Such books are omnipresent, anti-scientific and patronizing with glib titles like *Turtle Traders* and *Fortune's Formula.* Is there anything more pitiful than a person who says, "I have a way of beating the market. Here is my book."

- **Housing sector** as possessing superior economic bearing.
- **Prescience or perspicacity of FOMC meetings** and Fed economists supporting them. The level of insight and prediction is average.
- **Non-normal distributions** as a rejoinder to basic models of finance.
- **Various popular aspects of aggregate demand theorizing** like pent-up demand, sticky prices, etc. (Discussed above in "M&M for Skeptics").
- **Many "advanced methods,"** including, e.g., VARs ("vector autoregressives," models studied extensively by Ben Bernanke), neural networks, artificial intelligence, Mandlebroit's fractals, etc. are of minimal use, at least for understanding and taking action in economies and markets. Perhaps they have fruitful applications in fields like speech recognition but not in M&M, and not for beating the market.
- **Many economic indicators are arbitrarily defined or a product of opinions and guesswork** and, therefore, mostly useless for contemporary commentary. Other indicators are better defined and reflect quantities changing with the economy. The former category would include the (various) savings rates, the Beige book and capacity utilization. The personal savings rate, for example, is the difference between personal income and taxes, consumption, interest and government transfers. Changes in it do not reflect people changing their saving or spending except that perhaps over long periods of time it may reflect an overall trend. Better indicators might include the price of copper, fertility rates and the Baltic Dry Index. The last is a measure of the amount of dry [excluding wet items primarily oil] like iron ore, grains, etc. shipped. Commentary about the Baltic Dry Index is more rigorous than that invoking the savings rate.
- **Usefulness of diffusion indexes**: notably, the ISM Manufacturing and ISM Services Indexes. These surveys purport to discover real-time sentiment and informed speculations of the future by high-level business decision makers yet the indexes are useless.

Is there a point to proving that these social science methods don't exist? For one, if you can make a buck selling products based on any of these methods, no matter how questionable they may be, feel free to peddle your wares. If you are truth-seeker though, you are compelled to be more critical. Flawed science must ultimately lead to adverse results. Also, bad methods are patronizing. Many of the approaches involve studying people, judging what they value and presuming to improve their lives. We have studied people and society enough. We have surveyed them and analyzed their economic choices over and over. Is the marginal gain of more study even greater than the psychological cost of a populace feeling constantly scrutinized? Also, as I have pointed out many times before, the generational rift is grave. Young people will have a tougher time defending weak methods as year after year of data mount to demonstrates their flaws.

### III.15.B. Consumer Confidence

Because it is such a frequently invoked, yet intellectually mushy, concept—and since our economic policy system is such a confidence game—consumer confidence (there are a number of series mainly "consumer confidence" and "consumer sentiment" which we will refer to as "CC" in general) must be discussed at length. CC is a phantom, yet it is taken seriously. FOMC participants cite it copiously, as do the media and punditry. CC is probably the best "go-to" economic quantity when trying to explain an unexpected GDP growth number. I would like to propagate a new designation for the various consumer confidence indexes: APPE, for Attitudes Put to People by Economists.

The importance of CC is that our main economic objective, GDP, depends mainly on Consumption (the C in $Y = C + I + G$), which itself is enormous and unexplainable. C is the culmination of the spending intentions and actions of hundreds of millions of households and/or consumers. To explain C and, therefore, forecast GDP economic seers need to speak intelligently about people's economic intentions; so we have a number of projects asking people what their feelings about the economy are. In reality, CC is a ridiculous quantity: CC does not exist as a useful element of M&M. CC does not represent consumers' intentions. The seemingly endless comments relating CC to GDP, C, disposable income, employment, stock markets, etc. that have been made by economists and armchair economists alike have been made in vain.

## Consumer Confidence Series

Of course, CC does exist in the sense that we collect data on, analyze and discuss it copiously both in academia and in public. In my estimation, CC is among the grandest M&M clichés (along with lowering the rate, the business cycle, stimulation, big C, recovery, what the Fed Chair said, etc.). There are a variety of CC measures including two, older, well-established series and other newer ones. The two major series are the Consumer Sentiment Index, which is collected by the University of Michigan and began in 1946, and the Consumer Confidence Index, which is collected by the Conference Board and dates back to 1967. The two series are somewhat similar in the questions they pose. Often, though, the two series do not move together. There are other consumer confidence series including Consumer Comfort, which is a Bloomberg series, as well as other series on business confidence, investor confidence, confidence in specific areas or specific sectors like homebuilding, etc.

The data for the various CC series comes from surveys of households. The surveys are conducted by phone. They are offered in Spanish. The Consumer Sentiment Index interviews about 500 households and the Consumer Confidence Index about 5,000 households. The questions vary by survey. Consumer Sentiment asks five core questions. One is if the person thinks his household will be better off in a year. Another is if he thinks "business conditions in the country as a whole" will be better in a year followed by the same question asking about conditions in five years. The Consumer Confidence series asks similar questions. Also, both surveys about specific planned major purchases like furniture and appliances. Perhaps people have some sense of whether or not they will make a big purchase in the near future but the idea that people have insight on economic conditions in the future is dubious.

## Random Cause and Effect

CC does not track well with its basic theoretical economic link: It does not behave the way you would expect when going into, coming out of or during recessions. There is some rough, long-term correlation between CC and the state of the economy (being in a recession), but it is extremely imprecise, with many contrary points. It demonstrates little about people's feelings on the economy. CC does not track well with income and is utterly noisy concerning unemployment changes or lack thereof. CC will not provide reliable signals to time the stock market. It is generally volatile and very often contrary. You can get a big drop or increase in CC just when circumstances least warrant it. Also, CC does not precede spending. For example, during certain recessions, like 2001, CC did indeed go down; but consumers still bought cars, houses, etc. Often consumers keep spending even though they report low CC. The joke goes, "How much would people have spent if they were confident?"

CC moves in abrupt and quirky ways: It dropped dramatically at the onset of the U.S. recession in 1990. After that plummet, we could, perhaps, find a cause (an impending war) and conclude that CC does shape the economy. However, CC also drops and nothing happens: In September and October of 2005, consumer confidence dropped and people kept buying. The fact that CC moves generally with the economy, i.e., when the economy is strong it is up and vice versa, is not revealing because the movement is contemporary (i.e., not ahead) and minimal. CC frequently moves counter to what experts are thinking about the economy. Over any year, if you watch CC, it will frequently surprise. For example, 2013 was considered a recovery year by economists but CC was down substantially.

The basic thrust of CC as a predictor, explainer or tracker is useless. To reiterate, GDP depends upon C, which in turn depends upon consumer intentions so if we understood CC, we could predict C, and predict GDP. Then, of course, we could perform policy or budget appropriately; yet although CC, C and GDP may move together crudely over time, we never know CC ahead of time.

## Economists Feeding Consumer Confidence to the Masses

The vexatious facet of CC is the facile way we interpret confidence surveys as if ordinary people understand the economy like professional economists. Experts impute to people motivations and knowledge of external global and political events that the surveyed know very little about. Experts analyze CC numbers, and the press promulgates portrayals of people feeling good or bad about specific developments, like the state of the economy in Europe or about prospects for intricate budget negotiations that will happen months in the future, etc. Of course, such links are preposterous. People who are surveyed simply do not know much about the movement of the economy or how to relate those fluctuations to events and economic factors. There is a bifurcation concerning economic surveys: Although the people are assumed to understand economic issues, these same people display a lack of specific knowledge about economics. For example, in late 2014, only a quarter of people (24%) could pick Janet Yellen as head of the Fed from a list of four people. 48% simply said they did not know. 17% picked Alan Greenspan, and 11% picked the two other choices (who were both Supreme Court justices).[201]

The following CC-related quotes are attributed to various economists during the period 2004 to 2005, when the labor market was relatively stable. At that time, changes in unemployment were so minimal that very few people could have experienced them. Scott Hoyt of *Economy.com* notes, "A lot of it has to do with the labor market and the fact that we're not seeing the kind of picking up in jobs that consumers had originally expected." Few consumers look at labor market conditions, in general, though and Hoyt is imputing the thinking of economists to the attitudes of everyday people. *Associated Press* remarks, "The lack of confidence shows that consumers are puzzled by incremental improvements in the job picture." People are not puzzled by incremental improvements; however, professional economists who spend their lives scrutinizing macro data might be.

For another example, during 2004 and 2005, when outsourcing of jobs was a hot issue in the press, people's pessimism about the economy was attributed to this outsourcing. Of course, few individuals could have observed changes in the labor market due to job outsourcing—a process that has been happening throughout recent history and which happens slowly and only in certain industries. Few postal workers, food service workers, photocopier repair people, etc. have any experience in job outsourcing. Rather, they viewed the topic in the media and wanted to appear to be in the know. In later years, when outsourcing was just as common in the real economy but the topic dropped from discussion in the press, people were no longer seeing outsourcing as a cause of their economic discomfort. For a more current example, consider fall 2012 when we faced the Fiscal Cliff starting January 2013. Economists attributed changes in CC to

---

[201] "Who's in charge of the Fed? Don't bank on the public knowing the answer," by Seth Motel, Oct. 6, 2014. http://www.pewresearch.org/fact-tank/2014/10/06/whos-in-charge-of-the-fed-dont-bank-on-public-knowing-the-answer/

people's impending feeling of doom as a result of the cliff. Every person I talked to at that time, asked me, "What do they mean by the Fiscal Cliff?"

Analyzing CC on a short-term (like monthly) basis is a combination of guesses, rationalizations, prejudices and, as we pointed out, the assumption that average people scrutinize economic indicators as much as professional economists. On February 13, 2015, CC came out much lower than expected. For the previous few months it had been climbing and that was attributed to a supposedly improving economy, including presumably rising wages and also the specific factor of lower oil/fuel prices. Analysts tried to pooh-pooh the current CC decrease as temporary, attributing it to a knee-jerk reaction to a minor increase in fuel prices and sundry general factors like bad weather, overall sentiments on the stock and job markets and a few stabs at supposed trends (for example, energy workers feeling blue due to the decrease in oil price). In July 2015, the same scenario played out: CC dropped by a very large amount at a time when the media had been confirming the strength of the economy in conjunction with the U.S. Fed planning to raise interest rates due to a strong economy. Experts attributed the drop to people's outlooks to the job market and their sense of problems in Greece and China, yet all three of those reasons were items few consumers even knew about.[202]

Frequently when CC changes unexpectedly, expert commentary will be something like, "People are feeling the improvement in labor market conditions more than they are feeling the pain of higher food and energy prices." Such an analysis of a complicated economic tradeoff is surely the opinion of an economist who spends fifty hours a week analyzing such data. Then, economists and journalists (who are good at making minute distinctions) blithely put those distinctions into the mouths of the man on the street: "Confidence picked up to the point where consumers were in a better mood to spend but not too splurge," says one senior economist.[203]

To press CC to logical ends then, if indeed people are not seeing the economy's turns—yet economists are describing CC movements as if people are—what is the culpability of these economists? Are they cognizant of this reality but wishing to interpret for the public an "as if" type of story? Or do they simply not realize their fallacy? I would argue that they are so obsessed with their professional and intellectual standing that they cannot face reality. Then, to top it off experts are often puzzled about people's attitudes on CC but are sanguine that the public will soon change its opinion to reflect what is valid about the economy—as dictated by those experts. Here is another anecdote about people's sophistication on economic conditions. When I canvass my undergraduates about their confidence in the economy, they do not express personal economic experiences, or even the experiences of their families. (Of course, I am not formally surveying them and do not require answers, as in CC surveys. I don't know if that makes my case study incomparable with formal CC surveys.) For example, they do not say, "I buy and sell memorabilia on eBay and prices are high," or, "My mother has been working overtime every weekend for the last year." Rather, they cite articles they read in the press ("*The Wall Street Journal* had an article about..."). Furthermore, the articles they cite are usually editorials, columns or op-eds rather than pieces relating events, news and facts and figures. Also, they surmise what other people, usually far removed from themselves, feel about the economy. They like to assess people's reactions to high profile economic and financial news. For example, "People are feeling down due to lots of reports on the bad economy."

You might say that this idea that people do not grasp the macroeconomy is inconsistent with my other

---

[202] "Consumer Sentiment in U.S. Retreats From 11-Year High: Economy," by *Bloomberg News*, *Bloomberg.com*, February 13, 2015. http://www.bloomberg.com/news/articles/2015-02-13/consumer-sentiment-in-u-s-fell-in-february-from-11-year-high, and "Consumer Confidence in U.S. Drops by Most Since August 2011," by Erin Roman, *Bloomberg.com*, July 28, 2015. http://www.bloomberg.com/news/articles/2015-07-28/consumer-confidence-index-in-u-s-decreased-to-90-9-in-july.

[203] *Bloomberg.com*, January 27, 2012, "U.S. Economy Probably Grew on Spending."

claims that the crowd knows. The crowd does know micro situations and markets relevant and nearby to their own lives and livelihoods. The crowd does not, however, grasp trends in the broader economy.

## Explaining Consumer Confidence

Consumer confidence relays real-time assessment, reflecting how people feel today (e.g., "I am working now"). It is not an estimation of any future prospect—their own, their employer's or their community's. People have little, perhaps almost no, idea that economists and policy people envision a business cycle that has a certain time period to normal recovery and that such recovery is, as of some point in a recovery (like around 2012 to 2013), late or just taking hold, etc. Talking heads ponder why the recovery is different, but average people do not.

Indeed, CC might even depend on extremely short-term aspects of surveyed people's experiences, like if you were in heavy traffic an hour before you were interviewed. Some analysts believe CC can be explained variously by stock market movements, oil/gas prices and the weather. If CC does depend on the price of oil or the level of the stock market, then it would offer no more clue about the direction of the economy than either the price of oil or the level of the stock market. Also, CC may depend largely on attitudes of the elderly, whose opinions dominate the survey. Perhaps the elderly survey with more knowledge of economics simply because they have free time in which they watch the news.

CC comes primarily from observing news as presented on television. Every day, economists and other pundits show up at their jobs craving facts, trends, news or other information to talk about. As assorted, and sometimes random, facts and figures appear these analysts see relevance, broach theories and find patterns. People in the press contact the pundits, and they collectively concoct stories of grand and current cause and effect. People, especially the elderly, see those opinions in the press. These people feel compelled to be aware of the opinions of the experts such that, when contacted in CC surveys, they chirp back the sentiments they heard in the press. For CC to be meaningful there must be a train of events that goes something like this:

- STEP 1: EVENTS and NEWS in the economy and markets transpire.
- STEP 2: INSIGHT of PEOPLE forms through people's experiences with work, shopping, business, discussion with friends and family, soliciting services, etc.
- STEP 3: CC SURVEY is done collecting people's independent information as garnered in STEP 2.
- STEP 4: EXPERT ANALYSIS of the CC survey is done by economists, policy makers and the media.
- STEP 5: APPLICATION of the CC survey results by businesses, researchers and policy makers.

This should be a linear process:

In reality, that sequence is bogus. The entire CC project is a circular flow that has little to do with people. Most economists and certainly the financial press relish the idea of AD macro. They have a strong preconception that the typical "headwinds and tailwinds" that shape AD macro do indeed work that way. They look for these forces and communicate them to the media, which then recites them back. Average people do read this to some extent, but it only marginally impacts their thinking. Here is the real train of events:

- STEP 1: CONTINUOUS EXPERT ANALYSIS by academics, the press, business economists, policy makers, etc. is performed. Specialists broach ideas and discuss among themselves. Although they contest issues and trends, experts tend toward consensus of opinion (e.g., bad weather in early 2014 caused the economy to be weak). Their analysis reflects prevailing M&M intellectual prejudices with certain causes and effects getting significant press and becoming prevailing stories.
- STEP 2: CC SURVEY is done. Average people are surveyed but they have only sporadic and sundry personal experiences in the economy and otherwise know very little about the macroeconomy. Their main opinions of the economy come from what they hear in the news. People might be aware of large movements in the stock market or the price of gas.
- STEP 3: EXPERTS CONFIRM or RATIONALIZE the CC survey results. They match the random movements of CC with available economic news and conditions.

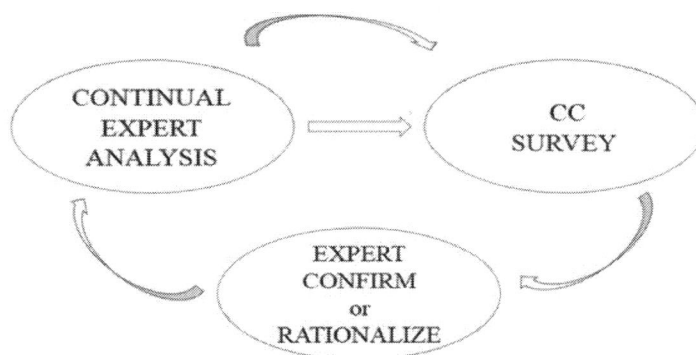

You might say there is a timing problem here by noting that the pundits opinions follow the survey results and, therefore, could not cause them; but the pundits opinions are continual.

## III.15.C. Prediction & Forecasting

Prediction is the act of making educated projections—sometimes just guesses—about the future. A prediction usually involves a broad idea or trend and probably without exact timing and quantification. Forecasting is similar but involves the use of historical data and precise statistical methods. Forecasting attempts estimates about the path, often within ranges, of specific quantities into the future. In M&M and related areas, like financial markets, we both predict and forecast; and we sometimes use the two terms interchangeably. Here are a variety of methods we use to divine the future:
- Prediction and forecasting are mostly guesswork with simply too many factors in the future that are unknown and variable. Even if you are forecasting some economic quantity given a specific event, like a U.S. Presidential election for example, you have to predict the result, predict the market reaction including the expectation of the market before the event, prediction the magnitude of the effect on your quantity and predict the time frame.
- The above statement itself is amateurish because it is obvious to any experienced practitioners that social and business science prediction and forecasting are mostly guesswork.
- Forecasting with sophisticated models, no matter how advanced, is generally no more useful than a "naïve" model, i.e., an extrapolation using a simple but informed basis.
- It is easy to find markets or quantities "out-of-equilibrium" (e.g. treasury bill rates at 0.05%, real estate in China, college tuition rates of increase over the last twenty years, private equity, biotech

stocks, etc.) and to predict that they will go back toward equilibrium. The key is timing, and the magnitude of the move back toward the old mean.

- The future is largely "priced in" or "factored in." Competitive forces set most asset values at about the right level such that future changes are roughly random. This makes it tough to predict a trend and, therefore, to perform government policy or beat the market in investing, etc.

### III.15.C.a. Facets of Predictions & Forecasts

Most readers are already aware of the limitations, but here are some additional thoughts and comments on forecasting and prediction:

- We do not call turning points or changes in rates of change ("inflections," as some say) in any of the cycles we believe exist, including in financial markets (like high-yield debt issuance) and in economic trends (like GDP). Nor can we estimate the duration or amplitude of these cycles. This failure includes private forecasters and forecasters at the U.S. Fed, who seemingly have a worse record of calling the economy. Often, forecasting specialists defend themselves by contending that they know everything you know and they also have their model, which can only give them an advantage. Even this rationalization is dubious.

- Forecasters cannot foresee big changes like 2008 or short-term turns unless there is some obvious cause. In the latter situation, of course, since everyone else witnesses the obvious short-term events as much as the forecaster does, his forecast is of little insight. That is part of the naïve model. For example, the supply-train disruptions following the 2011 tsunami that hit Japan would obviously impact Japanese GDP negatively in that quarter and for a little while longer. Another illustration is that it was common knowledge that taxes would rise substantially in January 2013, so we could add it to our naïve guesses about the economy just as well as the macro forecaster could add it to his macro model.

- One feature that demonstrates the relative value of naïve model forecasting is that if you ask a forecaster which information he covets it will likely be the "last data point." From Fed Chairmen down to the lowest budget forecasters in the smallest shops, we all crave that last number. Our Fed policymakers term their analysis as "data dependent," which refers to the same idea. I learned about the importance of the latest data point in my first research job after college. Our project was forecasting the New York State Welfare caseload utilizing a system of about 36 equations along with decades of monthly data. It was a relatively rich model. However, when we were asked for updates of forecasts, my boss would always ask me to solicit the latest data points of the two or three specific items we forecast. I thought such data was trivial given the tens of thousands of other pieces of data in our model. I finally learned that he was pegging the path of the model to move from those last data points because they were better estimates than anything that the model would have predicted. Discussions at FOMC meeting are similar with board members' comments frequently calling on the last piece of information. You might argue that this technique is appropriate. For example, if I wake up in the morning and the temperature has dropped 20 degrees from yesterday, I act on that and put warmer clothes on. In economic research though using the last data points largely implies your model, which is supposedly based on historical data, has little use.

- Forecasting and predicting in economics is circular/redundant, cliché and confined mainly to approximately ten macro aggregates; as a result, it is meaningless. Analysts expect that GDP will grow substantially if Consumption is strong; or that GDP will continue to grow because the housing market and stock market rose a lot recently; or that unemployment will go down so long as the economy continues to grow; etc. The other big macro aggregates in this tautology are confidence, the bond market, value of the dollar, interest rates, the trade deficit and the stock market. This "prediction" represents over 90% of newsprint.

- Often in the press and amateur economic commentary (and also in much of the professional commentary from the myriad economic consulting and forecasting firms) the analyst will deem one series a leading indicator of another series and impute to the leader a substantial forecasting ability. To forecast accurately though you need much more than a general trending together of two series with one moving perhaps a little bit before the other. Your leading indicator must also reveal turning points and it must lead by a sufficient and relatively consistent amount of time and in proportional magnitude: It cannot be down a little and then your following series be down a great deal. Also it must have those same properties when the series both start to reverse. The leading indicators that we like, such as the yield curve of the Index of Leading Economic Indicators, do not meet these conditions.

- We have so many specialists forecasting so many quantities and over so many varying time frames, that just by chance some may seem to succeed in forecasting. We hear results like "Best Forecaster for Asian currencies" two of the last three years.

- Forecasters themselves are careful not to claim that they can predict consistently and would not bet on their forecasts. The greatest boast of forecasters is that they made a small number of accurate calls and/or did a little better than average in general, and usually both. Alan Greenspan, who was a macro consultant for most of his career, makes this case in his autobiography. He cites a few cases were he made truly insightful calls, while maintaining that most major trends in the economy did not take him by surprise. Of course, a more clinical rundown of his record as a macro picker might have him a little less perspicacious. Another example is Laurence Meyer, head of consultancy Macroeconomic Advisors and one time Fed Board Governor (1996 to 2002). Meyer describes his record: "I…founded an economic forecasting firm… that has distinguished itself frequently through its forecasting accuracy and economic insights."[204] For another compelling example of this "better than most" assessment of experts' forecasting, read *Barron's* interviews in which the interviewed expert is almost always introduced as a successful caller of trends.

- Making a list of bloopers of forecasting and prediction is often done but it is silly and proves nothing. It is easy to find smart people making bad calls. For example, around 1991, noted economist Gregory Mankiw predicted that house prices in the U.S. would likely go down. His result was based on purposeful research that made sense but would turn out to be a big mistake.[205] Many great economists, including Paul Krugman and Lawrence Summers, made bad calls on the level of NAIRU during the 1990s. At the start of the Great Recession Ben Bernanke famously said that sub-prime defaults would not affect the rest of the economy. Another very famous and frequently made prediction from back in the 1990s was that crime in the U.S. was supposed to soar during the 1990s due to increased numbers of young people. In reality, crime went down—a lot. Perhaps the most notorious bad call in recent M&M was the "open letter" penned in November 2010 by numerous leading personages predicting rampant inflation given the extremely expansionary monetary policies. Such mistakes are understandable. The fatal flaws are more in how strenuously these experts cling to their results, and how they try to tweak or rationalize them, rather than just admitting that they made their best guess.

---

[204] *A Term at The Fed*, HarperCollins Publishers, 2004, p. xvi.
[205] *The Boston Globe* column January 31, 2003, p. D1.

- Making a bold prediction is risky. In the aftermath of 2008, well-reputed municipal bond analyst Meredith Whitney predicted that there would be hundreds of municipal bond defaults. They did not occur, and she was subsequently excoriated. There seemed to be great resentment directed at her, as if it were not sporting for someone like her to make such a call. Incidentally, it is not always this way. Many people like economist Edward Yardeni predicted widespread economic problems due to Y2K, yet nothing bad happened and pessimists were not too heavily criticized.

- Forecasters cluster around a moderate forecast and do not forecast far out of "consensus." To be way off in a forecast is apparently adverse for reputations in the forecasting business.

- Perennial forecasting is another facet. Some analysts are permanently negative, calling a recession again and again—and sooner or later they are right. We mock them saying that a broken clock will be right two times a day.

- Another facet is forecasting fatigue, followed by capitulation and reversal. For example, many analysts were calling for a double-dip recession following the recession of 2001. They saw broad weakness in the economy. The economy held up for many years, so they began touting a resilient economy even after the weaknesses of 2007 to 2008 came to fruition. For another example, around 2005 and 2006 forecasters saw the yield curve flatten and were calling a recession, but by the time recession came they had given up and even reversed their prediction of a recession. Some even took to renouncing the yield curve as the precursor to economic turns. This is perhaps the most embarrassing forecasting folly: to have a correct take, but reverse yourself just before the original call comes true.

- A very common fallacy of the accuracy of divination is the way forecasters reset their conjectures with each new piece of data, thereby making it look as though they predicted more accurately. To make an analogy, let's say on May 25 I ask you to forecast the temperature in New York City on July 15. It could be anywhere from about 70 to 95 degrees. If you can reset your forecast given the temperature on July 14, you could get much closer. If it were 92 on July 14 you could estimate 92 for July 15 and probably be pretty close. To give a real world example, certain parties forecast the number of hurricanes each season (I am referring primarily to the Caribbean/Atlantic area for the season starting June 1 of each year) based on some model constituted of recent climate events and trends. Forecasters initially might predict ten hurricanes for the season. If half way through the hurricane season, only one has hurricane has occurred, they reset their forecast lower, to six perhaps. If another four hurricanes transpire for a total of five the forecasters claim they were very close, in their prediction of six.

- Perhaps the most remarkable aspect of forecasting is that, despite widespread failure, predictors vociferously defend their abilities. This reflects a kind of intellectual pride on the part of forecasters. (Incidentally, the analog in active money management is just as ingrained in the beast. Despite overwhelming evidence that a person or investment process has not beaten the market, some continue to see themselves as successful.) Forecasters will defend their records by saying that their predictions were off only on timing, that their calculations will eventually prove correct or that they made forecasts of other major trends in the past.

- Forecasters will often explain moves in GDP growth (or whichever series, but GDP growth is the most common here), by invoking one-off's—like hurricanes, labor strikes, elections, short spending season, geo-political events, etc. Each one-off is typically applicable to two forecast iterations: "Expect GDP to be down this quarter due to...the big storm," they will say. Then, in the next period, they note, "GDP will rebound this quarter given some recovery from the big storm." Of course, sans the one-off, the forecaster's ability to discern regular economy movement is absent.

The first quarter of 2014 was supposedly marked by extremely bad weather in much of the U.S., and forecasts were way off. Virtually every forecaster and journalist invoked the weather as explanation/excuse. Just enough one-offs occur that a forecaster can spend his entire career using them to excuse constant errors.

- Worse are the economists and other experts (not including the media) who are asked to forecast the economy, but only cite others or the consensus.
- Many commentators are outright indignant at the persistence of forecasters forecasting the unforecastable. There is, of course, nothing wrong with forecasting economic and financial quantities and marketing them to whomever wants them.

## III.15.C.b. The Glib Forecast

Naïve models predict as well as sophisticated models. For example, if I asked any informed sports fan a year before an Olympic game to predict which nations would win medals he would, with just a little history of previous games, have little trouble making accurate predictions. The U.S., Russia, China and Germany would win many medals, he would say. He would assume that the home country of the Olympics that year would win more than its historical average—because that always happens.

Prior to the 2004 Summer Olympics in Athens, Greece, a couple of business school professors received great press for an Olympic medal predicting model with a reputedly high accuracy rate. The authors related performance to population, previous performance and wealth (in the form of per capita GDP). Supposedly, this same model had predicted exact medal totals for many nations in the previous Olympic games and was off by only one medal in many others. Their model would prove unsuccessful for the Athens Olympics. Of course, the authors contended high success, claiming for example that it was close on "23 out of 34" countries. In fact, it was way off on all countries with high numbers of medals, displayed perverse results on total medals v. gold medals, missed big changes, etc. The modelers triumphantly proclaimed, "The model performed well."[206] I use this Olympic medal prediction case because it is easy to comprehend how a naïve model is just as good as a complicated and quantitative one. A vast macro model predicting GDP, unemployment, etc. will likely have the same flaws but it is hard to see. Also, I like to illustrate how modelers fall in love with their works.

Another contender for dubious forecasting "value-added" is seen in various hurricane prediction projects. Probably the most well-known of these comes out of Colorado State University. Such calculations are no more accurate than simply extrapolating the average number of storms over the recent past. The forecasters get fairly favorable press, though. Just to give one more example of modeling no better than naïve modeling, one analyst claims he can predict divorce. He collects information on how often and how intensely people fight, what activities they engage in, how they view child rearing and money matters, etc. then runs some weighing algorithm. Given the same information verbally, any gossip could make a guess about the strength of a marriage without use of a computer.

These models demonstrate several concepts: (1) The uselessness of models relative to guesses or naïve models; (2) the stubbornness of researchers and other people who fancy themselves discerners and arbiters of issues; (3) the never-ending and always growing needs of media to report something people want to predict. You might say such endeavors are harmless—and I do not generally disagree; but I caution against any claim that it is easy to uncover information that was not already found by the market and by people at large. Also, I like to point out the desperation that certain people have to believe they have figured it all out. Returning to my story of personal experience forecasting the welfare case loads, our

---

[206] "Economists' Forecast Misses Olympic Gold," *The Wall Street Journal*, August 30, 2004, p. A2.

forecasts were not successful. In particular, we could not forecast turns. Simply using the last number of cases and extrapolating that for the coming year was as good a predictor as ours. Our client agreed. I asked why they hired us and the response was that simply needed the stamp of approval, which provided both a pretense of serious expertise and a way to fob off blame for errors in budgeting.

## III.15.D. Hiding the Truth & Tricking

In January 2012, a cruise ship sank off the coast of Italy with numerous fatalities. For over an hour after it was obvious to the captain and crew that the ship was indeed sinking, passengers were purposely misinformed that there was only an electrical malfunction that would be promptly fixed. Passengers were not told to report to muster stations. Why weren't they told that the ship was sinking? In this case, like in so many others, the people in charge were convinced that the passengers would have panicked and by hiding the truth, fewer lives would be lost. This is a widespread conviction of people in power about average people: People will panic so they must be tricked. Of course, nary a shred of evidence exists for this patronizing idea. Apparently, in the case of this cruise ship disaster, the passengers sensed a problem and independently reported to muster stations, with little or no panic and only routine pushing and shoving. Authorities in all institutions, including government, education, business, etc. hide the truth to "save" the people. What is the origin of this belief?

## III.15.D.a. Tricking in Life & Society

Tricking in private transactions is understandable. This is the way we get what we want in a competitive world. For example, I try to get a job beyond my skill level, sell you my defective used car, embellish my salary and job title to woo a member of the opposite sex, or—in general—use every trick in the book to get ahead. Sometimes we push our standards and morals. Protesters try to trick the police into over-reacting and get sympathy for their cause. Journalists try to trick authorities into saying something stupid. The cop tries to trick you by pretending to be on your side and not telling you that you are the main suspect. This kind of deception is, of course, a main element of business and corporate profitability. People are tricked by credit card companies into taking debt, by banks to overdraw checks, by fast food restaurants to eat too much, by car dealers, etc. This individual ruse is permissible since each involved party enters the negotiation warily, thus the playing field is even. It might seem dishonorable, but that is how we attain our goals. Some time ago I dabbled in fiction writing and learned that the writer hides clues in names, times, places, backgrounds, etc. designed in part to trick the reader. I wondered, is this what we do in the real world? But that was part of the fun for the reader.

Deception is different when it comes from the government or similar authority that is supposed to be working on your behalf. I recall a documentary on the demise of the old Soviet Union. A Russian soldier who had returned to Moscow after serving in the Soviet war in Afghanistan, remarked how at ease and happy he felt that the government was not hiding the truth. It wasn't that he was materially better off necessarily or that he had any expectation of getting an economic payoff. It was simply the notion of being told the truth. People appreciate the truth and desire it to make the best decisions for their lives, regardless of the economic or political realities that might be revealed.

It is not that tricks do not achieve a goal. Each person of authority must decide to what extent he will deceive. For example, if you are a teacher and you want to minimize student complaints about the course and grades, there are a number of methods you can employ: First, take attendance. It puts you in a position of additional authority. Give lower than warranted grades on the mid-term (or the earlier tests or quizzes in the semester). That limits students' expectations for their final grades. In corrected exam papers put random red marks along with the notations of points taken off (the -1's, -2's, etc.). Students will assume those marks indicate areas where more points could have been taken off, and thus will be averse to ask for the exam book to be regraded.

## III.15.D.b. Tricking in M&M & Financial Markets

Keynesian models are "trick the workers" prototypes. The Keynesian model assumes under-employed resources, including labor and capital, in the economy. Given this, some kind of stimulus must be done to restore the economy to full employment and get all the people who want to work working and all the factories operating. Private parties, supposedly, left to their own devices, will not realize that their future is prosperous enough that they should be spending, hiring and producing more. So in a way, in Keynesianism, workers and business owners are tricked into producing. Economists who believe that markets clear have an alternative story. They contend that slack is not unwarranted and that people chose to work based on a tradeoff between labor and leisure over time. A worker deems it is a desirable time to be out of the labor force because his skills are no longer valuable enough to merit his work effort. Similarly, if a factory is not operating, or not running at capacity, that is a correct decision of the management because it is due to a warranted lack of demand for the products made at that factory.

This applies to monetary policy too. Think of the economy's lenders and borrowers as willing to engage in a certain amount of commerce. For example, a potential homeowner is rejected for a mortgage because the interest rate at which he can borrow is too high, leaving him with a payment beyond his budget. Private lenders will not take a chance on him. Then, the central bank, "lowers the interest rate." With lower rates this homeowner can "swing the payment" and is offered a loan. M&M course instructors sometime say that, given the lower rates, bank lending officers call back customers they had recently rejected, and this commences a stimulating of the economy. That is the story of traditional monetary policy. Why don't bank lenders simply expect that the lower rate will cause higher inflation and, therefore, not want to lend at low rates? We do not entertain that case. Unconventional monetary policy also involves a kind of tricking. Under quantitative easing the Fed buys bonds, thereby lowering their yields and yields of similar securities and investments. Investors are then compelled, or tricked, into taking more risk by buying riskier assets to get back to a certain level of return.

As I taught M&M courses over the years, I could not downplay the fact that our M&M policy, both in practice and in our textbooks, was a never-ending con game. During the years of Alan Greenspan through Ben Bernanke and even into Janet Yellen as Fed Chairs, we have always had an attitude something like this: "Shhhh...don't let on to the public that economic problems are serious...that our society might/should face adversity. The public will overreact and cut back their commerce more than they should." In every episode of economic slowdown we faced, whether real or imagined, policy makers assumed that the general public would typically overcompensate toward less spending and generally never adjust economic activity correctly—and therefore had to be tricked. The reality of economic circumstances was hidden from the public, and M&M instruction reflects this. For example, commenting on Fed policy in 1998 (in response to the Russian government's sovereign debt default), my M&M textbook quipped: "Government officials had done what they were supposed to do: They had fixed a financial problem before it became serious enough for most of us to notice it."[207] Why didn't our government allow our people to

---

[207]Cecchetti, Stephen, 2008, *Money, Banking, and Financial Market*, 2nd edition. The 1998 example was removed in newer editions but only because it was replaced with the more current example of 2008 and not due to a change in the belief of the importance of policy.

suffer losses due to the default of Russia? Policy believers will contend that losses would have become unduly magnified due to overreaction. That assumption is debatable.

The transcripts of FOMC meetings reflect an inordinate amount of time spent discussing how to communicate an idea to the public. In other words, the public has to be appeased and calmed. FOMC decision makers are obsessed with the idea that their wording must be extremely careful. Policy leaders think they will control, or at least simplify, the situation if they use deception. They gainsay any suggestion that they are tricking and have minimal real control on the economy. Why doesn't the central bank head just tell the truth: " I am the Chairman of the Fed. I am a tweed coat professor with no real world experience. My academic work is impressive, but of limited use in the real world. The central bank has limited real power to shape the economy. We consider our economy to be in sub-optimal shape presently. I exhort people and businesses to engage in additional economic activity."

One of the curious aspects about this mainstream deception is that most people flatly deny that they themselves can be tricked. They will maintain that a central bank's rate lowering does not fool them. In fact many argue that they see through and even anticipate this move—and might even contend that others react as proscribed but surely not them. Average people are always assumed to be reactionary and to tend toward panic. As a result, they are being tricked for their own well-being. People in positions of power rarely doubt this assertion. For example, during the recent financial crisis, the Fed intervened in the money market funds market when a fund family faced reducing money funds values below a dollar—"breaking the buck." It was assumed that the people holding such funds would have done the equivalent of a bank run if the money funds went below a buck. You see the patronizing attitude in the FOMC transcripts. FOMC members recurrently broach panic and rarely applaud the financial resourcefulness of people. My worry is that this idea is growing in strength and prevalence and being reinforced by the field of behavioral economics.

## III.15.D.c. Conclusion: Why Do We Fool Our People?

We monitor our economy fanatically. Every development in the economy and markets requires scrutiny for its lessons and proscriptions for public policy. Our leaders posture themselves as called upon by the people to secure a greater GDP and allocate it more efficiently on our behalf. Their modus operandi is tricking the people to spend. At the macro level we have engaged in a multitude of new "tools" of bringing out spending, and the magnitudes are bigger than ever before. We are now positioned for behavioral economics: a major new foray into tricking our populace at a micro level. We collect more and more data, including extensive records of people's spending, taxes and financial transactions. What is it about human nature that each person assumes that others are weak, and why is our public policy so invasive at this time in history?

## III.15.E. Rhetoric

The dodge of poor verbiage for failure to comprehend your subject matter is not a new idea. Many great minds have pointed out that correct speaking and thinking go together. For example, George Orwell quipped, "The slovenliness of our language makes it easier for us to have foolish thoughts."[208] I heard many lectures on anti-cliché-talk in high school when required to read leading newsman Edwin Newman's books *Strictly Speaking* and *A Civil Tongue*,[209] in which he poked fun at the pompous and imprecise

---

[208] George Orwell, "Politics and the English Language," 1946. Essay.
[209] *Strictly Speaking: Will America Be the Death of English?* (G.K. Hall, 1975) and *A Civil Tongue* (Bobb-Merrill, 1976).

language by both prominent and everyday people. Where there is pompous language, there are misinformed people and demagogues. This language problem is particularly germane to M&M and has been highlighted by economists at least as far back as the 1970s. Economist Robert Lucas, one of the leading theorists of the 1970s New Classical revolution, composed a famous piece by stringing along Keynesian cliché after cliché.[210]

The fact that well-read people cite Orwell and others does not diminish the idiotic rhetoric problem. The very facile way we talk about the macroeconomy, very quickly invoking fluffy language devoid of science and specifics, hides our lack of knowledge of fundamental micro realities and uncertainties. It is remarkable how quickly a macroeconomist will go from citing specific data (e.g., the latest payrolls numbers, retail sales, etc.) to the "most-guess-like" statement on the system as a whole. Indeed, we must use analogies and estimations to describe broad trends in social systems but the rapidity, frequency and completeness with which pundits jump to the metaphorical when describing M&M belies the science. Why can't we admit that we have very limited insight on the macroeconomy?

Lax language is omnipresent and automatic in M&M. Experts invoke it with exceptional thoughtlessness. They do not even cull their clichés to reasonable timeliness or appropriateness. The authoritative *2012 Ibbotson SBBI Classic Yearbook* is a volume of facts and figures on markets and the economy, yet it summarizes monetary policy with cliché: "The Federal Reserve Bank remained active in trying to help jump start the economy in 2011" (p. 13). Discussions in other contemporary fields, such as race or health issues, typically demand more precise argumentation. Some of these terms are less fluffy than others. For example, economists often invoke the expression bottlenecks (in production or distribution or hiring) to explain either inflationary tendencies or, perhaps, the cause of a turndown in the economy. Bottlenecks at least offer some description of how pricing could go off a trend; conversely, kick-start, attaining escape velocity, tailwinds, etc. have very little.

Using one cliché might be permissible, but discussions of macroeconomics often contain effuse cliché, because the analyst is simply incapable of any insightful commentary. The sloppy language makes it possible to describe something that is un-describable, making it easy to feign knowledge of trends and causes and effects. As I have contended before, in other social sciences experts speak the same way; but, for example, when a political analyst says something like, "The Russian bear will back off…," the audience knows the analyst is making a general comment and has no specific model or hard science behind his statement. In contrast, when people hear analysts talk about 'tailwinds" in some macroeconomic context they think they could go to Harvard, MIT or the Fed where some definition and quantification of tailwinds could be put on the blackboard.

It is not that you cannot use such phrases, in general; but in most situations the context allows. If I say a person will "go the mile" to make his child happy you can visualize the kinds of tasks that person will do. When an economist says the economy faces "headwinds" and riffles off a list of economic factors or current events (weak stock market, low consumer confidence, bad weather, etc.), however, you have a harder time envisioning how those factors affect the massive macroeconomy. If you are told that the government is "priming the pump" with some big spending or that consumers are taking a "breather" following some event, you are hard-pressed to see why these economic forces manifest themselves and how they would be distinct from the functioning of the economy before the actions. Analysts use too many clichés that are neither supported by adequate facts nor operational descriptions. In short, the ratio of clichés to facts and insights is way too high.

---

[210] "A Review: Paul McCracken et al., Towards Full Employment and Price Stability, A Report to the OECD by a Group of Independent Experts," (OECD, June 1977) in *Studies in Business-Cycle Theory*, by Robert E. Lucas, Jr., MIT Press, 1981, pp. 262-270.

These clichés are recited by amateurs and professionals alike. Macro instructors who do not understand monetary policy commonly gets away with partial-explanations following by glibly-stated "drying up of liquidity," "injecting liquidity," "printing money" or "putting money into the system" as if such phrases suffice for an understanding of the theory of the mechanisms of the economy. Sans the fluffy talk, macroeconomists are often stifled. For example, when a new quarterly GDP number comes out substantially off of its expected level, unless there was some shock ('the hurricane will cut GDP this quarter") or some subsector of GDP behaving out of its trend, the experts cannot do much more than invoke the rhetoric: "The consumer is back." They must say something and cannot just admit, "I don't know. These data are essentially random."

It is impossible to define these fluffy terms. Imagine getting a question from a student: "What does jump-start really constitute?" You simply cannot answer this without equally imprecise language: "We think that it means to get something going faster than before and with persistence because prior to jump-starting it was moribund in some way. There is some point where added economic activity starts to feed on itself. We cannot really pinpoint the jump-start in a $18 trillion economy, but if $18 trillion rises to $18.5 trillion in a short enough period, we will have jump-started." Or suppose you are asked the question, "How does the housing market 'finds its footing'?" You could try to answer with an example, "Well, take the housing market in Florida. It boomed and then it busted. Now, we think it will settle into an equilibrium, meaning a level at true means given underlying factors like wages, population and interest rates. That level might be like we had in the 1990s and early 2000s, or not, and it might persist, or not." Here are some common—and vacuous—M&M terms and themes:

- **General**: Stimulate the economy is the most common term and somewhat official term for active policy. Spur, goose or jolt the economy are also popular.
- **Vehicles, motion and machines**: Hit a soft patch, hit a speed bump, pick up steam, stall, cruising altitude, stoke the engine, shift into high gear, the locomotive, the engine, cruise control, jump-start, kick-start, running on all cylinders (or pistons), put the foot on the accelerator, getting on track, stay on track, derail (or not derail), gain traction, attain escape velocity, liftoff, ignite or ignition, soft and hard landings, logjam, stoke the boiler, fuel, prime the pump, open the spigot and boil over.
- **Weather and nature**: Storm clouds, perfect storm, sow the seeds, green shoots, headwinds and tailwinds.
- **Nautical**: Buoyant, floating, stormy seas, all ahead full and on an even keel.
- **People/Body/Health**: On the mend, flexing its muscles, getting back on its feet, anemic, gains a sure footing or firmer footing, regaining its footing and recovering.

Certain terms get very popular at times. Winners for most mentions in the post-2008 period include "green shoots," "escape velocity" and "headwinds." Green shoots was extremely popular circa 2010 to 2012 in M&M press as we waited for the recovery. The green shoots were mostly certain minor blips in macro series that specialists were highlighting and extrapolating to reflect improving business activity like new business formations and new plant and equipment although it was not clear at the time that such business activities were increasing. Escape velocity was used incessantly in 2012 to 2014 (use of the phrase seemed to lessen by 2015), yet such an analogy is infuriating to an economist who believes in equilibrium over any long term. At any point an economy is growing and sometimes contracting. Is there a staggered nature to changes in rates of growth. For example, if the economy builds at 1.5%, can it get a little more growth but not much more—say no more than 2%? If the economy reaches a level like 2.8% growth, however, will it achieve a higher bracket of increase altogether and start to grow at 3% or higher? Finally, headwinds are continuously invoked since the economy was never considered to be fully recovered since 2008 and, since there was no singular reason, we simply called on a laundry list of adverse factors, like metaphorical "headwinds."

Sometimes more scientific terms are used. For example, to describe the apparently strengthening economic recovery, journalists and experts invoked the terms "breakout" and "inflection point"[211] after a revision of 3Q 2014 GDP growth to 5% from 3.9%. A better description might have been, "Quarterly GDP growth is a relatively random series around a mean, which may be tending lower over time. Each new observation is random." Because that does not sound informed it is not stated. Another line of fluffy language, which also reveals a lack of understanding, is the description of markets and financial market reactions to economic events with terms like confusing, manic, frustrating, contrary, anxious, irrational, exuberant, unexpected, surprising, etc. This is tantamount to admitting that the expert's underlying theories and convictions have little validity.

What is my recommendation for rectifying the glib language of M&M? The fluffy M&M talk is so embedded in the heads of anyone born before about 1990 that they have no choice but to continue to indulge. It is up to the next generation to think and speak more critically and minimize the cliché-ridden language. Any cliché should be accompanied by some facts or fundamental factors. For example, instead of saying that the housing market faces "headwinds" say it faces "headwinds including higher interest rate, fewer properties bought by investment funds and poor real wage growth." We must refrain from backing up one fluffy term with another—or stringing them along: "The housing market faces headwinds from declining pent-up demand due to lower consumer confidence." Instead we should use more prosaic descriptions like, "economic activity that feeds on itself," rather than "escape velocity." Finally—and perhaps most importantly—we should say, "We just don't know."

## III.15.F. Behavioral Economics

We have referred many times to the line of economics called behavioral economics ("BE"), aka experimental economics or, when applied to investing and markets, behavioral finance. BE is an attempt to incorporate both individual and group psychology into economic models with a goal to enhance the models and make them useful for public policy and business purposes. The policy objectives of BE include getting people to spend and save more efficiently, manage wealth more prudently and choose to live better lifestyles, including diet, work/leisure choice and mental and physical health. Business or private market applications of BE are various most notably investing to get higher returns without additional risk and using BE to market products. BE is microeconomic in its methods by drilling down to people, households and entities yet it is postured as critical of conventional microeconomics. BE advocates contend that it has implications for macro phenomena like productivity, GDP, labor markets, asset valuations, financial bubbles, etc.

BE is an area that I both dislike and fear. I dislike it because it portrays people as pathetic and wanting to be patronized. BE research is often done with trickery and misrepresentation. I fear BE because, in America, BE may support the next great invasion into and control of the lives of people. This increased government role can be achieved because Americans have been sold an economic motive as their prime goal. They now face heightened costs for items like health care, housing and retirement, and thus are economically more needy and gullible for assistance. If our economy fails to produce the high GDP growth that solved our economic problems in the past, we will search deeper and deeper for ways to fix people's economic lives. BE will then form that intellectual justification and provide the operational devices.

---

[211] "U.S. Economy Gains Momentum," *The Wall Street Journal*, Wednesday, December 24, 2014, front page story.

I comment on BE in four sections below: (1) some major ideas, (2) a rundown of popular BE devices, (3) sundry comments and (4) a proposal for future research. My commentary on BE is highly critical so I reiterate a variety of my disclaimers of potential personal motivating characteristics.

## III.15.F.a Elemental Flaws

First of all, among BE researchers there is an attitude that they have suffered intellectual persecution from the mainstream economics profession, and hence have suffered diminished opportunities and arbitrary rejection of their work. This is ridiculous. BE is omnipresent in journals, conferences, press coverage, awards, etc. Among the people who have complained about persecution are faculty with lifelong tenure at leading institutions.[212] In the popular press, BE is adulated, practically without reservation. It is considered right and valuable research—even courageous—that is performed by smart, concerned and cool scientists. It is presented as having valid lessons for improving the lives of our citizenry. *The Economist*, for example, relishes many of the findings in BE and generally never criticizes the field as a whole.[213] It is ironic, indeed, that you cannot find journalists critical of BE research, given that it is such an invasive and patronizing field. This makes sense though: BE is the lifeblood of journalism. Journalists' very reason-for-being hinges on the masses being repeatedly stupid and unable to cope with their lives.

The second bizarre aspect of BE is that it is perennially presented as new and only recently promulgated (almost always in the last decade). In reality, BE is not new at all. At every step in the development of economics, many of the best minds—including Adam Smith, Alfred Marshall, John Maynard Keynes, etc.—incorporated BE. Marshall's *Principles of Economics*, which first came out in 1890 and was the standard text for a long time, makes references to a variety of human motivations and to other economic ideas (like increasing returns) that do not apply to standard microeconomics. Keynes was known for a great variety of psychological takes on economics and markets like his beauty contest analogy to security picking.[214]

Present day BE advocates might agree that the age-old pioneers of economics were open-minded, but that after World War II economics became overly mathematical and doctrinaire, precluding modern BE research. This is also ridiculous. The study of economics sprawled in all directions and has generally been a relatively open and competitive discipline. Scholars can find forums for virtually any area. For example, empirical macroeconomic forecasting, which was deconstructed by theoretical economists in the 1970s, has always been a thriving area.[215] Throughout the post-World War II period much attention was given to the shortcomings of mathematical methods. Leading economists, like Paul Samuelson and Milton Friedman, utilized mathematical and non-mathematical methods. Scholars from all fields of economics either dabbled in or did significant work in what could be called BE. Strangely, the current BE advocates

---

[212] Even the top names in BE, who have generally received profuse and constant praise for their work, have been prone to complain of persecution. Leading BE scholar Richard Thaler is one example.

[213] The newsweekly runs articles on BE multiple times per year. Sometimes the articles are on specific BE ideas like a new finding or a book review. Sometimes BE will be invoked in a major way in an article on some other economics or business issue. Cites are easy to provide.

[214] For some commentary on Adam Smith as a behavioral economist try Nava Ashraf, Colin F. Camerer and George Lowenstein, "Adam Smith, Behavioral Economist," *Journal of Economic Perspectives*, Vol. 19, No. 3, Summer 2005, pp. 131-145.

[215] In the 1980s when I was graduate at University of Pennsylvania, the Economics department was well known for both its large group of Keynesian macro modelers and its equally large set of theorists who scorned Keynesianism.

trace one of their pivotal pieces, the 1979 "Prospect Theory" paper,[216] back to a 1953 piece by leading French economist Maurice Allais, winner of the Nobel Prize in Economics in 1988.

Even assuming that BE was not rediscovered until recently, this modern wave goes back far enough, easily to the 1980s. BE's great day of copious findings and research, if it is possible to peg one date, might be 1991 after notable sessions at the annual meeting of the American Economic Association were devoted to "Behavioral Finance."[217] Numerous powerhouse names in the field contributed, including Kenneth French, James Poterba, Josef Lakonishok, Andrei Shleifer, Richard Thaler, Robert Vishny, Daniel Kahneman and George Akerlof. Over the subsequent years, BE has remained very prominent in courses, books, symposia, etc. Indeed, BE has probably been the most mainstream area of economics recently. Any present day BE scholar will be frustrated on finding numerous cites and even collections of works, including research from fields other than economics. For example, if you stumbled upon *The Economic Mind: The Social Psychology of Economic Behavior*[218] you would be impressed by its summarizing of hundreds of BE studies. Upon realizing that it was published in 1986, you would be depressed though because all the research was already done.

Third, BE findings and accompanying jargon are sprawling and belie simple explanations or a general framework. BE is "all over the boards." Some of the BE terms/concepts are obvious, like hindsight biases, over-confidence, herding, extrapolation bias, impatience, recency effect, etc. Others can be guessed at, like anchoring (tending to relate present value to fixed point like the purchase price of an asset), myopic loss aversion (being averse to take losses because of some short-time thinking or scope) and herding (behaving like the crowd). More esoteric terms in BE are representative heuristic (judging the probability of an event by relating it to what you think are similar events, but which might essentially be incorrect), cognitive dissonance (discomfort from learning something different from what you always thought to be correct) and prospect theory (non-economic evaluation of losses and gains). Overall the BE theories represent almost all human behavior, and are therefore ad hoc and contradictory. Journalists and other analysts struggle with BE summaries, often presenting them in the form of a list but also having to cherry-pick no more than three or four BE biases lest their write-ups appear contradictory and frivolous.

Cognitive dissonance is the biggest catch-phrase in the BE business. Basically, this means that people act stupidly, then rationalize. Academics and pundits accuse average people of cognitive dissonance. Of course, rationalizing wrongheaded efforts, such as much academic work or predicting unpredictable events in M&M, is done by economists. They may not view themselves as committing cognitive dissonance and rationalize, "My research is being used by business."

Fourth, BE is extremely dependent on a researcher's use of verbal information (statements from survey questions or experiments) as characterizing people's preferences. For the data to be useful, people must be able to reveal their preferences honestly and consummately. This proposition is dubious if not preposterous. We have no way of quantifying what motivates people and data from surveys and experiments are largely, if not prohibitively, nonsense. Asking people their reasons for their actions and opinions of themselves is a futile procedure. One highly-touted BE result is that, in surveys, people claim grossly disproportionately to be above average. For example, psychologist Danny Kahneman polls an audience of financial planners concerning whether or not they "beat the market" in their investing programs. Since almost all claim they do and since only about half could, Kahneman concludes they are irrational or biased. Their affirmative answers are meaningless, however: They themselves do not believe

---

[216] "Prospect Theory: An Analysis of Decision under Risk," by Daniel Kahneman and Amos Tversky, *Econometrica*, Vol. 47, No. 2 (March 1979), pp. 263-292.
[217] The papers are in the May 1991 issue of *American Economic Review*.
[218] Adrian Furnham and Alan Lewis (St. Martin's Press).

their own answers; they just state them. In surveys, respondents have nothing on the line, so they can say anything. If Kahneman redesigned the query such that people had something on the line, their answers would change. For example, if he informed the audience that he had independently examined and ranked their investment performances, and then re-asked the question by pointing out that, if their responses were consistent with his finding, they would receive $1,000,000, then they would certainly answer differently.

### III.15.F.b. Stunts & Canards

The tone of BE is evident in certain of its most repeated demonstrations purporting to show that people make recurrent and significant mistakes in decisions. I offer several examples to demonstrate this reality:

**Selling the Dollar**

This exercise is attributed to economist Martin Shubik.[219] A dollar is auctioned with two conditions: 1) The highest bidder gets the dollar, and 2) the second highest bidder pays the amount he bid. This supposedly constitutes a test of open auctions, which microeconomists contend usually results in optimal outcomes. In this "auction," though, the bidding degenerates into an internecine pattern, in which parties become losers. For example, the first bidder bids $0.50 for the dollar. Then, the second bidder bids $0.75. They are now compelled to keep bidding against each other to avoid a loss until they have bid over a dollar for the dollar. Supposedly, professors have performed this game with their students and got the value of the final bids up to more than $3 for the dollar. There are flaws: The game's rules, despite that there are only two, are tricky. If, and generally only if, the game is broached and commenced *quickly* will the desired result of perverse bidding be achieved. If subjects are given even a little time for contemplation, they can determine the trick and will not play. The game will not work twice on the same audience. Also, it does not reflect a typical auction since bidders cannot drop out without penalty.

It is even worse than a trick because it typically involves a taunt. The auctioneer first must explain the game so rapidly that his audience cannot think it through. The, the auctioneer must adeptly perform a couple of prods. First, he taunts his subjects, "Hey, here's a dollar for, whatever, 25 cents, ten cents." Then if he gets one person to make an the auctioneer must prod the remaining subjects to challenge the initial bidder and take away his gain, "C'mon. This guy got a dollar for 25 cents. You can have it for 35 cents." Once the second bidder has spoken, like some huckster at the carnival you have pulled it off. I have done this dollar sale with my college students. Quickly enough, the few students who have partaken realize they have been suckered, start looking amongst themselves sheepishly and look to me to end the joke. Selling the Dollar might have demonstrated a general theoretical idea in 1971, but it is nothing more than a cheap stunt today.

This exercise points out a major flaw of BE simulations: They only get the desired result if done by surprise and infrequently to the same group (typically, only once). Also, it helps if your test subjects are a captive audience, like students in a classroom. BE proponents keep the discipline fresh by changing the simulations and alleged perverse economic findings. Media obliges by reporting novel experiments. For example, a professor at University of California Berkeley describes a simulation in which he gives pencils

---

[219]Shubik, Martin, "The Dollar Auction Game: A Paradox in Non-cooperative Behavior and Escalation," *Journal of Conflict Resolution,* Vol. 15, Number 1, March 1971, pp. 109-111.

to students in his class and then asks them to buy and sell the pencils. He concludes that people resist trade too much. This represents a slight twist on earlier findings.[220]

## The Lost Ticket

This BE experiment assumes a person shows up for an event and discovers she has lost her $10 ticket. Another person shows up for the event planning to buy a ticket, but upon opening his wallet, discovers he has lost $10. Both are, in a way, in the same situation, but according to surveys done of (hypothetical) cases like this, persons under the first circumstance go home, reluctant to buy a second ticket, while persons under the second circumstance buy a ticket. Once again this is flawed. It is a story supposedly valid in real cases but that may not be the case. Even if people do behave the "irrational" way there may be reasons. People judge situations by the entirety of circumstances, not just a singular outcome, and decisions change especially at the moment of making a commitment. Many people might feel that the ticket, at the point of loss, is not really worth $10.

## The "Linda Problem" of Cognitive Bias

A woman (named Linda in the original work) is described as smart, outspoken, very concerned about social issues and not married. Then, people are asked a pure statistical question about Linda. "Which is more probable? (1) Linda is a bank teller, or (2) Linda is a bank teller and is active in the feminist movement."[221] More people choose number 2, which is false. Statistically, the probability of both conditions must be lower than that of just one condition. Yet, number 2 is, indeed, a more right answer for most–almost all–real-world situations. Usually, in the real world, when you are given information, like in a conversation, it is intended to specifically address your objectives. Otherwise we would not be giving you the information. (In the Linda Problem, if a person asked me about a woman "Linda" and I knew the person to have certain interests, all I would tell him is information to his interests.) People know that the questions they are asked and the situations they are confronted with are not pure statistical situations presenting random data. Therefore, it is optimal to make educated guesses by speculating and extrapolating information. Pure statistical question are so rare in common human interactions that getting them wrong is optimal.

## Tie v. Car

In this scenario you are shopping for a necktie and see one for $25. You know though that a very similar tie is available at a store down the street for only $20, so you make the effort to save the $5. When it comes to buying a car, though, you can (supposedly) save a similar amount (or an even significantly greater amount like $250) by visiting another dealership. Paradoxically, and irrationally, you do not make that effort. Here are the flaws: The situation is not that simple. If you turn down the current car deal, you may not get it back on returning to that dealership. In many cases, you simply cannot find another car dealership. For example, models like BMWs may only be available at one dealership in the area. You will also face a significant time and effort cost. To get to the point of buying a car may take hours of

---

[220] *The Economist* January 14, 2006, p. 76, Economics focus column, "The aggro of the agora."
[221] Amos Tversky and Daniel Kahneman, "The Framing of Decisions and the Psychology of Choice." *Science*, 211 (1981), pp. 453-8.

negotiation. To walk from one store in a mall to another is of minimal cost, but to drive to another car dealership and complete a complicated negotiation may take half a day.

**Brainteaser Tests**

For a number of years, I used a textbook[222] that presented a typical BE exercise. It had pictures of four cards, each with a letter or number on the front that was visible to you. On the back there was another letter or number, not visible to you. You were given a set of rules about how the letters and numbers were arranged on either side, and then you are asked to identify what was on the hidden side. Supposedly, people consistently make the wrong deductions about what is on the other side. In this case, it supposedly demonstrates the Confirmation Bias. Semester after semester, though, as I re-prepared this exercise for the day's lecture, I repeatedly failed to do the deduction correctly, even having done it multiple times before and knowing that it was about the confirmation bias. I concluded that the exercise was simply difficult, regardless of my thinking biases, and that I, or anyone else, could have done it correctly if I had allowed enough time. I typically do not take the time to figure it out because there is no compelling reason (i.e., cost) to doing it incorrectly. Similarly, subjects doing this experiment just want to do it quickly.

This test/finding also conflicts with the way people go about making most decisions, which is by getting help from somebody with experience. Let's say you are facing a situation that involves selecting from a set of choices. For example, imagine you are on the computer using some new software or website. What do you do if you cannot figure it out promptly? You would likely get on the phone and ask a friend.

**Decisions Given Scenarios**

There are a multitude of these that purport to demonstrate inconsistency and other wrong choices, like aversion to loss. In these tests you must make a decision and are usually given two scenarios, each with two outcomes. One original example involves selecting public health programs involving 600 human lives at risk.[223] Subjects are asked about two cases:

Case 1: Program A: saves the lives of 200 people.
  Program B: a 1/3 probability of saving 600 lives and 2/3 probability of saving no lives.

Case 2: Program C: 400 people die.
  Program D: 1/3 probability of no deaths and 2/3 probability that all 600 will die.

Supposedly, those who are given Case 1 prefer A over B, but those who are asked Case 2 prefer D over C. Yet A and C are the same, and B and D are the same. The conclusion is that people are risk averse when it comes to gains, but risk seeking when it comes to losses. BE tests like this are done frequently in classrooms. They are succinct and give the appearance of being problems that should be solvable by average people. In reality, however, they are complicated, outside normal decision-making constraints and uncommon in the real world. Two choices, each with two outcomes, is a hard decision to make in short order. If the person being tested was allowed twenty minutes of quiet time, answers would be consistent. Another flaw of such tests is that they exclude the option of soliciting assistance. Normally, when a person

---

[222] Ross, Westefield, Jordan *Fundamentals of Corporate Finance*, 9th edition, 2009.
[223] Amos Tversky and Daniel Kahneman, "The Framing of Decisions and the Psychology of Choice." *Science*, 211 (1981), pp. 453-8.

faces a tough decision he turns to the person sitting next him or picks up the phone. Another option that is excluded is quitting. The person cannot deem the problem insufficiently important to even attempt to answer. Quitting is a fundamental facet of optimization. Also, the tests are either devoid of context or, if put into context, usually couched in terms of unfamiliar situations, like the life or death scenario used above. Another typical scenario is the fictional CEO of a company who must decide how to layoff workers: "Either a 50% chance of 3,000 workers losing their jobs, a 100% chance of 1,000 or..." If the test were designed around an activity that people commonly do and care about, like buying clothing given various sales offers, the results would be different.[224]

You are hard-pressed to think of real-life cases of these "decisions given scenarios." Sometimes offers from telemarketers or product solicitations in shopping malls are like them but most of those you either refuse or are experienced enough to figure out.

**Other BE Tests**

We could continue with these cornball BE tests: The probability of having an accident flying v. driving; the room with a million handguns, one of which is loaded; the nuts at the party; selling the jar of coins; the disease probability test; picking after elimination (aka, the *Let's Make a Deal* test); etc. BE experts may be puzzled by people's choices but each is explainable without the conclusion of behavioral pathologies. Some are simply hard decisions. Some do not afford people enough time to act correctly. Some only reveal bad decision making on an initial testing. Some are only simulations in which participants do not care about outcomes. Some are/were controlled such that probabilities do not matter, like game show host Monty Hall explained concerning the *Let's Make a Deal* test.

**III.15.F.c. Sundry BE Comments**

The list below details a variety of facets of BE:
- BE research frequently makes use of simulations, often done on campus with students, However, behavior in simulations is different from behavior in the real world. I have occasionally done experiments with students, typically investing and economic prediction tests. The students know they are being tested, which imparts an ulterior motive. Rather than try to perform the task, they try to please the tester. The simulations typically lack real costs. BE researchers will claim that offering real money, in large enough amounts, in BE experiments ensures that subjects try to perform economically optimally. The amounts typically offered are still paltry (in a rough range of $10 to $75 to partake) and, moreover, the experiments are still perceived as one-time events. Thus participants view them as optimizations not of money but of other objectives. I have generally found undergraduates unresponsive to monetary incentives.[225]

---

[224] One further point about BE experiments is that cases with much more sinister overtones are easy to cook up but are avoided by BE researchers. For example, if I told you that you could hit a button and get $500, but by hitting the button an impoverished child in a poor nation would die, would you hit that button? Your answer would almost surely be no. Then, if I told you that by making a $500 donation you could save a poor child's life, would you make the payment? The answer would be no. They are roughly the same propositions. BE researchers, however, do not use such examples because people get angry and will not concede that they are being inconsistent. They will denounce the experiment as deceptive and mean-spirited.

[225] I have primarily dealt with Tufts undergraduates who are, on average, from higher-income households, and my subjects typically do not respond to $50 or $100 payouts. Perhaps students from a different demographic do, but I doubt it. The average twenty-year old will protect his image over a half-day's pay .

- BE data are poor. For example, I recently witnessed a woman soliciting people at a food court. She was walking from table to table, with most everybody turning her away. When she came to me, I consented to talk with her and fulfill her request, which was a BE study. I somewhat recognized her particular BE test, so I could have answered it "correctly," but I just filled it out in a cursory way to be polite.

- BE research often depends on data from a process in which the BE researcher asks the questions and the subject, whose behavior is being judged, answers the questions. The privilege of asking the questions almost assures you that you "look smart" and "are right" while the other person "looks stupid" and "is wrong"—regardless of underlying facts. That is why the police always snap, "I'll ask the questions."

- Also, other data collected in BE tests are of poor quality. People habitually exaggerate certain data about their lives, like incomes, rates of return on investments, values of houses, mileage per gallon of gas of their cars,[226] etc. A man who makes $45,000 will say he makes $60,000. It makes him feel good about himself and the lying to the researcher causes him no discomfort. Also, many of the BE experiments are done with college students whose responses might tend to be especially boastful.

- One of the hallmark findings of BE is that the basic parable of microeconomics, which is that an optimal price is attained in an auction market, is proved incorrect—or at least flawed. BE specialists demonstrate auctions, oftentimes classroom experiments, in which pricing goes haywire, such as the price of a good being bid well above it true value. Yet in the real world, prices appear broadly consistent with the tenets of microeconomics. For example, costs at department stores, supermarkets, gas stations, etc. demonstrate mark ups consistent with the level of profit economists would expect in those industries.

- BE experiments require people to make snap decisions in situations that are foreign to them. Many of the simulations involve rare and relatively complicated scenarios. If you faced these multiple times you would indeed become adept at them. In fact, if subjects answered foreign questions correctly, an economist would conclude that they are not optimizing because they would have been spending too much time maintaining the ability to solve uncommon problems. This might sound outlandish but an example will help. If a thirty-year old waitress could solve a statistical problem like those we described above she would have not have been devoting enough time to tasks like working out at the gym, changing diapers, watching television, gossiping, dancing, etc.

- In general, the optimal strategy to a spot decision is getting it wrong. Unless spot decisions are common and/or costly, you may as well make wrong decisions.

- Many of the alleged flaws of human behavior are in reality the successes of their actions. For example, people get pleasure from being over-confident, sticking to their plans, making bets, etc.

- BE has a large element of political correctness. For example, BE analysts do not generally break down results by common subsets like race or sex. Surely there are differences but since the main thrust of BE is that people are flawed in the their basic decision making, only a finding that men and/or white people are more flawed would be acceptable. To find that "people x" are more prone to decision making incompetence would be politically incorrect. Perhaps the one major exception to this, which somewhat proves the case, is the incessant finding that women are better investors than men. Women engage is fewer of the knee-jerk reactions of investing and, therefore, supposedly gain higher rates of return.

---

[226] I typically find that people report implausibly high gas mileage. Many people pride themselves in motor vehicle frugality and the attaining of fuel economy in their vehicle is one of the appearances they seem to want to convey.

- BE researchers feign empathy to their research subjects: the average people of the world. The BE analyst admits, "Don't feel bad. I have biases too, just like you." One great BE economist confesses that he eats too many potato chips. But BE analysts do not want your judgement or your advice on how to live their lives. This reminds me of the stunt by the comedian who rang the doorbells of the religious proselytizers to confirm that proselytizers themselves do not want advice on the nature God.

- Various BE supporting stories related by prominent BE researchers from their personal experiences stretch credulity. One of Richard Thaler's favorites involves his dinner guests eating such a great quantity of nuts that they could not enjoy their meals. At a subsequent party, Thaler restricted the nuts: His guests could eat correctly and thanked him. Are Thaler's friends that ineffectual? Many of Dan Ariely's testimonials also appear bogus. One of his favorite stories is his buying of a sports car when he wanted a minivan, because the sports car offered a minor free item (oil changes). These stories may be altogether valid but they definitely appear contrived.

- Motivational stories by leading BE analysts are extremely patronizing: Stupidity is essentially omnipresent and only recently uncovered. For example, a famous story of Dan Ariely is that, while hospitalized for burns, he was subjected to needlessly painful bandage removal techniques. Apparently, he believes, bandage removal done primarily by nurses in hospitals has historically been done incorrectly. He did not argue that nurses are careless; indeed, Ariely characterizes them as kind and devoted to their patients. Rather, the pathology he is revealing is a societal and systemic problem. Ariely states that we are, "getting it wrong in a systemic way."[227] He contends to have proven his conclusions by doing pain studies. I have little experience to say he is right or wrong in this specific case but I would be very averse to go into a hospital, pastry shop or auto body shop and tell people how to do their job.

- One of the truly remarkable aspects of BE and its discussion in society is how extremely most "experts" accept BE ideas and how little they defend average people for their behavior. I could cite a multitude of cases. For example, a review of Thaler's new book by the usually sardonic financial writer Michael Lewis had only praise and no mocking.[228] Gossiping about the flaws of people dumber than yourself is fun.

- Various highly successful (non-BE research) people cite BE as a major contributor to their success. Great people, like big hedge fund moguls, refer to the studies of the behavioral researchers. Danny Kahneman's work in particular is frequently cited and often in a cavalier fashion: "As Danny Kahneman points out…" This demonstrates the great contempt that elites have for average people. Also, ironically, many successful people who cite BE end up failing or reverting to an average level of success. This is true in big-time investing. Their downfall can easily be attributed to their making the canonical errors of BE, like confirmation bias, anchoring, etc.

- BE research and findings of pervasive irrational investing and money management by average investors (called "retail investors") is exaggerated. As we pointed out before, research on bad investing ignores that people are investing for multiple purposes. An overall assessment of the investing success of average people is impossible to make, yet many of the major wraps on people are debatable. BE analysts often fault people for avoiding the stock market in favor of lower yielding cash. That is not clear. Many people avoided stocks during the 1990s when there was a

---

[227] "Dan Ariely: The Bandage-Ripping Mistake," Carnegie Council for Ethics in International Affairs, https://www.youtube.com/watch?v=NIRjYBX_9ls
[228] "The Economist Who Realized How Crazy We Are," BloombergView, May 29, 2015. http://www.bloombergview.com/articles/2015-05-29/richard-thaler-the-economist-who-realized-how-crazy-we-are

great bull market, and they were mocked by BE types as leaving profit on the table. Over the next twenty years, from the late 1990s through the present, equity markets' returns would be modest. It is easy to find long holding periods in which returns on cash did just as well as those on stock. The idea that retail investors time markets poorly is not scientific and is largely based on sundry tabulations of mutual fund investment patterns. People have lived through two extreme bear markets and a major recession since the year 2000 and their investment patterns are not clear.

- As we pointed out, much BE work involves questioning people on the spot and stumping or getting them to make the wrong answer. Yet any teacher knows that cold-calling students never really brings out their full faculties. In the college classroom, I can get students to provide wrong answers to obvious questions quite easily. Shyness is a major factor. Frequently, I ask my class a question and am certain many of the students know the answer but I get no responses. Many are simply averse to speak up.

- Much BE is simply moronic. Robert Fuller, one of the leaders in BE-based investing, posits that a person leaving a tip at a restaurant that he will never go to again is irrational, claiming that it violates the person's goal of wealth maximization. A tip is not typically a payment to ensure future service; it is a payment for a past service. Just to make the point further, have you ever forgotten to tip someone who you would not see again and felt terrible? Another common and offensive story of BE is that people, just before getting married, contend that they will never get divorced, even though, factually, about half of all marriages end in divorce. People do not say what they really feel in public. This is called common courtesy.

- Another one of the grand BE "findings cum buzz-phrase" is "hyperbolic discounter." People discount the future excessively. For example, offer a person $1,000 today or $1,200 a year from now and he will take the money today. Supposedly, people broadly behave like this and certain case studies, involving buyouts of workers with lump sums v. streams of payments, bear it out. Most people save, however, even at moderate rates of return. (Also, as we pointed out earlier in the M&M section on deflation, this hyperbolic discounting pathology conflicts with a pathology economists contend people have concerning deflation. In M&M many economists contend that people will defer consumption today if they think that prices will be lower next period.)

- The hallmark BE application in public policy is getting people to save more for retirement. The main recommendation is rather than having workers opt-in to employer savings programs, employees must opt-out. Some analysts claim that this policy has been successful but other evidence is that the policy backfires since people then subsequently change their spending behavior including borrowing against their savings.

- One of the oddest aspects of BE, as it is both proposed by BE experts and then hailed as innovative in the press, is that many of its most highly-touted proscriptions of nudging behavior have been known and used for a long time. For example, making parking tickets bright orange (to shame people into paying), requiring people to actively opt-out of organ donation, strategically placing products in a store or cafeteria to create more or less consumption of certain items (like putting healthy foods within easy reach in a school cafeteria), informing people that their peers have acted in a certain moral way (like informing tax scofflaws that their neighbors have paid), etc. are all practices that have been around for decades. People who have been using commonsense nudging methods in their fields for all these years must be offended when they read about the "discoveries" of BE experts.

- Related to the above point, in any profession there are and have been tricks of the trade. For example, here are some schemes to control students: (1) Grade examinations and other work done early in the semester harder. Then, students will have lower grade expectations and be less likely to grumble about a final grade.( 2) Offer choice on exams yet make the questions tougher, rendering the choice mostly useless. Students will be less likely to complain about grades if they had choice. (3) Rather than raising your voice and appearing imperious to control classroom chatter, talk softly such that students cannot hear and have to discipline their noisy classmates themselves. In general, ways of manipulating people are not hard to find. The question is whether or not you want to use them.

- People make correct decisions in their lives. It is easy to observe ignorance, laziness and failure of people but if you get close to most people you realize they are fairly adept at living their lives given their preferences and constraints.

- BE analysts often point out that people tend to live off of simple rules and the rules are wrong or, better stated, not optimal. People stick to rules that waste time and effort or forgo opportunities. Most rules people live by, however, are successful. Also, the overall package of rules people live by is probably quite efficient even if one or another rules is useless. It would be a waste of time to determine which rule(s) are not working. For example, many people drive about five to ten miles an hour over the speed limit, no matter where they are. It probably works. They go as fast as possible and minimize moving violations. Another rule many people use is paying their bills as soon as possible. In this case they forgo interest income. They may, indeed, overvalue the loss of late payments (which is probably nothing more than a late fee) and but there is nothing wrong with indulging a morbid fear if it makes you feel comfortable.[229]

- BE deprives people of the fulfillment of economic husbandry. Learning how to budget and how to deal with financial challenges of modern life, including making mistakes along the way, is a pleasurable activity to people in our economic society. BE master Dan Ariely hopes his research "enriches" people's lives, but it likely does not.

- A final tip on BE for young people is that, since it has become so hackneyed and picked-through, accusing other people of behavioral flaws has naturally become impolite and irrelevant.

### III.15.F.d. Next Stage: Analyzing the Behavior of Behavioral Economists

BE analysts have performed copious "research" to arrive at the obvious conclusion that people are indeed human. Noted BE researcher Cass Sunstein (Harvard Law School professor and holder of various high-level federal government positions) talks about using brain scans to push the field along.[230] A better improvement would be to leave the usual subject alone and collect a much less superficial dataset, attempting to reveal true motivations for choices and behavior. This could be achieved by surveying BE researchers and their colleagues who would not object to any invasion of privacy. Since I know I have all the biases of BE, I present my true confessions by listing my seemingly irrational behavior along with my explanation, or rationalization, of why it is rational to me.

---

[229] Think of the rules you live by. In teaching I refrain from commentary on race or sex regardless of how appropriate any remark might be. That rule has served me well. Another rule I live by is parking my car with the front sticking out to avoid backing out of parking spaces. I fear fender benders or hitting a person. Perhaps, you could demonstrate that I wasted time driving around parking lots and would not have had accidents regardless. It is irrelevant. My rule makes me feel safe.

[230] "Stay Alive: Imagine Yourself Decades From Now," by Cass Sunstein, *Bloomberg.com*, October 23, 2012, http://www.bloombergview.com/articles/2012-10-23/stay-alive-imagine-yourself-decades-from-now

- I have always been obsessed with sex, or women, to the point where I engage in what might appear to be non-optimal or even absurd behavior. I could provide endless examples. This obsession with sex and how we appear to the other sex is omnipresent and constant. Dan Ariely's purchase of the sports car rather than the minivan was probably a manifestation of desire rather than an error due to sales pricing come-ons.

- I show off a lot such that many of the activities I partake in I derive satisfaction from the broadcasting and demonstrating of the activity, rather than from the end results. Investing is a prime example. People are supposed to invest to maximize a total return, which is the highest return adjusted for risk (and perhaps other factors peculiar to their situations, like liquidity). They are assumed not to have any other objectives in investments. My investing activities have included a fair amount of non-total return goals. For example, my forays into commodities trading and options trading were, to a large extent, done to demonstrate how clever and daring I was. Although it is probably valid, most people would not admit, "Yeah, for ten years I invested in commodities and options even though I knew I wouldn't like make money. I was just trying to impress women."

- At times in my life I have faced numerous serious problems. At other times I have faced none or only minor problems. In the latter case, I raise importance of the minor problems to cause about as much discomfort as the serious problems. At times when I face serious problems I simply ignore the minor ones. In general, I maintain roughly the same mental state in good times and bad.

- I enjoy confrontation, especially when I believe I am right; but also sometimes even when I am wrong. For example, on occasion I get an email solicitation from someone demanding more that ne should, typically a request from a junior person presuming that I am obligated to perform a task for him. I politely explain the correct procedure but sometimes the person responds in a defiant manner. At this point, you would think, I would want him to retract his request and resolve our mutual issue efficiently. Typically, though, when I see the next email from this person, I hope he is defiant—just so I can fight a righteous fight.

- Similarly, at work, if a request is made of me that is not something I would typically do promptly, yet the requester is polite, I will handle it expeditiously. If a request is made for something that I am responsible to do and the requester is not polite, I might delay the task or even refuse the request.

- I lose my temper but do not consider that behavior to be sub-optimal, even given the various adverse outcomes of being rash. Behavioral economist Richard Thaler wishes there were some device that warns us not to send an angry email hastily, but I am glad to send rash emails. In fact, as I prepare to send a nasty email that I feel I might regret sending, in an odd way of proving to myself that I should be defiant, I make a point to send it even more quickly—before I can use my better judgment and suppress sending it.

- I am often very busy and crave a break, yet when I get free time, I don't know what to do with myself. I prefer duress. I contend that I have a hectic life with hard work, long hours, child care, doing other people's tasks, etc. and will say publicly that I wish my burdens were lessened. However, I am seemingly more content when I am burdened.

- I fantasize frequently, therefore wasting a lot of time. I have forfeited more potential income by daydreaming than through all the mistakes I made investing, etc.

- I love other people's failure, especially people making dopes of themselves and being gullible for foolish ideas. I like it when others make mistakes in M&M thinking.

- I often lie about my motivations. It is not that I really want to lie, but often relating the truth is so complicated that I must simplify to consummate the conversation. In other words, we won't get anything achieved with honest conversation. Remember this when assessing answers to surveys that support BE research.

- I often lie to myself and exaggerate my circumstances. Throughout my life, I overstated my salary or other achievement. I ponder why I do it and have never come up with an answer.
- I resent people accosting and questioning me about my motivations and dislike being surveyed. One specific facet of surveying that I dislike is being asked my race or sex, which I perceive—whether valid or not—as information collected to perpetuate anti-white and anti-male prejudice.
- I am sensitive to little failures and certain small losses and blow them out of proportion. For example, if I lost a ten dollar bill but soon after independently found another $10, I would still feel deprived. Losing something gives me great discomfort well beyond the monetary loss. The occurrence of losing something, or a similar mistake, hurts my ego and makes me feel weak or rapidly aging. BE analysts call this "loss aversion" and usually view it as contrary behavior.
- I scheme incessantly and analyze any opportunity that comes my way for whatever advantage it presents me. I don't think a day goes by that I do not ponder what I am, what I possess, what I lack and what I want. Nor do I hesitate to question my convictions. Perhaps BE economists can discern the Confirmation Bias in my actions, but I think past that.
- I am conniving and clever about issues that matter to me and not innocent like I might portray myself in public. For example, if the phone rang and I was told my wife was bludgeoned to death, I would feel grief. Then, within seconds I would surmise that I would be suspected. You might argue that any decent person would be so overcome with grief that pondering other implications could not possibly happen so quickly, but that is what happens on television shows. This facet of human nature is important in how people respond to surveys and questionings on sensitive matters.
- Many of my lifetime choices have been born of long-term bluster. For example, some time ago I noticed that many people were averse to gamble. One guy used to say, "I never gamble and when I do, I only bet on sure things." My modus operandi is to always gamble (in certain circumstances). It is not that I enjoy gambling and I do not believe I will be a net winner by gambling, but I love to demonstrate that I am more daring than the average person.
- I resent decisions being made for me, especially if they are appropriation of my choice given costs and benefits that only I know. For example, on occasion I am with a group of people and I am presented with the choice to purchase a frivolous and expensive item, like an expensive bottle of wine. If I make the choice and justify it however I wish I will feel contented and completely disregard the cost. If, though, under the same circumstances, one of my friends suggests that I make the purchase saying that the cost relative to my income is minor, I will resist the purchase and denounce it as too expensive. Any conventionally-measurable value of the purchase is irrelevant. A BE economist might contend that I am being irrational for valuing the good differently but, indeed, any conventional measure of the value of the good is irrelevant to my purchase. This example might sound cooked, but it happens frequently enough.
- I can often perform more efficiently when I am by myself and not being observed. For example, if I were to make a left turn in a car into heavy traffic, I would do it better if I were alone. The presence of others observing me changes my optimization. This may be important to keep in mind when doing BE experiments in which you are being extremely observed.
- When I was young, shyness caused me to forgo many opportunities. As I got older, I learned to overcome shyness. Perhaps, some suffer chronic shyness. Other people have no problem asserting themselves and even stick their necks out excessively creating problems for themselves. The same dichotomy applies to other common personality traits such as rashness, laziness, etc. In any case, I

think people are able to deal with their personality traits without the help of government or social scientists.

I could continue describing my preferences. Long ago the great microeconomists pondered people's preferences and concluded not to analyze them. "De gustibus non est disputandum," meaning do not question people's choices, is the phrase smart economists use. BE economists do not have greater insight or better methods and are in no position to understand people's optimizations unless they can account for preferences, like those I have described for myself. If they like, they can collect data on themselves and refrain from doing brain scans of average people.

## III.15.G. Surveys

We will face constant economic shortfalls, notably chronic government budget problems but also funding of education, health care, retirement, etc. They will give the appearance of being M&M problems that can be alleviated with policy and aggregate demand manipulation. Therefore, we will find it necessary to resort to shaping people's economic tendencies more and more. We will attempt to increase our GDP by growing C, which is, as we like to say, "two-thirds of our economy." To grow C, we must know, and be able to shape, people's intentions to spend; so we have to understand what makes people spend. Ultimately this leads to the use of surveys, and the raw truth is that surveys of what makes people choose their goods and services are all nonsense. Survey information represents another major flaw in our M&M system of making our economy big. Furthermore, as our demand policies prove to be unsuccessful and a contributing factor to our general economic decline the use of surveys will become discredited and perhaps relegated to status as unscrupulous and shameful methods of social science. It behooves young people to be prudent about how they participate in and use surveys.

## III.15.G.a. Surveys Compared to Choice or "Revealed Preferences"

There is a difference between what people say and what they do. In economics we talk about Revealed Preference, which is a microeconomic idea that people's choices demonstrate their preferences. Of course, this might sound obvious; but in economic and other social science analysis we need to measure the following: (1) people's preferences quantitatively and (2) their interest in goods and services they are not presently selecting. Therefore, we have to survey them or otherwise ask their intentions. What people say they do in surveys, polls, experiments, simulations, questionnaires, tests, etc. is useless. In the practice of microeconomics, revealed preference is an operational way of quantifying people' inclinations. Revealed preference is dominant over surveys and the other measures of people's choices as done in BE. Here are some examples of revealed preference being more insightful than experts' opinions and survey answers:

- **Choice of tasks and pastimes**: Let's say we observe two men who are very similar, including that they each earn $100 per hour in his occupation. One man mows his own lawn, while the other hires a person to do it at a rate of $20 per hour. What can we conclude? Some analysts conclude that the first man is irrational, wasting his time at the low-level task. Other analysts would recommend surveying the men to determine the factors behind their behavior. Both analyses are superfluous and demeaning. The man who mows his own lawn has demonstrated that there is some package of features of the task that yields utility equal to or greater than the disutility of the $80 per hour he forfeits. Perhaps he distrusts the quality of the work done for hire, enjoys the joint activity of getting exercise while mowing or values the gesture toward his wife at doing certain household chores while she does others that they cannot farm out. It may be a combination of all of those factors and myriad. Surveying is of very limited insight. The men themselves would have a difficult time explaining their actions.

- **Auto travel**: We drive alone. Highway lanes restricted to multiple passengers are notoriously empty. In cities with efficient public transportation, many people still choose to drive. According to surveys and the judgments of social scientists, people claim to want to drive with others,[231] yet actions indicate otherwise and people are averse to admit their desire to drive by themselves. Perhaps people do not enjoy the company of others as much as they say. Perhaps, in the cases of avoiding public transportation, people reveal that they dislike being close to other people. Perhaps people garner a sense of empowerment and independence by driving that they cannot have in any situation of their lives.

- **Work v. leisure**: Another example is people's claims of desiring more time off from work. Google magnate and social do-gooder Sergiy Brin (in various presentations circa 2014) claims that 100% of people report they want more time off from work. Even if we allow him some hyperbole, he is still gullible. What does he think people will say, "I would rather be at work, than have time off. My work gives me the greatest pleasure. I am in control at work and challenged among my peers in fulfilling ways. Spending time with my family and friends is boring. Often I have little control, which I dislike. I also dislike dealing with children and my spouse. At work I get to boss people around, and that makes me happy."

- **Spending time with children**: This is another case in which parents, in surveys, will contend they crave more time with their children. In many situations of choice, however, a parent might choose to do a dreary task, like washing dishes, over a "fun" child-related task, like reading the child a story.

- **College choice**: When accepted to many schools, prospective college applicants pick certain programs over others. This may be a better way of discerning school quality rankings, compared to conventional school rankings.[232]

- **Beliefs v. actions**: Many people report that they believe in ghosts. You can find many surveys that report this to be a large fraction (like 20%). Such beliefs reflect a great irrationality of the populace and a need to assist people in science and sensible thinking, according to analysts. Such outlandish and silly views are to be dismissed. People's actions do not reflect belief. For example, if you offered lodging in two similar hotel rooms, one with ghosts and one without, don't be too surprised if ghost-believers choose the cheaper room every time.

Analysts who rely on surveys, especially BE experts, find irrationality and foolishness among the populace but people's actions merely reveal the underlying preferences that provide self-esteem and comfort. The real pathology is the researcher who craves the existence of a vast retrograde citizenry so he can strut his superior intellect and pity.

### III.15.G.b. Surveys: The Insult & Folly

As a social scientist and observer of the popular discussion of current events, nothing is more infuriating to me than the incessant use of surveys and similar polls, questionnaires, tests, etc. to portray

---

[231] Behavioral economist Danny Kahneman contended in a 2004 presentation at Tufts University that people wanted to drive together.

[232] Avery, Christopher N., Mark E. Glickman, Caroline M. Hoxby and Andrew Metrick, "A Revealed Preference Ranking of U.S. Colleges and Universities," *The Quarterly Journal of Economics*, (2013), 128 (1), pp. 425-467.

people. Simply put, such exercises and the way in which they are presented in the media, mock people and diminish their actions and intentions. The single biggest finding of surveys is that people are dumb. Surveying may have legitimate applications in the marketing of products or in certain other specialized or straightforward tasks, but as for getting at what people really value in their lives and how they choose to live their lives, surveys are nonsense. Additionally, despite their folly, surveys get little or no condemnation.

## Major Survey Shortcomings

As we pointed out earlier about consumer confidence surveys, surveys demonstrate a basic causality problem. It should be that people report their sentiments from information they observe and information reported impartially in the news. Then, experts can analyze these unadulterated opinions and perhaps engage in policy. What most likely happens is that people are inundated with media and expert commentary on news events and then, when these people are surveyed, they simply mimic the opinions of the experts. Here are some other quirky facets of surveys:

- A common survey result is that people describe some facet of modern life as in severe condition in society as a whole but in their own lives that facet is fine. For example, people typically claim that crime is bad, but it is not a problem in their own lives. Another classic is that people contend the schools are poor, but the ones their kids go to are fine.[233]

- Surveys are often done on topics that average people know nothing about, including, for example, topics in M&M. People have been surveyed about the issue of whether or not the Federal Reserve Bank should be "audited" which is a ridiculous question to ask of a person.[234] These average people were not even informed of the specific type of audit that was being proposed. The proposed Fed audit was not a counting up of assets, liabilities, sales, etc. about which people have some sense. It was to be a review of monetary policy. In contrast, in 2015, for example, people were asked about the identity of the current Chair of the Fed and very few people could name her. Of course, analysts of surveys did not shy away from drawing conclusions from this survey. The lack of Fed personnel knowledge was deemed a severe shortcoming on the part of the populace to understand and contribute to public policy.

- In any survey involving personal questions or deep feelings and opinions of people (as opposed to surveys involving a product, current topic or some light topic like entertainment or sport) those being surveyed are immediately suspicious and offended—even if they do not let on. It is as if a person accosts you and says, "I am surveying you. I will be judging your life. I am attempting to demonstrate that you are retrograde in some capacity and inferior to a person like me. Also, you typically consent to people like me to rectify your problems." In such surveys, people's responses will typically prove points. Survey people about parenting, relationships, religion, social status, morality, etc. and you will likely get responses that serve to prove a point. Some questions are simply unanswerable. For example, asking, "Are you an atheist?" is a futile question. So are many questions relating to sex, race, homosexuality, faith, military service, etc. For example, a Mormon will assent if asked if he is religious and believes the tenets of Mormonism. Of course, he could never respond, "When I was young I craved regular sex and the only way I could get it was to get

---

[233] "I'm OK, you're not," *U.S. News & World Report*, December 16, 1996, pp. 24-32.
[234] "74% Want to Audit the Fed," Rasmussen Reports, November 8, 2013.
http://www.rasmussenreports.com/public_content/business/general_business/november_2013/74_want_to_audit_the_federal_re serve

married. Then, after having a child and another child, a house, a job, bills, etc., I got stuck in this Mormon community and circumstances dictated that I had to appear devout. To be honest, though, I never believed any of the religious trappings of Mormonism."

- Since many surveys make the questioned person feel incompetent and petty, defiant responses are common. Surveying people of modest means about money brings out financial bluster. That might explain many of the irrational beliefs people supposedly harbor about money, e.g., overly high rates of return on investments. Similarly, when you hear that a large fraction of people believe in ghosts, it might represent a reverse jab by the person being surveyed. Sometimes people answer incorrectly just to confound the surveyor. Other times they treat the survey with derision. A 2001 census done in Britain found many people writing in "Jedi Knight" to a question about religious affiliation.[235]

- People answer what they think the surveyor wants them to say and/or what makes the person being surveyed seem smart or cool. People wish to be "in the know." Also, people answer questions beyond their knowledge, usually mimicking the opinions of other people assuming that those people are better informed. For example, many surveys contend that people expect very high returns to their investments, which some analysts interpret as evidence of foolishness. The survey result does not necessarily reflect what people really believe nor how they act. In my conversations with people about investing, few seem to take such high rates of return as attainable. They themselves do not act on such assumed rates of return and do not plan retirement on these assumptions. They garner information about investment returns from the media and report them to surveyors to appear to know the topic.

- One of the most vile sub-varieties of surveying is the surveying of people's happiness by nationality (i.e., Americans v. Swedes v. Egyptians, etc.) relative to people's economic lots in life. Such surveying, and attendant assessment, is typically performed by Westerners with the subjects often being people from poor(er) lands. It is replete with estimations that people crave our standard of living and with stereotyping by nationality. Analysts explain drastic differences, for example contentment with life relative to income ranging from 10% to 80%, with glib comments like being surprised that Russians are happy and people of the Middle East are unhappy.[236]

- Surveys are often politically-loaded and designed and/or interpreted to make people appear nativist and reactionary. For example, most people believe in evolution and in other theories from science like the Big Bang. When surveyed in the context of bigger questions about life and man's ability to understand the mysteries of life though, people appeal to faith. Yet surveys emphasize extreme anti-scientific sentiments like, "Only 15 percent… [think] humans evolved from less advanced life forms," i.e. believe the science of evolution, or "Around a third of American adults accept the Big Bang theory."[237]

- Another pervasive problem in survey work is the difficulty of getting a random sample of the population. Most surveys work off of available subsets of interviewees, and oftentimes even a special, motivated subset of those. Not getting a representative sample renders the so-called "margins of error" reported in survey results as nonsense. The typical line in a newspaper article on a survey is something like, "The survey has a margin of error of 3.1 percentage points."[238] In this case a "telephone poll of 1,007 students" was done. A more accurate statement should be, "This

[235] "(British) empire's Jedis strike back on census," Associated Press piece in *The Boston Globe*, October 11, 2001, p. A3.
[236] "Money Buys Happiness Until It Doesn't," by Barry Ritholtz, November 10, 2014, *Bloomberg.com*, http://www.bloombergview.com/articles/2014-11-10/money-buys-happiness-until-it-doesnt
[237] "Academics warn of an assault on science," Reuters piece by Alan Elsner in *The Boston Globe*, October 31, 2005, p. C3.
[238] "Students surveyed think draft will resume" *The Boston Globe*, Associated Press, August 10, 2004, p. A9.

survey has a statistical margin of error which is minimal. Other, larger sources of errors in this survey include the following: the survey was done by telephone and we reached only those from certain phone lists; many people refused to cooperate; we suspect the ones who did answer were biased; the survey personnel were poorly paid and under time constraints; the survey questions are difficult to answer in a meaningful way; the ordering of the questions of the survey may yield different results."

- Relevant to M&M and the economic well-being of people is the level of knowledge that people have about finance and economics. There is a plethora of surveys demonstrating that Americans are financially illiterate. For example, a U.S. government survey done by FINRA asks a few simple questions, in True or False format, including this one, "A 15-year mortgage typically requires higher monthly payments than a 30-year mortgage but the total interest over the life of the loan will be less." (The survey is on www.usfinancialcapability.org/quiz.php.) Many people answer such questions incorrectly. Such knowledge, however, is not needed by people. It may seem like general knowledge that anyone should possess at all times, but it is specialized knowledge that people only need to know at certain times. When people are faced with such decisions in real life they are resourceful enough to find the answer or, more typically, to seek out the right person like the mortgage person at the bank. If he seems at all untrustworthy, people are clever enough to walk out the door and get a second opinion. You can make an analogy to other situations. For example, questions about rudimentary automobile maintenance would stump many people. They know, though, to go to the local gas station and ask.

- Surveys often show implausibly large changes of attitudes and journalists, and other promoters of the surveys usually imbibe the large change as valid. Examples of this are numerous and span many areas of survey results. Sometimes rampant change in survey results reveals dependence on current events and/or the media coverage of the events rather than grave underlying opinion. For example, only 1% of people cited "Race Relations" or "Racism" as an important issue in America in November 2014. The following month, 13% did—presumably due to intense media coverage of primarily one incident: the shooting of a black man by a white police officer in Ferguson, Missouri a few months earlier. Such changes also demean people, implying that they are fickle and prone to shift into extremism—and that they are generally ignorant. Here are a few survey results: A survey of high school seniors in 2000 has only 46% correctly distinguishing public from private pensions, while 64% "answered the question right" in 1997. In the same survey, only 21% knew they had to pay tax on savings interest, but 32% knew it four years earlier. A survey of back-to-school spending has households spending $436 in 1999 and $549 in 2000. A writer cites an IRS survey that notes, "Americans who believe it is acceptable to cheat on taxes rose from 11% in 1999 to 17% in 2003."[239]

- The act of surveying is hard and smart people learn to trick the survey. While doing surveys, I realized that often when I would answer an initial question affirmatively, I would get asked a series of other questions. For example, when asked, "Did you do business travel in the last six month?" A yes leads to multiple questions on that travel. To save time, I learned to deny activities. In this case, more intelligent people being surveyed will pick up this feature and will be more likely to lie.

---

[239] Sources: "As a Major U.S. Problem, Race Relations Sharply Rises," by Justin McCarthy, Gallup, Social Issues, December 19, 2014, www.gallup.com/poll/180257/major-problem-race-relations-sharply-rises.aspx?; "High school seniors flunk personal finance," Associated Press piece in *The Boston Globe*, April 9, 2000, p. K6; "Back-To-School Is Getting High Marks," *Business Week*, September 1, 2003, p. 38; "Fighting a New Cold War," *Business Week*, March 29, 2004, pp. 40-43; "Going Underground," by Jim McTague, *Barron's*, January 3, 2005, pp. 17-19.

Often, in a survey, I lock in a level of response: I give a high ranking initially and then have to rank everything else very highly. Sometimes, in such a situation, I feel sorry for the surveyor that I am giving the same answer every time, so I try to add some variability.

- Despite people's responses to surveys being contrary, duplicitous or self-serving, they are altogether consistent with maximizing utility. People are not obligated to reveal truths. They may, for example, tell a researcher that they believe in creationism or ghosts just to confound the researcher. There is no marginal cost to the person, and the marginal benefit of standing your ground is great.
- People who engage in surveying the public are relatively free to design and conduct their surveys. There are certain rules about soliciting people, the nature of questions and the disclosure of the purposes and results of surveys. Some survey outfits enforce very high standards on their work. In general, though, utilizing our populace as guinea pigs to explore any of a variety of questions or issues is not broadly criticized. People suffer significant psychological discomfort from the copious and random surveying done on them, most of which has some element of being non-voluntary. Surveying should be curtailed, and younger generations should avoid survey analysis.

# III.16. Methodology in Social & Business Science

This section addresses various methods upon which M&M and financial market analysis depend, focusing on ideas and models that are simultaneously prominent, important and often misapplied. If I had to choose the single, most important concept from all of the techniques and methods of social and business research, it would be the mean, or average. The average level, and its tendency to either stay at a certain level or depart from a former level, is dominant in M&M, financial analysis and life in general. It might sound simplistic, but show me any data series and all I want to know is, "What is its average, and will that average persist?" For an analogy, think of your baseball team. Its players go to bat, or to the pitcher's mound, with certain average tendencies, e.g., the hitter can hit a home run every twelve at-bats, and the pitcher can win twenty games. If they return to the playing field in the following year, and these mean tendencies are diminished they will win fewer games.

This is not a comprehensive coverage of method. Social and business science methods are so voluminous that non-professionals can easily trip themselves up if they try to master too many. Even a simple listing of methods is very extensive. Peruse commentary on the economy and financial markets and you will encounter regression, maximum likelihood, meta-analysis, alpha, beta, Monte Carlo, back-testing, neural networks, Bayesian inference, correlation, linear programming, fat tails, artificial intelligence, risk measures, etc. Each of those itself has a multitude of sub-categories, e.g., risk measures include the Sharpe Ratio, the Information Ratio, Jensen's alpha, Omega Ratio, Sortino Ratio, downside risk, Treynor Ratio, VaR (Value at Risk), etc. In addition, I have purposely omitted many quasi-scientific methods, such as technical analysis as done in investment research (the oscillators, bands, resistance levels, heads and shoulders, etc.), and advanced methods like neural networks. Some experts stand by them, but there is no bigger fool than the "finder of patterns in random information" fool. Some of the main pitfalls of research in business and social science include the following:

- It is very easy to do nonsense in empirical social science research. You will think that you have discovered a trend or a cause and effect and that your method is sound and your empirical work significant. You likely have discovered a false signal, however, and this is typically due to some basic methodological mistake.
- Similarly, it is very easy to find what you are looking for. Behavioral economists, for example, can easily affirm their theories by collecting examples of mistakes people make in economics or finance, claim the mistakes constitute a set, find statistical significance in some specification and apply an appellation like "confirmation bias," "anchoring," "recency effect," etc.
- Certain basic concepts (notably mean, variance, cycles and the randomness of future trends) are dominant. Despite all the advanced methods we use, for most questions on markets and the economy, we really fall back on guesses about means and variances (or standard deviations) of historical data series and assumptions of cyclical patterns. We otherwise concede that the future is a big unknown.
- It will become more and more difficult to present a variety of models and empirical results as if they contain novelty or findings exploitable for policy or otherwise taking action. For example, a pundit or portfolio manager during the period 1980 to 2010 could glibly support his research by appealing to cycles. This will be harder to do in the future, both at the intellectual level and at the practical level of peddling models and research services. This is a key insight for the young generation.

- Analysis of social and business science issues can be very patronizing of average people as if the analyst can discern and take advantage of flaws in people's behavior. Many of the findings of behavioral economics are like this: "The thinking is defunct. In our modern world, where most people are educated to some extent, it is very difficult to fix their lives."
- For most M&M and financial market analysis we inspect historical data series, typically simply graphing over time (with time, in years, days, etc. on the x-axis and the variable or variables being studied on the y-axis), and trying to discern correlations and causes and effects. If we cannot eyeball relations, we can apply statistical analysis of some sort, typically regression and let the computer find it. These processes may be entirely futile. Simply put, past trends of most M&M series do not persist. Movement is random. Nominal series, of course, trend with inflation but that is a relatively useless facet. Also series move given certain obvious factors underlying the trend. Such movement is also relatively useless since it is discernible by everyone and, therefore, factored in. For example, we know that the stock market goes up on average each year an amount equal to inflation and its real growth (which level is debatable, of course, but we can use consensus estimates). If you take those factors out what remains is mostly random.
- Trends must be related to fundamental microeconomic factors and not macro factors. Analysis that merely relates one macro quantity/trend (like GDP, consumption, employment, industrial production, etc.) to another is futile and, although such macro theorizing is omnipresent today, it will get harder and harder to spin credible macro stories in the future.

## III.16.A. General Probability & Statistics Issues

As stated before, despite the great volume of advanced methods, the simple average is the overwhelmingly important tool. In investing, for example, the most relevant quantity is the "expected return." In general, we scrutinize data and calculate average tendencies. Then we model and project assuming those means hold. As we saw in the history of our economy and financial markets, we looked at the recent averages (like unemployment, GDP growth, stock market returns, etc.) and assumed we must tend toward those levels. When the averages change, however, our methods and convictions break down.

## III.16.A.a. Mean, Standard Deviation, Skewness & Kurtosis

The following paragraph details the "moments" of a statistical distribution. The mean and standard deviation are the first and second moments and are pretty well understood by everybody. The mean is the sum of the observations divided by the number of observations. Most people also know other concepts of average including the median (the observation in the middle of the data) and the mode (the most common observation). Although most people cannot remember the exact formula for the standard deviation, some would get close. To get the standard deviation take the value of each observation, subtract it from the mean and square the result. Then, sum those squared differences and take that mean. That gives the variance. Next, take the square root of the variance and get the standard deviation. The variance represents a measure of the spread of data too, but the standard deviation gives you a measure in the same units as the mean. Skewness is the third moment and is the amount of asymmetry of a distribution. If the distribution is symmetrical, the skewness is zero. If the distribution has more observations on the right side, we have positive skewness, and vice versa. Kurtosis is the fourth moment and is a measure of how large the tails of a distribution are or how likely or how often you are to get an observation far away from the mean. Formulas for skewness and kurtosis are complicated. There are further moments but they have little intuition.

To illustrate these four moments, in returns to assets we want high expected returns (means) and low risk, which is typically measured as volatility or standard deviation. Skewness, by convention, is assumed to be positive. In investment returns you would want high (positive) skewness because it would mean tending to get high returns more frequently than low. Kurtosis represents the chance of getting a value way off of the mean, e.g., seven standard deviations from the mean. We want kurtosis to be small usually because we are averse to really bad outcomes—more than we desire really good outcomes. In street parlance, high kurtosis has many names: rare events, Black Swans (because they are very, very rare creatures), tail events, tail risk, non-normal distributions (because kurtosis is small in a normal distribution) and "once in a thousand year storms." In a normal distribution kurtosis is low/small, like in the first diagram where the tails are small. Normal distribution being more than two standard deviations away from your mean should happen less than 5% of the time. Somewhat naively, we assume stock market returns to be normally distributed. Then when we get a bad draw, like in 2008, we denounce everyone else's belief in the normality of stock market returns. Then the references to black swans, etc. become prominent in discussions and the press. Then we focus on it extremely, and to a certain extent ignore the mean and standard deviation. After some time we get "black swans fatigue" as we concede that the problem with rare events is that we cannot predict them, so we return to analyzing mean and standard deviation. We realize that if we think rare adverse events are going to happen with relative frequency, we should get out of any risky investing and put all of our wealth in risk-free or low risk assets.

In summary, in investment returns you want "high odd moments and low even moments." We want high mean returns, of course, and also high skewness because by convention skewness is assumed to be positive. Hedge fund returns, supposedly, deliver high skewness. We want low even moments because we want low spread of returns and returns devoid of great tail risk. To round out the discussion, what have the returns to U.S. stocks been historically? You can get all kinds of numbers depending on the start and end dates and which subset of the stock market you are looking at. For large company stock from about 1926 to the present the average return was around 11% per year in nominal terms. With inflation averaging about 3% the real return was around 8%. The standard deviation has been about 20%. There is some positive skewness and frequent extreme returns (like -37% in 2008) such that the tails are large but returns are close to a normal distribution. For small companies' stocks the mean is higher, about 16%, the standard deviation is about 32% and the distribution has a number of modes.

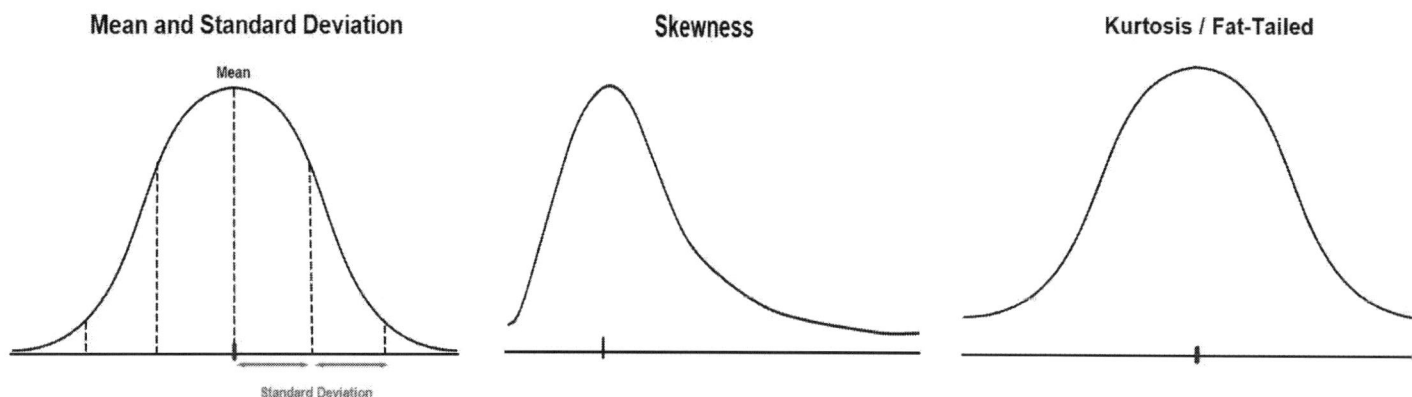

**Mean and Standard Deviation**    **Skewness**    **Kurtosis / Fat-Tailed**

## III.16.A.b. Unlikely Average

We rely on the average (mean or median, perhaps) and believe that the important quantities of our lives, including our macro series, tend toward average. How often do we say, "The average <insert any noun here> is …" Yet an average is often meaningless: Average salaries, for example, often reflect nothing typical. A person once asked me as an economist to give the average wage for an American and he was surprised when I could not give one number. I asked back, "Which kind of work, or group?" Take the legal profession, for example. The average lawyer might earn about $100,000 per year, but few lawyers earn anything around that. Lawyers break into the highly successful who earn many multiples of $100,000 and the rest, including the ambulance chasers, research lawyers, legal clerks, etc. For another example, consider the average cost of college. Some students go to private colleges while other go to public schools which are much cheaper. Some attend four-year schools while others go to community colleges. Some live on campus while others commute. Although almost all averages in social science have some element of imperfection, some are better than others. For example, the average earnings of firefighters in a big city would represent what a typical firefighter earns. Sometimes it might be easy to detect when an average comes from a distribution with obvious modes and adjust for them in your head. For example, the U.S. Census Bureau reports that 25.1 minutes is the average time a U.S. commuter spends getting to work.[240] You might surmise that a good fraction of people walk to work and, therefore, have very short commuting time, and the average for the remaining people who do commute is just a little higher than the reported average.

Many averages are combinations of other averages—for example, the affordability of a home. Following 2008, we often heard about affordability being at a very high level. We calculate housing affordability by taking average (median) income and comparing it to average (median) house price, then also, in some calculations, assuming an average mortgage rate, average loan term (30 years) and average down payment. This seems sensible but all of those averages were particularly hard to pin down during this time period for various reasons, so the sum of those averages would be even less reliable.

Averages can trick you in many ways. Here is one: Let's say that a law firm has two groups of workers: lawyers and paralegals. We are also told the average earnings of women are lower than those of men at this firm. Could it be that the female lawyers earn more than the male lawyers? If the paralegals earn less than the lawyers and most of the paralegals are women, then the overall average could be lower for the women even if the average female lawyer earns more than the average male lawyer. This is known as Simpson's Paradox. Bad averages abound in M&M, as the following examples illustrate:

- The average household retirement savings is often reported around $50,000 to $100,000. This is an odd amount to reconcile with what you know about the savings of your friends and family and with what amount you think retirement requires. The explanation is that few household have that amount. Most people have zero savings while a few have great sums.
- The same is true for the macro savings rate as reported monthly. It is a quantity that depends on asset value changes and its average level, which is reported as a rate of national income, like 4%, etc., is meaningless.[241] Yet M&M analysts make pronouncements about how average people suddenly became more or less thrifty.
- Average house values, or more pointedly house value increases, are misleading. In many recent years we have reported that house values rose substantially. It is accompanied by copious

---

[240] 2005 data cited widely in the press, e.g., on *cnn.com* September 1, 2006.
[241] We also discussed that the Savings Rate is poorly defined as savings due to it being a residual calculation of income minus spending.

commentary on how the "average" household realized this wealth and acted on it by spending more or less. House values and changes are very lumpy. They occur in certain housing markets and certain types of housing. The vast majority of homeowners simply have no concept of the value of the home going up or down.

We often hear that in surveys an outlandish percentage of people claim they are above average. We scoff at that, and BE economists use it as prima facie evidence of people's poor judgment. This is not altogether unlikely though if people perceive of the average as a mode or median average compared to a strict mean. For example, most people are pretty good drivers, rarely having an accident. Indeed, they are above average if the average is number of accidents and a small number of really bad drivers skew the average.

## III.16.A.c. Meandering Means & Stationarity

In social and business science, we rely on our historical means to persist. New data points come out higher or lower but each new point tends to regress around the mean. We use the term stationarity of a time series to describe a mean that is not drifting up or down. What if a data series is currently not regressing toward its assumed mean? What are the implications if a mean is drifting, or meandering, in either direction? A changing mean can represent a significant problem. For one, the assumed average is spurious. Also if the mean is not stationary then the standard deviation is useless. We can speculate that many of our M&M and financial market statistics have meandering means—especially since 2008. For example, as we pointed out about stock market returns, our hundred years of annual returns and their approximate 10% average might really represent just one observation of a golden age in the history of capitalism. That mean is now meandering down. The same could be hypothesized for interest rates, inflation, rates of increase in the price of houses, etc. If this is the case, the standard deviations from historical data, which we use for risk, are of limited use. In contemporary discussions of flaws of statistical analyses of economic and financial data, opinion focuses on the presence of fat tails. Yet the mean and its meandering might be the much more important statistical flaw.

## III.16.A.d. Rare Events

We talked about kurtosis in a relatively formal fashion, but we should examine rare events with greater detail. First of all, they are not as rare as we might assume. Also, rare events is often invoked as an excuse for purposeful risk taking. Average people have familiarity with rare events from public lotteries. Often we hear about a person who wins a big lottery pool two separate times. The dual winner will be written up in the press as an improbable case: "Overall, her chances of winning both games were a slim 1 in 3,669,120,000,000. "[242] Such a raw probability in this case is misleading. Indeed, the probability that somebody will win a big lottery payout twice if he starts playing today is very low, but the probability that someone, somewhere will win twice is not. In lotteries, many people play and make many bets. Some of them win and some win big pots. They continue to play and to play a lot, such that, on occasion, they win another big pot. Given the numbers of wages made expect to see double big winners from time to time— maybe multiple times per year, depending how low down you set the size of the big pot.

In a way, the first event of an unlikely sequence of events is a freebie. For example, you read in the newspaper that a golfer scored two holes in one in a row, and you are told it is a one in many million

---

[242] September 9, 2005, *Boston.com* piece.

chance because each hole in one is a one in one thousand chance. But if he had scored one hole in one, it would not be in the newspaper. In a sense, all you are testing is the probability of a player getting one hole in one. People often remark that an event is unlikely, both in personal situations and in the news. Today, though, when we are bombarded with online news, you realize how many people/events there are and why they are actually not unlikely. A famous bit of New England lore is the injury of Phineas P. Gage. In 1848, Gage, a 25 year-old railroad worker, had a large metal rod pierce his head. This was a major head injury that surely should have resulted in death, yet he survived for 13 years in relatively good shape. For one hundred years, his story was told and retold as if it were unlikely, but in the internet age we encounter a plethora of such incredible survival stories. We realize that such events are not unlikely.

Off events become excuses for economic policy and finance and investing. For example, the "storm" (either once in a thousand or hundred years)" was invoked by Alan Greenspan about the 2008 financial crisis (his term in testimony to Congress in 2008 was "once-in-a-century tsunami") and by countless money managers and investors who made big bets and lost money, like John Meriwether of Long-Term Capital Management back in 1998. These experts knew better though. They were aware of the principles of statistics and the histories of the quantities they were trying to take advantage of. They knew that non-normality in outcomes of investing and policy actions exists. Such inculcation has been in textbooks and in professional forums throughout their lifetimes. Don't be so foolish as to think happenings are that uncommon. Furthermore, do not be gullible for excuses given by professionals and other big-shots who are shocked that their policy or program did not work and opine, "It was a hundred year storm."

## III.16.A.e. Type II Errors, Backtesting, Data Snooping, Data Mining & Overidentification

The above terms refer to over-analysis of data which results in finding relationships that do not exist. More specifically, they refer to picking through data to find which statistical relationships work and then testing those with the same data that the relationships were originally found in or, alternatively, not testing them with fresh data or out-of-sample data.[243] They represent bad methods, and this is a grave problem in social and business science—and the faulty methodology dupes people.

Research is largely a search for relationships among data. We seek one or more variables that cause other variables, like temperature and humidity causing sweating. If one or more of our explanatory variables are known into the future with some accuracy, then perhaps we can forecast the variable dependent on those variables. As emphasized before, research—whether academic or business—should follow a certain procedure: Formulate a hypothesis; model it using accepted principles and frameworks from social or business science; test it with data that presumably measure the items being tested; examine results for hypothesized relationships and statistical significance and draw conclusions. The way we perform research and teach statistics and econometrics subverts this process. We "keep on trying." If your analysis, such as regression analysis, did not come out the way your initial theory implied you make a change such as adding a variable, removing a variable, lagging the data, de-trending the data, trying fitting a curve rather than a line, adding more data, using more or less aggregated data, etc. An alternative choice would be to test your initial specification and, if you reject your hypothesis, give up the research project. Of course, that diminishes your role as social scientist. The best practice is to estimate your model in one set of data (one time period if you are doing time series) and limit your tests to a few specifications. In other words, do not

---

[243] Certain of the terms have more specialized meanings. For example, data mining can refer to the using of high powered computers to examine the extremely large data sets available today to find minute trends. There is nothing necessarily or fundamentally wrong about this variety of data mining although it is easy to get carried away with techniques and engage in over-analysis.

change your model too frequently. Then, test your findings with data outside your data set. As we pointed out, such strict procedure is difficult to maintain in the real world.

In practice, the process is usually even less pure. People poke around until they find a hypothesis that suits their beliefs and that, for some reason, they feel they can prove. Then, various models are proposed to test the hypothesis. Various data are available; and if these initial selections and matches of the research procedure look fruitful or compelling, the project is undertaken. If the will is there, the researchers keep working on the project—ignoring adverse results, changing specifications, backtesting, data mining, etc.—until they pretty much prove what they believed in the first place. They maintain an illusion of unbiased results due to their hard work or earnest intentions or due to their use of advanced quantitative techniques. One of the damming demonstrations of this situation is that a large fraction of empirical work cannot be duplicated by other researchers.[244]

Another way of describing the situation of bias in research results, and a useful piece of jargon, is the "Type I/Type II" error. Consider a person on trial for a crime. There are four possible outcomes:

|  | Guilty | Not Guilty |
|---|---|---|
| **Found Guilty** | Accurate | Type II Error |
| **Not Found Guilty** | Type I Error | Accurate |

Two outcomes result in no error. The "Type I" error is when we do not find the result even though it really exists. The more grievous error in many cases is the "Type II" error, which occurs when we find the condition we are testing for, even though it is not there. We have too many Type II errors in research and society.

"False positive" is another term for a related concept of testing processes. This applies more commonly to tests or screens for medical conditions. For example, what is the chance you truly have a certain ailment if the test for that ailment is 95% accurate, the ailment affects 2% of the population and you have been tested and have a positive test result? Before analyzing the question more specifically most people think the answer is about 95%. If you break it down, though, there are really two situations/questions. First, what is the probability that, if you have the ailment, your test result is accurate? That is 95%. The second question is more common, what is the probability that, if you got a positive test result, you truly have the ailment? The correct answer is about 30% based on this reasoning: Assume 1,000 people are tested. Twenty of them should have the ailment and 980 should not. Of the 980 without the ailment, about 49 will produce a false positive. Of the twenty with the disease, one will produce a false negative. Altogether, there will be 69 positives, 49 of which are false positives or about 71% false positives and 29% correct tests.

### III.16.A.f. Cycles v. Secular Trends & Reversion

We talked about business cycles at length earlier and how they get vastly more credit than they should given cycles' minimal and erratic cyclicity. Perhaps there is no greater faux model/assumption/story of social systems than cycles. We invoke them in analyses of a wide variety of social and business

---

[244] "Is Economics Research Replicable? Sixty Published Papers from Thirteen Journals Say ' Usually Not'," by Andrew C. Chang and Phillip Li, Finance and Economics Discussion Series 2015-083. Washington: Board of Governors of the Federal Reserve System, http://dx.doi.org/10.17016/FEDS.2015.083.

phenomena and do so very cavalierly, as if no proof is needed. People will often say, "I'm a believer in cycles" or "We're now at this point in a cycle" as if such statements impart insight. Read the financial weekly *Barron's*, for example, to find a plethora of references to cycles. The columnists, the invited speakers, etc. rely heavily on cyclical forces to validate their investing and economic strategies. A cycle is a convenient device as if something desirable is moving in a way you can predict and take advantage of, rather than just random movements and noise.

The raw reality is that the vast majority of cycle talk simply does not describe a true cyclical force, i.e., a force that is moving in a pattern reasonably described by a cycle with some consistent length and degree of up and down (called amplitude). Also, even if a series displays up and down pattern or a growth and decline pattern, can we either predict, explain or relate it to some other force? If the answer is no, then it is not much of cycle. It is not too say that there are not wave movements. The bulk of movement of macro series is overwhelmingly determined by shifts rather than cycles. Plus, the timing is very variable, or, in cycle-speak, the amplitude (the vertical up and down) and the wavelengths (the horizontal span) are variable.

The standard business cycle that M&M and the concept of recession are based on supposedly happens every few years. Economists have also talked about longer cycles like the Kondratiev cycles (average about 50 years, ranging 40 to 60) and the Kuznets cycles (15 to 25 years). Also, there are shorter cyclical patterns like seasonal cycles (retail spending around Christmas). People invoke all cycles freely even to the point where they bump into and overlap with each other. For example, noted investor Ray Dalio (head of large hedge fund Bridgewater Associates) believes in both the standard business cycle and a longer "credit" cycle.

Of course, I would not deny that cyclical patterns appearing to have some regularity could be somewhat discerned in historical data series. Nor would I deny that certain sub-components follow very regular cycles such as calendar cycles. Overall, though, we are seeing patterns that appear cyclical but are not and, worse, we are making up stories where randomness exists. Rather than cycles with reasonable regularity of amplitude and length, what we are experiencing is some combination of the following four items, and our eye tricks us into seeing cycles:

- **Secular trends**: longer-term trends, representing changing means.
- **Shifts**: We sometimes say structural shifts or regime shifts (or Conjuncture, as we use in this book). They are abrupt substantial changes in means.
- **For nominal series common movement due to inflation**.
- **Random movements**: Even though random movements are random they cue up sufficiently that they can appear to be cyclical.

These four types of movements are usually not foreseen, not cyclical and not understood until years after they have become obvious to markets and average people. Almost all of the major M&M and financial market series in the past few decades were characterized by non-cyclical movement:

- Unemployment in the United States over the 1980s and 1990s went down secularly and remained low for a long time. The drop defied any cyclical trends. Then, pursuant to 2008, unemployment rose abruptly and stayed high.
- Stock markets surged in 1980s and 1990s. The P/E ratio rose from about ten around 1980 to about 20 in the 1990s and 2000s. The P/E can fluctuate significantly depending upon which subset of the market you use and since earnings change a fair amount year by year so those are rough average levels. The stock market downswings, or bear markets, tend to cluster, largely occurring during the

1970s and 2000s. The stock market was very high in 1999 and 2007 and then crashed. Incidentally, if you believe in cycles, it should be ready to crash now.

- The bond market rallied for about 30 years starting in the 1980s.
- Productivity in the U.S. was below long-run averages during much of the 1970s and then above averages during the late 1990s (again, annual productivity can fluctuate a lot, so those are rough trends).
- The trade deficit of the U.S. generally defied levels that would be implied by cyclical forces—in other words, hitting very high levels in the 2000s.
- Money velocity (the V in MV = PQ) meandered for long periods, tending down, and recently (since 2008) crashed.
- Money aggregates like M1 and M2 defied what cyclical forces would imply for many decades.
- After Japan's economy slowed in 1990, it was supposed to recover to some high(er) rate of growth, but it never did and stayed at low growth for twenty-five years. Japan's stock market crashed and generally stayed low despite many pundits predicting a return in the Japanese stock market due to a basic cyclical tendency.
- Unemployment in Europe was very low, then it rose during the 1970s rose to high levels and stayed there.
- Exchange rates often trend longer and further than cycles would imply.
- U.S. GDP growth is typically characterized as hovering around 3% per year, yet commencing in the mid-1980s through the 1990s GDP grew at more than 3% per year with a period in the late 1990s at about 4%. Now, over the last ten years growth has been closer to 2%.
- Inflation rose during the late 1960s through the early 1980s then declined for 25 years. Since 2008 inflation has tended lower than cyclical forces might dictate.
- Interest rates (nominal) were high, along with inflation and now they are low. Real interest rates are hard to measure but are not standardly cyclical.
- housing prices surged for ten years after decades of little change. Then price changes became negative (around 2007 to 2009). They have risen significantly lately. In the future house prices might decline steadily for decades and after 50 years analysts will look back and see a 25-year run-up in price following by a 25-year decline.

Thinkers have studied theories of cycles for a long time. Economist and mathematician Eugen Slutsky discovered, or at least formalized in a scholarly paper, the idea that random shocks can appear like patterns, i.e., cycles.[245] Intelligent people are able to appreciate that random events can cluster and many trends are just coincident, rather than cycles. For an example of cycle defiance, flip a coin forty times and plot the result over time. Do this exercise twenty times. Observe the 20 time series diagrams you have created and compare them to 20 time series diagrams of actual economic indicators like industrial production, GDP growth, consumer confidence, etc. Can you discern the two sets of plots?

### III.16.A.f.i. Cycles in Financial & Investment Analysis

References to how to invest following cycles abound in investing. Many investors, such as mutual fund managers, copiously cite cycles as part of the their portfolio selection. The most common claim is that

---

[245] Slutsky's paper appeared in publication in the Russian language in 1927. It was reprinted in English in a longer version in *Econometrica* in 1937 entitled "The Summation of Random Causes as a Source of Cyclic Processes."

they see the economy coming out of a recession and they therefore recommend buying stocks of "pro-cyclical" companies like car companies and retailers. Some highly successful investors, like Ray Dalio of Bridgewater Associates, attribute much of their success to the discerning of cyclical forces. Dalio propounds a theory of short cycles of five to eight years, and longer credit cycles of nearly one hundred years. A leading investment consultancy remarks on its philosophy of analysis on equity markets: It "comes down to a reliance on historical data and an expectation that valuations will eventually revert to their long-term averages."[246]

People think the existence of cycles is so simple that not only can you rely on conventional historical occurrences of them to continue but you can even relatively easily exploit cycles. in his investing book for average people, bond investing great Bill Gross has a box on "The Business Cycle" in which he talks about a standard business cycle being of three to five years in length. Gross advises, it is, "important to investors…being able to locate the current point of the business cycle, for instance, can provide entry and exit points for longer-term market-timing decisions."[247] Whether any person has ever got in and out of markets given business cycles is impossible to tell, of course.

Investing by cycle leads to guesswork and contradictory strategies. The prime rule of investing is to invest for the long run, which is in complete contrast to investing cyclically. If you do invest cyclically you must be able to judge the stage of the business cycle and assume that the stock market or at least the company you are investing in moves with that cycle. Also, since we usually discern a cycle turning point well after it has happened (e.g., we did not call the 2008 recession, which formally began in December 2007, until the latter half of 2008) we are confounded as to which action to take. For example, if companies that should do well as an economy recovers are doing well currently, should you conclude that the economy is in some stage of recovery or going into a recession? Investors also are confounded when trying to capitalize on cycles less large than the general business cycle. For example, in the high-yield debt and bankruptcy area we think we see a big increase in high-yield debt issuance followed by a surge in bankruptcies. We present time series of the two quantities and indeed the high-yield issuance surge seems to be followed by the amount of assets going into bankruptcy; but, for one, it just as easily could be the other way around, and, two, the span of timing and magnitudes are devoid of regularity.

In summary, if you interviewing for a job that involves the pretense of seeing cycles, comment that cyclical facets are omnipresent and discernible. Be prepared, however, that such knowledge of cycles will be useless and that you only will thrive if you can appreciate the sudden breaks and long trends of important economic and financial quantities. For that knowledge you must know your microeconomics.

### III.16.A.g. Economic (or Practical) Significance v. Statistical Significance

This distinction is extremely important and often ignored. This problem exists in M&M and related social and business science analysis and also any other statistical analyses, particularly those related to health.

In a study, you can determine statistical significance, which reflects the likelihood that something exists only by chance. For example, are people who consume a certain type of food heavier? If you take a sample of people, half of whom consume the food and half of whom do not, and compare the groups' weights you can perform statistical tests which reveal the chance that a difference in weight is significant. If you find that the difference is significant, you might conclude you have found something useful.

---

[246] Cambridge Associates, September 2006 report, "Monthly Resources: Capital Market Commentaries, Notes on Current Valuations and Investment Publication Highlights," p. 13.
[247] *Everything You've Heard About Investing Is Wrong!* by William H. Gross, 1997, Times Business, p. 47.

However, significance alone is not enough. The magnitude of the difference should be of practical importance. What if the flux in weight is a fraction of a pound? Then your result may be of no interest. Sometimes researchers will increase the level of statistical significance, from say a 5% chance that the relationship happened by chance to a 1% chance and contend they have a stronger result. That may not have any impact on the practical result, though. One key facet is that a large sample typically ensures statistical significance. Frequently in studies the number of observations is so large that "significant" correlation between variables is easily found. The finding then gets reported without reference to the magnitude. For example, with a large enough sample, it is easy to relate almost any health or diet practice to longevity. Typically, the finding is that people die younger due to the consumption of some food item, yet the magnitude of change in life expectancy might be trivial, like a day of added life. People are unlikely to abandon a preferred diet for one more day of life at age 87. Another area in which magnitude matters is returns on actively managed securities portfolios. Researchers find that certain actively managed securities portfolios beat passive strategies but the level is minute, like a quarter of a percent per year.[248]

### III.16.A.h. Forcing a Line

We frequently estimate a linear relationship between quantities. We can do this by eye or more precisely by regression analysis: fitting the line through the scatter of points by minimizing the sum of the squared deviations of the points from the line. A very common mistake in social and business science involves putting a line through data, as illustrated below:

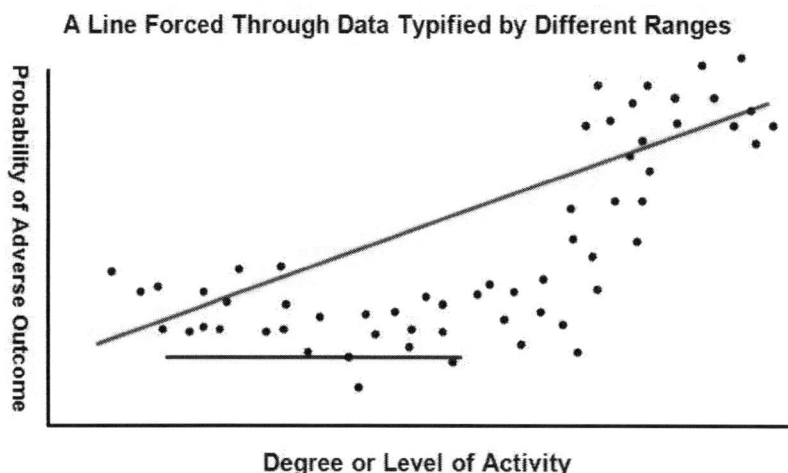

**A Line Forced Through Data Typified by Different Ranges**

Probability of Adverse Outcome

Degree or Level of Activity

If our relevant range of experience is exclusively in the left side of the x-axis (shown by the blue line), an increase in the degree or level of activity has no effect on the probability of the adverse outcome. For example, if your teenager plays computer games twenty minutes or sixty minutes a day, the effect on his schools grades will be the same. If he plays three hours day he is likely to suffer adverse conditions. Straight line regression gives the appearance that any increment in the activity is adverse. Such a situation applies to many of the activities that people enjoy, such as eating, drinking, using certain recreational drugs (like marijuana),

---

[248] There are many writings on the relationship between statistical significance and economic significance. For example, see "The Standard Error of Regressions," by Deirdre McCloskey and Stephen Ziliak, *Journal of Economic Literature*, 34 (March 1996), pp. 97-114.

sexual activity, watching television, using sunscreen, etc. For example, gross obesity may be associated with grave disease yet being a little overweight may have little adverse health effect. It applies frequently to economic analysis. For example, a pillar of M&M thinking is that stable GDP growth yields higher average GDP growth. The text I use states, "Stability leads to higher growth," citing an academic paper.[249] The research, however, shows something else: If you subdivide the data into types of countries (developed economies v. poor economies), then there is no relationship between stability and average growth.

## III.16.A.i. Number of "Obs"

Earlier we mentioned that we have merely a few examples of true M&M policy episodes. Small samples in statistical analysis of data are a fundamental problem. Statistics professors often tell the following ditty: A researcher was studying the behavior of chickens. He found that about 33% of the chickens exhibited one certain trait while another third exhibited a certain opposite characteristic but he could not comment on the behavior of the remainder of his sample because, "The third chicken ran away." Thirty observations is a rough cutoff for statistical analysis. With thirty observations, so long as the observations are not wildly different in value, the standard deviation gets small enough to make conclusions about your data. In the jargon we say. "you need about 30 obs to 'scrunch' the standard deviation down." For example, give me the prices of thirty recent house sales in a town and I can make a statement on the spread of prices in that area with some confidence.

Another concept of the number of observations concerns how to demarcate time series units. For example, for stock market returns or GDP growth rates we typically use annual data. That the Earth revolves around the Sun once a year may be irrelevant to either your investment horizon or the economic growth of a nation. For investing, returns over some weighted average of investing horizons, which would be longer than one year (maybe many years if not decades) might be better. Small samples are often used to make a case. Sometimes, samples of one, or even none (in a way), are used. Small samples abound in politics, sports, history and elsewhere. Writers for my local newspaper would need merely one or two cases of a corporate scandal to claim a trend. Political pundits remarked on the frequency of left-handed U.S. Presidents or that U.S. Presidents were more likely to be Governors than Senators. Pundits would make grandiose connections: "People are suspicious of Washington." Then, a Senator is elected President and the pundits change topics. "In President Obama's 2012 State of the Union speech he boasted the return of manufacturing jobs to America " or "The CEO of Master Lock told me that it now makes business sense for him to bring jobs back home." However, Master Lock was a rare case of the economic phenomenon he was hoping for. Many sports pundits comment on the relative superiority of European golfers over American ones based on infrequent events like the Ryder Cup, which the Europeans have won "three of the last four" and "eight of the last ten" (through 2014).

Big samples can be problematic also. We could also sub-divide our annual data into as many time periods as are available, which would be quarters in the case of GDP growth or days, or even minutes, in the case of market returns. For example, if you had twenty years of stock market returns, could you subdivide the data into monthly observations and have 240 observations? Could you thereby eliminate your small sample problem, or take daily data and have about 5,200 observations? This increases the number of observations which typically decreases the standard deviation (so long as the sub-divided data is not proportionally more volatile). Decreasing the standard deviation gives the appearance of greater significance. In many fields, like

---

[249] Stephen Cecchetti and Kermit Schoenholtz, *Money, Banking, and Financial Markets*, 2011, p. 380, citing Ramey and Ramey, *American Economic Review,* December 1995, pp. 1138-51.

investment research, it is easy to obtain large data sets. For example, millions of observations are available for trades of stocks, options, insider trades, etc.

We could just as readily aggregate time. For example, instead of using annual data use data demarcated by decades or centuries. This may demonstrate a key philosophical factor about the long-run average rate of return in markets and the economic growth of our country. At this point in history, do we really have merely one observation of a "20th century." Was the 20th century a unique period in which capitalism flourished? A key is how many "independent observations" you have. You can make mistakes in overcounting the number of independent observations. Victor Niederhoffer, a one-time outstanding commodities trader, is hyperbolic: "I am not a great believer in efficient markets, random walks, or rational expectations. My own trading especially refutes this….In statistical terms, I figure I have traded about 2 million contracts in my life thus far, with an average profit of $70….This average profit is approximately 700 standard deviations away from randomness, a departure that would occur by chance only about as frequently as the spare parts in an automotive salvage lot spontaneously assemble themselves into a McDonald's restaurant."[250] Soon after Niederhoffer's book came out, his fund got wiped out (putting average profit to about $0). His flaw was a simple stats error: Two million contracts traded is not the same as two million separate trades. Incidentally, his investment program was making roughly enough independent trades that his average profit was two or three standard deviations from zero in any time period; and, sure enough, chance eventually caught up with him.

M&M is largely a solitary observation science. The 20th century, with its growing population and constant economically implementable technological advances made it easy to grow economies along with a great increase in the level of government involvement. The same is true of the high returns to equity investment. The 20th century was a special century of private capital being able to garner monopoly rents and keep a large fraction of its profit. The 21st century will be an observation with lower means for GDP growth and stock market returns.

## III.16.A.j. Econometrics

Econometrics is statistical and mathematical applications to concepts and models of economics. It is a vast and complicated field ranging from simple regression to a plethora of advanced methods. Certain tools of econometrics are prominent in the press and in conversations among professionals. In econometrics the most fundamental facet is your specification, i.e., the model you are testing. In its most basic form it is a single equation with a variable to be explained as a function of a variety of independent variables that hypothetically can explain it. The analyst performs the regression or other economic method to find correlation and statistical significance.

If tests of the initial specification fail to find the theoretical relationship, the analyst can keep on trying new specs. As we pointed out though, such repeated analysis makes it easy to find wrong results. Listed below are some of the major facets of basic econometrics:

- If you add explanatory variables that are irrelevant to your specification, they will not bias your other results. Omitting a variable that is important is more problematic, and this biases your results.
- The main problem with your specification is correlation with no cause and effect. Let's say you notice that people drink plenty of Coke in the summer and they also wear shorts. Does wearing shorts cause them to drink Coke?
- The independent variables used to explain a variable are related to each other. We call this multicollinearity, and it is an extremely difficult statistical problem. Long ago an econometrics

---

[250] From Niederhoffer's autobiography, *The Education of a Speculator*, John Wiley & Sons, 1997, p. ix.

teacher told me, "There are a thousand ways to handle multicollinearity, yet there is no way to deal with it." To give an example, prominent economist Stephen Levitt applied econometrics to determine the reasons for the large drop in crime in America over the last few decades. He entertained all factors, including policing, imprisonment, the economy, etc., to isolate the really significant factors. His conclusion was that the legalization of abortion around 1970, which supposedly reduced the potential pool of criminals, was an important factor. Neither better policing nor imprisonment was significant. Yet such analysis depends on so many factors that they simply cannot be disentangled with econometrics. A straight-forward specification might do best. For example, a simple regression of crime against incarceration rates would yield a significant relationship. Omitted factors would change the impact of factors chosen. Levitt's specification left out variables, such as widespread surveillance, extensive medication of people and simple change in attitudes. The drop in crime ultimately may have had little to do with abortion.

- Instrumental variables ("IV") is a common and potentially effective technique to isolate cause and effect when the explanatory variables are related to each other. IV is simple in theory but difficult in practice because it is very hard to find satisfactory instruments. For example, let's say you want to find the effects of military service on earnings. You would make earnings a function of military service and other variables that determine earnings like education. Let's say you find a positive coefficient on military service. You would then conclude that being in the military results in higher earnings. You might worry, however, that people who join the military would tend to have certain predisposition to earnings, i.e., it is not military service causing the higher earnings. How could you isolate that effect? If, in your sample some of the soldiers were conscripts while others were volunteers, the conscripts would constitute a group untainted by propensity to join the military, and would be the instrument. You then engage in another regression with the instrument. IV depends on finding instruments. Economists rely on odd circumstances like lotteries, forces of nature, arbitrary calendar effects (like birth month), etc.[251]

- Serial correlation, or autocorrelation, is another major facet of econometrics/statistics. Time series data may tend to exhibit values that trend off of previous values. (The trending we are discussing here is not trending due to inflation.) Serial correlation, or patterns in data, indeed, is sought after by certain analysts such as technical analysts of stocks. Serial correlation is also a grave econometric problem generally leading to inefficient regression estimates. Not adjusting for serial correlation can result in finding spurious significance, i.e., not rejecting the null hypothesis when it should be rejected. It is a complicated econometric problem and there are methods to adjust for it, but it can also be an intractable problem.

- Vector autoregressions ("VARs") are time series econometric models used to explain one variable as a function of other variables. In a VAR there is no a priori theoretical assumption. VARs are

[251] A well-known relatively contemporary example of IV is the "streams" analysis of economist Caroline Hoxby ("Does Competition Among Public Schools Benefit Students and Taxpayers?" published in the *American Economic Review* in 2000; in working paper form it was out in December 1994). She wanted to test effects of school choice on achievement. She hypothesized that a larger number of school districts in a city would mean higher test scores since parents could move their children among the districts. A problem was that the number of districts itself depended on new districts being created or eliminated from schools being merged, shut down or opened due the quality of the schools. In other words, the number of districts would itself impact the quality of the schools in them. Hoxby's IV instrument was streams. Districts were formed around these natural barriers such that the number of streams would closely determine the number of districts. Using this control she eliminated the feedback effect and found that competition among districts had a positive effect. Her results were challenged. In particular, the way she mapped the streams was questioned. Regardless of the merits of the research, though, implementing IV requires an instrument that isolates effects.

common in M&M with output (GDP), money, interest rates, consumption, oil price and other macro aggregates. For example, making GDP growth a function of inflation and interest rates is one common VAR. We mentioned these above in the context that they are popular and require little theory. As previously noted, it is very easy to find trends that do not exist or to find effects that vary greatly in magnitude and even direction. Monetary policy has strong effects in one period; weak effects in another; opposite effects in some time periods.

### III.16.A.k. Accountability for Misunderstanding Probability and Statistics

One of the main contemporary statistics debates is not any technical or empirical matter. Rather, it is the culpability for failing to understand stats: Is it people and private parties, or the experts? Which party is, therefore, responsible for the economic losses that accrue from errant stats? Experts and the press characterize average people as easily and habitually fooled in statistical analyses. Of course, the experts fancy themselves savvy about stats and understanding of people's errant stats. The experts, however, make more mistakes. One odd aspect of the opinions of experts is that they typically mock each other. Wall Street contends that academics failed to explain the limitation of the normal distribution and sold them flawed statistical tools for managing portfolio risk. Academics like to tell us that they have been teaching stats correctly for over a hundred years, including the non-normality of series like stock market returns. Greedy practitioners misuse models. The media love to report research that suits their prejudices but which exhibits data mining and Type II errors.

Experts argue that average people overestimate rare events. Journalists love to invoke that dolts act on some probability: "…less likely than being hit by lighting." For example, in analysis of the major sniper attack that occurred in Washington DC in October 2002 (resulting in the deaths of ten average people), *The Economist* mocked people for being afraid and changing their routines to avoid the sniper attacks when the probability of being the victim of the sniper attacks was lower than that of any of variety of routine risks, like car accidents. *The Economist* projects simple mathematical constraints to people's behavior. People, though, are acting on a variety of motivations including empathy towards others and concern for their community.[252]

Another pervasive stats error committed by average people is misjudging relative probabilities in optimistic ways. A favorite story concerns lottery playing. Ask a man if he is likely to win a lottery game and he says, "Sure, I got a good chance." Ask him if he will suffer an equally probable adverse event like being hit by a car and he will say, "That's not about to happen." As we pointed out about surveys and the experiments of behavioral economics, people are purposely not providing analytic answers. Ask that same man, "Sir, in purely mathematical terms, do you think winning the lottery is more likely than being hit by a car?" He will respond, "I really don't know. They could equally unlikely."

Average people are not naïve about statistical matters. If I encounter a person making a statistics error and then explain his mistake he will readily comprehend the situation. His original mistake will be a product of reasonable decision making. For example, what was the loss to being very careful about daily activities during the times of the DC sniper? It is people in positions of power and influence who

---

[252]"The logic of irrational fear," *The Economist*, October 17, 2002. The article does a multitude of calculations showing that people were extremely overestimating their chanced of being killed by the sniper including that, "the sniper cannot continue at the same rate." Would any normal person say to his spouse, "Darling, first of all the probability of being shot by the sniper is very low. Let me give you some numbers. Also, the sniper cannot continue at the same rate?" This example is somewhat dated (2002) and I could easily find newer ones, but I include it because it is repugnant and reflective of the exploitative nature of much expert analysis of human nature. Tragedies and other highly emotional situations are not valid tests of people's decision making.

misestimate risks and are gullible for analyses that misestimate risk. It is the politicians and the media who find trends in observations of one or two, i.e., overestimating frequencies of rare events. Their errors lead us to engage in poor cost/benefit analysis in many public programs.

## III.16.B. Financial Market Methods

## III.16.B.a. Models of Financial Economics

These models of financial economics including the CAPM, Black-Scholes, the Sharpe Ratio, etc. are insightful and represent baseline approximations to reality. They are sometimes scapegoated for failures and excesses in markets.[253] The models are innocuous. How practitioners misused them or peddlers of financial services over-relied on for finalist statements is the villain. For example, if you measure your investment portfolio risk with the Sharpe Ratio, which does not factor in skewness and kurtosis, you should be aware of what you are assuming.

Students of M&M must understand financial markets because companies and their finance underlie GDP growth. This may have always been true but it more acute today. Our M&M ideas simply rely more and more on companies, their profits and the trading of the securities that represent the profit.

## III.16.B.b. Bond Market Concepts

The bond market is vast and its valuation today is so high it must represent the dominant economic force of our future. Equity market crashes are potent, but a bond market crash could be altogether bigger.

## III.16.B.b.i. "Bond Prices Vary Inversely with Rates"

We talked about this concept and cliché. It is worth reiterating. As interest rates declined for thirty years bond prices rose and we reveled in the bond price/interest rate dynamic and restated the truism as it worked in favor of greater wealth. If interest rates remain at current levels or rise, this relationship will be unfavorable. Will we continue to relish the statement or relegate it to a rarely mentioned concept?

## III.16.B.b.ii. Spreads

The difference between the average yield of one group of bonds (e.g., high-yield bonds) and that of another (e.g., 10-year U.S. notes) is the spread. The concept can be applied in a variety of ways invoking differences classes and categories of debt and equity and making comparison. The two main spreads types are risk spreads and term spreads. A risk spread relates yields of one asset to another usually a risky asset to a non-risky, for example, a high-yield bond v. a 10-year U.S. note. The term spread relates one type of debt varying by length of time to maturity, for example, a 3-month U.S. bill v. a 10-year U.S. note. The term spread is the yield curve. The concept of spreads is omnipresent in discussion of markets and M&M. Typically, analysts will know the level and trend of the spread more precisely than they know the absolute levels of the yields of the assets underlying that spread.

---

[253] In the aftermath of the 2008 financial crisis experts searched for blame. Prominent commentator and New York University professor Nassim Taleb broached suing the Swedish Central Bank for awarding Nobel prizes to academics like Harry Markowitz, Merton Miller and William Sharpe for their financial models which purported to measure risk. Taleb may have been primarily engaging in witty commentary yet, nonetheless, people frequently blame economic theories for real world folly. http://www.bloomberg.com/news/articles/2010-10-08/taleb-says-crisis-makes-nobel-panel-liable-for-legitimizing-economists

The fluctuating of certain spreads is supposed to reveal insight about markets and economies. The lower the spread, generally speaking, the less risk there is between the more and less risky. The recent policy of the our central bank, especially the rounds of QE, is all about changing spreads among the large asset classes, including treasuries and mortgage-backed bonds.

When spreads increase greatly we say they "blow-out," and it typically means that market participants have been selling the riskier bonds and buying the less risky. Typically, in a crisis, people want high quality debt and they engage in a "flight to quality." One notable historic example is August 1998 when Russia defaulted on its sovereign debt. People sold debt similar to Russian bonds, like Brazilian bonds, and bought U.S. treasuries. 2008 is another example. Initially people flocked to U.S. debt such that spreads to U.S. debt blew out greatly. Over time, as the Fed bought the bonds of assets like mortgage-backed bonds, the spread of mortgage-backed bonds to treasuries receded. Fed buying lowered rates in general which caused investors to seek higher-yielding debt, making its yields go down and the spread go down also.

### III.16.B.b.iii. The Bond Bull Market

The extraordinary bond bull market over the 1980s through the early 2000s is a main determinant of our exaggerated sense of economic output and our ability to take on debt. Bond markets of all kinds (high-yield, mortgage-backed, emerging markets, etc.) had returns in excess of their coupon averages and often very high rates of return. The Barclays U.S. Aggregate Bond Index, which represents investment grade bonds in the U.S., rose in 31 out of 34 years from 1980 through 2013 with an average return of 8.42%, a high of 32.65% and a low of only -2.92%. Inflation averaged about 3.4% so the real return was about 5% per year. That's quite a lot for quality bonds. The reason for the bond bull is largely that inflation decreased and interest rates decreased along with it. This scenario could not possibly happen again. The graph below of 10-year treasuries demonstrates the bond bull. For over thirty years rates tended down causing bond prices to rise.

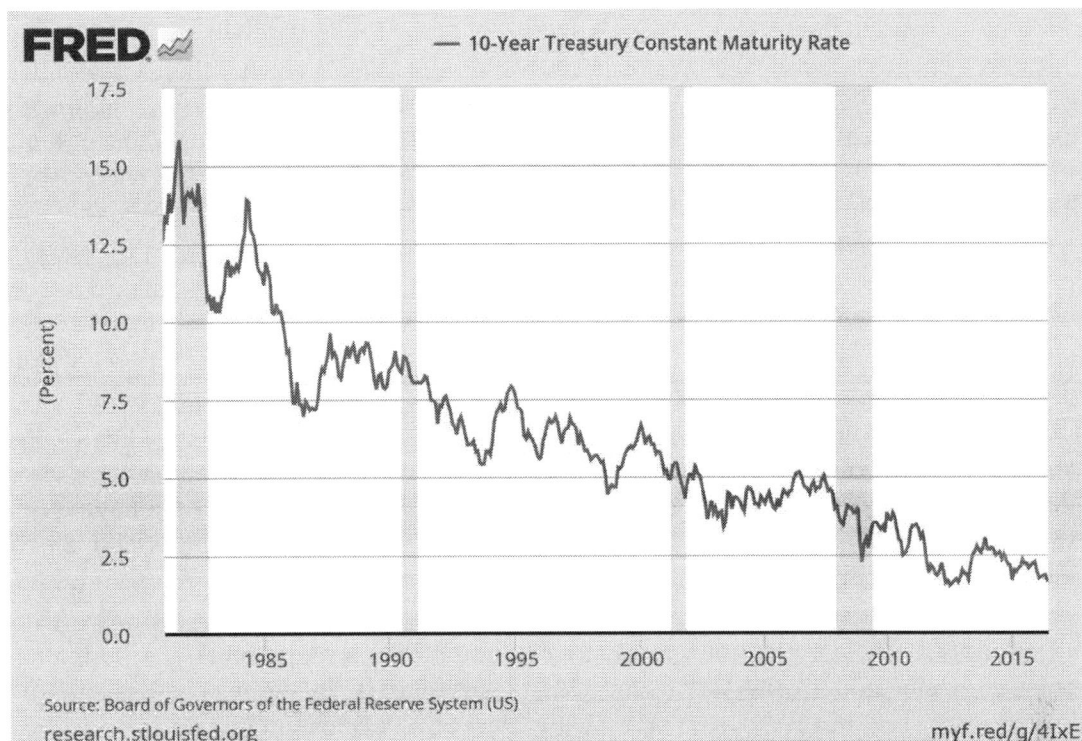

Source: Board of Governors of the Federal Reserve System (US)
research.stlouisfed.org                                    myf.red/g/4IxE

Before the bond bull, from about the late 1940s until 1980, we had a bond bear market. The gradual increase in inflation caused rates to increase and returns to bond portfolios were negatively affected by the price change component of bonds.

## III.16.B.b.iv. Duration and Convexity

Duration and convexity are common measures of the sensitivity of a bond, or a portfolio of bonds, to changes in interest rates; aka interest rate risk. Duration is like maturity except that maturity only captures one timing facet of a fixed income security. A longer maturity bond, everybody knows, has greater interest rate risk. If you were simply comparing two zero-coupon bonds (bonds that made only one future payment) the price of the longer maturity bond would be more sensitive to a change in interest rates than the shorter maturity bond.

Most bonds are not simple zero-coupon bonds. Duration takes into consideration the timing of all cash payments. Therefore it captures maturity, final payment and coupon payments and also, depending on the calculation, call features of the bond and other bond facets. Duration provides a measure of how long it will take a bondholder to recover his initial investment in a bond based on weighted present values of the cash flows of the bond. What you receive up to the point of your bond's duration recoups your layout, and what comes after that is seen as profit. Duration can also be a measure in percentage form showing the change in bond price given a change in yield.[254]

---

[254] There are three forms of duration used by bond practitioners: Macauley, modified and effective. Macauley duration, named after Canadian economist Frederic Macauley who developed the concept of duration in 1938, is a time measure usually in years. It is applicable to bonds with fixed cash flows. Macauley gives the number of years it takes to recover the cost of the bond. Modified duration is an extension of the Macauley measurement and is measured in percentage. Modified duration also applies

Duration has a complicated formula. It will generally be less than the maturity (although certain measures of duration can give the opposite result). For example a bond maturing in five years might have a duration of 4.2 years. In practice, for either your bond or your portfolio of bonds, you want to calculate the duration and then quantify how much a certain percentage change in general interest rates will change the price of your bonds with, of course, a rise in rates lowering prices and vice versa. The higher the duration the greater the changes in values when interest rates change. A bond portfolio manager's goal might be to structure a portfolio with a certain duration. In general for duration, the higher the coupons, the lower the duration; and the shorter the maturities, the lower the duration. Duration is a good measure of changes in value when there are small changes in interest rates. Also, other factors, like bonds being callable, qualify the interpretation of duration. Bond portfolio managers can adopt practice "immunization" of a portfolio, which is a matching of durations. This is typically done in big portfolios, like pension funds.

Convexity is another measure of relative risks and values of bonds. It measures the sensitivity of duration to changes in interest rates. Convexity reveals a little more about the relationship between bond prices and yields than duration does. Duration assumes a linear relationship between interest rate and bond prices. Convexity does not. The linear relationship dictates that an interest rate change of one percentage results in certain change in bond prices.

Convexity demonstrates a basic facet of bonds that changes in interest rates will change values of bonds but the amounts of changes vary depending upon characteristics of the bonds (or portfolios of bonds). They have varying convexities. For example, an increase in interest rates could decrease the value of one bond less than that of another bond, and a similar decrease in interest rates could increase the value of one bond more than that of another. The task is to compare bonds with different amounts of convexity, and then judge how much to pay to get the greater convexity. The straight line represents the duration relationship.

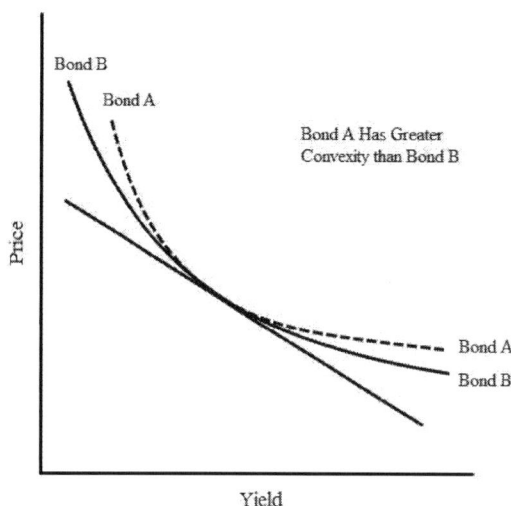

to instruments with non-fixed cash flows and is more popular in bond analysis. Modified duration is the percentage change in a bond price given a 100 basis point interest rate change. Effective duration extends the concept to measure duration of bonds that have embedded options or are callable. There are other duration calculations that address other features of fixed income. All durations show how sensitive changes in a bond's price are to changes in interest rates.

## III.16.B.c. The Fallacy of Compounding

The "magic of compounding" reflects a belief that returns to savings produce enhanced returns, devoid, in a sense, of sacrifice or risk. This belief is deeply clichéd. People, including many experts, chirp this "magic" without reflecting upon what they are promising or requiring. For example, we exhort the young to save due to compounding. However, it may not be in a young person's best interest to save. The magic of compounding is omnipresent in investment advice, investment advertisements, courses and coffee table conversation. Compounding's magic only exists to the extent that a person defers consumption—the cardinal sin of an economic agent. For example, if I advise my daughter not to spend $100 this year in order to have more a year from now there will be no compounding unless, when the year passes, she recommits to save both the original $100 and the interest she earned for another period. In other words, if we assume one time period there is no magic. This might seem irrelevant since most people save over a long period and do not view interest as something they want to use for consumption in the near future. However, they have to use their gains eventually since the ultimate purpose of saving is to spend the amount saved. The only question is how much you want to save.

The other main flaw of compounding is that burgeoning amounts depend critically on the rate of return you assume. At a high rate, compounding blows up; at a low rate, it does not. For most of my adult lifetime, at least in the 1980s through the early 2000s, we assumed high rates of return to stock portfolios, like 8% or 10%. Using those rates with typical investment horizons of thirty or forty years the terminal amounts became prohibitive. It was easy to tweak savings programs when the rates and time frames were so hefty. For example, increasing a return to 9% from 8% did not seem like a big change, compared to changing a rate today from maybe 2% to 3%. The change to 9%, though, would blow up your lifetime wealth.

Nor is compounding magical when you invest in assets that can have negative returns. For example, consecutive annual returns of 10%, 10%, 10% and -10% give you less than 20% due to the magic of compounding. Then, of course, when you withdraw your assets, you will also get compounding effects in reverse. This reality might become more ostensible as bigger population cohorts retire and withdraw savings.

The magic of compounding, combined with a high rate of return, is common today, yet society has seemingly wised up a little, perhaps due to the two major stock market shakeouts of 2000 to 2002 and 2008. I believe that in the 1990s compounding hype was more copious and more hyperbolic. Frequently you would get the story or the smallest of sacrifices leading to the largest of gains. "Do you buy a soda each workday? Fritter away $1 a day for 40 years and, when you're set to retire, you'll find that your account is short by $190,000. Ditto for the daily newspaper, cable TV, going out to dinner….By allowing yourself to spend discretionary money on little things, you will forever deny yourself the opportunity to spend money on big ones, like a home."[255] Today, though, we have finally toned down such hyperbolic numbers.

To demonstrate the effects of compounding many texts use the case of the purchase of the island of Manhattan. The Dutch supposedly bought it for about $24 in 1626, almost 400 years ago. To make a point some analysts contend the Dutch overpaid because if you blow up the $24 by any percent over 8% you will get an amount so large that it easily exceeds the current value of all the property in Manhattan. Of course, blow it up by something like 1%, which might more closely resemble an appropriate rate, and get virtually nothing. To belabor the issue, what is the appropriate rate of return, i.e., what rate would an investor with a

---

[255] "A Gen-X Financial Guide," *U.S. News & World Report*, October 20, 1997, p. 82.

long-term horizon have received over the last few centuries? Economic historians debate this with answers ranging from 0% to as much as 4%.

Compounding is not working for us any longer. That might seem like an odd statement when compounding itself is merely a mathematical concept. However, since lower rates to investments will likely prevail, we will get less of the good side of compounding. Then, we will see more of the bad side of compounding since the economic items that are growing at high rates are our debts and costs like pension, education and health care. To put the ditty in microeconomic terms–if you defer the drinking of a soda today and save the money for many periods at the going rate, you should obtain about the same amount of marginal utility in the future from whatever you do with the savings as you forfeit today.

### III.16.B.d. Rates and Their Potency

In 1999, investors were excited by a boldly entitled book *Dow 36,000* (Times Books, 1999), which proposed that the Dow Jones Industrial Index (which was around 10,000 to 11,000 during most of 1999) could logically be at 36,000—immediately. Authors James Glassman and Kevin Hassett theorized that stocks, if held for long periods in diversified portfolios, had little risk. Thus the prices of stocks should rise sufficiently to equilibrate the total return on stocks with the yield on safe bonds, like U.S. treasuries. Regardless of the ultimate merits of *Dow 36,000* (eventually, apparently, markets deemed that stocks did have risk and the Dow never hit 36,000), it demonstrates that rates of changes for certain key quantities are potent determinants of levels for markets and economic quantities. We have also seen the potency of small differences in the inflation rate and in interest rates. We can add to those other key rates including the risk premia, dividend yield and earnings growth rates.

Here is an analysis of rates[256]:

$$R = D/P — \Delta S + i + g + \Delta PE$$

Where

- R represents the total annual returns of the S&P 500 from 1926 to 2010;
- D/P is Dividend Yield;
- $\Delta S$ is Decrease in Number of Shares Outstanding (rate);
- D/P—$\Delta S$ together represent Income. They were about 4.1% combined, with most of that amount the Dividend Yield;
- i + g together are Earnings Growth with i as Inflation and g as Real Earnings Growth Rate; i was about 3% and g about 1.91%;
- $\Delta PE$ is the P/E repricing, meaning how much the P/E simply goes up or down, and was about 0.58%;
- R was about 9.5%.

The Equity Risk Premium is the amount R is greater than the risk-free rate of return, such as the 10-year treasury, which over that period was about 3.4%, giving an ERP of about 6%. What might the ERP be in the future? All of the components of the above equation are anybody's guess. Perhaps, $\Delta PE$ will add nothing since the P/E ratio is already so high that it will not be re-evaluated up.

The main point here is that these rates of the economy are hard to know, and relatively small changes in their magnitudes (3% v. 4%, e.g.) can mean big differences in economic outcomes. These major rates and ratios are best summarized in bullet points:

---

[256] From *Rethinking the Equity Risk Premium*, Research Foundation of CFA Institute, 2011, December 2011, Vol. 2011, No. 4, chapter by Richard C. Grinold, Kenneth F. Kroner and Laurence B. Siegel, "A Supply Model of the Equity Premium."

- **Equity risk premium**: Many analysts contend the equity risk premium was always too high historically, such as during the 1950s and 1960s. After the fact, stocks seemingly had little risk. This post hoc theorizing is dubious. You would have to measure how people perceived risk at the time. During the Cuban Missile Crisis, for example, the world, including equity investing, appeared very risky.

- **Inflation**: As previously discussed in our history of the U.S. economy, inflation has fluctuated greatly in the last few decades including years in the 1970s and 1980s when inflation was over 10%. A raw average of inflation over the period of 1960 to the present, about 4%, is misleading. Before 2008, I would have stated with confidence that inflation will be in the range of –0.5% to 2.0%. At that time our monetary policy was to keep inflation below about 2% and the strategy seemed successful. Given the deflationary factors of the world economy and our greatly expanded central bank policies since 2008 inflation could be very low including less than -0.5% or very high.

- **Interest rates (real)**: We have talked at great length about what the risk-free real interest is, perhaps no more than 0 to 1%. Other analysts would scoff and propose about 2 to 4% with some historical justification. People currently talk about the fed funds rate soon getting back to around 3 to 4% while we maintain inflation at or under our target of 2%, giving a real risk-free return of near 2%. This is dubious. If the fed funds rate gets to 4% inflation will likely be 4% too. (This is the case we have made throughout this text.)

- **GDP growth**: During the post-World War II period, the U.S. economy has grown at about 3% per year after inflation. During the latter half of the 1990s, it grew at about 4%. Since about 1990 it has grown about 2% per year. Growth in any of those ranges is possible, but low population growth along with low productivity growth could put U.S. GDP growth even lower.

- **Dividend yield**: The dividend yield is the dividend of a stock divided by the stock price. Some stocks do not pay dividends. Some pay high dividends. Most pay modest dividends. The average dividend yield has varied greatly ranging from about 3 to 7% up until about 1980, then tending down to nearly 1% around 2000 and currently (2010 to the present) about 2%.

- **P/E ratio**: Despite its simplicity the P/E ratio stands as the single most revealing stock market value measurement. Before the 1990s the P/E varied from about as low as 5 to as high as 25. For about a decade straddling the 1970s and early 1980s it was below 10. At that time conservative investors would have maintained that any stock with a P/E ratio over ten was expensive. Since the 1990s P/E's have been higher. Exact levels depend on which sub-set of the stock market you are looking at and which definition of earnings you are using. Currently (circa 2015), the conventional P/E is in the low 20's. Another calculation of P/E, called CAPE (cyclically adjusted price to earnings), looks at ten year average earnings and gives a much higher P/E. Many analysts prefer CAPE but critics of CAPE contend that the earnings from 2008, which were very bad, are included and CAPE is misleading.

- **Earnings yield**: Earnings are the main mover of stock prices of companies. The earnings yield is the inverse of the P/E ratio. The higher the P/E the lower the earnings yield.

- **Tax rates**: It is difficult to talk about "a" tax rate, since there are so many taxes and they apply to different incomes and wealth. In general, though, average and marginal tax rates should go up given continuing government deficits and growing government debt. Higher taxes detract from earnings, which impacts stock valuations and the P/E ratio. If we believe the thrust of this book, that future government obligations are grave and that GDP growth is lower than most analysts currently project, taxes will likely go up a lot.

To the extent possible, try to peg these rates to micro rather than macro factors. For example, GDP growth should depend on population, family formation, productivity, regulation, shocks, etc. Macro theories and relationships can be circular or spurious. For example, the idea that lower rates on bonds means that money must flow into the stock market, therefore increasing the prices of stocks and the P/E ratio, is a macro relationship that may hold only for a while or not at all.

## III.16.B.e. Risk

Risk is a major topic in social and business science and in everyday living. Analysis and measurement of risk in business and investing situations, you might call it Risk Management, is a vast business with numerous jobs for educated people. In money management (i.e., managing portfolios like mutual funds and hedge funds), since it is difficult to beat the market or even beat benchmarks, institutions sell their services by focusing on measuring and controlling risk. They contend they have high "risk-adjusted" rates or return. Of course, to make such a claim they must measure risk. It is not uncommon that companies might have a quarter or even a half of their professional employees specializing in risk. The list below details a variety of facets of risk:

- Risk is the possibility of an adverse or costly outcome. In the world of finance and investing we think of risk as not attaining an expected rate of return to an asset. Economists define and theorize risk in different ways. We relate risk to uncertainty. In one description we say that risk requires both uncertainty and having something on the line. For example, there is uncertainty about who will win the Kentucky Derby next year, but that does not represent risk to someone uninvolved in horse racing. Another description of risk and uncertainty is that risk is random outcomes that can be estimated with probabilities while uncertainty is random outcomes for which probabilities are not known.

- The above definition of risk suffices for general analyses, but we frequently refer to specific risks like interest rate, credit, illiquidity currency, political and model risk, etc. It is almost to the point where you can take any of the terms from an investing glossary and follow it with the word risk.

- Risk is tough to measure, and many intelligent people have been made to look negligent for either overestimating or underestimating it. Before 2008, many people argued that the stock or the housing markets were reasonably valued. Then those markets crashed and the people were scolded for ignoring risk. Errors in risk measurement are just as common by experts as average people. For decades experts mocked average people for holding their money in cash and thus forfeiting the higher returns of the stock market. Yet markets crashed twice in the last twenty years and people who held cash did pretty well. For an example of a typical sweeping statement, economist Steven D. Levitt says, "Most of us are…terrible risk assessors," in his popular book *Freakonomics*.[257] Here is another example, this time making a broad judgment of risk including a stereotype by nationality: "Experts seem to agree that Americans find it harder than most people to evaluate risks accurately."[258] These are flippant statements. People are very good at managing risks that are relevant to their lives. For example, most people drive throughout their lives with only minor accidents. People handle weather changes pretty well (how many times have you heard of friends suffering frost bite?). Most people eat well and use alcohol and tobacco wisely and those who ostensibly do not may be making a rational choice to risk gluttony or addiction.

---

[257] William Morrow, 2005, Steven D. Levitt and Stephen J. Dubner, p. 150.
[258] "The logic of irrational fear," *The Economist*, October 17, 2002.

- The financial press and punditry also pretend to be able to discern fundamental changes in risk or changes in the perception of risk by others. The prime example is swings in securities markets. When markets are volatile, the press imputes a mass and fundamental shift in investor sentiment on risk. People suddenly deem holding equities risky in the current economic environment. Virtually every time markets are suddenly volatile, the press will maintain that people's risk tolerance has changed fundamentally. Yet in most cases markets recover promptly and the talk in the media of the grave change in attitudes dries up.

- If you survey experts in economics or financial services they will list a plethora of ways of measuring risk such as standard deviation, correlation, Sharpe Ratio, Sortino Ratio, stress testing, maximum drawdowns, months to recovery, mean absolute deviation, Modigliani-Squared, Jensen's alpha, Omega Ratio, Treynor Ratio, VaR (Value at Risk)—to name a few. Yet almost all of these measures hinge on the standard deviation of returns from historical series of data. As a result, the standard deviation becomes the main measure of risk. Also, there is really no way to directly measure risk since risk is in the future; not in the past. Therefore, any risk we can measure is not the risk that is relevant. The most important risk may be the very small one of some very adverse outcome which, because such outcome is rare or has never happened, we have little or no data on. Some analysts contend risk is simply not quantifiable and a portfolio manager can only offer his clients estimates of how much loss they could suffer under different scenarios, some of which are not well-known. Another way of thinking about it is that risk is "how you got there." If your assets grow at only low rates yet you had little on the line, you managed risk well.

## III.16.B.f. The Efficient Market & Beating the Market

An analysis of the Efficient Market ("EM")[259] is a book unto itself, so we will simply do a high-level and impressionistic run down. EM is the idea that securities markets incorporate information relevant to the values of securities so well, or "efficiently," that the prices of securities are about as correct as current information can make them. The main implication of EM is that it is difficult to select a portfolio that beats the market. EM is believed by many, but it is also disbelieved and even dismissed and mocked by many others. Perhaps their case is justified, but few EM deniers either beat the market or even more oddly attempt to beat the market.

In my adult lifetime, especially in America, "beating the market" with active investing and money management (think mutual funds, hedge funds, buyout firms, private equity, institutional pools of money, etc.) is/was perhaps second only to "high tech" as the field of superlative endeavor and path to robber-baron-like wealth. The great investors prevailed with sheer brainpower, typically running companies with staffs of merely a handful or workers. As evidence, peruse a list of new owners of expensive professional sports teams.[260] The market beating successes are an illusion: EM prevails and the long list of successful investors is a product of fortune. These money masters and many people at large prefer to believe in the existence of the ability to beat the market though. It is a natural human desire to believe that you are special or outstanding. In financial markets, professionals want to believe that they can discern trends and facts and figures better than

---

[259] Most analysts and publications refer to this concept as the Efficient Market Hypothesis ("EMH"). I use EM since I am usually referring to a condition of financial markets (whether people believe it or not) rather than a concept that is being tested, i.e., a hypothesis.

[260] It is somewhat silly to compare disparate fields. Other areas like politics, sports, military, entertainment, journalism, etc. have their shares of individual success stories, but in recent decades the outsized gains of money managers is pretty hard to match.

others. EM nullifies that belief, however. EM diminishes more pretenders to exceptional standing in society today than the theory of evolution did in the decades after its introduction.

The idea of being special in investing prowess is palatable to leaders in other fields, like academia and journalism. Society's smart people like to confirm their superiority. Usually in any debate about EM you must review the arguments and empirical analyses. That exercise is defunct. EM has been debated ad infinitum. If you do not believe EM you can cite the great investors, the crazy markets and copious research by academics finding non-EM markets. If you do believe EM you can refer to Burton Malkiel's *A Random Walk Down Wall Street*, which first came out in the 1973 and is in its 15th edition as of 2015, or you can check other academic findings including the latest academic findings.[261]

You can believe EM or not, but for most situations, like when discussing investing at cocktail parties, EM is a one-sided debate. As an EM believer I invest mainly in index funds. Sometimes I pick individual stocks, sectors or countries, but I acknowledge that they are bets. I make some odds on plays like buying the dips. I spend some effort allocating my assets across cash, stocks and bonds, but my rules are pretty simple. I do not try to beat the market with strategies like the January Effect. EM deniers will never talk me down unless they can demonstrate that they can beat the market, which they cannot. If they claim they beat the market in the past or that great investors—like Warren Buffett beat the market—I doubt their claims and partnership with Buffett.

A few pensées on investing and markets are included below. They are eclectic and reflect my personal ideas and bias:

- A beginning investor might think it is easy to beat an average market return. After all, there are obvious and large differences in companies, industries and economies. How hard could it be to find well-run companies in growing sectors or industries and catch them when the economy is expanding? There might be some uncertainty and risk, but it should be pretty easy to make bets that will pay off most of the time. Isn't this what Warren Buffett did? Yet a beginner, within the first few days of researching investments, will realize that anything that looks "better" is expensive, i.e., the market has priced it in.

- About the best EM generalization (which I attribute to Paul Samuelson) is that markets are efficient at the micro level (Microsoft v Oracle stock, or Greek v. Swiss sovereign bonds) but markets vary from fundamental values and are not efficient at the macro level. Entire markets and asset classes can meander off of intrinsic values. This macro inefficiency though is tough to capitalize on.

- As you gain experience in investing, including even being employed as an investment professional, it is hard not to form the completely opposite attitude that it is impossible to find something cheap(er). Investing is an extremely competitive business.

- Warren Buffett is a man but is also a concept and cliché. Countless investors have tried to beat the market and failed dismally, yet they gainsay EM with a glib, "What about Warren Buffett?" Is there any other field in which one person is such a cynosure of an achievement that few others can emulate?

- It is somewhat comical when you think about how many highly-educated people are buying and selling the same securities. They buy and sell from each other. They are all looking for incorrectly valued securities (either under or overvalued). They all have similar training and education. They often collaborate. Few—if any—of them beat the market. What edge could anyone have? For example, in

---

[261] One succinct, pro-EM mustering is "The Efficient Market Hypothesis and Its Critics," by Burton Malkiel, *Journal of Economic Perspectives*, Volume 17, Number 1, Winter 2003, pp. 59-82. There are many other pieces of research related to issues of EM including more current material. One good piece is "Hedge Funds: A Dynamic Industry in Transition," working paper (draft July 28, 2015) by leading academics Mila Getmansky, Peter A. Lee and Andrew W. Lo. They assesses the success of hedge funds in beating the market and conclude it is a tough case to make.

late 2014 and early 2015, as a large drop in the price of oil caused a big shakeout in fortunes of energy sector companies, experts were alternatively buying or selling the stocks, high-yield debt and corporate grade debt of these energy companies. In press profiles, each expert would be described for his great experience, the billions and billions of dollars he represented, etc. and each would state his conviction that the market was a buy or a sell.

- Many managers are touted as having superlative records, "…returned 20% per year for 20 years" or "…30% per year for 30 years." Such runs may be, strictly speaking, valid in some cases, but they are often exaggerated in a variety of ways. Often one fund's results are presented while other funds that were unsuccessful are not reported. Often a fund will be successful for a long period when it has minimal assets but then when its size gets bigger its rates of return are no longer out of the ordinary.

- One of the most glaring interpretations in the popular press concerning money management is that market-beating success can be attained by beginners if they emulate the successful manages. In other words, if he beat the market by dint of hard work and earnest intentions, it is beatable. In other fields of endeavor, with similar chances of success, the media would focus on the rareness of the achievement.

- Judgment of success in money management is forgiving and favorably biased. Portfolio management is replete with extreme rationalizing, even fabricating, of market-beating performance. In few other endeavors do people fail to prevail yet claim they pulled it off. I would guess that of ten money managers who have no record of beating the market, five will be defiant. They will say, "Haven't beaten the market lately but over the long-term…," "Markets have been crazy but I am not…," "Beat my benchmarks…," "Never intended to compare to that market benchmark…," "Made money for the vast majority of my clients….," "Price of oil went way down, and nobody expected that…," "On a risk-adjusted basis…, " etc. This "bias the case in your favor" is more blatant in money management than in other areas. For example, a college sports coach who had no record of excellence for his program might highlight some tangential facet of his record, "I trained a lot of young people about how to lead good lives …." but he would not say, "I would have had a winning record except for the tough decade I coached in."

- One odd aspect of many investment pros is the way they juxtapose their macroeconomic view. Most portfolio managers will contend that divining the macroeconomy is futile for picking a portfolio, yet they ultimately resort to macro clichés. For example, the financial newsweekly *Barron's* profiles portfolio managers regularly. Typically each manager will wax philosophical about the macroeconomy but contend that his investing style is unaffected by trends in M&M. Rather, he will posture himself as a bottoms-up analyst. When he gives specific securities recommendations he will make some company or sector specific arguments but often will invoke some grand facet of M&M (e.g., rates, China, consumer confidence, consumer spending, the price of oil, etc.) as the main determinant of success or failure of the position.

- Another ironic facet ostensible among investment pros concerns Behavioral Economics ("BE"). Very often a portfolio manager's main argument for his investment prowess is that he is disinterested while the rest of society, including his peers, are irrational. In other words, he is switched onto BE. The other portfolio managers, of course, typically contend the same. Read interviews of portfolio managers in publications like *Barron's* and you will find copious citations straight from the lexicon of BE. They invoke the usual catchphrases with confirmation bias probably being the most popular and usual names with Daniel Kahneman probably the most popular. Many of these portfolio managers fail to beat their benchmarks. I have never heard one admit that he has failed due to committing BE pathologies.

- As for funds specifically based on principles of BE, for all the boasting of the great success of the field, they are not ostensibly successful. First of all, they are indistinguishable from value funds. Specific renditions, including by noted BE academic Richard Thaler, tout their attempts and successes with copious examples of perverse market and investor behavior, but they are unclear on the applied investing record.[262]

- The debate on the efficiency market is in a third and terminal phase. The initial phase, around 1970 to 1990, was the promulgation of the theory and empirical findings which mostly supported EM. This stage somewhat represented a triumph of academia over Wall Street. Then, the tide turned as a multitude of "flaws" in EM appeared, accompanied by copious "evidence" of biases and the widespread appearance of market beating practitioners. I would peg that period in the 1990s and early 2000s. Now, the EM debate is moot.

- Securities markets are well researched and information is widely and easily available. For contrast, for about ten years primarily during the 1990s I worked part-time as a securities research analyst. Our area was distressed (companies in bankruptcy, default or otherwise restructuring) and, to a certain extent at that time, the area was a niche lacking thorough research coverage of investable opportunities. Some research on distressed companies was available but not widely circulated. Research reports were largely produced by sell-side specialized brokers and only disseminated to their customers. My colleague, who was better connected with researchers and was also in another office, would call me and say, "Did you get the fax?" With excitement I would look over to the fax machine for an overflow of curly papers representing really exclusive research work. Similarly, before the internet certain data and other information, like court filings on corporate reorganizations, were hard to obtain. As the years went by, I would be excited as these data started to become readily available on the internet or Bloomberg. Yet I also felt professionally diminished that information that was once exclusive was now available to everybody. Today, a comprehensive report on a distressed situation, that might have taken me the better part of a week to compile in the 1990s, can be put together in a couple of hours or even minutes.

- Since 2008, in a wide variety of markets, largely due to government mandate, pricing of securities has become more extensive, frequent, standardized and publicly available. This is particularly true for fixed income and derivatives markets. It has made finding incorrectly priced securities harder.

- The major EM-defying strategies of my life were momentum, value, size and carry.[263] They "worked," in the sense that portfolios of securities with these attributes had higher rates of return, including adjusting for the portfolios' risk. Of course, it was not obvious at any point in the past that these strategies would work nor does it look likely they will work going forward. What are the stories for continuing success in beating the market? What could a top investor, like a hedge fund, offer? There are about a half-dozen stories bandied about: information advantage, undiscovered niches, quantitative system, enhanced beta, speed trading, holding for the long-term and holding when others have to get out, a large unexploited area, riskless arbitrage, macro trends, being nimble, being contrarian, being disciplined, finding cash flow, etc.

---

[262] *Barron's,* April 6, 2015 "Invest like Mr. Spock…," Thaler boasts the result of one BE-based "Value" fund but does not report that another fund, JP Morgan's Undiscovered Managers Behavioral Growth Fund (symbol UMGBX), was unsuccessful for ten years and closed in 2012, after roughly underperforming its benchmarks as much as the Value fund beat them.
[263] Momentum is the tendency of certain securities that have been going up in price to continue going up (or going down in value continuing to go down), for a certain period. Value is finding securities of companies that are cheap by some measure such as P/E ratio or book value. A portfolio of these stocks would have returned more—again, even after adjusting for risk. Size is that a portfolio of smaller companies will do better than a portfolio of larger companies, all other factors equal. Carry trades involve borrowing in one market in which rates are low, and investing the proceeds in another market in which rates are high(er). Carry trades are frequently done by borrowing and lending in different currencies.

✓ Niche: In investing, a niche is an asset class or other investing area/device that has a sufficiently small set of investment specialists or is relatively undiscovered by the mainstream investment community. The presumption is that miss-valued assets are more common in such niches. Twenty-five years ago many areas might have fit the description of a niche; today it is different. Niche markets might include, or have included, small company stocks, emerging markets, commercial real estate, private equities, bank loans, distressed debt, etc. Over the years, these niches have become heavily researched and traded. Distressed debt, which includes defaulted bonds, bankruptcies, companies undergoing turnarounds, etc. represented securities that were presumably shunned by many mainstream investors. Perhaps, therefore, distressed securities were underpriced. Now distressed is so heavily invested in that distressed bonds are traded more than many other classes of bonds. Such liquidity in a market itself may not guarantee that prices are always right, but at least it is hard to consider an area a niche when it is in the news every day. In distressed debt investing, bargains, like those that existed in the recent past, are no longer available. For example, in December 2001 Enron Corp. filed for bankruptcy. Leading up to the filing its numerous issues of bonds dropped precipitously in price, to 20 and 30 cents on dollar. Vulture investors swooped in and bought the bonds believing the Enron estate had much more value. Indeed over the years, the recoveries to the Enron debt were lucrative and numerous hedge funds made a fortune (and many hedge fund portfolio managers relished telling the tale of how they cleverly and bravely bought the debt of Enron when the situation looked grim). Today such sell-offs are rare. For example, in October 2011 MF Global filed for bankruptcy, yet its debt did not drop much in price. The same is true of virtually any distressed situation rendering the "buy when the blood flows" investment strategy ineffective. A curious aspect is the reluctance of veterans of the old ways to face current reality. In late 2014 and early 2015, oil prices plunged and a large set of levered energy companies faced distress. Experts comment with frustration, "Ironically, the greatest worry for some fund managers is that too many other investors will jump on the energy trade, pushing prices back up before they can exploit the oil-related selloff.[264]" All the problems of distressed investing from before—being able to raise capital, enduring high legal and administrative costs, having the patience to wait years for returns, etc.—now pale in comparison to that dastardly reality of competition. A feeling of indignation pervades the business.[265]

✓ Quantitative investing (or quant shops or algorithmic investing): These firms are numerous today. Most use conventional models based on economic theories enhanced with various statistical, mathematical and advanced computational systems. The data analyzed includes the usual economic time series, market data, other proprietary business and economic data and other, more esoteric data. For example, certain quant shops use data collected by satellites exhibiting the movement of people and goods or data from internet sources like social media websites. Quant operations can range from simple quantitative screens done at ordinary mutual fund houses or more complicated systems done at hedge funds. Their long-run overall record of success is impossible to discern for sure, but it appears dubious to me. A handful of quantitative mutual funds have good records, but many more do not. From time to time we hear about an especially advanced and mysterious subset of quant investing run by brilliant physicists, using methods

---

[264] "Bottom Fishers Play Energy Angle," by Matt Wirz, *The Wall Street Journal*, February 13, 2015, p. C1, C2.
[265] At this time, it remains to be seen if vulture investors will prevail. Undoubtedly, over the next few years some funds will turn up with high returns from energy investments. Others will not and others still will lose significantly, and their folly will be hidden from view.

unknown to average mutual fund or non-quantitative hedge fund managers. We also frequently hear of one of the brawniest money companies of all: Renaissance Technologies, the hedge fund with one of the best records in the business and run by a team of physicists. Presumably, though, Renaissance is not the only quant shop. In fact entire books have been written about the great physicists who have prevailed over markets, such as *The Physics of Wall Street* by physicist James Owen Weatherall.[266] If you read the book though you will find it has little to do with physics. The first half of the book broaches age old markets history describing primarily mathematicians and economists like Louis Bachelier, Paul Samuelson and Fischer Black. Nor does it have much to do with Wall Street or money managers. It is mostly theories of markets and lacks examples of successful money shops run by physicists. Much of the book is devoted to establishing that quants did not cause the financial system instability of 2008. Indeed, hedge funds and other big money houses do hire physicists, but only for their basic math training, and not for any special set of physics models. The quant field is now so full you have numerous, "My life as a quant," books.

✓ "Enhanced" beta (aka, smart beta, scientific beta, enhanced indexes, etc.): Enhanced beta is another pretense to beating the market. An enhanced beta portfolio strives to get the market return by buying the market as whole like an index fund and getting beta, but also doing some portfolio enhancement that supposedly adds more return without more risk. Another way of describing it is taking an index fund and changing the weightings of the holdings. In practice, enhanced beta is quantitative screens of stocks based on size, value, momentum and other factors that supposedly do better than index portfolios.

✓ (Being) nimble: This is another metaphor of investing advantage applied to sophisticated investors like hedge funds. Nimble refers to being able to decide promptly, sell or buy more quickly, perhaps buy and sell relatively illiquid securities quickly, take advantage of changes in rules and systems ahead of others, etc. Being nimble supposedly reflects a relative advantage against the non-nimble who are primarily retail investors, institutions and mutual funds.

✓ Speed trading: The use of advanced technology in the form of computers and network communications to perform very rapid securities trades has been popular in the press in the last few years. Technological innovations in investing may represent excess returns without commensurate risk for a while, but will probably not persist.

✓ Macro investing: There are dedicated macro shops that engage in a variety of strategies based on the fortunes of national economies, asset classes, commodities price, large sectors and other macroeconomic quantities. They typically involve bets on convergences of currencies and interest rates, inflation due to debt and deficit, sovereign defaults, commodities prices, consumer trends, etc. In today's world of central bank dominance of financial markets and economies, macro investing should be the area of most outsized returns. Ironically, however, the funds that engage in macro investing have done poorly. Another odd aspect of macro is that many active investors eschew macro, contending they pick companies, stock or situations without attempting to predict macro—which they perceive of as unpredictable. Yet, ask these investors to explain a certain stock pick and they will very frequently resort to something like, "depends on the price of oil," "depends on the GDP growth of China," "will go up if the economic recovery continues," "depends on consumer sentiment" or some other macro cliché. The bottom line is that M&M is very important to the investing community and as we have shown in this book M&M is very hard to discern.

---

[266] 2013. Houghton Mifflin Harcourt Publishing.

✓ Short selling: Long ago selling stock short was perceived of as unsporting and un-American. Investors should be on the positive side of capital and collectively partake in a growing economy and financial markets. That attitude is completely defunct and has been for decades. Short selling securities is widely praised and engaged in without hesitation. Stock short sellers are perceived of as watchdogs of frothy valuations. They are integral to the information-finding and price discovery functions of financial markets. Shorting is an extremely large and profitable business. Financial firms garner fees for short selling services. Many investors exclusively engage in shorting and very many investors, including a large fraction of hedge fund investors, are opportunistically long or short. The market is so active that any ostensibly profitable opportunities on the short side are costly in terms of the fees the security borrower has to pay. For example, for many years the stock of declining retailer Sears was a popular short. The cost to hold the Sears short was varied but was about 25% of the value of the stock. (If the Sears stock went from $40 to $30 per share in a year, you would have made little or no money.) Shorting is another market area that demonstrates EM.

- What do active portfolio managers actually do on a day-to-day basis? (The activities of passive investors, like those who run index funds, should be no mystery.) I am not referring to styles, models or trading strategies of investors but literally how and what they do. Most managers do not originate much research but collect and analyze research of others. They sit in offices and read, mostly material from or available on the internet. Some do quantitative work which they originate, i.e., it is not something pulled off of the internet. They also perform relatively simple and commoditized calculation. They converse with other analysts who are doing the same. There are exceptions, of course. Some experts visit companies and attend meetings and conferences. Some try to experience the businesses of the companies they are investing in in any way possible. Some money management operations take active roles in companies and, thereby, shape the very management of the company. Their principals perform roles of business executives. Primarily, the vast majority of pretenders to picking portfolios that beat markets do little more than read.

- There are numerous academic studies on EM. Many use mutual fund performance. Historically, few mutual funds beat the market. Mutual funds that do have long-run records of beating the market are generally not obvious as market beaters until their magic has worn off. Naysayers recommend looking at hedge funds, private equity, venture capital and other "alternative" investment vehicles not restricted in their investment programs like mutual funds are. In general, mutual funds cannot short stocks, use leverage or lock up capital for long periods. Mutual funds must also offer daily liquidity. Alternatives do not have such constraints. Therefore, many analysts contend the alternatives perform better. The stark reality is that alternatives simply do not outperform.

- Examine the outstanding hedge funds. Do they, or did they, beat the market? Supposedly they do—although many scholars doubt it. Some funds have good long-standing records of outperformance but those achievements are largely from the great day of hedge funds, from the late 1980s through the early 2000s. More recent returns are much less outstanding. Hedge funds' success is attributed to a variety of factors, including informational advantage in research, adroitness in trading, access to illiquid markets, hedging, time frames of holdings, and others. Sometimes the success of hedge funds is attributed simply to great investors who have some sixth sense. Hedge funds' historical success was most likely the result of one of the following: (1) insider trading; (2) selling far out-of-the-money options, which simply masks risk; (3) leverage, which simply masks risk; (4) luck or fortune (extraordinary recent decades of market returns ensured some success stories) and (5) selective reporting. (We will describe each of these below except #4, which is somewhat obvious.)

- Insider trading can generate a market-beating rate of return. The question is how prevalent it is, or was, in hedge funds. For many years I doubted one-time superstar hedge fund manager Steven Cohen and his record of beating the market by extreme amounts year after year. The majority of the financial press and people in the money business preferred to view his investment program as being a successful example of a market beater and refrained from mentioning insider trading.

- Selling or "writing" far out-of-the-money options is like selling insurance on unlikely events. Until the event happens you make money. Hedge funds using this strategy could garner frequent small gains, and rare big losses. They can borrow to magnify gains. If a big loss does occur, they can shut down the hedge fund and stop reporting results. To give an example, one of the greatest hedge fund masters of the 1980s and 1990s was Victor Niederhoffer. He was so successful he wrote a best-seller, *The Education of a Speculator*, in which he boasted his great investing acumen and mocked EM. His gig was selling naked far out-of-the-money put options on markets based on the assumption that markets would never go down very much as was the case in most of the 1990s. In 1997 though, big market drops wiped his fund out.

- Leverage is common but magnifies returns in both directions. If you are managing money and borrow against it three times and the market is up 10% you should be up about 40%. So long as the market goes up you are a success. When a down year, like 2008, hits, your losses will be magnified. Indeed, many hedge funds were wiped out or way down in 2008.

- Many times we have commented how we refrain from showcasing our failures. This is valid in surveys, in looking for work, in looking for love, etc. It is certainly true in the investing world. We will talk about "survivorship" bias as relates to professional investors in detail below. In all my years of personal investing I don't think I beat the market and I may likely have lagged it. However, I could very easily convince people that I did pick disproportionate winners simply by not mentioning my losers.

- Special situations is a catch-all term representing profitable investment opportunities in companies and securities that are undergoing some change or extraordinary conditions that might lead to temporary irregularity in the value of securities. For example, hedge funds scour the world, with lawyers in tow, looking for odd securities tied to governments with messed up finances. Recent places with such opportunities include Iceland, Ukraine, Argentina, Cyprus, Iran, Peru and Puerto Rico. They try to find a legal gimmick to get value. It is overwhelmingly a legal and political analysis. Others bet on political and policy events like Scotland leaving the United Kingdom (2014), the Swiss maintaining their currency peg (which they dropped in January 2015), etc. These are usually directional bets and are largely guesses. This investing often takes the form of a game in which there is a matching of wits and egos and/or political and social posturing. For example, the Fannie Mae/Freddie Mac investment, prominent around 2013 to 2015, involved big hedge funds touting the social importance of the mortgage-backing companies to America. Only through the housing finance giants could the all-important thirty-year mortgage be maintained. Thus, their investment was a public service to America. For another example of egos, during 2014, one big hedge fund shorted Herbalife, and publicly promoted its case, while other big investors took large long positions. Each side invoked social aspects too, with the short seller championing the case of the cheated workers of Herbalife.

- This highlights one of the truly comical features of the EM debate. Many experts are vociferous that the market is inefficient with obvious and overwhelming evidence. Some of these analysts also maintain their own historical success in beating the market. Yet, they themselves do not trade or, if they do, they funds are minimal and belie doubt of EM. Rather, they write books like the following: *Turtle Traders*, *Market Wizards* and *Fortune's Formula*. I have often wondered how seriously anti-EM book writers take themselves in confidential conversations. When writing his next book does the anti-EM person turn to his wife and say, "I am writing another book on beating the market. This time I am reviewing new compelling evidence," or "I am writing another book on beating the market. I don't have anything to say except the same old nonsense. But, hey, who cares, saps buy it!"

- Another comical facet of modern investing is that many of the brawniest investors, like big hedge fund investors, reveal and promote their investing ideas. There are regular conferences in which big name investors tout their best picks. You might think that they would be averse to telling their secrets but I suppose it make sense to promulgate an investing idea once you are mostly invested. Similarly, investors often explain their cases very publicly concerning large market and macro themes. Big investor Kyle Bass touted the shorting of Japanese debt for years. Again, I suppose once he has his position it makes perfect sense to enlighten the world, although it is odd to listen to his begging that others change their investments to support his idea. Other managers reveal not only one or two positions but their entire investing program. Their explanation sounds similar to what they would give potential investors who visited their offices. This does not make sense.[267]

- The era of wide-open asset valuation is over; virtually every asset that can be valued has been valued and valued at the highest value possible. Perhaps Michael Milken, the junk bond king of the 1980s, could study the junk bond market while a Wharton student in the late 1960s, discover the mispricing of the junk debt risk and then uncover a vast undervalued market; but you cannot. Since values are high you might resort to a selling strategy, i.e., "short-selling," but you will find that that market is also crowded such that compelling shorts are expensive to maintain.

- If you think about EM and individual security valuations and how they relate to M&M, it is both once-removed and closely connected. Stock pickers might value stocks and bonds by comparing across similar companies, sectors and other categories and not focusing on the macroeconomy. They might look at capital structure, management, tax aspects, insider trades, catalysts for default or takeover, etc. Most of them also probably eschew macroeconomic trends contending they are unpredictable and therefore impossible to factor in. The great mutual fund manager Peter Lynch said he devoted very little time to analyzing macro. Yet the basic securities valuation method is a thoroughly studied field. Soon enough analysts resort to arguments about the economy to support their picks. They work down from the big cliché components like housing, consumption, trade, unemployment, inflation, interest rates (and changes of interest rates), etc., to macro factors such as consumer confidence, Fed policy, Fed credibility, inflation expectations, etc. As pointed out above, it is odd how quickly stock pickers initially deny the ability to divine M&M, then resort to it.

- If you think about EM and market valuations and how they relate to M&M, it is a relatively simple story. Sometime during the 1980s asset values started to rise. Concurrently, certain central banks made support of their financial markets as their main economic function. Perhaps you can peg the

---

[267] "Picking Stocks by Watching Bonds," by Jon Asmundsson, *BloombergMarkets*, October 2015, pp. 100-102, profiles a portfolio manager with a strong performance record. He uses a relatively mechanical method of portfolio selection. In the article he reveals his tactic in sufficient detail that virtually any analyst could duplicate it: (1) Find companies with high-yield bonds outstanding; (2) Determine which of those have intentions to reduce debt; (3) Determine if they have sufficient cash to make the payments and (4) Make sundry checks like avoiding cyclical industries. Although each step involves some judgment and an imitator would never achieve the same exact portfolio, the imitator would be able to get close.

starting point in this process as the stock market crash of October 1987 when the Fed under Alan Greenspan supported the economy. Thereafter, the world engaged in a large increase in debt in developed countries who borrowed to maintain high standards of living and in developing countries who borrowed to build their economies. Developed countries overconsumed and developing countries overbuilt. All markets rose including real estate, bonds, equities, commodities, etc. EM's role was maintaining correct relative valuation among assets. The end result is the world we have now with zero interest rates and debt much greater than ever before.

### III.16.B.g. EBITDA, Non-GAAP, Pro Forma and the Commoditization of Financial Analysis

EBITDA is short for "earnings before interest, taxes, depreciation and amortization." This long and omnipresent acronym exemplifies investment research of the last few decades. Before EBITDA, and similar earnings measures like EBIT, cash flow, etc., became popular analysts worked primarily off of the earnings reported by companies in their formal financial statements. These formal data are GAAP, the Generally Accepted Accounting Principles, and refers to the set of accounting principles and standards that govern how companies formally present their accounting statements. GAAP earnings include every item which affects bottom line profits in any period even if certain items are temporary or special and not part of the recurring operations. Over the years analysts preferred to strip out special items to focus on the recurring operating earnings of companies as better reflective of their true value into the future. The non-GAAP measures, like EBITDA, reflect what a company can earn without certain non-cash and non-operating items, like depreciation or taxes. EBITDA, for example, applies to companies with debt in their capital structure and in theory removes extraneous factors related to the capital structure. For example, if a company paid for its physical plant some time ago with debt and the company does not need to reinvest in that plant, why count the depreciation or even the interest payments against earnings?

Companies propagate various non-GAAP earnings and future projections of earnings measures. These are not accounting statements that executives are required to sign their names to under threat of penalty as the GAAP measures are. The non-GAAP measures can be any of a wide variety of adjustments. Sometimes they are referred to as pro forma, "in the form of." Sometimes analysts use "adjusted EBITDA" which adjusted for non-recurring items such as stock-based compensation and amortizations of intangible assets. There is nothing necessarily wrong with use of any non-GAAP measure but if GAAP and non-GAAP vary systematically in one direction or the other it could be a sign of something amiss. For example, in recent years, like 2013 through 2016, the non-GAAP earnings measures have been more favorable. Of course, using non-GAAP measures is questionable. Eventually every item does matter to the bottom line of a company and certain non-recurring items are simply large or tend to recur.

Another prominent trend about analysis of financial data is the availability. GAAP and non-GAAP measures and extensive financial analysis in general are available to anyone with access to the internet. By one tally over one million research reports on securities of publicly traded stocks and bonds are done each year. Many are multiple pages and updated frequently. Some of the research is proprietary but most of it is available to the general public. The information is a commodity. Today the relative analysis of companies (for example, comparing IBM, Cisco, Apple, etc.) is so thoroughly done it is difficult to believe an analyst can find miss-valuations. Therefore the fortunes of stocks and bonds depend mostly on macroeconomic trends which leads to a point we have made a number of times: Fortunes of companies depend heavily on M&M. Assumptions of GDP growth, inflation, risk-free interest rates, price of oil, unemployment, etc. dominate analyses. If you scrutinize the portfolios of hedge funds and find many funds holding prominent companies like Apple you realize they are not making situation specific selections based on exclusive research but merely sector bets.

Listed below is a teaser of terms from financial analysis highlighting a few of the key items and ultimately how they relate to M&M. There are, of course, a great multitude of financial quantities. Some of them are formal quantities under rules of accounting and required to be reported in financial statements while others are quantities calculated to uncover the true value of an enterprise:

- Cash Flow is the net stream of revenues and expenses in and out of a project or business over a period. In financial analysis, it represents ongoing net value of a project. We can determine the value of an enterprise by projecting future cash flows and bringing them into the present.
- Free Cash Flow is Cash Flow minus expenses required to keep the company a going concern. Typically a company must pay for new capital and, in some cases, must pay a dividend. Free Cash Flow then represents a true extra amount of value that a company is creating.
- Capital expenditure or CAPEX is the spending by a company on plant, equipment and other investments to run the business over the long term. It is an important quantity to assess the future profitability of a company.
- EVA, or Economic Value Added, is an attempt to calculate a better net income, one that more closely resembles the concept of profit from economics. EVA is also a proprietary concept.
- Enterprise Value is the complete value of a company, or the amount required to buy the entire company. Enterprise Value includes the market capitalization (which is the number of shares times the share price) and the value of the debt and preferred equity. Cash and other marketable items like investments are subtracted.
- Multiples are quantities that relate the value of a security to the flows it can create. One common multiple is the P/E ratio. A more sophisticated multiple is the Enterprise Multiple, which is the Enterprise Value divided by the EBITDA. Analysts estimate multiples that apply to certain sectors or industries and then use them to judge the relative value of securities of different companies

It is relatively easy to calculate these items for many companies and then compare the relative value of the companies against each other and across industries, sectors, nationalities, etc. This is how analysts select undervalued v. overvalued securities. The levels, however, of all these quantities will depend on M&M. For example, an investment will be valuable if the Enterprise Multiple is low, all other factors equal. It will be lower if EBITDA is high, and EBITDA will be high is the economy is growing. It all goes to show how much our market valuations depend on M&M even if we pretend we do not watch the macroeconomy.

EBITDA and other non-GAAP earnings quantities exemplify an era, roughly from the 1980s through the present, in which such innovative analysis was the basis for highly profitable investment schemes and peddling of financial services. That era has come to an end. We have overused them and everybody knows about them.

## III.16.C. Other Items from Methodology in Social and Business Science

Among the myriad methods available I have selected common and more important methods, especially those that relate to M&M and financial markets.

## III.16.C.a. Extrapolation

If you extrapolate the level of a time series at some rate (which rate could be positive or negative) and continue extrapolating for many periods, the value can become very large—you might say hyperbolic. That obvious statement is often lost in analyses of M&M and financial markets. In government budget projections we assume quantities grow at constant rates, like GDP growing at 2% per year for seventy years and population growing constantly at a substantial rate. Under such assumptions, the U.S. becomes a land of many people who are very rich, yielding a large tax base from which we can raise great taxes and fund large liabilities. Such extrapolation may be a good baseline. It may also be the best we can do, i.e., we do not have any crystal ball that shows the path of any quantity into the future. Yet we should be circumspect about simple extrapolation.

A historical case of poor extrapolation was that done during the 1980s by many economy pundits of the size of Japanese economy. They had Japanese GDP exceeding that of the U.S. over the next couple of decades. It was an outlandish case given that Japan had about one-third the population of the U.S., but people were taking it seriously. An example of potentially bad extrapolation being used today (by certain economists including me) is the Fiscal Gap (which is a focal point of this entire manuscript). The Fiscal Gap of the U.S. is calculated to be an outlandish hundreds of trillions of dollars, by projecting, i.e., extrapolating, continual deficits and bringing those amounts into present value. Of course, long before our debt could blow up to such a great amount, events would transpire to flatten or even reverse the trajectory of deficit. Presumably, at some point, when U.S. debt became so high, the nation would not be able to continue to borrow. Although this seemingly weakens the Fiscal Gap as a strong indicator of extreme insolvency of the U.S., indeed the U.S is still insolvent and getting more insolvent.

Here is a simple example of the flaw of extrapolation. A woman takes up golf. Her first year her average score is 110. The second year she has improved five strokes to 105. She improves at about the same rate in her third and fourth years, getting her score down to 95. There is nothing outlandish about such progress for a golfer over the first few years of a career. Yet will she be golfing at scores of 70, 60 or lower in a few years?

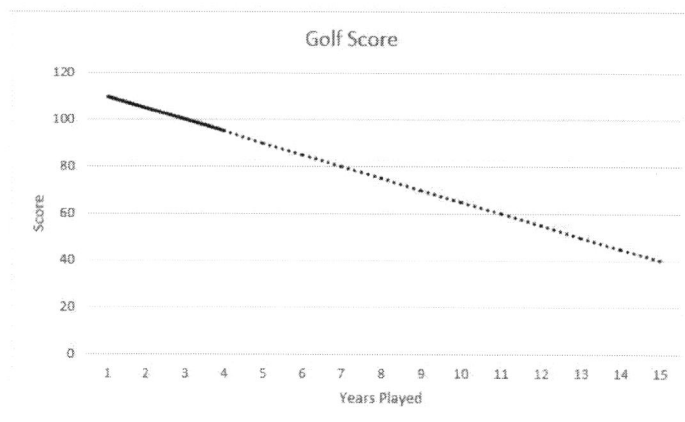

### III.16.C.b. Survivorship

One of the dominating aspects of analysis in modern economics and financial markets is survivorship: the concept that successes are recorded and misses are largely forgotten. Survivorship is an extreme problem in analysis of returns to mutual funds, hedge funds and other pools of investments. Here are a few observations about survivorship and money management.

- Forgetting failures is a pervasive tendency. In one college class I presented certain commodities trading tactics. When they were successful I brought them up every class. When they performed poorly, I did not.

- Similarly, in decades of working in the money management business, I have been surprised and sometimes shocked how readily people forget about unsuccessful attempts.
- Survivorship bias is common in databases of returns to investment pools. Some analysts say that, in the historical returns to hedge funds, if you remove the survivorship you will account for most of the alpha.
- Academics attempt to adjust databases to eliminate or at least minimize survivorship. This is easier in some data, like that of mutual funds, than in others, like private equity.
- Other varieties of bias in returns data are like survivorship. One is instant history bias, which is sometimes called backfill bias. In this case a money manager populates a database of performance with years of results of his most successful fund.
- Some analysts argue that it goes both ways. Successful investment funds may hide their performance since they may not want to raise money and may simply not want to draw attention to their wealth creation.

## III.16.C.c. Logarithms

Almost everybody was exposed to many math classes involving logarithms in both high school and college. The concept, though, is difficult to retain. Logarithms have multiple uses and interpretations. Logs are power terms in reverse. For example, $5^2 = 25$, then the log of 25 to the base 5 is 2. We frequently use logs with a base of ten, known as common logarithms. We also use logs with a base of e, which is a constant equal to about 2.718. We call this the natural log. It is applicable to many issues economics and finance such as compounding.

A data series plotted over time (i.e., with time on the x-axis) often will show a line with a slight slope, often virtually flat, but getting more and more curve and steeper in slope until the line bends drastically upward and becomes virtually vertical. This may be a totally valid demonstration but it is also virtually inscrutable and conveying of a wrong idea. This is a linear scale where the y-axis goes up on unit by unit basis. A much better scale would be a log scale which represents percent change. For example, a plot the Dow Jones stock market index starting in 1980 at $10,000 would be at $20,000 in 1990, $40,000 in 2000 and $80,000 in 2010. Each ten-year change would be the same percent but in plain dollars each increase would appear taller on a time series graph. If you took logarithms each two periods' change would appear the same. The log scale shows the rate of change over each period of time in consistent fashion and correctly demonstrates orders of magnitude:

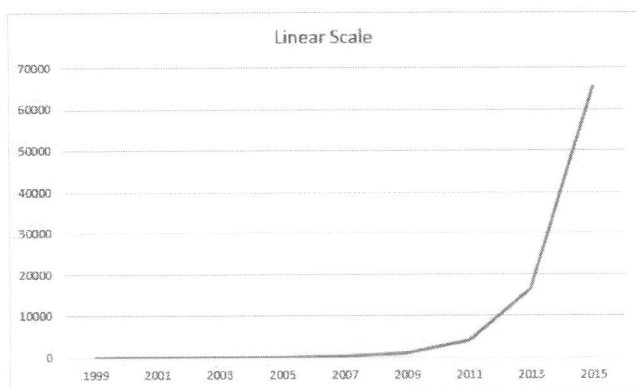

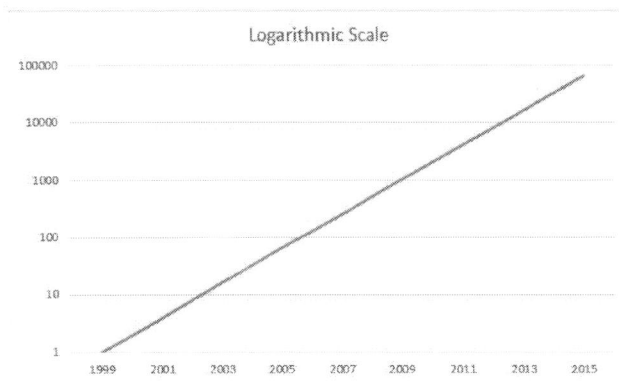

### III.16.C.d. Self-Fulfilling Prophesies

Even if some factor or method should have no effect in the real world, if people believe in it they act on it. Thus the factor or method does "work." We sometimes refer to this as a self-fulfilling prophesy. It applies to economics and to financial markets. Perhaps, for example, that the Fed's changing of interest rates really does not have real effects on the economy, yet if everyone believes it does, it will. Similarly, perhaps consumer confidence does not really exist and cannot be measured, yet it we collect and disseminate the data and people act on it, it will be a factor. In financial markets, a big area in which beliefs might play a role (according to some analysts) is technical analysis of stocks and markets. Perhaps market movements should not follow a Fibonacci sequence, head and shoulders, etc., but if people believe they do, then they do. In M&M theory self-fulfilling prophesies in one version go back to the 1970s and 1980s. A famous academic paper, "Do Sunspots Matter,[268]" modeled sunspots affecting the economy if people thought the sunspots mattered—even if, indeed, it was unlikely that sunspots really changed material conditions on planet Earth.

### III.16.C.e. An "Artifact of the Data" & Abrupt Changes in Series

Earlier, we hypothesized a structural break in our economy and presented a variety of series that changed abruptly. I contended that we have found a true break. In general though, when you hear about an abrupt change in the trend of some economic or financial quantity, examine it circumspectly. Look for the following: (1) a change in the method of data collection; (2) a change in the definition of the quantity or (3) even something conventional related to the data like who is collecting it, current political overtones, etc. Most of the time, the break will be "an artifact of the data." Examples abound in social, health and medical issues that depend on quantification by experts' opinions and also depend on reporting by people. For example, the prevalence of autism supposedly rose dramatically in the last decade. Yet the increase was likely just heightened reporting and delineating. (I am not judging whether such definitional changes are disadvantageous on net to society. The needs and preferences of today might require expanding sets and changing cutoffs and parameters. On the other hand, when comparisons over time really matter, you must be rigorous and precise in definition.)

When using data over long periods of time where the data has undergone numerous definitions, you have to research, case by case, whether or not the definition change renders the series non-comparable. In general, collectors of prominent economic data series, like GDP and most other government series, strive to make the data comparable, but conceptual issues are inevitable as are omissions.

### III.16.C.f. Ratios

If a ratio moves up or down, before making any conclusion, look at both the denominator and the numerator. For example, the P/E ratio could go up if the price of stocks went up, which might be a favorable circumstance, or if earnings went down, which would be unfavorable and indicate overpricing of stocks. Another example of a ratio is debt (or liabilities) to assets, or "leverage." In recent years we have been told that significant deleveraging for both households and businesses was occurring. We interpreted this as very favorable development for our future economic growth: since people were less leveraged they

---

[268] Karl Shell and David Cass, *Journal of Political Economy*, April 1983.

could borrow more and spend more and increase GDP. While the debt to asset ratio was going down, however, debt itself was not. Rather, assets like stock and housing values were rising in value. If people did not realize the increase in the numerator as much as the decrease in the denominator, they could be more indebted.

## III.16.C.g. Facile Economic Writings

There are many books on economics for average people. Some are decent musterings of certain topics. Many though are simplistic, patronizing and marked by clichéd economics. One pop econ book[269] contends that you can never get a good deal in the used car market, and then explains the lemons and plums model originated by economist George Akerlof.[270] This is silly. The used car market is efficient and fair. You will generally make a prudent purchase. Akerlof's model is clever but not easily applicable to the real world. The author overreaches by attempting to dazzle average people with clever devices applied to people's lives.

*Freakonomics*[271] is perhaps the most well-known pop econ book. It sells itself as iconoclastic and presenting of insights and surprises you never would have thought of. For example, the book notes:

- What do real estate agents have in common with the Ku Klux Klan? You tear your hair out trying to answer, assuming the relationship to be something specific or esoteric. His answer is that both groups, to further their objectives, try to hide information.
- The "rogue" economist tells us that real estate agents don't hold out for the highest price because they have little incentive given the nature of their commissions (e.g., a 5% commission on a sale of $400,000 is nearly as much as the commission on a $420,000 sale). You don't need econometrics to know that.
- He "discovers" many concepts that most people would not be at all surprised by including that parents engage in over-parenting, that there is corruption in sumo wrestling (which surprises him since it is such an ancient and procedural sport) and that Chicago public school teachers cheat.
- He engages in copious speculation of names accompanied with some number crunching to prove some picked-through story of trashy women named Brittany and Barbie.
- Another teaser question is why do drug dealers live at home with their mothers? Again, you look for some novel, unexpected connection. Like any other well-read person, you are aware that many young, low-income people live with their parents. You also know that most drug dealers are not big time operators making big money. You dismiss this connection as too obvious, though, and assume the *Freakonomics* writers, which include a leading academic economist, must have some other points. You are then disappointed to find that all Levitt has to say is that most drug dealers are poor and stay at home just to make ends meet. Depending on your level of sophistication, you might even become offended when Levitt suggests that he is one of the first to discover the world of inner city drug dealing claiming to have garnered information on ghetto life by having colleagues infiltrate the world of drug dealing. Such research was already done.
- Levitt's econometric analysis of crime perhaps his most famous case from *Freakonomics* concerning the drop in crime in the last few decades. He claims that the change in abortion availability that happened around 1970s reduced the number of potential crime prone people such

---

[269] *The Undercover Economist*, by Tim Harford, Random House Trade Paperbacks, 2005.
[270] Akerlof's 1970 academic paper (cited herein above) about information asymmetry.
[271] By Steven Levitt (a leading academic economist) and Stephen J. Dubner (a journalist), first published 2005, William Morrow and Company. There were additional *Freakonomics*-based books and a movie.

that crime decreased in the 1990s. He argues that other factors, like better policing, widespread incarceration and a strong economy, were not the reason. However, disentangling the effects of the myriad factors affecting crime in recent decades is impossible. As we pointed out before, it is very easy to get results you like when you do econometrics and statistics.

Under a shield of economics and econometrics *Freakonomics* patronizes. When left to their own devices, people are very good at running their economic lives: They Maximize Utility.

Made in the USA
Middletown, DE
06 February 2017